The Aesthetic Mind

# The Aesthetic Mind

*Philosophy and Psychology*

EDITED BY
Elisabeth Schellekens
and Peter Goldie

OXFORD
UNIVERSITY PRESS

# OXFORD
UNIVERSITY PRESS

Great Clarendon Street, Oxford, OX2 6DP,
United Kingdom

Oxford University Press is a department of the University of Oxford.
It furthers the University's objective of excellence in research, scholarship,
and education by publishing worldwide. Oxford is a registered trade mark of
Oxford University Press in the UK and in certain other countries

First Edition published in 2011
First published in paperback 2014

Published in the United States of America by Oxford University Press
198 Madison Avenue, New York, NY 10016, United States of America

British Library Cataloguing in Publication Data

Data available

ISBN 978–0–19–870592–5

# Contents

## Part IV.  Imagination and Make-Believe

## Part V.  Fiction and Empathy

## Part VI.  Music, Dance, and Expressivity

# Part VII. Pictorial Representation and Appreciation

# List of Figures

# Notes on Contributors

NOËL CARROLL is Distinguished Professor of Philosophy at the Graduate Center of the City University of New York. His most recent book is *On Criticism* (Routledge, 2008).

ZANNA CLAY is a primatologist at the School of Psychology in St Andrews. She studies the cognitive mechanisms underlying communication in a species of great ape, the bonobo. Being the closest living relatives to humans, the investigation of bonobo behaviour can provide important insights into the evolution of human behaviour, including empathy. Much of her fieldwork is conducted in DR Congo, where bonobos are endemic.

RODDY COWIE studied philosophy and psychology as an undergraduate (at Stirling and UCLA), and his Ph.D. (at Sussex) was on the relationship between human and machine vision. He was appointed Lecturer in Psychology at Queen's University Belfast in 1975, and Professor in 2003. His core research interest is in relationships between rational models of perception and experiences that are intensely subjective and seemingly counter to rational expectation. It has been followed through many areas—'impossible objects', misperceptions of movement, the subjective experience of hearing loss, and the perception and expression of emotion. His work on emotion included co-ordinating the EC's HUMAINE project, which aimed to lay the foundations for emotion-oriented technology. He also has long-standing interests in music and religion, as academic and practitioner.

GREGORY CURRIE teaches philosophy at the University of Nottingham. His latest book is *Narratives and Narrators* (OUP, 2010). He is currently working on the cognitive value of literature.

DAVID DAVIES is Professor of Philosophy at McGill University. He is the author of *Art as Performance* (Blackwell, 2004), *Aesthetics and Literature* (Continuum, 2007), and *Philosophy of the Performing Arts* (Blackwell, forthcoming), and the editor of *The Thin Red Line* (2008) in the Routledge series Philosophers on Film. He has published widely in the philosophy of art on topics relating to ontology, artistic value, literature, film, music, theatre, and the visual arts. He has also published articles on topics in metaphysics, philosophy of language, philosophy of mind, and philosophy of science.

STEPHEN DAVIES is Professor of Philosophy at the University of Auckland in New Zealand and an ex-President of the American Society of Aesthetics. His main research interests are in aesthetics and the philosophy of art. His books include *Musical Works and Performances* (Clarendon Press, 2001), *Themes in the Philosophy of Music* (OUP, 2003), *Philosophical Perspectives on Art* (OUP, 2007), and *The Philosophy of Art* (Blackwell, 2006). He is co-editor of *Companion to Aesthetics* (Wiley-Blackwell, 2009, 2nd edn.).

NORMAN H. FREEMAN is Emeritus Professor of Cognitive Development and Senior Research Fellow in the School of Experimental Psychology, University of Bristol. His main areas of research include drawing-production and children's theory of pictures. He has published two books on drawing, and over 100 refereed papers and invited chapters. Between 1988 and 1995 he was the Associate Editor for the *British Journal of Psychology* and the *British Journal of Developmental Psychology*. He is currently on the board of *Social Development*.

ROMAN FRIGG is a Reader in Philosophy at the London School of Economics and Deputy Director of the Centre for Natural and Social Science (CPNSS). He holds a Ph.D. in Philosophy from the University of London and an M.Sc. in Theoretical Physics from the University of Basel, Switzerland. His main research interests are in general philosophy of science and philosophy of physics. He has published papers on scientific modelling, quantum mechanics, the foundations of statistical mechanics, randomness, chaos, complexity theory, probability, and computer simulations, and he is currently working on a book on models and theories.

PETER GOLDIE is The Samuel Hall Chair at the University of Manchester. Before moving to Manchester, he was Reader in Philosophy at King's College London, and prior to that a Lecturer at Magdalen College Oxford. His main philosophical interests are in the philosophy of mind, ethics, and aesthetics, and particularly in questions concerning value and how the mind engages with value. He is the author of *The Emotions: A Philosophical Exploration* (OUP, 2000) and *On Personality* (Routledge, 2004), co-author of *Who's Afraid of Conceptual Art?* (Routledge, 2010), editor of *Understanding Emotions: Mind and Morals* (Ashgate, 2002) and *The Oxford Handbook of Philosophy of Emotion* (2010), and co-editor of *Philosophy and Conceptual Art* (OUP, 2007).

CATHERINE HOWARD is a postgraduate student at the University of New South Wales, Sydney. Her current research interests involve comparing cognitive and neurological approaches to artificial intelligence, and the role of functionalism within this volatile field. Her previous studies include cognitive psychology, neuropsychology, analytical philosophy, and the psychology of music.

MARCO IACOBONI is a neurologist and neuroscientist from the University 'La Sapienza' of Rome, Italy. He is Professor of Psychiatry and Biobehavioral Sciences at the David Geffen School of Medicine at UCLA, and Director of the Transcranial Magnetic Stimulation laboratory of the Ahmanson-Lovelace Brain Mapping Center. He investigates the neural basis of sensory–motor integration, imitation, and social cognition in humans using functional magnetic resonance imaging and transcranial magnetic stimulation. His recent book on mirror neurons and empathy is entitled *Mirroring People: The Science of Empathy and How We Connect with Others* (Picador, 2009).

MATTHEW KIERAN is Professor of Philosophy and the Arts at the University of Leeds. He is the author of *Revealing Art* (Routledge, 2004), articles on art and ethics, creativity, snobbery, and the values of art, editor of collections in aesthetics, and is working on aesthetic virtues and vices. He has given more public-orientated art world talks at The Tate, the Charles Parodi Lecture at the Miami-Basel Art Fair, and the National Icelandic Visual Arts Awards.

PETER LAMARQUE is Professor of Philosophy at the University of York. He has published extensively in aesthetics and the philosophy of literature, including *Truth, Fiction, and Literature: A Philosophical Perspective* (with Stein Haugom Olsen, Clarendon Press, 1994), *Fictional Points of View* (Cornell UP, 1996), *The Philosophy of Literature* (Blackwell, 2008), and *Work and Object: Explorations in the Metaphysics of Art* (OUP, 2010). He has edited or co-edited *Philosophy and*

*Fiction: Essays in Literary Aesthetics, Concise Encyclopedia of Philosophy of Language,* and *Aesthetics and the Philosophy of Art: The Analytic Tradition: An Anthology.* From 1995 to 2008 he was Editor of the *British Journal of Aesthetics.*

ROBERT LAYTON is Professor of Anthropology, University of Durham. His research interests include human social evolution and social change, the anthropology of art, and indigenous rights. He has conducted field research on social change in rural France, on art and on land rights in Aboriginal Australia, and on traditional arts in rural China. His publications include *The Anthropology of Art* (CUP, 1991, 2nd edn.), *An Introduction to Theory in Anthropology* (CUP, 1997), and 'Art and Agency: A Reassessment', *Journal of the Royal Anthropological Institute,* 9 (2003).

JERROLD LEVINSON is Distinguished University Professor of Philosophy at the University of Maryland, where he has taught since 1976. Levinson is the author of *Music, Art, and Metaphysics* (OUP, 1990), *The Pleasures of Aesthetics* (Cornell UP, 1996), *Music in the Moment* (Cornell UP, 1998), and *Contemplating Art* (Clarendon Press, 2006). He is also the editor of *Aesthetics and Ethics* (CUP, 1998) and *The Oxford Handbook of Aesthetics* (OUP, 2003), as well as past President of the American Society for Aesthetics, 2001–2003, and a longtime member of the Editorial Board of the *Journal of Aesthetics and Art Criticism.* Levinson has been a Visiting Professor at Johns Hopkins University, Columbia University, University of London, University of Canterbury, Université de Rennes, Université Libre de Bruxelles, Universidade de Lisboa, University of Kent, and Conservatorio della Svizzera Italiana. During 2010–11 he occupied an Internationale Chaire Francqui at the Katholieke Universiteit Leuven in Belgium.

DEREK MATRAVERS was an undergraduate at UCL, and obtained his Ph.D. in Cambridge. He was a British Academy post-doctoral Research Fellow, and a Junior Research Fellow at Darwin College, Cambridge. He is currently Professor of Philosophy at The Open University, Affiliated Lecturer to the Faculty of Philosophy in Cambridge, and a Bye-Fellow of Emmanuel College. He was a Visiting Professor at the University of British Columbia in 2009/10, and is currently working on a book on narrative and fiction.

I. C. McMANUS first developed an interest in experimental aesthetics while an undergraduate in Cambridge studying psychology and medicine. His research interests include cerebral lateralization and the education, training, and assessment of doctors. He is currently Professor of Psychology and Medical Education at University College London. He is a Fellow of the Royal Colleges of Physicians of London and Edinburgh, the Academy of Medical Sciences, and the International Association of Empirical Aesthetics. His books include *Right Hand Left Hand* (Phoenix, 2002).

AARON MESKIN is Senior Lecturer in Philosophy at the University of Leeds. He has published articles in the *Australasian Journal of Philosophy,* the *British Journal of Aesthetics,* the *Journal of Aesthetics and Art Criticism,* the *Journal of Aesthetic Education, Philosophy and Phenomenological Research,* and numerous collections. His current interests include the cognitive imagination, contextualism about aesthetic discourse, the ontology of multiple arts, and the philosophical issues raised by comics, videogames, and short stories. He co-edited *Aesthetics: A Comprehensive Anthology* (Wiley-Blackwell, 2007).

DAVID S. MIALL is Professor in the Department of English and Film Studies at the University of Alberta in Canada. Previous publications include, as editor, *Humanities and the Computer: New Directions* (Clarendon Press, 1990), *Romanticism: The CD-ROM* (Blackwell, 1997), and a monograph, *Literary Reading: Empirical and Theoretical Studies* (Peter Lang, 2006). He specializes in literature of the British Romantic period, and the empirical study of literary reading, a field in which he has collaborated with Don Kuiken (Department of Psychology) since 1990. He teaches courses in Romantic literature, Gothic fiction, literary computing, and empirical and historical studies of literary reading and literary aesthetics.

MARGARET MOORE recently completed her Ph.D. at Temple University and is now a research fellow with the AHRC aesthetics project 'Methods in aesthetics: the challenge from the sciences' at the University of Leeds. Her work focuses on topics in the intersection of the philosophy of music and the philosophy of mind, especially imagination and music cognition. She is also a flautist and violinist.

JESSE PRINZ is Distinguished Professor of Philosophy at the City University of New York, Graduate Center. His research focuses on the perceptual, emotional, and cultural foundations of human psychology. He is author of *Furnishing the Mind: Concepts and Their Perception Basis* (MIT, 2002), *Gut Reactions: A Perceptual Theory of Emotion* (OUP, 2004), and *The Emotional Construction of Morals* (OUP, 2007). He also has two forthcoming books: *The Conscious Brain* (OUP) and *Beyond Human Nature* (Penguin/Norton). He is currently working on the psychology of art.

LENA QUINTO is completing a Ph.D. on the emotional power of music, focusing on strategies and devices used by composers and performers to communicate emotion and induce emotional experiences. She has published several articles on music cognition, music and gesture, and the relation between music and speech.

MARK ROLLINS is Chair of Philosophy at Washington University in St. Louis, where he is also Professor of Philosophy and in the Philosophy–Neuroscience–Psychology Program and the Fox School of Art and Visual Design. He is the author of *Mental Imagery: On the Limits of Cognitive Science* (Yale UP, 1986) and *Danto and His Critics* (Blackwell, 1996), a new version of which will be published next year. He is currently completing a new book, *Perceptual Strategies and the Pictorial Arts*.

EDMUND T. ROLLS is at the Oxford Centre for Computational Neuroscience, Oxford (www.oxcns.org), and at the Department of Computer Science, University of Warwick, UK. He is a neuroscientist with research interests in computational neuroscience, including the operation of real neuronal networks in the brain; functional neuroimaging of vision, taste, olfaction, feeding, the control of appetite, memory, and emotion; neurological disorders of emotion; psychiatric disorders including schizophrenia; and the brain processes underlying consciousness. His books include *Emotion Explained* (OUP, 2005), *Memory, Attention, and Decision-Making: A Unifying Computational Neuroscience Approach* (OUP, 2008), and *The Noisy Brain: Stochastic Dynamics as a Principle of Brain Processing* (with G. Deco, OUP, 2010).

ELISABETH SCHELLEKENS is Chair Professor of Aesthetics at the University of Uppsala and Senior Research Fellow at the University of Durham. She is Co-Editor of the *British Journal of Aesthetics*, the author of *Aesthetics and Morality* (Continuum, 2007), and co-author of *Who's Afraid of Conceptual Art?* (Routledge, 2009). She was Post-Doctoral Research Fellow on the AHRC-funded project 'Towards an aesthetic psychology: the philosophy of aesthetic perception and cognition' between 2004 and 2006, the project which led to the publication of this collection of essays. Her main research interests include questions at the intersection of the philosophy of mind and aesthetics, meta-ethics, and Kant.

DOROTHY G. SINGER is retired Senior Research Scientist at the Department of Psychology, Yale University. She is also Co-director of the Yale University Family Television Research and Consultation Center affiliated with the Zigler Center for Child Development and Public Policy. She is also a Fellow of the American Psychological Association. Her research and publications are in the area of early childhood development, television effects on youth, and parent training in imaginative play. She has written numerous articles and books. She received the Distinguished Alumni Award from Teachers College, Columbia University in 2006, and, in 2009, the Award for Distinguished Lifetime Contributions to Media Psychology from the American Psychological Association.

JEROME L. SINGER is Professor Emeritus of Psychology at Yale University. He is a specialist in research on the psychology of imagination and day-dreaming and has authored articles on thought processes, imagery, personality, and psychotherapy as well as on children's play and the effects of television. Recent books include *The House of Make-Believe, Repression and Dissociation, Imagination and Play in the Electronic Age*, and *Imagery in Psychotherapy* (American Psychological Asssociation, 2001). His most recent position in the American Psychological Association has been President of Division 10, Creativity and the Arts. In 2008, he was awarded the Rudolf Arnheim Award from the American Psychology Association for Distinguished Contributions to the Psychology of Aesthetics, Creativity, and the Arts, and in 2009, the Paul Farnsworth Award for Lifetime Contribution and Service, Division 10, American Psychological Association.

KATHLEEN STOCK is a Senior Lecturer in Philosophy at the University of Sussex. She has published articles on various problems concerning the imagination and fiction, and also on definitions of art. She is currently completing a monograph on imagination and fiction. She is the editor of *Philosophers on Music* (OUP, 2007) and co-editor of *New Waves in Aesthetics* (Palgrave Macmillan, 2009).

WILLIAM FORDE THOMPSON is Professor of Psychology, Macquarie University. His 2009 book *Music, Thought and Feeling* (OUP, 2008) is a leading textbook on the psychology of music. He is past Editor of the journal *Empirical Musicology Review*, Associate Editor for the journals *Music Perception* and *Semiotica*, and past President of the Society for Music Perception and Cognition (SMPC). He has published over 80 articles and chapters on the perceptual, cognitive, and emotional aspects of music.

JONATHAN M. WEINBERG is Associate Professor in the Department of Philosophy at the University of Arizona. His research includes the intersection of cognitive science and both aesthetics and epistemology. In addition to contributions to several edited volumes, he has published in the *British Journal of Aesthetics, Nous, Philosophical Psychology, Midwest Studies in Philosophy, Philosophy of Science*, and *Philosophical Studies*. He is also an active researcher in the 'experimental philosophy' movement, attempting to apply the methods of the social sciences to questions about the malleability and variability of people's judgements about imagined thought-experiments.

DAHLIA W. ZAIDEL is a neuroscientist and Professor in the Department of Psychology and a member of the Brain Research Institute, in the University of California at Los Angeles (UCLA). She obtained her Ph.D. in 1982 at UCLA. She has been involved in brain research and publishing journal articles on hemispheric specialization, memory, facial beauty, and various issues on brain and art. She is the author of *Neuropsychology of Art: Neurological, Cognitive, and Evolutionary Perspectives* (Psychology Press, 2005).

# Introduction

*Elisabeth Schellekens and Peter Goldie*

Aesthetic and artistic experiences are remarkable case studies for anyone interested in the mind. Whether one is curious about the workings of highly complex neural systems, the depths of emotional sensitivity, our evolutionary past and distant ancestors' ability for thought, or what it means to lead a rich and virtuous life, the realm of the aesthetic provides plenty of food for thought and material for scrutiny.

That said, the precise means by which this material should be scrutinized remains a moot point. Different investigative perspectives have given rise not only to distinct methodological concerns about how best to address or tackle particular questions in aesthetics, but also how to separate enquiries into which questions are, in fact, central to understanding the aesthetic. What one discipline takes for granted may constitute an unwarranted presupposition in another. For example, whereas many scientists work with the assumption that aesthetic experiences are primarily experiences of beauty and generally have powerful emotional components, philosophers have long wondered about the link between aesthetic appreciation and emotion and the status of the beautiful as the paradigmatic aesthetic quality *par excellence*.

The central question driving this volume is this: how—if at all—can the empirical work of the sciences be integrated with the more a priori investigations which have traditionally characterized philosophy, and vice versa? More specifically, what role exactly does philosophy have to play in understanding aesthetic and artistic experience? So-called 'experimental philosophy' is now a significant part of normative ethics, and the philosophy of mind has for several decades been informed by work in the empirical sciences. But in aesthetics, these developments are at a much earlier stage, and many questions of principle have yet to be resolved. To some philosophers it is unclear whether empirical approaches are capable of adding anything significant to the debate at all, and whether neurology, social anthropology, or developmental psychology actually get to the heart of why aesthetic experiences matter to us. And to some scientists the many problems concerning our understanding of the aesthetic cannot ultimately be solved by 'armchair' philosophical analysis. How are we to make progress here?

This is the starting point of our discussion of what we are calling *aesthetic psychology*. While we do not claim to cover in this volume all aspects of aesthetic and artistic experience from every accessible angle, we aim to move forward on the question of what can or cannot be achieved in the context of co-operative work which focuses on both philosophical and empirical approaches to aesthetics. It is an opportunity for philosophers to air their views on alternative ways of analysing the aesthetic and to present arguments for why they see those disciplines as either threatening or helpful or both. It is also a chance for the sciences to engage philosophers in conversation about their methods and aims, and press them on exactly what the explanatory power of philosophical theories of the aesthetic amount to. For while sound philosophical accounts may still have their own tasks cut out for them alongside the results attained by the natural or social sciences, it also seems likely that the former will have to respect the boundaries of what is empirically possible.

The deeper one delves into these issues, the blurrier the disciplinary margins become. While philosophy is generally thought to be concerned with a priori conceptual analysis and the sciences tend to be in the business of developing and testing empirical hypotheses, it is clearly not the case that this contrast captures all instances of philosophical theorizing or scientific enquiry. What does the distinction between the two approaches fundamentally amount to, and where are overlaps not only possible but actually desirable? In an attempt to shed light on these concerns, we will focus on the following issues.

## The psychology of the aesthetic

The first theme to be debated offers a particularly good illustration of the broad conception of mind at work in this collection. Part I brings together anthropological, psychological, neurological, and philosophical ways of looking at what is distinctively aesthetic about some aspects of the mental, and raises a host of challenging questions about the kinds of minds we need for aesthetic appreciation. These questions fall, roughly, into three categories. First, there are queries about the function of art and aesthetic experience: What is art for? Why did we develop the ability to engage aesthetically with things in our environment? Is our aptitude for appreciating things aesthetically linked to the development of our moral character? Second, there are concerns about how this kind of engagement with the world has evolved: How is artistic activity connected to other aspects of our cognitive development?; Under what circumstances is our ability to discern aesthetic character shaped by neurology and physiology? Third, there are issues about the wider ramifications of this ability: Does aspiring to be good at appreciating things aesthetically somehow depend on having a certain kind of (moral) character?; Does physiological damage to our brain affect our artistic skills and creativity, and if so how? The idea underlying the discussions of Part I is that the mind—or the brain—is a constantly evolving thing, and to understand the aesthetic mind we must get a clearer idea of the various directions in which it continually progresses.

# Emotion in aesthetic experience

One notion that has attracted a lot of attention recently, perhaps especially among psychologists and philosophers, is emotion. The theme central to Part II is how to understand the relation between emotions and aesthetic experiences. Several alternatives are considered, ranging from the claim that all aesthetic experiences involve emotional responses to the idea that there are no necessary connections between those experiences and states such as pleasure or delight. The latter view gains support from cases where we seem to appreciate something aesthetically without experiencing that kind of enjoyment. What, for example, are we to think of artworks that evoke negative emotions, or which give rise to no emotional response whatsoever? The question touches on one of the most problematic topics of this collection, for while it might be possible for emotion and aesthetic experience to come apart in conceptual analysis, what are philosophers sympathetic to that view to make of the neuropsychological evidence indicating that aesthetic experiences not only do involve emotional components, but are valued (at least in part) precisely because they are pleasant? Added to this already loaded question, there is the further complication that even unpleasant sensations can lead us to care about specific artworks, such as when a negative response to an artwork contributes to our general emotional education. Clearly, the methodological controversy is in full swing here. For even if it is the case that we are genetically determined to find certain things pleasant and others unpleasant, and that these sensations lie at the root of what we find beautiful, what does that really tell us about why aesthetic experiences are so important to us?

# Beauty and universality

Part III examines the idea that, despite the many subjective elements of aesthetic and artistic experience, strong similarities of aesthetic taste nonetheless do occur across cultures and periods. Be it the notion of facial symmetry or the golden section, how deep does this seeming universality run and how are we to make sense of it? The question is pressing since if it can be established that human beings are, at least to a certain extent, predetermined to find some things beautiful and others not, then the way in which we judge objects of appreciation seems fundamentally threatened. In aesthetic appreciation we think of ourselves as free agents, assessing aesthetic character on a case-by-case basis—there is no rulebook to what is beautiful or not. What is more, the observation that there are at least some cross-cultural similarities and parallels encourages an understanding of beauty as a singular concept. But are there not different kinds of beauty; is natural beauty for example not to be distinguished from moral beauty which, again, is to be further distinguished from artistic beauty? If it is, what are the implications for empirical approaches to aesthetics which fail to draw distinctions of this kind? Perhaps, then, such approaches are better suited to explain certain instances of beauty or indeed components of aesthetic experience rather than others.

## Imagination and make-believe

One of the mental abilities that lies at the heart of many aesthetic experiences is the imagination. Whether we engage with artworks or admire scenes of natural beauty, we tend to exercise our imagination in at least one of many possible ways: we imagine Count Vronsky's despair when we read *Anna Karenina*, the powerful torrents of rivers in spring when we listen to the second movement of Smetana's *Ma Vlast*, the side of Canova's sculptures that we are not currently facing, that we are pursued by villains when we are engrossed in watching *Bullitt*, or the serene atmosphere that surrounded Monet when he painted his water-lilies. In Part IV, with a focus on this capacity for fantasy and make-believe, we return to some of the concerns raised in the opening section. Psychological studies of autistic children suggest, for example, that this capacity is closely linked not only to our ability for aesthetic creativity but also to the training of more general cognitive, social, and emotional skills needed in much of everyday life. But what about when we are somehow blocked from engaging imaginatively with an object, person, or situation? Whether it is voluntary or not, there are occasions when our mind seems to put certain restrictions on what is imaginable or not. Is it, for example, possible fully to put oneself in the shoes of someone who has inflicted unnecessary suffering on others and taken pride in that fact? In other words, are there limits to what we can imagine and, if so, are there empirical explanations why this might be so?

## Fiction and empathy

In Part V we turn to a closely related field of enquiry, namely fiction and empathy. Our propensity to empathize underlies much of our involvement with aesthetic and artistic objects, perhaps especially literary works. That said, what is empathy exactly and how does it arise? We all know from experience how attached we can become to fictional characters and how profoundly involved we can be with fictional scenarios. This phenomenon puzzles particularly those philosophers who are committed to the idea that responses of this kind go hand-in-hand with a belief in the existence of that which we respond to. How, one might ask, is it possible to identify with and develop deep bonds with persons or situations we know not to exist? According to neuroscience, a complex system of mechanisms known as the 'mirror neuron system' underlies our ability for at least some kinds of empathy with other people. Can these accounts be applied to empathy in fictional contexts, and do different kinds of empathy ground our appreciation of fiction in different contexts? The question extends to a broader concern about our aesthetic appreciation of fiction and the extent to which we should take psychological factors into account in understanding the ways in which we engage with works of literary art.

# Music, dance, and expressivity

At times, aesthetic experience translates directly into observable behaviour. Displaying or creating such experiences through and in dance movements or the physical effects of emotional expressivity is an important part of how we relate to music and sound, and highlights several interesting crossing points between what could be cast as abstract constitutive analysis and tangible trackable problem-solving. First, there is the relation between music and dance and the extent to which recent work in cognitive neuroscience can map that relation. If there are philosophical reasons why at least some dance can be understood as a performative interpretation of music, and empirical data support the idea that a dancer can transmit her feelings to the audience with the help of a mirroring response, then this might be one instance where interdisciplinarity leads to genuine progress. A second area which invites overlap is linked to the themes of Parts II and III and the possibility of cross-cultural associations. The relation in question here is that between music and emotional expressivity and the extent to which such expressivity can be appreciated from one culture to the next. Attempting to separate which aspects of that association are culture-specific and which are not is a complicated task, especially if some musical pieces can share certain organizational features without necessarily inviting similar experiences of the music's expressive qualities. In Part VI we see that these and other questions cannot be properly tackled without addressing the potential explanatory scope of various methodologies.

# Pictorial representation and appreciation

The final theme addressed in this collection centres around representation and pictures. Part VII poses the question driving this collection very directly: What, if anything, can psychology, cognitive science, and evolutionary biology tell us about the problems of pictorial representation? More specifically, why do viewers engage with pictures? What happens when we do? How is it distinct from engaging with non-pictures? Generally, answers to the first of these concerns appeal to the rewarding experiences that come from appreciating pictures, the visual delight to be had from viewing interesting or beautiful paintings. In order to resolve the second problem, several concepts such as 'seeing-in' have been introduced to help us make sense of the various more or less conscious processes that enable us to grasp and appreciate representations of that kind. Responses to the third query tend to rely on the accounts provided to find a way out of the second concern. Nevertheless, numerous issues about the relations between picture, artist, perceiver, and scene still require clarification. One of those has to do with the extent to which psychological or social factors can—or cannot—influence our perception and assessment of pictures. Being able to pinpoint what we bring to the table when we engage with pictorial representations and how crucial that cognitive baggage is to the aesthetic appreciation of pictures would no doubt take us one step closer to answering many of the questions raised above.

The present collection sprung from a research grant awarded by the Arts and Humanities Research Council in 2004–6. The research project, 'Aesthetic Perception and Cognition: Toward an Aesthetic Psychology', was based at King's College London and the University of Manchester, and led to a conference at the University of Durham in September 2006. Many but not all of the contributions to the volume were originally presented as papers at this conference. The editors remain most grateful to all the scholars who attended the conference as well as those who participated in the project in other ways.

# PART I

# The Psychology of the Aesthetic

# 1

# The Master of the Masek Beds: Handaxes, Art, and the Minds of Early Humans[1]

*Gregory Currie*

How old is art? People who disagree about what is to count as art will answer the question in different ways; even those with similar conceptions are unlikely to converge on a common century. For me, agreement within a few hundred thousand years would be progress. The answer I'm suggesting is: about half a million years ago. This is massively imprecise, but it's not blandly uninformative; on the contrary, it's an answer rejected by almost everyone whose views on this I understand. I don't say the answer is right; I'm not very confident about the answer. My point is that it is a serious candidate for an answer, and no one seriously considers it.

One reason this answer is not taken seriously may be that it has consequences many find unattractive. My candidates for first art are certain stone implements, called *handaxes*. A creature making these things around 800 thousand years ago (kya) had, so far as we know, limited social intelligence, no articulated language, no narrative, religion or symbol. To many it will seem absurd that anything produced within such a thin cultural and cognitive setting should count as art. I'll have this worry in mind throughout, giving it special attention in section 4. I'll also argue for the immense explanatory potential of handaxe production for issues which, while art-related, stand as independent markers of human achievement: practices of Gricean meaning-making, the imposition of style on human action, the development of symbolic culture. If you suspect that the question about art will turn out to be largely or wholly verbal, there may still be something here of interest.

I had better clarify one thing before I begin. I am arguing that the first art is an art of pure, unmeaningful beauty, and that our loss of a sense of the connection between art

[1] This research was supported by a generous grant from the Arts and Humanities Research Council of the UK. Earlier versions of this essay were read at a meeting of the Forum Scientiarum, University of Tübingen in 2009 and as a public lecture at Texas Tech University in the same year. I'm grateful to Nicholas Conard, Harald Fosse, Andrew Kania, Nick Humphrey, Catrin Misselhorn, and Kim Sterelny for discussion. My biggest debt is to John Ferrari, whose comments on an earlier version led to the addition of section 6.

and beauty and our insistence that what matters is meaning stand between us and a sense of the true significance of these objects. It would be wrong to take this as an argument for the enduring primacy of beauty over meaning in art, or even as a denial that beauty is sometimes highly meaning-dependent.

## 1. Acheulean technology

Thirty-five years ago the prehistorian J. Desmond Clark noted that 'The symmetry and refinement of some of the earlier Acheulean handaxes, which surely go beyond the utilitarian need, may reflect the first appearance of an aesthetic appreciation of form.'[2] Similarly hesitant references have been made since then, and occasionally before, to an aesthetic role for these stone artefacts produced from about 1.6 million years ago (mya) onwards. This has never gained the momentum that would turn it into a 'Here is the origin of art' thesis of the kind so often expressed concerning the European Upper Palaeolithic (UP) from 35kya onwards, with its exquisite carvings and grand painted caves. There are dangers in declaring this or that body of very ancient artefacts to be art; dangers that range from accusations of ethnocentricity, through the hubris of speculating in an environment almost devoid of signposts, to the possibility, once again, that the issue turns out to be largely or wholly verbal. Risking all these dangers, I want to give an airing to the idea that Acheulean tool-making has a place in the history of art, and in the process to draw attention to a remarkable body of work that was in production for a vastly longer time than any familiar art historical category such as Cubism, or even Western mimetic realism. It lasted more than one million years, outlived several human species, and spread from Africa to western Asia and parts of Europe. We call this handaxe technology the Acheulean, after St Acheul in France, the place where these objects were first recovered in modern times, though the form indisputably originated in Africa, perhaps in what is now southern Ethiopia.

These stone tools may also be called *bifaces*—two worked sides of a stone cobble or flake that meet at a sharp edge going all the way round. They are tear, cordate, or ovate in shape and sometimes worked to a high degree of symmetry.[3] They were created by a complex process of heavy and light striking with other objects: stone for the rougher shaping, bone and antler for the fine work. Because they were produced by reduction of a very durable material they have survived. Indeed, they exist in vast numbers, and carry a great deal of information about the techniques of making, techniques which

---

[2] At a lecture at the LSE which was my introduction to prehistory; if there was anything in the spoken version about the aesthetics of stone tools it made, I'm sorry to say it made no impression on me. The talk was published as 'Africa in Prehistory: Peripheral or Paramount?', *Man*, New Series, 10/2 (June, 1975): 175–98, and the quotation is from p. 190. Clark speaks of 'early' Acheulean handaxes; most authorities now emphasize the more refined appearance of later—post 500kya—instances. But note that one of the examples I discuss below is dated earlier, adding considerably to the uncertainty of my already vague estimate for the age of art. See below, section 2.

[3] See Thomas Wynn, 'Archaeology and Cognitive Evolution', *Behavioral and Brain Sciences*, 25 (2002): 389–438, p. 396.

modern stone knappers have been able reliably to reproduce.[4] At some sites the flakes removed in the process of reduction lie where they fell, making possible a painstaking refitting of the pieces and a (literal) blow by blow reconstruction of the making. Scholars have even drawn conclusions about the social relations between members of the community on the basis of the pattern of stone waste, sometimes called debitage. Despite talk of 'transitional artefact traditions', the current evidence suggests that the Acheulean emerged quite suddenly, against the background of a much less refined stone tool industry called the Oldowan which goes back to 2.6mya.[5]

So these objects are not utterly mysterious, even granted the huge temporal distance of their making from us, and the pathetically small quantity of contextual information we have to go on in interpreting them. There are, as we shall see, some well-articulated theories on offer to explain their flourishing. Before we get to that, it's worth focusing on the remarkable, the strangely satisfying beauty of these objects. Some of them seem to me among the most visually arresting human artefacts we have. Wide-eyed, untutored responses should not be our stopping place, but they are not a bad place to start.

## 2. Some bifaces

First, an example from Northern Cape, South Africa, dated at 750,000 BP and made from banded iron stone, remarkably symmetrical and crafted so as to show off variation in the material (Fig. 1.1). Moving out of Africa with a relatively late human diaspora, we have the Hoxne handaxe, presumed to be the product of our direct ancestor, *H. heidelbergensis*. It was discovered in 1789 by John Frere, a Suffolk landowner; it came, he surmised, from 'a very remote period indeed, even beyond that of the present world'.[6] Frere's handaxe is shaped as an elongated tear-drop, roughly symmetrical in two dimensions, but with a twist to the symmetry which has retained an embedded fossil (Fig. 1.2). In size and shape it would not have been a useful butchery implement, and is worked on to a degree out of proportion to any likely use.[7]

---

[4] It is estimated that there are about 100,000 handaxes at Swanscombe, a lower Palaeolithic site in England.

[5] See S. Semaw et al. 'The Oldowan-Acheulean Transition: Is There a "Developed Oldowan" Artifact Tradition?', in M. Camps and P. Cuhuan (eds.), *Sourcebook of Palaeolithic Transitions: Methods, Theories and Interpretations* (New York, Springer, 2009).

[6] 'Account of Flint Weapons Discovered at Hoxne in Suffolk', *Archaeologia*, 12 (1800): 204–5.

[7] There are other examples of notable deviation from symmetry. Thomas Wynn notes cleavers from the Tanzanian site of Isimila which 'appear bent, as if the whole plan symmetry, including the midline, had been warped into a series of curved, parallel lines. These are invariably extensively modified artefacts, whose cross sections are symmetrical, and the pattern is almost certainly the result of intention' (Wynn, 'Archaeology and Cognitive Evolution', p. 396). These cleavers are roughly contemporary with the Hoxne handaxe. For another twisted handaxe see British Museum object 1915 12–8, 265, dated at 400kya from Hitchen, UK. This object can be seen at http://www.britishmuseum.org/research/search_the_collection_database/ search_object_details.aspx?objectid=1635772&partid=1&searchText=palaeolithic&fromADBC=ad&- toADBC=ad&numpages=10&images=on&orig=%2fresearch%2fsearch_the_collection_database.aspx&cur- rentPage=5, though the photograph does not indicate the twist.

Figure 1.1  Handaxe banded ironstone, *c.*750,000 BP, McGregor Museum, Kimberley
See http://www.cope.co.za/Archaeo/masterhandaxe.htm

Figure 1.2  Hoxne handaxe, Lower Palaeolithic, *c.*400,000 BP, Hoxne, Suffolk, England
See http://images.google.co.uk/imgres?imgurl
=http://www.britishmuseum.org/images/
ps314332_m.jpg&imgrefurl=http://www.
britishmuseum.org/explore/highlights/high-
light_objects/pe_prb/h/hoxne_ handaxe.aspx
&usg=__GH6TyXHS8pXFYYpEpF5y9X2
eFy8=&h=225&w=225&sz=15&hl=en&start
=1&itbs=1&tbnid=c4ZGbnHJNcJw4M:
&tbnh=108&tbnw=108&prev=/images%3Fq%
3Dhoxne%2Bhand%2Baxe%26gbv%3D2%26hl%
3Den%26safe%3Dactive

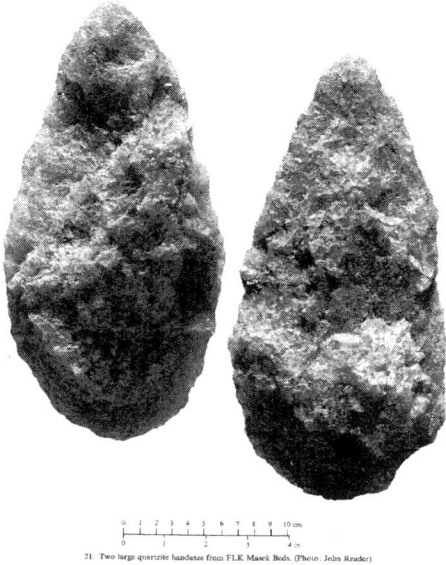

Figure 1.3 Handaxes from the Masek Beds, Olduvai. From M. Leakey (ed.), *Olduvai Gorge*, volume 5, Cambridge University Press, 1994

Astonishingly, given the depth of time involved, we occasionally glimpse the *oeuvre* of a single individual. At the Masek Beds, Olduvai Gorge, Tanzania, five finely shaped handaxes in white quartzite were found, measuring about 27 cm in length, dated between 600 and 400kya. (Fig. 1.3). This is very large; the average length for all handaxes is 13 cm and 90% are less than 18 cm in length.[8] Superposed drawings of their outline shapes show them to be almost perfect matches. Mary Leakey (great-great-great granddaughter of John Frere, by the way) describes them as 'elongate, with delicately trimmed tips. . . . In spite of the material being coarse grained, and intractable, these tools have been elaborately trimmed over both faces. . . . The close similarity in technique, size and form suggests the possibility that they may have been the work of a single craftsman.' Another analyst, not otherwise given to the language of connoisseurship, speaks of 'a highly accomplished knapper, in full control of a difficult raw material . . . a '*tour de force*'.[9]

---

[8] The largest handaxe discovered in Europe is the 'Furz Platt Giant', at 321 mm. It is in the Natural History Museum, London (for illustration see Chris Stringer and Peter Andrews, *The Complete World of Human Evolution* (London: Thames and Hudson, 2005), p. 225). As Marek Kohn says of it 'It is too large to be a serviceable tool for a hominid much less than twelve feet tall' (*As We Know it: Coming to Terms with an Evolved Mind* (London: Granta, 1999), p. 54). For another very large example see British Museum object 1938 12–15, 1, dated at 600kya. Larger handaxes have longer cutting edges but increases in length are bought at a high cost in weight; doubling cutting length means a six-fold increase in weight, and the Masek Beds specimens weigh more than 2 kilos each.

[9] From, respectively, M. Leakey 'The Masek Beds and Sites in Uncertain Stratigraphic Positions', D. A. Roe, 'A Metrical Analysis of Handaxes and Cleavers from Olduvai Gorge', and 'Summary and Overview', all in Leakey (ed.), *Olduvai Gorge*, volume V (Cambridge: Cambridge University Press, 1994), pp. 118–19, p. 207; see also ibid., plate 21.

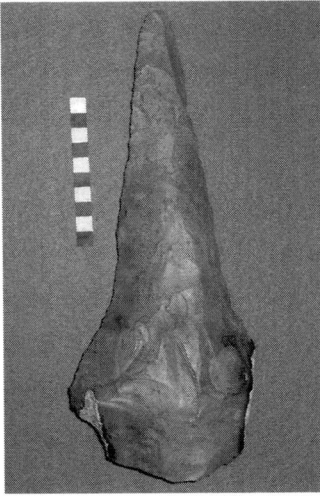

Figure 1.4  Ficron, Cuxton, England
See http://eprints.soton.ac.uk/41481/01/W-S_2004_
(Cuxton_handaxes).pdf

Rivalling the work of the Master of the Masek Beds, though in a less familiar genre, we have two implements from Cuxton in East Anglia found at exactly the same level; there is a suggestion, once again, that they were made by the same agent. One is an extraordinarily elongated dagger-like instrument (such things are called ficrons) measuring 30 cm in length, said to be 'exquisite, almost flamboyant' (Fig. 1.4). The other is a cleaver—a blunt-edged, less common version of the handaxe—of comparable size. Here again '[t]he workmanship is . . . extraordinary. Despite the large size, there are no mistakes such as step fractures across the wide expanse of the faces. The cross-sections along the long axis and across the handaxe are perfectly symmetrical. The cleaver edge, straight and perfectly orthogonal to the long axis, has been achieved by two immaculate opposing tranchet blows, one from each edge.'[10] Both weigh well over a kilo and are too large and heavy for a modern human male of normal size and strength to use.[11] They are provisionally dated at 240,000 BP.[12]

Finally, at Sima de los Huesos in Northern Spain, the remains of about thirty people belonging to the species *H. heidelbergensis* have been found, dating from 300kya; it is possible that the bodies were thrown into the pit for burial. Among them was one

[10]  Francis Wenban-Smith, 'Handaxe Typology and Lower Palaeolithic Cultural Development: Ficrons, Cleavers and Two Giant Handaxes from Cuxton', *Lithics*, 25 (2004): 10–21.

[11]  According to Merreck Poznasky many handaxes from Isimila Iringa, Tanganyika, are 16 inches in length and weigh up to 9 pounds ('Some Functional Considerations on the Handaxe', *Man*, 59 (1959): 42–44, p. 44).

[12]  Wenban-Smith, personal communication.

Figure 1.5  Handaxe, Sima de los Huesos, Spain 400,000 BP
See http://atapuerca.evoluciona.org/documents/00/en/gral_foto/content/inici/04_sima_de_los_huesos/
01_practica_funeraria.html

impressive handaxe of quartz (Fig. 1.5), not a material otherwise worked in this area, which some have speculated to be an early example of grave good.[13]

I have emphasized the visually arresting aspects of these objects. But they are engaging in other ways. Anyone who has held a handaxe will understand Steven Mithen's question:

Why does it feel so enthralling to hold a finely made symmetrical handaxe in one's hand? Why does a symmetrical handaxe look and feel so attractive? My guess is that the thrill of holding a finely made symmetrical handaxe is an echo of the Stone Age past, of a time when these objects played a key role in sexual display and to which our modern minds remain attuned.[14]

I shall say more about the answer Mithen gives later on; for now I simply note the strong tactile and kinaesthetic impression they make.[15]

[13] Eudald Carbonell and Marina Mosquera, 'The Emergence of a Symbolic Behaviour: The Sepulchral Pit of Sima de los Huesos, Sierra de Atapuerca, Burgos, Spain', Comptes Rendus Palevol, 5 (2006): 155–60. It remains a possibility that the handaxe was dropped into the pit by accident. For more on the possible role of Acheulean tools in symbolic culture see below, section 8.

[14] '"Whatever turns you on": A Response to Anna Machin, "Why handaxes just aren't that sexy"', Antiquity, 82 (2008): 766–9. There is sometimes a kindly person at the British Museum who will allow you to hold these artefacts.

[15] On the role of kinaesthetic impressions in art see my 'Empathy for Objects', in Peter Goldie and Amy Coplan (eds.), Empathy: Philosophical and Psychological Essays (Oxford: Oxford University Press, 2009).

## 3.  Art of the Acheulean?

Responses like these to artefacts from distant cultures often provoke warnings about ethnocentric foisting on others of aesthetic and artistic categories said to be the invention of recent Western societies.[16] Oddly, we don't hear parallel claims to the effect that preliterate societies past and present lack technology and religion, categories which are assumed to be elastic enough to take the strain of such cross-cultural comparison. A culture's technology may be seen as underpinned by magical forces, or as subject to the will of gods; religions may be polytheistic and suffused with magical elements in ways that make them very unlike the systematic and official doctrines some of us ascribe to today. Our art is not obviously more distant from that of the Stone Age than Anglicanism is from the religion of, say, the San people of southern Africa well into the twentieth century—a system of belief which, it has been suggested, is the best model we now have for religion in the Upper Palaeolithic (Lewis-Williams 2002). Why this so selective unwillingness to grant that art comes in varied forms and against radically different cultural backgrounds?[17] Further, those who insist on the impossibility of bringing the products of our own society and other, very different societies under a common category of art often ignore or deny a striking fact: the degree to which the aesthetic of another society is recognizable and appreciable without heroic efforts of cultural re-education. As John McDowell says, ' . . . it is remarkable, and heartening, to what extent, without losing hold of the sensitivities from which we begin, we can learn to find worth in what at first seems too alien to appreciate'.[18] These acts of recognition are difficult to explain without the assumption that we apply to the artistic cultures of others sensibilities nurtured within our own.

---

[16] See e.g., Randall White, *Prehistoric Art: The Symbolic Journey of Mankind* (New York: Harry N. Abrams, 2003), Chapter 2.

[17] A number of contemporary writers have also sought to reclaim for aesthetics the broader conception of art as encompassing the everyday; see the brief survey of this programme in Crispin Sartwell, 'Aesthetics of the Everyday', in J. Levinson (ed.), *The Oxford Handbook of Aesthetics* (Oxford: Oxford University Press, 2003). See also Arnold Berleant, *Art and Engagement* (Philadelphia: Temple University Press, 1991); J. David Lewis-Williams, *The Mind in the Cave: Consciousness and the Origins of Art* (London: Thames and Hudson, 2002); Stephen Davies, 'Non-Western Art and Art's Definition', and Denis Dutton, 'But They Don't Have Our Concept of Art', both in Noel Carroll (ed.), *Theories of Art Today* (Madison: University of Wisconsin Press). Davies asks us to include as art in the broad sense only objects where the aesthetic aspect is not highly localized, as it would be in a spade on which a tiny swirl has been carved in the handle; Acheulean tools surely meet this condition.

[18] John McDowell, 'Aesthetic Value, Objectivity and the Fabric of the World', in E. Schaper (ed.), *Pleasure, Preference & Value: Studies in Philosophical Aesthetics* (Cambridge: Cambridge University Press, 1983), p. 3. This view is, of course, consistent with also thinking that a detailed, authoritative appreciation and understanding of alien art forms requires a significant amount of knowledge, and perhaps experience, of the society concerned; see my 'Art and the Anthropologists', in Arthur P. Shimamura and Stephen E. Palmer (eds.), *Aesthetic Science: Connecting Minds, Brains, and Experience* (Oxford: Oxford University Press, 2010). See also Davies, 'Non-Western Art and Art's Definition', and Dutton, 'But They Don't Have Our Concept of Art', who illustrates the ways in which anthropologists have exaggerated the differences between the aesthetic practices and beliefs of different cultures.

We are free, of course, to use the word 'art' in more refined ways which make it inappropriate to speak of art before the UP, or before the Renaissance, or even before Duchamp. Some of these refined usages have their point, and it will be a waste of time to argue that one perspective should have a monopoly of the term. I am using 'art' in the broad but not wholly amorphous sense of that which is produced with the intention that it have aesthetic features. My usage is more or less the same as that employed by Franz Boas ninety years ago when he praised the work of most 'uncontaminated primitive manufacturers', saying that 'most objects of everyday use must be considered as works of art'.[19] And this apparently very broad sense of art is enough to generate significant battle-lines; when anthropologist Richard Klein says that the Acheulean 'produced nothing that could be mistaken for art',[20] he does not mean that the people who made Acheulean tools lacked an art world of curators, critics and Turner Prizes—the sorts of things that 'post-aesthetic' theorists of art consider so important.[21] He means art in a much looser and more traditional sense which includes the painted caves and carved statues of the Upper Palaeolithic (UP), a period which he contrasts very favourably with the supposedly art-free times before that. Klein is not alone in his view. Making the same contrast with the UP, Randall White says that '[f]or the first two and a half million years of the archaeological record the only artefacts of human beings and their hominid precursors were strictly utilitarian: stone tools and perhaps fragments of bone used for simple digging tasks'.[22]

How has the UP acquired this apparently unassailable status as first art? Perhaps the Acheulean's small-scale, non-representational objects have found it difficult to compete for attention with the spectacularly large cave depictions, and with sometimes exquisite representational carvings of the UP—though one might expect their very abstractness to appeal to a modern sensibility. Working in the UP's favour was the fact that the cave paintings were discovered at a time of intense reflection on and experimentation with modes of depiction. On visiting Altamira cave, with its combinations of naturalistic skill and confident deviations from naturalism, Picasso is reported to have said 'We have learned nothing', powerfully encapsulating the thought that these great works anticipate what European art has struggled to achieve in its painful path to—and beyond—pictorial realism. Thus the cave paintings were easily incorporated into a

[19] Franz Boas, *Primitive Art* (New York: Dover Publications, 2002, originally published 1927), pp. 23–4.

[20] Richard Klein and Blake Edgar, *The Dawn of Human Culture* (New York: John Wiley & Sons, 2002), p. 153.

[21] See e.g., George Dickie, *The Art Circle* (New York Haven, 1984); Noel Carroll, 'Identifying Art', in R. Yanal (ed.), *Institutions of Art* (University Park, PA: Pennsylvania State University Press, 1994). Dickie's 'institutional theory' is one of a range of theories designed to loosen the connection between art and the aesthetic; see also Arthur Danto, *The Transfiguration of the Commonplace* (Cambridge, MA: Harvard University Press, 1981).

[22] White, *Prehistoric Art*, p. 8. Similarly, a recent book on human evolution devotes its chapter on 'The First Artists' to the UP (Stringer and Andrews, *Complete World of Human Evolution*).

conception of 'high art' that spoke to classical and modernist sensibilities.[23] Then there are the dramatic stories of discovery, scepticism, and final vindication that go with the late nineteenth century's revelation of cave depiction, easing it naturally into the narrative form so often adopted when telling of the discoveries of Schliemann and Carter.[24] UP artefacts also benefit from the period's reputation as an unprecedented leap forward in cultural achievement across a range of activities which include a complex and articulated tool-kit, co-operative hunting, trading, and ritual and symbolic behaviours visible in grave goods and, by inference, many of the artistic products of the period. This picture is perhaps a too vivid one, and the UP has its detractors;[25] but on no one's account is the Acheulean comparable in cultural richness. The handaxe is basically a tool, and a simple one within a narrow and scarcely changing technology; aesthetic approaches to it naturally seem sentimental and unscientific.

## 4. Art, symbol, culture

I'll argue that an aesthetic approach to the Acheulean has nothing sentimental or unscientific about it. The primary difficulty for it is the close association scholars presume between art on the one hand and, on the other, culture, tradition, and the symbolic. In fact the thing which is currently threatening the view of the UP as first art is the discovery of evidence for symbolism in the Middle Stone Age, the latest being a report (January 2009) by the team working at Blombos Cave, Southern Cape, claiming to have found pieces of ochre with symbolic markings dated at 100kya. This is said to 'have challenged the notion that full-fledged symbolism, such as cave paintings, did not appear before about 40,000 years ago in Europe'.[26] The view that the marks on ochre at Blombos cave have symbolic significance is disputed, but I don't presume to join in that debate; I treat this as merely illustrative of the idea that symbolic activity is at least a necessary condition for art. As the same commentator puts it ' . . . art is an aesthetic expression of something more fundamental: the cognitive ability to

---

[23] While Altamira and Lascaux are dated late in the UP—around 13kya—recent discoveries at Chauvet cave in southern France suggest that this high art of the UP began earlier, at least as early as 30kya. See Jean-Marie Chauvet, Éliette Brunel Deschamps, and Christian Hillaire, *The Dawn of Art: The Chauvet Cave* (New York: Harry N. Abrams, 1998).

[24] See Whitney Davis, 'Beginning the History of Art', in *Replications: Archaeology, Art History, Psychoanalysis* (University Park, PA: Pennsylvania State University Press, 1996), p. 133, which outlines the debate sparked by Don Marcelino Sanz de Sautuolo's discovery at Altamira. Davis considers and rejects the case for regarding certain marked objects on the Middle Palaeolithic as precursors to the representational art of the UP. But why should the art-historical credentials of a period or practice depend on it being shown to merge with depictive art of the UP? See also below, Section 4.

[25] See S. McBrearty and A. Brooks, 'The Revolution that Wasn't: A New Interpretation of the Origin of Modern Human Behavior', *Journal of Human Evolution*, 39 (2000): 453–563.

[26] Michael Balter, 'Early Start for Human Art? Ochre May Revise Timeline', *Science*, 323/5914 (30 Jan. 2009), p. 569. See also C. S. Henshilwood, 'The Origins of Symbolism, Spirituality, and Shamans: Exploring Middle Stone Age Material Culture in South Africa', in C. Renfrew and Iain Morley (eds.), *Becoming Human: Innovation in Material and Spiritual Cultures* (Cambridge: Cambridge University Press, 2009).

construct symbols that communicate meaning, whether they be the words that make up our languages, the musical sounds that convey emotion, or the dramatic paintings that, 30,000 years after their creation, caused the discoverers of the Chauvet Cave to break down in tears'.[27] As long as this view prevails, and as long as we find no strong evidence for symbolic culture prior to 200kya, the claim to find an artistic element in the Acheulean technology will not be taken seriously.

But it can't, surely, be a necessary or conceptual truth that art depends on symbolic cultural practices. Take the case of the UP. Nicholas Humphrey has drawn attention to the often made assumption that the caves at Lascaux and Altamira show that the Magdalenian people were fundamentally like us, though living in a world remarkably different from ours.[28] As Humphrey points out, we have good evidence for the falsity of this assumption: pictures drawn by a profoundly autistic, language-less child, Nadia, which are remarkably like those at Lascaux, Altamira and the more recently discovered Chauvet cave, where depictions of horses, lions, and other creatures have been dated at 32kya. Someone looking only at Nadia's art might well conclude that she had a mind of extraordinary maturity, something we know is unfortunately not the case. Humphrey is not asking us to conclude that the people of the UP were autistic; his point is that there is no sound inference from their artistic production to the modernity of their minds.

Suppose that the people of the UP, for all that they were the same species as ourselves, were as different from normally developing modern-day humans as Nadia was from modern day children of her own age. Suppose they did not have a fully developed language, making do with an only partly articulated language for social communication, plus a suite of mimetic devices—imitative gestures and sounds—with which to communicate about the animal world. Suppose they did not have symbols or beliefs in a spirit world, no sense of tradition or collective memory. Suppose their painting and carving was the result of some turn taken by the arms race of sexual signalling—an idea I'll say more about later. What, in that case, should we say about their aesthetic products? Should we declare them to be fool's art—mere art look-alikes? Surely not. We should say instead that we have learned something surprising about the conditions under which their art was produced, that it is art without any of the standard cultural trimmings: symbol, tradition, general and reflective beliefs about the world and about value. Things would be different if we were invited to consider the possibility

---

[27] Michael Balter, 'On the Origin of Art and Symbolism', *Science*, 323/5915 (6 Feb. 2009), pp. 709–11. Notice that in this passage the communication of meaning and the generation of an emotional response are not distinguished.

[28] 'But what makes us so sure that Upper Palaeolithic humans were engaging in ritual, music, trading and so on at the level that everyone assumes? One answer that clearly will not do here is to say that these were the same humans who were producing symbolic art! Yet, as a matter of fact this is just the answer that comes across in much of the literature: cave art is taken as the first and best evidence of there having been a leap in human mentality at about this time, and the rest of the culture is taken as corroborating it.' Nicholas Humphrey, 'Cave Art, Autism, and the Evolution of the Human Mind', *Cambridge Archaeological Journal*, 8/2 (1998): 165–91; see especially pp. 165–6, where Humphrey cites Gombrich, Mithen, and others as having too easily accepted the inference from impressive artistic production to cultural and cognitive modernity.

that the cave paintings were the bizarre result of flooding, or bear-scratchings. Those would be genuine cases of fool's art: cases where things that look exactly like art turn out not to be art, because they are not the result of intentional activity. But in the present debate I am not questioning the assumption that the cave paintings were the deliberate products of agents; that much is true of Nadia's drawings.

Humphrey may be quite wrong about the facts here, as many people believe he is. It may be true, after all, that the culture of the UP was highly symbolic and its people fully linguistic. This would not affect the present argument, which uses the case as a thought experiment only. And while its assumptions may be contrary to fact, they don't represent bizarre possibilities of the cave-paintings-are-accidents kind. True, the people of the UP were, so far as we know, biologically indistinguishable from us. But that does not make it overwhelmingly probable that their minds were very similar to ours. Humphrey, following Dennett, suggests that 'the change from premodern to modern came about not through genetic changes in innately given "hardware" but rather through environmental changes in the available "software".... pre-modern humans became modern humans when their environment—and specifically the linguistic and symbolic environment inherited through their culture—became such as to reliably program their minds in quite new ways'.[29] Humans have sophisticated and powerful ways to change the world in which they live, and hence to change themselves; our biological sameness with the people of the UP is no reason to see them as possessing all and only all our cognitive capacities.

If this line of reasoning is correct, we don't have to think that the considerable uncertainty there is concerning the Acheulean cognitive and cultural context renders comparably uncertain the proposition that their art-like artefacts are art. We are free, instead, to view Acheulean products as evidence for the claim that an impulse to systematic aesthetic activity is a more basic feature of human kind than symbols, religion, and other emblems of modernity. Indeed, towards the end of this essay I'll suggest, in a speculative way, that aesthetic activity might itself explain the origin of symbolism.

Still, we cannot simply declare human beings to be essentially but mysteriously aesthetic creatures. We need a plausible evolutionary framework. The key idea here is the idea of a *reliable signal*.

## 5. Signals and sexual selection

Signalling among animals has traditionally been assumed to be a matter of common benefit, typified by signals that indicate to other members of the group that a predator

---

[29] 'But what makes us so sure that Upper Palaeolithic humans were engaging in ritual, music, trading and so on at the level that everyone assumes? One answer that clearly will not do here is to say that these were the same humans who were producing symbolic art! Yet, as a matter of fact this is just the answer that comes across in much of the literature: cave art is taken as the first and best evidence of there having been a leap in human mentality at about this time, and the rest of the culture is taken as corroborating it.' Nicholas Humphrey, 'Cave Art, Autism, and the Evolution of the Human Mind', *Cambridge Archaeological Journal*, 8/2 (1998): 165–91; see especially pp. 165–6, where Humphrey cites Gombrich, Mithen, and others as having too easily accepted the inference from impressive artistic production to cultural and cognitive modernity.

is near. On this view, signals evolve by refining their efficiency as channels of reliable communication. Rejecting this picture thirty years ago, Dawkins and Krebs pointed out that, except under unusual conditions of stable coincidence of interest, the evolution of signals is more likely to be a process of competition between deceptive senders and receivers refining their capacity to see through the deception.[30] Creatures thrive by manipulating their fellows by means of signals, and such manipulation often depends on sending a false message. This is particularly a feature of sexual selection, where it is in a creature's interest to persuade others that it is a more desirable mate than it actually is. Given that others need to know the truth about the creature's worthiness as a mate, and will not thrive by responding to false signals, how will signalling become entrenched when there is so much tendency to unreliability? An answer was suggested by the work of ethologist Amoz Zahavi.[31] He argued that certain kinds of activities serve reliably to signal the possession by the signaller of desirable traits because they constitute impediments, much as one can infer the relative skills of two golfers from their handicaps. Alan Grafen then showed that, on certain assumptions, a signal which is designed to advertise some quality will be evolutionarily stable only if it is a costly handicap, and costly in such a way that higher quality signallers pay lower costs for increases in the signal.[32] Because costs are lower for those whose quality is high, there is a reliable correlation between the quality indicated by the signal and the real quality of the signaller.

Might handaxes have functioned as expensive, and hence reliable, signals? Marek Kohn and Steven Mithen say they did: 'We propose that handaxes functioned not just to butcher animals or process plants but as Zahavian handicaps, indicating "good genes".' They go on:

Just as a peacock's tail may reliably indicate its 'success', so might the manufacture of a fine symmetrical handaxe have been a reliable indicator of the hominid's ability to secure food, find shelter, escape from predation and compete successfully within the social group. Such hominids would have been attractive mates...[33]

Successful axe production depends on a number of abilities, notably manual strength and dexterity. Given the many stages through which the working of the stone must go, with earlier stages keyed to later developments in order to give a finely wrought

---

[30] J. R. Krebs and R. Dawkins, 'Animal Signals: Mindreading and Manipulation', in J. R. Krebs and N. B. Davies (eds.), *Behavioural Ecology: An Evolutionary Approach* (Oxford: Blackwell Scientific Publications, 1984).

[31] See A. Zahavi and A. Zahavi, *The Handicap Principle: A Missing Piece of Darwin's Puzzle* (Oxford: Oxford University Press, 1997).

[32] See Grafen's elegant, insightful and immensely clarifying treatment in 'Biological Signals as Handicaps', *Journal of Theoretical Biology*, 144 (1990): 517–46, especially 2.2. Honesty is defined by Grafen roughly in this way: a signal of quality is honest when, given that one signaller, A, is of higher quality than another, the receiver's strategy in response to the signal will discriminate in favour of A. Honesty, thus defined, is nothing to do with intention.

[33] Marek Kohn and Steven Mithen, 'Handaxes: Products of Sexual Selection?', *Antiquity*, 73 (1999): 518–26, p. 521.

product, a number of other things are required: the capacity to hold and manipulate a mental image of the desired shape; steadfastness in carrying out a plan; the kind of mental flexibility we now assess as 'executive function', which is required for the maker to shift constantly between different methods and different tools for flake production, and to deal with unexpected flaws in the material. Success further advertises the superior spatial and perceptual skills necessary for the location of suitable materials, and the social skills and/or position necessary to compensate for the handicap of spending so much time on a non-social task. Because a stone knapper who has these qualities to a higher degree will find it easier to produce well-knapped stones than will someone with lesser relevant qualities, he or she will produce, on average, the better exemplars of the type. Thus the qualities of the knapper are reliably correlated with the qualities of the product.

One way to misunderstand the sexual selection hypothesis is as a claim to the effect that handaxes functioned to provide people with *rational grounds for thinking* that the maker was a good bet as a mate. Richard Klein describes the hypothesis in a way which suggests this interpretation:

When a female saw a large, well-made biface in the hands of its maker, she might have concluded that he possessed just the determination, coordination and strength needed to father successful offspring. Having obtained a mate, a male might simply discard the badge of his success, alongside others that had already served their purpose.[34]

In the same spirit, another critic questions 'whether the brains of protohumans such as *H. erectus* were capable of such sophisticated stratagems'.[35] But signals in sexual selection do not generally work by providing the receiver with grounds for an inference to the fitness of the signaller. For a start, sexual signals work in many species where there is no evidence that the creatures involved are capable of rational reasoning at all. Secondly, even in humans, sexual signals don't generally work that way: there is a good deal of variation in secondary sexual characteristics in humans and this is thought to be the result of sexual selection; when people find these characteristics, in some of their manifestations, highly attractive, the mechanism of attraction is not an inference from the features to thoughts about their owner's reproductive potential. Rather, people simply find certain bodily proportions sexually stimulating, without having any notion why. Note, however, that a lack of understanding of the function of handaxes as fitness indicators by no means entails (though it also does not rule out) a lack of understanding of the role of handaxe production in generating interest on the part of potential sexual partners. While peacocks and peahens presumably never reflect

---

[34] Klein and Edgar, *Dawn of Human Culture*, p. 107.

[35] Diane Bolger, 'Gender and Human Evolution', in Sarah Milledge Nelson (ed.), *Handbook of Gender in Archaeology* (Lanham, MD: AltaMira Press, 2006), p. 475. The same author says that 'one must question the efficacy to survival of dedicating such considerable time and effort to the manufacture of elaborate tools that afforded little practical value apart from their possible use as sex charms' (p. 475), as if sexual attractiveness was a marginal force in biological evolution.

on the role of elaborate tails in mate-attraction, axe-making hominids may well have done so, and may have engaged in strategic thinking about where and when to display their skills, to what extent, and under what conditions of open or disguised competition. Handaxe-making may have been, in Grafen's sense, an example of *strategic-choice* handicap: a handicap which works, not because only the fit are able to bear the handicap, but because the less fit will find more situations in which it is not worth their while to do so.[36] Decisions about the manner of making will be discussed again in the next section.

If the sexual selection hypothesis is right, handaxes were a curiously variable artefact. They are not 'pure signals', as may be the case with peacock tails. Many, quickly made, were used for butchery and perhaps other practical purposes, while we have seen examples of extraordinary craftsmanship and impracticality. A primary determinant of the degree to which a given handaxe seems to be aesthetically designed is its degree of symmetry. The continuation, over a long period of evolutionary time, of handaxes as instruments of sexual selection as well as practical implements argues a persistently high degree of variation in symmetry as between handaxes in a given assemblage. Do we find this variation? Archaeologists have compared assemblages in order to see what differences there are between them and what might be the explanation for such differences. Lycett and von Cramon-Taubadel first considered outline shape, which they measured in terms of relations between a number of (size adjusted) metrical variables. They found a general decrease in within-assemblage variation in shape with distance from the African origin of the technology. About half of this change they believe is explicable in terms of progressive loss of diversity as emigrant populations went through population bottlenecks: where numbers fell dramatically there might be only a very few skilled stone knappers left to copy, and the tool-making of the next generation would then reflect this reduced stock of methods. In extreme cases population would fall so low that the skill would simply be lost; this may be why the biface technology is absent in certain emigrant groups in Europe and Asia.[37] But symmetry turns out to be different; they found that there was not a significant negative correlation between distance from origin and within-assemblage differences in degree of symmetry. It looks as if some strong selection pressure was working to maintain diversity in symmetry, in those populations that managed to hang on to handaxe production, even along dispersal routes that involved multiple population bottlenecks.[38] I suggest that this pressure was the competing demands of practicality and sexual signalling.

---

[36] See again Grafen, 'Biological Signals as Handicaps'. See also Kohn, *As We Know it*, p. 140.

[37] Stephen J. Lycett and Noreen Von Cramon-Taubadel, 'Acheulean Variability and Hominin Dispersals: A Model-Bound Approach', *Journal of Archaeological Science*, 35 (2008): 553–62.

[38] Stephen J. Lycett, 'Acheulean Variation and Selection: Does Handaxe Symmetry Fit Neutral Expectations?' *Journal of Archaeological Science*, 35 (2008): 2640–8.

## 6. Interlude: perceptual bias

The hypothesis of sexual selection might be taken in a strong sense which sees it as an explanation of the emergence of symmetrical tools; on this strong reading, sexual competition selected for symmetrical handaxes, thus explaining the transition from less shapely Oldowan tools to increasingly symmetrical Acheulean ones. While this is an open question, I have no commitment to a strong version of the theory. It is possible instead that the symmetrical shape of the axe emerged first under the pressure of what is called sensory bias. Sensory bias operates when a phenotypic (in this case an extended phenotypic) feature emerges because it presents an appearance to which the creature's sensory apparatus gives a preferential response. Thus it is well known that creatures, including humans, respond preferentially to symmetrical faces, perhaps because facial symmetry is itself an indicator of good health.[39] Given that we are highly tuned to symmetrical stimuli, it is quite likely that there would be a gradual shift towards greater and greater symmetry, that handaxes made slightly more symmetrical than usual by accident would be preferentially attended to, retained, and copied. That symmetry in handaxe manufacture then became an instrument of sexual selection would then be a case of exaptation: a feature which evolved under one selection pressure is maintained, with perhaps heightened emphasis, because it comes to serve some other selective function.[40] It is possible that handaxes went through an intermediate stage where they functioned to increase reproductive advantage, not by serving as sexual signals but by serving as 'sensory traps': devices which, through sensory bias, encourage conspecifics to move closer to the trap's possessor, thereby increasing the possessor's chances of mating.

Do we have any evidence for the effect of perceptual bias in creating sexual signals in this way? We do. Some signals in sexual selection involve the co-evolution of the trait and the preference for the trait. But in other cases, the trait corresponds to a pre-existing preference. This has been shown to be the case with the terminal yellow band (TYB) on the tail of certain species of fish in the subfamily *Goodeinae*. The TYB mimics the appearance of a worm which these fish eat. Some species of *Goodeinae* lack the

---

[39] See the meta-analysis provided in G. Rhodes and L. Simmons, 'Symmetry, Attractiveness and Sexual Selection', in R. Dunbar and L. Barrett (eds.), *The Oxford Handbook of Evolutionary Psychology* (Oxford: Oxford University Press, 2007); see especially section 24.3.2. An alternative hypothesis is that symmetry in faces and elsewhere facilitates information processing, and there seems to be a correlation between the pleasure taken in perceptual stimuli and the ease with which they can be processed (for review see R. Reber, N. Schwarz, and P. Winkielman, 'Processing Fluency and Aesthetic Pleasure: Is Beauty in the Perceiver's Processing Experience?', *Personality and Social Psychology Review*, 8 (2004): 364–82).

[40] However, we need to avoid the implication that aesthetic sensibilities necessarily arise out of perceptual biases. Stephen Mithen says that 'Aesthetic traits . . . are physical or behavioural characteristics that exploit the perceptual biases of those looking for mates' (*The Singing Neanderthals: The Origins of Music, Language, Mind, and Body* (London: Phoenix, 2006), p. 178). It is perfectly conceivable that certain kinds of aesthetic sensibilities arise directly from the pressure of sexual selection, or, for that matter, out of shear cultural contingency. The claim that any particular aesthetic feature is marked out as such as a result of perceptual bias ought to be an empirical one.

TYB, so we can be sure that, within those species, the TYB does not serve as a sexual signal. Fish within these species are nonetheless attracted to the TYB of fish that have them, being apt to take bites out of the tail of a fish which has the TYB. However, fish belonging to species with the TYB had a much lower tendency to takes bites, though females of that species were attracted to the fish in proportion to the vividness of their TYB. This supports the view that the TYB began as a sensory trap but developed in some species into a signal of sexual selection. In those species the TYB no longer serves as a sensory trap, but as a costly signal.[41]

## 7. Makers and artists

How do these speculations about signalling help us to understand the ways people in the community of making would have found well-wrought handaxes appealing objects? These objects would not serve any purpose as sexual signals if, for example, the handaxes themselves were found sexually attractive, for in that case they would simply distract attention from the owner. But that is anyway an unlikely hypothesis. We need to think of them as attractive objects which, through being attractive, enhance the sexual attractions of their makers. Their being found to be beautiful objects well crafted by their makers is surely a very good way that they could fulfil this role. More precisely, the proposal is that handaxes served as sexual signals by being objects with a visual/tactile appearance such that (1) people tended to find that appearance attractive (but not sexually attractive), (2) where part of the attraction is the manifest skill of making something with that appearance, and (3) where the connection with the maker in (1) and (2) has the effect of enhancing the sexual attractiveness of the maker. On this account then, we have a process of artefact making which is sustained and elaborated because of its contribution to the fitness of the creatures who engage in the process, and which contributes to fitness via a mechanism which delivers aesthetic satisfaction—the satisfaction of form pleasing to sight and to touch. I emphasize once again that this is an account of the mechanism by which handaxes functioned as sexual signals, and not an account of the understanding that the people who made and admired them would have had of handaxes. In particular, admirers of these objects would have been aware of their aesthetic attraction—though they would not have thought in these terms, nor, perhaps, in any conceptualized way at all—and quite unaware of their fitness enhancing function.

But there is a danger in focusing too closely on the handaxes themselves, and not enough on the act of making. The danger threatens our understanding of their aesthetic role, but it is already evident when we ask about the ways in which handaxes would have contributed to signalling. If the handaxe itself is the signal, it does not provide very reliable information relevant to mate selection. Handaxes, being

---

[41] Constantino Macías Garcia and Elvia Ramirez, 'Evidence That Sensory Traps Can Evolve into Honest Signals', *Nature*, 434 (2005): 501–5.

disconnected from the body, cannot be reliably correlated with the maker; in this they are rather unlike peacock tails. There would be a great deal of benefit to be gained by stealing them, a pattern of behaviour which would then undermine the effectiveness of the signal. Kohn and Mithen respond to this by suggesting that the signalling occurs in the act of making, to which potential mates must attend. Note, however, that what is important about the making is that it is the making of a handaxe with certain visible properties, and the effectiveness of the act of making depends on the perceived attractiveness of the finished product. So we should think of the *making* as the signal, as long as we think of the act of making not merely as a series of physical manipulations but as a goal-directed process of which the product—the axe itself—is an intrinsic part. For the act is to be judged by the quality of its result. But is it to be judged wholly in that way? It is possible that the act of making serves not merely to identify the maker but to convey information about maker's quality: information not obtainable—or less easily obtainable—from inspection of the finished product together with knowledge of the maker's identity. Here there may be an important insight into the origin of *style*.

## 8. Performance art?

Throughout this section I'm grateful to John Ferrari for suggestions made in discussion, and for allowing me to read sections of a book he is preparing on art and communication.[42]

The maker creates a well-wrought handaxe by using certain skills and capacities: strength, fine motor control, high levels of executive function, imagination and memory. The handaxe is then a record, or trace, of the exercise, and hence the presence, of these skills and capacities. Indeed, a handaxe is especially notable as to some extent an *embodiment* of those skills and capacities, since its surface displays the marks of the individual blows that shaped it. And the maker's act of making is also an embodiment of those skills and capacities; the maker has a certain way of making which is evident in physical movements: a way of making that may be economical and elegant, or shows a surprising combination of strength and control, or displays intense concentration combined with an evident capacity to retain a memory-image of one side of the stone while working on the other—or perhaps it is unimpressive in all these respects and does not do much for the maker's reproductive prospects. And for all that makers know nothing of signalling and reproductive fitness, they may be very aware that episodes of making attract the attention of potential mates, and that there is *some* connection between the making and the subsequent mating. It would not then be surprising that makers did things to emphasize their making, to make it a more salient and impressive activity, and hence more likely to attract attention. Just to have some terms, let's say that the way a creature does something is its *mode* of doing; having a *style* is a matter of having a mode

---

[42] Provisionally titled *The Messages We Send*. My terminology does not always match Ferrari's, but the ideas are very largely his.

which is affected by practical reasoning that involves beliefs and desires about how the mode will affect observers. The situation I have just described is one in which there is a transition from mere mode of making to style; turning mode into style, the handaxe-maker deliberately alters characteristics of the signal. Would this transition be a form of deception, likely to destabilize the signalling system itself?

It might be dishonest if the signaller were hiding his intention, pretending to act merely for the purpose of producing a desirable handaxe but actually magnifying aspects of his performance to impress observers. But it need not be dishonest, even when driven by a covert intention, for the character of the performance still serves as a reliable indication of how the maker *can* behave—with what elegance, strength, economy, or whatever—irrespective of the maker's motive for behaving that way. Much then depends on whether there is an important (that is, fitness relevant) distinction between what one can do when driven by the desire for salience, and what one can do without that motive; if there is such a distinction then receivers of these signals will be less good at discriminating suitable mates and the signal will, indeed, be less than wholly honest.

There's another way covert magnification of the signal can remain honest. The capacity to turn mode into style might be a (to some extent) *general* capacity, one the agent can apply to a variety of circumstances. And a capacity deliberately to vary one's behaviour according to the demands of a social situation (call this trait T) may itself be a fitness-enhancing trait worth signalling to a prospective mate, whose progeny can then expect to inherit the trait and thrive as a result. In that case, the act of making may well evolve in such a way as to signal possession of T; increases in signal strength are cheaper for those who possess T to a greater degree, for they are better able to adjust their making in appropriate ways, thus satisfying Grafen's condition. Nor need the covert-ness of the signaller's intention to alter the signal prevent receivers from discriminating in favour of high-quality signallers; they have merely to find attractive the kinds of alterations to the making process which do derive from possession of T, and not find attractive those that do not.[43] Whether they in addition know that these are deliberate alterations is irrelevant.

That said, cognitive evolution did eventually give rise to an understanding among our ancestors of the style-generating intentions of makers (along, of course, with a vast range of their other intentions). We know that because we have that understanding ourselves. At this point, receivers would have understood, at least in many cases, that the act of making revealed something about the desires of the maker. And now a further step is possible: signallers can now indicate a differential interest in receivers, varying their imposition of style in such a way that they make it clear which receivers they are most interested in. At this point handaxes become instruments of meaning in something like Grice's sense; an intended effect of their making is achieved only if the

---

[43] Stated more carefully: they have merely to find those alterations to the making process more attractive which derive from possession of T to a greater degree.

receiver recognizes the intention.[44] In the next section I shall suggest another way in which handaxes, through the long period of cognitive evolution of the Old Stone Age, went from being instruments in a cognitively impoverished signalling game, to playing a role in cognitively—and this time culturally—sophisticated transactions.

## 9.  The origin of symbols

It may seem as if I have left out a promising alternative explanation of the way in which handaxes could have been sexual signals, one which draws upon an emerging body of work on indicators of social status.[45] Two pairs of jeans may have indistinguishable capacity to enhance bodily attractiveness, while presenting quite different signals concerning wealth, social status, or intimacy with fashion trends. And the effectiveness of these signals also does not depend on it being manifest that the wearer is the maker—by and large the opposite is true. Might handaxes have functioned similarly as status indicators? Let us call the hypothesis that they did the *Status Hypothesis* (*Status*), and the hypothesis, which I have been dealing with up to now, that handaxes were sexual signals the *Reproductive Fitness Hypothesis* (*Fitness*).

It is important to see, first of all, that acceptance of *Status* is not the same as acceptance of a symbolic role for handaxes. Like *Fitness, Status* need not be understood as assigning a signalling role to handaxes which depends on receivers understanding the mechanism of signalling. If handaxes functioned as *Status* suggests, they might have done so because people had a natural tendency (a tendency unmediated by knowledge or inference) to be more attracted towards those they understood to be the possessors of these objects, where this tendency was advantageous simply because, as a matter of fact and not because anyone knew this, possession of these objects was strongly correlated with fitness-enhancing traits like high status or capacity to dominate others.

*Status* is a hypothesis worth considering. But it is a mistake, I think, to see it as a rival to *Fitness*. Indeed, it seems to me best to assume that handaxes eventually acquired the role of status indicators *because* they had a prior history as fitness indicators. If finely wrought handaxes were not already serving as indicators of high quality in a mate, why would mere possession of such an object come to be associated with the powerfulness of the possessor? After all, the largest, most elaborately shaped and most finely pointed instances are not better tools than more workaday items, and don't serve to indicate that the possessor is going to be a better provisioner than other suitors (remember, we are assuming at this point that handaxes are not fitness indicators for their makers). In the

---

[44] This is not quite the meaning of Grice's classical formulation ('Meaning', *Philosophical Review*, 66 (1957): 377–88). In the situation envisaged, the signaller S intends receiver R to have as a reason for thinking that S is interested in R, that S intentionally adjusts the style of making; shorten this to 'S intends R to have as a reason for thinking P, that Q.' Q on its own provides R with a reason for believing P; R need not have as a reason for thinking P that S intended that R think that P.

[45] See e.g., Aimée M. Plourde, 'The Origins of Prestige Goods as Honest Signals of Skill and Knowledge', *Human Nature*, 19 (2008): 374–88.

more than one million years of handaxe production, hominids went through significant biological and, eventually, cultural change. As culture and cognition developed, and as emphasis on social differentiation increased, there may have been a shift in the function of these artefacts from being indicators of skill to indicators of status. If *Fitness* is correct, and the handaxe form went through a stage where it served as a fitness indicator of the maker, it could well have come to be thought a valuable and indeed mysterious object, one worth possessing. In the context of a long history of slowly emerging culture which it is fair to assume was going on in the Middle Stone Age it is plausible to see here a mechanism by which symbolic functions could be established. By some process of biological or cultural evolution—or more likely through a combination of both forces—people came to ascribe meanings to objects and to have their behaviour towards those objects and other things modulated through recognition of those meanings. John Searle imagines a wall, which once served as a physical barrier to entry to a certain place, crumbling over time but retaining its status as a barrier, not through its causal properties but because it has, by collective intentionality, the status of a barrier conferred on it.[46] The process of symbolization I am imagining is somewhat different: an object serves as a signal of some trait, and in virtue of this it confers on its maker a reproductive advantage; all this takes place without anyone understanding the processes involved. As brains grow, population rises, and articulated language comes into play, hominid cognition becomes more sophisticated, less tied to the here and now of experience and more able to reflect on general aspects of phenomena. It may then strike people that there is some connection between handaxes and sexual/social success. Being as ignorant of evolutionary theory as most of us are, these people would not have understood the nature of this connection; but they might see that there was some connection. One explanation would then be that these objects exerted hidden causal powers that involve action at a distance on agents; at this point we have the beginnings of a magical explanation, and it is reasonable to assume that the earliest symbols, at least those outside the realm of language, functioned within a set of assumptions about their magical powers. Handaxes may have been both the first art works and—later in their history—the first symbols.[47]

★

It's time to extract the central message from this long and speculative account. Acheulean handaxes are a valuable source of information about our very distant ancestors; many are also beautiful and finely crafted objects. Their credentials as aesthetic artefacts meshes with an evolutionary hypothesis which, while also speculative, draws only on well attested principles of perceptual bias, sexual selection, and reliable signalling. And if this hypothesis concerning their role in sexual selection is true, the way is open to a plausible story about how, later on, they provided our ancestors with the first symbolic objects.

---

[46] John Searle, *The Construction of Social Reality* (Harmondsworth: Allen Lane, The Penguin Press, 1995), Chapter 2.
[47] See also Kohn, *As We Know it*, p. 142 on 'pre-symbolic ritual'.

## 10. Art

It's also time to confess that there has been some strategic overstatement here. I end with a reflection on our use of the term 'art', mine included.

When we think in the broadest terms about art, we are confronted with a complex web of relations between ideas of beauty, design, display, individual achievement, tradition, communal meaning, and the institutions and practices we have developed which express and sustain these ideas. We can map this complexity in various ways, and one is to mark out a part of the territory as 'art'; there is currently a range of proposals before us about how best to do this. But none has, I think, managed to identify any particular subset of elements and relationships as primary—something that Grice managed to do with the similarly chaotic domain of meaning, finding a centre from which to impose intellectual order on the various things we call by that name. I don't believe we shall find a comparably satisfying solution to the problem of art; certainly we have not done so yet. Instead I treat the domain described above—the web of interconnections between beauty, design, and the rest—as a failed state, divisible in various more or less arbitrary ways but on which no centralizing order has been—perhaps can be—imposed. Proposals which present themselves as theories of what art is are better treated as attempts to elaborate a theory of one or other of these arbitrary divisions. At least some of these proposals have their uses, given some prior purpose to our investigations. It is interesting to think about the institutions of the art world, how they have evolved, how they function, and what art-making possibilities they give rise to; it is interesting to tell a story about how representational realism gave rise to abstraction, minimalism, and eventually to conceptualism; we may also have a legitimate interest in the enduring and apparently universal appeal of finely crafted objects, and wonder about the source of this interest. Engaging in any of these projects, it is tempting to say that we are concerned with art, if only to counter the attempts of others to monopolize the term for their own purposes; perhaps that is what I have been doing here. But in the end what matters is how interesting the project is and with what success it is carried out, rather than how we label it.[48]

So, is art half a million years old? Well, something pretty important within that complex and ungovernable web is: something important to tracing the history of

---

[48] There is an important issue here which I shan't try to settle though it's worth acknowledging. We might opt for what has been called 'art concept pluralism', insisting that *art* is a legitimate and coherent concept, but one definable in distinct, non-equivalent ways. In a more revisionary mood, we might argue that *art* is a rhetorically confusing and dialectically unhelpful notion (or non-notion), which ought to be replaced by a range of non-equivalent, non-competing and conceptually tractable notions fit for their various purposes. The first of these views is argued for by Uidhir and Brown, who gain comfort from what they see as a relevant parallel between *art* and the biological notion of *species* (Christy Mag Uidhir and P. D. Magnus, 'Art Concept Pluralism', *Metaphilosophy*, 42 (2011): 83–97). Advocates of the second view will also find support from a debate in biology: Griffiths argues that we should simply abandon the notion of *innateness* and use, as purposes dictate, one or other of a range of theoretically well-entrenched notions (Paul Griffiths, 'What is Innateness?', *The Monist*, 85 (2002): 70–85; see also Mateo Mameli and Patrick Bateson, 'Innateness and the sciences', *Biology and Philosophy*, 22 (2006): 155–88).

everything else that got, eventually, to be part of that web, something older than, and—if my speculations are right—causal antecedent to the symbolic culture so often taken to be the condition for art itself (as if there was such a thing). The products of this half a million or more years of aesthetic activity have no less a right to be called art than do Duchamp's ready-mades or Sol LeWitt's paragraphs. We ought not to think that the latter have a *better* claim to the label because they happen to have been created in more or less contemporary Paris or New York rather than in the African Old Stone Age. A better claim can be made out only by showing how that system of labelling picks out something with a stronger capacity to order the whole system than mine has. I have not yet heard an argument for that conclusion.

# 2

# The Fragility of Aesthetic Knowledge: Aesthetic Psychology and Appreciative Virtues

*Matthew Kieran*

It is a commonplace that collectors such as Larry Gagosian and Charles Saatchi have a big influence on the contemporary art market. Established investors and new collectors alike pay attention to their tastes. Indeed more generally across the arts, dealers, distributors, and commercial producers have a massive influence on taste in terms of what they put on, publish, or promote within the public domain. Public institutions and galleries are often not far behind and it is no coincidence that publicly funded work often bears all the hallmarks of marketplace trends. This is nothing new. While the forms of commercial support often differ, from the Florence of the Medici through Victorian Britain to the present day, patronage and the marketplace have often dressed up the accoutrements of power and social prestige in the finery of taste.

Analytic aesthetics has standardly been uninterested in such matters. An empirical concern with what influences people's actual taste is one thing, a philosophical interest in what constitutes good taste and the role of aesthetic expertise seems to be quite another. Nonetheless in what follows it will be argued that attention to empirical work on judgements of taste and appreciative claims presents a particular challenge to traditional aesthetics. Recent work in the empirical sciences suggests that we are extremely bad at recognizing when, where, and why we like something (or at least think we do). We think we know why we like the art we do. Yet all sorts of subconscious factors from status cues and subliminal familiarity to social signals influence appreciation and judgement. Working out how we can avoid such pitfalls will itself suggest the importance of a new approach within traditional aesthetics, one that puts character centre stage and involves elaborating the nature and role of particular aesthetic virtues and vices.

# 1. Aesthetic appreciation and justification

We take it as a mark or indeed constitutive of something's being aesthetically valuable that, at least under certain conditions, an object gives rise to pleasure in our appreciation of it. Thus where we derive pleasure from our appreciative engagement with a work we have defeasible reason to judge it to be good as art. We also recognize that our appreciation and judgements can go awry. The conditions under which we are apprehending something or the state we are in can distort aesthetic judgement and there is a crucial role for expertise (Hume 1993). Aesthetic appreciation draws on the cultivation of a wide range of perceptual capacities, cognitive-affective responses and relational knowledge. Hence appreciation is in principle always open to further refinement and discrimination.

A work's aesthetic features depend not merely on its directly perceivable non-aesthetic ones but also on its relational ones. What it is to identify a work as belonging to a certain appreciatively relevant category and thus what its relevant representational, expressive, and cognitive features are, often requires a large amount of relational knowledge (Walton 1970). Devoid of background knowledge we might be unable to identify and thus appreciate appropriately something as an Impressionist painting, a late Titian, an ironic pastiche of a particular literary style, or bluegrass music. Furthermore judgements of creativity and originality depend upon historical and comparative judgements.

Aesthetic objects designed to reward appreciative activity are typically complex and dense so small differences in tone, marking, or articulation can affect the aesthetic character of a piece. Hence the more discriminating and flexible an appreciator is, the more likely she will be able to pick up on aesthetically relevant features of a work—ones the less discriminating among us might miss. This is, after all, why we often pay attention to critics or friends whose judgement we trust. Expert appreciators can and sometimes do point us towards aspects of a work we may have missed in ways that transform our experience and judgement of the object concerned.

Whatever else is true the above is something that any adequate account of aesthetic value and appreciation must do justice to. Furthermore it is a desideratum of any such account that it precludes certain kinds of reasons as playing a justificatory role in underwriting aesthetic judgements. If someone judges a work to be artistically good because it is worth a certain amount of money, from a particular time, or people from a certain class like it then something has gone wrong. Aesthetic evaluations cannot be justified in virtue of reasons such as financial value, historical date of origination, or the preferences of certain social groups. This is not to deny that there might be complex relations between such things and the fundamental reasons that justify why a work is aesthetically good. It is just to say that at base such explanations cannot in and of themselves constitute justifying reasons. Thus to the extent that such factors contribute towards a subject's aesthetic appreciation as such and formation of a judgement that a work is good as art, both the appreciative activity and the judgement arrived at may be suspect. This is, no doubt, what prompted Hume to say that true critics must not only possess delicacy of imagination and sympathy but they must also be free from the dictates of prejudice and fashion. Thus far so unproblematic one might think. As long as we attend carefully to an aesthetic object and consciously reflect on the reasons why we like what we do then we should be in a good position to arrive at a good aesthetic judgement. We may lack the expertise that others possess but nonetheless it is presumed we can be sure enough that our appreciative activity and judgement is not being distorted by extraneous considerations. The problem is that as recent psychological work shows, we are often particularly bad at knowing when our appreciation and judgements are being driven by aesthetically irrelevant factors.

## 2. A challenge from psychology

Scientists at the California Institute of Technology and the University of Stanford recently conducted a distinctive wine tasting (Plassmann *et al.* 2008). Subjects were told they would be asked to sample five different cabernet sauvignons to study the relationship between tasting time and perceived flavours. The wine was administered via a set of tubes to a subject contained within an fMRI scanner. As each putatively different wine was administered to a subject it was identified by its supposed price, ranging from $5 to $90. However, there were only three different wines involved. Two wines were administered twice, one marked with its actual price ($5) and alternatively a 900% mark up ($45), another with its actual price ($90) and a 900% mark down ($10). All subjects reported being able to taste five distinct wines and the more expensive the price cue for a wine was the more subjects liked it. The pleasure apparently derived by the subjects in tasting the wine was significantly affected by its perceived price.

Subjects in the above experiment were screened for liking and occasionally drinking wine. It might be thought that perhaps the undue influence of perceived price was related to subjects' relative inexperience. However, the original inspiration for the experiment suggests this is not straightforwardly the case. A few years earlier Brochet (2001) conducted a renowned series of experiments with oenology students. One experiment involved asking fifty-four subjects to give their appraisal of a red and a white wine. Unbeknown to the subjects the 'red' wine was the same as the white, though its colour had been changed to red with a tasteless food dye. No one spotted the difference. Indeed subjects used descriptors typical of white wine in characterizing the taste of the unmodified wine and descriptors typical for red wine in relation to the coloured wine. In a related experiment Brochet asked subjects to appraise wine from a vin de table bottle and an expensive grand-cru one. The subjects' descriptions and appraisals diverged according to the nature of the bottle. Forty subjects thought the wine from the grand-cru bottle was worth drinking, while only twelve rated the wine from the vin de table bottle worth drinking. It was the same wine. Brochet had decanted a middle-of-the-road Bordeaux into both bottles. Even those with a fair degree of expertise enjoy wine more just because they think it is more expensive while assuming, falsely, this is because it is aesthetically superior.

Indeed, as remarked upon elsewhere (Kieran 2010; Prinz 2011), familiarity itself can afford pleasure and we often mistake the pleasures afforded by familiarity for something else. In an experiment at Cornell University, James Cutting taught an introduction to psychology module exposing subjects to slide reproductions of Impressionist paintings. He had previously established that students generally preferred the more commonly reproduced paintings over more rarely produced ones, even though many students could not remember having seen them before. During the psychology module Cutting then exposed subjects more frequently to the less publicly reproduced works and less frequently to the more widely reproduced ones. When the module finished students were then asked to rate Impressionist paintings. Despite having no reliable recall of whether or not they had seen the works before, the exposure effect meant that the previously established preference for more commonly reproduced works had disappeared (Cutting 2006).

We might not realize that features of the environment are doing any work or even that we have seen or heard of something before, and yet subconscious recognition can trigger greater pleasure and deceive us into thinking we are enjoying something more because it is highly aesthetically valuable—rather than being a function of status cues, the environment, or because we have seen something in a magazine or as a poster on a friend's wall. Identifying and evaluating aesthetically relevant features can be cued and significantly shaped by factors we are not consciously aware of. The fundamental problem is that in the aesthetic realm we are particularly susceptible to going awry because of the epistemic role that pleasure plays in relation to aesthetic judgement. It is all too easy to mistake the pleasures of status and recognition with pleasure gained in appreciation.

The recognition that pleasure plays a distinctive epistemic role in the aesthetic realm does not require commitment to substantive claims often taken to constitute or fall out of the autonomy of aesthetic judgement. One can hold that aesthetic knowledge is transmissible by testimony (contra Kant 2000: sect. 32–3), acquirable without first-hand experience (contra Wollheim 1980: 233), and that aesthetic judgement can be undermined as easily as some other kinds of judgements by others (contra Hopkins 2001) while nonetheless recognizing that pleasure in appreciation is a fundamental ground of aesthetic value. Appreciating a work involves deriving pleasure in the activity of apprehending and responding to aesthetically relevant features as realized in and through the work. Thus where someone takes pleasure in appreciating a work in aesthetically appropriate ways, there is a strong epistemic ground for judging it to be good. At the very least, pleasure is a first-personal epistemic route to an object's aesthetic value and it is a requirement of the adequacy of any putative account of aesthetic value that it recognize this to be so. Even on the weakest plausible conception of the role that pleasure in appreciation plays, namely that where pleasure is taken in appreciation it is a prima facie epistemic indicator of value, problems arise because, as the experiments show, we are extremely bad at identifying defeaters even in the first-person case.

## 3. Psychological and aesthetic explanations

Human beings are social animals and from an extremely early age onwards we define ourselves partly in terms of our relations with others. Indeed many of the most fundamental goods available to us are partly constituted by and through relations to others. Furthermore, intra-group hierarchical relations and in- and out-group identifications are central to our development and self-conceptions. It is not only important to us that we perceive ourselves to be and indeed are perceived by others to stand in social relations to various groups but that we have a certain social status or standing relative to others (Buss 2007: 355–83; Abrams and Hogg 1999).

As argued elsewhere one primary mechanism for realizing the drive for social status is defining oneself as superior relative to other individuals or groups. Indeed such a drive is likely to be exacerbated the greater the degree to which a culture emphasizes the importance of competition and individuality of self-expression. This explains the drive towards snobbery and unfortunately the aesthetic realm is particularly susceptible to snobbery (Kieran 2010). Snobbish judgements are ones where aesthetically irrelevant social features play a causal role in shaping someone's appreciative activity such that the judgement arrived at, alongside the relevant rationalizations, are to be more fundamentally explained in terms of the drive to feel or appear superior relative to some individual or group. The aesthetic realm is easily exploitable in such terms not just because it is a realm where expertise plays a large part, given one could in principle always be open to ever greater degrees of discrimination and relational knowledge, but due to the role that pleasure plays.

The end goal of the practice includes pleasure in the activity of appreciation. Hence pleasures derived for aesthetically irrelevant, social reasons can easily be confused with or dressed up as pleasures derived from proper and indeed more expert aesthetic appreciation. The situation is compounded by the lack of straightforward publicly available regulative norms. If someone is making mathematical or philosophical snobbish judgements it is easier to spot since it is hard to do these things well and not be guided by the right sorts of reasons. If you start trying to fool yourself or others you are more of an expert in mathematics, science, or etiquette than you really are, you'll be easily shown up much more quickly in these areas than in the aesthetic arena. The norm of first-person authority, due to the role of pleasure, explains why this is not straightforwardly the case in the aesthetic realm. Aesthetic evaluations are less easily amenable to public justification and more epistemically opaque than scientific, mathematical, and even philosophical ones. It need not be thought that only pleasure has this kind of epistemic role in the aesthetic realm, since there might be a range of sensations and emotions other than pleasure that do so, and, moreover, it might not even be distinctive of the aesthetic realm that this is so. After all, perhaps the emotions play a similar epistemic role in relation to certain kinds of moral, charientic, or social judgements. Rather the point is that the role of pleasure is sufficient to explain why an agent's aesthetic judgement is particularly susceptible to being driven by and confused with aesthetically irrelevant social factors.

The drive to cultivate and maintain a positive self-image both for one's self and with respect to the perceptions of others can manifest itself in other ways. Fundamental drives associated with cultivating satisfying social relations are also involved in explaining the nature of situational cues and the role of social influence. The drive towards conformity, for example, is important in establishing membership of certain groups (Latane 1981: Latane and Bourgeois 2001). Actions at odds with the attitudes of a group identified with often bring social costs with them. The extent to which this is so and how it is manifested will itself depend upon variables such as the relevant norms operating within the groups identified with and how significant the group is to the person concerned. Indeed there is a tension between the drive for conformity in order to establish group membership and non-conformity in order to establish superiority.

The issues are complex but nonetheless the point is that our basic social drives—especially for reasons concerning social group identification and status—are commonly realized through defining ourselves as belonging to some groups rather than others and as superior relative to other individuals or groups. Hence we are particularly susceptible to being influenced by factors that enable us to appear more knowledgeable or discriminating than we really are. The thing about taste is that it is so much easier to deceive one's self or others that you are getting things right—taking the pleasures of recognition or status to be those of refined appreciation. Hence the huge amounts of money, market research, and promotion multinational corporations spend on branding and product placement.

Traditionally, we assume that we know when and why we're making the aesthetic judgements we do. It is the taste of the wine, the look of the painting, or the profundity of the text. However, if the science is sound, then this is not quite right. It can be extremely difficult to tell why we like something since we are often being pushed one way or another by situational cues and social influences we are not even aware of. Ordinarily people are much more influenced by subconsciously processed environmental features and social considerations in forming aesthetic judgements than we realize. Even aesthetic experts or rather those with some expertise—despite being such—are often more influenced than they think. Moreover, expertise brings with it a greater capacity for rationalization. At least for those who know something but are not ideal critics (many of us) there will be a tendency to go awry due to irrelevant subconscious factors much more often than is presumed. This does not underwrite aesthetic scepticism as such but it does underwrite the following—if we are interested in aesthetic appreciation and justifying our judgements we need to be much more careful about attending to what is driving our appreciation and why.

## 4. Facilitators versus distorters

It is tempting to think that the tricks our minds can play on us simply distort aesthetic appreciation and judgement. Yet matters are not so straightforward. First, while being driven by snobbery or conformity may often constitute an appreciative vice, it is important to realize that judgements issuing from such are not necessarily wrong. Second, the cultivation of expertise and appropriate appreciation in some given aesthetic area often involves making use of the very situational and social markers we are concerned with. Although far from infallible in lots of contexts such factors can be useful heuristic guides. This is not to say that high prices in the art markets, the environment of a gallery, or social convergence in judgements are finely discriminating guides to artistic value. After all, we are familiar enough with the recognition that today's 'genius' may be tomorrow's also ran. Fashionably pricey art can end up seeming pretty mediocre taken out of its social context. In 1882 Edwin Long, the one-time doyen of the Victorian art world, sold his *Babylonian Marriage Market* for a record-shattering 6,300 guineas at Christie's. Yet we hardly hear of him now and why indeed should we? The huge, laboured, static canvases of biblical scenes that were his stock in trade and upon which his reputation was built are far from compelling. Nonetheless, those influencing the art market, setting up galleries or who take some interest in appreciating art tend to know a fair amount. The marketplace, gallery, or social convergences of opinion are often rough guides to something. It is no surprise that in seventeenth-century Amsterdam, Rembrandt was one of the most popular and indeed expensive of contemporary artists. Financial and social indicators are far from infallible, but they are not worthless. The high cost of a bottle of wine or work of art, the setting in which we are presented with them, or social opinion are grossly simplistic if taken as having a direct relation to the appreciative worth of an object. Nonetheless when construed in terms of whether a wine is worth tasting or a work worth looking at they can be useful markers.

How useful such rough indicators are depends upon the level of expertise someone already has. If someone has only just started drinking coffee or is new to the visual arts, then a nice looking café with a Gaggia machine or an art gallery that people are going on about are not bad places to start from. There is some reason to believe that people who have some expertise and interest have gone to the trouble of presenting for appreciation the kind of coffee or art they think has some value.

Indeed, more often than not there are a cluster of markers and the valences involved might not all point in the same direction. When looking for somewhere to have a coffee you might come across two cafés virtually opposite each other. While one of them looks nicer than the other (pro), with fancy coffee signs in the window and espresso china, and is slightly more expensive (pro), it might be virtually empty when compared with the one across the road (con). How to weigh such considerations will depend upon one's estimation of the likely explanation. Perhaps the more crowded café seems to be populated by students who have less money to spend, or perhaps the empty one seems more like a chain.

Nonetheless, to the extent that such contingent markers do more work in shaping our judgements than we think they remain problematic. Drinking coffee surrounded by the superficial sheen of the more expensive place might afford pleasure even though the taste of the coffee affords little and I might mistake the former cause of my pleasure for the latter. Yet it is important to recognize that, especially from the viewpoint of the naïve or recently inducted, such markers are often useful albeit extremely rough and ready guides. Indeed, even where the naïve coffee drinker knows that she derives pleasure via an appropriate aesthetic route from the taste of the coffee, such markers can sometimes give reason to be agnostic about or undermine the aesthetic judgement the pleasure apparently underwrites. The fact that the café's popularity has recently become a thing of the past and a renowned London coffee blog reveals people's dissatisfaction with it might give reason to suspect that the appropriate but naïve pleasure taken in the coffee is insufficiently refined. Thus though the pleasure taken may incline one to judge that the coffee is superb, various markers conjoined with the recognition that one is not particularly well versed in coffee drinking may rather underwrite the judgement that it is not bad.

The situation can be more rather than less problematic where we are concerned with someone who has some knowledge and expertise. A little knowledge can often be a dangerous thing. The more aware someone becomes of the complexity of potentially aesthetically relevant features and relations regarding an aesthetic object and their markers the more ways there are in which someone's appreciation and judgement can go wrong. First, in contrast with the barely inducted naïve appreciator, if someone is fairly used to drinking decent coffee or appreciating art then the usefulness of markers such as an Illy sign or being a much talked about gallery goes down. Second, as aesthetic expertise and knowledge is acquired there is a natural tendency to fixate upon and fetishize the aspects the subject has acquired knowledge and expertise about along with their attendant markers—sometimes at the expense of carefully attending to other features of the object or indeed the resultant responses.

It is not uncommon, for example, to find someone who has begun to acquire some appreciation of wine to fixate upon region, appellation, and year. In general as one acquires a passion for and some expertise in any given aesthetic area, it is all too easy and very tempting to allow the pleasures of exercising the expertise one has acquired to overgeneralize or shape one's judgements for the reasons glossed above—we feel pleasure in the recognition that we can classify works or draw on knowledge that others may lack so that we can belong to groups we identify with or indeed feel superior to. If anything, without undue care those with some expertise and knowledge are more likely to be prey to underlying irrelevant social and situational factors driving their aesthetic pronouncements because they are more likely to think, in contrast with the naïve appreciator, that they really know something that in turn justifies their judgement. A little knowledge and expertise exponentially increases the capacity for effective rationalizations. It is easier to be an effective snob if one can talk with some knowledge concerning whatever one is being snobbish about.

## 5. Self-insulation and appreciative virtues

How can we avoid such pitfalls? We can be motivated to appreciate a work for a host of non-aesthetic reasons ranging from the desire for distraction or the desire for social status to the desire to improve one's mind and gain knowledge. Nonetheless we must come to be motivated in the activity of appreciation to attend to and respond to the work's aesthetically relevant features for appropriate sorts of reasons in order for our appreciation to be aesthetically virtuous and properly ground our aesthetic judgements. Indeed this must be the governing motivation in our appreciative activity. Where this is not the case then our appreciative activity is likely to go awry in fixing on irrelevant features or responding inappropriately for non-aesthetic reasons.

Fair Francesca may be motivated to appreciate wine over beer or go to the Hans Bellmer exhibition instead of the Chapman brothers show due to social reasons. Yet as long as her responses to what it is she engages with are guided by an interest in the object's aesthetically relevant features then her appreciation is, at least in this respect, unproblematic. By contrast, Flawed Frederick's judgement that Andy Goldsworthy's work is no good is driven by a desire to appear superior to those who like what is popular. Furthermore, the drive for superiority causally explains why his appreciation fixes on elements of the works with mass appeal and thereby derides the obvious technical engineering feats involved while failing to apprehend the ways in which the work can be sculpturally light and minimal. Indeed Frederick's overblown praise for contemporary artists that are deliberately superficially difficult and devoid of mass appeal is to be similarly explained.

If someone's motivation for social status feeds through into appreciative activity and plays a causal role in explaining why aesthetically irrelevant social features shape responses to and the formation of aesthetic judgements about the work concerned, we have a case of appreciative vice. It is one thing to come to engage with and be interested in works for non-aesthetic reasons. It is quite another for such motivations to feed through into and drive someone's aesthetic appreciation and judgement. Awareness that we have social drives and biases that can distort aesthetic appreciation and judgement should itself help to put us on our guard with respect to our own aesthetic pronouncements and those of others. But is there anything else more concrete we can do to insulate ourselves from being prey to such errors?

We can look out for the tendency to go in for selective attention, comparison bias, confabulation, or pejorative characterizations. We can critically reflect on the particular biases someone is especially prone to and look out for the fetishizing of heuristics, use of aesthetic principles out of context, or a tendency to overgeneralize for aesthetically irrelevant reasons. In doing so we should consider the situation and ask what, aesthetic interest apart, might be doing the work in driving appreciation and judgement. Where there is a social drive or desire that might be doing some work such problematic strategies might be indulged in for the sake of self-aggrandizement in ways that could render our own judgement or the testimony of others epistemically and appreciatively suspect.

Cultivating critical awareness about such strategies might help us to insulate ourselves against the effects of undue social influences in striving to become what Hume terms a true critic. We should seek to cultivate critical sympathy for what an artist is trying to do, be able to take up different points of view in imagination, be perceptually and emotionally discriminating, free from the dictates of prejudice and fashion, seek out comparative experiences, compare our own appreciation with that of others, and seek to give appropriate reasons which underwrite our aesthetic judgements. Yet such critical awareness is not enough since, apart from anything else, such critical awareness could enable someone to exploit aesthetic judgement even more effectively for social reasons. What is also crucial is that the motivation to appreciate an aesthetic object for its own sake must govern the activity of appreciation. This is perfectly consistent with appreciating an object for other reasons since appreciation need not be *solely* for its own sake. Motivation can and often does make a difference to what we attend to, why, and how we come to form our judgement. Thus aspiring to be a good aesthetic appreciator depends upon cultivating a range of aesthetic virtues, several of which we will briefly consider in order to elucidate how this is so.

One important appreciative virtue is humility. Humility involves having a modest sense of the nature of one's appreciative activity in striving to do justice to a work rather than taking one's self to be the measure of the work. It also involves openness to the appreciative activity and judgements of others while simultaneously acknowledging that irrelevant factors might be shaping one's own appreciation and judgement. Pride in aesthetic expertise can not only blind us to aesthetically relevant features but can tempt us into falsely dismissing the possibility that we are influenced by market value, fashion, or gallery presentation. The self-aggrandizing estimation of one's appreciative activity and judgement that constitutes aesthetic pride also explains the ways in which the opinions of others are often too easily dismissed as the result of lack of expertise. Humility, by contrast, involves remaining open to the possibility that the appreciative activity of others may have picked up on something worth considering and thereby reveals something importantly new about a work. This is not to say that humility involves the abjection of one's own responses in favour of others or the assumption that one cannot but be unduly influenced. Humility does not involve thinking less of ourselves than others. This would be to err too far the other way. Rather it involves recognizing that we may be unduly influenced and that others may possess appreciative responses and indeed virtues we may lack—and where they do so, we should recognize them.

Another closely related appreciative virtue is critical self-honesty. Aesthetic self-deception is a constant temptation for the reasons given above and thus critical self-honesty is required in order to be appreciatively virtuous. One must never be afraid to admit one's judgement might be incomplete or wrong. Indeed one should be prepared to admit where one has hastily overgeneralized, been dismissive, or failed to attend carefully enough either to one's appreciative activity or the grounds for appreciative judgements arrived at. It is all too easy to allow drives and desires concerning our self-image and how we would like to be seen by others to drive our appreciation and concomitant rationalizations. All this achieves, however, is both a lack of fidelity to the formal object of appreciation and an undermining of the possibility of strengthening the motives and capacities required for virtuous appreciation. It is related to an abjection of one's self in favour of the views of others. What is required is the genuine motive to appreciate a work for what it is worth irrespective of whether or not in so doing one exposes one's self to the ridicule of others.

Articulating the importance of honesty in this way naturally leads into acknowledging the importance of another appreciative virtue. Courage is crucial in having the fortitude to be true to one's own responses and not cave in to received opinion or social influence without appreciative justification. It also involves being able to refrain from taking one's self or one's own appreciative activity too seriously at the right time. Where it turns out one has been unduly influenced one should have the capacity to laugh at oneself rather than give in to the temptation to reach for rationalizing explanations. Courage is also required to maintain critical sympathy and openness. It is all too easy to consider works in terms of preconceived schemas and assumptions. Yet the mere fact that a work does not conform to our expectations does not automatically show that it is no good. Hence the need to think about what an artist is attempting to do and what reasons might drive an artist to think that what is being presented for appreciation rewards such. Indeed courage thus links up with the virtue of patience. Worthwhile works often require discipline and perseverance. Aesthetic appreciation is sometimes hard and it is often tempting to reach for quick and easy judgements because we are tired or lazy. Yet at least where there are reasons for thinking it worth persevering we should do so or at the very least withhold from dismissive judgements.

While recognizing the role of the aesthetic virtues (and vices) is amenable to an Aristotelian particularist understanding of the nature of appreciation and judgement, such that it is a matter of an appropriate response, at the right time, in the right degree, towards the right kind of features in a way that is at odds with the notion of aesthetic principles, it need not disavow the possibility of aesthetic principles. It could be held that there are or could be aesthetic principles that govern virtuous appreciation and judgement while nonetheless recognizing that virtuous appreciation naturally accords with whatever the appropriate aesthetic principles are. The greater the security and strength of the aesthetic motivation in our appreciative activity the less likely we are to be susceptible to irrelevant social influences and the more likely we are to fix on appropriate aesthetic features which figure in the right sort of roles to underwrite aesthetic judgement and claims.

The challenge presented by experiments in the psychology of taste can be met if we pay attention not just to the strategies that cultivate greater critical self-awareness but also to motivation itself and thus the importance of aesthetic virtue. Aesthetic education should not only focus on appropriate aesthetic engagement and judgement on particular occasions but should also explicitly seek to cultivate the aesthetic virtues. More generally, as individuals we should strive to be sensitive to our own aesthetic virtues and vices as part of our aesthetic development and self-realization. If we do so then in both epistemic and appreciative terms we will thus be less likely to go awry and come much closer to the right sort of achievement qua aesthetic appreciator.

# References

Abrams, Dominic and Michael A. Hogg (1999). *Social Identity and Social Cognition*. Oxford: Blackwell.

Brochet, F. (2001). 'Tasting: Chemical Object Representation in the Field of Consciousness', Prix Coup de Cœur, Académie Amorin. Unpublished ms. available at http://www.academie-amorim.com

Buss, D. (2007). *Evolutionary Psychology: The New Science of the Mind*, 3rd edn. Boston: Allyn and Bacon.

Cutting, James E. (2006). 'The Mere Exposure Effect and Aesthetic Preference', in P. Locher, Colin Martindale, and Leonid Dorfman (eds.), *New Directions in Aesthetics, Creativity and the Psychology of Art*. New York: Baywood, pp. 33–46.

Hopkins, R. (2001). 'Kant, Quasi-Realism and the Autonomy of Aesthetic Judgement'. *European Journal of Philosophy*, 9: 166–89.

Hume, D. (1993 [1757]). 'Of the Standard of Taste', in his *Selected Essays*. Oxford: Oxford University Press, pp. 133–53.

Kant, I. (2000 [1793]). *Critique of the Power of Judgment*, trans. P. Guyer and E. Matthews. Cambridge: Cambridge University Press.

Kieran, M. (2010). 'The Vice of Snobbery: Aesthetic Knowledge, Justification and Virtue in Art Appreciation'. *Philosophical Quarterly*, 60: 243–63.

Latane, B. (1981). 'The Psychology of Social Impact'. *Scientific American*, 36: 343–65.

——and M. J. Bourgeois (2001). 'Successfully Stimulating Dynamic Social Impact', in J. P. Forgas and K. D. Williams (eds.), *Social Influence: Direct and Indirect Processes*. Hove: Psychology Press, pp. 61–78.

Plassmann, H., J. O'Doherty, B. Shiv, and A. Rangel (2008). 'Marketing Actions can Modulate Neural Representations of Experienced Pleasantness'. *Proceedings of the National Academy of Sciences of the United States of America*, 105: 1050–4.

Prinz, J (2011). 'Emotion and Aesthetic Value', in E. Schellekens and P. Goldie (eds.), *The Aesthetic Mind: Philosophy and Psychology* (Chapter 5, this volume). Oxford: Oxford University Press.

Walton, K. (1970). 'Categories of Art'. *Philosophical Review*, 79: 334–67.

Wollheim, R. (1980). *Art and Its Objects*, 2nd edn. Cambridge: Cambridge University Press.

# 3

# Neuroscience, Biology, and Brain Evolution in Visual Art

*Dahlia W. Zaidel*

Self-knowledge, insight into all phases of life and mind, springs from artistic imagination. That is the cognitive value of the arts.

(Langer 1962: 82)

Symbolic cognition is one of the hallmarks of the human mind. Visual artists are able to create something new on canvas, something that did not exist previously and does not actually exist in reality, even when, at times, it closely resembles reality, precisely because of this abstract and symbolic cognition. What the creation expresses is what is on the artist's mind, which includes conscious and unconscious experiences, political and cultural events, beliefs, fears, desires, emotions, and much more. The list is endless. Above all, the composition communicates a message from artist to viewer. Art is a communicative system able to relay ideas in ways not afforded in language alone.

The neuroscientific basis of art is a puzzle if only we consider that some symbolic behavior has been observed in animals as well, including non-human primates (Addessi *et al.* 2008; de Waal and Tyack 2003). Admittedly, not full-blown pervasive symbolic behavior as is observed in humans, but symbolic nevertheless. And, yet, animals do not produce art (one exception perhaps is the bowerbird (Diamond 1982; Miller 2000; Zaidel 2009, 2010). The fact that they do not would suggest that a certain threshold of symbolism capacity, abstraction, and referential cognition must be reached before art can be produced (to say nothing of other neuroanatomical and neurochemical underpinnings). Whatever that threshold level might be, and regardless of when and how in evolutionary times it was reached, it could have given rise to additional human communicative systems as well, namely language, body language, hand gestures, and facial expressions. The precursors must have been in place for millions of years, since non-human primates have their own vocalization language, body language, hand gestures, and facial expressions (Premack 2007; Remedios *et al.* 2009). Other critical brain capacities, then, ones that are unique to humans, must play significant roles in art production.

We often think of human language as the prime example of symbolic cognition. While the neurological basis of language has been extensively studied in the past 150 years, and quite a bit is now known and understood regarding how it is organized in the brain, attempts to zero in on the neuroanatomical underpinning of art are greatly hampered by absence of clear definitions of the components of pictorial art (or any art). Neuroscientists and neuropsychologists need reducible (defined) components to be able to link them to neural regions and pathways. Currently, except for spatial organization required in pictures, a function specialized in the right parietal lobe, there is no simple way of achieving such definitions. On the other hand, the whole of pictorial production may indeed be more significant than its parts, and general components may be sufficient. Skills, talent, and creativity are good examples of such components.

Several intriguing and relevant issues to the neuroscience of art are discussed in this chapter. (1) Brain regions and visual sensory considerations: The appearance of art stems from both sensory properties, namely the eyes themselves, and central properties, namely brain regions specialized in processing spatial cognition, color knowledge, and aesthetics. (2) *Homo sapiens* evolution: When did the symbolic cognition threshold reach a level that triggered abundant art production by *Homo sapiens* and what else happened simultaneously by way of cognitive changes? (3) Biology and sexual selection strategies: The display feature of pictorial art might be explained in biological motivation terms, ones that involve neural motivational systems in the brain particularly associated with mate selection strategies (Miller 2000, 2001; Zahavi 1978; Zaidel 2010).

## 1. Peripheral sensory influences

Vision is influenced by neurological events, starting with the eye itself and ending in the vision processing regions of the brain. In this regard, several scenarios with potential effects on the appearance of art can be drawn. The first concerns the clarity of the artist's sensory vision arising from physical structures within the eye, such as the crystalline lens and retina. Distortions and fuzziness in the composition can be caused by the shape and elasticity of the lens, or they can be caused by abnormal or diseased arrangements of the photoreceptors in the retina, and other eye-related causes.

Consider visual processes and the use of colors in paintings. The first stage in seeing colors resides in retinal photoreceptors known as cones, which are situated in the back of the eyeball, and are in fact specialized neurons (Hubel 1995). The fovea is located in the retina and through its anatomical and physiological makeup facilitates focused vision. The cones enable us to see colors with chemical reactions triggered by the lightwaves entering the eye and hitting the fovea. The chemical reaction initiates neuro-signals to the vision processing regions in the cortex, via several subcortical synaptic stations. In the occipital lobes reside the primary visual areas where neuronal computations are performed on the signals arriving from the synaptic stations and resulting in conscious perception of colors. But suppose, for example, there is abnormality in the cones in the first place, as in colorblindness (color deficiency). In such cases colors are not perceived normally. More of one cone receptor type than another or a complete absence of a receptor skews the lightwave information reaching the brain, particularly the vision processing regions in the occipital lobes. The condition is caused by genetic transmission of a mutation on the maternal X chromosome, typically affecting males. In colorblindness cases, some colors end up being seen as shades of gray. A colorblind artist can be the best painter in the world but when it comes to colors, the eye's physiological condition impacts the choice of colors (Lanthony 2001). Several such artists have been identified (for review see Zaidel 2005). With non-colorblind artists, it is not known why artists apply their own unique coloring techniques (Van Gogh and Matisse, for example) or the nature, organization, and dynamics of the cones across non-artists. Whatever colors are applied by individual artists, colorblind or not, they reflect, in part, the physiological and anatomical status of the cones.

Other eye-related issues affect pictorial representation. An eye disease such as retinal degeneration where the neurons in the retina degenerate (e.g., Degas), or a cataract in the crystalline lens (e.g., Monet, Cassatt), or normal aging of the eye (e.g., Rembrandt, Titian) (Jackson and Owsley, 2003; Spear, 1993) would all prevent lightwaves from impacting the cones in a normal fashion. Fuzzy vision, abnormal perception of colors, and inaccurate perception of details can result from such eye diseases. Moreover, the cones being specialized neurons are actually an extension of the brain and are affected by neurotransmitters present in brain tissue. For example, dopamine, a major neuro-transmitter in the brain, has many receptors on the cones themselves and too much or too little of this neurotransmitter impacts the way some colors, particularly blue, are seen and applied pictorially (Djamgoz et al. 1997; Masson et al. 1993).

## 2. Brain and aesthetic sensations

The organization of our psychological capacities in the brain is traditionally inferred from consequences of damage to the brain. To my knowledge, there have been no reports of loss of aesthetic responses following any type of brain damage. Alterations in visual aesthetics following brain damage have been documented in a single published case, again to the best of my knowledge. A few cases of dementia where there was moderate brain atrophy have been described for musical preference alterations (reviewed in Zaidel 2005). A man suffering from temporal lobe epilepsy and who underwent left anterior temporal lobectomy reported changes in his music, literature, and painting preferences (Sellal et al. 2003). Before surgery he preferred rock music, science fiction literature, and abstract paintings; after surgery his taste shifted to polyphonic singing, novels, and realistic paintings. This neurological case is unusual.

In the absence of a critical mass of evidence for aesthetic alterations, there is too little to go on to reach conclusions. Importantly, a study of aesthetic preference in Alzheimer's patients found no statistically significant difference in preference between the patients and the normal controls, despite presence of major cognitive deficits in the patients (Halpern *et al.* 2008). Collectively, the large-scale absence of aesthetic preference alterations following brain damage, of any etiology or localization, as well as absence of reports for loss of aesthetic reactions, suggests a diffuse functional representation of aesthetics processing in the brain (see discussion, Zaidel 2005: 159–60).

Across historical times aesthetic reactions appear remarkably stable. Consider modern-day preference for ancient or cross-cultural art. Art created in one side of the world by cultures speaking languages and adhering to customs no one can understand on the other side of the world can nevertheless trigger aesthetic reactions in that side. Context is a critical clue to understanding the nature of art, and still without understanding the context of a distant culture we react aesthetically to its art. This suggests a context-free, culture-free neuronal foundation for aesthetic reactions, perhaps one rooted in ancestral biological motivational systems linked to reproduction (discussed in subsequent paragraphs of this chapter). It should be mentioned, however, that we do not have evidence of aesthetic reactions, per se, in animals; aesthetic assessment may be uniquely human.

A few neuroimaging studies investigated preference for paintings. The results implicate brain activity in several regions and little agreement among the studies (reviewed in Nadal *et al.* 2008). Some of these studies have discussed involvement of the motivational system known as the "reward pathway." The system consists of the forebrain bundle, lateral hypothalamus and its "pleasure center," and the excitatory neurotransmitter dopamine. However, recent animal work demands reconsideration of the role the "reward pathway" and dopamine play in motivational behavior (Burgdorf and Panksepp 2006; Panksepp 2005). The limbic system, dorsolateral prefrontal cortex, and other subcortical regions as well as the endorphins, and the inhibitory neurotransmitter GABA are also involved in experiential pleasure and positive affect. Thus, it is not unreasonable to expect aesthetics and its pleasure-related reactions to have brain origins other than the "reward pathway." Moreover, not all aesthetic experiences are linked to pleasure in a straightforward way: For example, horror and tragedy in art do not lead to clear-cut pleasure. In the context of aesthetics, then, reward and pleasure are not necessarily the same thing.

## 3. Brain damage effects in artists

Visual artists with brain damage can shed light on the relationship between art and brain regions. This is accomplished through examination of the post-damage works and comparing to pre-damage output. The issues concern any alterations, loss of talent, skill, or creativity. Approximately forty cases with unilateral damage or with diffuse damage have been described thus far in the neurological literature, and a review of the majority of these cases indicates that on the whole artists go on producing art despite the damage and, importantly, independently of its laterality or localization (Zaidel 2005). So this suggests that artistic talent, skill, and creativity, to say nothing of ideas, concepts, and symbolic cognition, are generally diffusely represented in the brain and no single "center," region, or pathway controls art-related cognition and production.

Furthermore, no specific technique or style alterations are associated with localization of the damage, or its etiology. Artists accustomed to using the abstract art *genre* (style) adhere to it following damage, and the same is true of the realistic style pre- and post-damage. This implies that the neurological foundations of *genre* are diffusely represented, and through redundancy of functional representation survive regional damage (Zaidel 2010). Some brain-damaged artists develop techniques to compensate for loss of perceptual and cognitive specialization. However, these techniques are subtle and difficult to group into coherent categories.

Specific art-related alterations can nevertheless be explained in terms of loss of perceptual and cognitive specialization controlled by particular brain regions, although similar deficits are observed in non-artists suffering from damage in the same brain regions. One example is loss of accurate depictions of spatial relations, particularly as they apply to three-dimensional space (3-D). These deficits are observed following damage in the right parietal lobe (De Renzi 1982). Another example is the phenomenon of hemi-neglect. The condition typically occurs following damage in the right hemisphere, in the parietal lobe, and manifests in hemi-neglect of the left half of space where the left half of the canvas would be largely unfilled. The neglect symptoms often have short time duration, lasting approximately six weeks or so in the majority of cases. Regardless, the essence of pictorial art does not lie in its spatial layout alone, certainly not in two-dimensional (2-D) depictions of 3-D space, so functions specialized in the right parietal lobe cannot be regarded as the core essence of pictorial art. Instead, the cognitive functions specialized in both cerebral hemispheres should be regarded as being involved in the whole artistic process, and only future research could decipher the balance of individual hemispheric contributions.

## 4. Biological motivations in art production

The energy put into an artistic creation, its purpose and function, the continued experimentation and innovations by artists, and the impact on the observer, have all been interpreted against a background of biological motivation. Specifically, it has been proposed that art, whether visual or not, serves as means for the display of talent, skill, and the artist's genetic quality (Miller 2000, 2001; Zahavi 1978). According to this view, the need to exhibit art is rooted in mate selection display strategies for the purpose of procreation and promulgation of their species. Such courtship displays, the most famous of which is the stunning display of the peacock's tail, have driven sexual selection in evolutionary dynamics (Cronin 1992; Darwin 1871). Just as the peacock fans out his tail to reveal perfections and imperfections stemming from genetic fitness, disease, parasites, and strength, so do artists reveal quite a bit about their cognitive prowess, which includes skill, talent, and creativity, by exhibiting their compositions. Art is produced principally in order to display to others.

This biological motivational background of art is consistent with its communicative essence. There is a mutually receptive interaction between the producer and the viewer emanating from an earlier biological level than the symbolic and abstract. Courtship signals in animals are meant to attract attention and maintain interest long enough for procreation; the displays are varied, as they are spectacular. They characteristically involve body parts and motor control that historically evolved to advertise fitness in the most optimal ways. The male bird of paradise not only displays fitness, health, and genetic quality in his elaborate feathers and acrobatics, but also in the various shades of color reflected from his feathers. All of this is meant to expose quality level for the critical assessment by potential female mates aiming for healthy offspring (Gould and Gould 1989). The position adopted in this chapter is that the foregoing is a reasonable way to explain how the motivation behind exhibition and display in animals drives the motivation for display of human art, and attract our attention to the message.

## 5. *Homo sapiens* and evolutionary cognitive and neurological changes

Extensive symbolic and abstract cognition is associated with *Homo sapiens*. The fossil record points to Africa where *Homo sapiens* first emerged around 150,000–200,000 years ago (Mellars 2006b; Relethford 2008). There is archaeological and genetic DNA evidence that anatomically modern humans migrated away from Africa to other parts of the world at least a couple of times. The first migration, around 100,000 years ago, did not spread extensively throughout Europe and Asia. However, traces of symbolic cognition associated with this group have been uncovered in sites located both in South Africa and in Israel, including symbolic burials, red ochre pigments of different shades, which had to be transported into cave shelters over long distances, as well as ornamentations (Hovers *et al.* 2003; Jacobs *et al.* 2008; Mellars 2006b). The second migration out of Africa around 60,000–65,000 years ago did lead to a wider dispersion throughout Europe and Asia (Behar *et al.* 2008; Mellars, 2006b). This migration brought with it from Africa more sophisticated tool technology than the first migration. In the intervening years since the first migration, cognitive and neurological changes are assumed to have proceeded in Africa based on archaeological evidence of finer, more sophisticated tools. Locations in South Africa, in particular, have revealed refined hand tools and ornamentations at more advanced levels than other regions in this continent (Henshilwood and Marean 2003; McBrearty and Stringer 2007), and it is the South Africa ancestors that are believed to have formed the second migration (Mellars 2006a). In the absence of substantially large archaeological and fossil data from the period of the intervening years, it is only speculation as to what led to the cognitive and neurological changes. One explanation rests on substantial evidence for serious climatic events in Africa, particularly droughts lasting for over 100,000 years, leading to isolation of human groups who nevertheless survived by harvesting new sources of food and living along seacoasts where seafood was abundant (Jacobs *et al.* 2008; deMenocal 2011). Both the nutrients available in such food and the methods to harvest it could have contributed greatly to the increased symbolic and advanced technology.

However, archaeological evidence for full-blown art production is lacking from these sites in Africa and other places in the world. Developed art does not appear on the modern human scene until around 35,000–45,000 years ago, and when it does appear, it is in Western Europe. And therein lies the mystery: the time gap between the appearance of *Homo sapiens* and the emergence of abundant practice of art. In addition, given that anatomically modern humans had spread to so many regions by then, why was art produced abundantly only in Western Europe? What was the role of humans' closest relatives, the Neanderthals, who were already present in Western Europe for more than 300,000 years when *Homo sapiens* arrived, in the big art explosion (Balter 2009)? Presently, these remain outstanding questions. Clearly, cognitive and neuroanatomical changes occurred gradually over biological time, altering and modifying in the context of natural selection and adaptation to the environment (Zaidel 2010).

As mentioned in the initial paragraphs of this chapter, cognitive and neurological thresholds must be reached in order to produce art. This level may not be unique to art; it could include many forms of communication as well. In the debate concerning the role and emergence of art in human societies not all agree with the biological reproductive link arguments (described in section 4). Another point of view links art principally to a simultaneous development of sophisticated grammatical language, with the latter leading the way. This view implies that the hallmark of symbolic cognition in humans was triggered first and foremost by language development. According to the language-symbol argument, the primary brain alteration was linguistic cognition with art being secondary or a byproduct. One proposal for the genetic trigger for language development is the FOXP2 gene (Enard *et al.* 2002). However, doubts have been raised about any unique role of FOXP2 in human language since this gene is found in animals as well (Fisher and Scharff 2009). In sum, a major change in the brain of the anatomically modern humans, associated with the period of the initial abundant art in Western Europe, is hypothesized by some evolutionary scholars (Klein and Edgar 2002).

However, not everyone agrees with this view of a sudden and major brain change (Holden 2004), including the present author. The debate is ongoing. The dynamics of biological changes are slow and gradual over time; they are subject to evolutionary adaptive changes and natural selection forces (Hernandez *et al.* 2011). The anatomical and physiological precursors of humans' sophisticated grammatical language with its combinatorial syntax had to have been in place for millions of years before 45,000 years ago (McBrearty and Stringer 2007; Remedios *et al.* 2009; Zaidel 2005, 2009). Besides, there is no convincing evidence that the earliest *Homo sapiens* lacked language; they may very well have had elaborate grammatical language. However, what could have happened around 45,000 years ago in Western Europe is some critical change in the behavior of the anatomically modern *Homo sapiens* that facilitated consistent production of art, a practice that has increased since then and gone unabated to this day. The critical behavior is likely to have a genetic and neuroanatomical basis. For example, it has recently been suggested that there was an increase in group size, intra-group cooperation, spike in altruism leading to group cohesion, and as a result long-term survival of talented, skilled individuals, were all pivotal changes (Bowles 2009; Mace 2009; Powell *et al.* 2009). These possibilities are highly plausible and could serve as new insights into speculations and debates on the origins of art practice.

# References

Addessi, E., Mancini, A., Crescimbene, L., Padoa-Schioppa, C., and Visalberghi, E. (2008). Preference transitivity and symbolic representation in capuchin monkeys (cebus apella). *PLoS ONE*, 3: e2414.

Balter, M. (2009). New work may complicate history of Neanderthals and H. sapiens. *Science*, 326: 224–5.

Behar, D. M., Villems, R., Soodyall, H., Blue-Smith, J., Pereira, L., Metspalu, E., Scozzari, R., Makkan, H., *et al.* (2008). The dawn of human matrilineal diversity. *American Journal of Human Genetics*, 82: 1130–40.

Bowles, S. (2009). Did warfare among ancestral hunter-gatherers affect the evolution of human social behaviors? *Science*, 324: 1293–8.

Burgdorf, J. and Panksepp, J. (2006). The neurobiology of positive emotions. *Neuroscience and Biobehavioral Review*, 30: 173–87.

Cronin, H. (1992). *The Ant and the Peacock*. Cambridge: Cambridge University Press.

Darwin, C. (1871). *The Descent of Man, and Selection in Relation to Sex*. London: John Murray.

deMenocal, P. B. (2011). Climate and human evolution. *Science*, 331: 540–2.

De Renzi, E. (1982). *Disorders of Space Exploration and Cognition*. New York: Wiley.

De Waal, F. B. M. and Tyack, P. L. (eds.) (2003). *Animal Social Complexity: Intelligence, Culture, and Individualized Societies*. Cambridge, MA: Harvard University Press.

Diamond, J. (1982). Rediscovery of the yellow-fronted gardener bowerbird. *Science*, 216: 431–4.

Djamgoz, M. B. A., Hankins, M. W., Hirano, J., and Archer, S. N. (1997). Neurobiology of retinal dopamine in relation to degenerative states of the tissue. *Vision Research*, 37 (Special Issue: Vision and Neurodegenerative Diseases): 3509–29.

Enard, W., Przeworski, M., Fisher, S. E., Lai, C. S. L., Wiebe, V., Kitano, T., Monaco, A. P., and Paabo, S. (2002). Molecular evolution of FOXP2, a gene involved in speech and language. *Nature*, 418: 869–72.

Fisher, S. E. and Scharff, C. (2009). FOXP2 as a molecular window into speech and language. *Trends in Genetics*, 25: 166–77.

Gould, J. L. and Gould, C. G. (1989). *Sexual Selection*. New York: Scientific American Library.

Halpern, A. R., Ly, J., Elkin-Frankston, S., and O'connor, M. G. (2008). "I know what i like": Stability of aesthetic preference in Alzheimer's patients. *Brain and Cognition*, 66: 65–72.

Henshilwood, C. S. and Marean, C. W. (2003). The origin of modern human behavior. *Current Anthropology*, 44: 627–51.

Hernandez, R. D., Kelley, J. L., Elyashiv, E., Melton, S. C., Auton, A., Mcvean, G., Project, G., Sella, G., and Przeworski, M. (2011). Classic selective sweeps were rare in recent human evolution. *Science*, 331: 920–4.

Holden, C. (2004). The origin of speech. *Science*, 303: 1316–19.

Hovers, E., Ilani, S., Bar-Yosef, O., and Vandermeersch, B. (2003). An early case of color symbolism: Ochre use by modern humans in Qafzeh Cave. *Current Anthropology*, 44: 491–522.

Hubel, D. H. (1995). *Eye, Brain, and Vision*. New York: W. H. Freeman.

Jackson, G. R. and Owsley, C. (2003). Visual dysfunction, neurodegenerative diseases, and aging. *Neurological Clinic*, 21/3: 709–28.

Jacobs, Z., Roberts, R. G., Galbraith, R. F., Deacon, H. J., Grun, R., Mackay, A., Mitchell, P., Vogelsang, R., *et al.* (2008). Ages for the Middle Stone Age of Southern Africa: Implications for human behavior and dispersal. *Science*, 322: 733–5.

Klein, R. G. and Edgar, B. (2002). *The Dawn of Human Culture*. New York: Nevraumont.

Langer, S. K. (1962). *Philosophical Sketches*. Baltimore: Johns Hopkins University Press.

Lanthony, P. (2001). Daltonism in painting. *Color Research & Application*, 26: S12–S16.

Mace, R. (2009). On becoming modern. *Science*, 324: 1280–1.

Masson, G., Mestre, D., and Blin, O. (1993). Dopaminergic modulation of visual sensitivity in man. *Fundamentals of Clinical Pharmacology*, 7: 449–63.

McBrearty, S. and Stringer, C. (2007). The coast in colour. *Nature*, 449: 793–4.

Mellars, P. (2006a). Going East: New genetic and archaeological perspectives on the modern human colonization of Eurasia. *Science*, 313: 796–800.

—— (2006b). Why did modern human populations disperse from Africa ca. 60,000 years ago? A new model. *Proceedings of the National Academy of Sciences USA*, 103: 9381–6.

Miller, G. F. (2000). *The Mating Mind: How Sexual Choice Shaped the Evolution of Human Nature*. New York: Doubleday.

—— (2001). Aesthetic fitness: How sexual selection shaped artistic virtuosity as a fitness indicator and aesthetic preferences as mate choice criteria. *Bulletin of Psychology and the Arts*, 2: 20–5.

Nadal, M., Munar, E., Capó, M. A., Rosselló, J., and Cela-Conde, C. J. (2008). Towards a framework for the study of the neural correlates of aesthetic preference. *Spatial Vision*, 21: 379–96.

Panksepp, J. (2005). Affective consciousness: Core emotional feelings in animals and humans. *Consciousness and Cognition*, 14: 30–80.

Powell, A.,Shennan, S., and Thomas, M. G. (2009). Late Pleistocene demography and the appearance of modern human behavior. *Science*, 324: 1298–1301.

Premack, D. (2007). Human and animal cognition: Continuity and discontinuity. *Proceedings of the National Academy of Sciences USA*, 104: 13861–7.

Relethford, J. H. (2008). Genetic evidence and the modern human origins debate. *Heredity*, 100: 555–63.

Remedios, R., Logothetis, N. K., and Kayser, C. (2009). Monkey drumming reveals common networks for perceiving vocal and nonvocal communication sounds. *Proceedings of the National Academy of Sciences USA*, 106: 18010–15.

Sellal, F., Andriantseheno, M., Vercueil, L., Hirsch, E., Kahane, P., and Pellat, J. (2003). Dramatic changes in artistic preference after left temporal lobectomy. *Epilepsy and Behavior*, 4: 449–51.

Spear, P. D. (1993). Neural bases of visual deficits during aging. *Vision Research*, 33: 2589–2609.

Zahavi, A. (1978). Decorative patterns and the evolution of art. *New Scientist*, 19: 182–4.

Zaidel, D. W. (2005). *Neuropsychology of Art: Neurological, Cognitive, and Evolutionary Perspectives*. New York and Hove, UK: Psychology Press.

—— (2009). Brain and art: Neuro-clues from intersection of disciplines. In M. Skov and O. Vartanian (eds.), *Neuroaesthetics*. Amityville, NY: Baywood, pp. 153–70.

—— (2010). Art and brain: Insights from neuropsychology, biology and evolution. *Journal of Anatomy*, 216: 177–83.

# 4

# Fact and Fiction in the Neuropsychology of Art

*Roman Frigg and Catherine Howard*[1]

The time-honoured philosophical issue of how to resolve the mind/body problem has taken a more scientific turn of late. Instead of discussing issues of the soul and emotion and person and their reduction to a physical form, we now ask ourselves how well-understood cognitive and social concepts fit into the growing and changing field of neuropsychology. One of the many projects that have come out of this new scientific endeavour is Zaidel's (2005) enquiry into the neuropsychological bases of art.[2]

Zaidel's book is widely considered to be a landmark piece in the field, and for this reason it deserves careful consideration. Her approach to the neuropsychology of art combines neurological, evolutionary, and cognitive perspectives. One aspect of this programme is the study of brain damage in established artists: the relationship between art and certain brain regions is investigated through an examination of the difference between pre- and post-damage works of a painter suffering brain damage. This aspect of Zaidel's programme is the focus of this essay. Our conclusion will be critical: the methods used are inappropriate to the subject matter, and progress in the study of neuropsychology of art is more likely to be made if the topic is approached in a different way. We should emphasize, however, that we do not reach this conclusion because we generally have a sceptical perspective on reductionist programmes such as Zaidel's. In our view there is no good reason to believe that we could not, at least in principle, one day have a thorough understanding of the physiology behind our ability to create, imagine, enjoy, and recognize art. The aim of Zaidel's project is a good one.

In her investigation Zaidel uses a range of established artists (i.e., artists who are recognized as such by art history and society broadly construed) from a range of time

---

[1] The authors are listed alphabetically; the paper is collaborative. To contact the authors write to r.p.frigg@lse.ac.uk and z3192298@student.unsw.edu.au

[2] Related research programmes are those of Vilayanur S. Ramachandran and Semir Zeki. For a critical discussion of these see Hyman (2010).

periods and artistic persuasions as objects of study. Our main criticism is that this focus is mistaken for two reasons. First, to address the questions that neuroscience can reasonably be expected address, there is no need to focus on established artists. In fact, art school undergraduates would be no less valuable subjects. Second, the choice of historical figures as subjects forces Zaidel to extract her data from sketchy and incomplete historical records (incomplete in that they do not provide detailed information about the exact nature of brain damage suffered), which rarely, if ever, provide data that are fit for purpose. Studying 'ordinary' art students rather than established historical figures also makes this problem go away. And this is what we recommend should happen: rather then relying on gappy historical records, data should be gathered on living painters using state of the art technology, and these painters can be chosen arbitrarily since nothing depends on their standing in the art world.

## 1.  Learning from brain damage in established artists

Zaidel investigates the neuropsychology of art by looking at subjects who have suffered brain damage and then exploring the artistic implications of this damage. To do so she has collected anecdotal and historical data about artists throughout history. Zaidel's research is extensive, and covers artists from all areas of art: the visual arts, literature, music composition and performance, and even film. Zaidel's goal is to find what common elements span these varied concepts of art, and ultimately to find out how our brains process, create, and recognize works from any field *as art*. However, Zaidel is not just interested in any old piece; her focus is works of art that have been produced by established artists, that is ones whose status as artists is confirmed both by professional art history as well as society at large and whose works remain recognized and hallowed as art throughout time and within recognized and prestigious establishments. In other words, in her study of the neurology of art, Zaidel is interested in studying artists and works that belong within the upper echelon of the artistic world: 'Art', with a capital A, as we shall call it.

In this chapter we aim to give an account of the method Zaidel uses to achieve her goal. For the sake of clarity, we will limit ourselves to those studies relating to visual artists, specifically painters. We will also limit these examples to painters who have suffered specific neurological damage. Despite the fact that Zaidel argues from a range of conditions, both physical (such as defective colour vision) and neurological (such as brain damage caused by strokes), we limit our attention to neurological conditions since these are more pertinent to the issue at stake and help us bring into focus her claims regarding the role of neurology in the study of art.

We will use two of Zaidel's examples to examine her method (this is for ease of presentation only; our points could just as well be made using other cases). The first is the case of the Bulgarian painter Zlatio Boyadjiev (pp. 30–1).[3] In 1951 Boyadjiev, then 48 years old, suffered a stroke within the left hemisphere of his brain. This left Boyadjiev with permanent right hand paralysis (his dominant hand) and mixed aphasia. After his stroke, Boyadjiev learned how to use his left hand to paint. After gaining proficient skill at this new task, he continued to produce work that was acclaimed by critics and exhibited in museums. His ability to realistically depict figures was unchanged. However, compared to the pre-stroke period his use of colours became less exuberant and less varied; the perspective was less convergent (with some pieces lacking depth altogether); a left–right mirror symmetry became typical of many of his compositions; and there were fewer figures present in each piece (creating a feeling of less overall complexity in the piece).

The second example is that of portrait painter William Utermohlen (pp. 43–4). From the age of 57 onwards, Utermohlen experienced a slow deterioration of global cognitive ability due to the onset of Alzheimer's disease. An MRI scan revealed generalized cortical atrophy with no asymmetry. As the disease progressed, Zaidel notes that Utermohlen's trademark use of realistic depictions tapered off, and a use of more abstract techniques ensued. Facial distortions were introduced into his portraits; perspective and depth were slowly lost over time; and although colour and form were still used, colour was left unblended and paint was applied with broad brush strokes which gave the paintings an air of patchiness. Eventually he gave up colour altogether and resorted to just sketching with a pencil.

The thrust of these examples (and many others in the book) is to correlate alterations in artistic style with alterations in the brain, and then draw a conclusion about which parts of the brain are involved in the production of artworks. In more detail, the method consists in the following steps:

1. Examine an artist's work before damage.
2. Examine the same artist's work after having suffered brain damage.
3. Identify aesthetically relevant aspects in the artist's work that have changed.
4. Assume that these changes appear exclusively due to the brain damage.
5. Identify the nature of the brain damage suffered.
6. Conclude that the change in the brain is responsible for the change in artistic style and that therefore the part of the brain affected by the disease is responsible for the production of the pre-stroke style.

In Zaidel's case studies the last stage is often left implicit, but the overall discussion clearly indicates that such an 'attributive' step is the aim of the exercise. In the first case, for instance, the conclusion clearly is that damage to the left hemisphere was responsible for the changes in Boyadjiev's style. This, then, provides us with a possible clue as to

---

[3] Unless indicated otherwise, page numbers in this chapter refer to Zaidel's (2005).

where in the brain certain artistic capabilities are located. For want of a better term, we refer to this method as the *method of diachronic difference*, MDD for short.[4]

In this chapter, we aim to closely scrutinize Zaidel's method and argue that it suffers from serious problems. Our criticisms fall into two categories. The first is Zaidel's application of MDD. The second criticism focuses on the use of MDD as an adequate cornerstone for research of this nature. Here we will examine similar projects that have tried to use MDD in this fashion, and the problems that subsequently arose affecting their study. We will argue that Zaidel's study of brain damage in artists is not immune to these same problems. Finally, we propose an approach that avoids these pitfalls and may lead to a great wealth of interesting information regarding neurology, aesthetics, and art.

## 2. Aiming too high

The first problem we will deal with is Zaidel's use of MDD. Our problem becomes palpable as soon as we are pressed to lay out what the above examples really show. Upon closer inspection this seems to be rather little. The first example suggests that there is a connection between brain damage to the left hemisphere and the absence of perspective as well as an unimaginative use of colour; the second case suggests that there is a connection between abstraction and the malfunctioning of the cortex as a whole. Even if one grants that these findings generalize to other cases—which is by no means clear; in fact, Zaidel (p. 31) herself points out that the loss of the ability to produce perspectival representations is often associated with lesions of the right rather than the left hemisphere—they are too unspecific to give us serious hints about the connections between the workings of the brain and the production of art. Unless the brain damage is clearly located, we cannot draw useful conclusions about which parts or functional units of the brain are involved in the production of art, which undermines the very project of a neuropsychology of art. Locating a capability somewhere in the left hemisphere, or even the entire cortex, is not specific enough to provide serious clues about the neurological underpinnings of art. And this problem is by no means restricted to the two examples we have chosen. The book gathers together a large collection of cases, but only few, if any, receive detailed treatment. For the most part the descriptions are short and coarse.

By and large the brevity of the discussion is owed to the fact that historical records provide only limited information. Zaidel places great emphasis on investigating established artists—Otto Dix, Louis Corinth, and Willem de Kooning are but a few of the eminent artists discussed—and where she considers lesser(-known) artists she is careful to choose only those who are of some art-historic interest. The basic problem is that our knowledge about the conditions of these artists is, as a matter of fact, limited. For

---

[4]  This name echoes Mill's 'method of difference' (1843, Book 3, Ch. VIII, Sec. 2). We add 'diachronic' to make explicit that we are comparing properties at different times.

one, diagnostic techniques of the kind we have today were not available at the time and hence we often only have the crudest of descriptions of their neurological conditions; for another, medical records often contain only limited information about brain damage suffered by an artist. Although Zaidel is not to blame for the sketchiness of available historical records, there is a serious question about whether such records are able to form the basis of a research programme in neuroscience. They are not. Far more detailed knowledge of the neurological conditions of patients would have to be available in order to form a sound basis of an investigation of the functioning of the brain in the production of art. Current neuroscience has evolved to the point where we understand in great detail the structures of various regions of the brain and the interconnections between them. In fact, we now have a very detailed map of the brain telling us even how individual columns (a small bundle of neurons operating as a unit) work and in which functions of the brain they are involved. When studying specific brain damage to attribute artistic skills and practices to brain regions, we can only make useful claims through locating damage on this finely drawn chart. It is no longer reasonable to make significant claims with a loose description of the location of the relevant damage; locating damage in the right or the left hemisphere, or even in the visual cortex as a whole, no longer furthers our understanding of the functioning of the brain in general, or the neurology of art in particular.[5]

The focus on eminent historical figures should also be given up for another, and independent, reason. In order to see what this reason is, let us first give a more abstract characterization of MDD:

1. Examine a person's capability of doing $X$ before brain damage.
2. Examine the same person's capability of doing $X$ after the person has suffered brain damage.
3. Identify relevant differences in the person's capability of doing $X$ before and after having suffered brain damage. Call this difference $\Delta X$.
4. Assume that the brain damage suffered is the only cause of $\Delta X$.
5. Identify the nature of the brain damage suffered. Call the difference between the brain's condition before and after brain damage $\Delta C$.
6. Conclude that $\Delta C$ is the cause of $\Delta X$.

This method suffers from all the well-known difficulties of inductive reasoning,[6] but these do not concern us here; we assume that they can be circumvented successfully in

---

[5] Section 3 of Zaidel's contribution to this book may be read as suggesting that the aim of the investigation is not so much correlating certain artistic skills (or loss thereof) with certain precisely circumscribed parts of the brain, but rather to show that artistic talent, skill, and creativity are diffusely located in the brain and do not have a particular centre. Even if this is the goal, the problems remain the same: our failure to precisely locate certain conditions does not imply that they have no precise location.

[6] Let us mention but some: the inductive step of generalizing from the sample investigated to the entire reference class is notoriously problematic; the assumption that there are no confounding factors (premise 4) is highly problematic in the current context and has to be accepted as an article of faith; and neurological data

the relevant cases because our criticism of Zaidel's approach is orthogonal to concerns about induction. The point we want to emphasize is that there are at least two conditions on X for a legitimate application of MDD. The first condition we call the *requirement of specificity*. It must be clear what it means to do X—there cannot be any ambiguities about the concept itself—and we need operational criteria to unequivocally decide on any given occasion whether a person is doing X or not. If there are ambiguities about X, or if in an experiment we cannot decide whether the person really does X, then looking for the neurological foundations of X is an ill-defined problem.

The second condition we call the *requirement of individuality*. This condition requires that whether the person under investigation does X (or fails to do so) only depends on that person's mental state and not on other persons' mental states.[7] Let us illustrate this with an example. Whether John feels pain depends only on the state of his brain (and possibly his nervous system); other people's mental activities play no part in John's being in pain. By contrast, whether John is behaving politely is not only a function of his brain state. Behaving politely depends on other people's preferences and on social norms which are beyond the control of the individual. For instance, while in traditional Islamic cultures it is impolite to eat with your left hand, it is impolite in most Western societies not to use both hands to eat. If John eats with both hands, he is behaving politely or impolitely depending on the cultural beliefs of people around him. But John's action is the exactly the same in either case—he is eating with both hands—and hence the mental actions that guide his behaviour must be the same too.[8] For this reason, the concept of behaving politely cannot be studied from a neuroscience point of view, because the subject matter of such an investigation is an individual's brain state. It is a necessary condition for activity X to be open to neurological investigation that the execution of X be a function only of the individual's state of mind, and not of what happens in the person's social environment.

The X at stake in Zaidel's investigation is 'producing a work of Art'. Unfortunately producing a work of Art clearly fails to satisfy the first condition, and, at least given current views concerning the nature of art, it does not satisfy the second condition either. As regards the first condition, it is a matter of fact that there is no agreement

---

are nearly always messy, even when experiments are conducted under strict control, and hence the neurological condition itself is in part speculative.

[7] Doing X may also depend on facts about the world, as long as they do not depend on other persons' beliefs and desires. For instance, if we assume externalism to be true, then it must be the case that there are objects in the world for a person to have object-involving thoughts. This dependency on facts is harmless in the context of the current discussion. What is at issue here is dependence on other persons' mental states.

[8] One can, of course, investigate a person's disposition or willingness to respect a given set of social rules or the execution of a particular action that is in line with the rules (e.g., keeping at a certain distance when talking to someone). But this is not the same as investigating behaving politely *per se*: someone can be willing to respect rules and yet fail to do so, or keeping a certain distance to your interlocutor may be polite in one context but not in another one.

about what defines a work of Art.[9] Classical definitions which construe art as imitation or representation (Plato), a medium of transmission of feelings (Tolstoy), intuitive expression (Croce), or significant form (Bell) are believed by many to be seriously defective. More recent approaches include functionalism (Beardsley), proceduralism (Dickie), or approaches emphasizing historical reflexivity (Danto). For our current concerns the relative merits of these approaches are immaterial. The salient point is that there is a plethora of different schools of thought and that producing a piece of art means something different to each of them. Hence there is no unanimous view of how a piece of art is to be identified, which undermines any attempt to identify the neurological basis of the production of art.

Assume now, for the sake of argument, that this dispute could be resolved. Of course we can only speculate about how the conflict will be resolved, but at least given the state of play in the current discussion, this resolution is unlikely to be in line with MDD. Most contemporary definitions of art in one way or another explicitly appeal to social practices and the role of institutions (this is explicit, for instance, in Dickie's institutional theory) in order to define art: what turns an artefact into a work of art is neither a particular property of the object itself nor a specific characteristic of its process of production, but rather the role it plays in certain social practices. This suggests that art is more like behaving politely than like feeling pain, and hence does not lend itself to a neurological investigation at all since it fails on account of the requirement of individuality.

Although Zaidel does not discuss this point, there is implicit acknowledgement of it in her discussion, since any reference to artistic value (or any of its cognates) are conspicuously absent from her discussion of *actual cases* (as opposed to programmatic statements). The discussion of specific bodies of work focuses on the use of perspective, the choice of colour, the level of abstraction, the curviness of lines, the smoothness of boundaries, the thickness of layers of paint, the characteristics of brush strokes, the presence of symmetries, the distortion of objects, the choice of motives, and the like. What Zaidel is really examining is how neurological damage affects the specific representations that are being processed by the artists, and how in turn the damage affects their ability to create their brushstrokes and accurately represent what they desire on their canvas. These (and related) aspects no doubt play a role in the appreciation of an artwork, but they are not specific to Art with capital A and it seems unnecessary to restrict attention to these 'upper echelon artists' if all that is at stake are specific technical aspects of their work. To discuss, say, the use of perspective we don't have to look at geniuses of the calibre of van Gogh; the canvases produced by Sunday painters, primary school teachers, distraught managers seeking relaxation in painting, and commercial painters producing pieces that are sold on tourist markets are not less valuable as 'data points'. Once we limit our attention to a specific aspect of pictorial

---

[9] For a survey of the various positions held in this debate see Davies (2005).

representation (like the use of perspective), it just doesn't matter any more whether the pieces we look at count as Art, or whether they are merely canvases produced for any number of other reasons. In other words, the fact that the subjects studied were established artists seems to play no role at all in the conclusions that we are supposed to draw from the cases!

This is not merely an academic point. In fact, its practical implications can hardly be overstated. It is the focus on eminent figures that forces Zaidel to use uncontrolled and sketchy data extracted from artists' histories as a basis for claims concerning a low level neurological story for a change in aesthetic perception of an artist's work, and we have argued above that this is detrimental to her research programme. Once we recognize that there is no necessity to focus on established artists and that the neurological studies could just as well be carried out on the participants in the painting class at the local community college, we free the investigation from the straitjacket of historical records and open up the possibility of gathering detailed and reliable data using cutting edge technology. And this is exactly what we think should happen. Rather than keep relying on notoriously gappy historical records, data should be gathered on living painters, irrespective of their standing (or even participation) in the art world. In fact, this is the only way forward if we really want to understand the neurological basis of how visual representation works.

In sum, the $X$ in the investigation should not be 'producing a work of Art', but a particular skill like 'producing a perspectival ink drawing' or 'producing a representation that is truthful with respect to colour'. This shift not only makes the problems with specificity and individuality go away (and hence allows us to use MDD); it also gives investigators the possibility to choose contemporary subjects who have no recognition in the art world (and who may not even aspire to so being recognized) on which data can be generated using cutting edge technology. It is such data rather than sketchy historical records that should be used in a study of the neurology of art.

## 3.  Qualms about top-down approaches

Before outlining in more detail (in Section 5) what we regards as a more promising approach to neuroaesthetics, we would like to have closer look at a parallel case: the debate over the neurological underpinnings of the cognitive notion of a visual representation, which also suggests that the focus on Art is a red herring.

Let us start by setting the stage. There are two possible approaches to cognitive neuroscience: the traditional top-down approach, and the more controversial bottom-up approach, where, in this context, by 'top' we mean the level of mental phenomena as we experience them (seeing a house, feeling sad, wanting to sleep, etc.) and 'down' refers to the level of brain states (patters of neuron firings, etc.). The difference between the two is best illustrated through a slightly revised version of Dennett's bridge analogy, in which he describes top-down cognitive neuroscience as 'reverse engineering' (Dennett 1998: 255). Consider someone who has no knowledge of engineering, but who takes an interest in the workings of a particular bridge. This person could start by looking at the bridge and identifying certain functional units like the deck, the pillars, the pillar foundations, the anchorage blocks, the suspenders, and the suspension cables. There are certain ways in which these fit together and understanding how the bridge works involves understanding how these parts fit together: the pillar foundations carry the pillars, the suspensions are fixed at the top of the pillars, the suspension cables are connected to the suspensions and they carry the platform. These macro concepts provide a good description of the bridge and the person can now tell what each of the bridge pieces do, which parts are integral to structural integrity, etc. But this does not yet satisfy the person; she also wants to know why and how the parts can perform their function. So she starts looking at the materials used and the way they are connected: the foundation blocks are made from concrete, the pillars are metal bars riveted together in particular way, the deck is a combination of stone and steel, etc. The more she knows about the constitution of each part, the better she understands how these parts work and why the entire bridge holds together. In sum, the person *first* develops a well worked out macro-theory of the bridge, and *then* asks what kind of micro-constitution allows the various parts identified in the macro-theory to work in the way they do.

This approach contrasts with a bottom-up method. This method does not require a well worked out macro-theory in order to start investigating the micro level; in fact, it tells us not to have one—and if we happen to have one to put it to the side for the time being. The way forward, on this view, is not to look for the micro underpinnings of a finished macro-theory, but to start tampering with the micro structure directly and observe how changes at the micro level bear on broad issues we are interested in. In the case of the bridge, for example, the bottom-up method denies that we *first* have to describe the bridge in macro terms like 'pillar' and 'foundation' and *then* ask what the constitution of a pillar and a foundation is; instead it invites us to ponder directly what effect it would have on the stability of the bridge if we replaced, say, rivets by screws, used wood instead of steel in certain places, etc. This would lead to an understanding of the effect of micro changes on the functioning of the bridge, but without presupposing a particular macro conceptualization of it.

Starting the investigation with the notion of Art, and a view about what art is and how it has to be understood, amounts to adopting a top-down approach: it presupposes a clear understanding of the phenomenon under investigation and then asks how the different elements of our understanding of Art are realized at the neurological level.[10] It is easy to see why a top-down approach seems appealing for Zaidel's project. For one, the top-down method seems generally tidier and more systematic than the somewhat messy and anarchic bottom-up approach. For another, especially in a field

---

[10] In fact, she is specifically evoking common cognitive science methodology and not the straight neurological methodology the title of her work implies.

in which there already exists a body of knowledge it would seem to be natural to take this knowledge into account.

Is this the right choice? This is not the first time that a problem of this nature has been presented to the philosophical community. A similar issue has been well discussed throughout the philosophical and cognitive neuroscience literature about the long-standing debate between Kosslyn and Pylyshyn concerning the cognitive notion of visual representation (VR). We will now discuss this case in some detail, which brings us to the conclusion that, first impressions notwithstanding, a bottom-up methodology seems to be more appropriate for neuroaesthetics than a top-down approach.

VR is defined in this discussion as what it involves for someone to imagine something (Pylyshyn 2003); that is, what it involves for someone to have an image of something in her head. As imagining something is a cognitive concept, evoking such things as images and imagining and thought (not traditionally language used in strict neuropsychology), the cognitivists, most recently encouraged by Pylyshyn, were the first to try and create a 'cognitive map' or theory that would help explain this common experience. This theory of VR would outline precisely what is happening when we imagine something visually; it would, as it were, provide us with the anatomy of visual representation, detailing which kinds of cognitive capacities are involved in imagery, how they fit together, and how they relate to the capacities involved in other tasks such as verbal expression. To come back to Dennett's analogy, this theory of VR would be like the description of the bridge in terms of concepts like 'pillar' and 'platform'. Such a theory is regarded by cognitivists as the indispensable starting point of every investigation into how VR functions at the level of the brain—without such a macro-theory, so the cognitivists think, one cannot even begin addressing this issue.

However, Pylyshyn quickly ran into a problem. Due to cognitive theory being so dependent on semantic content, there seemed to be no real way to create one static theory that would account for all forms of VR. For instance, if a cognitivist decided to examine the cognitive aspects that were evoked when you imagined a man walking along the beach at sunset, you could be said to evoking cognitive semantic concepts such as water, sand, outdoors, humans (man), sunset, etc. But if you were to imagine a fresh plate of sheet metal being produced by a machine in a factory, you would evoke semantic concepts that involve industrial centres, machinery, fire, ore, coal, etc. A cognitive theory of VR would consist of a general schema of which both concrete cases would be an instance (in pretty much the same way in which the trajectories of planets orbiting around the sun and of heavy objects falling from towers are instances of the Newtonian laws of motion). Unfortunately it turned out that there seems to be no way to collate these two very distinct and different visual representations into any one unified cognitive theory. In fact, it turns out that it is not even clear what format such a theory should have—an issue that was the source of a rousing debate: in even considering the problem of visual representation, Pylyshyn states that you are automatically evoking the argument that 'thought' is pictorial (as opposed to linguistic) in format. However, understanding the 'format' of 'thought' does not seem possible until you have a better idea of what you are looking at, and as the cognitivists seem unable to agree what VR really is on a cognitive level, a unified theory of VR seems unattainable.

This has severe consequences. Due to this inability to assume any format, no upper ground was solidified as a basis for a top-down cognitive to neurological explanation of the cognitive/phenomenal aspects of VR. For Pylyshyn, if there is no solid 'upper ground' theory of VR, then a top-down neurological explanation of VR simply does not exist and not only has the project of a neurological reduction failed, but there seems no viable starting point for researching and understanding the complexities of VR at all.

Art seems to be much like VR in that it is a multilayered, highly complex and context-sensitive concept, and hence it is unlikely that there will ever be a unifying theory about Art that would provide the starting point for a neurological top-down reduction.[11] As a consequence, Pylyshyn's conclusion concerning the prospects of a neurological reduction of VR seems to carry over to Art unscathed: it can't be done!

This leaves two options: biting the bullet and regarding reduction as impossible, or choosing an alternative methodology. Neurologist Kosslyn opted for the latter. He decided to forgo all cognitive definitions, explanations, and assumptions of VR and worked to develop a theory of VR from the bottom-up perspective. In essence this means that research is guided not by a high-level theory but by practical issues; more specifically, a subject is confronted with a particular task and then it is observed which parts of the brain are involved in tackling that task. This can be done either by observing the subject's brain in an MRI or CT scanning device while she deals with the task, or by observing subjects suffering from a particular brain condition and then comparing them with healthy subjects. Consider, for example, Maguire et al.'s (2006) study of navigation. In order to find out what role the hippocampus plays in our ability to navigate in spaces that we have become acquainted with a long time ago, a taxi driver with bilateral hippocampal lesion as well as several control taxi drivers were asked to navigate in an interactive virtual reality simulation of central London. The investigation found that the hippocampus is not required for general orientation relying on main roads, but that it plays a role when it comes to navigating in areas off the main roads. The salient point here is that no cognitive theory of navigation—let alone a complete and accurate one—is presupposed; the investigation bypasses this step and simply asks what is and what is not important when a subject is actively participating in the activity you wish to study.

Through use of this method, Kosslyn discovered that the reason why VR intuitively seems to be so similar to vision is that the areas of the brain used for VR share

---

[11] In her review of Zaidel's book, Franz (2006) seems sympathetic to the idea that Zaidel's research question does not seem well defined, which could be one of the reasons why it is so hard for Zaidel to develop an easy to state research programme. Brown (2006) also feels that the cognitive aspects of Zaidel's approach have not been given enough justice, which could be another reason why a top-down methodology does not seem to fit her current project.

two-thirds of the cortical space of normal vision. In fact, visual representations are actually represented within the visual cortex in a way very similar to how the visual cortex processes normal sight: the difference between VR and normal sight seems simply to be the origin of the information processed. In the case of normal vision, the information comes directly through our eyes from the real world. In the case of VR, the information is taken from our memory systems and then collated throughout the visual cortex (Kosslyn *et al.* 2003). Despite not having a theory of visual representation, Kosslyn was, through bottom-up exploration of the issue, able to find out how it worked and develop a working theory that helps us understand more about this phenomenon.

Since Art is much like VR, this case shows the dangers involved in subscribing to a top-down method: we may be lead to nihilism where interesting insights could be gained by using other methods because a misplaced focus on Art (and the high level theory attached to it) comes to stand in the way of progress that could be made in our understanding of neurological processes that are involved in aesthetic judgements.

## 4. The neuropsychology of art revised

The arguments in Sections 3 and 4 converge towards the same point: the focus on Art is a dead end for neuroaesthetics. Progress is more likely to be made if the investigation, first, focuses on 'local' themes rather than Art; second, uses controlled laboratory environments to generate data rather then trying to extract information from historical records; and third also pays attention to aspects of the appreciation of art. Let us address these points one at a time, beginning with the second.

As we have pointed out in Section 3, the focus on established artists is both unnecessary and detrimental to the project of neuroaesthetics. The project of gathering information about eminent historical figures from historical records is doomed to failure from the start because these records do not provide information which meets the needs of modern neuroscience as regards precision, detail, and specificity. Instead neuroscientists interested in aesthetics should investigate the workings of the brain of persons engaging in art-related practises no matter what their standing (or even participation) in the art world and observe their brains while they do so using all means available in a modern laboratory (for instance MRI, fMRI, PET, EEG, and MEG). This is because relevant issues can be investigated using any subjects with some artistic talent or interest: one does not need the great artists; simple art school students would do. The data collected would be far stronger and more controlled than those gleaned from partial and possibly misleading medical records, and they would provide a more solid and reliable basis for an understanding of the brain processes involved in art-related activities.

Studying living subjects would have two further advantages. First, although attributing changes in the production of art to a specific change in the brain is a first step, it is no more than that. A complete investigation on the neuropsychology of art would need to include a way of obtaining information regarding brain activity throughout all stages of the artistic process. It would be helpful to understand how each region is involved in first conception, then first sketches, then filling out the colour and the idea all the way to the final draft, and then work completion. It may even be useful to examine the difference in response to the artist looking at the final work. This would give us data representing a holistic approach to the neuropsychology of art, and a rough sketch as to how the system as a whole is structured. If a rough sketch of the whole system can be obtained, then any information we can gather regarding specific system damage can be discussed in its context.

Second, studying broken systems is a difficult job that neurologists excel at: one could claim that the majority of modern neuroscience is based on breaking and examining the brain.[12] However, other methods have become available in recent years: we now have the technology and knowledge to bypass studying broken systems and instead focus on watching the brain function correctly. That is, we no longer need to break aspects of the brain to find out what they do, we can watch the brain work as a whole system uninterrupted while real artists work using the above-mentioned technologies.

Let us now return to the first of the above issues: what questions should be addressed by neuroaesthetics. There seem to be at least three kinds of questions that neuroscience could meaningfully address (needless to say, this list is in no way exhaustive). The first family of questions concerns technical aspects in the execution of a piece of visual art. Neuroscience is well equipped to study the effects of the use of perspective, colour, shading, symmetries, distortions, thickness of lines, and many more, for instance by observing what happens in a person's brain when they produce or see, say, a drawing using one-point perspective and comparing it to the brain of people who do (or are not able to) see or produce such images. Indeed, there already is a wealth of information available about some of these issues. For instance, the functioning of the visual cortex and the eye itself have been studied extensively, which can lead to studies that help us understand the physical (and emotional) response we feel when looking at certain colours, or certain shades, or certain oblique lines.

Some studies help us make leeway on these difficult topics. For instance, extensive studies have already been carried out on how our brain uses ganglion cells to see and interpret colour, light, and shading (Livingstone and Hubel 1988), how our brain can see and distinguish between different types of colour (Martin 1998), and how we physiologically pick up movement and lines within our visual field (Merrigan and Maunsell 1993). Understanding vision in this way could well be the first step to understanding how these specific images or specific colours/tones/shades affect other neural centres engaged in memory or emotion, ultimately helping us understand the neurology of how art affects us.

---

[12] For a closer examination on the problems presented by studying broken systems, see Glymour (1994).

The second group of issues centres on the phenomenon of creative impulse. One person looks at a sunset and simply wants to enjoy its beauty while another person sees the same sunset and is compelled to recreate it in drawing or painting, or capture the emotion that it evokes in some way. Is there a difference in the brain function of these two persons? Studying the difference between what someone with creative impulse does with their perception in comparison with someone who does not have any creative drive at all may give us a starting point to understanding the creation of art.[13]

The third group of questions focuses on the appreciation of art. Although the emphasis in studying art usually is on the artist, the audience plays an important role too—pieces of art are produced with the intention that they be appreciated *as such*. This can lead to the study of those who call themselves 'art appreciators'. What goes on in the brain of someone who appreciates, say, a drawing *as a piece of art* as opposed to regarding it simply as a provider of information about the spatial arrangement of certain objects? One could study this difference, for instance, by investigating the difference between a subject observing a picture just as a picture (for instance a photograph in a newspaper article) and compare this to the neurological effect of them observing that same photograph as a work of art in an art exhibition. This in itself would give us some clue as to how the brain processes and recognizes art in different forms, and allow us to examine different perspectives of someone experiencing art.

None of these three areas of study amounts, in itself, to the study of art, but it is plausible that studies such as these will give us vital information that could, at some later point, also contribute to the neurological study of the more cognitive, phenomeno-logical, and aesthetic aspects of art. Finding the necessary neurological conditions for artistic skill (technique), creative impulse, recognition, and appreciation may very well be the key to truly understanding the neuroscience of art, and potentially also help us understand how our capability to produce art relates to (and depends on) our general cognitive capacities for everyday survival activities such as general motor skills as well as auditory, spatial, and visual mechanisms.[14]

# References

Brown, Steven (2006), 'Bringing Science to Art'. *Trends in Cognitive Sciences*, 10/8: 356–7.

Davies, Stephen (2005). 'Definitions of Art', in Berys Gaut and Dominic Mciver Lopez (eds.), *The Routledge Companion to Aesthetics*. 2nd edn. London: Routledge, pp. 227–40.

---

[13] Zaidel seems to agree with this at least. In her introductory discussion of what she considers to be artistic she includes anything that can be seen as using a creative impulse as being artistic (even to some degree science). Studying this creative urge in its own right could be seen as a worthwhile starting point.

[14] We would like to thank Chris Bertram, Martin Frigg, Andrew Goldfinch, Peter Goldie, Julian Reiss, and Elisabeth Schellekens for helpful comments on earlier drafts. Thanks also go to Dahlia Zaidel for her feedback and her forbearance.

Dennett, Daniel (1998). 'Cognitive Science as Reverse Engineering: Several Meanings of "Top-Down" and "Botton-Up"', in *Brainchildren: Essays on Design and Mind*. Boston: MIT Press, pp. 249–60.

Franz, Liz (2006). 'Arts and Minds'. *Lancet* (April): 302.

Glymour, Clark (1994). 'On the Methods of Cognitive Neuropsychology'. *British Journal for the Philosophy of Science*, 45: 815–35.

Hyman, John (2010). 'Art and Neuroscience', in Roman Frigg and Matthew Hunter (eds.), *Beyond Mimesis and Convention: Representation in Art and Science*. New York: Springer, pp. 245–62.

Kosslyn, Stephan M., Giorgio Ganis, and William L. Thompson (2003). 'Mental Imagery: Against the Nihilistic Hypothesis'. *Trends in Cognitive Sciences*, 7/3: 109–11.

Livingstone, Margaret and David Hubel (1988). 'Segregation of Form, Colour, Movement, and Depth: Anatomy, Physiology, and Perception'. *Science*, 240: 740–9.

Maguire, Eleanor, Rory Nannery, and Hugo Spiers (2006) 'Navigation around London by a Taxi Driver with Bilateral Hippocampal Lesions'. *Brain*, 129: 2894–2907.

Martin, Paul R. (1998). 'Colour Processing in the Primate Retina: Recent Progress'. *Journal of Physiology*, 513: 631–8.

Merrigan, William H. and John H. R. Maunsell (1993). 'How Parallel are the Primate Visual Pathways?' *Annual Review of Neuroscience*, 16: 369–402.

Mill, John Stuart ([1843] 1973). *A System of Logic: Ratiocinative and Inductive*, ed. John M. Robson. Toronto: Toronto University Press.

Pylyshyn, Zenon (2003). 'Return of the Mental Image: Are There Really Pictures in the Brain?' *Trends in Cognitive Sciences*, 7/3: 113–18.

Zaidel, Dahlia W. (2005). Neuropsychology of Art: Neurological, Cognitive, and Evolutionary Perspectives. New York and Hove, UK: Psychology Press.

# PART II

# Emotion in Aesthetic Experience

# 5

# Emotion and Aesthetic Value

*Jesse Prinz*

Aesthetics is a normative domain. We evaluate artworks as better or worse, good or bad, great or grim. I will refer to a positive appraisal of an artwork as an aesthetic appreciation of that work, and I refer to a negative appraisal as aesthetic depreciation. (I will often drop the word "aesthetic.") There has been considerable amount of work on what makes an artwork worthy of appreciation, and less, it seems, on the nature of appreciation itself. These two topics are related, of course, because the nature of appreciation may bear on what things are worthy of that response, or at least on what things are likely to elicit it. So I will have some things to say about the latter. But I want to focus in this discussion on appreciation itself. When we praise a work of art, when we say it has aesthetic value, what does our praise consist in? This is a question about aesthetic psychology. I am interested in what kind of mental state appreciation is. What kind of state are we expressing when we say a work of art is "good"?

This question has parallels in other areas of value theory. In ethics, most notably, there has been much attention lavished on the question of what people express when they refer to an action as "morally good." One popular class of theories, associated with the British moralists and their followers, posits a link between moral valuation and emotion. To call an act morally good is to express an emotion toward that act. I think this approach to morality is right on target (Prinz 2007a). Here I want to argue that an emotional account of aesthetic valuation is equally promising. There are important differences between the two domains, but both have an affective foundation. I suspect that valuing of all kinds involves the emotions. Here I will inquire into the role of emotions in aesthetic valuing. I will not claim that artworks express emotions or even that they necessarily evoke emotions. I will claim only that when we appreciate a work, the appreciation consists in an emotional response.

I will begin by arguing that emotions are involved in appreciation, and then I will look more specifically at which emotions are involved. Two methodological caveats are in order before we begin. First, I will not survey the important philosophical theories of appreciation here. Instead, I will make an effort, where possible, to ground my conclusions in empirical findings. This is an exercise in naturalized aesthetics. Second, I will focus on fine art (including film). These two methodological choices reflect limitations of time and expertise, and nothing more. I hope that the proposals here can further the dialogue between scientists and philosophers who share an interest in aesthetic psychology, and I hope that everything I say about fine art can be extended to the other arts as well.

# 1. Affective appreciation

## 1.1 An affective theory of appreciation

I want to begin by offering some reasons for thinking that appreciation is an emotional state. I don't think there are any knock-down arguments for that conclusion. Rather, one can defend it by argument to the best explanation. The hypothesis that appreciation has an affective foundation systematizes a number of observations that are hard to make sense of otherwise. I will also consider three objections.

I will divide the evidence into several categories. First, there is evidence that emotions co-occur with art appreciation. For me, this conclusion can be readily derived from introspection. When I view artworks and arrive at an evaluation it seems to be perfectly obvious that I am having an emotional response. Good art can be thrilling, and bad art can be depressing. An experience with art can be invigorating, stimulating, and exhausting. Obviously, appeals to introspection are not decisive. My introspective experiences may differ from yours. Fortunately, introspection is not the only way to support the conjecture that emotion co-occurs with appreciation. Further support comes from neuroimaging. In an fMRI study, Kawabata and Zeki (2004) found that beautiful pictures correlated with activations in orbitofrontal cortex and anterior cingulate gyrus, both of which are associated with emotion. Vartanian and Goel (2004) correlated aesthetic judgments with left cingulate gyrus as well. Using MEG, Cela-Conde et al. (2004) observed cingulate activations for both positive and negative aesthetic appraisals. And Jacobsen et al. (2006) correlated aesthetic judgment with activations in both anterior and posterior cingulate, as well as temporal pole, which has also been associated with emotion (e.g., Greene et al. 2001). Some of these authors also observed brain activity associated with motor-response, which might indicate engagement of the action tendencies associated with emotion (Frijda 1986). Kawabata and Zeki found bilateral activation in somato-motor cortex, Vartanian and Goel reported decreases in right caudate response when participant viewed ugly pictures, and Cela-Conde et al. found responses in prefrontal dorsolateral cortex at late latencies, an area associated with selection of action. Each of these studies is different, and each raises as many questions as it answers, but all suggest that some of the areas that show up in emotion studies are also major players in aesthetic response.

Introspection and neuroimaging support the conclusion that emotions arise when we have positive aesthetic experiences. One can also show that different affective states correlate with different aesthetic preferences. Mealey and Theis (1995) asked people to rate the attractiveness of various landscape paintings after asking them to report their moods. Anxious moods correlate with preferences for pictures of enclosed spaces and angry moods correlate with preferences for open spaces. White *et al.* (1981) showed that physical attractiveness judgments could be directly influenced by emotional induction. In their study emotionally evocative film clips were shown to increase assessments of physical attractiveness. Isen and Shalker (1982) were able to show a similar affect on aesthetic appraisals of photographs. They showed that participants who found a coin on the chair in the laboratory (planted by the experimenters) gave higher positive ratings to snapshots taken on their college campus. These studies establish a link between mood and aesthetic appreciation, and, given the close link between moods and emotions it is plausible that emotion induction would have an impact as well.

More enduring links between affective states and preference can also be demonstrated by comparing people who have different personality traits. For example, Furnham and Walker (2001) found that thrill-seeking and conscientiousness both correlate with a taste for representational art, while neuroticism and disinhibition correlate with high ratings for abstract paintings and pop art. Pop art was disliked by people who rate high on agreeableness. In another study, Rosenbloom (2006) showed that thrill-seekers use more colors when they paint and show a preference for "hot" colors. These personality traits can be interpreted, at least in part, as emotional dispositions, and, consequently, these findings point to a link between emotion and preference.

The link between emotion and preference can also be established by exploiting the well-known fact that repeated exposure to a stimulus induces positive affect (Zajonc 1968). Cutting (2006) exploited this fact in a study of aesthetic preferences for Impressionist paintings. During the course of a semester, he used both widely reproduced and rarely reproduced Impressionist paintings in the background of slides used while teaching his introduction to psychology course. He has independently shown that students prefer the frequently reproduced images, even if they could not recall having seen those images in the past. While teaching his class, he showed the infrequently reproduced works at a greater frequency and, at the end of the semester, he tested his students' preferences. They couldn't reliably recall whether or not they had seen any of the works before, but they now showed a strong preference for the images that had been shown with greater frequency over the course of the semester. The standard explanation of the mere exposure effect is that familiarity (even without recollection) induces positive affect, and positive affect increases preference. If this interpretation is right, Cutting's result adds further support to the claim that preference is linked to affective states.

Such findings indicate that emotions play a role in directing our aesthetic preferences. There is also evidence that, when emotions are diminished, there is a corresponding reduction in aesthetic interest. People who lack strong positive emotions tend to have less appreciation for aesthetic experiences than others. In a standard scale for measuring anhedonia, people with low positive affect are found to agree with the statement "The beauty of sunsets is greatly overrated" (Chapman *et al.* 1976). People who score high on alexithymia scales (characterized as having low emotional expressivity quite broadly) often have comparatively little interest in art, and are likely to prefer movies for their superficial entertainment value rather than their deeper meaning (Bagby *et al.* 1994).

The hypothesis that appreciation has an emotional basis also helps to explain variability in taste (Prinz 2007b). It is often noticed that beauty (and aesthetic worth more generally) is in the eye of the beholder. This platitude expresses both subjectivism and relativism. Folk aesthetics explicitly recognizes that aesthetic merits depend on us. Relativism is also borne out by more empirical findings. We have already seen that individuals with different personalities have different preferences. It is also easy to demonstrate group differences. For example, aesthetic preferences may vary between Eastern and Western cultures, with Westerners preferring to depict focal individuals and Easterners preferring more encompassing scenes. Masuda *et al.* (2008) asked Japanese and American subjects to take a photo of a seated model, and the Americans took close-ups while the Japanese took shots showing the model's entire body and much of the surrounding scene. There are also aesthetic differences dividing European cultures and African cultures. For example, among the Yoruba, one of the cardinal aesthetic virtues is shininess (Thompson 1973). Of course, Europeans do appreciate African art, but they may do so for different reasons than the Africans who produce that art. As Clifford Geertz (1976: 1498) put it, "Most [Europeans], I am convinced, see African sculpture as bush Picasso." To take one more vivid example of aesthetic relativism, preferences differ between members of the art world, and individuals who are less involved in the arts. In an amusing demonstration of this, Komar and Melamid surveyed ordinary people and found that they like landscapes with water, animals, and famous people—hardly common themes in contemporary art galleries (see Wypijewski 1999). One explanation for such differences is that aesthetic preferences are based on emotions, and emotions can be conditioned differently in different cultural settings. Differences in taste are easier to pin on differences in passions rather than differences in beliefs—it's far from clear what the relevant beliefs would be.

Curiously, the platitude that beauty is in the eye of the beholder is contradicted by other aspects of folk aesthetics. In some ways, people are objectivists about art. We tend to think that artworks would be beautiful even if no one continued to admire them (Nichols and Folds-bennett 2003), and we also tend to think that some people have better taste than others. There are aesthetic experts, and we sometimes defer to them when, for example, we invest in art or decorate our homes. On the face of it, this objectivist tendency is difficult to reconcile with the widespread recognition of aesthetic relativism, and it is also ostensibly difficult to reconcile with the conjecture that appreciation has an emotional basis. On closer examination, however, it turns out that aesthetic objectivism actually provides further grounds for equating appreciation with an emotion. The reason for this is that we tend to project our emotions out onto the world. Suppose that a painting makes us feel good, and then we are asked whether the painting would still be beautiful if people didn't react to it. When we imagine the case, we continue to imagine the painting, and as long as we imagine the painting, we get that good feeling. That leads us to think the painting is intrinsically good. And if artworks can be intrinsically good, then there may be objective aesthetic facts. Ironically, the very thing that makes tastes subjective and relative, also dupes us into thinking that aesthetic worth is objective.

In a test of this hypothesis, Nichols and Prinz (unpublished data) administered a questionnaire about whether artworks are objectively good to a group of undergraduate students, and we also gave the same group of students a questionnaire used by clinicians to measure anhedonia. People who are anhedonic have a diminished capacity to experience positive emotions. If objectivism is a consequence of projecting the positive emotions elicited by artworks onto the world, then anhedonic individuals should be less prone toward objectivism. This is exactly what we found. They were less likely than the comparison group to judge that artworks would no longer be beautiful if people stopped judging them to be beautiful. A non-affective theory of aesthetic appraisal would not predict this result.

The findings surveyed so far suggest that emotions arise during aesthetic appreciation, influence aesthetic preference, and may even be necessary for appreciating art. One can also argue for the emotional basis of appreciation by arguing against competing hypothesis. If appreciation is not affective, then what is it? The most obvious answer is that it is a rational process (or the output of a rational process). There is good reason for doubting this view. Here as elsewhere, reasons seem to underdetermine values. Suppose one studies a painting and discerns every fact about its genesis form and content. No deduction from these features seems to be sufficient for determining that the work is good. One might find that the work is compositionally balanced, original, and skillfully executed. One cannot infer that the work is good on this basis unless one values balance, originality, and skill. The value of these things cannot be a further descriptive fact about them, because for any descriptive fact there can be a question about whether it is worthy of appreciation. So it seems much more plausible that appreciating a work depends on the emotional responses we are disposed to have to its many features. This argument echoes a long tradition in the literature on value theory (cf. Hutcheson on art, and Hume on morals).

None of the evidence that I have been considering is decisive, but it can be systematized by supposing that appreciation is an emotional state. More specifically, I propose the following model. We need to distinguish two stages in the appraisal process. There is an initial response to the work, and an assessment of the work, which is informed by that response. The first stage often involves emotions, but need not; purely cognitive processes can occur during our response to art. The second stage necessarily involves emotions, I believe. It is the point at which we step back and judge, on the basis of the first stage, that a work is good or bad. Let's consider the two stages in a bit more detail.

The response stage is the stage at which we perceive the work and react to its features. Some of those reactions are passive. Some elements may elicit emotions because they resemble emotionally significant things in the real world, some combinations of form may satisfy us, irritate us, or draw our attention. In many cases the response is driven by perceptual factors that we are totally unaware of. For example, judgments of beauty are strongly affected by prototypicality. A more beautiful face is a more average face, and likewise for other objects (Hekkert and Van Wieringen 1990; Langlois and Roggman 1990). In addition, we have implicit biases for certain compositional features. Most of us are right-handed, and right-handers like works that have their focal objects on the right, and, in the case of portraits, we like to see the left cheek more than the right, (otherwise we would have to turn leftward to look the sitter in the eyes). It turns out that 73 percent of works have a right-handed bias (Grusser *et al.* 1988), though the pattern is not found among artists (such as Leonardo da Vinci) who are known to have been left-handed.

The response stage can also be affected top-down by knowledge. If we know that a picture was produced in a certain way (say, made out of human hair), it might excite us more. Beliefs can also affect attention and interpretation. For example, there has been a dramatic change in how people view the *Mona Lisa* (Boas 1940). Writing in Leonardo's time, Vasari described the painting as remarkable for its realism, and he described its sitter as a pretty young woman with a light expression and innocent smile. This all changed with the rise of Romanticism. Romantic critics viewed the painting as otherworldly and unreal, and they described the sitter as a femme fatale with eyes that track the viewer and a mysterious smile. We have inherited the Romantic construal and it affects how we experience the work. For example, we attend to the eyes and spooky landscape in the background. This results in a feeling of intrigue, vulnerability, and gratifying unease.

The second stage of aesthetic appraisal is assessment. We consider the responses evoked by the work in light of our aesthetic values. I think an aesthetic value is a rule stored in long-term memory that can be schematized: if a work W has feature F, then, to that extent W is good to degree N. For example, we may value words that evoke certain emotions or works that surprise us or impress us with their technical skill. We also bring in more background knowledge at this stage: Is the work original? Does it respond in interesting ways to other works in the history of art? Such explicit forms of deliberation may be comparatively rare, however. Research shows that when we explicitly reason about our preferences, we make bad choices that we come to regret (Wilson *et al.* 2003). There is also evidence that explicit reasoning is post-hoc (Johansson *et al.* 2005). People will come up with explanations for why they prefer one of two images even when experimenters secretly swap the two images, so that people end up generating reasons for preferring a picture that was not the one they in fact selected as preferable minutes earlier. This suggests that assessment often involves unconscious rules.

I think assessment is an affective process. All of the good-making features of a work are added together and combined with bad-making features, and the result is an overall level of goodness (or badness), which is what we report when we verbally appraise the work as good or bad. I propose that units of goodness that are tabulated in this way are affective. Any feature that we regard as good, whether consciously or unconsciously, contributes a bit of positive emotion. The evaluative rules that we apply generate positive emotions. In the scheme, "if a work W has feature F, then, to that extent W is good to degree N" the "good to degree N" is constituted by a positive feeling of degree N. There are also negative emotion rules (corresponding to features that we depreciate), which contribute negative emotions. Each feature that we assess in this way contributes to the total emotional state that results from our encounter with the work, and the valence and intensity of that total emotional state ordinarily constitutes our aesthetic appraisal.

## 1.2 Three objections

I will refine this model below, but first I want to consider four objections.

First, even if emotions often arise in the context of aesthetic evaluation, it seems perfectly obvious that they are dispensable. Consider the experienced art dealer who can quickly distinguish bad art from good. Such a dealer, well aware of the latest trends, might go to an art fair or gallery and buy some work by an unknown young artist because it resembles work that is doing well on the market. Recognizing such resemblances (or recognizing technical mastery, originality, composition, or almost any other feature that might contribute to a work's value) requires visual perception and some background knowledge about other works; it does not seem to require emotion. It is very plausible that some dealers are so accustomed to assessing art that they rarely react strongly to works, but they retain an eye for quality. They can appreciate that a work is good dispassionately.

Despite appearances, the dispassionate dealer is not a counter-example. Two possible replies are available, depending on the details of the case. First, it could always be argued that dispassionate dealers do not actually appreciate the art that they buy; they merely recognize that it will be appreciated by others. We might say that the dispassionate dealer is jaded, and is merely working like an anthropologist who keeps track of trends without having any genuine convictions about which trends are really good. We might say that the dealer is giving lip service to aesthetic praise, and has confused aesthetic worth with market value. Alternatively, it might turn out that dispassionate dealers are actually disposed to experience emotions of appreciation; it just happens that those emotions do not arise because they are over-practiced at aesthetic appraisal. When such dealers assess a work as good they are in effect recognizing that they would have a positive response to it if they weren't so harassed.

The second objection that I want to consider has to do with our ability to filter out misleading emotions when we make aesthetic judgments. I suggested earlier that appreciation is a positive emotional response to an artwork. But consider cases where a work induces negative emotions, such as sadness, fear, indignation, or disgust. In the latter category, one might include Mark Quinn's *Lucas*—a bust of his three-day-old child cast in liquidized placenta. One can appreciate such works even though they are repellent. In addition, there are countless bad works that induce positive emotions: works that are derivative, saccharine, or silly. One might be amused or charmed by paintings in the Museum of Bad Art, while still judging that they are bad (consider *Pauline Reclining* or *Love is Being Out on a Limb Together*). In sum, good art can elicit negative emotions, and bad art can elicit positive emotions. Appreciation seems to transcend these feelings, and must therefore have a non-emotional foundation.

I think this objection is important because it reveals something about the complex interaction of emotions during aesthetic appraisal, but it ultimately rests on a non sequitur. The fact that we can positively praise works that elicit negative emotions (and conversely) does not entail that such works fail to elicit positive emotions. A single work of art can elicit emotions that are both positive and negative. One might have a positive emotion precisely because the work so successfully elicits a negative emotion. Someone who appreciates the Quinn sculpture might be enthralled by the concept of depicting a baby out of the very materials that kept the baby alive *in utero*. The use of this medium—fragile, organic, and unprecedented in the history of art—might strike the viewer as clever, and the attribution of cleverness might lead to a positive emotion, and hence to a positive appraisal of the work. Another viewer might regard Quinn's choice of materials as an exercise in gratuitous shock value—banal, superficial, commercial, and vulgar. In that case, the initial disgust response elicited by the placenta will be followed by a feeling of disgust at the artist and his work: a depreciating appraisal.

In the case of "Bad Art," one might begin by noticing how inelegant and inept the works are. The awkward lines and distorted proportions, the unnecessary details, the hokey sentiments—all of this may lead to a negative feeling. But the failure to conform to aesthetic standards might be so extreme and so charmingly innocent that one might be amused. One might explicitly compare bad works to good counterparts: *Pauline Reclining* evokes Modigliani, and, if viewed with irony, *Love is Being Out on a Limb Together* has many of the virtues of a David Shrigley drawing. Sometimes these comparisons amplify the negative appraisal (ugliness is even more apparent when juxtaposed with beauty), and sometimes it mitigates the negative appraisal (why celebrate Shrigley, while scoffing at *Love is Being Out on a Limb?*). This complex unfolding of emotions raises some interesting questions. For example, one might wonder which of the many conflicting emotions qualifies as the appraisal. I will return to this question below. For now the main point is that there are resources for addressing the objection under consideration. The fact that we can appreciate works that elicit negative emotions (and conversely) does not entail that appreciation is not a positive affective state.

Another objection concerns my claim that emotions are part of the assessment stage, and not just the response stage. In arguing that appreciation has an emotional basis, I cited evidence that emotions arise when we appraise art and exert an influence on our appraisals. Such findings are ambiguous. They show that emotions are part of the appraisal process but they don't necessarily show that appreciation is itself an emotion. An alternative possibility might go like this. When we consider a work, it elicits various emotions in us, and then, partially on the basis of those emotions, we judge whether the work is good or bad. The judgment that a work is good or bad is not an emotion, but rather dispassionate. In other words, emotions might lead to appreciation rather than constituting appreciation. In terms of the model proposed above, the emotions may be part of the response process rather than the outputs of the assessment process. The data don't distinguish between cause and constitution.

I certainly admit that emotions can play a role in causing appreciation (e.g., we can appreciate a work because it moves us, for example), but I also want to insist that emotions constitute appreciation. My main reason for this conclusion is that it accounts for the phenomenology, evaluative nature, and motivational consequences of aesthetic appraisal. If the units used to assess art were not affective in nature, then it's not clear why we should call them units of goodness. To dramatize this point, imagine that units of goodness were jellybeans. We could say a unit of goodness is a green jellybean and a unit of badness is a red jellybean. Now imagine that a work is tabulated to get a jellybean score of 32 green and 16 red. Greens win. But what makes this green jellybean count as good, rather than bad? What makes the score qualify as an evaluation of the work rather than a mere quantification of its properties? It seems that, in order to qualify as evaluative, the units could not be arbitrary markers, like jellybeans. Emotions are not arbitrary. They are intrinsically valenced. If the units of goodness are feelings, we can explain why assessment qualifies as a form or evaluation. We can also explain why we are drawn to good works, why we seek them out, why we surround ourselves with them, why we pay for them and treasure them. We do this even when they also elicit negative emotions, such as disgust. Somehow, those feelings must be out-weighed, and they can only be outweighed, it seems, by other feelings that have a positive valence.

A final objection, which I owe to Peter Goldie, presses further on my claim that assessment is an affective process. This claim seems hard to reconcile with the fact that we often give reasons for our appraisals of art. The view just sketched, wherein we assess by tabulating units of positive emotion, seems insufficiently cognitive. We don't justify our positive appraisals of art by just saying how good they make us feel; we offer arguments. This suggests that a cognitive process is at work, even if emotions play some role.

I do not want to deny that we give reasons when justifying assessments, but I think this can be explained on the two-stage model. When we give reasons, I think we are reconstructing as best we can our implicit aesthetic rules. That is, we are trying to articulate what it is about the work that led us to appraise the work positively. Recall that aesthetic rules have the form: "If a work W has feature F, then, to that extent W is good to degree N." Thus, to justify praise, we list what we take these features to be. If a work struck me as good in virtue of its balanced composition, I will point to balance in trying to persuade others to share my evaluation. It would be useless for me to persuade them by citing my positive emotions. I can only persuade others by pointing out good-making features of the work. But it's perfectly compatible with this observation that to see a feature as good is a matter of feeling positively towards it. My proposal is that when we give reasons for appraising a work as good, we are implicitly assuming that the audience to whom we are speaking will have similar aesthetic values. That means that, once we point out the features we value, they too will have a positive emotional response to the work. If I show someone that Pollock's action paintings have a balanced distribution of colors, that person might reconsider her initial dismissal of the work, and come to feel positively about it. Upon seeing the balance, she'll experience the same positive emotions that I do, and agree that the work is good. Giving reasons is a matter of making emotion-eliciting features more salient to our conversation partners.

The arguments in this section are not demonstrative, but I hope that I have at least made it plausible that appreciation is an emotional state. I think that conclusion is the best explanation for what goes on during aesthetic appraisal.

## 2. What is appreciation?

### 2.1 Aesthetic emotion

I have been defending a model of aesthetic appraisal according to which appreciation is constituted by a positive emotional response. But this formulation is under-specified. What exactly is this positive emotion? This is not an easy question to answer, but I think we can make some progress on it. In this section, I will narrow down the possibilities by arguing against some tempting proposals.

To begin, let's consider three possibilities. The first is that appreciation is a biologically basic emotion dedicated to aesthetic evaluation. I find this implausible. It is not so implausible that we have a biologically basic emotional response to attractiveness (that might help us pick nutritious foods, opulent habitats, and ideal sexual partners), but aesthetic appreciation is not the same thing as attractiveness. An attractive thing can be disvalued aesthetically (a forgery, some soft pornography, a cliché sunset), and an unattractive thing can have aesthetic value (e.g., some Dubuffet paintings). Attractiveness is just one factor that may be assessed when deciding whether an artwork is good. Might we have evolved an emotion for aesthetic appreciation in addition to the emotions underlying attractiveness judgments? I doubt it. I can't develop the case here, but I don't think that the production and appreciation of art is an evolved response. It seems to appear relatively recently in the history of our species, and makes no obvious contribution to fitness. There is also considerable variability in what people aesthetically value, suggesting that it is not a biologically fixed response.

If appreciation is not biologically basic, then it is derived from other emotions. Here there are two possibilities. One is that appreciation is not one emotion, but many—perhaps an open-ended range of positive emotions that arise during the experience of art. The other possibility is that appreciation reduces to a single emotion, or perhaps a small class of emotions. I think a more unified theory would be better, all else being equal. If there were multiple different emotions that factor into appreciation, it would be harder to explain how we add them all up together to make an overall assessment of a work. It would also be hard to find coherence in the phenomenon of evaluating art. Aesthetic goodness would vary from work to work, and comparison would be difficult. Granted, there are some difficulties in comparing artworks, because the features by which we assess often seem incommensurable. Two works can be good for different reasons. But we do seem to be able to make comparisons. We can compile a list of favorite paintings, for example, and we can decide which postcard to buy at the museum shop. For such reasons, I think we should assume that appreciation has a kind of emotional uniformity until forced to conclude otherwise.

If appreciation is a single emotion (or small family of emotions) and not *sui generis*, then presumably it reduces to or derives from some other emotion. In other words, in trying to determine what appreciation is, we should try to identify it with an emotion that also arises outside of aesthetic contexts. Let me consider some candidates.

In the previous section, I described appreciation as a positive emotion. That might immediately bring to mind pleasure (for discussions of aesthetic pleasure, see Levinson 1996; Walton 1993). It might be proposed that appreciating an artwork is a matter of taking pleasure in it. This proposal has some intuitive appeal, because encounters with art often are pleasurable, but it also faces some serious objections. Some artworks are depressing, terrifying, or disturbing (the point has been made by others): consider Käthe Kollwitz's *Mother and Child* or Goya's *Disasters of War*. This is even more so when we move from pictures into film. Consider de Sica's *Shoeshine*, Bresson's *Mouchette*, Buñuel's *Los Olvidaos*, or Resnais' *Night and Fog*. It would be a gross mischaracterization of the phenomenology to call these works pleasurable.

Pleasure seems so unapt in such cases that one wonders whether I was too hasty in describing appreciation as a positive emotion. In some cases, encounters with great art are a largely negative experience. This objection trades on an ambiguity, however. "Positive" does not necessarily mean pleasant. Elsewhere I have argued that emotional valence is quite independent of good feelings. Valence has to do with appetitive dispositions. More precisely, a positive emotion is one that we will work to seek out or sustain. Positive emotions are positive reinforcers. We certainly seek out art. In economic terms, we are willing to incur costs to have aesthetic experiences. We invest money, time, and effort. This suggests that art induces emotions that are appetitive, and hence positive valenced in that technical sense, even if the emotions are not always pleasurable.

With this in mind, let's consider another candidate. Perhaps appreciation is a kind of admiration. Admiration is, strictly speaking, a social emotion—one that we would direct at the creator of a work rather than the work itself. It is intuitively plausible that art elicits admiration. When we see good art, we quickly turn our thoughts to the artist.

When you see a Caravaggio, you see it as a Caravaggio. You don't merely say this painting is great; you say this painter is great. It is also clear that we would withdraw praise if we discovered that an object of appreciation was not intentionally created. A pattern in concrete might strike us as genius if we think it is created intentionally by Tapies, but it may not be worthy of aesthetic praise if it turns out to be an unintentional accident. Preissler and Bloom (2008) have shown that two-year-olds regard something as an artwork only if they have reason to believe it was created intentionally. Spilled paint is art, and hence a candidate for aesthetic appraisal, only if it was spilled on purpose.

Admiration has an advantage over pleasure: it is not necessarily pleasurable. Admiration can even involve feelings of subordination, which can be unpleasant. It is nevertheless a positive emotion in the technical sense. We seek to experience things we admire. There may even be roots of this response in other species. Many mammals have social status hierarchies, and studies show that a macaque monkey will actually forgo a food award just to look at pictures of an alpha male (Deaner *et al.* 2005)!

Nevertheless, several serious problems arise if we equate appreciation with admiration. First, as a social emotion, admiration may be too intellectually demanding to explain many cases of appreciation. Young children and individuals with autism may appreciate art without having the capacity or tendency to think about the fact that art works are intentionally created by someone. Second, admiration often seems to be a *consequence* of appreciation rather than a constituting part. We admire an artist because we appreciate the work. Third, admiration sometimes comes prior to appreciation. We find a work impressive, which involves appreciating what the artist has accomplished, and that leads us to appreciate the work. Fourth, admiration renders it difficult to have an aesthetic appreciation of nature and other objects that were not products of intentional creation. Fifth, admiration seems to be an odd emotion to attribute to an artist, who, in the course of creating a work, appreciates that it is good; self-admiration seems arrogant and requires a curious split in the self (the admirer usually looks up to the person admired). Sixth, appreciation generally seems directed toward the artwork, not toward its creator. Seventh, while looking at some works of art we don't dwell much on who in particular created them (think of decorative arts, or arts created by large groups or artisans, like the tomb reliefs in Egypt's Valley of the Kings). For all these reasons, I think it would be a mistake to equate appreciation with admiration.

Another possibility, which may seem somewhat more promising, would be to equate appreciation with interest. When we look at good works of art, we often attend to them with great interest. Good works can be stared at and contemplated at length. They often repay these efforts, by leading us to new insights and discoveries. Moreover, like admiration, interest does not necessarily feel pleasurable. Horror and despair can warrant interest.

I think interest is on the right track, but also problematic. For one thing, interest need not be a form of praise. Sometimes bad works interest us because they are so bad. Another problem is that interest is most readily applied while we are experiencing a work, while appreciation often takes place afterwards. This is especially true in the performing arts. We might be so engaged by a performance—so interested in it—that we don't step back and evaluate it. Then, after it's over we reflect and conclude that it was a good work. Finally, some good works are actually difficult to sustain interest in. Consider slowly paced films, like Tarkoksky's *Solaris* or Antonioni's *Red Desert*. Such works are challenging to watch, because our minds may wander, our attention may wane, our patience may go thin. But they are often great precisely because of their pacing. The Iranian director, Abbas Kiarostami puts it this way:

> [T]here are films that nail you to your seat and overwhelm you to the point that you forget everything, but you feel cheated later. These are the films that take you hostage. I absolutely don't like the films in which the filmmaker take their viewer hostages and provoke them. I prefer the films that put their audience to sleep in the theater. (Akrami 2000)

There may well be a sense in which such films are nevertheless interesting, but the term "interest" implies that good works engage us more than bad works, and that simply isn't the case. It might be better to say that appreciation warrants attention, even if the works that we appreciate do not always attract or sustain interest easily.

I have considered three possible candidates for reductively explaining the emotion of appreciation, and I found all of them wanting. But I also think each captures something that a correct account should try to preserve. Appreciation is not a form of pleasure, but like pleasure it is positive valenced. Appreciation is not admiration, but admiration may capture something right about the upward directionality of appreciation: good works strike us as elevated. Appreciation is not interest, but good works warrant attention.

Integrating these lessons, I want to offer another proposal. Perhaps we can identify appreciation with a kind of wonder. Wonder is no longer widely discussed in emotion theory, but it once had a privileged place. It was widely discussed and celebrated in medieval thought (Bynum 1997) on through to the Enlightenment (Datson and Park 1998). Wonder in included on Descartes' (1649) list of basic emotions, and, indeed, he describes it as the most fundamental. For Descartes, wonder is a kind of surprise, and intense wonder is astonishment. I'm hesitant to adopt this characterization, because I think we can respond with wonder to something that is familiar. One might feel wonder when looking in a lover's eyes no matter how often one has done it before. "Wonder" is synonymous, as I understand the term, with marvel. So the proposal is that to value a feature of an artwork is to marvel in it. This marveling can vary in intensity. When the response is very strong, we call it "amazement" or "awe." Neither of these terms, unlike Descartes' "astonishment," implies novelty or the unexpected. A great painting, like Goya's *Third of May*, might amaze us each time we see it. What is crucial is not how the work violates our expectations, but how it captivates us.

It is unknown whether wonder is itself a biologically basic emotion. One possibility is that it evolved as a kind of reward signal when attending to things that are valuable to survival. The wonder experienced when staring into a lover's eyes may be an example of this. We can also experience wonder when we look at newborn babies. This may be a mechanism that helps motivate us to care for them. In addition there is the wonder we experience when we see certain natural scenes. Perhaps paying attention to nature, especially when it is complex, unusual, or grand, was advantageous in the past. These are wild speculations, of course. I think it is a bit more plausible that wonder is a culturally elaborated extension of a biologically basic emotion. Perhaps positively valenced attention is a basic emotion, and that state takes on a distinctive character though enculturation.

I think the principal difference between mere positively valenced attention and wonder is that wonder is also to be characterized as a feeling of reverence. The object of wonder is an object of veneration. When we contemplate artworks, this veneration usually lacks religious significance, but perhaps not entirely. Artworks are often treated as sacred, and artists are sometimes viewed as if they were endowed with magical powers. Like other sacred objects, we also want to come into contact with wondrous things, and the destruction of an object of wonder is regarded as a more significant loss than the destruction of objects that merely please us. Artworks are more like people in this respect. We see them as unique and irreplaceable (no mere copy will do). If the *Mona Lisa* burnt in a fire, we'd sooner visit the ashes than a perfect replica. This may be a culturally driven phenomenon. In Western culture, like many others, artworks were once widely used in ritual contexts, and the secular appreciation of art is informed by that history. If so, wonder has biological roots, but it is also a product of culture. If appreciation is wonder, then appreciation is a biocultural response.

Wonder captures the features of pleasure, admiration, and interest that seem central to appreciation. Like pleasure, it is a positive emotion, though not always pleasant. Like admiration, it involves a feeling of elevation: the wondrous thing has an elevated status, and we are elevated by it. Like interest, wonder is a kind of regard, though whereas interest can be characterized as a way of looking, wonder might be better characterized as a way of seeing: we see things with wonder (or, alternatively, we see the wonder in things). Wonder also warrants attention. Something wondrous is worthy of attention and reflection.

For these reasons, I think wonder nicely captures what goes on when we positively appraise artworks. I think it is the best candidate for the emotion underlying aesthetic appreciation. This is just speculation, of course, and preliminary speculation at that. I have not provided a complete analysis of wonder, and further evidence is needed to establish that wonder is the basis of appreciation. It remains possible that appreciation involves a more open-ended range of emotions. I have also said nothing about depreciation. Is that a single emotion too? If so, which one? I leave these tasks for another occasion. For now I simply present the wonder hypothesis as a possibility worthy of further investigation. Before concluding, I will address one more objection.

*2.2 Aesthetic wonder*

I have been pursuing a reductionist account of appreciation. I have suggested that appreciation reduces to some emotion that is not specific to the domain or aesthetic appraisal. And in particular, I proposed that appreciation is a form of wonder. The problem with pursuing a reductionist account is that this approach makes it difficult to see what is *distinctive* about aesthetic responding. Wonder arises in non-aesthetic contexts. I already mentioned the wonder that can be experienced when staring in a lover's eyes or at a newborn child. One can experience wonder when looking at a bee-hive, at a tornado, or at an intellectual achievement. As Peter Goldie points out (personal communication), we can even have a non-aesthetic experience of wonder when looking at art; we marvel at Michelangelo's stamina when looking at the Sistine Chapel ceiling. If wonder plays all these non-aesthetic roles, how can aesthetic appreciation simply reduce to wonder? We can certainly appreciate tornados and newborns aesthetically, but we need not, and, crucially, when we are having a response of wonder to a baby or a storm, we are not necessarily at that moment having an aesthetic response. It seems something has gone wrong.

The answer to this worry is quite simple, I think. Aesthetic appreciation is a form of wonder, but it is not the case that all forms of wonder are forms of aesthetic apprecia-tion. Elsewhere I have defended the view that we can generate new forms of emotion by re-calibrating previously existing emotions to new classes of elicitors (Prinz 2007a). "Re-calibration" is simply setting up a mechanism in our long-term memory that links the emotion to a specific set of stimuli, which may not have been disposed to elicit the emotion before. *Schadenfreude* is joy re-calibrated to suffering; guilt may be a blend of anxiety and sadness re-calibrated to situations in which we have harmed a loved one; accidie is despondency re-calibrated to religious worship; patriotism is pride re-calibrated to one's nation and symbols thereof. And so on. In each of these cases, we first construe a class of stimuli is a way that naturally elicits the more fundamental emotion, and thereby set up an association between those stimuli and that emotion. Representations of those stimuli are stored in memory, in what I call an elicitation file, and, on future occasions, encounters with a stimulus of the right kind elicit the emotion. Then we introduce a verbal label to refer to that fundamental emotion as elicited by the kinds of things represented in the elicitation file. I want to say that aesthetic appreciation is wonder that has been re-calibrated to artworks and things that we construe as artworks.

The solution comes easy enough, but it immediately leads into one of the largest and thorniest questions in all of aesthetics: What exactly is an artwork? Fortunately, I don't need to provide an answer here. I think ordinary consumers of art probably have no good theories about what artworks are. They could not make much progress on questions about the ontology of art. Philosophers have spent centuries on this question without arriving at consensus. From the perspective of aesthetic psychology, the question isn't about the essence of art. Rather, it's about how we recognize something as an artwork. Posed this way, the question is just one instance of a more general question about how we classify things. Most people couldn't tell you the essence of a tiger or even of gold. But, we are all pretty good at identifying things. Likewise, we usually have little difficulty recognizing something as an artwork. With tigers, gold, and artworks, we probably use similar mental tricks. In particular, we probably store representations of category exemplars, and then, when we encounter a new object we compare it to exemplars we already possess. We may also store information about where category instances are likely to occur: tigers are found in jungles and zoos, gold is found in jewelry, and artworks are found in museums (or on stages and screens). We use all of this information to classify. In some cases, classification is difficult: Is a happening an artwork? It's hard to tell, because it's unlike the most familiar exemplars. We can construe a happening as an artwork by focusing on the features it shares with paradigm cases. We can also view a perfume mixture, a meal at a restaurant, or a natural landscape as artworks in a similar way. When we do this, we may be making a mistake, but that doesn't matter. For present purposes, they key thing is that, in the absence of any adequate theory of what artworks are, we can classify things as art, and we have a stored mental file of exemplar representations that helps us do that.

So the story that I am telling can be summarized as follows. When we encounter an artwork, we first classify it as such by comparison to memories of other artworks. Then we respond to it. Then we assess it. Each merit induces a small amount of wonder, and the sum of all the wonder is the degree to which we appreciate the work. Because wonder so induced is calibrated to things that we classify as artworks, it can be referred to as "aesthetic wonder" or, if I am right, "appreciation."

## 3.  Conclusions

In this discussion, I have been investigating the nature of aesthetic appreciation. A lot of the work on appreciation has focused on the question of what we appreciate, rather than on the nature of appreciation itself. Of course, there has been some important work on the topic in the past. Major contributors to aesthetics have made relevant proposals, including Hutcheson and Kant. My goal here has not been to review the philosophical literature. Rather, this has largely been an exercise in naturalized aesthetics, with a focus on what we can learn from contemporary cognitive science and philosophical psychology. This exercise led me to draw two main conclusions. First, appreciation is an emotional state, and, second, it may be a form of wonder. Both of these conclusions are hostage to empirical fortune. Little work has been done to tease apart the emotions that are involved in aesthetic response and the emotions that are involved in aesthetic appraisal, and, to my knowledge, there has been no empirical exploration of the role of wonder in appreciation of art. The second part of this chapter is even more speculative than the first. If the conclusions do not hold up, I hope at least that progress on the nature of appreciation will be made in the course of refuting them.[1]

[1]  I am grateful to Peter Goldie, Jenefer Robinson, and Angelika Seidel for probing and valuable comments.

# References

Akrami, J. (2000). *Friendly Persuasion: Iranian Cinema after the Revolution.* Jam-Hi Productions.

Bagby, R. M., J. D. A. Parker, and G. J. Taylor (1994). The twenty-item Toronto alexithymia scale-1: Item selection and cross-validation of the factor structure. *Journal of Psychosomatic Research*, 38: 23–32.

Boas, G. (1940). The *Mona Lisa* in the history of taste. *Journal of the History of Ideas*, 1: 207–24.

Bynum, C. W. (1997). Wonder. *American Historical Review*, 102: 1–26.

Cela-Conde, C. J., G. Marty, F. Maestu, T. Ortiz, E. Munar, A. Fernandez, M. Roca, J. Rossello, and F. Quesney (2004). Activation of the prefrontal cortex in the human visual aesthetic perception. *Proceedings of the National Academy of Science*, 101: 6321–5.

Chapman, L. J., J. P. Chapman, and M. L. Raulin (1976). Scales for physical and social anhedonia. *Journal of Abnormal Psychology*, 85: 374–82.

Cutting, J. (2006). The mere exposure effect and aesthetic preference. In *New Directions in Aesthetics, Creativity and the Arts*. Amityville, NY: Baywood Publishing Co., pp. 33–46.

Datson, L. and K. Park (1998). *Wonders and the Order of Nature*. New York: Zone Books.

Deaner, R. O., A. V. Khera, and M. L. Platt (2005). Monkeys pay per view: Adaptive valuation of social images by Rhesus macaques. *Current Biology*, 15: 543–8.

Descartes, René ([1649] 1988). *The Passions of the Soul.* In J. Cottingham, R. Stoothoff, and D. Murdoch (trans. and eds.), *Selected Philosophical Writings of René Descartes*. Cambridge: Cambridge University Press.

Frijda, N. H. (1986). *The Emotions*. Cambridge: Cambridge University Press.

Furnham, A. and J. Walker (2001). Personality and judgments of abstract, pop art, and representational paintings. *European Journal of Personality*, 15: 57–72.

Geertz, C. (1976). Art as a cultural system. *Modern Language Notes*, 91: 1473–99.

Greene, J. D., R. B. Sommerville, L. E. Nystrom, J. M. Darley, and J. D. Cohen (2001). An fMRI investigation of emotional engagement in moral judgment. *Science*, 293: 2105–8.

Grusser, O. J., T. Selke, and B. Zynda (1988). Cerebral lateralization and some implications for art, aesthetic perception, and artistic creativity. In I. Reutschler, B. Herzberger, and D. Epstein (eds.), *Beauty and the Brain: Biological Aspects of Aesthetics*. Boston, MA: Springer-Verlag, pp. 257–93.

Hekkert, P. and Van Wieringen, P. (1990). Complexity and prototypicality as determinants of the appraisal of cubist paintings. *British Journal of Psychology*, 81: 483–95.

Isen, A. M. and T. E. Shalker (1982). The effect of feeling state on evaluation of positive, neutral, and negative stimuli: When you "accentuate the positive," do you "eliminate the negative"? *Social Psychology Quarterly*, 45: 58–63.

Jacobsen, T., R. I. Schubotz, L. Hofel, and D. Y. Von Cramon (2006). Brain correlates of aesthetic judgment of beauty. *NeuroImage*, 29: 276–85.

Johansson, P., L. Hall, S. Sikstrom, and A. Olsson (2005). Failure to detect mismatches between intention and outcome in a simple decision task. *Science*, 310: 116–19.

Kawabata, H. and S. Zeki (2004). Neural correlates of beauty. *Journal of Neurophysiology*, 91: 1699–1705.

Langlois, J. H. and Roggman, L. A. (1990). Attractive faces are only average. *Psychological Science*, 1: 115–21.

Levinson, J. (1996). *The Pleasures of Aesthetics: Philosophical Essays*. Ithaca, NY: Cornell University Press.

Masuda, T., R. Gonzalez, L. Kwan, and R. E. Nisbett (2008). Culture and aesthetic preference: Comparing the attention to context of East Asians and European Americans. *Personality and Social Psychology Bulletin*, 34: 1260–75.

Mealey, L. and P. Theis (1995). The relationship between mood and preferences among natural landscapes: An evolutionary perspective. *Ethology and Sociobiology*, 16: 247–56.

Nichols, S. and T. Folds-Bennett (2003). Are children moral objectivists? Children's judgments about moral and response-dependent properties. *Cognition*, 90: B23–B32.

Preissler, M. A. and P. Bloom (2008). Two-year-olds use artist intention to understand drawings. *Cognition*, 106: 512–18.

Prinz, J. J. (2007a). *The Emotional Construction of Morals*. Oxford: Oxford University Press.

——(2007b). Really bad taste. In M. Kieran and D. Lopes (eds.), *Knowing Art: Essays in Aesthetics and Epistemology*. Dordrecht: Springer, pp. 95–107.

Rosenbloom, T. (2006). Color preferences of high and low sensation seekers. *Creativity Research Journal*, 18: 229–35.

Thompson, R. F. (1973). Yoruba artistic criticism. In W. L. D'azevedo (ed.), *The Traditional Artist in African Societies*. Bloomington, IN: Indiana University Press, pp. 19–59.

Vartanian, O. and V. Goel (2004) Neuroanatomical correlates of aesthetic preference for paintings. *Neuroreport*, 15: 893–7.

Walton, K. (1993). How marvelous! Toward a theory of aesthetic value. *Journal of Aesthetics and Art Criticism*, 51: 499–510.

White, G., S. Fishbein, and J. Rutstein (1981). Passionate love and the misattribution of arousal. *Journal of Personality and Social Psychology*, 41: 56–62.

Wilson, T. D., D. T. Gilbert, and D. B. Centerbar (2003). Making sense: The causes of emotional evanescence. In I. Brocas and J. D. Carillo (eds.), *The Psychology of Economic Decisions. Volume 1: Rationality and Well-Being*. New York: Oxford University Press, pp. 209–33.

Wypijewski, J. (1999) *Painting by Numbers: Komar and Melamid's Scientific Guide to Art*. Berkeley: University of California Press.

Zajonc, R. B. (1968) Attitudinal effects of mere exposure. *Journal of Personality and Social Psychology*, 9: 1–27.

# 6

# Beauty is Felt, Not Calculated; and it Does Not Fit in Boxes

*Roddy Cowie*

## 1. Frameworks for the description of emotion

The framework that is used here comes from an earlier essay called 'Forms of Emotional Colouring that Pervade Everyday Life' (Cowie 2010). It is meant to reflect ideas about emotion that are widely held rather than to state a distinctive position, though given the nature of emotion research, there is at least some dissent over almost every point.

Probably the most controversial feature of the framework is that it does not give priority to the most commonly used approach to describing emotion, that is, description in terms of categories such as fear, anger, and so on. The basic image that is used instead is one that is widespread in empirical research. Emotions are thought of as syndromes involving various kinds of component (feelings, percepts, expressions, characteristic actions, and so on). Not all of the components, but many of them, vary continuously. Instead of reflecting divisions into natural kinds, words are seen as a particular way of summarizing that underlying, multidimensional, continuum.

That kind of image has been elaborated in a number of different ways. Pennebaker and Chung (2007) draw out the similarities between describing emotion in words and transforming an analogue signal into a digital code They imply that verbal description could in principle fully capture the experience, but would involve what they describe as 'overrepresentation'. The usual case is 'moderate representation', which loses information, but allows cognitive processes to access the information that matters. At first sight, the description in 'Forms of Emotional Colouring' appears more radical. It describes the relationship between everyday category words and a 'landscape' defined by the underlying continuous variables. It suggests that category names point to particularly distinctive regions in that landscape. The regions that they describe accurately are like points of reference in a continuously varying landscape rather than national territories which partition a continent without overlap or remainder. That might seem to go well beyond Pennebaker and Chung, until one registers that the descriptions they are talking about are not simply categorizations: they are narratives which include causal words (such as 'because' and 'reason'), and insight words (such as 'understand' and 'realize'). It is part of their account that even those, which include much more than simple category names, usually omit detail.

Views like that go against a strong intuitive disposition to believe that emotion is fundamentally categorical. It is clear that people naturally conceptualize emotion in terms of apparently discrete categories, such as fear and anger, at least when they are thinking about it in abstract rather than confronting examples. However, the arguments against that intuition are varied and substantial. One line of research deals with the perception of other people's emotions. When people imagine other people's behaviour, they do so in such a way that it will contain clear instances of discrete categories. However, when they are presented with evidence in the form of recordings of naturally occurring emotional episodes, they discover that what they see and hear rarely fits any single standard category (Cowie and Cornelius 2003; Devillers *et al.* 2005; Vaudable *et al.* 2010). Objective studies of emotion-related behaviour reinforce the point by showing that even partly natural material does not show the clusters of expressive features that people believe implicitly are the way emotion is expressed, and that they use to act emotion (Scherer and Ellgring 2007a, 2007b). Pennebaker and Chung come from a different tradition which is concerned with the effects of verbalizing one's own emotional state. It is therapeutically important that assigning it to categories actually changes it—which strongly suggests that what existed before the exercise was not categorical. The idea that emotions have a componential structure also explains something that is a problem for strictly categorical accounts, which is that people can quite easily make judgements about levels of similarity and contrast between two emotions: some share many components, others very few. Feldman Barrett (2006) provides a fuller review of the empirical work in this area.

Philosophers are familiar with the distinction between the epistemological question of whether people perceive emotion in terms of distinct categories and the ontological question of whether it does actually fall into those categories. Many neuroscientists in particular believe that the various things called emotion actually arise from a modest number of naturally distinct systems (Ledoux 1996). Individual pieces of research often appear to support that view, but a series of meta-analyses suggest that there is little convincing evidence of discrete systems in the evidence as a whole (Murphy *et al.* 2003; Phan *et al.* 2002). In contrast, there is a good deal of evidence for systems related to arousal, valence, reinforcement, and other constructs that relate to dimensions or components of emotion.

If individual emotion categories like fear and anger are superimposed on an underlying reality which is continuous, it would be strange if the category 'emotion' itself were not similar. A great deal of evidence suggests that that is the case. A well-known formalization of the idea uses 'prototype theory', which proposes that the category 'emotion' is defined by central exemplars, and membership becomes progressively less clear as distance from those exemplars increases (Fehr and Russell 1984; Shaver *et al.* 1987). A particularly direct demonstration comes from evidence that there is a substantial gap between states where raters judge that the person they are observing is completely unemotional, and states where they judge that he or she is exhibiting emotion in a strict sense (Cowie 2010). This is to say that a large part of life is occupied by states which are neither completely unemotional, nor emotions in the core sense of the word.

The issue is by no means closed, and there is no obvious way to resolve it beyond doubt. But in that situation, there are good reasons for leaning towards the continuous option. It is a long-established rule that *natura non facit saltus*—nature does not make abrupt leaps. Clearly, there are exceptions to the rule. Nevertheless, it seems a fair principle that continuity should be regarded as the default, so that the onus of providing evidence falls on those who propose discontinuities. As indicated above, the evidence is not there.

Perhaps the most basic argument, though, is that category names *per se* are not very interesting or useful descriptions of emotion. The most interesting descriptions, and the most practically useful, are at the level of components: they articulate what people feel, do, perceive, think, and so on, under the influence of emotion. There is a good deal of convergence on the kinds of descriptor that are useful for that purpose, and they do not lead naturally to categorical conceptions. Perhaps they could be recast in terms that do result in a categorical structure, but it is difficult to see how; and as indicated above, there do not seem to be compelling reasons to try.

On that basis, it is not the main priority of this chapter to decide whether aesthetic responses are or are not emotional. The main question is how they stand in relation to phenomena that are manifestly emotional. The conclusion that they belong to a single natural kind is one possible outcome, but given what it already known about emotion, it should not be considered a particularly central issue. The fundamental issue is whether the attempt to set them within a single frame of reference helps to illuminate aesthetic responses.

'Forms of Emotional Colouring' groups the resources needed to describe emotional life under ten headings. They are introduced briefly here, and then the next section considers how they apply to aesthetic responses. They are drawn directly from 'Forms of Emotional Colouring', and readers are referred to that essay for the justifications and sources behind the choice.

*Units*. Discussions are often conducted as if abstract concepts like 'fear' were the only conceivable units of analysis for emotion. However, concrete instances have at least an equally good claim to be considered as units. These include short-lived, relatively homogeneous 'episodes', and longer 'eras' over which enduring emotions are part of the person's make-up, even if they are not always active.

*Dimensions*. Psychologists routinely describe both concepts and instances of emotion in terms of dimensions derived from statistical analysis. A well-constructed recent study (Fontaine *et al.* 2007) identified four.

- *Valence* describes the individual's global sense of how positive or negative a situation is.

- *Activation* describes the strength of the individual's disposition to act or to avoid acting.
- *Potency* describes the individual's sense that he or she has or lacks the power to deal with relevant events.
- *Unpredictability* describes the individual's sense that events are or are not proceeding according to expectation.

*Engagement* refers to a fifth dimension, which is clearly important in some contexts, but less often discussed. It is the individual's sense that events are a matter of concern to him or her. Ortony (2002) used the term 'caring', but engagement (as opposed to detachment) seems less loaded.

*Feeling*. The term 'feeling' has two senses which can be separated conceptually, though it is commonly assumed that they are related in reality. First, it refers to the visceral experiences that William James identified as central to emotion. Second, it expresses something about the cognitions involved in emotion. For example, the valence that matters for emotion is not the individual's actuarial calculation of the balance between threats and opportunities: it is a felt evaluation, which may well be at odds with actuarial judgement. The same is true of all the dimensions listed above, and the appraisals considered below.

*Appraisal*. Appraisal is a distinctive form of perception, which psychological accounts consider central to emotion. It involves a selective grasp of a situation, which highlights what is relevant to the subject's 'weal or woe' (Arnold 1960). Sophisticated accounts of appraisal such as Scherer's (2009) identify multiple issues that appraisals address, including intrinsic pleasantness; novelty; relevance to the subject's goals and needs; implications for the future events, relationships, etc; the subject's power to affect the situation and/or to adjust to its consequences; and the normative significance of events and actions (including moral significance). Clearly there is substantial overlap between the themes of appraisal and themes raised in connection with dimensions and feeling. What appraisal theory adds is that these themes are inherent in perceptual experience as well as other modalities.

*Action tendency*. Plato's metaphor of the charioteer depicts emotion as harnessed to action in a way that intellect is not. The idea was reinstated in the modern era in Frijda's concept of 'action tendencies' (1986). He (and others) argues that tendencies to act in certain ways are part and parcel of particular emotions—the urge to flee is part of fear, the urge to attack is part of anger, and so on. As Cowie and Cornelius (2003) pointed out, action tendency can be thought of as an expansion of the activation axis in dimensional descriptions. Describing activation specifies that there is a tendency to some action: describing an action tendency specifies what the action in question is.

*Expression*. It is a very characteristic feature of emotional episodes that people experiencing them tend to act in ways that communicate information about the episode—they laugh, smile, weep, shout, whisper, tremble, gesticulate, and so on.

*Emotional modes of action and cognition.* Emotion affects not only what people do, but also the way they do it, so it can be recognized from the way people walk, knock, or drive a car. Intuitively the principle seems to apply to thought as well as to overt action, and evidence confirms that emotion affects various cognitive processes, including attention, judgement of risk, sustained logical problem-solving, memory, and so on.

*Connectedness.* An emotional episode is typically richly connected in the sense that describing it adequately depends on referring beyond the person who has an emotional experience to various significant objects and significant others. One of the marks of emotion in the strong sense is that it has an object. An episode is likely to be prompted by one or more events, recent or in the distant past. Connections with people are particularly rich: it may involve them as prompts, objects, recipients, audiences, critics, and so on.

*Impressions of emotion.* What happens in a large proportion of emotional episodes depends quite fundamentally on the fact that people form impressions of each other's emotions and act on them.

*Global labels.* It is a feature of the area that people have a wealth of names for states distinguished by the kinds of property that have just been listed. These names are involved in registering consciously what is happening, understanding it and judging what it permits and excuses, communicating about it, and much more.

It is worth separating out one other theme which is touched on very briefly in 'Forms of Emotional Colouring' (in the context of expression), but which is very prominent in the field of emotion at large. It is the tension between theories that consider emotion as a product of evolution and those that consider it as a product of culture. The point here is not to weigh the alternatives. It is that something about emotion means that both views have strong attractions. It is possible to read Darwin and feel convinced that his evolutionary ideas tap something fundamental about emotion; and also to read Harré (1989) and feel equally convinced that his social constructivism comes near the heart of the matter. One might say that the fingerprints of both evolution and culture seem to be conspicuous in a way that they are not in other areas of psychology.

## 2. Approaching the description of aesthetic responses

This section uses the headings introduced in the previous section to follow through first, matches between emotion and aesthetic response; and then, mismatches. Within each part, it considers issues in the same order as the previous section, with occasional exceptions.

*Parallels between emotional and aesthetic responses*

*Units.* The decision to take aesthetic responses as the topic reflects the fact that choosing units is a substantial issue. The term identifies a type of unit that psychology can engage with richly; whereas questions about abstract aesthetic concepts give it much less purchase. The fact that it makes sense to consider that kind of unit is a non-trivial link to emotion. The link is reinforced by the fact that there are similar issues of dual timescale. Our response to beauty involves both episodes of brief, intense response, and eras of sustained appreciation.

Much of what follows here reflects a related point. It is useful to consider aesthetic responses and emotional episodes as units because in both cases, the phenomena are multilayered and interconnected, and abstracting risks dismissing issues that are actually essential. There is a provocative similarity between comments on that issue in the two domains. For example, Scherer (2009) argues that the defining characteristic of emotion is that multiple systems (which are broadly linked to the themes sketched in the last section) are drawn into surges of synchronized activity. That is strikingly reminiscent of descriptions of aesthetic experience based on Kant, such as Goldman's: 'the full engagement of our mental (perceptual, cognitive, affective) capacities and the felt intensity of the experience that results' (2001: 262).

It is interesting to ask whether similar issues arise over units of analysis for other psychological phenomena, such as drives, or learning, or reasoning, or communication. If not, it marks an interesting structural similarity between the aesthetic and emotional domains.

*Feeling.* It makes sense to move from there to the issue of feeling. This is flagged in the description from Goldman above; and intuitively, it would seem to be the link between aesthetic response and emotion that most people notice immediately. It involves both sides of the distinction drawn earlier.

Feeling in the sense of visceral reaction is one of the obvious hallmarks of aesthetic response in the short term. It is a cliché to say that art is breathtaking, or heart-stoppingly beautiful, or raises the hairs on the back of your neck; but the clichés are clearly grounded in fact. Intense experiences of beauty affect very much the same autonomic systems as intense emotions.

As with emotion, the issue of visceral reaction is conceptually distinct from a second point, which is that aesthetic responses are felt rather than achieved by a process of rational symbol manipulation. The judgement that something is beautiful need not be accompanied by gross visceral reactions, but it is still not the outcome of a calculation. Even if there were a formula that could discriminate objects that were generally considered beautiful from objects that were not, someone who could only make the discrimination by taking measurements and applying the formula would not have experienced beauty, and would not understand it. In contrast to most thought experiments, there are real cases where something quite similar happens. It is possible to appreciate the technical sophistication of a piece of music, for instance, by considering the chord progressions; but it is another matter altogether whether the sound will turn out to be beautiful. If the felt response does not materialize, the piece falls short, however well constructed it may be.

It is natural to believe that the two senses of 'feeling' are connected, but the issue is actually not at all clear. It is just the kind of issue that psychology would typically try to resolve by collecting more detailed evidence about the systems involved in various kinds of feeling, emotional and aesthetic.

A subtler issue is raised by a point that Sibley (1965: 34) made in memorable style:

merely to learn from others, on good authority, that the music is serene, the play moving, or the picture unbalanced, is of little aesthetic value: the crucial thing is to see, hear, or feel.

The parallels to the second point above are obvious. However, Sibley's conclusion is that the aesthetic response is a kind of perception. It will, therefore, be asked whether the issue is that the response should be felt or that it should be perceived. There is an answer which is too interesting to censor. One of the most distinguished living visual scientists, Irving Biederman, has highlighted the fact that brain areas associated with high-level visual processing are rich in neurotransmitters that are associated with pleasure (Biederman and Vessel 2006). That offers a very useful way to bolster the argument against reifying conceptual lines. Much as one might want to distinguish perception and valenced feeling, neither experience nor neuroscience actually reveals a sharp division.

*Appraisal*. The point that has just been made is intimately linked to appraisal. As Sibley insisted, beauty is experienced perceptually. The archetypal experience of beauty is that something is seen or heard as beautiful. However, it is a perception infused with significance, not simply an account of shapes, sizes, or potential functions. That is what appraisal is. It is worth noting that the experience is not simply concerned with intrinsic pleasantness; both power and moral significance are often deeply implicated. Describing a work as powerful is part of the standard vocabulary of criticism; and although a beautiful person is not necessarily good, few would deny that the existence of beauty is experienced as good, and its destruction is experienced as appalling.

*Dimensions*. Considering dimensional descriptions yields another set of similarities. Valence is clearly relevant to aesthetic responses as well as emotion. Beauty is manifestly a valenced concept. Of course there are paradoxical cases, such as Yeats's 'terrible beauty', but the poetic tension arises precisely because the contrasting valences of beauty and terror are so strongly entrenched. Engagement is also strongly linked to beauty. By default, saying that something is beautiful implies that it matters. Again, there are paradoxical cases—for instance, the developer who proclaims indifference to the beauty of the butterflies that his project will exterminate; but again, the telling point is that the combination carries a sense of something deeply awry.

Predictability is a more delicate case. It has become widely accepted that beauty involves a balance between simplicity and complexity: for instance, Haught takes Whitehead as his authority for the view that 'the beautiful precariously balances the order and novelty brought together in the aesthetic object' (2000: 72). Ideas of that kind were formalized within psychology using information theoretic concepts related to predictability and randomness (Attneave 1954; Garner 1974). It has to be said that the evidence from formal studies is not easy to interpret (Rolf 2004), but it remains an interesting conjecture. If it were confirmed, it would imply that weighing predictability underpinned emotional and aesthetic responses.

At first glance, activation does not seem to be a relevant dimension. However, there are opinions that it would be ill-advised to ignore. Wordsworth famously described poetry as 'emotion recollected in tranquillity'; and Yeats described the poet's ideal state as 'colder and dumber and deafer than a fish'. It seems credible that at least some aspects of the aesthetic response thrive on low activation.

There is an obvious, but puzzling link between these arguments and Kant's contention that aesthetic judgements are disinterested. At first sight, the dimension most closely related to disinterestedness would seem to be engagement. But as noted above, it would be very strange to deny that beauty matters. Conversely, it makes sense to link low activation to aesthetic response, but low activation and disinterest would seem to be logically quite separate. This is not so much a problem as a reminder that dimensional descriptions have limitations that are not always intuitive. In particular, they are not intentional. Disinterestedness, of course, is: the point is that what the subject cares about are not his or her own interests.

*Action tendencies.* It seems equally clear that aesthetic responses may involve action tendencies. The most obvious candidate is a tendency to contemplate, not only perceptually but also intellectually (that is taken up shortly). However, other actions are common, if not universal. My reaction to beautiful music is to sing, play, or plagiarize it; different members of my family will react to a beautiful landscape by photographing it or by engaging in conservation. All of these seem to be concerned with making what is beautiful a permanent part of the individual's world. Common reactions to human beauty may fit the same description.

*Emotional modes of action and cognition.* The general point that aesthetic responses impact on cognition is also hardly in dispute. It is part of the Kantian position noted earlier that beauty engages the intellect, and critics tend to be particularly insistent that artefacts do not qualify as art unless they give people something to think about. It is less straightforward to say how closely the effects parallel those that occur in emotion. Intuitively, it seems that there may be quite substantial similarities. It would be surprising if aesthetic responses could not be shown to affect attention and risk-taking, at least in the case of human beauty. It is harder to gauge whether the same would apply to music or visual art, for instance. Some of the effects of beauty on thought seem to be rather like the effects that Eysenck *et al.* (2007) have demonstrated with anxiety, where affective factors draw intellectual processes to revisit and revisit particular themes. It is easy to find prima facie evidence of effects on memory. An informal poll of colleagues asked about the events for which they had 'flashbulb memories'—vivid, concrete recall of a specific situation. These are thought to be associated with a 'consequential (or emotionally arousing) event' (Brown and Kulik 1977: 73). They reported flashbulb memories attached to aesthetic events (glossed as 'hearing an amazing performance, seeing a great picture, etc') about as often as to world events (9/11, Kennedy's death, etc.), which are the standard examples of flashbulb memories; and much more often than to sporting or religious events. That kind of gross observation cannot be interpreted with any precision, not least because the exact nature of flashbulb memories is hotly debated (Winograd and Neisser, 1992). What it suggests is a link worth following up. The follow-up is another area where the experimental psychologist's standard procedure of collecting evidence seems to be eminently appropriate.

The last parallel to be considered involves the tension between cultural and evolutionary approaches. There is an ambivalence over aesthetic responses which is strikingly like the ambivalence that occurs with emotion. It is clearest in two areas: human beauty and aesthetic response to landscape.

In the case of human beauty, different cultures show substantial and well-documented differences in their standards of physical beauty (e.g., Tovée *et al.* 2006), and it is highly tempting to conclude with Jackson: 'physical attractiveness itself has no inherent value. The culture imparts value to it' (1992: 36). On the other hand, a mass of evidence indicates that some characteristics are associated with impressions of beauty across cultures, and can be interpreted as signs that a potential mate is healthy. So Grammer *et al.* conclude: 'Human beauty standards reflect our evolutionary distant and recent past and emphasize the role of health assessment in mate choice' (2003: 385). The tension leads to ingenious arguments like the proposal by Tovée *et al.* that the systems underpinning judgements of human beauty have evolved to take account of local variations in the signs of health and reproductive fitness.

Responses to landscape are similarly confusing. There is a body of research on 'charged experiences' of landscape (Cowie 2002), aesthetic and emotional; and it documents a multitude of cultural effects on aesthetic judgements. For example, in the eighteenth century, Gerhart Schoning passed through the Romsdal Mountains in Norway and described them as the ugliest piece of nature he had ever encountered; but he praised the wheatfields beyond for their aesthetic beauty (Keller 1994). Nowadays the Romsdal Mountains are a tourist attraction, and the wheatfields are considered boring. The counterbalance is a reasonably credible argument that the core of response to landscape is recognition of functionally important features which Appleton (1975) calls prospects and refuges, or more generally that 'charged experiences reflect a kind of seeing that assesses where we fit into an environment and what we should do in it. This may be likened to perceiving affordances on a grand scale' (Cowie 2002: 141). A resolution like the one proposed by Tovée *et al.* seems possible.

What is important here is not the resolution, but the tension, and the fact that the tension is very reminiscent of the situation in research on undeniably emotional phenomena.

The list of parallels that has been outlined is hard to ignore, and it suggests that there are important senses in which aesthetic and emotional responses lie close in the space of human experience. However, considering only positive evidence is a capital mistake, and there are other issues to consider.

*Contrasts between emotional and aesthetic responses*

*Units*. It has been noted that ideas about relevant units of analysis that were proposed in the context of emotion also seem relevant to the aesthetic domain. However, aesthetic responses also have structural features which seem to contrast with core examples of emotional episodes and eras.

The core point is that the judgement of beauty seems to have a very particular kind of time course—not unparalleled (ethical judgements, for instance, have obvious similarities), but unlike most emotional experiences. The sense that something is beautiful may be given in the first felt response, but if so, it is then subject to evaluation; and the conclusion may be that the appeal is purely superficial. The opposite trajectory also occurs: some things evoke a limited response at first, or even a negative one, but come to be judged beautiful. Art history relishes examples of that kind, from 'take away that nasty green thing' to the first audience response to Stravinsky's *Rite of Spring*. There seems to be no fixed timescale for the changes: they may take seconds or decades.

Allied to that, there is a contrast in expected long-term trajectory. It is an important feature of healthy emotional responses that they subside over time (in contrast to pathological states), and re-evoking them repeatedly produces extinction. In contrast, it seems to be part of what we mean by beauty that if something is beautiful, it is always beautiful. Decay in our sense that something is beautiful is described as 'palling', and it indicates that it was never truly beautiful.

There are partial parallels that are unequivocally emotional. In particular, the sense that something is terrifying seems to be close in many respects. But examples from other domains may well be closer—such as the judgement that someone is kind.

It is natural to think of time-course differences as signs of a distinctive interplay between cognitive and affective factors. The philosopher's instinct may be to brush the signs aside and try to grasp the core. However, empirical psychology can point to a huge range of topics where engaging with the details of time course has provided rich insights into underlying structures. A similar strategy may be appropriate here.

*Dimensions*. Turning to the issue of dimensions, there is sound empirical work that raises provocative questions. It deals with responses to music. Zentner and his collaborators (2008) have used standard psychological techniques to identify what they describe as dimensions of emotional response to classical music. Since the technique involved participants listening to a piece and rating how well a range of terms described their response, it seems fair to assume that the responses captured by their dimensions are at least partly aesthetic. Analysis, using standard statistical techniques, extracted nine dimensions. Three, which they called 'joyful activation', 'power', and 'tension', are recognizably variants of the standard affective dimensions. Four more, 'sadness', 'tenderness', 'nostalgia', and 'peacefulness', seem to reflect the idea raised earlier that there is a particular connection between art and low activation—they bring out subdivisions in the space of tranquil response in ways that are blurred in analyses based on everyday life or concepts. The remaining two, 'wonder' and 'transcendence', deserve more thought.

Wonder is interesting partly because it is one of the emotions that some theorists have proposed could be equated with aesthetic response (Prinz 2007). The Zentner study encapsulates a reasonable response. It confirms that wonder is a significant issue in responses to music. However, what the study finds is a dimension of wonder, which is to say that one of the factors that most effectively distinguish responses to different pieces is that they involve different levels of wonder. It is a major part of some responses, little or no part of others. In addition, wonder is only one of nine or so dimensions. Those points do not settle the argument, but they pinpoint questions that need to be answered before it is reasonable to accept that wonder is more than one emotion-related aspect of the aesthetic response among many.

The dimension of transcendence is interesting because it points to an obvious doubt about the overlap between the space of emotion and the space of aesthetic response. Even using the term 'emotion' broadly (which 'Forms of Emotional Colouring' does), transcendence falls outside the domain that most people think of as an emotion. The domain it falls within is spirituality; and research on religious experience, predictably, does find dimensions of that general sort (Hood 2001). Religion is an elephant in the seminar room that discussions of aesthetics contrive to avoid surprisingly often, but an unbiased observer can hardly fail to notice how salient art is in religious life, and how much outstanding art is inspired by religion. The point has also been made that 'charged' responses to landscape often have at least overtones of religion (Cowie 2002).

The general bias of this chapter is to avoid categorization, and the issue of spirituality and emotion does not need to be addressed in terms of categories. It seems reasonable to say that human feeling extends over a massive domain. The term 'emotion' is most comfortably applied to the region of it that can, as Darwin pointed out, be linked rather directly to evolutionary function. Spiritual feelings are, on the face of it, rather far removed from that region. The Zentner study makes the point that aesthetic responses often seem to be located nearer the realm of spirit than the realm of evolution.

*Appraisal*. There is a link between that point and another set of contrasts, involving appraisal. It was part of Arnold's original formulation of the concept that appraisals dealt with matters relevant to our 'weal or woe'. That feature does not seem as central to aesthetic response. The beauty of the snowflake or the sunset is of no material relevance to us. While we are responding to it, it is a marvel, and what is important is that such a marvel exists, not what it can do for us. Of course, self-interest is not easily kept out of human affairs, but its route into aesthetic response is perhaps less direct than its route into the more Darwinian zones of the domain of feeling.

A second contrast involving appraisal seems to be related. It is often said that aesthetic response is to the pattern of things, not to their function. It is fascinating for perceptual psychology to consider the different ways in which we may be aware of pattern, and which are relevant to aesthetic experience (identifying the chord sequence in a song is surely not); but that is not for this chapter. The point here is that appraisal in the usual sense is almost the opposite: it is awareness of significance to the exclusion of structural and surface attributes.

*Connection, expression, impressions.* A different cluster of contrasts involves three of the headings from the last section—connection, expression, and impressions. The point has been made that an emotional episode is typically richly connected, particularly with people. Key types of connection depend on the fact that people express their own emotion, and form impressions of other people's.

One type of connection seems if anything more mandatory than with emotion. The domain of emotion in a broad sense includes states that seem to be objectless (moods, so-called 'free floating anxiety', and so on). At first sight, the idea of an objectless aesthetic experience seems not to make sense. One can imagine Oscar Wilde disagreeing. The point is intriguing, but perhaps not central.

More basic is the cluster of issues involving other people. At first sight, aesthetic responses seem to be primarily between the subject and the object. It is at least not obvious how easily we can assess that another person's response to something is aesthetic.

There is an obvious objection. It is natural to think that we can tell whether someone is entranced by a painting or wondering why he paid the entrance cost, and even more so whether the audience at a concert is rapt and still, or waiting as politely as possible for the event to end. But although we can certainly detect engagement, it is not so obvious whether we can tell that the response is aesthetic. The watcher in the gallery may see nothing to recommend the picture aesthetically, but be deeply engaged in working out where the scene is, or identifying the myth that the painter was depicting, or deciding whether the perspective is consistent. Experiments might show that there was a difference, but if so, it would surely not be comparable to the differences between clear-cut emotions.

There is a case for thinking that the concert case is different. Live performance is strongly associated with audiences, and audiences are integral to atmosphere. Hence, though it may be difficult to articulate what the signs are, there must (so the argument runs) be signs that skilled performers detect and engage with. They may well be collective rather than individual—matters of synchrony and symmetry—but they are there. The argument has force, but there is a response which is not frivolous. It is to say that what audience creates is an emotional climate where aesthetic responses are possible. From the standpoint of an occasional performer in churches, it can be genuinely difficult to know whether the audience responded to the music aesthetically or entered a kind of reverent meditation where they barely heard it. People may recognize the issue from the other side if they have sat in concert halls or churches, felt the solemnity and intensity of the people round them, and been unable to fathom why these people should respond in that way to the events that were unfolding. Emotional tone clearly is transmitted: it is not at all so clear that the aesthetic element is.

These questions about connection are among the most practical in the area. The effort to promote aesthetic responses is a central issue in galleries, museums, concert halls, and classrooms, and increasingly in their electronic counterparts. If one cares about promoting aesthetic response, then one should care about understanding how these environments work, and what they can and cannot achieve. From a psychologist's point of view, the area is one that begs for empirical research—not least because it is not obvious what the outcome might be. Research in the area is actually beginning to gather momentum (Camurri 2009), and the results will be interesting philosophically as well as practically.

The final contrast also relates to communication. Something about emotional states seems to invite labelling, and the labels play an active part in emotional life. The pattern is conspicuously different for aesthetic responses. At the crudest, we might expect there to be words meaning something like 'beauty-struck' or 'ugly-struck', but they seem not to exist; and unlike a host of coining and imports in the domain of emotion, when they are coined, they do not have the quality of being words that we always wanted but never had. In contrast, there is a huge range of words purporting to describe aesthetically significant qualities of things, to which new members are added daily—dreamy, feisty, harmonious, mellifluous, pure, spiky, and so on indefinitely.

*Assembling evidence*

A feature of the kind of argument that has been used in this section, which is shared with 'Forms of Emotional Colouring', is that ideas about the characteristics of aesthetic responses are evaluated against examples. It follows that selecting relevant examples has a critical role. Choosing examples on an ad hoc basis, as has been done here, is clearly far from ideal. It would be much more appropriate to assemble them systematically, but that is not a straightforward job,

It takes very little thought to see that the range of potential examples is very large, and its boundaries less than clear. Examples may make the point better than abstractions.

I look at the stars, and if I am purely concerned with locating Jupiter or the Milky Way, it may be an experience that is totally factual rather than aesthetic. I will often oscillate between that and a sense of enjoyment and admiration, which may or may not be considered aesthetic. That may or may not shade into an experience with a different quality, profoundly positive, and profoundly important to me, where the beauty of the stars is my primary concern—presumably an archetypal kind of aesthetic experience. That kind of experience in its turn occasionally drifts off into an even more rarefied dimension. I can experience a kind of Pythagorean ecstasy—a pure engagement with the music of the spheres. At that stage, I am not aware of caring. There is a fundamental coolness about the relationship—I simply am caught up in the patterns of the stars. That kind of experience might or might not be considered aesthetic. Most of these may be tinged to a greater of lesser extent with a sense of the sublime, that is, sensing the vastness and destructive power of the stars.

All of these contrast significantly with the experience of looking at van Gogh's *The Starry Night*, because there, it is an issue whether the artefact qualifies as art, and admiration of the artist is a large part of the experience. I may or may not consider the experience aesthetic when I am focused on the technical innovations that give the picture its distinctive power. Different again is contemplating mathematical models of the way stars resonate, and realizing that an awe-inspiring phenomenon flows from an elegant underlying pattern (http://plus.maths.org/latestnews/sep-dec08/stellarch-oir/). All of those contrast again with the experience of singing 'How brightly shines the morning star', however much the music evokes the shimmer of starlight. The reference to singing rather than listening is deliberate: the experience of producing things of beauty (or things that feel beautiful at the time) seems to feature rather little in discussions of aesthetic experience, but it is surely common enough to be an integral part of debate.

It would be an interesting and useful project to move from the kind of description that has just been given to a systematic listing of experiences that sample the whole range of aesthetic responses in at least a roughly representative way. It would be surprising if it did not show several kinds of variability. Some instances would be archetypal, others marginal. Some would probably be considered archetypal by one community, and excluded altogether by others (contemplating Damien Hirst's pickled cow is a likely candidate). Some would probably be rated differently according to the set induced by instructions or context. That kind of variability could be documented as a fact of the domain rather than considered a problem: it is only a problem for those who are wedded *a priori* to the idea that was questioned at the beginning of this chapter, that the domain of aesthetic response is inherently categorical. For others, it would simply re-emphasize the artificiality of imposing category boundaries.

# 3. Conclusion

It is natural to ask whether aesthetic responses are or are not emotional. If one had to answer 'yes' or 'no', the conclusion from this chapter would probably be that they are not. They are akin to emotion in fundamental ways, the most fundamental being that they are felt, not calculated. It is natural to hypothesize that that quality betrays the involvement of systems that are old in evolutionary terms, concerned with the value and significance of things, with rather direct access to the control of involuntary responses and voluntary actions. However, the conclusion that they are the same kind of thing as emotion would only follow if we believed that those systems have rather few functions, and rather few ways of engaging with reflective cognition.

Considering relationships item by item, there is a substantial list of differences between archetypal emotions and archetypal aesthetic responses. They involve distinctive kinds of perception, but not the same kinds; different relationships with intellect and communication; and different relationships to self-interest. These are substantial differences.

On the other hand, the preferred answer to the 'yes–no' question is clearly that neither answer is really appropriate. Putting the question in that way presupposes boundary lines that have no obvious warrant in nature. It may also reflect a tendency to underestimate the scale and diversity of the domain that is involved. If we assume that the domain is small, we will naturally assume that things which belong in it must be similar. If the domain is vast, that kind of assumption is obviously inappropriate. On reflection, it is not surprising that our intellects are prone to underestimate the domain to which emotion belongs, because one of the hallmarks of the domain is that it abounds with signs that life is directed and coloured by processes and capacities whose workings are not naturally open to the intellect. Considering that the aesthetic is inseparable from that domain not only highlights its scale, but also acts as a useful counterbalance to the tendency to portray the domain as a realm of simple associative processes and brute self-interest.

This chapter has tried to indicate that descriptive resources developed for research on emotion may provide useful ways of describing that wider domain, so that it is possible to see both what unifies it and how diverse it is. Clearly the resources as presented here are in a relatively crude form, and need to be refined. That interacts with the need for sound empirical work, which has been stressed throughout. Either enterprise may throw up difficulties that are deeper than this chapter has understood. However, the effort seems to be worth making.

## References

Appleton, J. (1975). *The Experience of Landscape*. London: Wiley.

Arnold, M. B. (1960). *Emotion and Personality: Vol. 2. Physiological Aspects*. New York: Columbia University Press.

Attneave, F. (1954). 'Some Informational Aspects of Visual Perception'. *Psychological Review*, 61: 183–93.

Biederman, I. and E. A. Vessel (2006). 'Perceptual Pleasure and the Brain'. *American Scientist*, 94: 247–53.

Brown, R. and J. Kulik (1977). 'Flashbulb Memories'. *Cognition*, 5/1: 73–99.

Camurri, A. (2009). 'Non-Verbal Full Body Emotional and Social Interaction: A Case Study on Multimedia Systems for Active Music Listening'. *INTETAIN*, 9/1: 9–18.

Cowie, R. (2002). 'Charged Experiences of Natural Environments'. *Current Psychology*, 21: 133–43.

——(2010). 'Describing the Forms of Emotional Colouring that Pervade Everyday Life', in P. Goldie (ed.), *Oxford Handbook of Philosophy of Emotion*. Oxford: Oxford University Press, pp. 63–94.

——and R. Cornelius (2003). 'Describing the Emotional States that are Expressed in Speech'. *Speech Communication*, 40: 5–32.

Devillers, L., L. Vidrascu, and L. Lamel (2005). 'Challenges in Real-Life Emotion Annotation and Machine Learning Based Detection'. *Neural Networks*, 18: 407–22.

Eysenck, M. W., N. Derakshan, R. Santos, and M. G. Calvo (2007). 'Anxiety and Cognitive Performance: Attentional Control Theory'. *Emotion*, 7: 336–53.

Fehr, B. and J. A. Russell (1984). 'Concept of Emotion Viewed from a Prototype Perspective'. *Journal of Experimental Psychology: General*, 113: 464–86.

Feldman Barrett, L. (2006). 'Are Emotions Natural Kinds?' *Perspectives on Psychological Science*, 1: 28–58.

Fontaine, J., K. Scherer, E. Roesch, and P. Ellsworth (2007). 'The World of Emotions is Not Two-Dimensional'. *Psychological Science*, 18/12: 1050–7.

Frijda, N. H. (1986). *The Emotions*. Cambridge: Cambridge University Press.

Garner, W. R. (1974). *The Processing of Information Structure*. Potomac, MD: Lawrence Erlbaum Associates, Inc.

Goldman, A. (2001). 'The Aesthetic', in Berys Nigel Gaut and Dominic Lopes (eds.), *The Routledge Companion to Aesthetics*. Abingdon: Routledge, pp. 255–66.

Grammer, K., B. Fink, A. P. Møller, and R. Thornhill (2003). 'Darwinian Aesthetics: Sexual Selection and the Biology of Beauty'. *Biological Reviews*, 78/3: 385–407.

Harré, R. (ed.) (1989). *The Social Construction of Emotions*. Oxford: Blackwell.

Haught, J. F. (2000). *What is God? How to Think about the Divine*. Mahwah, NJ: Paulist Press.

Hood, R. (2001). *Dimensions of Mystical Experiences: Empirical Studies and Psychological Links*. New York: Rodopi.

Jackson, L. A. (1992). *Physical Appearance and Gender: Sociobiological and Sociocultural perspectives*. Albany, NY: SUNY Press.

Keller, C. (1994). 'Theoretical Aspects of Landscape Study', in T. Collins (ed.), *Decoding the Landscape*. Galway: Centre for Landscape Studies, pp. 79–98.

Ledoux, J. (1996). *The Emotional Brain: The Mysterious Underpinnings of Emotional Life*. New York: Simon & Schuster.

Murphy F. C., I. Nimmo-Smith, and A. D. Lawrence (2003). 'Functional Neuroanatomy of Emotion: A Meta-Analysis'. *Cognitive, Affective, & Behavioral Neuroscience*, 3: 207–33.

Ortony, A. (2002) 'On Making Believable Emotional Agents Believable', in R. Trappl, P. Petta, and S. Payr (eds.), *Emotions in Humans and Artifacts*. Cambridge, MA: MIT Press, pp. 189–212.

Pennebaker, J. W. and C. K. Chung (2007). 'Expressive Writing, Emotional Upheavals, and Health', in H. S. Friedman and R. C. Silver (eds.), *Foundations of Health Psychology*. New York: Oxford University Press, pp. 263–84.

Phan K. L., T. D. Wager, S. F. Taylor, and I. Liberzon (2002). 'Functional Neuroanatomy of Emotion: A Meta-Analysis of Emotion Activation Studies in PET and fMRI'. *NeuroImage*, 16: 331–48.

Prinz, J. (2007). 'Emotion and Aesthetic Value'. Paper presented at the American Philosophical Association Pacific Division Meeting, San Francisco, CA, April.

Rolf, R. (2004). 'Processing Fluency and Aesthetic Pleasure: Is Beauty in the Perceiver's Processing Experience?' *Personality and Social Psychology Review*, 8/4: 364–82.

Scherer K. (2009) 'Emotions are Emergent Processes: They Require a Dynamic Computational Architecture'. *Philosophical Transactions of the Royal Society, Series B*, 364: 3459–74.

——and H. Ellgring (2007a). 'Are Facial Expressions of Emotion Produced by Categorical Affect Programs or Dynamically Driven by Appraisal?' *Emotion*, 7: 113–30.

————(2007b). 'Multimodal Expression of Emotion: Affect Programs or Componential Appraisal Patterns? *Emotion*, 7/1: 158–71.

Shaver, P., J. Schwartz, D. Kirson, and C. O'connor (1987). 'Emotion Knowledge: Further Exploration of a Prototype Approach'. *Journal of Personality and Social Psychology*, 52: 1061–86.

Sibley, F. (1965). 'Aesthetic and Non-Aesthetic'. *Philosophical Review*, 74: 135–59. Reprinted in Frank Sibley, *Approach to Aesthetics: Collected Papers on Philosophical Aesthetics*, ed. J. Benson, B. Redfearn, and J. R. Cox. Oxford: Clarendon Press, pp. 33–51.

Tovée, M., V. Swami, A. Furnham, and R. Mangalparsad (2006). 'Changing Perceptions of Attractiveness as Observers are Exposed to a Different Culture'. *Evolution and Human Behavior*, 27/6: 443–56.

Vaudable, C., N. Rollet, and L. Devillers (2010). 'Annotation of Affective Interaction in Real-Life Dialogs Collected in a Call-Center'. Proceedings of Emotion 2010: Third International Workshop on Corpora for Research on Emotion and Affect, pp. 47–52.

Winograd, E. and U. Neisser (eds.) (1992). *Affect and Accuracy in Recall: Studies of Flashbulb Memories*. Cambridge: Cambridge University Press.

Zentner, M., D. Grandjean, and K. R. Scherer (2008). 'Emotions Evoked by the Sound of Music: Characterization, Classification, and Measurement'. *Emotion*, 4: 494–521.

# 7

# The Ethics of Aesthetic Bootstrapping

*Peter Goldie*

The claim that the emotions are implicated in our aesthetic appreciation is certainly contentious. I do not want to argue directly for the claim here, although I believe it to be true. What I want to do, rather, is to assume that it is true, and that, in our engagement with literature and film, with music and painting, we embark on a 'sentimental education' (Robinson 2005).

This education of our sentiments is particularly problematic, I believe, when concerned with those artworks which we often call an 'acquired taste'. Here I think that the emotional strategy of aesthetic bootstrapping plays a vital role. Very roughly for now, aesthetic bootstrapping is the strategy of cultivating our emotional responses to artworks by feigning those emotions, to ourselves and to others, in the hope and expectation that they will, in due course, become genuine.

I will proceed as follows. First, I will outline three elements which are involved in the strategy of emotional bootstrapping, beginning with an example to do with food and drink—gustatory bootstrapping—and then turn to the aesthetic case, to aesthetic bootstrapping. Then I will seek to provide a justification of the strategy on the grounds, roughly, that the aim of the strategy, namely appreciation of what is aesthetically good, is a reasonable aim, and that the strategy is often the most effective way of achieving that aim. Here I will draw an analogy with ethics and specifically with a familiar kind of bootstrapping that is involved in ethical education. Lastly, I turn to a number of criticisms and problems that are faced by the idea of aesthetic bootstrapping: that the strategy is irrational because it involves self-deception; that the strategy is not to be trusted because it begins with the testimony of others, and thus is not to be relied on; that aesthetic bootstrapping is phoney or pretentious; that it can easily be allied to a certain kind of snobbery; and, finally, that it is often difficult, or even sometime impossible, to know whether one is yet a full appreciator of an aesthetic object, or whether one is still, at least in part, an aesthetic bootstrapper.

# 1. The three elements of emotional bootstrapping

Let me start then, not with aesthetics, but with good food and wine, and specifically with native oysters from Galway and cold, crisp Chablis from Burgundy. When I was a child, I liked childish things, and Galway natives and Chablis were not among their number. Oysters were disgusting (just look at them!) and wine was bitter and horrid (just taste it!). But as I grew older I came to know that oysters and Chablis were an 'acquired taste': they were good, and, furthermore, good together. How did I know that they were good? Simply on the basis of trustworthy testimony from reliable sources, with further support from the fact that they have passed the test of time. And yet to my uneducated palate they still aroused the same negative feelings. Testimony and the test of time were not enough on their own to convert me. So what was I to do? How could I get from where I was to where I wanted to be: from not liking what I knew I ought to like (because I knew it was good), to liking it and *finding* it good?

The answer was to be found in an emotional strategy of gustatory bootstrapping. Robert Solomon argued for many years (1973, 2007) that we can choose our emotions. As he put it, we can 'practice' our emotions, we can 'cultivate' them as 'strategies for living well' (2007: 190). Although we cannot simply decide to have an emotion, we can, however, decide to do any number of things which will lead us in that direction (2007: 190, 197). First of all, of course, following in the footsteps of Blaise Pascal, I can put myself 'in situations that I know or hope will inspire [the sought-for] emotion' (2007: 198). But simply eating oysters and drinking Chablis would not be sufficient to do the trick in my case; disgust and distaste would still arise, and it was far from clear how long I would be willing to go on before deciding to give it up as not worth the candle—particularly because the activity was not without expense. Not all food and drink is an acquired taste, of course, and what is an acquired taste for one person may not be for another; some people might take to Chablis like a duck to water.

So, mere exposure to the relevant object not being enough in my case, what I had also to do was deploy some further necessary elements in the emotional strategy. The second thing that I had to do was, to put it bluntly, to *pretend* to like these things—to engage in what Ronald de Sousa (1987) has called *self-feigning*. Self-feigning is a form of self-deception 'in which an expression of emotion designed to be deceptive is read back to the subject through bodily feeling and misleadingly induces the very emotion it was intended to counterfeit' (1987: 235–6). Robert Solomon says this about anger: you can '*act as if* you have an emotion, act angrily, for instance, from which genuine anger may follow' (2007: 197). And Solomon quotes William James's famous advice, about how to stop being gloomy, to cheer yourself up, and to feel more kindly towards others. This is what James said:

we must assiduously, and in the first instance cold-bloodedly, go through the *outward movements* of those contrary dispositions which we prefer to cultivate. The reward of persistency will infallibly come, in the fading out of the sullenness or depression, and the advent of real cheerfulness and kindliness in their stead. Smooth the brow, brighten the eye, contract the dorsal rather than the ventral aspect of the frame, and speak in a major key, pass the genial compliment, and your heart must be frigid indeed if it do not gradually thaw! (1981: 1077–8)

This step in my strategy of gustatory bootstrapping was along very similar lines to those recommended by James, although with different emotions and a different end in view. After the first step of choosing the relevant objects for appreciation—the oysters and the Chablis, rather than the fishcakes and the Coke (which I would have preferred and which were not for me an acquired taste)—I then sit up straight and consume them with a keen gaze and licking lips, making genial admiring remarks to others about how good they taste. What is being feigned, then, is gustatory appreciation, which characteristically manifests itself in expressive behaviour of this kind.

There is a third element in the strategy, one which has to be effected at the same time as the second, which concerns one's attentional focus while engaged in the self-feigning. If I were to focus my attention on how horrible the oysters looked, the strategy might not get any further than mere pretence. Instead, what I needed to do was to attend carefully to what I knew to be the good properties of the objects of my hoped-for feelings—their taste—and not to attend to those not-so-good properties of the objects—especially the oysters' visible properties, which I found so repellent. Of course the first part of this element of the strategy is, as is well known, more in one's control than the second; as de Sousa puts it, 'it is easier to attend at will than to withdraw one's attention at will' (1987: 243).

After a while, the emotional strategy paid off. My heart did indeed gradually thaw, and now I really do like oysters and Chablis. I no longer need to pretend to like them, to act as if I like them. Of course the idea that our emotions are under our control certainly does not imply that we can change them just like that, and gustatory boot-strapping typically takes a certain amount of perseverance; as I noted above, quite how much will depend on a number of variables.

Let me now consider aesthetic bootstrapping, which takes very much the same form, although of course with different objects. I have to confess to having adopted in my youth a rather similar strategy in respect of those aesthetic objects that are 'acquired tastes'. When I was finding my way into art, it was the easily won aesthetic delights that first appealed to me: Vivaldi's Four Seasons, Constable's The Hay Wain, and so on. Just as with the oysters and the Chablis, I knew from reliable, trustworthy sources that there was more than that to be won, and I knew from these sources—at least roughly—what the putative objects of appreciation were (Beethoven's late quartets for example, and the landscapes of Nicholas Poussin). But even with all this knowledge, I still was not able to appreciate them as I knew I should—to perceive them in the right way, and to have the right affective responses to them. As Frank Sibley tells us, in relation to what is now known as the Acquaintance Principle, 'Merely to learn from others, on good authority, that the music is serene, the play moving, or the picture unbalanced is of little aesthetic value; the crucial thing is to see, hear, or feel' (Sibley 1965: 34–5). (And one might add, remembering the oysters and the Chablis, the crucial thing is to *taste*.)

So, to get me from where I was to where I wanted to be, in came aesthetic bootstrapping, deploying just the same three elements of the emotional strategy. I put myself in contact with the right aesthetic objects, I engaged in self-feigning, and I focused my attention on the right properties of those objects, relying at this early stage of the strategy merely on testimony, and my knowledge that the objects have passed the test of time. And again, sure enough, the heart gradually thawed. I was able to move from being able only to make 'second-hand' judgements based on the testimony of others ('Beethoven's late quartets have tremendous emotional depth'; 'Degas' pictures of Paris café life capture the loneliness of the city with an unrelenting gaze'), to being able to make these judgements based on first-hand acquaintance. Thus I became able to satisfy the Acquaintance Principle: I could appreciate them as good because they are good, and because I saw and felt them to be so, and not merely because others told me they are so.

I have made these points in relation to my own experiences, but I believe that they apply quite generally—although, as with food and drink, quite which aesthetic objects will require aesthetic bootstrapping will vary across individuals and across time, and across a number of other variables. One interesting variable is the novelty of a work relative to what has gone before. Sherry Irvin has a nice discussion of the role of bootstrapping in relation to our aesthetic understanding of significant new artworks, which can be particularly difficult to come to appreciate in the right way. In such cases, as Irvin puts it, 'there is a crucial element of trust, or faith, in the development of aesthetic understanding. To make effective aesthetic judgements in uncharted terrain, we must rely, at least temporarily and defeasibly, on acknowledged sources of aesthetic superiority to lead us incrementally further in aesthetic comprehension' (2007: 297).

## 2. Habituation, familiarity, and the ethical analogy

As is often the case with aesthetics, there is an analogy with ethics, but one which can only be taken so far. In bringing up a child to be ethical, to begin with the motivations will very likely not be internal to the activity. For example, the child might take an interest in the well-being of his younger sister not for her own sake, because he loves her, but in order to please his parents, or to receive some kind of reward from them. As Myles Burnyeat has so well argued in his discussion of Aristotle's notion of moral education, what is required is habituation:

I may be told, and may believe, that such and such actions are just and noble, but I have not really learned for myself (taken to heart, made second nature to me) that they have intrinsic value until I have learned to value (love) them for it, with the consequence that I take pleasure in doing them. To understand and appreciate the value that makes them enjoyable in themselves, I must learn for myself to enjoy them, and that does take time and practice—in short, habituation. (1980: 78)

In aesthetics too, habituation, or what one might better call familiarity, is necessary to enable us to come to appreciate aesthetic objects for their own sake. Friedrich Nietzsche made just this point in relation to music, as Kathleen Higgins has reminded us. Nietzsche says this:

First one has to *learn to hear* a figure and melody at all, to detect and distinguish it, to isolate it and delimit it as a separate life. Then it requires some exertion and good will to *tolerate* it in spite of its strangeness, to be patient with its appearance and expression, and kindhearted about its oddity. Finally there comes a moment when we are *used* to it, when we wait for it, when we sense that we should miss it if it were missing; and now it continues to compel and enchant us relentlessly until we have become its humble and enraptured lovers who desire nothing better from the world than it and only it.

But that is what happens to us not only in music. That is how we have *learned to love* all things that we now love . . . Even those who love themselves will have learned it in this way; for there is no other way. Love, too, has to be learned. (1974: 334)

So love of something—or of someone Nietzsche adds—takes practice and time before we can love it for itself. Moreover, bootstrapping can be involved in the ethical case, very much as I have argued it can be in the aesthetic case. For example, a new colleague might arrive in your place of work, an unfamiliar figure who seems really not to be your 'type' at all, and to have many idiosyncrasies which you find far from appealing (she is, your other colleagues pointedly inform you, an 'acquired taste'). Perhaps here some Jamesian-style bootstrapping is needed to come to appreciate this person with whom you will need to co-operate over the years to come: first, pretend to like her, act well towards her, focus on her better features, and then ultimately you might come to fully appreciate her for her own sake as a person and as a colleague, and not merely instrumentally, in order to facilitate a smooth-running department.

## 3. Problems with aesthetic bootstrapping

Aesthetic bootstrapping is not without its difficulties and problems. I will discuss five. The first is that aesthetic bootstrapping is irrational, because it involves self-deception. When I pretended to like oysters and Chablis, I was not only fooling other people about my preferences and tastes, I was fooling myself. However, what I was doing was *strategically* rational. Bootstrapping was the best strategy of getting from where I was (not liking oysters and Chablis) to where I wanted to be (liking them); best because it was a faster and more reliable strategy than the alternative of mere perseverance; and, at least in the aesthetic case, the objective is after all aiming at properly appreciating something of real value—it is no chimera. (In this respect, there is an important disanalogy with gustatory bootstrapping, for here the aim is simply to get yourself to *like* the food and the drink, whereas in art appreciation the aim is to get yourself to appreciate the artwork for the *right reasons*.[1])

This leads directly to the second concern about aesthetic bootstrapping. How can I be so confident that these putative objects of appreciation really are good? Am I not simply relying on the testimony of others? Indeed I am, and I do need to be justified in my confidence in their testimony; I should not simply be blindly following the herd wherever it charges off to. Yet of course, there do remain risks. One might set out to appreciate some aesthetic object on the grounds that it is so well spoken of by so many reliable people, and yet it is not really worthwhile at all, in spite of its reputation. I have bitter memories of the hours I spent in the 1960s watching *Last Year in Marienbad* (Alain Resnais, 1961), time after time, including watching the credits right through to the end, convinced that this really was a great movie, and that all I had to do was to keep plugging away at the emotional strategy. The test of time has an important place here as a further constraint on what aesthetic objects are suitable objects for selection for the strategy.

Now, the second concern leads us to the third, that appreciation of an object that is achieved through bootstrapping is phoney or pretentious. In the gustatory example, is my liking for oysters and Chablis, as it now is, phoney? In other words, am I *still* pretending? Of course I might be, and there are questions of self-knowledge which I will come to shortly. But I would agree with Solomon here, when he insists that just because an emotion is 'manufactured' (2007: 198) to begin with, as mine was, it does not simply follow from this that the fully developed emotion is phoney. What might begin as phoney aesthetic appreciation, grounded in the testimony of others, can ultimately become proper appreciation, grounded in a proper understanding of the aesthetic merits of the artwork concerned.[2] Irvin puts it like this: 'The sort of trust I have in mind is not blind trust of infinite duration . . . Once I place this provisional trust, it provides me with directions to pursue in my continued looking and perhaps helps me to see features and relationships that I was unable to detect before. Ultimately, whether or not my trust was warranted will be determined largely by the nature of my own aesthetic experience (which has perceptual, cognitive and affective components)' (2007: 298).

Even if we need not worry too much about phoniness, closely allied to being phoney is being snobbish in one's tastes, and this is my fourth concern. Matthew Kieran's discussion of the vice of snobbery is highly instructive here. Kieran defines aesthetic snobbery thus:

A snobbish judgement or response is one where aesthetically irrelevant social features play a causal role in S's appreciative activity in coming to judge the value of *x qua* aesthetic object,

---

[1] This touches on deep questions about the objectivity of artistic value which I cannot of course go into here.

[2] The ethical analogy is again instructive here: just because one's initial motivations for coming to be ethical are external to ethics does not imply that one's mature ethical motivations have to remain external.

so that how they are formed, along with any concomitant rationalization, is explained more fundamentally in terms of S's drive to feel or appear superior in relation to some individual or group. (2010: 244)

It should be immediately clear that someone who engages in aesthetic bootstrapping certainly need not be a snob. As Kieran puts it, 'Snobbish judgements arise out of vice rather than virtue because at the most general level the motivation is wrong—the fundamental guiding desire is the desire for social esteem rather than appreciation of the work' (2010: 255). And this need not be the case with the bootstrapper. For example, my reasons for attempting to appreciate *Last Year in Marienbad* need not have included a desire to feel socially superior in any way. My motivations might have been pure, in the sense that I believed the film to be of genuine aesthetic value, and I wanted to appreciate it as such. No doubt both snobbery and aesthetic bootstrapping are endemic in aesthetics, and they can appear together in individual cases, but they are not the same phenomenon, and there is no necessary connection between them.

I think that the greatest concern with aesthetic bootstrapping is the difficulty of self-knowledge that it presents, and this is my first concern. As Kieran points out, snobbery is easy to get away with, and, partly for this reason, 'it is often not obvious whether we are being snobbish, either in the first- or the third-person case' (2010: 263). I think that the problem of self-knowledge is perhaps even more acute with aesthetic bootstrapping than it is with snobbery. Let me explain.[3]

I am concerned at this point with aesthetic bootstrapping in what one might call later life, not in the young. When we are younger and more innocent, it may be readily apparent, both to ourselves and to others, that we are pretending to like oysters and Chablis, or pretending to like *Measure for Measure*. Like many of you, I expect, I have taken teenagers to smart restaurants, to the theatre, to art exhibitions, to concerts, to the opera, and so on, and have put certain much-loved books their way. And I am pretty convinced that I observe them deploying the same kind of emotional strategy as I deployed in *my* youth. They would rather be eating pizzas or watching *Trainspotting* (again), but still they pretend, not just for the sake of their hosts, but also as a strategy: they know what is good.

I might at this point say, rather patronizingly, that I *used* to be like that once. But I am not so sure that I should take such a superior attitude. For aesthetic bootstrapping is something that can, and often does, continue well into maturity. Not all one's aesthetic development comes so naturally that one can move with facility, and without artifice, from those aesthetic delights that are already won to those further aesthetic

---

[3] There is an issue of self-knowledge that I will not discuss, and that is the question of knowledge of one's taste. Daniel Dennett (1988) has a nice example of two long-serving coffee tasters for Maxwell House. They both now agree that they no longer like the taste of the coffee. Yet one says that the coffee tastes the same, but he no longer likes it; the other says that his taste buds have changed, so the coffee now tastes different to him. It would be interesting to see how this applies to the aesthetic case. Thanks to Matthew Kieran for discussion here.

delights that are yet to be won. And in the mature person, the strategy is not obvious in at all the same way as it is with the young.

Perhaps I have already revealed to the reader quite enough about myself, so let us imagine a person, P, who is keen to come to appreciate Wagner's operas. For many years, P has sincerely believed, on the grounds of reliable, trustworthy testimony and the test of time, that Wagner's operas are proper objects of profound aesthetic appreciation. However, he was far from satisfying the Acquaintance Principle. In fact for many years, knowing that they are an 'acquired taste', he avoided even trying to engage in bootstrapping. Then finally, P at last decided that he was 'ready' for Wagner. So he put the three elements of aesthetic bootstrapping into play: going to Wagner operas, self-feigning or pretending to enjoy them, and focusing his attention on what he knew to be the excellences of the works. Now P is sincere in his belief that he enjoys Wagner operas in the way required by the Acquaintance Principle. But still, nagging doubts arise from time to time in P's mind. Is all his self-feigning really now in the past? Does he really appreciate Wagner operas as much as he appears to do and as he believes he does? For of course, as we all know, there are longueurs in Wagner operas, and at these times P sometimes finds himself wondering just whether it really is worth all the effort: so many hours, so much expense, so many other things that one could be doing. It is especially at these times that P's doubts arise, as to whether he has really come to appreciate Wagner operas for their own sake, as proper objects of aesthetic appreciation, for there might still be a significant element of self-feigning in his motivational structure, which reveals itself at just these moments.

Should the 'true appreciator' (Kieran 2010: 255) in aesthetics have a purity of motive, appreciating the object solely for its aesthetic value, untainted by snobbish motives, untainted by pretence, or is it sufficient for it to be 'the governing end in the activity of appreciation' (Kieran 2010: 261)? So far as snobbery is concerned, Kieran rightly argues that self-knowledge is problematic. But with the snob, the motive to 'feel or appear superior in relation to some individual or group' is quite distinct from the motive to appreciate an artwork for its own sake in that they have quite distinct ends. In contrast, aesthetic bootstrappers such as P have as their motive appreciation of the work for its own sake, but while they are engaged in the strategy, during the bootstrapping process, they are pretending to have this motive. So the possibility of failure of self-knowledge is in that respect greater: just when is the feigning process really over—if ever—and how is one to tell what is the 'governing end'? (Compare Solomon's example of pretending to be angry, and then becoming angry: quite where pretence ends and real anger begins is often far from obvious.)

Again the ethical analogy is instructive. Immanuel Kant held that the ideal in ethical action is purity of motive—what he held to be the thought of one's duty—so that the ethical action with true moral worth is necessarily done for the sake of duty alone, not out of inclination, and also not out of inclination and duty with duty as the 'governing' motive. Perhaps, though, purity of motive is unreasonably demanding in ethics, as it might well be in aesthetics. David Hume certainly thought so. In his *Enquiry Concerning the Principles of Morals* (1978), he asked this rhetorical question: 'Now, where is the difficulty in conceiving, that this may likewise be the case with benevolence and friendship, and that, from the original frame of our temper, we may feel a desire of another's happiness or good, which, by means of that affection, becomes our own good, and is afterwards pursued, from the combined motives of benevolence and self-enjoyment?'

Whatever the right answer in the ethical case, whether purity of motive is necessary or just having the appropriate governing motive, there remains a deep irony: what one's motives are matters in ethics, and yet the acting subject can never be sure about his own motives. Kant writes movingly about this in his *Groundwork*:

It is indeed at times the case that after the keenest self-examination we find nothing that without the moral motive of duty could have been strong enough to move us to this or that good action and to so great a sacrifice; but we cannot infer from this with certainty that it is not some secret impulse of self-love which has actually, under the mere show of the Idea of duty, been the cause genuinely determining our will. We are pleased to flatter ourselves with the false claim to a nobler motive, but in fact we can never, even by the most strenuous self-examination, get to the bottom of our secret impulsions; for when moral value is in question, we are concerned, not with the actions which we see, but with their inner principles, which we cannot see. (1964: 407)

In aesthetics too, we can never be sure just what our motivations are, and whether or not there remains an element of pretence in our exclamations of delight at the contemplation of acquired tastes.

## 4. Conclusion

I have put forward a number of problems with aesthetic bootstrapping, placing special emphasis on the difficulties of self-knowledge. And yet I have also suggested that aesthetic bootstrapping is often the most effective way of coming to appreciate artworks that really are of genuine value. There is a tension which I do not wish to dissolve: motive matters in aesthetic appreciation, but, as Kant insisted in the ethical case, 'it is absolutely impossible for experience to establish with complete certainty a single case in which the maxim of an action . . . has rested solely on moral grounds and on the thought of one's duty' (1964: 407). I believe that the same might well be true in aesthetics: being a truly virtuous appreciator with a motive which is purely aesthetic, might be as elusive an ideal as being a truly virtuous moral agent. But still, it is something to which we can aspire, even if we never get there, and aesthetic bootstrapping is often a good place to start.[4]

---

[4] In writing this chapter, I have learned much from Ronald de Sousa, Kathleen Higgins, and Matthew Kieran, and especially from Robert Solomon, who is much missed. Thanks also to Elisabeth Schellekens for her helpful comments.

# References

Burnyeat, Myles (1980). 'Aristotle on Learning to be Good', in A. O. Rorty (ed.), *Essays on Aristotle's Ethics*. Berkeley: University of California Press, pp. 69–92.

Dennett, D. (1988). 'Quining Qualia', in A. Marcel and E. Bisiach (eds.), *Consciousness in Modern Science*. Oxford: Oxford University Press.

de Sousa, Ronald (1987). *The Rationality of the Emotions*. Cambridge, MA: MIT Press.

Hume, David (1978). *Enquiries Concerning Human Understanding and Concerning the Principles of Morals*, ed. L. A. Selby-Bigge. Oxford: Oxford University Press.

Irvin, Sherry (2007). 'Forgery and the Corruption of Aesthetic Understanding'. *Canadian Journal of Philosophy*, 37: 283–304.

James, William (1981). *The Principles of Psychology*. Cambridge, MA: Harvard University Press.

Kant, Immanuel (1964). *Groundwork of the Metaphysics of Morals*, trans. H. J. Paton. New York: Harper Torchbooks.

Kieran, Matthew (2010). 'The Vice of Snobbery: Aesthetic Knowledge, Justification, and Virtue in Art Appreciation'. *Philosophical Quarterly*, 60: 243–63.

Nietzsche, Friedrich (1974). *The Gay Science*, trans. Walter Kaufmann. New York: Random House.

Robinson, Jenefer (2005). *Deeper Than Reason: Emotion and its Role in Literature, Music and Art*. Oxford: Oxford University Press.

Sibley, Frank (1965). 'Aesthetic and Nonaesthetic'. *Philosophical Review*, 74: 135–59.

Reprinted in Frank Sibley, *Approach to Aesthetics: Collected Papers on Philosophical Aesthetics*, ed. J. Benson, B. Redfearn, and J. R. Cox. Oxford: Clarendon Press 2001, pp. 33–51. Page numbers refer to this edition

Solomon, Robert (1973). 'Emotions and Choice', *Review of Metaphysics* 28, reprinted with appendix in his *Not Passion's Slave: Emotions and Choice*. Oxford: Oxford University Press, 2003.

——(2007). *True to Our Feelings: What our Emotions are Really Telling Us*. Oxford: Oxford University Press.

# 8

# The Origins of Aesthetics: A Neurobiological Basis for Affective Feelings and Aesthetics

*Edmund T. Rolls*

In this chapter a theory of the origins of aesthetics is described. This has its roots in emotion, in which what is pleasant or unpleasant, a reward or punisher, is the result of an evolutionary process in which genes define the (pleasant or unpleasant) goals for action (Rolls 2005b). It is argued that combinations of multiple such factors provide part of the basis for aesthetics. To this is added the operation of the reasoning, syntactic, brain system which evolved to help solve difficult, multistep, problems, and the use of which is encouraged by pleasant feelings when elegant, simple, and hence aesthetic solutions are found that are advantageous because they are parsimonious, and follow Occam's Razor. The combination of these two systems, and the interactions between them, provides an approach to understanding aesthetics that is rooted in evolution and its effects on brain design and function.

I start by considering how affective value is generated in the brain as a solution to the problem of how genes can specify useful goals for actions. This is more efficient and produces more flexible behaviour than by specifying the actions themselves. Then, in Sections 5 and 6, I develop this theory further into a theory of the origins of aesthetics.

## 1. Emotions as states elicited by rewards and punishers

Emotions can usefully be defined (operationally) as states elicited by rewards and punishers that have particular functions (Rolls 1999, 2005b). The functions are defined below, and include working to obtain or avoid the rewards and punishers. A reward is anything for which an animal (which includes humans) will work. A punisher is anything that an animal will escape from or avoid. An example of an emotion might thus be happiness produced by being given a reward, such as a pleasant touch, praise, or winning a large sum of money. Another example of an emotion might be fear produced by the sound of a rapidly approaching bus, or the sight of an angry expression on someone's face. We will work to avoid such stimuli, which are punishing. Another example would be frustration, anger, or sadness produced by the omission of an expected reward such as a prize, or the termination of a reward such as the death of a loved one. Another example would be relief, produced by the omission or termination of a punishing stimulus such as the removal of a painful stimulus, or sailing out of danger. These examples indicate how emotions can be produced by the delivery, omission, or termination of rewarding or punishing stimuli, and go some way to indicate how different emotions could be produced and classified in terms of the rewards and punishments received, omitted, or terminated. A diagram summarizing some of the emotions associated with the delivery of reward or punishment or a stimulus associated with them, or with the omission of a reward or punishment, is shown in Fig. 8.1.

Before accepting this approach, we should consider whether there are any exceptions to the proposed rule. Are any emotions caused by stimuli, events, or remembered events that are not rewarding or punishing? Do any rewarding or punishing stimuli not

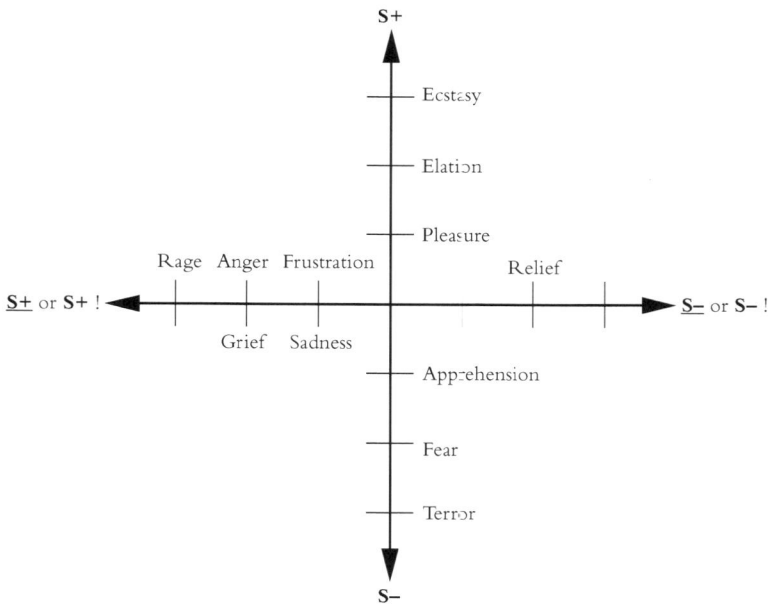

Figure 8.1 Some of the emotions associated with different reinforcement contingencies are indicated. Intensity increases away from the centre of the diagram, on a continuous scale. The classification scheme created by the different reinforcement contingencies consists of (1) the presentation of a positive reinforcer (S+), (2) the presentation of a negative reinforcer (S−), (3) the omission of a positive reinforcer (S+) or the termination of a positive reinforcer (S+!), and (4) the omission of a negative reinforcer (S−) or the termination of a negative reinforcer (S−!)

cause emotions? We will consider these questions in more detail below. The point is that if there are no major exceptions, or if any exceptions can be clearly encapsulated, then we may have a good working definition at least of what causes emotions. Moreover, it is worth pointing out that many approaches to or theories of emotion (Strongman 1996) have in common that part of the process involves 'appraisal' (Frijda 1986; Lazarus 1991; Oatley and Jenkins 1996). In all these theories the concept of appraisal presumably involves assessing whether something is rewarding or punishing. The description in terms of reward or punishment adopted here seems more tightly and operationally specified. I next consider a slightly more formal definition than rewards or punishments, in which the concept of reinforcers is introduced, and show how there has been a considerable history in the development of ideas along this line.

The proposal that emotions can be usefully seen as states produced by instrumental reinforcing stimuli follows earlier work by Millenson (1967), Weiskrantz (1968), Gray (1975, 1987), and Rolls (1986a, 1986b, 1990, 1999, 2000, 2005b). (Instrumental reinforcers are stimuli which, if their occurrence, termination, or omission is made contingent upon the making of a response, alter the probability of the future emission of that response.) Some stimuli are unlearned reinforcers (e.g., the taste of food if the animal is hungry, or pain); while others may become reinforcing by learning, because of their association with such primary reinforcers, thereby becoming 'secondary reinforcers'. This type of learning may thus be called 'stimulus-reinforcement association', and occurs via a process like classical conditioning. If a reinforcer increases the probability of emission of a response on which it is contingent, it is said to be a 'positive reinforcer' or 'reward'; if it decreases the probability of such a response it is a 'negative reinforcer' or 'punisher'. For example, fear is an emotional state which might be produced by a sound (the conditioned stimulus) that has previously been associated with an electric shock (the primary reinforcer).

The converse reinforcement contingencies produce the opposite effects on behaviour. The omission or termination of a positive reinforcer ('extinction' and 'time out' respectively, sometimes described as 'punishing') decreases the probability of responses. Responses followed by the omission or termination of a negative reinforcer increase in probability, this pair of negative reinforcement operations being termed 'active avoidance' and 'escape' respectively (Rolls 2005b).

This foundation has been developed (see Rolls 1986a, 1986b, 1990, 1999, 2000, 2005b) to show how a very wide range of emotions can be accounted for, as a result of the operation of a number of factors, including the following:

1. The *reinforcement contingency* (e.g., whether reward or punishment is given, or withheld) (see Fig. 8.1).
2. The *intensity* of the reinforcer (see Fig. 8.1).
3. Any environmental stimulus might have a *number of different reinforcement associations*. (For example, a stimulus might be associated both with the presentation of a reward and of a punisher, allowing states such as conflict and guilt to arise.)

Table 8.1 Examples of primary reinforcers, and the dimensions of the environment to which they are tuned

These reinforcers, rewards and punishers, are gene-defined goals for action, and are associated with affective states.

**Taste**

| | |
|---|---|
| Salt taste | reward in salt deficiency |
| Sweet | reward in energy deficiency |
| Bitter | punisher, indicator of possible poison |
| Sour | punisher |
| Umami | reward, indicator of protein; produced by monosodium glutamate and inosine monophosphate |
| Tannic acid | punisher, it prevents absorption of protein; found in old leaves; probably somatosensory rather than strictly gustatory |

**Odour**

| | |
|---|---|
| Putrefying odour | punisher; hazard to health |
| Pheromones | reward (depending on hormonal state) |

**Somatosensory**

| | |
|---|---|
| Pain | punisher |
| Touch | reward |
| Grooming | reward; to give grooming may also be a primary reinforcer |
| Washing | reward |
| Temperature | reward if tends to help maintain normal body temperature; otherwise punisher |

**Visual**

| | |
|---|---|
| Snakes, etc. | punisher for, e.g., primates |
| Youthfulness | reward, associated with mate choice |
| Beauty | reward |
| Secondary sexual characteristics | rewards |
| Face expression | reward (e.g., smile) and punisher (e.g., threat) |
| Blue sky, cover, open space | reward, indicator of safety |
| Flowers | reward (indicator of fruit later in season?) |

**Auditory**

| | |
|---|---|
| Warning call | punisher |
| Aggressive vocalization | punisher |
| Soothing vocalization | reward (part of the evolutionary history of music, which at least in its origins taps into the channels used for the communication of emotions) |

**Reproduction**

| | |
|---|---|
| Courtship | reward |
| Sexual behaviour | reward (a number of different reinforcers, including a low waist-to-hip ration, and attractiveness influenced by symmetry and being found attractive by members of the other sex) |
| Mate guarding | reward for a male to protect his parental investment; jealousy results if his mate is courted by another male, because this may ruin his parental investment |

*(continued)*

Table 8.1 Continued

| | |
|---|---|
| Nest building | reward (when expecting young) |
| Parental attachment | reward |
| Infant attachment to parents | reward |
| Crying of infant | punisher to parents; produced to promote successful development |

**Other**

| | |
|---|---|
| Novel stimuli | rewards (encourage animals to investigate the full possibilities of the multidimensional space in which their genes are operating) |
| Sleep | reward; minimizes nutritional requirements and protects from danger |
| Altruism to genetically related individuals | reward (kin altruism) |
| Altruism to other individuals | reward while the altruism is reciprocated in a 'tit-for-tat' reciprocation (reciprocal altruism); punisher when the altruism is not reciprocated |
| Group acceptance | reward (social greeting might indicate this) |
| Control over actions | reward |
| Play | reward |
| Danger, stimulation, excitement | reward if not too extreme (adaptive because practice?) |
| Exercise | reward (keeps the body fit for action) |
| Mind reading | reward; practice in reading others' minds, which might be adaptive |
| Solving an intellectual problem | reward (practice in which might be adaptive) |
| Storing, collecting | reward (e.g., food) |
| Habitat preference, home, territory | reward |
| Some responses | reward (e.g., pecking in chickens, pigeons; adaptive because it is a simple way in which eating grain can be programmed for a relatively fixed type of environmental stimulus) |

4. Emotions elicited by stimuli associated with *different primary reinforcers* will be different. A list of some primary reinforcers to illustrate some of the different affective states that can be produced by them is provided in Table 8.1.

5. Emotions elicited by *different secondary reinforcing stimuli* will be different from each other (even if the primary reinforcer is similar).

6. The emotion elicited can depend on whether an *active or passive behavioural response* is possible. (For example, if an active behavioural response can occur to the omission of a positive reinforcer, then anger might be produced, but if only passive behaviour is possible, then sadness, depression or grief might occur.)

By combining these six factors, it is possible to account for a very wide range of emotions (for elaboration see Rolls 2005b). It is also worth noting that emotions can be produced just as much by the recall of reinforcing events as by external reinforcing stimuli; and that cognitive processing (whether conscious or not) is important in many emotions, for very complex cognitive processing may be required to determine whether or not environmental events are reinforcing. Indeed, emotions normally consist of cognitive processing which analyses the stimulus, and then determines its reinforcing valence; and then an elicited mood change if the valence is positive or negative. In that an emotion is produced by a stimulus, philosophers say that emotions have an object in the world, and that emotional states are intentional, in that they are about something. We note that a mood or affective state may occur in the absence of an external stimulus, as in some types of depression, but that normally the mood or affective state is produced by an external stimulus, with the whole process of stimulus representation, evaluation in terms of reward or punishment, and the resulting mood or affect being referred to as emotion.

It is worth raising the issue that some philosophers categorize fear in the example as an emotion, but not pain. The distinction they make may be that primary (unlearned or innate) reinforcers (for example pain) do not produce emotions, whereas secondary reinforcers (stimuli associated by stimulus-reinforcement learning with primary reinforcers) do. (An example is fear, which is a state produced by a secondary reinforcing stimulus such as the sight of an image associated by learning with a primary reinforcer such as pain.) They describe the pain as a sensation. But neutral stimuli (such as a table) can produce sensations when touched. Thus whether a stimulus produces a sensation or not does not seem to be a useful distinction that has anything to do with affective or emotional states. It accordingly seems to be much more useful to categorize stimuli according to whether they are reinforcing (in which case they produce emotions or affective states, produced by both primary and secondary reinforcers), or are not reinforcing (in which case they do not produce emotions or affective states such as pleasantness or unpleasantness). Clearly there is a difference between primary reinforcers and learned reinforcers; but this is most precisely caught by noting that this is the difference, and that it is whether a stimulus is reinforcing that determines whether it is related to affective states and emotion. These points are considered in more detail by Rolls (2005b), who provides many examples of primary versus secondary reinforcers, all of which elicit affective states.

## 2. The functions of emotion

The functions of emotion also provide insight into the nature of emotion. These functions, described more fully elsewhere (Rolls 1990, 1999, 2005b), can be summarized as follows:

1. The *elicitation of autonomic responses* (e.g., a change in heart rate) and *endocrine responses* (e.g., the release of adrenaline). These prepare the body for action.
2. *Flexibility of behavioural responses to reinforcing stimuli.* Emotional (and motivational) states allow a simple interface between sensory inputs and action systems. The essence of this idea is that goals for behaviour are specified by reward and punishment evaluation. When an environmental stimulus has been decoded as a primary reward or punishment, or (after previous stimulus–reinforcer association learning) a secondary rewarding or punishing stimulus, then it becomes a goal for action. The person can then perform any action (instrumental response) to obtain the reward, or to avoid the punisher. Thus there is flexibility of action, and this is in contrast with stimulus–response, or habit, learning in which a particular response to a particular stimulus is learned. The emotional route to action is flexible not only because any action can be performed to obtain the reward or avoid the punishment, but also because the person can learn in as little as one trial that a reward or punishment is associated with a particular stimulus, in what is termed 'stimulus–reinforcer association learning'.

To summarize and formalize, two processes are involved in the actions being described. The first is stimulus–reinforcer association learning, and the second is instrumental learning of an operant response made to approach and obtain the reward or to avoid or escape from the punisher. Emotion is an integral part of this, for it is the state elicited in the first stage, by stimuli which are decoded as rewards or punishers, and this state has the property that it is motivating. The motivation is to obtain the reward or avoid the punisher, and animals must be built to obtain certain rewards and avoid certain punishers. Indeed, primary or unlearned rewards and punishers are specified by genes which effectively specify the goals for action. This is the solution which natural selection has found for how genes can influence behaviour to promote their fitness (as measured by reproductive success), and for how the brain could interface sensory systems to action systems, and is an important part of Rolls' theory of emotion (1990, 1999, 2005b).

Selecting between available rewards with their associated costs, and avoiding punishers with their associated costs, is a process that can take place both implicitly (unconsciously), and explicitly using a language system to enable long-term plans to be made (Rolls 2005a, 2008b). These many different brain systems, some involving implicit evaluation of rewards, and others explicit, verbal, conscious, evaluation of rewards and planned long-term goals, must all enter into the selector of behaviour (see Fig. 8.2). This selector is poorly understood, but it might include a process of competition between all the competing calls on output, and might involve the anterior cingulate cortex and basal ganglia in the brain (Rolls 2005b, 2008b) (see Fig. 8.2).

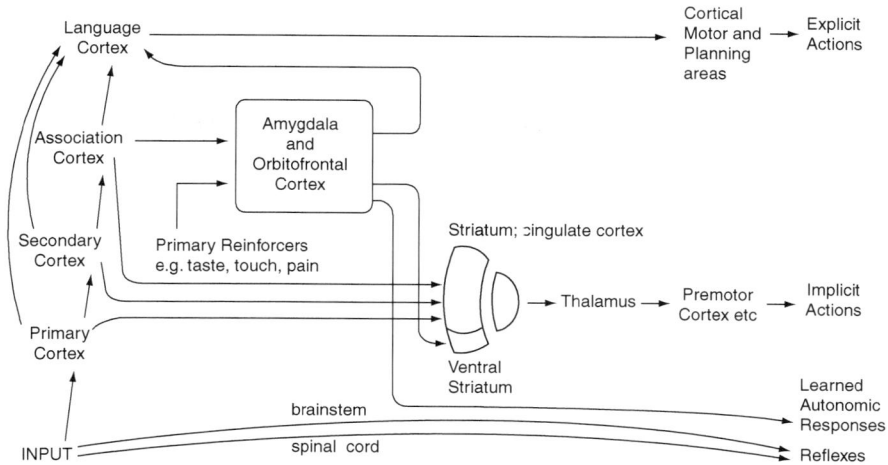

Figure 8.2 Dual routes to the initiation of action in response to rewarding and punishing stimuli. The inputs from different sensory systems to brain structures such as the orbitofrontal cortex and amygdala allow these brain structures to evaluate the reward- or punishment-related value of incoming stimuli, or of remembered stimuli. The different sensory inputs enable evaluations within the orbitofrontal cortex and amygdala based mainly on the primary (unlearned) reinforcement value for taste, touch, and olfactory stimuli, and on the secondary (learned) reinforcement value for visual and auditory stimuli. In the case of vision, the 'association cortex' which outputs representations of objects to the amygdala and orbitofrontal cortex is the inferior temporal visual cortex. One route for the outputs from these evaluative brain structures is via projections directly to structures such as the basal ganglia (including the striatum and ventral striatum) to enable implicit, direct behavioural responses based on the reward- or punishment-related evaluation of the stimuli to be made. The second route is via the language systems of the brain, which allow explicit decisions involving multistep syntactic planning to be implemented

3. Emotion is *motivating*, as just described. For example, fear learned by stimulus-reinforcement association provides the motivation for actions performed to avoid noxious stimuli.

4. *Communication*. Monkeys, for example, may communicate their emotional state to others, by making an open-mouth threat to indicate the extent to which they are willing to compete for resources, and this may influence the behaviour of other animals. This aspect of emotion was emphasized by Darwin (1872), and has been studied more recently by Ekman (1982, 1993). He reviews evidence that humans can categorize facial expressions into the categories happy, sad, fearful, angry, surprised, and disgusted, and that this categorization may operate similarly in different cultures. As shown elsewhere, there are neural systems in the orbitofrontal cortex, amygdala, and overlying temporal cortical visual areas that are specialized for the face-related aspects of this processing (Rolls 2005b, 2007c; Rolls et al. 2006).

5. *Social bonding*. Examples of this are the emotions associated with the attachment of the parents to their young, and the attachment of the young to their parents.

6. The current mood state can affect the *cognitive evaluation of events or memories* (see Oatley and Jenkins 1996). This may facilitate continuity in the interpretation of the reinforcing value of events in the environment. A hypothesis that back projections from parts of the brain involved in emotion such as the orbitofrontal cortex and amygdala implement this is described in *Emotion Explained* (Rolls 2005b).

7. Emotion may facilitate the *storage of memories*. One way this occurs is that episodic memory (i.e., one's memory of particular episodes) is facilitated by emotional states (Rolls 2005b, 2008b). A second way in which emotion may affect the storage of memories is that the current emotional state may be stored with episodic memories, providing a mechanism for the current emotional state to affect which memories are recalled. A third way that emotion may affect the storage of memories is by guiding the cerebral cortex in the representations of the world that are set up (Rolls 2008b).

8. Another function of emotion is that by enduring for minutes or longer after a reinforcing stimulus has occurred, emotion may help to produce *persistent and continuing motivation and direction of behaviour*, to help achieve a goal or goals.

9. Emotion may trigger the *recall of memories* stored in neocortical representations. Amygdala back projections to the cortex could perform this for emotion in a way analogous to that in which the hippocampus could implement the retrieval in the neocortex of recent (episodic) memories (Rolls 2008b; Rolls and Stringer 2001).

## 3.  Reward, punishment and emotion in brain design: an evolutionary approach

The theory of the functions of emotion is further developed in *Emotion Explained* (Rolls 2005b). Some of the points made help to elaborate greatly on 3 above. Rolls (2005b) considers the fundamental question of why we and other animals are built to use rewards and punishers to guide or determine our behaviour. Why are we built to have emotions, as well as motivational states? Is there any reasonable alternative around which evolution could have built complex animals?

Rolls (2005b) argues that a role of natural selection is to guide animals to build sensory systems that will respond to dimensions of stimuli in the natural environment along which actions can lead to better ability to pass genes on to the next generation, that is to increased fitness. The animals must be built by such natural selection to make actions that will enable them to obtain more rewards, that is to work to obtain stimuli that will increase their fitness. Correspondingly, animals must be built to make responses that will enable them to escape from, or learn to avoid, stimuli that will reduce their fitness. There are likely to be many dimensions of environmental stimuli along which responses can alter fitness. Each of these dimensions may be a separate reward/punishment dimension. An example of one of these dimensions might be food reward. It increases fitness to be able to sense nutrient need, to have sensors that respond to the taste of food, and to perform behavioural responses to obtain such reward stimuli when in that need or motivational state. Similarly, another dimension is water reward, in which the taste of water becomes rewarding when there is body fluid depletion (see Chapter 6 of *Emotion Explained*).

With many reward/punishment dimensions for which actions may be performed (see Table 8.1 for a non-exhaustive list!), a selection mechanism for actions performed is needed. In this sense, rewards and punishers provide a *common currency scale* for inputs to response selection mechanisms. Evolution must set the magnitudes of each of the different reward systems so that each will be chosen for action in such a way as to maximize overall fitness. Food reward must be chosen as the aim for action if a nutrient is depleted; but water reward as a target for action must be selected if current water depletion poses a greater threat to fitness than the current food depletion. This indicates that each reward must be carefully calibrated by evolution to have the right value in the common currency for the competitive selection process. Other types of behaviour, such as sexual behaviour, must be selected sometimes, but probably less frequently, in order to maximize fitness (as measured by gene transmission into the next generation). Many processes contribute to increasing the chances that a wide set of different environmental rewards will be chosen over a period of time, including not only need-related satiety mechanisms which decrease the rewards within a dimension, but also sensory-specific satiety mechanisms, which facilitate switching to another reward stimulus (sometimes within and sometimes outside the same main dimension), and attraction to novel stimuli. Finding novel stimuli rewarding is one way that organisms are encouraged to explore the multidimensional space in which their genes are operating.

The implication of this comparison is that operation by animals using reward and punishment systems tuned to dimensions of the environment that increase fitness provides a mode of operation that can work in organisms that evolve by natural selection. It is clearly a natural outcome of Darwinian evolution to operate using reward and punishment systems tuned to fitness-related dimensions of the environment, if instrumental goal-directed actions are to be made by the animals, rather than just pre-programmed responses and movements such as tropisms and taxes. This view of brain design in terms of reward and punishment systems built by genes that gain their adaptive value by being tuned to a goal for action offers I believe a deep insight into how natural selection has shaped many brain systems, and is a fascinating outcome of Darwinian thought.

We thus have part of a theory of how value is placed on some stimuli. Value will be placed according to whether the stimuli activate our reward or punishment systems, themselves tuned during evolution to produce goals that will increase the fitness of our genes. Moreover, we have seen that these gene-defined goals may include a wide range of reinforcers, including many involved in social behaviour, and define some of the things that make people and objects attractive. Before building in the direction of aesthetics, we need to take into account a second way in which humans by reasoning can define a wider range of goals, or at least can place different value on goals as a result of reasoning. I now compare these two routes to action (see also Rolls 2003, 2005b).

## 4. Dual routes to action: gene-defined goals, and syntactic reasoning

The first route is via the brain systems that have been present in non-human primates such as monkeys, and to some extent in other mammals, for millions of years, and have built in the brain a system for defining these goals. Achieving these goals feels pleasant or unpleasant. The goals may be primary reinforcers, or stimuli associated with them by learning. This value assessment may be based on a number of different factors. One is the previous reinforcement history, which involves stimulus–reinforcement association learning, and its rapid updating especially in primates using the orbitofrontal cortex. A second is the current motivational state, for example whether hunger is present, whether other needs are satisfied, etc. A third factor that affects the computed reward value of the stimulus is whether that reward has been received recently. If it has been received recently but in small quantity, this may increase the reward value of the stimulus. This is known as incentive motivation or the 'salted-nut' phenomenon. The adaptive value of such a process is that this positive feedback of reward value in the early stages of working for a particular reward tends to lock the organism onto behaviour being performed for that reward. A fourth factor is the computed absolute value of the reward or punishment expected or being obtained from a stimulus, e.g., the sweetness of the stimulus (set by evolution so that sweet stimuli will tend to be rewarding, because they are generally associated with energy sources), or the pleasant-ness of touch (set by evolution to be pleasant according to the extent to which it brings animals of the opposite sex together, and depending on the investment in time that the partner is willing to put into making the touch pleasurable, a sign which indicates the commitment and value for the partner of the relationship). After the reward value of the stimulus has been assessed in these ways, behaviour is then initiated based on approach towards or withdrawal from the stimulus. A critical aspect of the behaviour produced by this type of system is that it is aimed directly towards obtaining a sensed or expected reward, by virtue of connections to brain systems such as the basal ganglia and cingulate cortex (Rolls 2009) which are concerned with the initiation of actions (see Fig. 8.2).

Now part of the way in which the behaviour is controlled with this first route is according to the reward value of the outcome. At the same time, the animal may only work for the reward if the cost is not too high. Part of the value of having the computation expressed in this reward-minus-cost (or 'net reward') form is that there is then a suitable 'currency', or net reward value, to enable the animal to select the behaviour with currently the most net reward gain (or minimal aversive outcome).

The second route in humans and perhaps closely related animals involves a computation with many 'if...then' statements, to implement a plan to obtain a reward. In this case, the reward may actually be *deferred* as part of the plan, which might involve working first to obtain one reward, and only then to work for a second more highly valued reward, if this was thought to be overall an optimal strategy in terms of resource usage (e.g., time). In this case, syntax is required, because the many symbols (e.g., names of people) that are part of the plan must be correctly linked or bound. Such linking might be of the form: 'if A does this, then B is likely to do this, and this will cause C to do this . . . '. The requirement of syntax for this type of planning implies that an output to language systems in the brain is required for this type of planning (see Fig. 8.2). Thus the explicit language system in humans may allow working for deferred rewards by enabling use of a one-off, individual, plan appropriate for each situation.

The question then arises of how decisions are made in animals such as humans that have both the implicit, direct reward-based, and the explicit, rational, planning systems (see Fig. 8.2) (Rolls 2008b). One particular situation in which the first, implicit, system may be especially important is when rapid reactions to stimuli with reward or punishment value must be made, for then the direct connections from structures such as the orbitofrontal cortex to the basal ganglia may allow rapid actions (Rolls 2005b). Another is when there may be too many factors to be taken into account easily by the explicit, rational, planning, system, when the implicit system may be used to guide action. In contrast, when the implicit system continually makes errors, it would then be beneficial for the organism to switch from automatic, direct, action based on obtaining what the orbitofrontal cortex system decodes as being the most positively reinforcing choice currently available, to the explicit conscious control system which can evaluate with its long-term planning algorithms what action should be performed next. Indeed, it would be adaptive for the explicit system to regularly be assessing performance by the more automatic system, and to switch itself in to control behaviour quite frequently, as otherwise the adaptive value of having the explicit system would be less than optimal.

There may also be a flow of influence from the explicit, verbal system to the implicit system, in that the explicit system may decide on a plan of action or strategy, and exert an influence on the implicit system that will alter the reinforcement evaluations made by and the signals produced by the implicit system (Rolls 2005b).

The second route to action allows, by reasoning, decisions to be taken that might not be in the interests of the genes, might be longer-term decisions, and might be in the interests of the individual. An example might be a choice not to have children, but instead to devote oneself to science, medicine, music, or literature. The reasoning, rational, system presumably evolved because taking longer-term decisions involving planning rather than choosing a gene-defined goal might be advantageous at least sometimes for genes. But an 'unforeseen' consequence of the evolution of the rational system might be that the decisions would, sometimes, not be to the advantage of any genes in the organism. After all, evolution by natural selection operates utilizing genetic variation like a Blind Watchmaker (Dawkins 1986). In this sense, the interests when the second route to decision-making is used are at least sometimes those of the 'selfish phenotype'. (Indeed, we might euphonically say that the interests are those of the 'selfish phene' (where the etymology is Gk. *phaino*, 'appear', referring to appearance, hence the thing that one observes, the individual).

Hence the decision-making is between a first system where the goals are gene-defined, and a second rational system in which the decisions may be made in the interests of the genes, or in the interests of the phenotype and not in the interests of the genes. Thus we may speak of the choice as sometimes being between the 'Selfish Genes' (Dawkins 1989) and the 'Selfish Phenes' (Rolls 2011, b, a).

Now what keeps the decision-making between the 'Selfish Genes' and the 'Selfish Phenes' more or less under control and in balance? If the second, rational, system chose too often for the interests of the 'Selfish Phene', the genes in that phenotype would not survive over generations. Having these two systems in the same individual will only be stable if their potency is approximately equal, so that sometimes decisions are made with the first route, and sometimes with the second route. If the two types of decision-making, then, compete with approximately equal potency, and sometimes one is chosen, and sometimes the other, then this is exactly the scenario in which stochastic processes in the decision-making mechanism are likely to play an important role in the decision that is taken. The same decision, even with the same evidence, may not be taken each time a decision is made, because of noise in the system, and this makes the decision-making probabilistic (Rolls and Deco 2010).

The system itself may have some properties that help to keep the system operating well. One is that if the second, rational, system tends to dominate the decision-making too much, the first, gene-based emotional system might fight back over generations of selection, and enhance the magnitude of the reward value specified by the genes, so that emotions might actually become stronger as a consequence of them having to compete in the interests of the selfish genes with the rational decision-making process.

Another property of the system may be that sometimes the rational system cannot gain all the evidence that would be needed to make a rational choice. Under these circumstances the rational system might fail to make a clear decision, and under these circumstances, basing a decision on the gene-specified emotions is an alternative. Indeed, Damasio (1994) argued that under circumstances such as this, emotions might take an important role in decision-making. In this respect, I agree with him, basing my reasons on the arguments above. He called the emotional feelings gut feelings, and, in contrast to me, hypothesized that actual feedback from the gut was involved. His argument seemed to be that if the decision was too complicated for the rational system, outputs are sent to the viscera, and whatever is sensed by what they send back could be used in the decision-making, and would account for the conscious feelings of the emotional states. My reading of the evidence is that the feedback from the periphery is not necessary for the emotional decision-making, or for the feelings, nor would it be computationally efficient to put the viscera in the loop given that the information starts from the brain, but that is a matter considered elsewhere (Maia and McClelland 2004; Rolls 2005b).

Another property is that the interests of the second, rational, system, although involving a different form of computation, should not be too far from those of the gene-defined emotional system, for the arrangement to be stable in evolution by natural selection. One way that this could be facilitated would be if the gene-based goals felt pleasant or unpleasant in the rational system, and in this way contributed to the operation of the second, rational, system. This is something that I propose is the case, as considered further in the next section.

The operation of the reasoning system—how its multistep plans may be corrected by higher order thoughts, and how this higher order thought process appears to be closely related to consciousness—is developed elsewhere (Rolls, 2003, 2004, 2005a, 2005b, 2007b, 2007d, 2008a). When I write here about aesthetic (and emotional) feelings, the conscious feelings I refer to are of the type considered in those sources.

# 5. A theory of aesthetics

## 5.1 Introduction to and outline of the theory

We thus have part of a theory of how value is placed on some stimuli. Value will be placed according to whether the stimuli activate our reward or punishment systems, themselves tuned during evolution to produce goals that will increase the fitness of our genes. Moreover, we have seen that these gene-defined goals may include a wide range of reinforcers, including many involved in social behaviour, and define some of the things that make people and objects attractive. We have seen that humans by reasoning can define a wider range of goals, or at least can place different values on goals as a result of reasoning, and use this as a second route to action. We have also seen that cognition can influence the representation of affective value in the orbitofrontal cortex. The analysis of the evolutionary basis of reward value provides a fundamental and Darwinian way to understand emotion (Rolls 2005b).

I now explore whether the same approach can provide a neurobiological basis for understanding aesthetics. Now that we have a fundamental, Darwinian, approach to the value of people, objects, relationships, etc., I propose that this provides a funda-mental approach to understanding aesthetics. I propose that while the gene-specified rewards and punishers define many things that have aesthetic value, the value that we place on items is enhanced by the reasoning, rational, system, which enables what produces aesthetic value to become highly intellectualized, as in music. However, even here I argue that there are certain adaptive principles that influence the operation of our rational system that provide a systematic way to understand aesthetics.

I emphasize at the outset that this does not at all reduce aesthetics to a common denominator. Genetic variation is essential to evolution by natural selection, and this is one reason why we should expect different people to assign aesthetic value differently. But rational thought, which will lead in different directions in different people, partly because of noise caused by random neuronal firing times in the brain (Rolls and Deco 2010), and because of what they have learned from the environment, and because different brain areas will be emphasized in different people, will also be different between individuals, so that the rational system will also contribute to differences between individuals in what is considered aesthetic.

Indeed, although the theory presented here on the origin of aesthetics is a reductive explanation, in that it treats the underlying bases and causes, it should not be seen at all to 'reduce' aesthetics. Far from it. When we understand the underlying origins and bases of aesthetics, we see that the processes involved are elegant and beautiful, as part of a Darwinian theory. But the approach also provides important pointers about how to enhance aesthetics. For example, by understanding that verbal level cognitive factors that can be produced by reasoning have a top-down modulatory influence on the first cortical area where value (reward) is made explicit in the representation, the orbito-frontal cortex (De Araujo *et al.* 2005; Grabenhorst *et al.* 2008; McCabe *et al.* 2008), we can see ways in which we can enhance our aesthetic feelings. (For example, if love be the thing, then it can be heightened by explicitly choosing the musical treatment of it in *Tristan and Isolde*.)

I should also emphasize that aesthetic value judgements will usually be influenced by a number of different value factors, so that while accounting for an aesthetic judgement by just one of the value factors I describe is and will often seem too simple, it does seem that aesthetic value judgements can be understood by combinations of some of the factors I describe.

I also emphasize that this is a theory of the origin of aesthetics. I provide generic examples, but of course cannot cover all factors that influence value. An indication of the range of factors that can provide a basis for aesthetic judgements is shown in Table 8.1, but this is by no means complete. These examples are gene-defined goals for action, and we are built to want to obtain these goals (the basis for motivation), to treat them operationally as rewards or punishers, and to have pleasant or unpleasant affective feelings when they are delivered (the basis of emotion) (Rolls 2005b). It is argued here that these factors contribute to aesthetic judgements, that any one stimulus will often have multiple such attributes, and that these factors are afforced by operations of the reasoning system.

I emphasize that rewards, of which examples are provided in Table 8.1, contribute to what makes stimuli or brain processing positively aesthetic, beautiful; and that the punishers contribute to what makes stimuli or processing in the brain aesthetically negative, lacking beauty, ugly, or distasteful. Both rewards and punishers are needed for the theory of aesthetics.

The overall theory of the origin of aesthetics I propose is that natural selection, whether operating by 'survival or adaptation selection', or by sexual selection, operates by specifying goals for action, and these goals are aesthetically and subjectively attractive or beautiful (Rolls 2005a), or the opposite, and provide what I argue here is the origin of many judgements of what is aesthetic. Examples of these rewards and punishers, many of which operate for 'survival or adaptation selection', and many of which contribute to aesthetic experience, are shown in Table 8.1.

In contrast to my theory, Miller (2000, 2001) emphasizes the role of sexual selection. Understanding the mechanisms that drive evolution to make certain stimuli rewarding or punishing can help us to understand the origin of aesthetics, and I therefore summarize the characteristics of these two evolutionary processes in Sections 5.2 and 5.3.

I note first that the term 'natural selection' encompasses in its broad sense both 'survival or adaptation selection', and sexual selection. Both are processes now understood to be driven by the selection of genes, and it is gene competition and replication into the next generation that is the driving force of biological evolution (Dawkins 1986, 1989). The distinction can be made that with 'survival or adaptation selection', the genes being selected for make the individual stronger, healthier, and more likely to survive and reproduce; whereas sexual selection operates by sexual choice selecting for genes that may or may not have survival value to the individual, but enable the individual to be selected as a mate or to compete for a mate in intra-sexual selection, and thus pass on the genes selected by intra-sexual or inter-sexual selection to the offspring. More generally, we might have other types of selection as further types of natural selection, including selection for good parental care, and kin selection.

### 5.2 'Survival' or 'adaptation' selection (natural selection in a narrow sense)

Darwin (1871) distinguished natural selection from sexual selection, and this distinction has been consolidated and developed (Fisher 1930; Hamilton 1964; Zahavi 1975; Dawkins 1986; Grafen 1990a, 1990b; Dawkins 1995; Hamilton 1996; Miller 2000). Natural selection can be used in a narrow sense to refer to selection processes that lead to the development of characteristics that have a function of providing adaptive or survival value to an individual so that the individual can reproduce, and pass on its genes. In its narrow sense, natural selection can be thought of as 'survival or adaptation selection'. An example might be a gene or genes that specify that the sensory properties of food should be rewarding (and should taste pleasant) when we are in a physiological need state for food. Many of the reward and punishment systems described here and by Rolls (2005b) deal with this type of reward and punishment decoding that has evolved to enable genes to influence behaviour in directions in a high-dimensional space of rewards and punishments that are adaptive for survival and health of the individual, and thus promote reproductive success or fitness of the genes that build such adaptive functionality. We can include kin-related altruistic behaviours because the behaviour is adaptive in promoting the survival of kin, and thus promoting the likelihood that the kin (who contain one's genes, and are likely to share the genes for kin altruism) survive and reproduce. We can also include reciprocal altruism as an example of 'survival or adaptation' selection. Tribalism can be treated similarly, for it probably has its origins in altruism. Resources and wealth are also understood at least in part as being selected by natural selection, in that resources and wealth may enable the individual to survive better. As we will see next, resources and wealth can also be attractive as a result of sexual selection. (I note that natural selection in a broad sense includes 'survival or adaptation' selection, sexual selection, selection for good parental care, etc.)

## 5.3 Sexual selection

Darwin (1871) also recognized that evolution can occur by sexual selection, when what is being selected for is attractive to potential mates (*inter-sexual selection*), or helps in competing with others of the same sex (*intra-sexual selection*, e.g., the deer's large antlers, and a strong male physique). The most cited example of mate selection (inter-sexual selection) is the peacock's large tail, which does not have survival value for the peacock (and indeed it is somewhat of a handicap to have a very long tail), but, because it is attractive to the peahen, becomes prevalent in the population. Indeed, part of the reason for the long tail being attractive may be that it is an honest signal of phenotypic fitness (or 'fitness indicator'), in that having a very long tail is a handicap to survival (Zahavi 1975), though the signalling system that reveals this only operates correctly if certain conditions apply (Grafen 1990a, 1990b; Maynard Smith and Harper 2003). The inherited genes for a long tail may be expressed in the female's sons, and they will accordingly be attractive to females in the next generation. Although the female offspring of the mating will not express the male father's attractive long-tail genes, these genes are likely to be expressed in her sons. The female has to evolve to find the characteristic being selected for in males attractive for this situation to lead to selection of the characteristic being selected for by the choosiness of females. Indeed, the fact that the female who chose a long-tailed male has children following her mating with genes for liking long-tailed males, and for generating long tails, is part of what leads to the sexual selection. The fact that the long tail is actually a handicap for the peacock, and so is a signal of general physical fitness in the male, may be one way in which sexual selection can occur stably (Zahavi 1975; Grafen 1990a, 1990b).

The peacock tail example is categorized as sexual selection because the long tail is not adaptive to the individual with the long tail, though of course it is useful to the male's genes to have a long tail if females are choosing it because it indicates general physical fitness. However, sexual selection can also occur when a revealing or index signal or fitness indicator is not associated with a handicap, but is hard to fake, so that it is necessarily an honest fitness indicator (Maynard Smith and Harper 2003). An example occurs in birds that may show bare skin as part of their courtship, providing a sign that they are parasite resistant (Hamilton and Zuk 1982). Revealing bare skin in women can be beautiful and may have its origins partly in this, as well as in perhaps displaying secondary sexual characteristics (such as breasts) that may be attractive to men (with an origin as indicators of sexual maturity and of maternal readiness). (Note that this account is very different to that of Sigmund Freud.)

The mechanisms of mate choice evolution include the following (Andersson and Simmons 2006):

(i) Direct phenotypic effects. Female preference for a male ornament can evolve as a result of direct phenotypic benefits if the ornament reflects the ability of the male to provide material advantages, such as high-quality territory, nutrition, parental care, or protection.

(ii) Sensory bias. Female preference favouring a male ornament can initially evolve under natural selection for other reasons, for instance in the context of foraging or predator avoidance. Males evolving traits that exploit this bias then become favoured by mate choice (Ryan 1998).

(iii) Fisherian sexy sons. If there are genetic components to variance in female preference and male trait, a female choosing a male with a large trait bears daughters and sons that can both carry alleles for a large trait, and for the preference for it. This genetic coupling might lead to self-reinforcing co-evolution between trait and preference (Fisher 1930; Mead and Arnold 2004). (Sexual election may be identified when females choose sexy mates so that the female's sons will be sexy and attractive. Survival selection may be identified if the choice helps the female's daughters as well as sons.)

(iv) Fitness indicator mechanisms ('good genes' or 'handicap mechanisms') suggest that attractive male traits reflect broad genetic quality (Zahavi 1975; Grafen 1990a, 1990b). Female preference for such traits can provide genetic benefits to those of her offspring that inherit favourable alleles from their father.

(v) Genetic compatibility mechanisms. As well as additive genetic benefits reflected by indicator traits, there might be non-additive benefits from choosing a mate with alleles that complement the genome of the chooser. Examples have been found for instance in major histocompatibility complex (MHC) genes, which may be associated with odour preferences for potential mates (Dulac and Torello 2003). These genes are involved in the process by which a cell infected with an antigen (from a virus or bacterium) displays short peptide sequences of it at the cell surface, and the T lymphocytes of the immune system then recognize the fragment, and build an antibody to it. This MHC gene system must maintain great diversity to help detect uncommon antigens, with an advantage arising from mating with an individual with different MHC genes. At least some of the MHC genes are very closely associated with gene-specified pheromone receptors, with individual pheromone receptor cells often expressing one or a few MHC genes in a complex with specific V2R-specified receptors (Dulac and Torello 2003). Thus, a mate may be found attractive (and beautiful) based on odour, and a mechanism such as this may operate in humans (see Rolls 2005b).

The evolution of mate choice is based either on direct selection of a preference that gives a fitness advantage (mechanisms i–ii) (i.e., there is a survival or adaptation advantage); or on indirect selection of a preference as it becomes genetically correlated with directly selected traits (mechanisms iii, iv) (i.e., the trait has no advantage, and might be thought of as a useless ornament) (Andersson 1994; Mead and Arnold 2004). In addition, rather than favouring any particular display trait, mate choice might evolve because it conveys non-additive genetic benefits (mechanism v). These mechanisms are mutually compatible and can occur together, rendering the evolution of mating preferences a multiple-causation problem, and calling for estimation of the relative roles of individual mechanisms (Andersson, 1994).[1]

Some characteristics of sexual selection that help to separate it from survival selection are as follows:

First, the sexually selected characteristic is usually sexually dimorphic, with the male typically showing the characteristic. (For example the peacock but not the peahen has the long tail.) This occurs because it is the female who is being choosy, and is selecting males. The female is the choosy one because she has a considerable investment in her offspring, whom she may need to nurture until birth, and then rear until independent, and for this reason has a much more limited reproductive potential than the male, who could in principle father large numbers of offspring to optimize his genetic potential. This is an example of a sexual dimorphism selected by inter-sexual selection. An example of a sexual dimorphism selected by intra-sexual selection is the deer's antlers. Sexual dimorphism usually reflects sexual selection, but may not, with an example being that the female may be cryptic (hidden against the background, camouflaged) when incubating eggs, in order to be a good parent.

Second, sexually selected characteristics such as ornamentation helpful in identification are typically species-specific, whereas naturally selected characteristics may, because they have survival value for individuals, be found in many species within a genus, and even across genera.

Third, and accordingly, the competition is within a species for sexual selection, whereas competition may be across as well as within species for natural (survival) selection.

Fourth, sexual selection operates most efficiently in polygynous species, that is species where some (attractive) males must mate with two or more females, and unattractive males must be more likely to be childless. Polygyny does seem to have been present to at least some extent in our ancestors, as shown for example by body size differences, with males larger than females. This situation is selected because males compete harder with each other in polygynous species compared to monogamous, where there is less competition. In humans, the male is 10 per cent taller, 20 per cent

---

[1] I note that even in the Fisherian case, iii, for 'runaway' to occur there must be a critical proportion of females in the population with the preference, and this is only likely to occur if the ornamental characteristic has some survival value. For example, a slightly longer tail may have helped flying, even if that characteristic later showed runaway. Further, runaway can refer to the characteristic, or to the proportion of individuals (males) with the characteristic. Overall, the implication is that there may be some 'use' or survival value even in characteristics that later become sexually selected by a Fisherian process. Further, I note that runaway may occur with a Fisherian process, but not with a handicap, which is self-limiting.

heavier, 50 per cent stronger in the upper body muscles, and 100 per cent stronger in the hand grip strength than the average female (Miller 2000).

Fifth, the sexually selected characteristics are often apparent after but not before puberty. In humans, one possible example is the deep male voice.

Sixth, there may be marked differences between individuals, as it is these differences that are being used for mate choice. Sexual selection thus promotes genetic diversity. In contrast, when natural or survival selection is operating efficiently, there may be little variation between individuals.

Seventh, the fitness indicator may be costly or difficult to produce, as in this way it can reflect real fitness, and be kept honest (mechanism iv above).

However, sexual selection is not as pure as was once thought: females are less choosy, and more promiscuous, than was once thought (Birkhead 2000).

Overall, Darwinian natural or survival selection increases health, strength, and potentially resources, and survival of the individual, and thus ability to mate and reproduce, and to look handsome or beautiful. Inter-sexual sexual selection does not make the individual healthier, but does make the individual more attractive as a mate, as in female choice, an example of inter-sexual selection. Intra-sexual sexual selection does not necessarily help survival of the individual, but does help in competition for a mate, for example in intimidation of one male by another (Darwin 1871; Kappeler and van Schaik 2004). The behaviours and characteristics involved in sperm competition, which itself may influence what is judged to be attractive and beautiful, are produced by intrasexual sexual selection (Rolls 2005b; Andersson and Simmons 2006).

It turns out that many of the best examples of inter-sexual sexual selection are in birds (for example the peacock's tail, and the male lyre bird's tail). In mammals, including primates, the selection is often by size, strength, physical prowess, and aggressiveness, which provide for direct physical (and other types of) competition, and are examples of intra-sexual selection (in males) (Kappeler and van Schaik 2004).

It has been suggested that sexual selection is important for further types of characteristic in humans. For example, it has been suggested that human mental abilities that may be important in courtship such as kindness, humour, and telling stories, are the type of characteristic that may be sexually selected in humans (Miller 2000). Before assessing this (in Section 5.8), and illuminating thus some of what may be sexually selected rewards and punishers that therefore contribute to human affective states and aesthetics, we should note a twist in how sexual selection may operate in humans.

In humans, because babies are born relatively immature and may take years of demanding care before they can look after themselves, there is some advantage to male genes of providing at least some parental care for the children. That is, the father may invest in his offspring. In this situation, where there is a male investment, the male may optimize the chance of his genes faring well by being choosy about his wife. The implication is that in humans, sexual selection may be of female characteristics (by males), as well as of male characteristics (by females). This may mean that the differences between the sexes may not be as large as can often be the case with inter-sexual

sexual selection, where the female is the main chooser. One example of how sexual selection may affect female characteristics is in the selection for large breasts. These may be selected to be larger in humans than is really necessary for milk production, by the incorporation of additional fat. This characteristic may be attractive to males (and hence produce affective responses in males) because it is a symbol relating to fertility and child rearing potential, and not because large breasts have any particular adaptive value. It has even been suggested that the large breast size makes them useful to males as a sign of reproductive potential, for their pertness is maximal when a (young) woman's fertility and reproductive potential is at its highest. Although large breasts may be less pert with age, and it might thus be thought to be an advantage for women not to have large breasts, it may be possible that this is offset by the advantageous signal of a pert but large breast when fertility and reproductive potential is at its maximal when young, as this may attract high status males (even though there may be disadvantages later) (Miller 2000). Thus it is possible that inter-sexual selection contributes to the large breast size of some women. The fact that the variation is quite large is consistent with this being a sexually selected, not survival-selected, characteristic. Thus sexual selection of characteristics may occur in women as well as in men, and may contribute to aesthetic judgements.

### 5.4 Beauty in men and women

Given this background in the processes that drive evolution to make certain stimuli and types of brain processing rewarding or punishing, in this section I examine how they contribute to what factors make men and women aesthetically beautiful.

What factors are decoded by our brains to influence the attractiveness and beauty (reward value) of men and women? This can affect their selection as possible mates, and the factors are not necessarily the same for selection of a long-term vs. short-term partner (Rolls 2005b). I note that many of these factors may operate unconsciously, and that we may confabulate a rational verbal account about why we judge that something is beautiful. We may not realize that the following factors can influence our aesthetic judgements.

### 5.4.1 Female preferences: factors that make men attractive
Factors that across a range of species influence female selection of male mates include the following:

**Athleticism**. The ability to compete well in mate selection (including being healthy and strong), as this will be useful for her genes when present in her male offspring. Athleticism may be attractive (rewarding) also as an indicator of protection from male marauding (single females are at risk in some species of abuse, and forced copulation, which circumvents female mate choice), from predators, and as an indicator of hunting competency (meat was important in human evolution, although the hunt may also have been co-opted by sexual selection as a mating ritual giving the males a chance to show off). Consistent with these points, women show a strong preference for tall, strong, athletic men (Buss and Schmitt 1993).

**Resources, power and wealth**. In species with shared parental investment (which include many birds and humans), having power and wealth may be attractive to the female, because they are indicators of resources that may be provided for her young. Women should desire a man who shows willingness to invest resources (which should be defensible, accruable, and controllable) in his partner. (An expensive diamond engagement ring taken by a woman and kept guarded close to her on a finger meets these criteria. At the same time, the ring is a signal to her partner and to others that she is committed, which itself is attractive to her partner.) Women place a greater premium on income or financial prospects than men (Buss 1989). Further, in a cross-cultural study of 37 cultures with 10,047 participants, it was found that irrespective of cultural/political/social background, women consistently placed more value on financial resources (100 per cent more) than men (Buss 1989, 1999). Women value a man's love as an indicator of resource commitment.

**Status**. Both now and historically, status hierarchies are found in many cultures (and species, for example monkeys' dominance hierarchies, and chickens' pecking order). Status correlates with the control of resources (e.g., alpha male chimpanzees take precedence in feeding), and therefore acts as a good cue for women. Women should therefore find men of high status attractive (e.g., rock stars, politicians, and tribal rulers), and these men should be able to attract the most attractive partners. Consistent with this, cross-culturally women regard high social status as more valuable than do men; and attractive women marry men of high status (Buss 1989, 1999). Status may be attractive because of direct effects (e.g., as an indicator of resources for children), or because of indirect effects (because high status implies good genes for offspring).

**Age**. Status and higher income are generally only achieved with age, and therefore women should generally find older men attractive. Cross-culturally women prefer older men (3.42 years older on average; and marriage records from 27 countries show that the average age difference was 2.99 years) (Buss 1989).

**Ambition and industriousness**, which may be good predictors of future occupational status and income, are attractive. Valued characteristics include those that show a male will work to improve their lot in terms of resources or in terms of rising up in social status. Cross-culturally, women rated ambition/industriousness as highly desirable (Buss 1989).

**Testosterone-dependent features** may also be attractive. These features include a strong (longer and broader) jaw, a broad chin, strong cheekbones, defined eyebrow ridges, a forward central face, and a lengthened lower face (secondary sexual characteristics that are a result of pubertal hormone levels). High testosterone levels are immuno-suppressing, so these features may be indicators of immuno-competence (and thus honest indicators of fitness). The attractiveness of these masculinized features increases with increased risk of conception across the menstrual cycle (Penton-Voak et al. 1999). The implication is that the neural mechanism controlling perception of attractiveness must be sensitive to oestrogen/progesterone levels in women.

Another feature thought to depend on prenatal testosterone levels is the 2nd/4th digit ratio. A low ratio reflects a testosterone-rich uterine environment. It has been found that low ratios correlate with female ratings of male dominance and masculinity, although the relationship to attractiveness ratings was less clear (Swaddle and Reierson 2002).

**Symmetry** (in both males and females) may be attractive, in that it may reflect good development *in utero*, a non-harmful birth, adequate nutrition, and lack of disease and parasitic infections (Thornhill and Gangestad 1999). Fluctuating asymmetry (FA) reflects the degree to which individuals deviate from perfect symmetry on bilateral features (e.g., in humans, both ears, both feet, both hands and arms; in other species, bilateral fins, bilateral tail feathers). Greater asymmetry may reflect deviations in developmental design resulting from the disruptive effects of environmental or genetic abnormalities, and in some species is associated with lower fecundity, slower growth, and poorer survival. A low fluctuating asymmetry may thus be a sign of reproductive fitness (Gangestad and Simpson 2000). In humans, more symmetrical men reported more lifetime partners ($r = 0.38$), and more extra-pair partners; and women's choice of extra-pair partners was predicted by male symmetry (Gangestad and Simpson 2000). Moreover, women rate men as more attractive if they have high symmetry (low FA). Intellectual ability (which may be attractive to women) is also correlated with symmetry (Gangestad and Thornhill 1999).

**Dependability and faithfulness** may be attractive, particularly where there is paternal investment in bringing up the young, as these characteristics may indicate stability of resources (Buss 1999). Emotionally unstable men may also inflict costs on women, and thus women rate emotional stability and maturity as important. For example, jealousy might lead to abuse.

**Risk-taking** by men may be attractive to women, perhaps because it is a form of competitive advertising: surviving the risk may be an honest indicator of high quality genes (Barrett *et al.* 2002).

Characteristics that may not be adaptive in terms of the survival of the male, but that may be attractive because of inter-sexual sexual selection, are common in birds, perhaps less common in most mammals, though present in some primates (Kappeler and van Schaik 2004), and may be present in humans (see Section 5.3). An example of a sexually selected characteristic that may not increase the survival of the individual, but that may be attractive to females and thus increase the fitness of the male in terms of whether his genes are passed on to the next generation by reproduction, is the peacock's tail. These characteristics may in some cases be an honest indicator of health, in the sense that having a large gaudy tail may be a handicap.

**Odour.** The preference by women for the odour of symmetrical men is correlated with the probability of fertility of women as influenced by their cycle (Gangestad and Simpson 2000). Another way in which odour can influence preference is by pheromones that are related to MHC genes, which may provide a molecular mechanism for producing genetic diversity by influencing those who are considered attractive as mates, as described in Section 5.3.

It is important to note that physical factors such as high symmetry and that are indicators of genetic fitness may be especially attractive when women choose short-term partners, and that factors such as resources and faithfulness may be especially important when women choose long-term partners, in what may be termed a conditional mating strategy (Buss 1999, 2006). This conditionality means that the particular factors that influence preferences alter dynamically, and preferences will often depend on the prevailing circumstances, including the current opportunities and costs.

*5.4.2 Male preferences: what makes women attractive and beautiful to men* Males are not always indiscriminate.[2] When a male chooses to invest (for example to produce offspring), there are preferences for the partner with whom he will make the investment. Accurate evaluation of female quality (reproductive value) is therefore important, and a male will need to look out for cues to this, and find these cues attractive, beautiful, and rewarding. The factors that influence attractiveness include the following (see also Barrett *et al.* 2002):

**Youth**. As fertility and reproductive value in females is linked to age (reproductive value is higher when younger, and actual fertility in humans peaks in the twenties), males (unlike females) place a special premium on youth. It is not youth *per se* that men find attractive, but indicators of youth, for example neotenous traits such as blonde hair and wide eyes. An example of this preference is that male college students preferred an age difference on average of 2.5 years younger (Buss 1989). Another indicator of youth might be a small body frame, and it is interesting that this might contribute to the small body frame of some women in this example of sexual dimorphism.

**Beautiful features**. Features that are most commonly described as the most attractive tend to be those that are oestrogen-dependent, e.g., full lips and cheeks, and short lower facial features. (Oestrogen caps the growth of certain facial bones.) Like testosterone, oestrogen also affects the immune system, and its effects might be seen as 'honest indicators' of genetic fitness.

For example, when subjects were able to evolve a computer generated image into their ideal standard of female beauty, the beautiful composite had a relatively short lower face, small mouth, and full lips (Johnston and Franklin 1993).

There is some agreement across cultures about what constitute beautiful features. For example, in meta-analyses of 11 studies, it has been demonstrated that (a) raters agree about who is and is not attractive, both within and across cultures; (b) attractive children and adults are judged and treated more positively than unattractive children and adults, even by those who know them; and (c) attractive children and adults exhibit more positive behaviours and traits than unattractive children and adults (Langlois *et al.*

---

[2] In fact, males are probably rarely indiscriminate, in that producing sperm and performing sexual behaviour do have costs (Pizzari *et al.* 2003), including, for example, the risk of catching disease.

2000). In an fMRI study, it was found that attractive faces produce more activation of the human medial orbitofrontal cortex (where many pleasant stimuli are represented (Rolls and Grabenhorst 2008)) than unattractive faces (O'Doherty *et al.* 2003).

Further, small babies were even shown to gaze for longer at slides of the more attractive woman when shown pairs of pictures of women that differed in attractiveness (Langlois *et al.* 1987, 1991). In another study, 12-month-olds interacted with a stranger. The infants showed more positive affective tone, less withdrawal, and more play involvement with a stranger who wore a professionally constructed attractive than unattractive mask; and played longer with an attractive than an unattractive doll (Langlois *et al.* 1990). These results extend and amplify earlier findings showing that young infants exhibit visual preferences for attractive over unattractive faces. Both visual and behavioural preferences for attractiveness are evidently exhibited rather early in life.

Women appear to spend more time on fashion and enhancing beauty than men. Why should this be, when in most mammals it is males who may be gaudy to help in their competition for females, given that females make the larger investment in offspring? In humans, there is of course value to investment by males in their offspring, so women may benefit by attracting a male who will invest time and resources in bring up children together. But nevertheless, women do seem to invest more in bearing and then raising children, so why is the imbalance so marked, with women apparently competing by paying attention to their own beauty and fashion? Perhaps the answer is that males who are willing to make major investments of time and resources in raising the children of a partner are a somewhat limiting resource (as other factors may make it advantageous genetically for men not to invest all their resources in one partner), and because women are competing to obtain and maintain this scarce resource, being beautiful and fashionable is important to women. Faithful men may be a limited resource because there are alternative strategies that may have a low cost, whereas women are essentially committed to a considerable investment in their offspring. These factors lead to greater variability in men's strategies, and thus contribute to making men who invest in their offspring a more limited resource than women who invest in their offspring.

Given that men are a scare resource, and that women have such a major investment in their offspring that they must be sure of a man's commitment to invest before they commit in any way, we have a scientific basis for understanding why women are reserved and more cautious and shy in their interactions with men, which has been noticed to be prevalent in visual art, in which men look at women, but less vice versa (Berger 1972).

**Body fat**. The face is not the only cue to a woman's reproductive capacity, and her attractiveness, and beauty. Although the ideal body weight varies significantly with culture (in cultures with scarcity, obesity is attractive, and relates to status, a trend evident in beautiful painting throughout its history), the ideal distribution of body fat seems to be a universal standard, as measured by the waist-to-hip ratio (which cancels out effects of actual body weight). Consistently, across cultures, men preferred an average ratio of 0.7 (small waist/bigger hips) when rating female figures (line drawings and photographic images) for attractiveness (Singh and Luis 1995). Thornhill and Grammer (1999) also found high correlations between rating of attractiveness of nude females by men of different ethnicity. At a simpler level, a low waist-to-hip ratio is an indication that a woman is not already pregnant, and is thus a contributor to attractiveness and beauty.

**Fidelity.** The desire for fidelity in females is most obviously related to her concealed ovulation (see next paragraph and Rolls 2005b), and therefore the degree of paternity uncertainty that males may suffer. Males therefore place a premium on a woman's sexual history. Virginity was a requisite for marriage both historically (before the arrival of contraceptives) and cross-culturally (in non-Westernized societies where virginity is still highly valued) (Buss 1989). Nowadays, female monogamy in previous relationships is a sought-after characteristic in future long-term partners (Buss and Schmitt 1993). (Presumably with simple genetic methods now available for identifying the father of a child, the rational thought system (Rolls 2005b) might place less value on fidelity with respect to paternity issues as paternity can be established genetically, yet the implicit emotional system may still place high value on fidelity, as during evolution, fidelity was valued as an indicator of paternity probability.) The modern rational emphasis might be especially placed on valuing fidelity because this may indicate less risk of sexually transmitted disease, and perhaps the emotional value and attractiveness of fidelity will be a help in this respect.

**Attractiveness and the time of ovulation.** Although ovulation in some primates and in humans is concealed,[3] it would be at a premium for men to pick up other cues to ovulation, and find women highly desirable (and beautiful) at these times. Possible cues include an increased body temperature reflected in the warm glow of vascularized skin (Vandenberghe and Frost 1986), and pheromonal cues. Indeed, male raters judged the odours of T-shirts worn during the follicular phase as more pleasant and sexy than odours from T-shirts worn during the luteal phase (Singh and Bronstad 2001). Women generally do not know when they are ovulating (and in this sense ovulation may be double blind), but there is a possibility that ovulation could unconsciously affect female behaviour. In fact, Event-Related Potentials (ERPs) were found to be greater to sexual stimuli in ovulating women, and these could reflect increased affective processing of the stimuli (Krug et al. 2000). This in turn might affect outward behaviour of the female, helping her to attract a mate at this time. Another possibly unconscious influence might be on the use of cosmetics and the types of clothes worn, which may be different close to the time of ovulation.

In most species, females invest heavily in the offspring in terms of providing the eggs and providing the care (from gestation until weaning, and far beyond weaning in the

---

[3] Perhaps so that males may be uncertain who the father is of a baby, and thus not threaten infanticide (Rolls 2005b).

case of humans). Females are therefore a 'limited resource' for males allowing the females to be the choosier sex during mate choice. In humans, male investment in caring for the offspring means that male choice has a strong effect on intra-sexual selection in women. Female cosmetic use and designer clothing could be seen as weapons in this competition, and perhaps are reflected in extreme female self-grooming behaviour such as cosmetic surgery, or pathological disorders such as anorexia, bulimia, and body dysmorphic disorder. The modern media, by bombarding people with images of beautiful women, may heighten intra-sexual selection even further, pushing women's competitive mating mechanisms to a major scale.

### 5.5 Pair-bonding, love, and beauty

I extend in the next few sections the background provided in Sections 5.2 and 5.3 in the processes that drive evolution to make certain stimuli and types of brain processing rewarding or punishing, to other stimuli, events, and types of brain processing that produce aesthetic judgements.

Attachment to a particular partner by pair-bonding in a monogamous relationship, which in humans becomes manifest in love between pair-bonded parents, and which occurs in humans in relation to the advantage to the man of investing in his offspring, may have special mechanisms to facilitate it. Species in which attachment has been investigated include the prairie vole. In monogamous species of prairie voles, mating can increase pair-bonding (as measured by partner preference). Oxytocin, a hormone released from the posterior pituitary, whose other actions include the milk let-down response, is released during mating (Lee *et al.* 2009). Exogenous administration of oxytocin facilitates pair-bonding in both female and male prairie voles (Carter 1998). In female prairie voles, antagonists of oxytocin interfere with partner preference formation. In female prairie voles, the endogenous release of oxytocin is thus important in partner preference and attachment. Thus oxytocin has been thought of as the 'hormone of love'. Oxytocin gene knock-out mice fail to recognize familiar conspe-cifics after repeated social exposures, and injection of oxytocin in the medial amygdala restores social recognition (Winslow and Insel 2004). In males, the effects of oxytocin are facilitated by vasopressin, another posterior pituitary hormone whose other effects include promoting the retention of water by the kidney. In the case of vasopressin, it has been possible to show that the vasopressin V1a receptor (V1aR) is expressed in higher concentration in the ventral forebrain of monogamous prairie voles than in promiscuous (i.e., polygamous) meadow voles, and that viral vector V1aR transfer into the forebrain of the meadow mouse increases its partner preference (i.e., makes it more like a monogamous prairie vole) (Lim *et al.* 2004; Young 2008). Thus a single gene may be important in influencing monogamy vs. promiscuity in voles. Stress, or the administration of the hormone corticosterone which is released during stress, can facilitate the onset of new pair bonds (Devries *et al.* 1996).

Are similar mechanisms at work in humans to promote pair-bonding and love? There is as yet no definitive evidence, but in humans, oxytocin is released by intercourse, and especially at the time of orgasm, in both women and men (Meston and Frohlich 2000; Kruger *et al.* 2003). It has also been reported that women desiring to become pregnant are more likely to have an orgasm after their partner ejaculates (Singh *et al.* 1998).

An implication is that there may be hormonal, and other biological, mechanisms that promote a bifurcation in a state space (Rolls and Deco 2010), and have an effect of cementing attraction and love of a particular person after the process has been started. This may have an effect on (partly!) blinding a person to a partner's imperfections, and may thus contribute to each individual's judgements about the beauty of a partner, an aesthetic judgement.

Given this Darwinian approach rooted in selfish genes (Dawkins 1989), should we describe the aesthetic state of love as selfish? I suggest that the answer is that although individual acts can be truly altruistic (and non-adaptive), even the altruism implied by love must have its origins in selfish genes, which shape human behaviour to in this case produce a state that promotes the production of and survival of offspring. Overall, for a characteristic (such as falling in love, or reciprocal altruism, or kin altruism) that is influenced by genes to remain in a breeding population, the characteristic must be good for the (selfish) gene or it would be selected out. Even love guided by rational thought must not overall detract too much over generations from the wish to produce offspring, or it would tend (other things being equal) to be selected out of the gene population.

## 5.6 Parental attachment: beautiful children

Many mammal females make strong attachments to their own offspring, and this is also facilitated in many species by oxytocin. One model is the sheep, in which vaginal-cervical stimulation and suckling, which release both oxytocin and endogenous opioids, facilitate maternal bonding (Keverne *et al.* 1997). Oxytocin injections can cause ewes to become attached to an unfamiliar lamb presented at the time oxytocin is released or injected, and oxytocin antagonists can block filial bonding in sheep. Perhaps oxytocin had an initial role in evolution in the milk let-down reflex, and then became appropriate as a hormone that might facilitate mother–infant attachment.

In humans the evidence is much more correlative, but oxytocin release during natural childbirth, and rapid placing of the baby to breast feed and release more oxytocin (Uvnas-moberg 1998), might facilitate maternal attachment to her baby. Prolactin, the female hormone that promotes milk production, may also influence maternal attachment—and how beautiful a mother thinks her child is. It is certainly a major factor in humans that bonding can change quite suddenly at the time that a child is born, with women having a strong tendency to shift their interests markedly towards the baby as soon as it is born (probably in part under hormonal influences), and this can result in relatively less attachment behaviour to the man. In men, oxytocin may also be involved in paternal behaviour (Wynne-Edwards 2001).

Another aspect of parental care is that there is competition between the mother and child, for example over weaning (Trivers 1974). The mother may wish to devote resources to preparing for her next offspring (by building herself up); and continuing to breast feed delays the onset of fertility and cycling. In contrast, it is to the offspring's genetic advantage to demand milk and attention. The infant's scream can be seen as part of trying to wring resources out of its mother, potentially to an extent that is unfavourable for the mother's genes (Buss 1999).

As described above, females generally have a greater investment in their offspring, and tend to provide more parental care and perhaps become more attached than fathers. This situation is not as extreme in humans as in most other mammals, because human offspring are born relatively immature, and a father who helps to rear the offspring can help to increase the reproductive fitness of his genes.

Lack of parental care in stepfathers is evident in many species, and can be as extreme as the infanticide by a male lion of the pups of another father, so that his new female may come into heat more quickly to have babies by him (Bertram 1975). Infanticide also occurs in non-human primates (Kappeler and van Schaik 2004). In humans, the statistics indicate that stepfathers are much more likely to harm or kill children in the family than are real fathers (Daly and Wilson 1988).

The tendency to find babies beautiful is not of course restricted to parents of their own children. Part of the reason for this is that in the societies in which our genes evolved with relatively small groups, babies encountered might often be genetically related, and the tendency to find babies beautiful is probably a way to increase the success of selfish genes. One may still make these aesthetic judgements of babies in distant countries with no close genetic relationship, but this does not of course mean that such judgements do not have their evolutionary origin in kin-related advantageous behaviour.

### 5.7 Synthesis on beauty in humans

We see that many factors are involved in making humans attractive, and beautiful. All may contribute, to different extents, and differently in different individuals, and moreover we may not be conscious of some of the origins of our aesthetic judgements, but may confabulate reasons for what we judge to be aesthetic.

When there is a biological foundation for art, for example when it is figurative, and especially when it is about human figures, there may be a basis for consensus about what is good art—art that stimulates our rational system, and at the same time speaks to what we find beautiful due to our evolutionary history. However, if art becomes totally abstract, we lack the biological foundation for judging whether it is aesthetically beautiful, and judgements may be much more arbitrary, and driven by short-term fashion. Some abstraction away from very realistic and figurative in art can of course have advantages for it allows the viewer to create in their own experience of a work of art by adding their own interpretation.

There is an important point here about the separation between art and the world. Objects of art can idealize beauty, and enhance it. An example is the emphasis on thin bodies, long limbs, and athletic poses found in some Art Deco sculpture, for example in the works of Lorenzl. Here what is beautiful can be made super-normal, one might say in the literal sense super-natural. Another example is in the emotion in the music of *Tristan and Isolde*. We see that art can emphasize and thus idealize some of the properties of the real world, and lose other details that do not enhance, or distract. This abstraction of what we find beautiful due to evolution can be seen in some semi-figurative/semi-abstract art, as in some of the line drawings of humans by Matisse and Picasso. It is also found in the sculptures of human forms of Brancusi. What I argue is that if art goes too abstract, then it loses the aesthetic value that can be contributed by tapping into these evolutionary origins. Interesting cases are found in the sculptures of Barbara Hepworth and Henry Moore. In the case of Barbara Hepworth, I now see that she often retains sufficient figurative contribution to her sculpture to tap into evolutionary origins, and I show Fig. 8.3 as an example of a work that after all seems to have some relation to a male and female. Much of the sculpture of Henry Moore is clearly figurative, and where it becomes apparently very abstract it may lose what is gained by tapping into evolutionary origins, but may gain by association and interpretation in relation to his more figurative work. Where art becomes very abstract, as in some of the work of Mark Rothko, perhaps those especially interested are those who have expertise themselves in what is being achieved technically, such as the painting of colours by Rothko.

Figure 8.3 *Two Forms* (January) 1967. Barbara Hepworth

*5.8 Sexual selection of mental ability, survival or adaptation selection of mental ability, and the origin of aesthetics*

Miller (2000, 2001) has developed the hypothesis that courtship provides an opportunity for sexual selection to select non-sexual mental characteristics such as kindness, humour, the ability to tell stories, creativity, art, and even language. He postulates that these are 'courtship tools, evolved to attract and entertain sexual partners'. One mechanism of sexual selection (see Section 5.3) views organisms as advertisers of their phenotypic fitness, and Miller sees these characteristics as such signals. From this perspective, hunting is seen as a costly and inefficient exercise (in comparison with food gathering) undertaken by men to obtain small gifts of meat for women, but at the same time to show how competitive and fit the successful hunter is in relation to other men. Conspicuous waste, and conspicuous consumption, are often signs in nature that sexual selection is at work, with high costs for behaviours that seem maladaptive in terms of survival and natural selection in the narrow sense. The mental characteristics described above are not only costly in terms of time, but may rely on many genes operating efficiently for these characteristics to be expressed well, and so, Miller suggests, may be 'fitness indicators'. Consistent with sexual selection, there is also great individual variability in these characteristics, providing a basis for choice.

One mental characteristic that Miller suggests could have evolved in this way is kindness, which is very highly valued by both sexes (Buss 1999), and is usually judged as aesthetically pleasing. In human evolution, being kind to the mother's children may have been seen as an attractive characteristic in men during courtship, especially when relationships may not have lasted for many years, and the children might not be those of the courting male. Kindness may also be used as an indicator of future cooperation. In a sense kindness thus may indicate potential useful benefits, consistent with the fact that across cultures human females tend to prefer males who have high social status, good income, ambition, intelligence, and energy (Buss 1999). Kindness may also be related to kin altruism (Hamilton 1964) or to reciprocal altruism (Trivers 1971), both of which are genetically adaptive strategies.

Although the simple interpretation of all these mental characteristics is that they indicate a good provider and potential material and genetic benefits (and thus would be subject to natural or survival selection), Miller (2000) argues that at least kindness is being used in addition as a fitness indicator and is being sexually selected.

Morality can be related in part to kin and reciprocal altruism, which influence survival, and make many of the behaviours described as moral also attractive, because of their evolutionary adaptive value (Ridley 1996; Rolls 2005b). In addition, moral behaviour may bring reproductive benefits and be attractive through the social status that it inspires or by direct mate choice for moralistic displays during courtship (Miller 2000). The suggestion made by Miller (2000) is that the status of moral behaviour helps to attract mates, because it may reflect fitness as the moral behaviour may have costs. In turn, the same effects may influence aesthetic judgements.

Miller (2000, 2001) also suggests that art, language, and creativity can be explained by sexual selection, and that they are difficult to account for by survival selection. He suggests that art develops from courtship ornamentation, and uses bowerbirds as an evolutionary example. Male bowerbirds ornament their often enormous and structurally elaborate nests or bowers with mosses, ferns, shells, berries, and bark to attract female bowerbirds. The nests are used just to attract females, and after insemination the females go off and build their own cup-shaped nests, lay their eggs, and raise their offspring by themselves with no male support. In this sense, the bowers are useless ornamentation that do not have survival value. Darwin (1871) himself viewed human ornamentation and clothing as outcomes of sexual selection. Sexual selection for artistic ability does not mean of course that the art itself needs to be about sex. This example helps to show that sexual selection can lead to changes in what is valued and found attractive, in areas that might be precursors to art in humans. In Miller's (2001) view, the fine arts are just the most recent and pretentious manifestations of a universal human instinct for visual self-ornamentation, which in turn is a manifestation of sexual selection's universal tendency to ornament individuals with visual advertisements of their fitness. Thus, the human capacity for visual artistry is viewed as a 'fitness indicator', evolved like the peacock's tail and the bowerbird's bower for a courtship function. So although inherently useless, the bower or work of art is seen as attractive because it is difficult to produce, and might only be made by a brain that is very competent in general, and thus the bower or work of art may act as a fitness indicator.

A useful point (Miller 2001) is that although artworks are now commodified and spread wide so that we may not know the artist producing the ornament, when we seek the evolutionary origins of art, we should remember that any artwork our prehistoric ancestors would have been able to see, would have probably been made by a living individual with whom they could have interacted socially or sexually. The artist was never far from his or her work, or else the work could not have functioned as the artist's extended phenotype.

Miller (2000) also suggests that language evolved as a courtship device in males to attract females. Miller (2000) further suggests that creativity may be related to systems that can explore random new ideas, and also is a courtship device in males to attract females. My view, elaborated here and elsewhere (Rolls 2005b, 2008b; Rolls and Deco 2010), is that language and creativity have functions that have survival value, and thus are not just sexually selected.

Indeed, a criticism of the approach of Miller (2000) is that many of these characteristics (e.g., language, creative solutions, originality, problem-solving) may have survival value, and are not purely or primarily sexually selected. For example, syntax and language have many uses in problem-solving, planning ahead, and correcting multiple step plans that are likely to be very important to enable immediate rewards to be deferred, and longer-term goals to be achieved (Pinker and Bloom, 1992; Rolls, 2005b, 2008b). In relation to aesthetics, I argue that when syntax is used successfully to solve a difficult problem, we feel aesthetic pleasure, and I argue that the generation of pleasure generated by the survival value of good ideas contributes to the appeal of those ideas, and that sexual selection of the ideas as mental ornaments is not the only process at work in aesthetics.

Moreover, the notion (Miller 2000, 2001) that art has to do with useless ornaments (useless in the sense that sexual selection is for characteristics that may not have 'survival' value, but may be attractive because they are 'indicators of fitness') does not have much to say about the utilitarian arts such as simplicity of design in architecture. Perhaps the structure of a piece of music can appeal, and be pleasing, because it taps into our syntactic system that finds that elegant and simple solutions to problem-solving produce pleasure. As I argue elsewhere in this chapter, interest in social relations and knowledge about them is adaptive as it may help to understand who is doing what to whom, and more generally to understand what can happen to people, and much fictional literature addresses these issues, and is not primarily ornamental and without inherent value. Thus although Miller (2000, 2001) may well be right that there are aspects of art that may be primarily ornamental and useless, and are just indicators of general mental fitness, though attractive to members of the opposite sex in courtship, I suggest that much art has its roots in goals that have been specified as pleasurable or unpleasurable because of their adaptive or survival value, whether as primary reinforcers, other stimuli associated by learning with these, or rewards of a more cognitive origin that accrue when difficult cognitive, syntactic, problems are solved (see Table 8.1).

Another problem with Miller's approach is that traits that become sexually selected often have survival value in the first place, so it is often not possible to fully dissociate sexual selection from survival or adaptation selection (Andersson 1994; Andersson and Simmons 2006).

Another potential problem with Miller's approach is that some of the processes involved in sexual selection favour fast runaway evolution, because sexual preferences are genetically correlated with the ornaments they favour (see Section 5.3). Why does mental capacity not develop more rapidly, and with larger sex differences, in humans, if Miller (2000) is right? Why is there not a faster runaway? Miller suggests a number of possible reasons.

1. There is a high genetic correlation between human males and females, with 22/23 chromosomes the same.
2. The female's brain must evolve to be able to appreciate the male's mental adornment—and might even be one step ahead to judge effectively. Further, similar or partly overlapping brain mechanisms may be used to produce (in males) and perceive (in females). In addition, male self-monitoring (and female practice) may help appraisal. Males may even internalize females' appreciation systems, to predict their responses.
3. There is mutual choice in humans: males choose females because human males do make a parental investment; and females compete for males. Indeed, the

selection of a long-term partner is mutual, and this tends to reduce sex differences. Consistent with this, Buss (1989, 1999) has shown that, in contrast, human sex differences are more evident in short-term mating. It is likely in fact that sexual selection works mainly through long-term relationships, because of concealed ovulation in women. This means that only in a relatively long-term relationship is it likely that a man will become the father of a woman's child, because only if he mates with her regularly is there a reasonable probability that he will hit her fertile time.

Miller might predict that men should be specialized to have artistic creativity, to provide an ornament that women might find attractive because it is a fitness indicator. Evidence on this is difficult to evaluate, because there have been fewer opportunities available for women in the past, as argued for so beautifully by Virginia Woolf in *A Room of One's Own* (1928), and I come to no conclusions, but have the following thoughts. Whereas Virginia Woolf argues about circumstances, one can consider in addition the possibility that women's and men's brains have been subject to different selective pressure in evolution, and that this might contribute to differences in the ways in which they are creative. In terms of artists, composers of music, poets, and writers of drama and non-fiction, there appears to be on average a preponderance of men relative to women. This is on average, and there are individual women who given the distribution around the average are undoubtedly highly creative in these areas, and have made enormous contributions. If this is the case (and it might take a long time into the future to know, given the imbalance of opportunity in the past), does this mean that sexual selection is the underlying process? I suggest that this would not necessarily be the case. Such a 'sexual dimorphism' could occur by natural (adaptation) selection, not by sexual selection, in that women might have specialized for an environmental niche to emphasize child rearing, cultivation including food gathering and preparation, fashioning of clothing, and creating peaceful order among siblings and parents. On the other hand, men might have specialized for an environmental niche to emphasize spatial problem-solving, useful for producing and using tools, building shelters, creating structures, etc., and navigational problem-solving useful for hunting, all of which would be good for survival. Interestingly, the same (narrow) natural selection pressure might have provided a survival advantage for men to have a stronger physique which is likely be advantageous when manufacturing items useful for survival such as shelters. Thus interestingly, one of the predictions of sexual selection, sexual dimorphism, including human mental problem-solving as well as physique, could in this case have its origin at least partly in adaptation and survival.

There is, however, a possible exception to the generalization that at least in the past men have been more likely to be creative in 'art' than women, and this is the area of literary fiction, where there are many women with high reputations as novelists (e.g., Jane Austen, George Eliot, Virginia Woolf). If women take more to this area of creative art, might this be because of the adaptive value of gossip to women, so knowing about who is doing what to whom, and having an interest and expertise in this, could be adaptive, perhaps helping a woman, and her children, to survive better (Dunbar 1996)? If this were the case, there might even be a prediction that women might be relatively more excellent, on average, in areas of fiction, such as novels, where this interest and expertise in mind-reading and gossip might be especially engaged. (The fact that autism, which is associated with problems with mind reading, is several times more prevalent in men than in women (Baron-Cohen 2008) does fit with this general approach about adaptations suitable for different environmental niches.) More generally, the evolutionary survival value approach might argue that women have adapted to relational, social, caring, and problem-solving activities, and the novel, particularly the novel of manners, is ideally suited to displaying these specializations. Indeed, the specialization for a caring role is consonant with Carol Gilligan's argument in *In a Different Voice* (1982: 73) that women's sense of morality concerns itself with the activity of 'care and responsibility in relationships'.

The overall point I make is that natural selection, sometimes operating by 'survival or adaptation selection', and sometimes by sexual selection (and sometimes both, see above), operates by specifying goals for action, and these goals are aesthetically and subjectively attractive or beautiful (Rolls 2005b), or the opposite, and provide what I argue here is the origin of many judgements of what is aesthetic. Many examples of these rewards and punishers, many of which operate for 'survival or adaptation selection', and many of which contribute to aesthetic experience and judgements, are shown in Table 8.1.

## 5.9 Fashion and memes

We have seen that sexual selection can provide runaway selective pressure for what is not something that is produced by 'survival or adaptation' selection. In a sense, a fashion or useless ornament (which may indicate fitness) can be selected for genetically.

However, fashions are strong characteristics of many human aesthetic judgements, and we may ask if there are further reasons for this that are not to do with genetic variation (which necessarily takes place over generations), but that operate over time-scales of months to years. Such fashions (for example in clothing) may occur because they fit adaptations of the human mind, themselves the result of adaptive pressure in evolutionary history. For example, the human mind will be attracted towards new ideas (of clear adaptive value, for it is only by exploring new ideas that advantage may be gained partly as a result of finding a match with one's own genetically influenced capacities) (Rolls 2005b). In this way, there may be runaway changes that do not necessarily make the individual better adapted to the environment. Of course, many factors, again frequently of evolutionary origin, influence fashion, including its cost (of which the label is an indicator), which helps to make it attractive as it indicates wealth, resources, and status, and the elegance and simplicity of the idea, which as argued below, the human mind finds attractive because simplicity often is a good indicator of a correct and useful solution to a problem. It is argued that memes (Blackmore 1999), ideas that follow some of the rules of fashion, fit these properties of the human mind.

## 5.10 The elegance and beauty of ideas, and solving problems in the reasoning system

Solving difficult problems feels good, and we often speak about elegant (and beautiful) solutions. What is the origin of the pleasure we obtain from elegant ideas? What makes them aesthetically pleasing? It is suggested that solving problems should feel good to us, to make us keep trying, as being able to solve difficult problems that require syntactic operations may have survival value (Rolls 2005b). But what is it that makes simple ideas and solutions (those with fewest premises, fewest steps to the solution, and fewest exceptions for a given level of complexity of a problem) particularly aesthetically pleasing, so much so that physicists may use this as a guide to their thinking? It is suggested that the human brain has become adapted to find simple solutions aesthetically pleasing because they are more likely to be correct (Rolls 2005b), and this is exactly the thrust of parsimony and Occam's Razor. (Occam's Razor is the principle or heuristic that entities and hypotheses should not be multiplied needlessly; the simplest of two competing and otherwise equally effective theories is to be preferred. The principle states that the explanation of any phenomenon should make as few assumptions as possible, eliminating those that make no difference in the observable predictions of the explanation or theory.)

This finds expression in art: for example in the structure of a piece of music; in the solution of how to incorporate perspective into painting (which took hundreds of years and was helped by the camera obscura); and in the interest by Vitruvius and Leonardo in the proportions of the human body (tapping into our gene-based appreciation of that) to provide rules for proportions in architecture. Of course, focus on intellectual aspects of art can lead to art that we may find fascinating and revealing, if not conventionally physically beautiful, as in some of the work of Francis Bacon. Factors such as cultural heritage and familiarity with the rules of a system can also make a style of architecture more appealing than something very unfamiliar. Some of the history of ecclesiastical architecture in England from the eleventh to the fifteenth century (from Norman through Early English and Decorated to Perpendicular) can also be seen as solutions to difficult architectural problems, of how to increase the light and feeling of space in a building, and its impression of grand and daring height.

## 5.11 Cognition and aesthetics

Not only can operation of our reasoning, syntactic, explicit, system lead to pleasure and aesthetic value, as just described, but also this cognitive system can modulate activity in the emotional, implicit, gene-identified goal system. This cognitive modulation, from the level of word descriptions, can have modulatory effects right down into the first cortical area, the orbitofrontal cortex, where affective value, including aesthetic value, such as the beauty in a face, is first made explicit in the representation (O'Doherty et al. 2003; De Araujo et al. 2005; Grabenhorst et al. 2008; McCabe et al. 2008; Rolls and

Grabenhorst 2008). Indeed, cognition and attention can be used to enhance the emotional aspect of aesthetic experience, as described in Section 5.1.

The human mind may create objects such as sculpture and painting in ways that depend to different extents on the explicit reasoning system and the more implicit emotional system. I know at least one sculptor who intentionally reduces cognitive processing by turning off attention to cognitive processing when creating works of art, and then follows this with an explicit, conscious, reasoning stage in which selections and further changes may be made, with the whole creation involving very many such cycles.

Because cognition can by top-down cortico-cortical back projections influence representations at lower levels, it is possible that training, including cognitive guidance, can help to make more separate the representations of the representations of stimuli and their reward value at early levels of cortical processing (Rolls 2008b; Rolls and Treves 1998; Rolls and Deco 2002). This top-down effect may add to the bottom-up effects of self-organization in competitive networks that also through repeated training help representations of stimuli to be separated from and made more different to each other (Rolls 2008b; Rolls and Treves 1998; Rolls and Deco 2002). These effects may be important in many aesthetic judgements that are affected by training, including the appreciation of fine art, architecture, and wine.

## 5.12 Wealth, power, resources, and reputation

As described above, wealth, power, resources, and status are attractive qualities, aesthetically attractive, because resources are likely to be beneficial to the survival of genes. Reputation is similar, in that guarding one's reputation can be important in reproductive success: trust is important in a mate, or in reciprocal altruism, and hormones such as oxytocin may contribute to trust (Lee *et al.* 2009). This provides some insight into the history of Western art, in which individual and family portraits frequently have as one of their aims the portrayal of wealth, power, and resources. The clothes and background are consistent with a contribution of these underlying origins. Commissioned portraits thus frequently emphasize beauty, status, wealth, and resources. Interestingly, because self-portraits are rarely commissioned, they are less likely to emphasize these characteristics (Cumming 2009), and of course can also reflect subjective knowledge of the person portrayed. An additional property that can add value judged as aesthetic to a portrait is that an image of someone dear is associated with that person, and what that person means to the viewer, and the attraction of photographic images illustrates this. Religion and its accompanying states aiming often at everlasting happiness must also be recognized as drivers of art.

## 5.13 The beauty of scenery and places

Many topological features of landscapes may be aesthetically attractive because they tap into brain systems that evolved to provide signals of safety, food, etc. Open space may be attractive because potential predators can be seen; cover may be attractive as a place to hide (Appleton 1975); a verdant landscape may be attractive because it indicates abundant food; flowers may be attractive as predictors of fruit later in the season. The colour blue is preferred by monkeys, and this may be because blue sky, seen from the canopy, is an indicator of a safe place away from predators on the ground (Humphrey 1971). A clear red/orange sunset may be attractive as a predictor of good weather, and of safety overnight without bad weather. These factors do not operate alone to produce beauty, but may as origins contribute to aesthetic beauty which I argue is multifactorial, influenced by many of the factors described in this theory of the origin of aesthetics.

### 5.14 The beauty of music

Vocalization is used for emotional communication between humans, with an origin evident in other primates (Rolls *et al.* 2006). Examples include warning calls, warlike encouragement to action, and a soothing lullaby or song to an infant. It is suggested that this emotional communication channel is tapped into by music, and indeed consonant vs. dissonant sounds differentially activate the orbitofrontal cortex (Blood *et al.* 1999; Blood and Zatorre 2001), involved in emotion (Rolls 2005b). Of course, the reasoning system then provides its own input to the development, pleasure, and aesthetic value of music, in ways described in Sections 5.10 and 5.11.

What may underlie the greater pleasure and aesthetic value that many people accord to consonant vs. dissonant music? I suggest that consonance is generally pleasant because it is associated with natural including vocal sounds with a single source that naturally has harmonics. A good example is a calm female voice. Dissonance may often occur when there are multiple unrelated sources, such as those that might be produced by a catastrophe such as an earthquake, or boulders grinding against each other (or strings on a violin that are not tuned to be harmonics of each other). Further, a human voice when angry might have non-linearities, in for example the vocal cords due to over-exertion, and these may be harmonically much less pure than when the voice is calm and softer.

### 5.15 Beauty, pleasure, and pain

If a mildly unpleasant stimulus is added to a pleasant stimulus, sometimes the overall pleasantness of the stimulus, its attractive value, and perhaps its beauty, can be enhanced. A striking example is the sweet, floral scent of jasmine, which as it occurs naturally in *Jasminum grandiflorum* contains typically 2–3 per cent of indole, a pure chemical which on its own at the same concentration is usually rated as unpleasant. The mixture can, at least in some people (and this may depend on their olfactory sensitivity to the different components), increase the pleasantness of the jasmine compared to the same odour without the indole. Why might this occur? One investigation has shown that parts of the brain such as the medial orbitofrontal cortex that represent the pleasantness of odors (Anderson *et al.* 2003; Rolls *et al.* 2003b; Grabenhorst and Rolls 2009) can respond even more strongly to jasmine when it contains the unpleasant component indole, compared to when it only contains individually pleasant components (Grabenhorst *et al.* 2007). Thus one brain mechanism that may underlie the enhancement effect is a principle that brain areas that represent the pleasantness of stimuli can do this in a way that is at least partly independent of unpleasant components, thereby emphasizing the pleasant component of a hedonically complex mixture.

A second factor that may contribute to the enhanced pleasantness of the mixture of jasmine and indole is that the indole may produce a contrast effect in the brain areas that represent the pleasant components of the mixture. An indication of this was found in increased activations in the medial orbitofrontal cortex (which represents the pleasantness of many stimuli) when the jasmine-indole mixture was being applied, compared to just the jasmine alone (Grabenhorst *et al.* 2007). To the extent that the pleasantness representation may drive hedonic experience separately from unpleasantness representations (Grabenhorst *et al.* 2007), and this might be facilitated by paying attention selectively to the pleasantness of a stimulus vs. its unpleasantness (Rolls *et al.* 2008), then a factor might be the increased activation of pleasantness representations if there is a component to the stimulus that is unpleasant, and can enhance the pleasantness representation by a contrast effect. Another example of pleasantness enhancement of pleasant by unpleasant stimuli occurs when an odour become more pleasant if it is preceded by an unpleasant (compared to a pleasant) odour, an effect represented in the human orbitofrontal cortex (Grabenhorst and Rolls 2009).

A third factor is that the interaction between the pleasant (jasmine) and unpleasant (indole) components makes the complex hedonic mixture (jasmine + indole) capture attention (which in turn may enhance and prolong the activation of the brain by the complex hedonic mixture), and evidence for the capture of attentional mechanisms in the brain by the pleasant-unpleasant mixture has been found (Grabenhorst *et al.* 2011).

These principles may of course operate in most areas where pleasant and unpleasant stimuli combine. Examples might include the pleasure we get from demanding terrain (high cliffs, high mountains, high seas); from spicy food that activates capsaicin (hot somatosensory) as well as gustatory and olfactory receptors (Rolls 2007a); from tragedy in literature, though empathy makes a large contribution here; from difficult feats, such as those performed by Odysseus (Rolls and Deco 2010), etc.

Let us consider the paradox of tragedy. For Aristotle, tragedy purged one of anxieties (Herwitz 2008). Somehow the depiction of tragedy in drama, which raises unpleasant emotions such as sadness at the tragedy, can also as drama afford pleasure. Hume's explanation was that the beauty of the language and the eloquence of the artist's depictive talents are the source of pleasure (Hume 1757; Yanal 1991). Is there more to say about this? *Schadenfreude*, gloating pleasure at the distress of an envied person, is associated with activation of brain areas that respond to pleasant stimuli (Shamay-Tsoory *et al.* 2007; Takahashi *et al.* 2009), and I suggest is related to the evolutionary origin of competition between individuals, and winning the competition. It is probably not an important factor in the appreciation of tragedy in drama. What may be more important is first that we (and this is especially strong in women) always want to know what is happening to whom, and gossip has evolutionary value (Dunbar 1996) in that this can provide information about how others are likely to treat you, and more generally, about the things that can happen to people in life, and from which we can potentially learn. Second, the ability to empathize with another's emotions, and indeed to be good at this and find it rewarding, may also be important in communities, in order to facilitate kin or reciprocal altruism (Ridley 1996). Third, the ability to have a theory of other people's minds is adaptive in facilitating prediction of their behaviour (Frith and Singer 2008), and fascination with this should again in an evolutionary context be rewarding, and be associated with pleasure. It is suggested that these three factors are at least important contributors to the pleasure that people find in tragedy in drama. The same factors, I suggest, are also important contributors to the popularity of novels. In the cases of both drama and novels, we know that they are fiction, or at least are not happening to the spectator or reader, and this helps to make them particularly rewarding ways to learn about social relations and life events, because there is no risk to the spectator or reader.

Knowing that the work of art (music, literature, painting, sculpture) is a fiction may also account for why the 'aesthetic' emotions are not as long-lasting, and are not as motivating, as goals in real life.

*5.16  Absolute value in aesthetics and art*

The approach described here proposes that what we find aesthetic has its roots and origins in two main processes: gene-specified goals, rewards and punishers; and the value that is felt when our reasoning system produces. and understands, elegant and simple solutions to problems. What implications does this have for absolute aesthetic value? The implication is that while there is no absolute aesthetic value that is independent of these processes, we will nevertheless find considerable agreement between individuals, especially when the aesthetic value being judged has its roots in the two main processes described. However, as described here, there will be variation for good evolutionary reasons between what different individuals find of value, and there will be variation in individuals' thought processes caused by their cultural heritage, and by noise in the brain which is an important component to creativity (Rolls and Deco 2010). For these reasons, and because aesthetic value is multifactorial (i.e., is influenced by multiple conscious and unconscious processes), we must expect variation in aesthetic value across people, time, and place, with no absolute aesthetic value.

# 6.  Is what is attractive, beautiful and aesthetic?

I wish to counter a possible objection to the theory of the origin of aesthetics described here. The possible objection is that some of the goals specified by our genes, such as the reward value and pleasantness of a high energy. high fat diet, might seem rather unsavoury, and not quite aesthetic. The point I make is that it is not just the gene-specified rewards and punishers that make stimuli have aesthetic value. My proposal is that the reasoning (rational) system also contributes to aesthetic value, in a number of ways. It makes rather longer-term goals attractive. It introduces the further goal that innovation is attractive, as this is likely to help solve difficult problems and move the person into a new part of state space where the person may have an advantage. It introduces the use of syntactic relational structure to provide another way of computation, and problem-solving with this reasoning system is encouraged by simple elegant solutions being rewarding and having aesthetic value, as described above. These factors would help the sophisticated structure in a Bach partita and fugue to contribute to what we judge as aesthetically pleasing, because such music taps not only into our emotional systems, but also into the systems that provide intellectual pleasure because difficult and complex structural problems are posed, and solutions to these difficult structural problems are provided, which as described provides aesthetic pleasure.

In this sense, aesthetic value may have its roots partly in gene-specified rewards (and punishers), but also in the pleasure that the rational system can provide when it is posed, and finds, elegant and simple solutions (which by parsimony are likely to be correct) to complex problems. For this reason, emotions may not be perfectly aligned with aesthetic value. Although both have their origin in gene-specified rewards, emotions may be produced by any one of a large number of reinforcers, whereas aesthetic value usually includes contributions of the reasoning (rational) system, as just described.

Art as a whole is a larger issue than aesthetics and beauty. The content of art might I suggest be seen as the result of multiple separate trajectories through a state space in which each trajectory is guided by the origins of aesthetics (products of adaptations for survival and of sexual selection for useless, sometimes handicapping ornament, and rational thought to develop structure in which an elegant and simple solution is pleasing), and depends on each previous trajectory, the history of art in each culture. Each trajectory is not itself deterministic, because it is influenced by noise (Rolls and Deco 2010) (as is Darwinian evolution). Thus the particular future trajectories cannot be predicted. In each trajectory though a number of factors guide, including new-ness (which is biologically attractive as argued above), wildness (as in Beethoven's late string quartets), as well as what we rationally find aesthetic (as described above), and what survival and sexual selection have also provided in us as some of the origins of aesthetics.

## 7. Comparison with other theories of aesthetics

Much research I have performed shows that there is a perceptual representation of objects formed in cortical areas that is kept separate from the representation of the affective value of objects, which happens further on in processing, in brain regions such as the orbitofrontal cortex (and in an area to which it projects, the anterior cingulate cortex) and the amygdala (see Fig. 8.2). For example, in the inferior temporal visual cortex there is a representation of objects that is independent of whether an object is associated with reward vs. punishment, or is made rewarding or not by hunger (Rolls *et al.* 1977, 2003a). In the primary taste cortex in the insula and frontal operculum, there is a representation of what taste is present, and of its intensity, that is independent of its reward value as altered by hunger vs. satiety, and that is correlated with the subjective intensity but not subjective pleasantness of taste (Rolls *et al.* 1988; Yaxley *et al.* 1988; Grabenhorst and Rolls 2008; Grabenhorst *et al.* 2008; Rolls *et al.* 2009). In the primary olfactory (pyriform) cortex, activations are correlated with the subjective intensity but not subjective pleasantness of odor (Rolls *et al.* 2003b, 2008, 2009). On the other hand, the affective value of taste, olfactory, visual, thermal, tactile, and auditory stimuli is represented in the orbitofrontal cortex. This is shown by neuronal responses that are modulated by hunger or occur to stimuli when they are associated with a reward, and by correlations of brain activations with subjective ratings of pleasantness but not intensity (Rolls *et al.* 1989; Critchley and Rolls 1996; Kringelbach *et al.* 2003; Rolls 2005b, 2007a; Rolls and Grabenhorst 2008; Rolls *et al.* 2009).

There are good functional and adaptive reasons for separate representations of objects and of their affective value. We can still see and recognize objects (including tastes, smell, the sight of objects, etc.) even when they are not rewarding to us, for example if they are foods and we are not hungry. (We do not go blind to objects when they are not rewarding or punishing.) Moreover, it is adaptive to be able to learn about where we have seen objects, people, etc., even if they are not currently rewarding, so that we can find them later when they are needed. Thus there is strong neuroscientific evidence, and sound biological arguments, for separate representations of perceptual objects and of their affective value. Baumgarten (1750) expressed this thought in his book *Aesthetica* when he suggested that sensation, the use of the five senses, is separate from sensibility, which is something more, a 'kind of intuition/cognition/formulation of the thing which judges it beautiful', and in doing so gave rise to the term aesthetics (Herwitz 2008). Before this, abstract questions such as 'What is beauty?' 'What is art?' had not been treated in philosophy, although before this Aristotle had discussed the social role of drama as purging us of ever-present anxiety, and Plato had dismissed poetry as obfuscating by sending the mind reeling into hypnotic trances instead of focusing on rational deductions and argument (Herwitz 2008).

David Hume (1777) takes a broad view of taste (which engages beauty), and argues for five standards of ('delicacy of') taste that might be shown by experts: 'Strong sense, united to delicate sentiment, improved by practice, perfected by comparison, and cleared of all prejudice, can alone entitle critics to this valuable character; and the joint verdict of such, wherever they are to be found, is the true standard of taste and beauty.' Hume's difficulty is that he believes taste is objective, because delicacy is the probing instrument for truth; but instead, taste is a circular and constructivist enterprise (Herwitz 2008). My approach has in contrast a clear foundation for aesthetics in brain function and its evolutionary design, with clear views about how it includes rational thought which provides its own pleasures, and about how art can idealize beyond the normal world by building on these foundations and origins.

Immanuel Kant (1724–1804) distinguishes between liking something and finding it beautiful. According to Kant when I find a painting beautiful this is not conditioned by any causal relation between its properties and my pleasures. For Kant, a judgement of beauty carries the weight of 'ought', that others should judge it beautiful too, so his theory has moral implications. His judgement of beauty is a 'disinterested' judgement, one that is not peculiar to him. He wants the beauty to be in the person, but not causally dependent on the properties of the object in the world such as the pleasure it produces (Kant 1790). He thus appears to be committed to an objective and universal view of art, although exactly how this view is arrived at is not at all clear. The biological and neuroscientific view that I propose indicates that in contrast art is not universal or objective, but instead can be judged good art if it taps into many of the human rational and gene-based reward systems (see further Section 6), with therefore individual differences expected, as described in Section 5.16.

Darwin (1871) recognized that evolution can occur by sexual selection, when what is being selected for has no inherent adaptive or survival value, but is attractive to potential mates (inter-sexual selection), or helps in competing with others of the same sex (intra-sexual selection). His view was that natural beauty arose through competition to attract a sexual partner. His process of sexual selection through mate choice—the struggle to reproduce, not to survive—drove the evolution of visual ornamentation and artistry, from flowers through bird plumage to human self-adornment. Many have developed or ascribed to this idea (including Veblen 1899; Gombrich 1977; Zahavi 1978; and Dutton 2009; see Miller 2001), and Miller (2000, 2001) has proposed a sexual selection theory of art. The implication of this theory is that art has to do with what are frequently useless ornaments (useless in the sense that sexual selection is for characteristics that do not have 'survival' value, but are usually just attractive because they are handicaps and are indicators of fitness). I agree that useless handicapping ornament produced by sexual selection does play a role in aesthetics. However, the sexual selection theory does not therefore have much to say about the utilitarian arts such as simple design in architecture. Perhaps the structure of a piece of music can appeal, and be pleasing, because it taps into our syntactic system that finds that adaptive, survival value-related, elegant, and simple solutions to problem-solving produce plea-sure. As I argued above, interest in social relations and knowledge about them is adaptive and has survival value as it may help to understand who is doing what to whom, and more generally to understand what can happen to people, and much fictional literature addresses these issues, and is not purely ornamental and without inherent value. Thus although Miller may well be right that there are aspects of art that may be primarily ornamental and useless, though attractive to members of the opposite sex in courtship, I suggest that much art has its roots in goals that have been specified as pleasurable or unpleasurable because of their 'survival or adaptive' value, whether as primary reinforcers, other stimuli associated by learning with these, or rewards of a more cognitive origin that accrue when difficult cognitive, syntactic, problems are solved. I also emphasize that some of the characteristics emphasised by sexual selection may have some inherent survival value (mechanisms i–ii in Section 5.3).

To end, my theory (Rolls' theory) of aesthetics thus specifies the roles of Darwinian 'survival or adaptive' selection and sexual selection in aesthetics. It is thus thoroughly Darwinian. A key idea is that many of the things that provide pleasure, or its opposite, do so because they are, or are related to, the gene-specified goals for action. Motivational states arise when trying to obtain these goals, and emotional or affective states when these goals are obtained, or are not obtained. These states are associated with affect and value, and with subjective pleasantness or unpleasantness, because it is an efficient way in which genes can influence their own (reproductive) success ('fitness'), and much more efficient and effective as a Darwinian process than prescribing that the animal should make particular responses to particular stimuli (Rolls 2005a). The theory is that aesthetic value has its roots partly in these gene-specified rewards that have survival or adaptive value; but also in the pleasure that the rational system can provide when it is posed, and finds, elegant and simple solutions (which by parsimony are likely to be correct and hence adaptive) to complex problems; and to some extent in sexual selection. What makes good art can be influenced by many factors, as described here, so is complex and multifaceted, and these factors must include whether the effect of the art is for good or for harm. It also follows that attempts in aesthetics to produce a systematic account based on consistent explicit beliefs will not succeed, for many factors that are not necessarily consistent with each other are involved in aesthetic values, and because some of these factors operate at least partly unconsciously and non-propositionally/non-syntactically, that is, using computational systems in the brain that do not involve reasoning.[4]

# References

Anderson, A. K., K. Christoff, I. Stappen, D. Panitz, D. G. Ghahremani, G. Glover, J. D. Gabrieli, and N. Sobel (2003). 'Dissociated Neural Representations of Intensity and Valence in Human Olfaction'. *Nature Neuroscience*, 6: 196–202.

Andersson, M. (1994). *Sexual Selection*. Princeton: Princeton University Press.

——and L. W. Simmons (2006). 'Sexual Selection and Mate Choice'. *Trends in Ecology & Evolution (Personal Edition)*, 21: 296–302.

Appleton, J. (1975). *The Experience of Landscape*. New York: Wiley.

Baron-Cohen, S. (2008). *Autism and Asperger Syndrome: The Facts*. Oxford: Oxford University Press.

Barrett, L., R. Dunbar, and J. Lycett (2002). *Human Evolutionary Psychology*. Basingstoke: Palgrave Macmillan.

Baumgarten, A. G. (1750). *Aesthetica*.

Berger, J. (1972). *Ways of Seeing*. Harmondsworth: Penguin.

---

[4] I am grateful to M. S. Dawkins, B. K. Scott, and P. Wheatley for helpful discussions, and to Peter Goldie for good advice.

Bertram, B. C. R. (1975). 'Social Factors Influencing Reproduction in Wild Lions'. *Journal of Zoology*, 177: 463–82.

Birkhead, T. (2000). *Promiscuity*. London: Faber and Faber.

Blackmore, S. J. (1999). *The Meme Machine*. Oxford: Oxford University Press.

Blood, A. J. and R. J. Zatorre (2001). 'Intensely Pleasurable Responses to Music Correlate With Activity in Brain Regions Implicated in Reward and Emotion'. *Proceedings of the National Academy of Sciences of the United States of America*, 98: 11818–23.

Blood, A. J., R. J. Zatorre, P. Bermudez, and A. C. Evans (1999). Emotional Responses to Pleasant and Unpleasant Music Correlate With Activity in Paralimbic Brain Regions'. *Nature Neuroscience*, 2: 382–7.

Buss, D. M. (1989). 'Sex Differences in Human Mate Preferences: Evoluntionary Hypotheses Tested in 37 Cultures'. *Behavioural and Brain Sciences*, 12: 1–14.

——(1999). *Evolutionary Psychology: The New Science of the Mind*. Boston, MA: Allyn and Bacon.

——(2006). 'Debating Sexual Selection and Mating Strategies'. *Science*, 312: 689–97.

——and D. P. Schmitt (1993). 'Sexual Strategies Theory: An Evolutionary Perspective on Human Mating'. *Psychological Review*, 100: 204–32.

Carter, C. S. (1998). 'Neuroendocrine Perspectives on Social Attachment and Love'. *Psychoneuroendocrinology*, 23: 779–818.

Critchley, H. D. and E. T. Rolls (1996). 'Hunger and Satiety Modify the Responses of Olfactory and Visual Neurons in the Primate Orbitofrontal Cortex'. *Journal of Neurophysiology*, 75: 1673–86.

Cumming, L. (2009). *A Face to the World: On Self-Portraits*. London: Harper.

Daly, M. and M. Wilson (1988). *Homicide*. New York: Aldine de Gruyter.

Damasio, A. R. (1994). *Descartes' Error*. New York: Putnam.

Darwin, C. (1871). *The Descent of Man, and Selection in Relation to Sex*. London: John Murray (reprinted in 1981 by Princeton University Press).

——(1872). *The Expression of the Emotions in Man and Animals*, 3rd ed. Chicago: University of Chicago Press.

Dawkins, M. S. (1995). *Unravelling Animal Behaviour*. Harlow: Longman.

Dawkins, R. (1986). *The Blind Watchmaker*. Harlow: Longman.

——(1989). *The Selfish Gene*, 2nd ed. Oxford: Oxford University Press.

de Araujo, I. E. T., E. T. Rolls, M. I. Velazco, C. Margot, and I. Cayeux (2005). 'Cognitive Modulation of Olfactory Processing'. *Neuron*, 46: 671–9.

De Vries, A. C., M. B. De Vries, S. E. Taymans, and C. S. Carter (1996). 'The Effects of Stress on Social Preferences are Sexually Dimorphic in Prairie Voles'. *Proceedings of the National Academy of Sciences of the United States of America*, 93: 11980–4.

Dulac, C. and A. T. Torello (2003). 'Molecular Detection of Pheromone Signals in Mammals: From Genes to Behaviour'. *Nature Reviews*, 4: 551–62.

Dunbar, R. (1996). *Grooming, Gossip, and the Evolution of Language*. London: Faber and Faber.

Dutton, D. (2009). *The Art Instinct*. Oxford: Oxford University Press.

Ekman, P. (1982). *Emotion in the Human Face*, 2nd edn. Cambridge: Cambridge University Press.

——(1993). 'Facial Expression and Emotion'. *American Psychologist*, 48: 384–92.

Fisher, R. A. (1930). *The Genetical Theory of Natural Selection*. Oxford: Clarendon Press (2nd edn. New York: Dover, 1958).

Frijda, N. H. (1986). *The Emotions*. Cambridge: Cambridge University Press.

Frith, C. D. and T. Singer (2008). 'The Role of Social cognition in Decision Making'. *Philosophical Transactions of the Royal Society of London*, 363: 3875–86.

Gangestad, S. W and J. A. Simpson (2000). 'The Evolution of Human Mating: Trade-offs and Strategic Pluralism'. *Behavioral and Brain Sciences*, 23: 573–87; discussion 587–644.

——and R. Thornhill (1999). 'Individual Differences in Developmental Precision and Fluctu-ating Asymmetry: A Model and its Implications'. *Journal of Evolutionary Biology*, 12: 402–16.

Gilligan, C. (1982). *In a Different Voice*. Cambridge, MA: Harvard University Press.

Gombrich, E. (1977). *Art and Illusion: A Study in the Psychology of Pictorial Representation*, 5th edn. London: Phaidon Press.

Grabenhorst, F. and E. T. Rolls (2008). 'Selective Attention to Affective Value Alters How the Brain Processes Taste Stimuli'. *European Journal of Neuroscience*, 27: 723–9.

————(2009). 'Different Representations of Relative and Absolute Value in the Human Brain'. *NeuroImage*, 48: 258–68.

————(2011). 'Value, Pleasure, and Choice Systems in the Ventral Prefrontal Cortex'. *Trends in Cognitive Sciences*, 15: 56–67.

————and A. Bilderbeck (2008). 'How Cognition Modulates Affective Responses to Taste and Flavor: Top-down Influences on the Orbitofrontal and Pregenual Cingulate Cortices'. *Cerebral Cortex*, 18: 1549–59.

————and C. Margot (2011). 'A Hedonically Complex Odor Mixture Captures the Brain's Attention'. *NeuroImage*, 55: 832–43.

——————M. A. A. P. Da Silva, and M. I. Velazco (2007). 'How Pleasant and Unpleasant Stimuli Combine in Different Brain Regions: Odor Mixtures'. *Journal of Neuroscience*, 27: 13532–40.

Grafen, A. (1990a). 'Biological Signals as Handicaps'. *Journal of Theoretical Biology*, 144: 517–46.

——(1990b). 'Sexual Selection Unhandicapped by the Fisher Process'. *Journal of Theoretical Biology*, 144: 473–516.

Gray, J. A. (1975). *Elements of a Two-Process Theory of Learning*. London: Academic Press.

——(1987). *The Psychology of Fear and Stress*, 2nd edn. Cambridge: Cambridge University Press.

Hamilton, W. (1964). 'The Genetical Evolution of Social Behaviour'. *Journal of Theoretical Biology*, 7: 1–52.

Hamilton, W. D. (1996). *Narrow Roads of Gene Land*. New York: W. H. Freeman.

——and M. Zuk (1982). 'Heritable True Fitness and Bright Birds: A Role for Parasites?' *Science*, 218: 384–7.

Herwitz, D. (2008). *Aesthetics*. London: Continuum.

Hume, D. (1757). *Four Dissertations: Of Tragedy*.

——(1777). *Selected Essays: Of the Standard of Taste*.

Humphrey, N. (1971). 'Colour and Brightness Preferences in Monkeys'. *Nature*, 229: 615–17.

Johnston, V. S. and M. Franklin (1993). 'Is Beauty in the Eye of the Beholder?' *Ethology and Sociobiology*, 14: 183–99.

Kant, I. (1790). *Critique of Judgement*.

Kappeler, P. M. and C. P. Van Schaik (2004). 'Sexual Selection in Primates: Review and Selective Preview', in P. M. Kappeler and C. P. Van Schaik (eds.), *Sexual Selection in Primates*. Cambridge: Cambridge University Press, pp. 3–23.

Keverne, E. B., C. M. Nevison, and F. L. Martel (1997). 'Early Learning and the Social Bond'. *Annals of the New York Academy of Science*, 807: 329–39.

Kringelbach, M. L., J. O'Doherty, E. T. Rolls, and C. Andrews (2003). 'Activation of the Human Orbitofrontal Cortex to a Liquid Food Stimulus is Correlated with its Subjective Pleasantness'. *Cerebral Cortex*, 13: 1064–71.

Krug, R., W. Plihal, H. L. Fehm, and J. Born (2000). 'Selective Influence of the Menstrual Cycle on Perception of Stimuli with Reproductive Significance: An Event-Related Potential Study'. *Psychophysiology*, 37: 111–22.

Kruger, T. H. C., P. Haake, D. Chereath, W. Knapp, O. E. Janssen, M. S. Exton, M. Schedlowski, and U. Hartmann (2003). 'Specificity of the Neuroendocrine Response to Orgasm during Sexual Arousal in Men'. *Journal of Endocrinology*, 177: 57–64.

Langlois, J. H., L. Kalakanis, A. J. Rubenstein, A. Larson, M. Hallam, and M. Smoot (2000). 'Maxims or Myths of Beauty? A Meta-Analytic and Theoretical Review'. *Psychological Bulletin*, 126: 390–423.

——J. M. Ritter, L. A. Roggman, and L. S. Vaughn (1991). 'Facial Diversity and Infant Preferences for Attractive Faces'. *Developmental Psychology*, 27: 79–84.

——L. A. Roggman, and L. A. Rieserdanner (1990). 'Infants Differential Social Responses to Attractive and Unattractive Faces'. *Developmental Psychology*, 26: 153–9.

——————R. J. Casey, J. M. Ritter, L. A. Rieserdanner, and V. Y. Jenkins (1987). 'Infant Preferences for Attractive Faces: Rudiments of a Stereotype'. *Developmental Psychology*, 23: 363–9.

Lazarus, R. S. (1991). *Emotion and Adaptation*. New York: Oxford University Press.

Lee, H. J., A. H. Macbeth, J. H. Pagani, and W. S. Young Iii (2009). 'Oxytocin: The Great Facilitator of Life'. *Progress in Neurobiology*, 88: 127–51.

Lim, M. M., Z. X. Wang, D. E. Olazabal, X. H. Ren, E. F. Terwilliger, and L. J. Young (2004). 'Enhanced Partner Preference in a Promiscuous Species by Manipulating the Expression of a Single Gene'. *Nature*, 429: 754–7.

Maia, T. V. and J. L. McClelland (2004). 'A Reexamination of the Evidence for the Somatic Marker Hypothesis: What Participants Really Know in the Iowa Gambling Task'. *Proceedings of the National Academy of Sciences of the United States of America*, 101: 16075–80.

Maynard Smith, J. and D. Harper (2003). *Animal Signals*. Oxford: Oxford University Press.

McCabe, C., E. T. Rolls, A. Bilderbeck, and F. McGlone (2008). 'Cognitive Influences on the Affective Representation of Touch and the Sight of Touch in the Human Brain'. *Social, Cognitive and Affective Neuroscience*, 3: 97–108.

Mead, L. S. and S. J. Arnold (2004). 'Quantitative Genetic Models of Sexual Selection'. *Trends in Ecology & Evolution* (Personal Edition), 19: 264–71.

Meston, C. M. and P. F. Frohlich (2000). 'The Neurobiology of Sexual Function'. *Archives of General Psychiatry*, 57: 1012–30.

Millenson, J. R. (1967). *Principles of Behavioral Analysis*. New York: Macmillan.

Miller, G. F. (2000). *The Mating Mind*. London: Heinemann.

——(2001). 'Aesthetic Fitness: How Sexual Selection Shaped Artistic Virtuosity as a Fitness Indicator and Aesthetic Preferences as Mate Choice Criteria'. *Bulletin of Psychology and the Arts*, 2: 20–5.

O'Doherty, J., J. Winston, H. Critchley, D. Perrett, D. M. Burt, and R. J. Dolan (2003). 'Beauty in a Smile: The Role of Medial Orbitofrontal Cortex in Facial Attractiveness'. *Neuropsychologia*, 41: 147–55.

Oatley, K. and J. M. Jenkins (1996). *Understanding Emotions*. Oxford: Blackwell.

Penton-Voak, I. S., D. I. Perrett, D. L. Castles, T. Kobayashi, D. M. Burt, L. K. Murray, and R. Minamisawa (1999). 'Menstrual Cycle Alters Face Preference'. *Nature*, 399: 741–2.

Pinker, S. and P. Bloom (1992). 'Natural Language and Natural Selection', in J. H. Barkow, L. Cosmides, and J. Tooby (eds.), *The Adapted Mind*. New York: Oxford University Press, pp. 451–93.

Pizzari, T., C. K. Cornwallis, H. Lovlie, S. Jakobsson, and T. R. Birkhead (2003). 'Sophisticated Sperm Allocation in Male Fowl'. *Nature*, 426: 70–4.

Ridley, M. (1996). *The Origins of Virtue*. London: Viking.

Rolls, E. T. (1986a). 'Neural Systems Involved in Emotion in Primates', in R. Plutchik and H. Kellerman (eds.), *Emotion: Theory, Research, and Experience. Vol. 3. Biological Foundations of Emotion*. New York: Academic Press, pp. 125–43.

——(1986b). 'A Theory of Emotion, and its Application to Understanding the Neural Basis of Emotion', in Y. Oomura (ed.), *Emotions. Neural and Chemical Control*. Basel: Karger, pp. 325–44.

——(1990). 'A Theory of Emotion, and its Application to Understanding the Neural Basis of Emotion'. *Cognition and Emotion*, 4: 161–90.

——(1999). *The Brain and Emotion*. Oxford: Oxford University Press.

——(2000). 'Précis of *The Brain and Emotion*'. *Behavioral and Brain Sciences*, 23: 177–233.

——(2003). 'Consciousness Absent and Present: A Neurophysiological Exploration'. *Progress in Brain Research*, 144: 95–106.

——(2004). 'A Higher Order Syntactic Thought (HOST) Theory Of Consciousness', in R. J. Gennaro (ed.), *Higher-Order Theories of Consciousness: An Anthology*. Amsterdam: John Benjamins, pp. 137–72.

——(2005a). 'Consciousness Absent or Present: A Neurophysiological Exploration of Masking', in H. Ogmen and B. G. Breitmeyer (eds.), *The First Half Second: The Microgenesis and Temporal Dynamics of Unconscious and Conscious Visual Processes*. Cambridge, MA: MIT Press, pp. 89–108.

——(2005b). *Emotion Explained*. Oxford: Oxford University Press.

——(2007a). 'The Representation of Information about Faces in the Temporal and Frontal Lobes'. *Neuropsychologia*, 45: 125–43.

——(2007b). 'A Computational Neuroscience Approach to Consciousness'. *Neural Networks*, 20: 962–82.

——(2007c). 'The Affective Neuroscience of Consciousness: Higher Order Linguistic Thoughts, Dual Routes to Emotion and Action, and Consciousness', in P. Zelazo, M. Moscovitch, and E. Thompson (eds.), *Cambridge Handbook of Consciousness*. Cambridge: Cambridge University Press, pp. 831–59.

——(2007d). 'Sensory Processing in the Brain Related to the Control of Food Intake'. *Proceedings of the Nutrition Society*, 66: 96–112.

——(2008a). *Memory, Attention, and Decision-Making: A Unifying Computational Neuroscience Approach*. Oxford: Oxford University Press.

——(2008b). 'Emotion, Higher Order Syntactic Thoughts, and Consciousness', in L. Weiskrantz and M. K. Davies (eds.), *Frontiers of Consciousness*. Oxford: Oxford University Press, pp. 131–67.

——(2009). 'The Anterior and Midcingulate Cortices and Reward', in B. A. Vogt (ed.), *Cingulate Neurobiology and Disease*. Oxford: Oxford University Press, pp. 191–206.

——(2011a). *Neuroculture*. Oxford: Oxford University Press.

——(2011b). 'Consciousness, Decision-Making, and Neural Computation', in V. Cutsuridis, A. Hussain, and J. G. Taylor (eds.), *Perception–Action Cycle: Models, Algorithms and Systems*. Berlin: Springer, 287–333.

——and G. Deco (2002). *Computational Neuroscience of Vision*. Oxford: Oxford University Press.

————(2010). *The Noisy Brain: Stochastic Dynamics as a Principle of Brain Function*. Oxford: Oxford University Press.

——and F. Grabenhorst (2008). 'The Orbitofrontal Cortex and Beyond: From Affect to Decision-Making'. *Progress in Neurobiology*, 86: 216–44.

——and S. M. Stringer (2001). 'A Model of the Interaction between Mood and Memory'. *Network: Computation in Neural Systems*, 12: 111–29.

——and A. Treves (1998). *Neural Networks and Brain Function*. Oxford: Oxford University Press.

——N. C. Aggelopoulos, and F. Zheng (2003a). 'The Receptive Fields of Inferior Temporal Cortex Neurons in Natural Scenes'. *Journal of Neuroscience*, 23: 339–48.

——H. D. Critchley, A. S. Browning, and K. Inoue (2006). 'Face-Selective and Auditory Neurons in the Primate Orbitofrontal Cortex'. *Experimental Brain Research*, 170: 74–87.

————J. V. Verhagen, and M. Kadohisa (2009). 'The Representation of Information about Taste and Odor in the Orbitofrontal Cortex'. *Chemosensory Perception*, 3: 16–33.

——F. Grabenhorst, C. Margot, M. A. A. P. da Silva, and M. I. Velazco (2008). 'Selective Attention to Affective Value Alters How the Brain Processes Olfactory Stimuli'. *Journal of Cognitive Neuroscience*, 20: 1815–26.

——S. J. Judge, and M. Sanghera (1977). 'Activity of Neurones in the Inferotemporal Cortex of the Alert Monkey'. *Brain Research*, 130: 229–38.

——M. L. Kringelbach, and I. E. T. de Araujo (2003b). 'Different Representations of Pleasant and Unpleasant Odors in the Human Brain'. *European Journal of Neuroscience*, 18: 695–703.

——T. R. Scott, Z. J. Sienkiewicz, and S. Yaxley (1988). 'The Responsiveness of Neurones in the Frontal Opercular Gustatory Cortex of the Macaque Monkey is Independent of Hunger'. *Journal of Physiology*, 397: 1–12.

——Z. J. Sienkiewicz and S. Yaxley (1989). 'Hunger Modulates the Responses to Gustatory Stimuli of Single Neurons in the Caudolateral Orbitofrontal Cortex of the Macaque Monkey'. *European Journal of Neuroscience*, 1: 53–60.

Ryan, M. J. (1998). 'Sexual Selection, Receiver Biases, and the Evolution of Sex Differences'. *Science*, 281: 1999–2003.

Shamay-Tsoory, S. G., Y. Tibi-Elhanany, and J. Aharon-Peretz (2007). 'The Green-Eyed Monster and Malicious Joy: The Neuroanatomical Bases of Envy and Gloating (Schadenfreude)'. *Brain*, 130: 1663–78.

Singh, D. and P. M. Bronstad (2001). 'Female Body Odour is a Potential Cue to Ovulation'. *Proceedings of the Royal Society B-Biological Sciences*, 268: 797–801.

——and S. Luis (1995). 'Ethnic and Gender Consensus for the Effect of Waist-to-Hip Ratio on Judgment of Women's Attractiveness'. *Human Nature: An Interdisciplinary Biosocial Perspective*, 6: 51–65.

——W. Meyer, R. J. Zambarano, D. Farley, and D. F. Hurlbert (1998). 'Frequency and Timing of Coital Orgasm in Women Desirous of Becoming Pregnant'. *Archives of Sexual Behavior*, 27: 15–29.

Strongman, K. T. (1996). *The Psychology of Emotion*, 4th edn. London: Wiley.

Swaddle, J. P. and G. W. Reierson (2002). 'Testosterone Increases Perceived Dominance But Not Attractiveness in Human Males'. *Proceedings of the Royal Society: Biological Sciences*, 269: 2285–9.

Takahashi, H., M. Kato, M. Matsuura, D. Mobbs, T. Suhara, and Y. Okubo (2009). 'When Your Gain is My Pain and Your Pain is My Gain: Neural Correlates of Envy and Schadenfreude'. *Science*, 323: 937–9.

Thornhill, R. and S. W. Gangestad (1999). 'Facial Attractiveness'. *Trends in Cognitive Science*, 3: 452–60.

——and K. Grammer (1999). 'The Body and Face of Woman: One Ornament that Signals Quality?' *Evolution and Human Behavior*, 20: 105–20.

Trivers, R. L. (1971). 'Evolution of Reciprocal Altruism'. *Quarterly Review of Biology*, 46: 35–57.

——(1974). 'Parent–Offspring Conflict'. *American Zoologist*, 14: 249–64.

Uvnas-Moberg, K. (1998). 'Oxytocin May Mediate the Benefits of Positive Social Interaction and Emotions'. *Psychoneuroendocrinology*, 23: 819–35.

Vandenberghe, P. L. and P. Frost (1986). 'Skin Color Preference, Sexual Dimorphism and Sexual Selection: A Case of Gene Culture Coevolution'. *Ethnic and Racial Studies*, 9: 87–113.

Veblen, T. (1899). *The Theory of the Leisure Class*. New York: Macmillan.

Weiskrantz, L. (1968). 'Emotion', in L. Weiskrantz (ed.), *Analysis of Behavioural Change*. New York and London: Harper & Row, pp. 50–90.

Winslow, J. T. and T. R. Insel (2004). 'Neuroendocrine Basis of Social Recognition'. *Current Opinion in Neurobiology*, 14: 248–53.

Woolf, V. (1928). *A Room of One's Own*.

Wynne-Edwards, K. E. (2001). 'Hormonal Changes in Mammalian Fathers'. *Hormones and Behavior*, 40: 139–45.

Yanal, R. J. (1991). 'Hume and Others on the Paradox of Tragedy'. *Journal of Aesthetics and Art Criticism*, 49: 75–6.

Yaxley, S., E. T. Rolls, and Z. J. Sienkiewicz (1988). 'The Responsiveness of Neurons in the Insular Gustatory Cortex of the Macaque Monkey is Independent of Hunger'. *Physiology and Behavior*, 42: 223–9.

Young, L. J. (2008). 'Molecular Neurobiology of the Social Brain'. *Hormones and Social Behavior*, 198: 57–64.

Zahavi, A. (1975). 'Mate Selection: A Selection for a Handicap'. *Journal of Theoretical Biology*, 53: 205–14.

——(1978). 'Decorative Patterns and the Evolution of Art'. *New Scientist*, 19: 182–4.

# PART III

# Beauty and Universality

# 9

# Beauty is Instinctive Feeling: Experimenting on Aesthetics and Art

*I. C. McManus*

Any psychologist attempting to analyse the how and the why of human aesthetics, particularly in the presence of colleagues who are philosophers, cannot help but remember the daunting words of Wittgenstein, who in his 1938 *Lectures and Conversations on Aesthetics, Psychology and Religious Belief* said that:

People still have the idea that psychology is one day going to explain all our aesthetic judgments, and they mean experimental psychology. This is very funny—very funny indeed . . . Aesthetic questions have nothing to do with psychological experiments, but are answered in an entirely different way (Wittgenstein 1970: III, §7)

He did not mince his words, and earlier he had said:

People often say that aesthetics is a branch of psychology. The idea is that once we are more advanced, everything—all the mysteries of Art—will be understood by psychological experiments. *Exceedingly stupid as the idea is, this is roughly it.* (Wittgenstein 1970: II, §35; my emphasis)

Worse still, Wittgenstein is not the only one with such views,[1] Dickie (1962: 285) also stating bluntly, 'My thesis is that psychology is not relevant to aesthetics.'

Fortunately there are views in the opposite direction, perhaps put in its most minimal form by Zangwill (2009: 19), who said, 'There is surely some scope for

---

[1] Unpacking Wittgenstein's comments on psychology is far from easy, and I am not the right person to do it, but it is worth realizing that such comments are present from the *Tractatus* (4.1121) through to the last page of the *Philosophical Investigations* (II.xiv, 232e), where Wittgenstein famously talks of 'the confusion and barrenness of psychology . . . For in psychology there are experimental methods and *conceptual confusion*' (emphasis in original), with a very similar phrase to the latter occurring also in the *Remarks on the Philosophy of Psychology* (I.1039). It is probably relevant that Wittgenstein had himself carried out psychological experiments in Cambridge (Wittgenstein and Muscio 1912; Monk 1990: 49–50). One possibility is that Wittgenstein was not antagonistic to the experimental methods of psychology as such, but was concerned about the too easy way in which theoretical explanations of those experiments slide across into an analysis of what are essentially unknowable private objects of mind (see Candlish 2002 and also Harré and Tissaw 2005).

empirical research. It would be odd if there were not.' Even before Wittgenstein was lecturing on aesthetics, his early disciple, Frank Ramsey, who was also a reviewer and explicator of the *Tractatus* (Ramsey 1923), in a talk to the Apostles, in February 1925, pointed out that, aesthetics and literature 'always excites us far more than anything else' (Ramsey 1990: 247), but that the arguments around them are often 'feeble', and in part that was because there was, 'very little to say about *the psychological problems of which aesthetics really consists*, e.g., why certain combinations of colours give us such peculiar feelings' (my emphasis). In the absence of such crucial information, discussion and argument resorted to, 'What we really like doing [which] is...to compare our experience[s]' (Ramsey 1990: 248). While not providing answers to philosophical questions, the empirical findings of psychology can surely set limits on the possible nature of such answers, preventing an over-reliance on any single individual's intuitions and introspections (but see Sosa 2007 for the problems of so-called experimental philosophy).

When psychologists do study 'the psychological problems of which aesthetics really consists', the answers they provide can often be either disconcertingly vague or disconcertingly specific for those looking for clean, hard, empirical conclusions which can readily generalize and hence assist the logical argumentation of philosophy. The difficulty is one that underpins so much psychology, as was elegantly pointed out in the 1950s by Kluckhohn (Kluckhohn and Murray 1953: 35), in his pithy statement that:

Every man is in certain respects a) like all other men, b) like some other men, c) like no other men.

This is undoubtedly true of aesthetics. The point was shown in a review of a 2009 exhibition of the works of J. W. Waterhouse (1849–1917) at the Royal Academy in London, where the reviewer, Frank Whitford (2009), suggested that, 'those with sophisticated tastes may not be able to respond positively to Waterhouse', with art historians condemning him as 'parochial, academic, eclectic, with a tendency towards cliché...whose fate it was eventually to be (almost) erased from art history'. And yet, and yet, and at first it seems to be said with near despair, 'Waterhouse and his kind are what many people enjoy looking at', with *The Lady of Shalott* being 'one of the nation's favourite paintings' (Whitford 2009: 20). However, as Whitford then goes on to point out, 'there are today not one but many art publics, each with its preferences and needs'. It is one of those publics that has made a painter such as Thomas Kinkade one of the most successful in North America, his pictures apparently being displayed in one in twenty homes (Schroeder 2006), although his particular style, and kitsch in general, are rarely ever discussed in serious art journals (but see Wilson 2006), or in psychological accounts (but see Winston 1995), or philosophical discussion (but see Carroll 1998). Systematic measurement of aesthetic activities shows that people not only vary in the extent of their aesthetic interests but also in the focus of that interest, both in broad direction, with personality being a major determinant of extent of both quantity and type of aesthetic interest (McManus and Furnham 2006).

Variation in taste is often forgotten in writings both on philosophical aesthetics and psychological aesthetics, the latter so often presenting averaged values as typifying a population as a whole. Tastes, though, obviously differ, and the average rarely summarizes the population well—if half the population prefers coffee and the other half prefers tea, it is not the case that a coffee–tea mix would satisfy everyone and provide a reasonable summary of taste for hot drinks. The Latin maxim may say, 'De gustibus non est disputandum'—there is no point in arguing about taste—but to a psychologist, where there is variation, there must also be a reason for that variation. As Gustav Theodor Fechner, the founder of experimental aesthetics, put it:

Es ist eine alte Rede, dass sich über den Geschmack nicht streiten lässt; indes streitet man doch darüber, ja über nichts mehr als den Geschmack; es muss sich also doch darüber streiten lassen [It is an old saying that there is no accounting for taste, nevertheless people argue about it, about nothing more than taste; it must thus be possible to argue about taste]. (Translation, Jacobsen 2004: 41)

Of course responses to art and aesthetic stimuli do not only differ between people, but also differ within individuals, developing and evolving over time, so that just as I would hate to have to wear the clothes that I wore when I was twenty, so I would hate to be condemned to a life of the pictures, the music, and the food that I liked at that age.

The consequence for psychology is that analysis needs to be at many levels, from universals, through commonalities, to idiosyncrasies. Art and aesthetic responses occur at each level, and the real challenge is to account for them all. Tempting as it might be to equate 'aesthetics' and 'art' (particularly what might be called 'high art' or the art of the contemporary critics) aesthetic phenomena encompass a much wider range than that, and require explanation.

## 1. Big theories

A recent trend in psychology that has attracted much public attention is the advent of what might be called 'grand theories' of art, theories that are trying to do for art and aesthetics what TOEs ('theories of everything') try to do in physics. This chapter will not be considering in much detail the two main contenders, Evolutionary Psychology and Neuroaesthetics, believing that they fail at many levels. Evolutionary Psychology has particular difficulty in explaining why people differ, its successes mostly occurring in those domains where people are broadly very similar (Buss 2009). Pinning down precisely what Neuroaesthetics says is more difficult, with a broad philosophical interpretation being that the claims are 'astonishing', 'aesthetically uninformative', 'supposedly explanatory', 'surely unrealistic', and 'further undermined', so that ultimately, 'there is little to show so far' (Currie 2003: 707). Showing that the contemplation of art objects results in brain activity is hardly a surprise, even if the red blobs on the brain scans provide a veneer of serious science; invocation of hypothetical 'aesthetic cells' (Solso 2003) provides no theoretical leverage on deep problems; and claiming that 'the artist is in a sense, a neuroscientist, exploring the potentials and capacities of the brain, though with different tools' (Zeki n.d.) might flatter artists, but provides little else in the way of serious analysis. High technology is no substitute for a serious dissection of phenomenology and psychological processes, mental architecture being replaced by hypothesized neuroarchitecture with little explanatory gain. Perhaps the most interesting question for psychology is why such theories are so popular, and one possibility is that they seemingly make what was otherwise complex seem to be easy, reducing it to one or two simple principles. But then as H. L. Mencken said, 'there is always an easy solution to every [complex] human problem—neat, plausible and wrong' (Mencken 1917).

The problems of grand theories of aesthetics were perhaps never better shown than by Sir Ernst Gombrich in his devastating twelve-line critique of Ramachandran and Hirstein's 'The Science of Art: A Neurological Theory of Aesthetic Experience' (1999). In his dry response, Gombrich commented that, 'Even a fleeting visit to one of the great museums might serve to convince the authors that few of the exhibits conform to the laws of art they postulate' (Gombrich 2006). Grand theory is surely premature, and in another devastating criticism of Ramachandran and Hirstein, the philosopher John Hyman has suggested that, 'There are lessons here...The lesson about neuroscience is that it should concentrate on specific problems about the visual arts instead of the grandiose question, what is art?' (Hyman 2006: 45). Echoing Frank Ramsey, Hyman argues for more data, more evidence, a better understanding of psychological processes, before theories try to explain such complex phenomena as art and aesthetics. The empirical research I report later in this chapter will follow precisely that line.

## 2. Beauty

In the same issue of the *TLS* that reviewed the Waterhouse exhibition, there was also a review of an exhibition at Tate Modern in London of the contemporary Danish artist Per Kirkeby (1938–) (Binding 2009). There is a revealing aside in which the reviewer comments that, 'Kirkeby has said he is nervous of the word "beauty", though he does not deny valuing or seeking it.' It could be argued that much of modern art and the aesthetics of modernism arose from similar problems with that word 'beauty', many refusing to see that it merits consideration or discussion as a concept. Nevertheless, when the psychologist Thomas Jacobsen (2004) asked 311 non-art students to write down the adjectives that they understood by the word 'aesthetic', some 590 different adjectives were produced, but no less than 92 per cent of the subjects included the word 'beautiful', with 42 per cent of subjects using 'ugly', the second most frequent word. Art and aesthetics for most people are about beauty, whatever artists and critics may say (and such data would seem to provide problems for Wittgenstein's assertion that, 'in real life, when aesthetic judgements are made, aesthetics adjectives such as "beautiful"... play hardly any role at all' (Wittgenstein 1970: 3). To a practising psychologist, perhaps one of the most useful philosophical and art historical discussions into beauty's relationship to art is that of Arthur Danto (2003). In *The Abuse of Beauty*, Danto takes the line that beauty is just one of many emotional and cognitive states that artists can manipulate to obtain effects, and that its abuse before the twentieth century by artists was in their near total obsession with beauty to the exclusion of most other emotions. It is a convincing argument in many ways, but also has the effect of reinstating beauty as having a role within the arts and aesthetics. The philosopher Nick Zangwill has gone further, arguing that it is useful to think of beauty as 'one among many aesthetic properties', but that one mustn't 'lose sight of beauty's special-ness' (Zangwill 2003: 325).

Defining beauty is another matter, and the critics C. K. Ogden and I. A. Richards and the artist, James Wood, in *The Foundations of Aesthetics* (1922) identified sixteen separate uses of the word, while more recently Crispin Sartwell (2006) referred to 'six names of beauty'. The poet Denis Donoghue (2003), at the beginning of his *Speaking of Beauty*, says that 'a theory of beauty would be a good thing to have', but then shows the problems for any such theory, and continues by listing the range of phenomena that would need to be included, for:

we continue to say without much hesitation that such-and-such and so-and-so are beautiful: tulips, roses, certain women, certain men, children, a page of Chinese written characters, an African mask, a mathematical process, a piece of music, the view from Portofino, a certain sunset, a full moon, some animals (but not the rhinoceros), most birds, kingfishers, dragonflies, the air at Brighton, Alexander Kipnis' voice, the weather when noon's a purple glow. (Donoghue 2003: 25)

Much of the problem of definition arises because, as the quotation in my title says, 'beauty is instinctive feeling'. That comment was scribbled down in July 1838 on page 32 of his *M Notebook*, by Charles Darwin,[2] long before *The Origin of Species* was written, and long also before Darwin had considered the nature of beauty more formally in *The Descent of Man, and Selection in Relation to Sex*, where he talks of 'the pleasure given by certain colours, forms, and sounds, and which may fairly be called a sense of the beautiful' (Darwin 1874: Chapter 3). Darwin does not deny the possibility that simple forms of the perception of beauty are present in species other than man, although, 'In man, however, when cultivated, the sense of beauty is manifestly a far more complex feeling, and is associated with various intellectual ideas.' Certainly it seems likely that other species, particularly apes and primates, might exhibit what Ruskin called, the 'animal consciousness of the pleasantness I call *aesthesis*' (*Modern Painters*, Pt III: I.II. §6),

---

[2] See http://www.darwin-online.org.uk/content/frameset?viewtype=side&itemID=CUL-DAR125.-&pageseq=1

and such preferences have been elegantly demonstrated in experiments with rhesus monkeys by Nicholas Humphrey (1972).

The knowing of what counts as beauty is often immediate, immune to justification, reflection, explanation or rationalization, and mostly opaque to introspection. For Danto (2003: 89), 'Beauty is really as obvious as blue; one does not have to work at seeing it when it is there.' As Darwin correctly intuited, beauty is indeed 'instinctive feeling'. People readily make judgements of beauty, be it of art objects or natural objects, and those judgements just feel correct. Beauty therefore is not special but quotidian, for, 'beauty . . . is part of the everyday world of purpose and desire, history and contingency, subjectivity and incompleteness [which is] the only world there is' (Nehamas 2007: 35). Whether confronted by Sophia Loren or the frescos of Ghirlandaio, 'their beauty rushes upon you. There is no space for appraisal. You are open-mouthed, dazed into a wholly unself-regarding act of worship' (Inglis 2007).

Of course judgements of beauty are not the only assessments that can be made about art objects, and the Danish psychologist Bjarne Sode Funch (1997) has unpacked phenomenological responses to art in much more detail, and as he points out, it is the immediacy and the ease of judgements of beauty which mak its assessment, expressed typically as preference or choice, so suitable for laboratory studies of experimental aesthetics. The nature of preference itself has been surprisingly neglected in philosophical theory, despite, as Von Wright (1963: 5) commented, what he calls 'intrinsic preference' being, 'of pivotal importance to theory of value in general and to its three principal branches—aesthetics, economics, and ethics'. Whatever the theoretical problems of understanding the nature of preference, subjects in experiments rarely find difficulty in answering questions such as, 'How much do you like this image?', 'Which of these pair of images is the more beautiful?', or 'Adjust this object so that it looks as nice as possible', and they carry out such tasks quickly and reliably, and they concern themselves little with philosophical niceties about the precise meaning of 'nice', 'like', 'beautiful', or 'better'. Of course not all responses to art are immediate, and sometimes, as with T. J. Clark (2006) looking at Poussin's *Landscape with a Man killed by a Snake* and *Landscape with a Calm* most days over a six-month period, it can be extremely intense. Having said that though, every intense viewing has to start with a first glance, and if that first glance is not attracted and then held by something—a something that as often or not is beauty—then sustained viewing is unlikely to take place. The average viewer in an art gallery looks at each individual picture for less than a second, and unless that first impression attracts, then there will not be any second impressions (Smith and Wolf 1996).

Beauty is therefore a key component of many aesthetic responses. While it is probably true, as the sculptor Anish Kapoor recently said, that, 'The power of a work [of art] comes from its ability to accrue layers of meaning—whether poetic, political or historical' (Kent 2009: 42), it is nevertheless the lush, sensuous, gorgeous, beautiful surfaces of Kapoor's sculptures that draw people in and keep them returning, so that they can perceive those meanings (even if, as Danto suggests, it could presumably have been any other emotional response). Zangwill (2003) empha-sizes the importance of Kant's distinction between *free* and *dependent* beauty (*freie Schönheit* and *anhängende Schönheit*) (Kant 1952: §16), the latter relating only to how an object works in relation to some external function, whereas free beauty is intrinsic to the object as such. Judgements of free beauty are precisely those made by subjects in experiments on aesthetics, assessing the 'visual pleasure' that Crispin Sartwell identifies in Monet's paintings of water lilies, which 'capture and provide *pleasure in mere seeing*' (Sartwell 2006: 20, my emphasis). And from such perceptions of the sensory qualities of the object itself, more complex aesthetic responses are built. As Zangwill says, 'the foundation of our sophisticated aesthetic life is the primitive enjoyment of beauty', so that, 'if we did not appreciate the free beauties of arrangements of colours and shapes, then we could not appreciate the more sophisticated dependent beauties of representa-tional content' (Zangwill 2001: 336).

Donoghue also does battle with the precise meaning of beauty for much of his book, and eventually, towards the end, he concludes that, 'form and beauty seem to be one and the same . . . [so that] I don't see any difference between beauty and formal perfection' (2003: 107). Later he asserts that, 'form is the distinguishing characteristic of art' (2003: 121). Art criticism has, almost since its inception, distinguished form and content, assessing not only what is said but how it is said. In many ways it is form, rather than content, that, in psychological terms, can be seen as separating aesthetic responses to a work of art from other responses, be they intellectual, emotional, spiritual, political, or whatever. Despite its many powerful meanings and effects, the ultimate and lasting effect of Picasso's *Guernica* comes from its formal properties as a work of art, rather than its content as a piece of journalism or as a propaganda document, however much it is also both of those. The primacy of form is perhaps most obvious in photography, perhaps particularly war photography (Sontag 2004), where despite the horror of the content, it is nigh on impossible for a good photographer not to incorporate the aesthetics of form derived from high art, 'To photograph [is] to compose . . . and the desire to arrange elements in the picture [does] not vanish' (Sontag 2004: 47–8), the result being that, 'beauty can encompass even ugliness, even terror, even evil' (Sartwell 2006: 151).[3] By concentrating on formal properties, designers such as Denman Ross (1907) and psychologists such as Rudolf Arnheim (1974, 1982) have

---

[3] Sontag (2004: 23) does point out that for 'the photography of atrocity, people want the weight of witnessing without the taint of artistry', so that the pictures 'seem more authentic when they don't have the look that comes from being "properly" lighted and composed' (2004: 23–4). However, even if amateur photographers might be better placed to achieve that effect, news and picture editors themselves make choices between multiple images, so that the likely result is that the better composed images are used more often. The beauty of the tragic can be seen well in the now rarely reproduced photographs of 'the falling man' jumping from the doomed World Trade Center (Junood 2003). Sontag comments that, 'To acknowl-edge the beauty of photographs of the World Trade Center ruins in the months following the attack seemed frivolous, sacrilegious . . . But they *were* beautiful . . . Photographs tend to transform . . . and as an image something may be beautiful . . . as it is not in real life' (2004: 67–8, emphasis in original). As Sontag had put it previously, photography results in 'the aestheticising of reality' (Sontag 1979: 176).

searched for the underlying principles of aesthetic organization that underpin works of art whose surface content is widely diverse, covering most of human life and experience. If experimental aesthetics is to be successful it surely has to be identifying the deep structures of form, rather than the surface structures of content. As for the need to try and do that, as Danto said, 'There is doubtless a psychology of everyday aesthetics to be worked out, and if there are what might one call laws of aesthetic preference, it would be greatly to our advantage to learn what they are' (Danto 2003: 7).

## 3. Three studies

The three empirical studies I will describe here are used to illustrate various principles of experimenting on aesthetics, and some of the conclusions that might inform philosophical discussion. The first study goes back to the very foundations of experimental aesthetics, and returns to Fechner's extreme reductionist paradigm examining the aesthetics of simple geometric figures such as rectangles. Such minimal objects are as far as it is possible to go while still considering the study to be about aesthetics, but they run the risk of not really seeming to be about anything to do with art proper. The second study therefore looks at the paintings of Piet Mondrian (1872–1944), the Dutch neo-plasticist painter, whose works are simultaneously of the highest aesthetic quality, and yet are geometrically simple enough to be manipulated in laboratory experiments. Finally, the third study looks at how people crop photographs, the great advantage of the task being that it is genuinely aesthetic, but it is also familiar to most people and yet does not require technical ability, and there is a sense in which it is genuinely aesthetic objects that are being *produced* rather than merely *perceived*.

## 4. Rectangles and the Golden Section

In one of the first attempts at 'grand theory' in aesthetics, the Pythagoreans and then Vitruvius argued that beauty could be found in particular numerical ratios, particularly of integers (Wittkower 1971) (and Wittgenstein himself seems to have used ratios of 1:1, 1:2, 2:3, 3:4, 4:5, and 5:6 when designing his house in the Kundmanngasse (Leitner 2000; Wijdeveld 1994)). In the Renaissance, Pacioli in particular, but also Leonardo and Dürer, suggested that the ratio known to Euclid as 'extreme and mean ratio' (Herz-Fischler 1998), to Pacioli as the Divine Proportion, and later called the Golden Section, Golden Ratio, Golden Proportion, or Golden Number, underpinned aesthetic beauty. Euclid showed that there is only one rectangle which can be constructed so that when a square is removed from one end, the rectangle remaining is in the same proportion as the original, the longer side being 1.618034 . . . times the length of the shorter. The number 1.618 . . . , also known as $\phi$, is, like $e$ and $\pi$, an irrational number which crops up in a range of unexpected situations in mathematics, putting it under Donoghue's heading of 'a mathematical process' showing beauty, as with the gnomically elegant formulae:

$$\Phi = 1.61803... = 1 + \cfrac{1}{1 + \cfrac{1}{1 + \cfrac{1}{1 + \cfrac{1}{1 + \cfrac{1}{1 + \cfrac{1}{1 + ...}}}}}} = \sqrt{1 + \sqrt{1 + \sqrt{1 + \sqrt{1 + \sqrt{1 + \sqrt{1 + \sqrt{1 + ...}}}}}}}$$

Adolph Zeising's *Neue Lehre von den Proportionen des menschlichen Körpers* (1854) made strong claims about the universal aesthetic significance of the Golden Section across a range of artistic masterpieces, and those claims interested Fechner. His major innovation, though, was not to look for the proportions found in works of art (and given enough points of significance in a painting, there are almost inevitably some in the ratio 1:1.618 . . . or indeed any other proportion (Broadbent 1980), making such studies a methodological quagmire, full of danger and artefactual significance—see for instance the almost certainly spurious claim (Duckworth 1962) that the Golden Section occurs throughout Virgil's *Aeneid* (Fischler 1981). Fechner cut that Gordian knot by showing people rectangles of different proportions and asking them which they preferred. Ten white rectangles of different height–width ratios but similar area were laid at random on a black table, and several hundred subjects were asked which they saw as the most attractive. To Fechner's surprise, the modal response was at the Golden Section. However, 24 per cent of subjects chose rectangles far removed from the Golden Section, suggesting substantial variation in the answers to Fechner's simple question. Fechner's results are often quoted very uncritically (e.g., Livio 2002), and are treated as divine gospel in a host of websites and other places which are little short of numerological mysticism (see for instance http://goldennumber.net/). Studies in the fifty or so years following Fechner mostly reported broadly similar findings, although psychologists became less and less convinced of any special attractivity for the Golden Section rectangle (Höge 1997). The controversy still continues, but its most striking aspect is that the argument is still couched almost entirely in terms of whether the average population response is or is not at the Golden Section, this single numerical ratio continuing to be fetishized, primarily because of the mathematical elegance of 1.618 . . .

My own research into experimental aesthetics, begun while an undergraduate, looked at the aesthetics of rectangles and other simple geometric figures. There were undoubted methodological problems with Fechner's study, not least range effects, so that, when rectangles are presented in the range 1:1 to 2.5:1, there is an implicit suggestion that the preferred one should be towards the middle of the range (Godkewitsch 1974; Piehl 1976). A second problem is that choosing one item from ten does not allow one to construct the 'preference function', which may well be multimodal. These and other problems are mostly solved by the method of paired comparisons, where on any one trial a subject makes a simple preference judgement between two items, randomly placed to right or left (and as Walter Pater said, 'Beauty,

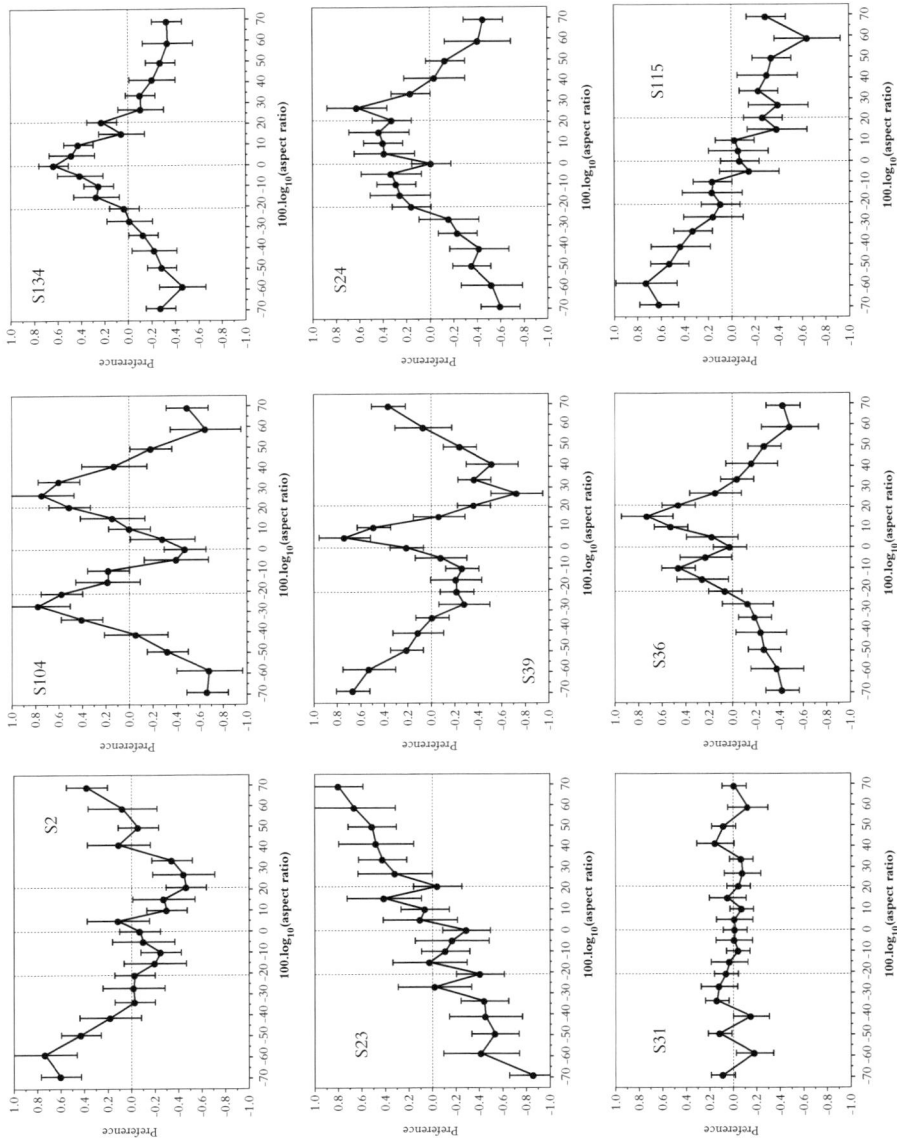

Figure 9.1 Examples of nine disparate sets of rectangle preferences (from McManus, Cook, and Hunt, in press)

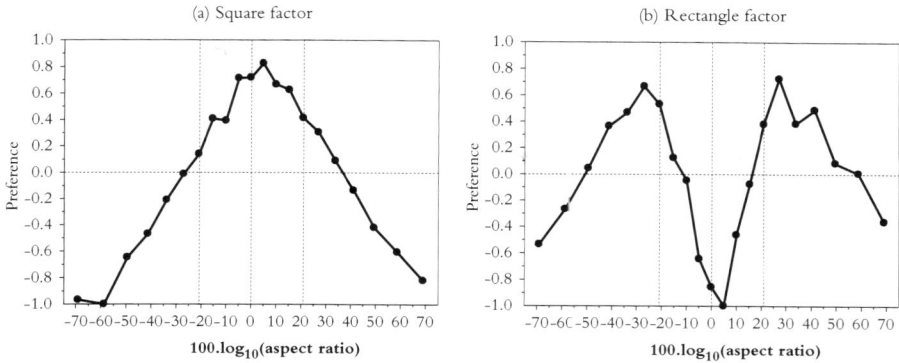

Figure 9.2 The two main underlying factors for the rectangle preferences, reconstructed from the Q-mode factor analysis (see text)

like all other qualities presented to human experience, is relative' (Tinio and Leder 2009: vii)). Such data allow the construction of preference functions *for each individual subject*. Then it is immediately obvious that there are very large individual differences, some preferring rectangles near the Golden Section, some preferring squares, some preferring long thin rectangles, some preferring horizontal but not vertical rectangles, or vice versa (McManus 1980). There are population preferences but they are extremely weak compared with the strong individual preferences, which are mostly stable over the short, medium, and long-term (more than two years later; McManus 1980). The graphs in Fig. 9.1 show some of the wide variety of rectangle preferences that we have found in our subjects, with most subjects showing statistically significant preferences (although S31 is indistinguishable from random responding) (McManus *et al.* 2010). As in my earlier study (McManus 1980), the technique of Q-mode factor analysis can be used to look for underlying commonalities in the preferences. There are at least two common factors, which are reconstructed in Fig. 9.2. Each subject's individual preferences can be seen as a mixture of these and perhaps other factors, which might include a horizontal–vertical asymmetry component. Several things are noteworthy in Fig. 9.2. The preference for the square is not precisely at the square but is shifted slightly to a more horizontal rectangle, probably due to the horizontal–vertical illusion (McManus 1978), suggesting that it is perceived squareness rather than mathematical squareness that underpins the judgement. Secondly, the rectangle factor is quite broad in its distribution and is *not* precisely at the Golden Section, the mode being for slightly more extreme rectangles (both horizontally and vertically, meaning the effect is not just due to the horizontal–vertical illusion). Some people do like rectangles, but there is no special status for the Golden Section rectangle. One possibility is that some people are searching for a 'canonical' rectangle—the sort of rectangle that would be drawn in a mathematics textbook to show the typical, general, almost Platonic, idea of a rectangle (McManus and Weatherby 1997).

Despite the venerable provenance for studying rectangle preferences, I invariably find that if I tell people that I study aesthetics, and then say that I look for preferences for white rectangles on a black background, there is a sense of disconnection, a worry that such studies cannot say anything about what is *really* art, or about the high-level aesthetic phenomena that fill art galleries and concern critics and artists themselves. And that concern does not seem entirely unjustified. Reductionism is a standard *modus operandi* for scientists, not because they believe the world is simple, but to a much greater extent because they realize they themselves, as well as their methods, are simple, so that the rich complexity of many phenomena is not available to formal analysis, particularly in laboratories. Fechner was working in such a tradition, but he also realized experimental aesthetics must in part address real works of art (and an early study was on the Dresden *Madonna* that was attributed to Holbein). There are though immediate problems, for real works of art are finite in number, their makers are often dead, or when alive will not manufacture hundreds of similar exemplars for a scientist's convenience, and manipulating a Rembrandt portrait runs the risk at best of hubris, and at worst of destroying the aesthetics of the image. The second study described here circumvents some of those problems by studying the works of Piet Mondrian's mature period, whose austere paintings with their white background, horizontal and vertical black lines, and areas of solid primary colour, are ideal for aesthetic research, being both undoubtedly high art of the highest aesthetic quality, recognized by critics, gallery goers, and the market alike, and yet are straightforward to simulate and manipulate on a computer screen.

## 5. The paintings of Mondrian

On 23 February 2009, a painting by Mondrian, *Composition with blue, red, yellow and black*, of 1922, sold for 21.9 million euros. The price, according to an article in the *International Herald Tribune* (1 August 2009), was 'understandable up to a point', because, 'The condition of the picture was superb *and the balance in the geometrical composition remarkable*' (my emphasis).

What is it about *Composition with blue, red, yellow and black* that might make its geometrical composition remarkable? The painting is abstract, and its impact must come from the positioning of the lines and colours. The corollary has to be that altering the precise positions of those lines should alter the geometry, and, in all probability, make it worse rather than better. Mondrian's working habits suggest that he was working towards some optimal combination of lines and colours, detailed analyses of his transatlantic paintings showing how, often over a period of years, he moved lines by small amounts, he added extra lines, he removed or added areas of colour, until eventually the painting was finished (or at least sold) (Cooper and Spronk 2001). This feels very like what scientists call a 'hill-climbing' procedure, small changes being made until some form of optimization occurs, no better result being achievable. If that is what Mondrian was doing, then perturbing the lines in the image should reduce the

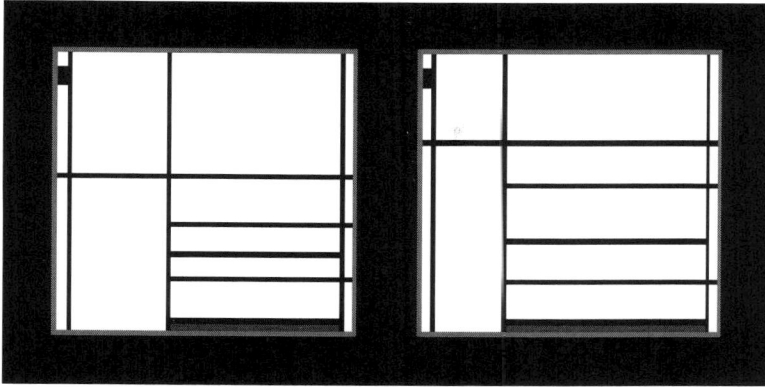

Figure 9.3 Two computer-generated Mondrian-like images, one of which, on the left, reproduces as exactly as possible the lines and colours of Mondrian's *Composition with Red and Black* of 1936 (Museum of Modern Art, New York), and the other, on the right, is a pseudo-Mondrian in which the positions of the black horizontal and vertical lines have been randomly 'nudged' (see McManus *et al.* 1993 for a description of the algorithm)

quality of the image. That is what we did in our experiment (McManus *et al.* 1993), the results being replicated several times since.

Figure 9.3 shows two images, both generated on a computer, one based on a real Mondrian and the other being a pseudo-Mondrian in which all of the lines have been randomly 'nudged' to move them from their original positions. Don't look at the caption yet, and try to assess what is different in these images. Is the balance in the geometrical composition of one somehow more remarkable than in the other? Now look at the caption and see if that is the one which is based on the real Mondrian. Our first study asked 52 people to make such preference judgements, using pairs of images based on 25 Mondrian paintings, with overall there being 75 binary choices for each subject. Imagine someone doing this with their eyes closed, so that they cannot see the images. In the long run, making 75 choices, they should be correct on average 37.5 times, just as if one tosses a coin 75 times one should in the long run get a head on 37.5 occasions. That is the null hypothesis. The key question is whether real subjects are correct more than 50 per cent of the time. The simple answer is that on average the real Mondrian was preferred to the pseudo-Mondrian on 54 per cent of occasions. The effect is not large, but statistically it is highly unlikely by chance. A real Mondrian therefore has something in its composition that makes it better, more attractive, more liked, more balanced, or whatever term one wishes to use. Look again at Fig. 9.3, and try and describe what feels different about the real Mondrian. No rational explanation seems possible, but there is something that can only be described as a feeling, an instinctive feeling, that one is better than the other. The effect is reminiscent of the type of beauty found in beautiful faces, where no one individual feature is responsible for the effect (and indeed some individual features may not be perfect) but the entire ensemble seems lovely, every piece perfectly related to the others in some way. The beauty lies in the configuration of the components, not in the beauty of the elements themselves. Even if a Mondrian can be seen as composed of rectangles, the ultimate effect does not lie in the simple aggregate of those rectangles, but in their configuration and interrelation.

The Mondrian study also forces other conclusions. As with the rectangle experiment, the average of 54 per cent does not properly summarize the findings, for some people seem particularly good at the task, being correct on nearly 80 per cent of trials, whereas others are not distinguishable from chance (and might as well have had their eyes closed), and there is a small group who are significantly much *worse* than chance—they consistently choose the pseudo-Mondrian. If the first group can be thought of as having excellent taste, the eye of the connoisseur, the latter group must be thought of as having bad taste. Beyond that, at present though, we know little about what characterizes these extreme groups. Not their personality, their interests in art, or any other measures we have yet found. But any workable theory of aesthetics has not only to explain why on average people can distinguish a real Mondrian from a fake, but also why some are better at it than others, and a few are terrible at it. There is also the deeper question, that Zangwill (2009: 19) has posed: 'what would be wrong with someone who lacked an aesthetic sensitivity?' We don't know at present, but it is an important question to ask.

In his studio, Mondrian created his paintings, by experimentally moving lines around, trying the effect, looking for some kind of optimum. The subjects in our experiments do not do that, but can merely compare. The third study was designed to make the participants in our experiments far more creative in their actions, dynamically selecting and choosing in much the same way that an artist might do.

## 6.  Photographic cropping

Fechner described three main ways of studying aesthetics scientifically, of which the most frequently used was the *Method of Choice*, where subjects choose between alternative stimuli, as in our studies on rectangles and Mondrian paintings. Subjects in laboratories are happy making such choices, although interestingly it can be harder to persuade practising artists to choose between alternatives, the artists typically saying that they do not wish to judge, and that they can see strengths and virtues in each of the images shown. Fechner's second method was the *Method of Use*, where one looks at objects produced in the world (and Fechner studied the proportions of visiting cards, crosses in graveyards, and doorways, and the canvases on which paintings were painted, none of which showed any evidence of the Golden Section being used preferentially). The method has several problems, not the least being that practical constraints (the objects are dependent, in Kant's sense) often override the purely aesthetic (so that the proportions of doors are constrained by the ergonomics of ingress and egress, rather than by aesthetics).

Fechner's third method, the *Method of Production*, has been little used, requiring subjects to *produce* aesthetically satisfactory objects, typically by drawing or painting, skills which most ordinary participants simply do not have at a sufficiently high level, and which are difficult to constrain satisfactorily in practising artists. Photography solves those problems. Almost everyone in the modern world not only has experience of looking at photographs and judging their quality, but also of pointing a camera and choosing the best view of a particular scene. We believe that photography, and particularly photographic cropping, could be an ideal research paradigm within experimental aesthetics, being both familiar enough for subjects to use it easily, constrainable enough to mean that experiments can look in detail at particular questions, rich enough, as there is almost no limit to the types of image that can be studied, and, most crucially, it is also acceptable to experts in photography as it feels realistic and a part of normal professional practice (McManus *et al.* forthcoming). As John Szarkowski has put it, 'The central act of photography [is] the act of choosing and eliminating' (Szarkowski 1966: 9), with the photographer asking, 'what shall he include, what shall he reject?' (Szarkowski 1966: 70), making photography 'a system of visual editing. At bottom, it is a matter of surrounding with a frame a portion of one's cone of vision, while standing in the right place at the right time' (Sontag 1979: 172; Szarkowski 1976). The outcome is what Henri Cartier-Bresson called, 'a precise organisation of forms which give [an] event its proper expression' (Cartier-bresson 1999: 42).

The task is shown in Fig. 9.4. In the *viewing phase* (Fig. 9.4a) the entire screen shows an image, which also contains a yellow *inclusion box*. This box shows what is, in some sense, the subject of the photograph, and it must be included in the final crop. Using the inclusion box is not essential but it does prevent crops of what, in effect, are entirely different scenes. The subject then clicks the mouse, most of the screen goes black, and the *crop window* appears (Fig. 9.4b), which can be moved using the mouse, and is a quarter the area (half the linear extent) of the full image, in the same aspect ratio. The inclusion box is no longer visible, but the software prevents the cropping window being moved so that the box is not fully included. The feeling of the experiment is similar to that of a photographer looking through a viewfinder and seeing a cropped portion of the visual world (and photography can be seen as a cropping of the visual world at a particular instant—what Susan Sontag has called 'a thin slice of space [and] time' (Sontag 1979: 22)). The subject moves the cropping window around, until the result looks 'best' (again, the instructions are purposely vague), when the mouse is then clicked, and the next viewing window appears. In a typical experimental block a subject may crop about 40 images, on average looking at the viewing window for about one or two seconds, and then cropping the image in about four to nine seconds. Subjects find the task interesting and natural, they have no problems in understanding what is required, and they say that it is fun to do. Wittgenstein would surely also have recognized the validity of the task, for it seems he obsessionally cropped photographs himself: 'Wittgenstein would devote hours to shaving off tiny slivers from the small photos he took before he would be satisfied with some kind of balance achieved' (Pascal 1981: 42). There is something here of the immediate judgements that he described when one designs a door, and says, 'Higher, higher, higher...oh, all right'

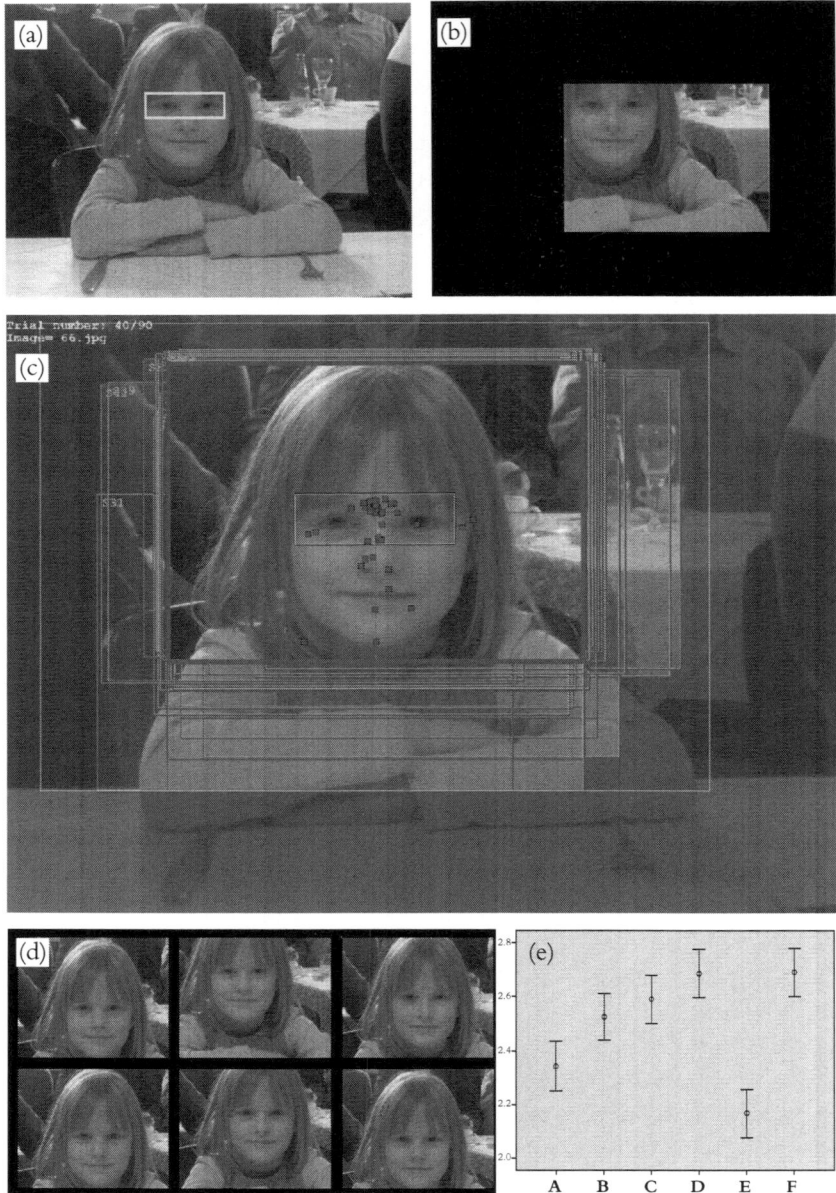

Figure 9.4 Example of an image used in the cropping experiment. (a) the viewing window with the inclusion box in yellow; (b) the cropping window, in which the inclusion box is no longer visible, and only a portion of the image can be seen through the cropping window; (c) a composite image showing the crops of 40 non-expert subjects—see text for further details; (d) six croppings of the image made by a maximally disparate set of subjects; (e) preferences of 21 judges for a set of croppings of 20 different images made by six croppers, A–F

(Wittgenstein 1970: 13), judgements in which in some sense there is a minimization of what Wittgenstein called 'aesthetic reactions e.g., discontent, disgust, discomfort' (Wittgenstein 1970: 13).

Figure 9.4c shows a typical *composite image*, which summarizes data from 40 non-expert subjects cropping Fig. 9.4a. The small yellow box at the centre is the inclusion box, and the larger yellow window is the possible range of crop windows given the inclusion box. Each subject's chosen crop is shown both in outline as a pastel coloured box, and by a small red square at the centre. The 'average' crop is shown by the large red box, which is at the median horizontal and vertical position chosen by all the subjects.

Without going into details, the key psychophysical features of the task are that it is reliable (when subjects re-crop 40 images without having been told that they will have to do so, they make very similar choices), and there are individual differences (people differ in their choices, as seen in Fig. 9.4d, but they are consistent). A key result, that some people are *better* croppers than others, was shown by presenting a new set of subjects (the 'judges') with sets of crops made by six different croppers, chosen as maximally different across their range of crops. Figure 9.4e shows one example, the six images being arranged randomly, and judges ranking them from Best, through Good, to Poor, and Worst, which are scored as 4, 3, 2, and 1. Figure 9.4f shows that the crops produced by croppers D and F were most preferred, while the crops produced by A and E were least preferred, the differences being highly significant statistically. That result confirms the task is genuinely an aesthetic one, and that there are individual differences in ability at cropping. A further study, showing photographs in colour, in monochrome, and 'thresholded', showed that colour, perhaps surprisingly, had little influence on crop location, whereas removing meaning, as in the thresholded images, whose content cannot be recognized by naive observers, moves the crop position dramatically. The latter implies that cropping cannot be merely a matter of patterns of light and shade (and the *Oxford Companion to the Photograph* includes tonal mass, and balance, as two of the features of good composition), but instead depends at least in part on the *meaning* of the image, on certain objects being particularly salient beyond their mere patterns of light and shade (although of course that does not mean, all other things being equal, that good crops do not also depend on patterns of light and shade). A final study used expert subjects studying on the MA Photography course at the Royal College of Art, and showed that experts are not only willing and able to carry out the task, but also that they systematically crop in different ways, being more variable in the possible crops they consider, and being more willing to choose crops that differ in their vertical position, from those of non-experts.

## 7. Conclusions

There are no grand conclusions from this overview of several sets of empirical work, except to conclude that there is an utter failure of grand theories of evolutionary psychology or neuroaesthetics to explain the wide variety or responses shown by subjects when making aesthetic preferences for rectangles or Mondrian paintings, or when cropping photographs. Grand theories are surely hopelessly premature in their grandiosity, and empirical studies constrain and test such theories by forcing attention on detail (and the devil for any theory is always in the details). The experimental stimuli are often simple, and the responses equally simple, but the participants are in little doubt that what they are doing is aesthetic, and that needs explaining.

In our experimental situations, subjects are by and large, as Nick Zangwill (2003: 336) has put it, 'responding aesthetically to no more than what confronts [their] senses', responding to the *free beauty* of the stimuli, which a stimulus has, 'just in virtue of how it is at that time' (Zangwill 2003: 332). Even if, as Danto said, 'the idea of beauty is a "mangled, sodden thing"', as he then continues, 'the *fact* of beauty is quite another matter' (2003: 29, emphasis in original); and that fact manifests in the judgements that are being made. Of course there is much more to high art and aesthetics than free beauty alone, for as Zangwill says, 'we become more sophisticated . . . But sophisticates should not deny the existence and importance of the primitive aesthetic response. The foundation of our sophisticated aesthetic life is the primitive enjoyment of free beauty' (Zangwill 2003: 336). Zangwill's 'primacy conjecture' puts simple judgements of beauty at centre-stage theoretically, for: 'without a conception of free beauty, no other beauty would be available to us. We can conceive of [dependent beauty] only because we can conceive of [free beauty]' (Zangwill 2003: 334–5). Experimental aesthetics, at least in the studies I am describing here, can be seen as an empirical exploration of the nature of free beauty. It might also meet the criteria of Zangwill (2009: 19) for a successful form of empirical research, in that, '(1) researchers operate with a concept of the aesthetic that allows them to distinguish aesthetic experiences from other experiences; and (2) that there is shrewd experimental design that is sensitive to the features of aesthetic experience that distinguish it from other kinds of experience.' In these three studies the task is explicitly aesthetic, and the design, with their close comparison of highly similar stimuli, means that there are few other psychological states that might be invoked to explain the behaviour. Demand characteristics might be one, but they would almost certainly result in a lack of long-term consistency (and subjects are generally reliable across time).

Near the end of *Speaking of Beauty*, Dennis Donoghue, in a chapter mainly concerned with Ruskin and his ideas on art, quotes a long passage from Walter Pater's *Studies in the History of the Renaissance* (1873). Donoghue emphasizes that Pater is attacking not only Ruskin, but also, 'the German Professors of aesthetics, who thought that they must define the principles of art before addressing its particles' (Donoghue 2003: 151). Pater was writing at much the same time as Fechner, but it is unlikely that Pater had read Fechner, and one hopes, Pater would not have included Fechner as one making that mistake, for his intention was to study aesthetics, 'von Oben *und von Unten*' (Fechner 1876: 1) (my emphasis). Pater concludes by suggesting what I think is precisely the right research program for psychological studies of art and aesthetics, one which I hope the studies in this chapter have shown in action:

To define beauty not in the most abstract, but in the most concrete terms possible, not to find a universal formula for it, but the formula which expresses most adequately this or that special manifestation of it, is the aim of the true student of aesthetics. (Pater 1873: vii)

When that has been done adequately will then be the time for grand theories.

# References

Arnheim, R. (1974). *Art and Visual Perception: A Psychology of the Creative Eye. The New Version.* Berkeley, CA: University of California Press.

——(1982). *The Power of the Center: A Study of Composition in the Visual Arts.* Berkeley, CA: University of California Press.

Binding, P. (2009). 'Landscapes of Deep Time'. *Times Literary Supplement* (7 August), p. 20.

Broadbent, S. (1980). 'Simulating the Ley Hunter'. *Journal of the Royal Statistical Society, A*, 143: 109–40.

Buss, D. (2009). 'How Can Evolutionary Psychology Successfully Explain Personality and Individual Differences?' *Perspectives on Psychological Science*, 4: 359–66.

Candlish, S. (2002). 'Testing Wittgenstein's Dismissal of Experimental Psychology against Examples'. *Noetica.* Available from http://www.scribd.com/doc/88252/Wittgenstein-on-Psychology.

Carroll, N. (1998). *A Philosophy of Mass Art.* Oxford: Clarendon Press.

Cartier-Bresson, H. (1999). *The Mind's Eye: Writings on Photography and Photographs.* New York: Aperture.

Clark, T. J. (2006). *The Sight of Death: An Experiment in Art Writing.* New Haven, CT: Yale University Press.

Cooper, H. and R. Spronk (2001). *Mondrian: The Transatlantic Paintings.* Cambridge, MA: Harvard University Art Museums.

Currie, G. (2003). 'Aesthetics and Cognitive Science', in J. Levinson (ed.), *The Oxford Handbook of Aesthetics.* Oxford: Oxford University Press, pp. 706–21.

Danto, A. C. (2003). *The Abuse of Beauty: Aesthetics and the Concept of Art.* Chicago: Open Court.

Darwin, C. (1874). *The Descent of Man and Selection in Relation to Sex*, 2nd edn. London: John Murray.

Dickie, G. (1962). 'Is Psychology Relevant to Aesthetics?' *Philosophical Review*, 71: 285–302.

Donoghue, D. (2003). *Speaking of Beauty.* New Haven: Yale University Press.

Duckworth, G. E. (1962). *Structural Patterns and Proportions in Virgil's Aeneid: A Study in Mathematical Composition.* Ann Arbor: University of Michigan Press.

Fechner, G. T. (1876). *Vorschule der Aesthetik.* Leipzig: Breitkopf & Haertel.

Fischler, R. (1981). 'How to Find the "Golden Number" without Really Trying'. *Fibonacci Quarterly*, 19: 406–10.

Funch, B. S. (1997). *The Psychology of Art Appreciation.* Copenhagen: Museum Tusculanum Press, University of Copenhagen.

Godkewitsch, M. (1974). 'The "Golden Section": An Artifact of Stimulus Range and Measure of Preference'. *American Journal of Psychology*, 87: 269–77.

Gombrich, E. H. (2006). 'Concerning "The Science of Art"'. *Journal of Consciousness Studies*, 7: 17.

Harré, R. and M. A. Tissaw (2005). *Wittgenstein and Psychology: A Practical Guide*. Aldershot: Ashgate.

Herz-Fischler, R. (1998). *A Mathematical History of the Golden Number*. Mineola, NY: Dover.

Höge, H. (1997). 'The Golden Section Hypothesis: Its Last Funeral'. *Empirical Studies of the Arts*, 15: 233–55.

Humphrey, N. K. (1972). '"Interest" and "Pleasure": Two Determinants of a Monkey's Visual Preferences'. *Perception*, 1: 395–416.

Hyman, J. (2006). 'In Search of the Big Picture'. *New Scientist* (15 August), pp. 44–5.

Inglis, F. (2007). 'Sublime Sights to Behold'. *Times Higher Education Supplement* (22 June), p. 22.

Jacobsen, T. (2004). 'Individual and Group Modelling of Aesthetic Judgment Strategies'. *British Journal of Psychology*, 95: 41–56.

——K. Buchta, M. Kohler, and E. Schroger (2004). 'The Primacy of Beauty in Judging the Aesthetics of Objects'. *Psychological Reports*, 94: 1253–60.

Junood, T. (2003). 'The Falling Man'. *The Observer (London), Review* (7 September), pp. 1–3.

Kant, I. (1952). *The Critique of Judgement*, trans. J. C. Meredith. Oxford: Oxford University Press.

Kent, S. (2009). 'Material World'. *RA Magazine* (Autumn), pp. 40–7.

Kluckhohn, C. K. M. and H. A. Murray (1953). *Personality in Nature, Society, and Culture*. New York: Knopf.

Leitner, B. (2000). *The Wittgenstein House*. New York: Princeton Architectural Press.

Livio, M. (2002). *The Golden Ratio: The Story of Phi, the Extraordinary Number of Nature, Art and Beauty*. London: Review/Headline.

McManus, I. C. (1978). 'The Horizontal–Vertical Illusion and the Square'. *British Journal of Psychology*, 69: 369–70.

——(1980). 'The Aesthetics of Simple Figures'. *British Journal of Psychology*, 71: 505–24.

——and A. Furnham (2006). 'Aesthetic Activities and Aesthetic Attitudes: Influences of Education, Background and Personality on Interest and Involvement in the Arts'. *British Journal of Psychology*, 97: 555–87.

——and P. Weatherby, P. (1997). 'The Golden Section and the Aesthetics of Form and Composition: A Cognitive Model'. *Empirical Studies of the Arts*, 15: 209–32.

——B. Cheema, and J. Stoker (1993). 'The Aesthetics of Composition: A Study of Mondrian'. *Empirical Studies of the Arts*, 11: 83–94.

——R. Cook, and A. Hunt (2010). 'Beyond the Golden Section and Normative Aesthetics: Why do Individuals Differ so Much in Their Aesthetic Preferences for Rectangles?' *Psychology of Aesthetics, Creativity, and the Arts*, 4: 113–26.

——A. Zhou, S. l'Anson, and L. Waterfield (2011). 'The Psychometrics of Photographic Cropping: The Influence of Colour, Meaning, and Expertise' *Perception*, 40: 332–57.

Mencken, H. L. (1917). 'The Divine Afflatus'. *New York Evening Mail* (16 November).

Monk, R. (1990). *Ludwig Wittgenstein: The Duty of Genius*. London: Jonathan Cape.

Nehamas, A. (2007). *Only a Promise of Happiness: The Place of Beauty in a World of Art*. Princeton, NJ: Princeton University Press.

Ogden, C. K., I. A. Richards, and J. Wood (1922). *The Foundations of Aesthetics*. London: George Allen & Unwin.

Pascal, F. (1981). 'Wittgenstein: A Personal Memoir', in R. Rhees (ed.), *Ludwig Wittgenstein: Personal Recollections*. Oxford: Blackwell, pp. 26–62.

Pater, W. (1873). *Studies in the History of the Renaissance*. London.

Piehl, J. (1976). 'The "Golden Section": An Artefact of Stimulus Range and Demand Characteristics'. *Perceptual and Motor Skills*, 43: 47–50.

Ramachandran, V. S. and W. Hirstein (1999). 'The Science of Art: A Neurological Theory of Aesthetic Experience'. *Journal of Consciousness Studies*, 6: 15–51.

Ramsey, F. P. (1923). 'Review of *Tractatus Logico-Philosophicus*'. *Mind*, 32: 465–78.

——(1990). *Philosophical Papers* , ed. D. H. Mellor. Cambridge: Cambridge University Press.

Ross, D. W. (1907). *A Theory of Pure Design: Harmony, Balance, Rhythm*. Boston: Houghton Mifflin.

Sartwell, C. (2006). *Six Names of Beauty*. New York: Routledge.

Schroeder, J. E. (2006). 'Aesthetics Awry: The Painter of Light and the Commodification of Artistic Values'. *Consumption, Markets and Culture*, 9: 87–99.

Smith, J. K. and L. F. Wolf (1996). 'Museum Visitor Preferences and Intentions in Constructing Aesthetic Experience'. *Poetics*, 24: 219–38.

Solso, R. L. (2003). *The Psychology of Art and the Evolution of the Conscious Brain*. Cambridge, MA: MIT Press.

Sontag, S. (1979). *On Photography*. Harmondsworth: Penguin.

——(2004). *Regarding the Pain of Others*. London: Penguin.

Sosa, E. (2007). 'Experimental Philosophy and Philosophical Intuition'. *Philosophical Studies*, 132: 99–107.

Szarkowski, J. (1966). *The Photographer's Eye*. New York: Museum of Modern Art.

——(1976). 'Introduction', in *William Eggleston's Guide*. Cambridge, MA: MIT Press.

Tinio, P. P. L. and H. Leder (2009). 'Natural Scenes are Indeed Preferred, but Image Quality Might Have the Last Word'. *Psychology of Aesthetics, Creativity and the Arts*, 3: 52–6.

von Wright, G. H. (1963). *The Logic of Preference*. Edinburgh: Edinburgh University Press.

Whitford, F. (2009). 'Damozels, not Demoiselles'. *Times Literary Supplement* (7 August), pp. 19–20.

Wijdeveld, P. (1994). *Ludwig Wittgenstein, Architect*. London: Thames & Hudson.

Wilson, A. (2006). 'America's Most Wanted'. *Modern Painters* (July–August), pp. 94–7.

Winston, A. S. (1995). 'Simple Pleasures: The Psychological Aesthetics of High and Popular Art'. *Empirical Studies of the Arts*, 13: 193–203.

Wittgenstein, L. (1970). *Lectures and Conversations on Aesthetics, Psychology and Religious Belief*. Oxford: Blackwell.

——and B. Muscio (1912). 'Experiments on Rhythm (Demonstration)'. *British Journal of Psychology*, 5: 356.

Wittkower, R. (1971). *Architectural Principles in the Age of Humanism*. London: Tiranti.

Zangwill, N. (2001). *The Metaphysics of Beauty*. Ithaca: Cornell University Press.

——(2003). 'Beauty', in J. Levinson (ed.), *The Oxford Handbook of Aesthetics*. Oxford: Oxford University Press, pp. 325–43.

——(2009). 'Aesthetic Experience', in T. Bayne, A. Cleeremans, and P. Wilken (eds.), *The Oxford Companion to Consciousness*. Oxford: Oxford University Press, pp. 16–19.

Zeising, A. (1854). *Neue Lehre von den Proportionen des menschlichen Körpers*. Leipzig: R. Weigel.

Zeki, S. (n.d.). *Statement on Neuroesthetics*. http://neuroesthetics.org/statement-on-neuroes-thetics.php [Accessed 3 October 2009]. Document undated but probably April 2003.

# 10

# Beauty is Not One: The Irreducible Variety of Visual Beauty

*Jerrold Levinson*

'The saying that beauty is but skin-deep is but a skin-deep saying.'

Herbert Spencer, "Personal Beauty" (1854)

## I

When you look at (a) Matisse's *Red Studio*, (b) a cycloid or a parabola, (c) a gently flowing river or a rose in bloom, (d) a Ming vase or a Mies van der Rohe chair, (e) the face of Michelle Pfeiffer or the body of Halle Berry, and think to yourself "How beautiful!", is the judgment you are making in each case substantially the same judgment? Does your experience in each case testify to substantially the same property of the object in question? My answer, which I attempt to defend here, is a resounding "no."

Such an answer certainly has precedents. Consider what the early twentieth-century British theorist Clive Bell has to say about beauty in his celebrated book on art:

When an ordinary man speaks of a beautiful woman he certainly does not mean only that she moves him aesthetically ... Indeed, most of us never dream of going for aesthetic emotions to human beings, from whom we ask something very different. This 'something', when we find it in a young woman, we are apt to call 'beauty'. We live in a nice age. With the man-in-the-street 'beautiful' is more often than not synonymous with 'desirable' ... I have noticed a consistency in those to whom the most beautiful thing in the world is a beautiful woman, and the next most beautiful thing a picture of one ... Clearly, the word 'beauty' is used to connote the objects of quite distinguishable emotions.[1]

However, it's fair to say that the weight of theoretical opinion is rather on the other side, favoring the sameness of beauty across its manifestations.[2] In opposition to that

---

[1] *Art* (London: Chatto & Windus, 1914), p. 15.

[2] Such a consensus is noted recently by one contemporary researcher: "Running as a common thread through the discourses on beauty, from pre-Socratic times onward, is an aesthetic based on proportion and number ... Common to all these theories is the idea that the properties of beauty are the same whether we are

widespread sentiment, my aim in this chapter is to show, rather more in sympathy with Bell, that there really are different species of beauty, and thus that the genus of beauty has only a superficial unity. I aim to show that, most notably, natural beauty, artistic beauty, and physical beauty are three quite different phenomena.

For simplicity, and because it is the original home of beauty understood literally, my attention in this chapter is restricted to the *visual* realm, that is, to beauty that is accessible to *sight*. My topic is thus *visual beauty*. I am here interested in beauty as a *specific* positive aesthetic attribute, one traditionally associated with harmony, order, and pleasingness, and not in beauty understood as aesthetic excellence in general; rough equivalents for beauty in this narrow sense are thus charm, prettiness, loveliness, gorgeousness. Beauty in the sense I am interested in is distinct, furthermore, from aesthetic attributes such as profundity, imaginativeness, expressiveness, and so on, which do not turn on the notion of affording pleasure in visually beholding. Finally, beauty in the narrow sense I am targeting is also distinct from more closely related aesthetic attributes such as gracefulness, delicacy or elegance; these either contribute to beauty in the narrow sense, or else are themselves even narrower species of beauty.

There is, of course, already precedent for distinguishing different positive aesthetic responses in the traditional opposition, firmly established by the eighteenth century, between the beautiful and the sublime.[3] The response associated with the latter clearly includes an affective and/or cognitive element absent in the response associated with the former. In a nutshell, the sublime is disturbing and unsettling, whereas the beautiful is delighting and invigorating.[4] Paradigms of sublime objects are raging torrents, towering mountains, bottomless chasms, ocean tempests, grizzly bears, the nighttime sky with its multitude of stars, and the appearance of Zeus as a ravishing swan in the eyes of Leda as described in Yeats's poem of that name. Paradigms of beautiful objects, by contrast, are flowers, trees, sunsets, lakes, valleys, dresses, vases, necklaces, and a range of human beings.

But what do all such paradigms of visual beauty have in common? The essential feature of all species of visual beauty, as already hinted, is a connection with pleasure in viewing, beholding, or contemplating: visually beautiful things are things it is pleasurable to view, things that are pleasurable to view precisely in virtue of how they look or appear visually, and not, say, in virtue of their being instrumentally valuable or cognitively intriguing to us.[5] In other words, visually beautiful things

---

seeing a beautiful woman, a flower, a landscape, or a circle" (Nancy Etcoff, *Survival of the Prettiest* (New York: Doubleday), p. 15).

[3] See, most importantly, the writings of Burke, Addison, Kant, Schiller, and Schopenhauer.

[4] Of course that contrast, as befits what can fit in a nutshell, is too crude. For some beauty is aptly described as *thrilling*, which would seem to range it more with cases of the sublime.

[5] A definition in this spirit is given in a recent dictionary of philosophical ideas: "Belleza: caratteristica di tutto quanto viene percepito con un'approvazione e un piacere immediati, disgiunti da ogni scopo esterno alla percezione stessa." ["The characteristic of everything that is perceived with immediate approbation and pleasure, apart from any external aim or interest."]Ermanno Bencivenga, *Parole che contano* (Milan: Mondadori, 2004), p. 24.

are things we derive pleasure merely from beholding, whose mere appearance pleases us, and which we are inclined, all things being equal, to continue beholding.[6]

I try to forestall in this formulation the objection that there are surely different sorts of visual pleasure, and thus that the beautiful cannot be adequately captured simply as that which provides such pleasure, by underlining that what is in question where the beautiful is concerned is pleasure that comes merely from looking or that is rooted in mere appearance.[7] The beautiful so conceived falls squarely in the tradition of theorizing beauty that is associated with Kant.

Before proceeding, though, I must briefly acknowledge another tradition of theorizing beauty, initiated by Plato, that makes of it a richer affair, or sets for it a higher standard. This is a tradition according to which beauty is not simply that which gives us pleasure to behold, but rather that which inspires us, ennobles us, summons us to transcendence and offers us, in Nietzsche's words, not just pleasure in contemplation but a vivid "promise of happiness."[8]

My view is that although this is a power or an effect of some beautiful objects, of certain sorts, in some conditions of reception, it does not characterize all such objects or occasions of beholding. The more earthbound, quasi-Kantian[9] conception of beauty articulated above is thus more apt for covering the full range of things that are found visually beautiful. Or so it seems to me.

My thesis, again, is that there are several fundamentally different species of visual beauty. How, though, is the real difference between different species of visual beauty to be established? What criterion of real difference of beauties should we appeal to? Compare human weight, animal weight, and inanimate weight. Clearly, these are all the same thing, namely, weight, or the downward force exerted by a body in virtue of the pull of gravity upon it. That the weight is attributable to a person, an animal, or an object makes no difference. What is attributed is the same property in each case. In other words, it's all weight.[10] So why, then, think that there is a multiplicity of kinds of visual beauty? Surely the mere great diversity of things that display visual beauty does not impel us to any such conclusion.

---

[6] That said, is a thing's visual beauty precisely the same as its *power* to give pleasure to viewers who behold it? Or is a thing's visual beauty rather a complex kind of *appearance*, dependent on lower-level visual features, an appearance that *has* the power to produce pleasure in viewers? I will here remain neutral on this difficult metaphysical issue.

[7] Thus the perverse pleasure in dwelling on the sight of car crashes, featured in the J.G. Ballard novel *Crash*, would not necessarily testify to the visual beauty of such crashes, because the pleasure is represented as rooted in and deriving from more than appearances *per se*.

[8] See the recent passionate study by Alexander Nehamas, *Only a Promise of Happiness* (Princeton: Princeton University Press, 2007).

[9] It is at most quasi-Kantian, for at least two reasons. First, no credence is given to the idea of beauty as the symbol of *morality*. Second, not all the varieties of beauty that I acknowledge are such as call for *disinterested* contemplation; most notably physical beauty, as I conceive it, calls for contemplation of the most interested sort.

[10] This is the basis of the old joking riddle, "Which weighs more, a pound of gold or a pound of feathers?"

On the other hand, perhaps the parallel with weight does not extend as far as all that. For there is no temptation to say of a weighted person, animal, or object that each is weighted, or has weight, *in its own way*. But when it comes to the beauty exhibited by a person's face, a tidepool, a Cezanne still life, and a suspension bridge by Santiago Calatrava, it is almost impossible to avoid remarking that each is, indeed, *beautiful in its own way*. Beauties in the different categories differ in how they strike us as beautiful, in a way that weighted things do not in respect of their weight. Beautiful women, beautiful paintings, and beautiful bridges differ in the respective beautiful appearances they present; apart from all producing immediate visual pleasure in the viewer, their beautiful appearances seem to be of radically different sorts.

For the moment, and without as yet much in the way of theoretical defense, it seems to me that there are at least six fundamentally different properties of visual beauty. I will label these *abstract beauty, artistic beauty, artifactual beauty, natural beauty, physical beauty*, and *moral beauty*, the last two being modes of *human beauty*.[11] Furthermore, within most of those six categories are subcategories of beauty of sufficient importance as almost to merit recognition themselves as distinct categories of beauty.

## II

Let us begin by distinguishing the beauty of patterns or configurations by themselves, what we may label *formal beauty*, a subcategory of abstract beauty, and the beauty of such patterns or configurations as they occur in works of abstract art such as the canvases of Klee, Mondrian, Barnett Newman, Kenneth Noland, or Frank Stella, which is a species of *artistic beauty*.[12] It is not hard to show that formal beauty and this sort of artistic beauty, though it is easy to conflate them, are distinct. In the case of artworks, such patterns or configurations are not appreciated merely for their geometric or spatial properties, but also for what they may represent, symbolize, exemplify or express. As Arthur Danto puts it, "At a minimum, art has a content that must be grasped; it is, in contrast with skies and flowers, about something."[13] A giant red rectangle broken only by a black off-center vertical in a painting by Newman has an import difference from that it possesses as a mere configuration; as a painting it speaks of oneness and infinity. And a stripe painting by Noland or Stella has an import not found in the mere pattern it contains, bearing a message of streamlined cool and machinelike

---

[11] To forestall misunderstanding, I don't mean to deny that *animals* can display physical beauty in the sexual-attraction-based sense I have in mind. However, that would be a physical beauty that we are not well positioned to directly estimate, since the constitutive responses of desire and attraction are presumably not evoked in us by members of other species. In any event, I am here only interested in *human* physical beauty, and so that qualification should be understood as attaching to occurrences of "physical beauty" in what follows.

[12] Formal beauty is the most important subcategory of abstract beauty in the visual realm, but is not coincident with it, however, because of the existence of *qualitative* beauty, that is, the beauty of colors *per se*.

[13] "Beauty and Beautification," in P. Brand (ed.), *Beauty Matters* (Bloomington: Indiana University Press, 2000), p. 66.

efficiency.[14] Thus, even if both the pure patterns or configurations and the paintings that contain them are all beautiful, the beauty of the latter seems a different property from the beauty of the former, since in part a function of meanings and how they are embodied visually.

Put otherwise, the beauty of patterns or configurations in art is always *dependent* beauty, in the sense we owe largely to Kant. That is, it is beauty that depends upon the object being perceived *under some concept*, in this case, a concept of the object as an artwork, something with a potential significance. As one writer has it, "In order to see a thing as having dependent beauty, one must see it as a thing of a certain kind."[15] Once one construes something as an object of a certain kind and not simply an abstract sensory presentation, it takes on a different appearance, and displays properties it would otherwise lack. An object viewed under some object concept is seen as *for* something, as having *arisen* in a certain way, as having some characteristic *activity*, or the like. It is seen, in short, as having an *identity*, often of a purposive or functional sort.[16]

Much the same can be said when one considers patterns as found in works of craft, such as oriental rugs. Such patterns are appreciated, first, in relation to the design of the rug as a whole; second, in relation to the function of a rug as a floor covering to be viewed from above and trod upon; and third, in relation to the natural forms, of vegetation or whatnot, that such patterns are often derived from and still lightly evoke. So the beauty of rug patterns, in Kant's terms, is also a kind of dependent, rather than free, beauty.

Before proceeding further we may note that even the beauty of abstract forms may not always be entirely free, that is, unmediated by object concepts mobilized by the viewer. Take the curves known as cycloids and catenaries. These strike me as beautiful curves, but perhaps their generating concepts—the former the trajectory of a point on the circumference of a circle rolling on a straight line, the latter the shape assumed by a chain suspended from its endpoints under the force of gravity—enter tangentially into my impression of them as beautiful. Still, I take it that formal beauty is normally not conceptually mediated to any appreciable degree, and may hence be considered more or less free beauty in the sense Kant had in mind, thus distinguishing it and the other species of abstract beauty, namely qualitative beauty, such as that possessed by shades of color, from all the other varieties of visual beauty with which we are concerned.

---

[14] See Leo Steinberg, "Other Criteria,", in *Other Criteria: Confrontations with Twentieth-Century Art* (New York: Oxford University Press, 1972).

[15] Nick Zangwill, "Beauty," in J. Levinson (ed.), *Oxford Handbook of Aesthetics* (Oxford: Oxford University Press, 2003), p. 332.

[16] For a good discussion of dependent beauty understood specifically as functional beauty, see Stephen Davies, "Aesthetic Judgements, Artworks, and Functional Beauty," *Philosophical Quarterly*, 56 (2006): 224–41. However, Davies's claim that all beauty is in effect functional, and so dependent, beauty, is not one to which I can subscribe.

# III

Consider now the *physical beauty* of human beings. I will argue that such beauty is virtually equivalent to *sexual beauty*, though the two are *not entirely* coincident. At any rate the *core* of human physical beauty, I contend, is sexual beauty, and I will be concerned to underline the consequences of that for my main thesis, the irreducible variety of visual beauty.

The next thing to note about physical beauty, by which I mean the physical beauty of adult men and women, is that we have once again to do with a mode of *dependent* beauty, beauty that is perceived as such only when its possessor is seen *as* a human being, a creature of a certain sort, as one recent writer makes plain in his discussion of the topic:

The aesthetics of human beings is somewhat anomalous from the point of view of the usual division of the objects of aesthetic interest into art and nature . . . Neither art nor nature will do as a model for thinking about the beauty of human beings . . . Personal beauty is clearly dependent beauty. A person is beautiful not as an abstract sculpture, but as a human being.[17]

So human physical beauty, like almost every other sort of beauty, is dependent beauty. But in what does its specificity reside, apart from its dependence on a concept of the human necessarily deployed by the beholder in registering such beauty? The specificity of physical beauty, I suggest, understood as comprising both facial and bodily beauty, is its power to induce, in appropriate viewers, pleasure in viewing of a certain kind, namely, pleasure in which feelings of *attraction or desire* are involved.

As many have noted, the perception of human physical beauty impels us toward the beautiful object. We are drawn to it, transfixed by it, and long to possess it.[18] Not to put too fine a point on it, we want, if only subconsciously, to mate with, have intercourse with, or make love with, the person who displays it. The evolutionary reasons for this are both readily apparent and widely known. Here is a recent summary of the case for physical beauty as a sexually rooted biological adaptation:

The argument is a simple one: that beauty is a universal part of human experience, and that it provokes pleasure, rivets attention, and impels actions that help ensure the survival of our genes. Our extreme sensitivity to beauty is hard-wired, that is, governed by circuits in the brain shaped by natural selection. We love to look at smooth skin, thick shiny hair, curved waists, and symmetrical bodies because in the course of evolution the people who noticed these signals and desired their possessors had more reproductive success. We are their descendants.[19]

---

[17] Zangwill, "Beauty," p. 336.

[18] Some of the peremptory and commanding character of human beauty is conveyed by this telling remark: "But what is beauty? . . . It's when someone walks in the door and you almost can't breathe" (Etcoff, *Survival of the Prettiest*, p. 7). Or in this one as well, though less approvingly: "The glamorous body's allure is not a spiritual radiance, but a sexual magnetism that pulls the enchanted viewer off course" (Kathleen Higgins, "Beauty and Its Kitsch Competitors," in Brand (ed.), *Beauty Matters*, p. 93). Note also that one of the most common terms for a high degree of human, especially female, beauty is the word "stunning."

[19] Etcoff, *Survival of the Prettiest*, p. 24.

Now one may be inclined to object that human physical beauty should not be understood as having an essential connection with desire, because that would be to equate physical beauty and sexual attractiveness, yet it is widely thought that these are not the same thing: someone might be physically beautiful without being sexually attractive, and sexually attractive without being physically beautiful. My response to this is to deny at least the first half of the datum, which strikes me as not a little sanctimonious. Viewed honestly, I suggest, there cannot be physical beauty without sexual attractiveness to an appropriate class of perceivers.

As remarked at the outset, sexual attractiveness is the *core* of physical beauty. But it is not quite the whole of it, for though they are closely linked, there is an asymmetry between them. The physical beauty of men and women, I submit, presupposes sexual attractiveness, so that a person cannot be physically beautiful without being at the same time sexually attractive, at least to an appropriate class of perceivers. But sexual attractiveness seems not to strictly presuppose physical beauty, and can sometimes emerge, for various reasons, where physical beauty is absent. But then what characterizes those cases, arguably a minority, of sexual attractiveness *without* physical beauty? More or less this: the desire to draw near to and to interact with the person—the desire for sexual intimacy—but not also pleasure in visually beholding the person's visual appearance for its own sake.

I must now address, however inadequately, the thorny issue of who are the appropriate viewers for a subcategory of human sexual beauty. For the beauty of women the default answer, one might suggest, albeit with trepidation, is adult heterosexual men, and perhaps within that class, the subclass that is of the same race as the woman in question. One will be quick to object that this is too limiting, and unnecessarily so, since the beauty of a white woman, say, might very well be adequately gauged by a homosexual white man, a heterosexual black man, or a woman of any race.[20] That may be true, but the point is not who is *capable* of judging of such beauty, but rather whose pleasurable reaction of desire or attraction should be taken as *criterial* of the species of human beauty in question. And on a response-dependent and sexual-desire-linked conception of human beauty, the appropriate primary reference class would seem to be roughly as indicated.[21]

---

[20] As for how individuals not in the class criterial of a given kind of human beauty might reliably judge of it, there are a number of possibilities. One is that even if one is not of that class, one's response tendencies may be nonetheless sufficiently *similar* to those of individuals in that class. Two is that one may *simulate* the responses of individuals in the criterial class by vividly imagining being someone of that sort, by putting oneself imaginatively into their bodies and minds. Three is that one may *infer* those responses on the basis of knowledge, either tacit or explicit, of how such individuals respond to such and such visually perceivable features of human beings.

[21] That said, one might go on to allow that a person whose appearance induced a pleasurable reaction of desire or attraction in those *outside* the class criterial of the kind of beauty in question was, in a sense, *even more* beautiful, in giving evidence of a broader power to affect human sensibility in a positive manner. But it should be underlined that inducing such reactions *only* in members of the criterial class does not in any way count *against* a person's beauty, that is, does not count against a person's being wholly or entirely beautiful. Alternatively, one might agree to relativize the subcategories of human beauty to specific reference classes

I have not yet said anything, it will be noted, about the much noted social construction of sexual beauty, of the role that cultural context and tradition play in shaping norms of human physical beauty. I have no interest in denying such a role, or the variability in norms that results from it. As is well known, for instance, standards of fleshiness for womanly beauty have fluctuated markedly over the ages and from one society to another, and that this often reflects certain underlying political and economic realities. Here I would only insist that such variability, viewed from a distance, is not really all that great, and that certain features, such as symmetry, smoothness, youthfulness, occupy a non-negotiable place in what makes for human physical beauty, in contrast to the immense variability in the forms of artistic beauty, for which no such roster of non-negotiable features could plausibly be drawn up.

It may help to dissipate some of the resistance to the idea of closely tying physical beauty and sexual desirability if one distinguishes *judging* or *estimating* a person to be physically beautiful and *experiencing* or *registering* a person's physical beauty. The latter plausibly requires feeling the sexual appeal of the person, whereas the former does not. But even such judging arguably presupposes that feelings of sexual attraction exist on the part of members of the appropriate reference class for the human beauty in question, even if the judger does not himself or herself have such feelings on viewing the person in question. For otherwise, it is unclear what the substance of the judgment could be.

It has been suggested that when someone judges a person physically beautiful to whom he or she does not feel attracted the substance of the judgment is just that the person is an *exemplary specimen* of humankind. But that cannot be right, for it would be to effectively make the judgment a judgment of perfection, not a judgment of beauty, and one from which the character of immediate pleasure in appearance would appear to have evaporated. The beauty that putatively attaches to men and women who are exemplars of the kind *human being*, where such exemplariness is independent of and unrelated to sexual attractiveness, is, I think, a myth.

Resistance to the idea that physical beauty is roughly tantamount to sexual attractiveness also stems, in part, from the fact that we are often presented with *mixed cases*, that is, with individuals who exhibit a conjunction of physical beauty and some *other* kind of human beauty, such as *moral* beauty, or *athletic* beauty, or *natural* beauty of an animate sort, on all of which I will soon touch briefly. Thus when we judge such individuals beautiful our judgment is not entirely addressed to physical beauty, and we may in addition be unaware of the mixed nature of beauty judgment we are making, and hence of the proportion that narrowly concerns physical beauty. In any case,

---

of viewers, recognizing reference classes other than the default one for a given subcategory of beautiful person. This would lead to recognizing, for example, not the beauty of white women *per se*, but rather, the beauty of white women for white heterosexual men, the beauty of white women for black heterosexual men, the beauty of white women for Asian homosexual women, and so on. But such manifold beauties, thus relativized, would still count as objective properties of appearance.

I would deny that human physical beauty can be detached from sexual attractiveness, and attribute some of the hesitation on this score to the fact that physical beauty is often conjoined or admixed with beauties of other sorts, which complicates matters.

Finally, it might be objected to the rough identification I have proposed of physical beauty and sexual attractiveness that if one accepts that one loses the possibility, which seems a coherent one, of explaining *why* one is sexually attracted to a person precisely *by* citing their being physically beautiful. But that is not, on reflection, surprising, if physical beauty and sexual attractiveness are intimately connected in the way I have suggested. It would be like explaining why one desires to eat a certain dish by citing its appetizingness; that is, it would be to offer a pseudo-explanation, since appetizingness is naturally understood in terms of a disposition to induce just such a desire in eaters.

## IV

The human beauty I have been concerned with so far, namely the physical beauty of adult men and women, is tantamount to, or at least necessarily intertwined with, desirability or attractiveness, and so is roughly equatable with sexual beauty. But there is admittedly human beauty of *other* kinds, such as that displayed by young children, which is presumably non-sexual. Such beauty may be assimilated, I suggest, to natural beauty of an *animate* sort, such as that exhibited by swans or gazelles. Another sort of human beauty, again presumably non-sexual, is what one can label *athletic* beauty, perhaps also a species of natural beauty, one that we share with animals such as panthers or horses.

But there is also the human beauty of a wizened sage or kindly grandmother, which fits under neither physical beauty nor natural beauty. If admitted, those are examples of what I will here label *moral beauty*. Moral beauty covers appearances that we behold with pleasure because of traits of character or virtue that seem visually manifest in a person's outward form. Such beauty is sometimes also labeled "inner beauty," "spiritual beauty," or "'beauty of soul."[22]

Note that the admirable qualities manifest in a person's appearance that make for what I have labeled *moral beauty* are not necessarily *narrowly* moral ones. So, to be sure, honesty, benevolence, fairness, and generosity figure there; but so also do courage, strength, determination, loyalty, perspicacity, and the like. And for moral beauty to count as a species of visual beauty, it should be underlined, the pleasure must derive from beholding such traits *as seemingly manifest* in a person's appearance. It is not a matter of *rationally assessing* such traits as good, and so according their possessor moral

---

[22] Something like this sort of human beauty is evoked in the following passage from a recent essay on our topic: "Human beauty is not only skin deep; instead, it emerges from a condition of integration that encompasses body and soul, however the latter term is understood … One sees the beautiful person as radiant, and this radiance depends on a wholeness that we take to include the person's inner life" (Higgins, "Beauty and Its Kitsch Competitors," pp. 104–5).

approval. Nor is it a matter of whether the person presenting such traits in appearance *actually possesses* them as personal qualities, that is, is in fact a virtuous, noble, or soulful person. So moral beauty as characterized here is no guarantee of moral worth, though part of its appeal is no doubt the *suggestion* that such worth obtains.[23]

## V

We have seen some reasons to think that formal beauty and artistic beauty are not the same thing, that formal beauty and physical beauty are not the same, and that physical beauty and artistic beauty are not the same. These reasons include: (a) differences in the bases, or features causally responsible for, a given beauty; (b) differences in what viewers attend to or focus on in finding a given object beautiful; and (c) differences of an internal sort in the experience of the given beauty. I will return to these grounds of difference among beauties later on, after reviewing four other kinds of visual beauty.

Consider next *natural beauty*, such as that of landscape, seascape, fauna, and flora. It seems clear that this is, once again, like all beauty other than abstract beauty, a species of dependent beauty, beauty that is mediated by our sense of what the objects of nature are, how they arose, what processes of change they are subject to, and how they are disposed in relation to human beings. The shapes and colors we find most appealing in a landscape are not necessarily those we find most appealing as abstract forms, nor those we find most appealing in a human face or a work of art. Our response to such shapes and colors is mediated by our awareness of what those shapes and colors represent, and especially if the speculations of some evolutionary psychologists are correct, of whether such a scene is congenial to human flourishing. But natural beauty is clearly not the same as sexual beauty, since it does not induce desire for physical possession, and is plausibly not the same as either artistic or artifactual beauty, since although mediated by concepts, assessments of intention and purpose play no part in finding something to be naturally beautiful, or beautiful as a part of nature.[24]

Natural beauty as dependent on a conception of the object in question, one with a characteristic place or role in the natural scheme, but not one that we credit with powers of design at a high level, is nicely captured in this example of Malcolm Budd's:

What is the object of delight . . . when we take an aesthetic delight in birdsong as birdsong? . . . We delight in the seemingly endless and effortless variety of a song thrush's song . . . but not as the product of artistry . . . The object of aesthetic delight is the sounds as issuing naturally from a living, sentient creature, more specifically, a bird.[25]

---

[23] It hardly needs underlining that *physical* beauty does not necessarily betoken moral worth, but here is a reminder anyway, from a song of Hall and Oates: "the beauty is there, but a beast is in her heart . . ." (*Maneater*).

[24] Unless, of course, theistic assumptions are being made according to which nature is the product of a supremely powerful and intelligent Grand Designer.

[25] "The Aesthetic Appreciation of Nature," *British Journal of Aesthetics*, 36 (1996), pp. 211–12.

It is important to underline that when I speak of the response to natural beauty I mean the beauty response proper to nature *as* nature, where the thought of the object of perception as natural permeates and regulates the response, as in Budd's example. Of course a portion of nature, such as a scene of mountain aspens in the fall, *might* be regarded as if it were just an abstract array of colors and shapes, or alternatively, as if it were some sort of monumental artwork. And so regarded, it might strike one as beautiful. But that would not be a perception or registering of the scene's properly *natural* beauty.

A subcategory of natural beauty worthy of special note is that of animals, including human beings, in motion—what one might denominate *athletic* beauty. Such beauty resides in the suppleness, grace, speed, and assurance of the bodily movements involved.[26] In any case it seems clear that athletic beauty, whether animal or human— that is, whether displayed by panthers and horses or by boxers and footballers—is distinct from the physical beauty of face and body discussed earlier, which a beautiful human being displays even when entirely motionless.

# VI

Turn now to *artifactual* beauty, that is, the beauty of non-art artifacts, including craft objects, such as the oriental rugs mentioned earlier. Artifactual beauty is not precisely identifiable with artistic beauty, since although both are highly dependent on the categories under which the object in question is conceptualized, and on assessments of intention and purpose and of the adjustment of means to ends, in the beauty of artworks, though not that of non-art artifacts, there is always a dimension of *content*, and a sense of the fittingness of such content to the form in which it has been embodied. In other words, viewed as art, the perceivable form of an artwork is apprehended, not in relation to the fulfillment of basic human needs, nor in relation to the satisfaction of utilitarian ends, nor again as merely abstract patterning, but as something which potentially has something to *say* through such form. When that saying seems to us fine, and when apprehending its vehicle gives us pleasure, we regard such an artwork as *beautiful*.

---

[26] As found in the motion of one of today's premier tennis players, athletic beauty is the theme of a recent celebratory article, "Federer as Religious Experience," by David Foster Wallace: "The human beauty we're talking about here is beauty of a particular type . . . [whose] power and appeal are universal. It has nothing to do with sex or cultural norms . . . A top athlete's beauty is next to impossible to describe directly" (*New York Times Sports Magazine*, September 2006, p. 48). Despite the disclaimer about its indescribability, Wallace does take pains to describe at least some dimensions of Federer's athletic beauty: "Federer's forehand is a great liquid whip, his backhand a one-hander that he can drive flat, load with topspin, or slice . . . His serve has world-class pace and a degree of placement and variety no one else comes close to; the service motion is lithe and uneccentric, distinctive only in a certain eel-like all-body snap at the moment of impact. His anticipation and court sense are otherworldly, and his footwork is the best in the game . . . " (p. 49).

The beauty of an artwork is thus plausibly something different from, if related to, the beauty of a non-art artifact, such as an automobile, wardrobe, hammock, or hammer.[27] But artifactual beauty is also not simply a matter of the *formal* beauty of the shapes or patterns that such an artifact embodies or contains. Consider a set of silverware. Such silverware might be considered less beautiful not because of the forms, colors, or textures it presents, or even the relationships among them, but because the pieces simply appear too heavy, and thus likely to be unwieldy in practice. The thought of their impracticality, the imagining of their less-than-effortless employment, impacts negatively on their perceived beauty as artifacts designed for a specific use.

A case worthy of extended discussion, but which I cannot accord it here, is that of architecture. Do good works of architecture possess artifactual beauty or artistic beauty? That depends, in part, on whether all works of architecture are works of art, and more specifically, on whether they always have content of an order comparable to that possessed by paintings, symphonies, novels, and films, so that appreciative interest can carry to the manner in which that content is embodied by the work's specific form. I am inclined to say that much architecture is art, and possesses content, and hence may display artistic beauty, while some architecture is simply artifact, and so capable of displaying at most artifactual beauty. But is it fair, after all, to say that non-art artifacts wholly lack significant content? What about the original Brillo Boxes, designed for commercial purposes, and arguably carrying a message of a positive sort, one intended to boost sales? Well, those are borderline cases, being examples at least of *commercial* art, and hence different from paradigm non-art artifacts such as hammers, chairs, and rugs.

# VII

I must now tentatively acknowledge yet another category of beauty, which I will label *accidental beauty*, and which does not seem assimilable to any of the six types which I have so far recognized. Instances of accidental beauty are simply accidental arrangements of elements, man-made or natural, that one just comes across and finds somehow absorbing or compelling.

Take, as an example, the look of a city from on high, as from the roof of a skyscraper. Such a cityscape, though the byproduct of numerous individual creative acts, was not envisaged or designed by anyone, and yet is often visually arresting. Or consider a portion of such an urban environment, haphazardly framed, containing persons, vegetation, artifacts, et cetera, but which strikes one as harmonious, or singular, or

---

[27] The beauty of useful objects, of course, can be far from negligible, as this encomium to tools succinctly suggests: "Indeed, few objects are so simply and obviously beautiful as a well-made tool, the purpose of which is by necessity inscribed in its design" (Crispin Sartwell, *Six Names of Beauty* (New York: Routledge, 2004), p. 7).

redolent of some hidden meaning.[28] Such phenomena, it is clear, are neither artistically beautiful, nor artifactually beautiful, nor naturally beautiful; that is, they are not beautiful in the way of art, or artifact, or nature. They thus seem to exemplify another category of the beautiful, not reducible to the others.

But a reservation is certainly in order as regards this putative seventh category of visual beauty. Since there is very likely *even less* convergence among perceivers about the beauty of such world-portions or thing-arrangements than there is for the other categories of beauty we have noted, the ground for regarding such beauty as an *objective property* of the items in question is accordingly shakier. In these cases it may just be a matter of beauty *experiences*, idiosyncratic and unpredictable, without correlated beautiful *objects*. That said, we may at least provisionally admit into our scheme beauties of this sort, conditional on the emergence of a requisite degree of intersubjective convergence.[29]

## VIII

In order to consolidate some of what I have so far suggested, I now pass in review some paradigms of visual beauty, and attempt to highlight what is characteristic of our perception or experience of each. With formal beauty, such that of an arabesque or dodecahedron, our attention is directed to and held by line, shape, and volume, without any concept of what is before the eyes necessarily being in play, at least on a reflective level.[30] With artifactual beauty, such as confronts us in a chair of modern design, say by Breuer or Rietvelt, our attention is drawn to line, shape, and volume, but in relation to the form of the human body, and with the idea of supporting, echoing, and conforming to it in mind. Pleasure is taken partly in the chair's form as such, but partly in imagining employment of the chair as it was meant to be employed. And with artistic beauty, such as presented by Brancusi's emblematic sculpture *Bird in Space*, our attention is drawn to shape, volume, line, flow, and texture, but all in relation to what is represented, namely, a bird, and to what is expressed, namely, the elegance, grace, and dynamism of such a creature. Pleasure is partly taken in the sculpture's form as such, but partly in an awareness of the relation of form to content

---

[28] A comparison suggests itself between this domain of accidental beauty and certain Surrealist ideals, such as Lautréamont's evocation of the fortuitous meeting of sewing machine and an umbrella on an operating table.

[29] Here is how P. D. Magnus, who drew my attention to this peculiar mode of visual beauty, describes his experience of a street scene in which such beauty was manifest to him: "I am not impressed by a single artifact that is elegantly functional. I am not impressed by a solitary building or park that is the work of a single architect. Rather, it is the whole haphazard assemblage of things that impresses me" (personal communication, 2006). And here is Aldous Huxley, testifying in 1954 to something in the same vein: "And all at once I saw what Guardi had seen and... had so often rendered in his paintings—a stucco wall with a shadow slanting across it, blank but unforgettably beautiful, empty but charged with all the meaning and the mystery of existence" (*The Doors of Perception* (New York: HarperCollins, 1990), p. 61).

[30] Apart from the caveat already noted in discussing the beauty of conceptually definable abstract forms.

in the sculpture, which is in this case a particularly intimate one. Similar comments would apply, say, to Edward Steichen's photograph *Pear on a Plate*, modulo the difference in medium.

Moving now to natural beauty, consider a stand of Rocky Mountain aspens in fall, or Mount Fuji in winter. In such cases our attention is directed on shape, line, mass, and color, but in relation to natural processes and natural norms. Our pleasure is in a significant part pleasure in the perfection of portions of nature as exemplars of their kind. The appreciation of colors in a natural scene, most pointedly, is always mediated by our sense of the naturalness of the color for the thing in question, for instance, the beauty of vast expanses of varied green when perceived as foliage, rather than as something whose identity is indeterminate, and the panoply of whites and grays on a mountainside understood as reflective of atmospheric and geological conditions, rather than as a mere pattern without significance.[31]

As regards physical beauty, the movies and the media are lavish in providing specimens. I recall just a few, of yesterday and today: Greta Garbo, Natalie Wood, Catherine Deneuve, Romy Schneider, Cindy Crawford, Halle Berry, Emmanuelle Beart, Olivia Wilde, Cary Grant, James Dean, Jude Law, Denzel Washington, Brad Pitt, Johnny Depp, Matt Damon. When we respond to the beauty of such individuals, it's clear that shape, form, line, and volume are appreciated, not for their own sakes, but as answering to human sexual desire, and as triggering the imaginative pleasure of its satisfaction. The experience of human physical beauty on the part of a member of the reference class for such beauty always involves, however mutedly or obliquely, desire for physical possession of or interaction with the person found beautiful. Furthermore, as recent research has overwhelmingly shown, such beauty also has a fairly narrow set of underlying or properties. In particular, where facial beauty is concerned, properties such as symmetry, smoothness, large lips, and large eyes, and as regards other facial features, average size and average distances between features.[32]

Consider next moral beauty, such as that evinced by the Dalai Lama, the novelist Doris Lessing, the man depicted in Rembrandt's painting *The Jewish Bride*, or the protagonist of Bresson's film *Un condamné à mort s'est echappé*. Such beauty consists in admirable qualities which seem to be manifest in a person's appearance. With moral beauty it is the soul, as it were, that appears through the shapes, lines, and volumes of the face, which are thus not dwelt on for their own sakes, as with instances of formal beauty, but instead as emblems of good character.

---

[31] Difficult cases, though, are those of black tulips or blue roses, those somewhat perverse products of the horticultural imagination, which are often considered beautiful despite involving colors that are decidedly unnatural. But in such cases, as in more ordinary ones, the beauty such flowers appear to have is a function of perceiving their colors against a background awareness of the colors normal for such flowers, an awareness those unusual specimens are expressly designed to unsettle.

[32] See, for instance, J. Langlois and L. Roggman, "Attractive Faces Are Only Average," *Psychological Science*, 1/2 (1990); B. C. Jones, L. M. DeBruine, and A. Little "The Role of Symmetry in Attraction to Average Faces," *Perception and Psychophysics*, 69/ 8 (2007); and a number of studies cited in Etcoff, *Survival of the Prettiest*.

Finally, recall our provisionally admitted category of accidental beauty, such as that presented by some adventitiously framed portion of the partly natural, partly man-made world in which we usually find ourselves: if this be beauty, then clearly its perception is permeated by thoughts of the constituent things involved, of the manifold associations and connotations brought into play, and of their interaction with the formal elements of the scene before us. Accidental beauty is thus perhaps a beauty more dependent, in Kant's sense, than any other.

# IX

It is time again to take stock. As suggested earlier, three possible grounds seem to emerge for distinguishing beauties from one another in virtue of differences in the beauty responses each provokes. First, there are the features of the object on which the given response is *directed* or on which the response is *focused*. Second, there are the properties *causally responsible* for, or that *structurally underpin*, the given response. Third, there is the *phenomenology* of the given response, or alternatively, the thoughts, feelings, and desires that characteristically enter into the response. Call these the *intentional, structural*, and *phenomenological* grounds for distinguishing beauty responses, and thus species of beauty corresponding to them. Let us see how they apply in relation to the categories of visual beauty we have distinguished.

Consider the property of bilateral symmetry. This clearly contributes to, and is arguably a *sine qua non* of, human beauty. But it is hardly a *sine qua non* of, and does not always contribute to, artistic beauty, such as that of paintings, whether representational or non-representational. So we have reason to regard human beauty and artistic beauty as distinct, that is, as different beauty properties, at least with respect to the second ground above, or as regards their structural underpinnings. Human beauty and artistic beauty surely also diverge as well with respect to the third ground, or phenomenologically: the response to the former necessarily involves desire, at some level, while the response to the latter necessarily includes thoughts about meaning.

If one emphasizes that third ground one will likely be disinclined to identify any variety of dependent beauty with any other. That is because of the quite different sorts of thoughts involved in the response to or apprehension of different sorts of dependently beautiful things, thoughts centered on design (as with artifactual beauty), or function (as with natural beauty), or desirability (as with physical beauty), or content (as with artistic beauty). The difference in these thoughts gives some reason to think the beauties perceived through, and only through, such thoughts are themselves different.

As for the first ground noted above, the intentional focus of the response, with both physical beauty and artistic beauty, in contrast to abstract beauty, the response centers on more than visual form as such. Yet those two cases importantly differ. In the case of physical beauty such form is normally seen past unreflectingly, giving way immediately to an image of the desirable person, while in the case of artistic beauty such form is not rightly seen past, but is rather dwelt on in relation to any figurative or expressive meaning that results.

Let me now formulate some specific grounds of difference that might serve to bring into clearer relief the distinctness of the seven species of beauty with which I have been concerned. One of these specific grounds of difference is of the intentional sort, one is of the structural sort, but the remaining four are of the phenomenological sort:

(a) apprehension of the beauty presupposes a conception of the object *as a thing of a particular kind*, and not simply attention to the object's visual form;
(b) apprehension of the beauty involves estimation of *purpose or use* in relation to form;
(c) apprehension of the beauty involves estimation of *meaning or content* in relation to form;
(d) apprehension of the beauty involves estimation of *moral character*;
(e) apprehension of the beauty involves *desire for and attraction to* the object;
(f) the beauty depends on a relatively *narrow range of underlying properties*.

Abstract beauty exhibits none of the above marks, thus emerging as in some sense the purest of beauties. Natural beauty exhibits (a), the characteristic of all dependent beauties, but none of the others. Artifactual beauty exhibits (a) and (b), while artistic beauty exhibits (a) and (c), reflecting in each case the specific sort of dependent beauty at issue. Physical beauty exhibits (a), dependent as it is on a concept of the human, but also both (e) and (f), which sharply distinguishes it from all the other species of beauty. Moral beauty exhibits (a), but then distinctively, also (d). Finally, accidental beauty exhibits (a), since it requires at least recognition of object identities within the world portion being contemplated, but perhaps none of the other marks. And yet it is not the same as natural beauty, which also exhibits of those marks only (a).

What I have said so far perhaps suffices to establish, at least loosely, that the beauties ranged under my seven categories are quite different things. But let me now pose a harder question, one I have been studiously avoiding: are there really distinct beauty *properties* corresponding to those different sorts of beauty? It is difficult to say, and not only because identity criteria for properties remains among the murkiest matters in metaphysics. But here are a few remarks in favor of a positive answer.

The same property, we know, may have different bases on which it supervenes, and thus one might propose that even in light of the differences among beauties on which we have dwelt, visual beauty is the same property in all cases despite supervening on different subvenient bases in the different cases. Fair enough. But if the *base* properties are really *quite* different, as between physical and natural beauty, and if those largely visible base properties seem almost to *constitute* the resultant beauty, rather than simply disappearing from view in favor of the beauty that emerges, then it seems that one has some reason to consider the beauty properties in question distinct.

Similarly, if perception of a given beauty exhibits a different *intentional focus*, in one case involving a structure in relation to an expressive end, as with artistic beauty, in another a structure in relation to a utilitarian purpose, as with artifactual beauty, and in a third a structure just as a formal configuration, as with abstract beauty, that would also seem some reason to consider the beauty properties in each case distinct. Lastly, if experience of a given beauty, such as physical beauty, exhibits a *phenomenology*—involving, say, certain feelings or desires—which does not characterize the experience of some other beauty, such as artistic beauty, then again we seem to have some reason to consider the beauty properties in question to be distinct.

The main point of this chapter might perhaps now be restated by way of a simple comparison between our chief concern, visual beauty, and a more basic visual phenomenon, such as redness. Of course there is a great range of things that are red, that exhibit the characteristic red appearance. But the experience of that redness, and the way the redness presents itself, is fundamentally the same, despite differences in size, shape, texture and so on of the object that is red.[33]

It is quite otherwise with the range of things that are visually beautiful. For the experience of that beauty, and the way the beauty presents itself, differs dramatically across the different varieties of beauty. This difference manifests itself in terms of what the experience is focused or directed on; in terms of the conative, affective, or cognitive complexion of the experience; in terms of the underlying perceptual properties in which it seems to inhere and from which it seems to arise; or in all three ways at once. In sum, the varieties of visual beauty are importantly different, and are not to be assimilated to one another.

# X

I note two issues for further reflection on this vexed topic. The first issue is whether having made a case for there being six or so fundamentally different varieties of visual beauty, there is any principled way to stop at those six or so, rather than going on to recognize an indefinite number of further beauties, appealing to the same sorts of reasons for distinguishing the six or seven already recognized, but turning on even finer differences in the experiences or concepts involved. Why not recognize painterly, photographic, sculptural, and architectural beauty as distinct kinds of artistic beauty? And why not recognize, say within painterly beauty, Matisse-beauty, Seurat-beauty, Vermeer-beauty, and so on? I see no obvious answer here. But on the other hand, there is perhaps no harm in such recognition, though the theoretical gain to be reaped from it is unclear.

The second issue is this. Some modes of visual beauty borrow from and echo other modes of visual beauty. For example, the artistic beauty of Art Nouveau architecture, such as Albert Guimard's Paris metro entrances or Victor Horta's Brussels townhouses, which unmistakably reflect floral and vegetal shapes, or the physical beauty of human

---

[33] One might try to make something out of the differences in how the red of a glass bottle, or an oil slick, or a patch of sky, are experienced, but that would surely come to little in this context.

beings such as that of the leonine man or swanlike woman, whose look or bearing clearly evokes the natural beauty of the respective animals. Is this a problem for the thesis of the irreducible variety of visual beauty? I don't believe so, but it reminds us that the different varieties of beauty do not exist in waterproof compartments, and may intermingle more than I have so far suggested.

Finally, what are some lessons we might draw from the existence of real diversity in the realm of visual beauty, from the conclusion that the genus of visual beauty has only a superficial unity? Well, an obvious one is this: we should not expect persons responsive to and interested in one species of visual beauty to necessarily be responsive to and interested in another such species. This consequence of real diversity among visual beauties should not be surprising if we recall that such non-uniformity of response or interest is often the case across the arts rooted in different sensory media. Thus someone could be passionate about symphonies and indifferent to paintings, or thrilled by poetry and bored by theater, or wild about film and unmoved by sculpture. There are several examples of great writers, persons presumably well attuned to literary beauty, who were singularly unstirred by music, such as, I believe, Vladimir Nabokov and Iris Murdoch. It is easy enough to recognize that literary beauty, musical beauty, and painterly beauty, though they have something in common, namely a pleasurable appeal to perception and/or imagination, are yet importantly different things. It should not be too much of a stretch, then, to recognize this as true as well for artistic beauty as opposed to other varieties of visual beauty, such as physical or natural or abstract beauty, and thus to expect that a taste for one may very well not carry over into a taste for the other. Let me end, then, by simply affirming my title: beauty is not one.[34]

[34] Thanks to audiences at Grand Valley State University, University of Leuven, University at Albany, Trinity University, University of London, University of Southampton, University of Leeds, University of Tübingen, and the Centre de Recherches sur les Arts et le Langage, for valuable comments on and reactions to this paper. I thank, in particular, Hans Maes, Alessandro Giovannelli, Stacie Friend, Katalin Farkas, Anna Ribeiro, Aaron Ridley, Genia Schonbaumsfeld, Jean-Marie Schaeffer, Peter Rinderle, Catrin Missenhorn, and P. D. Magnus.

# 11

# Aesthetics: The Approach from Social Anthropology

*Robert Layton*

## 1. Scope and method in anthropology

Anthropology is a broad subject, with biological anthropology investigating aspects of human evolution ranging from anatomy to health, while social anthropology investigates the variety of human societies and cultures and their place in the international social order. Social anthropology offers several approaches to the cross-cultural study of aesthetics or the appreciation of beauty, in particular by examining both cross-cultural constants and variability in the appreciation of beauty, and the social functions served by the creation of beautiful objects that range from body decoration to pottery and cave art. The French sociologist Durkheim (1858–1917) was hugely influential upon the constitution of social anthropology. Durkheim's key axiom was that the social sciences study what he called 'social facts', in other words, the emergent properties of social interaction. In *The Rules of Sociological Method* (1938 [1901]) Durkheim argued that French language, currency, and laws exist independently of any particular individual; they are brought into being through social interaction. They should, therefore 'not be confused with biological phenomena, since they consist of representations and actions; nor with psychological phenomena, which exist only in the individual consciousness' (1938: 3). Durkheim did not dismiss the value of biological or psychological explanations for human behaviour, but insisted that sociology has a distinct, additional role to play in explaining human society and culture.

In the generation following Durkheim, the anthropologists Radcliffe-Brown and Malinowski working in Britain developed one aspect of Durkheim's method, known as Functionalism. Functionalists explain the presence of a social custom in terms of its contribution to social order. Working at a time when little was known about the history or archaeology of non-literate societies, the Functionalists warned against speculative explanations for the presence of a custom in terms of its origin. Subsequent authors (e.g., Giddens 1984) have rejected the a-temporal nature of Functionalism, taking their lead from Marx's analysis of the dynamics of social systems through time, but retained the premise that social practices must be studied within the context of the emergent social system.

In France, other anthropologists developed the second aspect of Durkheim's sociological method, which was to explain the meaning of a custom in terms of its place in a culturally specific cognitive system. This is the Structuralist approach. The Structuralists also warned against speculative history. Van Gennep, for example, explained 'marriage by capture' as a dramatization of the bride's separation from her unmarried life in her natal home, and not as a survival from an imagined past when men stole mates by force. Van Gennep argued that all rites of passage that accompany a change in social stratus have a three-part structure, in which the initiate is separated from their old position in society, and passes through a liminal phase before re-entering society in their new role. Thanks to Bourdieu and Derrida in France, and the *Writing Culture* School in the United States, Structuralism has mutated into interpretative anthropology, which questions whether the more or less arbitrary cultural constructs of an exotic culture can be reliably translated into the familiar terms of the anthropologist's tradition. Particularly since Bourdieu (1977 [1972]), anthropologists sometimes prefer to write of 'habitus' rather than culture. Bourdieu argued that, even within a cultural community, each individual constructs his or her own habitus, deduced from observing the actions and words of the preceding generation. Identifying the factors that cause individual habituses to converge towards a cultural consensus thus becomes an important object of research.

These divergent trends in social anthropology were in fact anticipated by the sociologist Weber (1947 [1925]) who, drawing on German philosophy, distinguished between explanation and understanding. A customary practice is explained in terms of general laws that exist independently of its practitioners, but its cultural meaning must be interpreted by gaining intersubjective understanding with members of the culture. It is likely that the German-born anthropologist Boas independently introduced the distinction between explanation and understanding to US social anthropology (see Layton 1997: 184–6).

The scope of social anthropology's contribution to *explanation* in the study of aesthetics and its context within the sciences can be delineated with reference to Tinbergen's (1963) 'four questions'. Tinbergen's questions were directed at the explanation of animal behaviour. He showed that functional and historical explanations can be subdivided into four issues. Transposed into social science these can be phrased as

*Ultimate questions*

- What the custom does, i.e. its functional consequences for those who practise it.
- How the practice developed (evolved) through time.

*Proximate questions*

- What causes or prompts performance of the custom (fear of attack by rivals, hunger).

- How social practices develop in the individual (a question that might appeal both to evolutionary psychology and cultural learning).

Much of Tinbergen's own research concerned the postures and calls of individual herring gulls interacting with mates, offspring, and rivals. Effective communication was vital, but not only was Tinbergen concerned simply with observable behaviour between such dyads, the presumption was that the ritualized behaviour was genetically motivated. Moreover, since he was studying how pairs of gulls interact as individuals, Tinbergen was not concerned with the politics of co-ordinated action that is often an aspect of art and ritual in small-scale societies. What, then, can anthropology contribute to the study of function and evolution of aesthetics beyond the explanations offered by evolutionary biology?

*Question 1: The social functions of aesthetics*

In his book *Primitive Art*, the US anthropologist Franz Boas illustrated numerous cases of symmetry and rhythm in the art of small-scale societies, and concluded 'we cannot reduce this world-wide tendency to any other ultimate causes than to a feeling for form, in other words, to an aesthetic impulse' (Boas 1955: 58). Building on Boas's approach, Dorothy Washburn (1983) edited a collection of papers that persuasively demonstrates the recurrent expressions of symmetry and rhythm in the art of small-scale societies.

Other writers have, however, drawn attention to the problematic status of aesthetics as a universal category, showing the risk of imposing our own conceptual categories on other cultures. When dealing with unfamiliar human cultures, interpretation is needed, as well as explanation, to appreciate what other cultures regard as beautiful. Local aesthetic values may combine apparently universal qualities with others that emerge from the specific features of local society.

Robert Thompson found that among the Yoruba of Nigeria, evaluations of form in sculpture ranged from 'almost universal' criteria such as delicacy of form, shining smoothness, and careful and symmetrical composition, to culturally specific qualities such as the facial scarification that indicated a person had been socialized like a tended field, not unmarked like the wild forest (Thompson 1973; cf. Lawal 1993). Davies (2007a) points out that some aspects of Balinese aesthetics are readily translatable. *Taksu* denotes the charismatic power of a great performer, *becik* denotes unity and balance between elements and technical excellence. Other qualities appear more culturally specific. The proportions for a traditional Balinese house are based on the bodily parts of its occupants. Balinese art and music show a desire to avoid blank spaces (cf. Bateson 1973). In order to translate Balinese aesthetics, Davies searches for the closest parallels in our familiar society: Balinese competitive musical performances are like European sporting contests; Balinese audience etiquette resembles European audience response to popular rather than classical music. This search for the most apt translation is well established in anthropology, having been used by such founding fathers as Malinowski

(1922) in his study of inter-island trade among the Trobriands of the Pacific. Traditional trade in subsistence goods is underwritten by the exchange of highly valued arm bands and necklaces between the leader of a canoe party bringing goods to an island, and the local leader who guarantees peaceful trade. In seeking to convey why these seemingly useless objects were highly valued he compared them to sporting trophies or crown jewels.

A recurrent theme in the anthropological literature on aesthetics is that what we construe as aesthetically pleasing is understood in other cultures as a manifestation of spiritual agency. Anthony Forge, who carried out fieldwork among the Abelam of New Guinea, contended that Abelam artists, although lacking an aesthetic vocabulary, can discuss form and proportion in their work, but that ordinary members of the community interpreted form and design differently. 'The skilful artist who satisfies his aesthetic sense and produces beauty is rewarded not for the beauty itself but because the beauty . . . is regarded by the rest as power' (Forge 1967. 82–3). Howard Morphy later showed in greater detail how, among the Yolngu of northern Australia, artists are clearly concerned to produce effects on the senses which Europeans would interpret as aesthetic, but 'what Europeans interpret at a general level as an aesthetic effect Yolngu interpret as a manifestation of ancestral power' (Morphy 1989: 23). Each Yolngu clan owns a distinctive design that depicts the travels of its totemic ancestor. The design is a tangible link between living people and the time of the ancestors. One of the most appreciated qualities of sacred paintings among the Yolngu is a shimmering finish they are given by the delicate addition of fine, cross-hatched lines that give the painting a brilliance conveying the creative power of the ancestor embodied in the work.

Alfred Gell put forward a more comprehensive argument against the universal validity of Western aesthetics, based on similar case studies to those cited here. Gell asserted that 'the "aesthetic attitude" is a specific historical product of the religious crisis of the Enlightenment and the rise of Western science . . . [that brought about] the separation between the beautiful and the holy' (Gell 1998: 97). In India, as in the Ancient World, he argued, aesthetics is subsumed within the philosophy of religion, whereas 'we have neutralised our idols by reclassifying them as art' (Gell 1998: 97).

Taking a Functionalist stance, Gell argues that the proper job of anthropology is to investigate the purposes that art is used for in society, rather than its psychological foundations. He contends that the anthropology of art should be interested in how aesthetic principles are mobilized in the course of social interaction. While Westerners attribute outstanding artistic work to the personal inspiration of the artist, the Trobriand Islanders of Melanesia attribute such skill to superior magic. 'Melanesian aesthetics is about efficacy, the capacity to accomplish tasks, not "beauty"' (1998: 94). Gell's general conclusion is that art is deployed to extend the maker, owner or user's agency, using agency in the sense specified by Giddens, for whom agency is the capacity to modify other people's actions. Gell argues that art objects 'stand in' for people, evoking the same reactions that the maker or owner's personal presence would. An interesting example of this phenomenon is the use of life-size two-dimensional photographs of policemen in shops and offices to reduce theft. Gell's examples are largely taken from non-Western culture. The necklaces and arm bands that Trobriand exchange with their ceremonial partners on other islands circulate widely beyond the original owner, but carry his prestige with them. A Hindu or Buddhist statue stands in for the deity it embodies.

Gell does not, in fact, reject design universals, but attributes their ubiquity to their common social functions. Acknowledging later work by Washburn and Crowe (1988), he argues that 'There exists what amounts to a "universal aesthetic" of patterned surface; the same symmetry configurations... turn up all over the world' (Gell 1998: 160). Gell attributes two functions to the formal qualities of decorative art. Decorative patterns weave their spell because 'we can never quite understand the complex relationships they embody' (Gell 1998: 80). They also dazzle, attract, or frighten the viewer.

### Question 2: The evolution of aesthetics

Hypotheses concerning the evolution of aesthetics rely on the Darwinian axiom that biological evolution proceeds through competition for reproductive fitness between organisms displaying slight variations in genetically guided behaviour. Geoffrey Miller (2000) hypothesized that art evolved as a form of ritual display performed by males to attract mates. Male bowerbirds build large, elaborate structures decorated with flowers, fruits, leaves, butterfly wings, and feathers of other birds. These structures attract females and influence their decision to mate with particular males. Miller suggested that serial monogamy and female choice in Pleistocene human populations provided selection pressure for analogous creative displays by human males, giving rise to art and dance. The evolutionary parallel between bowerbird displays and human art are, however, likely to be as partial as the parallels between bird song and human speech. Miller has also committed the fallacy against which the Functionalist anthropologists reacted, of explaining the known (contemporary art) in terms of an unknown (the imagined role of art in early human evolution). His approach recalls Freud's explanation for the incest taboo, in which Freud locates the origins of totemism and food avoidances in the killing of the original father of an imagined primal human family band, by his sons (Freud 2001 [1913]: 164).

Sillitoe has described how men among the Wola of Highland New Guinea take their inspiration from the displays of male bowerbirds and birds of paradise. They incorporate the birds' feathers into the headdresses they wear when dancing at inter-village feasts, in order to attract men from other villages as partners in the exchange system that creates alliances between politically autonomous villages and helps reduce the threat of war. They seek thus to appropriate the birds' behaviour to themselves in response to the particular functional context of living in a politically uncentralized society prone to inter-village raids on garden crops (see below). Birds of paradise attract less colourful birds of the same species that watch, 'like spectators come to our full-dress dances' (Sillitoe 1988: 304). Wola men find the behaviour of the gardener bowerbird particularly appealing, since it not only mimics the squealing of the pigs that are killed at exchange feasts but also decorates its dance ground with, among other things, pigs' droppings.

Viewed from a Western perspective, however, the Wola are less well-informed about the birds' reproductive biology. The men who dance at feasts have abstained from sex, to avoid debilitating contact with women. They interpret the displaying male birds as practising abstinence, while the dull plumaged females are thought by the Wola to include males who have been less virtuous as well as females. Sillitoe's elucidation of Wola ritual thus relies on a Structuralist interpretation of the specific meaning of bird displays in Wola culture, which starts with a binary opposition between us and them, in which 'they' are potential allies but also potential enemies. The Wola draw a structural analogy between this human situation and the natural opposition between the bower-bird and its audience. By identifying with the male bowerbird, the dancers express their desire to win their audience as allies.

Miller's argument, shorn of its pseudo-history, can to some extent be rescued if it is treated as an application of 'costly signalling theory' to art. Zahavi (1975) explained the evolution of the male peacock's tail as a signal of reproductive health. Those males that can sustain the longest, brightest tails are signalling their fitness relative to other males with shorter or duller tails, just as are the bower birds with the most effective displays. The most successful males are those that achieve the best 'trade-off' between the competing evolutionary pressures to reproduce while avoiding predators. This, I think, offers a better functional parallel with the displays of Wola men (who hope both to impress other men and attract women) although surely not a universal explanation for the social functions of art (cf. Davies 2007b: 108–9).

A more persuasive explanation for the evolutionary origins of aesthetics is provided by the large and growing body of research on facial symmetry and reproductive health. One of the earliest to work in this field was Thornhill who, with others, has argued in various papers (e.g., Thornhill and Gangestad 1999), that facial symmetry in humans is an indication of reproductive health, and we have therefore evolved to recognize and value symmetry. Further facial features recognized cross-culturally as signalling good health include evenly coloured, smooth pliant skin, clear eyes, and shiny hair (Symons 1995, cited in Thornhill and Gangestad 1999). Lie et al. (2008) have looked in closer detail into the genetic link between resistance to parasites and facial attractiveness.

Although there is evidence that other values such as wealth, status, and capacity for work also influence judgements of marital worth in small-scale societies (e.g., Borgerh-off-Mulder 1990), there is cross-cultural support for the association of reproductive health and aesthetics. The Mende of Sierra Leone expect women to be beautiful, delicate, pretty, and groomed (Boone 1993: 304), but they also expect them to be kind, patient, and loving. Overwhelming beauty is considered dangerous because a beautiful Mende girl may become arrogant and narcissistic. Thompson investigated aesthetic judgements of sculpture among the Yoruba of West Africa. He found that shining smoothness, anatomical accuracy in the placement of body parts, careful and symmetrical composition, and the depiction of people in the prime of life were all criteria used in the evaluation of sculpture. Biebuyck (1973) found that the Lega of central Africa value ivory carvings that have been oiled and polished to make them shiny or glossy, a technique that 'is called *kubongia*, meaning to bring in harmony, to produce unison . . . the reference is to beauty', and they enhance their own bodies in the same way (Biebuyck 1973: 179).

Again, however, I would caution that even if the facial attractiveness hypothesis provides an explanation of *why* we have evolved the capacity to value symmetry, it doesn't necessarily explain *how* that capacity is used in recent human cultures. McManus's demonstration that we can intuitively recognize and appreciate symmetry and balance in art, with reference to the Golden Section (McManus and Weatherby 1997) demonstrates how a cognitive capacity that may have evolved in the context of sexual selection is now used in other fields of experience such as the appreciation of Mondrian's abstract paintings (cf. Davies's 2007b criticism of Dissanayake's evolutionary theory of art).

## 2. Archaeological evidence for the origin of aesthetic expression

The oldest stone tools, first found at Olduvai Gorge and hence known as 'Olduwan choppers' have no apparent preconceived shape. Around one and a half million years ago they were replaced by the Acheulean industry, whose so-called 'handaxes' are more or less pear-shaped, showing clear bilateral symmetry that was apparently achieved by design. Handaxes were produced in Africa and Eurasia for an extraordinarily long time, until about two hundred thousand years ago, predominantly by a pre-modern human species, *Homo erectus*. An estimated one in a hundred, or perhaps even one per fifty shows symmetry and regularity seemingly beyond practical requirements (Corbey *et al.* 2004).

Whether this can be attributed to the makers' appreciation of pure beauty, or whether it served some further, social purpose is unknown. The archaeologists Kohn and Mithen (1999) have suggested handaxes were made by men whose ulterior motive was to attract mates through a demonstration of technical virtuosity. It is difficult to see how the hypothesis could be tested although, to be fair to Kohn and Mithen, they do predict that such sexual displays are more likely to have occurred in certain environments than others, allowing a test of sorts.

The most likely point of origin for our species, i.e., fully modern humans, is Africa. While rock art appears suddenly, and seemingly fully formed, in the earliest modern human societies of the Upper Palaeolithic to reach Europe, this phenomenon is almost certainly the outcome of a long process of further behavioural and cognitive evolution that spanned 200,000 years and occurred in Africa, after *Homo erectus* had spread into Europe and Asia (McBrearty and Brooks 2000).

D'Errico (1992) accepts perforated and ochre covered shells associated with 100,000-year-old burials of anatomically modern humans at Qafzeth in modern Israel as evidence for personal ornaments. Some of the oldest evidence for the use of ochre comes from the Howieson's Poort industry of South Africa, between 50,000 and 75,000 years ago (Barham 1998). Excavation of a site from this period at Blombos Cave on the South African coast has uncovered an increasing number of pieces of ochre on which a flat surface had been prepared that was then decorated with cross-hatched parallel lines. Since these lines are deliberate yet apparently non-utilitarian, the Blombos material invites interpretation in terms of a Boasian impulse or feeling for form. These engravings are approximately 70,000 years old (*Science*, 10 January 2002).

The oldest secure dates for representational rock art come from the paintings in the French cave of Chauvet, where paintings of two rhino and a bison have been dated to *c*.30,000 B.P. (Clottes 2001). The Upper Palaeolithic cave art of France and Spain spans a continuous period from 30,000 to 12,000 B.P. Remarkably, the distinctive animal style is already in full flower at Chauvet. Although animals are rarely juxtaposed or combined, one particularly notable composition at Lascaux (*c*.11,000 years old) shows two opposed bison whose legs and tails overlap symmetrically. An early theory for Upper Palaeolithic art, prompted by the ancient artists' undeniable skill in form and representation, was that it was a case of art for art's sake. This theory, however, was soon rejected on the grounds that ancient hunter-gatherers would not have taken the time to walk deep into limestone caves prompted merely by what was at that time supposed to be a disinterested creative urge. Some powerful social function would be required. Since then, a series of alternative explanations have been advanced: that the art was practised as a form of totemism, or sympathetic magic, or shamanism. These hypotheses can be tested by comparing the distribution of animal motifs, within and between caves, with distribution patterns in recent hunter-gatherer rock art where such functions are documented, but the results are inconclusive (see Sauvet *et al.* 2009).

Elsewhere in the world, fallen slabs bearing paintings excavated at Apollo 11 shelter in southern Namibia have been dated to between 19,000 and 26,000 B.P. (Wendt 1974). The geometric rock art of Southern Australia may date from 10,000 years B.P. and continues today in the so-called 'dot' or 'Papunya' tradition which, like the Yolngu art studied by Morphy, depicts the travels of ancestral beings during the creation period. Since, however, there has been change in both the ecological context of the art (from open air sites to rock shelters) and its compositional qualities (from apparently unconnected figures to narrative compositions), there is no reason to assume its cultural context and function have remained constant (Clegg 1983; Layton 1992: 236).

Two of the most compelling differences between humans and other species, from an evolutionary perspective are:

(a) Many species engage in social behaviour, but the complexity of human social organization is exceptional;

(b) Learning is important in many species, but the importance of cultural transmission is also exceptional in humans.

These differences are particularly apparent when addressing questions 3 and 4, and it is here that much social and cultural anthropological research into art and aesthetics has been concentrated. Here we see the relevance of Durkheim's argument that sociology differentiates itself from biology and psychology through its study of the emergent properties of social interaction. The importance of the concept of habitus is demonstrated in the study of how individual cultural learning tends to converge on a local cultural consensus.

*Question 3: What causes or prompts performance of the custom*

The societies of highland Papua New Guinea, which have been used to illustrate this chapter, are particularly vulnerable to inter-village warfare. Their swidden cultivation systems do not provide sufficient surplus to sustain a social elite of permanent rulers, as the anthropologist Marshall Sahlins demonstrated in a classic comparative study of the egalitarian political systems of Melanesia with social rank in Polynesia (Sahlins 1974). Horticultural societies lack the flexibility of hunter-gatherers to evade disputes, because they are tied to the gardens in which they have invested months of effort cultivating crops. These crops offer a tempting prize to neighbouring villages. But horticulturalists also lack the strength of politically centralized societies in the co-ordination of warfare. Like the horticultural societies of the Amazon discussed by Jorg Helbling (1999), the New Guinea highlanders live in politically independent villages and rely on alliances built through marriage exchange with neighbouring villages to lessen the risk of attack. Helbling argued that each village must convey the impression that they are 'tough guys' rather than trusting suckers. If their partners in an exchange relationship betray them, the effect of military defeat would be so devastating that it would be too late to punish the partners as many of those who were betrayed will be dead, or forced to flee (Helbling 1999: 108–9; see also Layton 2006).

In response to such political insecurity, New Guinea Highland society is characterized by exchange festivals at which the host village seeks to impress allies and potential enemies with the coherence of its social organization, to attract marriage partners who will cement alliances, and to indebt guest villages through the lavishness of the feast provided. The aesthetics of display are thus part of co-ordinated social action that emerges from, and is prompted by, their specific ecological and social context.

The host clansmen at a festival aim to signal their coherence as a potential fighting force through uniformity of body decoration. Michael O'Hanlon gives an excellent account of the lengths to which the men of villages in the Wahgi Valley go to present a united front at ceremonial feasts. Their headdresses must remain in place without slipping. An impressive display is one in which the dancers achieve a glossy appearance and uniformity in decoration. If they are successful, onlookers will say, 'their skin glows . . . none of them will die' (O'Hanlon 1989: 119). This goal cannot be achieved if there are unresolved disputes within the clan, or allies who are angry that their debts have not been repaid. The fear is that the audience will say, 'the plumes on their shields are not properly dark . . . the warriors' legs aren't treading the ground firmly' (O'Hanlon 1989: 128), thus appearing weak enough to be defeated. During preparation for a display, clansmen try to resolve any simmering disputes within the clan by confessing guilt or anger towards one another and may be advised by friendly onlookers to return to their 'magic war house' and talk further. O'Hanlon gives a graphic description of a ceremonial display where the opposing 'phalanxes' of hosts and guests parade across the dance ground, each attempting to drown the others' performance with the volume of their own drumming, to project group strength and well-being, while watching crowds press forward to within a foot or two of the dancers. Girls in the audience attracted by a dancer will snatch his drum and lead him to the margins to engage in courtship. 'There are often excited surges and rushes in the crowd as young spectators hurry to watch some stalwart girl belabour and chase off a rival' (O'Hanlon 1989: 98).

It is not difficult to notice evolutionary precedents for this behaviour, but the overall situation is more complex than seen in the social behaviour of other species. I return to this point in the conclusion.

*Question 4: How do social practices develop in the individual?*

While the preceding sections of the chapter provide evidence for evolutionary under-pinnings for aesthetic expression in small-scale societies, they also provide evidence for the emergence of diverse cultural traditions, whose values and techniques are transmit-ted by learning. Alland (1983) investigated children's art in six cultures. He found that each sample showed an internal unity of style, but that there were marked differences between samples. Sixty per cent of the Balinese sample included representational figures, but only 15 per cent of the Micronesian sample. The Balinese children tended to fill the whole page, while Taiwanese children preferred to construct a picture consisting of several discrete elements. In each case, the children had clearly begun to learn the aesthetic of adult art within their own culture. O'Hanlon's study of ceremonial art in the Wahgi Valley demonstrates the intensity of negotiation and discussion that precede a collective performance at exchange festivals in New Guinea, which achieves a consistency of self-decoration among men who may start by con-structing rather different assemblages of plumes and body paint.

Numerous peasant communities on different continents supplement the household's agricultural output with art or craft manufacture. The functionality of this practice was famously demonstrated by the Russian economist Chayanov (1966), who argued that the agricultural year includes periods demanding peak labour inputs alternating with slack seasons between planting and harvesting. Peasant families will redirect their labour into craft production during the slack season. Chayanov predicted that the less land was available to a household, the more it would rely on craft production. This makes households crucially dependent on the successful sale of crafts in local or distant markets.

Margaret Ann Hardin (1983) explored convergence in aesthetic judgements among members of a Mexican pottery-making village with a population of about 300. Two types of pottery were produced in the village, a plain red ware for domestic use and a green-glazed, elaborately decorated ware. Both types were sold at the local market during two annual fiestas, where the green-glazed ware earned at least 50 per cent higher prices. The local style of decoration consisted of bands containing flowing floral or geometric motifs separated by horizontal borders. Although all potters had learned to build up the design in a standard sequence, there was substantial variation in the quality of potters' work, depending on both skill and knowledge of design possibilities. Hardin selected a range of pots which she asked the most prolific local potters, who produced pots all year round, to evaluate. She found that leading artists in the village of San José agreed that the best work was finely painted, with motifs that fitted neatly within the borders of the design and did not overlap with each other (Hardin 1983: 13, 22). Crucially, because the pots were sold in a local market, buyers' preferences influenced potters' goals, facilitating the emergence of a local aesthetic consensus.

A more complex situation was described by Harry Silver (1981) among modern wood carvers in the traditional West African kingdom of Asante. The village studied by Silver had been established by the king of Asante during the nineteenth century, to house a craft guild that specialized in producing royal regalia according to designs authorized by the king. The king's control over design weakened during the colonial era, and a market in traditional crafts began to develop. By the time of Silver's fieldwork, a three-tiered class system had emerged among village carvers. The most prosperous class produced innovative work that depicted traditional Asante proverbs and modern activities, but in a non-traditional, 'naturalistic' style. A successful innovation could be sold for a high price, but innovation was risky, and only wealthy artists could bear the risk of failure. Middle-ranking carvers avoided this risk by copying the successful innovations of high-ranking, respected carvers, thus presumably increasing supply in relation to market demand and driving the leading craftsmen to create yet further innovations in order to preserve their high economic status. Low-ranking carvers, such as unsuccessful adults and children who were still learning to carve, were desperate to earn income but had no prestige to risk losing. They catered for the less discerning, mass market created by European tourists and supplied work that played upon European fantasies about the 'primitive fierceness' of African culture. To do so they drew on well-known but non-Asante traditions of African carving. For them, the pressure to earn a living overrode the stigma of stepping outside local traditional conventions. Thus, while variations in skill existed among carvers in all three classes, the interaction of a complex market environment and a complex cultural tradition allowed carvers to adapt more or less successfully to three distinct socio-economic niches that either promoted or discouraged artistic innovation.

## 3. Conclusion

The evidence from studies of facial attractiveness leaves little doubt that aesthetic appreciation of symmetry is grounded in our evolved psychology, but that is only part of the story. The evidence is persuasive because it is experimentally demonstrable among living people. Geoffrey Miller's imaginative reconstruction of the environment in which art originally became adaptive, however, shows that the Functionalists' warning about the dangers of speculative history remains valid. If the Wola model their ceremonial headdresses and dancing on the behaviour of the bowerbird and birds of paradise, this is not because their rituals are a survival from humanity's original condition, but because they have noted the same analogy between human and bird behaviour that inspired Miller. Different analogies with bird behaviour are noted by other New Guinea Highland communities. The people of Mt. Hagen told Andrew and Marilyn Strathern that men use the resin of the *kilt* tree in their ceremonial wigs, 'for it helps men to get women . . . It is the brightness of the *kilt* tree's red flowers which attract flocks of birds to it, and we attract women in the same way' (Strathern and Strathern 1971: 89–90). The bowerbird analogy is not unique.

If human rituals were as simple as those of the herring gulls studied by Tinbergen, the evolution of psychological dispositions would play a large part in any analysis. The complexity of human culture and social organization demands that analysis goes beyond psychology. As Durkheim argued, society and culture have emergent properties that impinge upon the individual's inherent psychological and biological predispositions, determining when and how they are evoked. New Guinea Highland ceremonial displays clearly have a direct effect on the participants' reproductive success: a well-performed ceremony attracts marriage partners and deters potential enemies. The pressure to succeed, however, is particularly acute because of the distinctive challenges to social order faced by politically uncentralized horticulturalists. The displays are, moreover, not played out between individuals (at least, not until Wahgi girls pluck men from the dance), but depend upon a socially co-ordinated choreography.

Successful artists and craftsmen in peasant societies can enhance their household's prosperity and material well-being, and thereby their likelihood of raising children to maturity, but the decorations that potters of San José place on their green-glazed wares are not a simple advertisement of their reproductive health. The link is established indirectly by the production cycle of a peasant economy, in which the peak labour periods of planting and harvesting are separated by slack seasons where the family's labour power is under-used, and the presence of a market economy in craft goods. The more complex situation that Silver described among Asante wood-carvers shows the socially constructed environment plays a vital, perhaps pre-eminent role in determining the adaptiveness of alternative strategies for the display of artistic skills.

# References

Alland, A. (1983). *Playing with Form: Children Learn to Draw in Six Cultures*. New York: Columbia University Press.

Barham, L. (1998). 'Possible Early Pigment Use in South-Central Africa'. *Current Anthropology*, 39: 703–10.

Bateson, G. (1973). 'Style, Grace and Information in Primitive Art', in A. Forge (ed.), *Primitive Art and Society*. Oxford: Oxford University Press, pp. 235–55.

Biebuyck, D. (1973). *The Lega: Art, Initiation and Moral Philosophy*. Berkeley, CA: University of California Press.

Boas, F. (1955). *Primitive Art*. New York: Dover.

Boone, S. A. (1993). 'Radiance from the Waters: Mende Feminine Beauty', in R. L. Anderson and K. L. Field (eds.), *Art in Small-Scale Societies: Contemporary Readings*. Englewood Cliffs, NJ: Prentice Hall, pp. 303–8.

Borgerhoff-Mulder, M. (1990). 'Kipsigis Women's Preferences for Wealthy Men: Evidence for Female Choice in Mammals?' *Behavioural Ecology and Sciobiology*, 27/4: 255–64.

Bourdieu, P. (1977 [1972]). *Outline of a Theory of Practice*, trans. R. Nice. Cambridge: Cambridge University Press.

Chayanov, A. V. (1966). *The Theory of Peasant Economy*, ed. D. Thorner, B. Kerblay, and R. E. F. Smith. Madison, WI: University of Wisconsin Press.

Clegg, J. (1983). 'Correlations and Associations at Sturt's Meadow', in M. Smith (ed.), *Archaeology at ANZAAS 1983*. Perth: Western Australian Museum.

Clottes, J. (ed.) (2001). *La Grotte Chauvet: l'art des origins*. Paris: Seuil.

Corbey, R., R. Layton, and J. Tanner (2004). 'Archaeology and Art', in J. Bintliff (ed.), *A Companion to Archaeology*. Oxford: Blackwell, pp. 357–79.

Davies, S. (2007a). 'Balinese Aesthetics', in S. Feagin (ed.), *Global Theories of the Arts and Aesthetics*. Malden: Blackwell, pp. 21–9.

—— (2007b). 'Ellen Dissanayake's Evolutionary Aesthetic', in *Philosophical Perspectives on Art*. Oxford: Oxford University Press, pp. 103–18.

D'Errico, F. (1992). 'Technology, Motion, and the Meaning of Epipalaeolithic Art'. *Current Anthropology*, 33: 185–201.

Durkheim, E. (1938 [1901]). *The Rules of Sociological Method*, trans. S. Solovay and J. Mueller. New York: Free Press.

Forge, A. (1967). 'The Abelam Artist', in M. Freedman (ed.), *Social Organization: Essays Presented to Raymond Firth*. London: Cass, pp. 65–84.

Freud, S. (2001 [1913]). *Totem and Taboo: Some Points of Agreement between the Mental Lives of Savages and Neurotics*, trans. J. Strachey. London: Routledge.

Gell, A. (1998). *Art and Agency: An Anthropological Theory*. Oxford: Oxford University Press.

Giddens, A. (1984). *The Constitution of Society*. Cambridge: Polity Press.

Hardin, M. A. (1983). 'The Structure of Tarascan Pottery Painting', in D. Washburn (ed.), *Structure and Cognition in Art*. Cambridge: Cambridge University Press, pp. 8–24.

Helbling, J. (1999). 'The Dynamics of War and Alliance among the Yanomami', in G. Elwert, S. Feuchtwang, and D. Neubert (eds.), *Dynamics of Violence*. Berlin: Dunker and Humblot, pp. 103–15.

Kohn, M. and S. Mithen (1999). 'Handaxes: Products of Sexual Selection?' *Antiquity*, 73: 518–26.

Lawal, B. (1993). 'Some Aspects of Yoruba Aesthetics', in R. Anderson and K. Field (eds.), *Art in Small-Scale Societies: Contemporary Readings*. Englewood Cliffs, NJ: Prentice Hall, pp. 309–16.

Layton, R. (1992). *Australian Rock Art: A New Synthesis*. Cambridge: Cambridge University Press.

——(1997). *An Introduction to Theory in Anthropology*. Cambridge: Cambridge University Press.

——(2006). *Order and Anarchy: Civil Society, Social Disorder and War*. Cambridge: Cambridge University Press.

Lie, H., G. Rhodes, and L. Simmons (2008). 'Genetic Diversity Revealed in Human Faces'. *Evolution*, 62: 2473–86.

Malinowski, B. (1922). *Argonauts of the Western Pacific: An Account of Native Enterprise and Adventure in the Archipelagoes of Melanesian New Guinea*. London: Routledge.

McBrearty, S. and A. Brooks (2000). 'The Revolution that Wasn't: A New Interpretation of the Origin of Modern Human Behaviour'. *Evolution*, 39: 453–563.

McManus, I. and P. Weatherby (1997). 'The Golden Section and the Aesthetics of Form and Composition: A Cognitive Model'. *Empirical Studies of the Arts*, 15: 209–32.

Miller, G. (2000). *The Mating Mind*. New York: Doubleday.

Morphy, H. (1989). 'From Dull to Brilliant: The Aesthetics of Spiritual Power among the Yolngu'. *Man*, 24 (n.s.): 21–40.

O'Hanlon, M. (1989). *Reading the Skin: Adornment, Display and Society among the Wahgi*. London: British Museum.

Sahlins, M. (1974). *Stone-Age Economics*. London: Tavistock.

Sauvet, G., R. Layton, T. Lenssen-Erz, P. Taçon, and A. Wlodarczyk (2009). 'Thinking with Animals in Upper Palaeolithic Rock Art'. *Cambridge Archaeological Journal*, 19: 319–36.

Sillitoe, P. (1988). 'From Head-Dress to Head-Messages'. *Man*, 23 (n.s.): 298–318.

Silver, H. (1981). 'Calculating Risks: The Socio-Economic Foundations of Aesthetic Innovations in an Asante Carving Community'. *Ethnology*, 20: 101–14.

Strathern, A. and M. Strathern (1971). *Self-Decoration in Mount Hagen*. London: Duckworth.

Symons, D. (1995). 'Beauty is in the Adaptations of the Beholder: The Evolutionary Psychology of Human Female Attractiveness', in P. R. Abramson and S. D. Pinkerton (eds.), *Sexual Nature/Sexual Culture*. Chicago: University of Chicago Press, pp. 80–118.

Thompson, R. F. (1973). 'Yoruba Artistic Criticism', in W. L. d'Azevedo (ed.), *The Traditional Artist in African Societies*. Bloomington: Indiana University Press, pp. 19–61.

Thornhill, R. and S. Gangestad (1999). 'Facial Attractiveness'. *Trends in Cognitive Science*, 3/12: 452–60.

Tinbergen, N. (1963). 'On Aims and Methods in Ethology'. *Zeitschrift für Tierpsychologie*, 20: 410–33.

Van Gennep, A. (1960 [1905]). *The Rites of Passage*, trans. M. B. Vizedom and G. L. Caffee. London: Routledge.

Washburn, D. (ed.) (1983). *Structure and Cognition in Art*. Cambridge: Cambridge University Press.

——and D. Crowe (1988). *Symmetries of Culture: Theory and Practice of Plane Pattern Analysis*. Seattle: University of Washington Press.

Weber, M. (1947 [1925]). *The Theory of Social and Economic Organisation*, trans. A. R. Henderson and T. Parsons. London: Hedge and Co.

Wendt, W. E. (1974). '"Art mobilier" aus der Apollo-11 grotte in Südwest-Afrika'. *Acta Praehistorica et Archaeologica*, 5: 1–42. A report was published in English in *South African Archaeological Bulletin*, 31 (1976): 5–11.

Zahavi, A. (1975). 'Mate Selection: A Selection for a Handicap'. *Journal of Theoretical Biology*, 53: 205–14.

# 12

# Experiencing the Aesthetic: Kantian Autonomy or Evolutionary Biology?

*Elisabeth Schellekens*

One of the reasons many philosophers are sceptical about empirical approaches to aesthetics is the perception that philosophically loaded terms are employed in rather liberal ways. This scepticism is founded on the impression that the concepts at the heart of aesthetic analysis—such as beauty, art, or emotion—seem often to be applied without sufficient attention being paid to exactly what things or events these concepts refer to, or to the ambiguities that frequently surround the instantiation of many such concepts. To be sure, the greater part of this scepticism is not motivated by an *a priori* rejection of the application of scientific methodologies to questions in aesthetics. A consistent theme nonetheless is the way that the notions deployed in empirical analyses seem inadequate to the task of capturing the full depth and breadth of the relevant aesthetic experience.

The very notion of the aesthetic itself is not immune to this charge. In the wider sense of the word, we are happy to call 'aesthetic' that which is sensorily enjoyable, beautiful in some sense, or that which gives rise to a certain kind of valuable experience. And it is more often than not in this wider sense that we find the term deployed in the empirical literature. Unfortunately, many philosophers are not satisfied with this, especially in the context of evidence-based investigations, because such a broad conception of the aesthetic seems insensitive to concerns to do with how we are to separate the aesthetic from the non-aesthetic, what the value we ascribe to it actually amounts to, or indeed why we seem to care so deeply about our aesthetic experiences, our aesthetic tastes, and so on. Furthermore, the question needs to remain open of whether there really is such a category to begin with. Is there, in fact, anything uniquely aesthetic, and if so, what is it? Since there is no universal agreement on what things count as aesthetic, or indeed whether there can be a negative aesthetic, these questions call for examination. Indeed, from a traditional philosopher's point of view, an account that proclaims to have explained the aesthetic without at the very least considering these concerns is unlikely to make any significant progress in the field.

The scepticism felt towards empirical accounts on this issue is often justified since claiming that empirical data reveal something fundamental about the aesthetic without stating what that notion really means leaves much of the job undone.[1] What exactly is being explained here, and is there a clear sense in which the empirical sciences aren't simply hand-picking or moulding the very concept their data are supposed to be elucidating? It is especially interesting to note, then, that the discipline which tends to level this complaint can hardly be said to present a united front on these questions either. In fact, philosophers are still a long way from sharing a cohesive account of the aesthetic, and attempts to define it have taken numerous forms. Focusing primarily on aesthetic *experience*, theories tend to vary between emphasizing features internal to that experience (such as a certain kind of attitude or pleasure)[2] or external to it (such as the properties of the object or event that the experience is of).[3]

Either strategy meets with serious difficulties. Whether the characteristics singled out are unity, intensity, complexity,[4] or pleasure,[5] or indeed any combination of them, these features encounter substantial problems when we try to cast them as unique to *aesthetic* experience (not the least, neither seems to occur in all instances of the experiences we think of as aesthetic). Similarly, appealing to beauty or any other individual aesthetic property in order to define aesthetic experience relies on too narrow a conception of what aesthetic experiences take as their subject or indeed the manifold of qualities that gives rise to them. After all, it is perfectly possible to have aesthetic experiences which do not involve, for example, beauty.

The lack of resolution on this point in turn raises the question of whether *experience* is the best starting point for an account of the aesthetic. Immensely broad in scope and hugely rich in components, the kind of experience philosophers have been trying to pin down affords both subjective and objective elements, the combination of which doesn't necessarily lend itself particularly well to comprehensive definitions. This is not merely the neo-Wittgensteinian point that some concepts resist definition in terms of necessary and sufficient conditions.[6] Rather, it is the thought that aesthetic experience itself may not allow for one distinguishing feature other than its being, simply put, aesthetic. And for obvious reasons, such a plain observation is not very helpful in this context. Perhaps, then, we ought to consider the possibility that in trying to locate the uniquely aesthetic, we should first be looking for a description (or definition if you like) of something other than experience on which to base our attempts to delimit the notion of the aesthetic.

---

[1] There are, of course, empirical accounts that are less ambitious and don't make any systematic claims about the notion of the aesthetic as such. For example, a study showing how children learn perspective in drawing doesn't necessarily beg any questions about what is and what is not aesthetic about perspective.

[2] Beardsley 1958 and Dewey 1934.

[3] Beardsley 1982 and Dickie 1988. For more on this topic, see also Walton 1993; Levinson 1996; Zangwill 1999; Sharpe 2000.

[4] Beardsley 1958.

[5] Levinson 1996.

[6] For more on this point, see for example Weitz 1956.

One appealing candidate for this task is aesthetic judgement, where such judgement is conceived on broadly Kantian lines as a deliberative process which rests on pleasurable experience and enjoys a special form of autonomy in virtue of its perceptual and non-inferential nature. Much points to the idea that this autonomy might be the source of that which is unique to the aesthetic. After all, as Kant himself suggests in the *Critique of the Power of Judgement*, aesthetic judgements seem fundamentally different from 'cognitive judgements', 'moral judgements', or indeed 'judgements of the agreeable' in this respect: despite being rooted in the subject of experience (more specifically first-hand perception and pleasure), these judgements harbour objectivist aspirations of widespread applicability.[7]

Generally speaking, if the autonomy of aesthetic judgements is to be a viable candidate for distinguishing such judgements from other forms of judgement, then we need to establish whether such autonomy is even possible to begin with. For one thing, might eighteenth-century philosophy about the exercise of aesthetic taste and judgement not have been superseded by recent empirical explanations concerning how and why aesthetic preference, appreciation, and assessment seem to have developed over time? On many of these accounts, that which we think of as the autonomy of the aesthetic is shown to be underpinned by universal principles or rules of thumb to do with our biological and physiological evolution. Minor individual differences aside, our attributions of aesthetic character or value to things around us is first and foremost a matter of what we as a species are physically attracted to, and this in turn seems to leave little room for the non-inferential understanding of aesthetic judgement that philosophers have tended to rely on.

The main aim of this chapter is, then, to examine the following question: can we maintain a commitment to the autonomy of aesthetic judgements in the context of a collaborative discourse with the empirical sciences? In other words, is a philosophical commitment to aesthetic autonomy compatible with the data provided about how and why we make aesthetic judgements?

# I

The driving force of empirical aesthetics (hereafter EA) is the idea that art, beauty, and the aesthetic can be explained by the findings of evolutionary biology, developmental and cognitive psychology, social anthropology, and neuroscience.[8] That is, the role, purpose, and importance of art and beauty are to be accounted for within a framework of psychological evolution and neurological development. On this line, the aesthetic

---

[7] See especially sections 1-8 of Kant 2001.

[8] See, for example, Dissanayake 2000; Humphrey 1999, 2008; Ramachandran and Hirstein 1999; Ramachandran and Rogers-Ramachandran 2006; Solso 2003; Tooby and Cosmides 2001; Turner 2006; Zaidel 2005; Zeki 1999a, 1999b.

gains most of its worth from the function it has performed, and continues to perform, in the course of that development.

Now, adherence to this method does not automatically divide philosophy from science. In fact, a number of prominent philosophers advocate a shift of emphasis away from pure conceptual analysis towards a methodology strongly informed by empirical data.[9] Similarly, some scientists are doubtful of the idea that their disciplines can reveal much about why, and more importantly what, humanity gains from its engagement with beauty and art.[10] Rather than driving a wedge between two disciplines or methodologies as such, then, the main disagreement about the validity and scope of EA centres around the question of whether the aesthetic is to be considered a generally pleasant and enjoyable effect of various physiological and biological processes in which terms they are to be explained, or whether it carries sufficient independent explanatory weight to deserve examination aside from those processes.

Broadly speaking, concerns about the fundamentally reductive commitments implicit in this kind of empirical approach can take three main forms:

*Experiential.* If aesthetic experience is to be cast in the terms of EA, the aesthetic seems to amount to little more than an epiphenomenal notion. This worry can, in turn, take two expressions.

*Evaluative worry*: If the aesthetic is to be explained in empirical terms, then it is not really aesthetic value as we know it that is being examined, for such value resists the causal explanations proposed by the empirical sciences. EA thus seems to dispense with the notion of the aesthetic altogether.

*Phenomenological worry*: If the aesthetic is to be cast in empirical terms, then the phenomenology of aesthetic experience, central to our conception of it, becomes more or less irrelevant. According to EA, then, the content of my experience—qua aesthetic experience—does not actually reflect anything real.

*Ontological.* If we adhere to the empirical project, it seems difficult to retain an independent ontological status for the aesthetic. For the metaphysical assumption implicit in EA is that aesthetic character or aesthetic properties are fundamentally to be understood in terms of the material properties on which they causally depend or supervene. EA thus seems to reduce the features we focus on in aesthetic experience to non-aesthetic properties (where such a move is not warranted).

*Epistemological.* On the empirical account, there is neither much room to expand the idea that art and the aesthetic may yield a form of understanding other than about our evolutionary development and neurophysiological systems, nor a commitment to the claim that aesthetic perception and judgement-making is not regulated by certain impulses and patterns rooted in our biological nature. For EA, which features will give rise to aesthetic experiences and which characteristics

---

[9] For example, Jesse Prinz and Shaun Nichols.
[10] For example, Raymond Tallis and Roger Penrose.

we will deem beautiful seem predetermined by (non-aesthetic) facts about our brain and its evolutionary past, and this seems to go against the way in which aesthetic perception and judgement-making proceeds on a case-by-case basis. EA thus disregards the autonomy of aesthetic judgement and that of the experiences we base them upon.[11]

As sketched here, these worries have been given a somewhat exaggerated form. Nonetheless, they capture an attitude which underlies much of the scepticism referred to earlier, and which can motivate the suspicion that philosophical analysis and empirical methodologies just don't seem to join up in this context. In what follows, my intention is to concentrate on the third worry in order to further our investigation into aesthetic autonomy and its compatibility with EA.

# II

At the heart of the epistemological worry about EA is the idea that aesthetic judgements are fundamentally perceptual, and as such enjoy an independence that sets them apart from non-aesthetic judgements. As Frank Sibley puts it, we have to 'see the grace or unity of a work, hear the plaintiveness or frenzy in the music, notice the gaudiness of a colour scheme, feel the power of a novel, its mood, or its certainty of tone'. Aesthetic judgements cannot be made on the basis of testimony, nor predicted or inferred from previous experience of non-aesthetic features. Unless we 'perceive for [our]selves . . . aesthetic judgement [is] beyond [us]'.[12] Similarly, according to Alan Tormey, 'we require critical judgements to be rooted in "eye-witness" encounters, and the epistemically indirect avenues of evidence, inference, and authority that are permissible elsewhere are anathema here'.[13] In an epistemological context, then, the autonomy of the aesthetic thus primarily turns into a question of the unpredictability and non-inferential character of aesthetic judgements.[14]

The notion of aesthetic autonomy takes one of its most famous expressions in Kant's aesthetic theory. In the *Critique of the Power of Judgement*, Kant explains that genuine aesthetic judgements must be grounded in a subject's perception of the object and the accompanying feeling.

---

[11] Obviously, not all the worries enumerated here necessarily apply to every theory that falls under our heading of EA. For example, it is not because one is committed to the view that the experience of certain aesthetic features can be reduced to specific physiological or neural states (such as in the first and second worry) that one must conclude that these experiences cannot yield any form of relevant information (such as in some versions of the third worry).

[12] Sibley 2001a: 34.

[13] Tormey 1973: 39.

[14] While there are a handful of philosophers who have recently questioned the importance of aesthetic judgements being grounded in *first-hand* perceptual experiences (Budd 2003 and Livingston 2003), they nonetheless uphold the autonomy and non-inferential character of aesthetic judgements. What is questioned is whether the perception must be experienced by oneself (or whether it could also be the experience of another reliable aesthetic subject).

There can

> be no objective rule of taste that would determine what is beautiful . . . For every judgement
> from this source is aesthetic; i.e. its determining ground is the feeling of the subject . . . To seek
> a principle of taste that would provide the universal criterion of the beautiful . . . is a fruitless
> undertaking, because what is sought is impossible and intrinsically self-contradictory. (Kant
> 2000, §17, 5: 231)

One of the cornerstones of most aesthetic theories, ranging from Kant to Tormey, is
this idea that judgements of beauty cannot be rule-based and must result from
independent subjective experiences. Can this philosophical understanding of beauty
and aesthetic experience—whereby we are subjects of autonomous aesthetic experiences and makers of independent aesthetic judgements—be squared with EA according to which we follow neurologically set paths of aesthetic preferences grounded in
sexual impulse? As we shall soon see, the answer to this question will largely depend on
exactly which property-relations are targeted by the generalizations described by
EA and, similarly, which property-relations are affected by the claim to aesthetic
autonomy. But before examining these relations in greater detail, let us look at what
proponents of this seeming threat to aesthetic autonomy actually hold.

One of the most aggressive empirical theories of aesthetic judgement is that developed by Vilayanur Ramachandran and William Hirstein.[15] According to this theory,
there is indeed a set of universal rules that underlies all artistic experience. Defining art
and aesthetic experience must centre around three questions: (i) What are the 'rules
of art'?, (ii) Why did these rules evolve and have the form that they do?, and (iii) What
is the brain circuitry involved? In order to answer these concerns, Ramachandran and
Hirstein put forward 'Eight Laws of Artistic Experience' that 'artists either consciously
or unconsciously deploy to optimally titillate the relevant visual areas of the brain',[16]
and that are said to provide the cornerstone of a neurobiological account of beauty and
art. Of these eight, the two main laws are:

> **'Perceptual grouping'.** This law is grounded in the enjoyable process of construct-
> ing an aesthetic object out of the data presented to the senses as an exercise of
> perceptual problem-solving. When a random collection of spots are grouped into a
> dog or a human face, for example, our so-called 'discovery' leads to a pleasant
> sensation, and this in turn indicates that there are neurological links between the
> processes that uncover such correlations and the limbic areas which give rise to the
> pleasurable 'rewarding' sensations associated with 'feature binding'.

---

[15] Ramachandran and Hirstein 1999. Social anthropologist Nick Humphrey, for example, has also argued
that human aesthetic preferences have evolved in the context of courtship and mate choice. According to
Humphrey, when we are excited by beauty, whether in painting, music, sculpture, or literature, we are
responding to features in the beautiful object that reveal the hand of a *human artist*. So, when we are excited
by beauty in the things around us, we are in fact being titillated by cues from the environment that we are in
the presence of a potentially good mate. For more on this topic, see Humphrey 1999 and 2008.

[16] Ramachandran and Hirstein 1999.

'Peak Shift Effect'. This law is illustrated by the way in which the female figure is represented by classical Indian sculptors, for example, namely as a caricature of the female shape. Artists are thus said to amplify the 'very essence' of being feminine in order to more powerfully activate the same neural mechanisms that would be activated by the presence of the real object, and these amplifications operate as 'super stimuli'. The representation of beauty in art is thus founded on exaggeration, and the physiological response that it gives rise to.

On this view, then, beauty and the aesthetic earn their function and worth from relating directly to the categories of natural and sexual selection which we are programmed to exemplify. These categories are the same for all normal perceivers under normal circumstances and apply whether a particular perceiver has engaged first-hand with a specific object of aesthetic of appreciation or not. Likewise, it applies regardless of any small variation that such an object may manifest. In other words, on this account, there seems to be no reason not to suppose that we can draw certain inferences from the presence of specific properties in objects of aesthetic appreciation if we know that those properties are generally linked to our aesthetic preferences (which, in turn, are rooted in principles of sexual attraction).

Now, to return to our philosophical perspective, and if aesthetic judgements are to be non-inferential, there cannot be law-like connections between two (kinds of) properties in so far as the ascription of one (kind of) property follows from the presence of another. The two kinds of connection in question here concern the relations between

(a) a non-aesthetic property (e.g., red, square) and an aesthetic property (e.g., beautiful, dumpy);
(b) a (thick) aesthetic property (e.g., dumpy) and a (thin)[17] aesthetic property (e.g., beautiful).

If the autonomy of aesthetic judgements as it is generally understood is to be upheld, what cannot be allowed are law-like regularities in the first of these relations. In other words, the autonomy of aesthetic judgements requires that we cannot infer that a thing has an aesthetic property such as beauty from the mere fact that it is of a certain size or colour, shape or size, say.

That said, and surprisingly perhaps, conceiving relation (a) along these lines does not necessarily commit one to a similar understanding of (b). In fact, the philosopher Monroe Beardsley famously argued that unity, intensity, and complexity operate as criterial rules for overall aesthetic worth.[18] and many philosophical

---

[17] For more on the distinction between thick and thin concepts see. for example, Williams 1985.

[18] According to Beardsley, an artwork must have these three features in order for it to be aesthetically valuable. For Beardsley, they are features that 'always contribute positively to the value of a work' (1962: 485).

theories have taken seriously the idea that at least some aesthetic properties, including grace, harmony, or vivacity, do almost invariably tend to count in favour of something's overall positive aesthetic value.[19] At the very least, then, we need to be clearer about the exact relation that our views about the possibility of aesthetic inference apply to.

Separating these two relations has at least two advantages. First, it helps us gain a better grasp of what a commitment to aesthetic autonomy actually involves at the level of property relations. Second, it may have ramifications for the extent to which our two approaches can be held to represent genuinely conflicting views. For if (a) and (b) can allow for different accounts of the degree to which the connections between aesthetically relevant properties are law-like (or not), and there can be some strong regularities at (b) without necessarily denying aesthetic autonomy at (a), the question comes into focus of which relation exactly it is that is targeted by EA.

# III

In a nutshell, Ramachandran and Hirstein's theory holds that:

1. When a heterosexual man sees a curvaceous womanly figure under suitable conditions he will be sexually aroused.
2. The experience of seeing a curvaceous woman's figure can be translated into looking at a (curvaceous) female figure in an artwork.
3. Looking at the artistic representation of a (curvaceous) woman is sufficiently similar to looking at a real (curvaceous) womanly figure.
4. Therefore, a heterosexual man looking at (curvaceous) womanly figures in artworks will be aroused. He will find the artistic representation attractive and thus deem it aesthetically rewarding.

Over time, complex evolutionary processes have led this originally heterosexual male impulse to apply more broadly, eventually making its way into our conception of beauty and aesthetic value in general. The result of these processes is, then, some form of sublimated version of what was initially the reflection of a basic biological need.[20]

Let us now re-cast (a) and (b) in terms more explicitly in line with EA as relations between

---

[19] In a similar vein, Sibley has also defended the view that there can be general reasons for some aesthetic judgements even though he describes Beardsley's position as unnecessarily 'extreme and heroic' (2001b: 104). For Sibley, certain aesthetic qualities count as 'inherently general aesthetic merits' although they can constitute 'a defect . . . in the context of a given work' (2001b: 108).

[20] According to Ramachandran and Hirstein, the 'Laws of Aesthetic Experience' are deployed either consciously or unconsciously.

(a′) a non-aesthetic property (being curvy) and an aesthetic property (being sexually attractive, being beautiful);

(b′) a (thick) aesthetic property (being sexually attractive) and a (thin) aesthetic property (being beautiful).

The first issue to address is the classification of sexual attractiveness as an aesthetic property. Being sexy[21] is a sensory quality, and although some aesthetic properties are sensory, the reverse isn't necessarily the case. For example, while being soothing can count as aesthetic, being chewy tends not to. Also, sensory properties might more naturally be cast as aesthetic properties when applied to certain things. So, while a soothing piece of music might be described as aesthetic, a soothing bowl of chicken soup might not.[22] Similarly, while being sharp can be an aesthetic property in the context of a poem, in describing a person as sharp we tend to have another kind of quality in mind.

When we call a man or a woman sexually attractive, do we make an aesthetic judgement about that person or not? Of course on the one hand, finding someone attractive is simply about wanting to mate or procreate with them. And this desire might well be rooted in the fact that we are 'hard-wired' to deem attractive the potential partner which seems to be the fittest, healthiest, and generally best equipped at ensuring survival. On this reading, taking sexual attractiveness to be an aesthetic property might be rather stretching a point. On the other hand, in practice, finding someone attractive operates in a considerably more intricate and complex way, and most of us would probably agree that being sexy or finding someone attractive is intimately bound up with factors that fall outside the set of features highlighted by Ramachandran and Hirstein. Having an infectious laugh, being self-confident (or not), dressing in a certain kind of way, having a certain kind of humour, speaking with a certain tone of voice, moving in a certain way, having a certain glint in the eye, to name but a few factors, all contribute to whether a person can be said to be attractive or not. What is more, those factors—together with other aesthetically relevant features— don't always add or up or combine in such a way as to warrant saying that that same person is beautiful (or not).

Although much remains to be said on this topic, let us assume for the sake of our argument that being sexually attractive can in some meaningful sense be classified as an aesthetic property when ascribed to persons. This leaves us with two further concerns: first, can we predict from the fact that a woman is curvy that she is attractive (a′); second, can we predict from the fact that a woman is sexually attractive that she is beautiful (b′)?

---

[21] I will use the term 'sexy' as shorthand for being sexually attractive.

[22] Being smooth to the touch can be an aesthetic property in certain contexts too: touching a marble sculpture, for example, can add to the aesthetic experience of the work.

While it seems unlikely that we can *infer* the presence of beauty from the ascription of sexual attractiveness, it is only fair to admit that when we deem someone beautiful we often find that person attractive. In other words, although the relation between the two qualities might not be such that we can posit invariable inferential rules between them, there do seem to be strong regularities here, perhaps not entirely unlike those stressed by Beardsley with respect to how properties such as unity, intensity, and complexity do tend to go hand in hand with positive aesthetic value.[23] At the very least, if one were to find a person attractive without also finding them beautiful in some sense, a further explanation might be required in order to back up this discrepancy.

What about our first question: can we predict from the fact that a woman is curvy that she is also attractive? Obviously sexual preferences vary, and merely being curvy could not serve as a guarantee for sexual attractiveness. Having said that, it is also true that most women generally considered to be attractive, and certainly paradigmatic examples such as Marilyn Monroe, Naomi Campbell, or Scarlett Johansson, tend to be curvy. But these regularities might be disturbed by a sufficient amount of exceptions such that no law-like structures can be determined here. After all, not only are some attractive people not at all curvy. There are also instances where someone might be considered 'too curvy' to be attractive. In any case—and as the examples above indicate—being curvy is more often than not accompanied by some other aesthetic feature or features (such as having gorgeous eyes, a slender neck, or flowing hair) which, together, lead to the opinion that the person in question is indeed attractive.

To my knowledge, no proponent of EA (including Ramachandran and Hirstein) would argue that the generalities at the root of their theory of aesthetic judgement turn aesthetic perceivers and judgement-makers into mindless robots who merely follow the biological patterns scientists are in the process of uncovering for us. The empirical data in question here are not parts of a fully conscious reasoning process but, rather, relate to factors typical of our responses to perceptual stimuli which can be said to underlie our aesthetic reactions.

To think that EA necessarily threatens the possibility of aesthetic autonomy thus rests on two misconceptions of EA's project and claims: first, any law-like regularities that might form a part of empirical explanations of aesthetic judgement run so deeply that we are not directly aware of them (and so would only count as inferences at a considerable stretch); second, it is not obvious from the literature on EA that any such patterns are specifically said to link non-aesthetic properties to aesthetic properties (rather than some aesthetic properties to other aesthetic properties) where it is only at this level that law-like regularities might threaten the notion of aesthetic autonomy as discussed here.

---

[23] Beardsley 1962.

# IV

The extent to which our traditional philosophical conception of aesthetic judgements may or may not easily be reconciled with the data provided by EA will depend on several factors. These include the question of what, exactly, we take the autonomy of aesthetic judgements to consist in, and whether attractiveness can be cast as an aesthetic property in any meaningful sense. Most importantly, however, it will depend on whether the non-inferential character of the aesthetic must be upheld in all property relations and whether or not it must be said to hold 'all the way down', so to speak. If philosophers are committed to the claim that there cannot be *any* regularities whatso-ever—be it conscious or unconscious—between non-aesthetic and aesthetic proper-ties, then they will have to deny the possibility of some form of generalities occurring in relation (b) too—and, as we have already seen, some philosophers have argued against that view.[24] If, on the other hand, philosophers can make room for some form of regularities in (b), and the only law-like patterns that EA can be said to pinpoint operate at that same level, it may be possible to allow for some rules of thumb in aesthetic judgements without for that matter forsaking either aesthetic autonomy as such or the findings of EA (assuming that EA does indeed call for law-like patterns at this level).

It has not been the aim of this chapter to examine every aspect of aesthetic autonomy, nor indeed to establish definitively whether, all things considered, philo-sophical conceptions of the aesthetic are fundamentally at loggerheads with empirical accounts of that same concept. Nor has it been to try to map out in any comprehensive sense the areas in which philosophical and scientific enquiry can be mutually informa-tive. Rather, the goal has been to identify a potentially fruitful point of contact and to examine whether, in seeking to clarify what the aesthetic refers to exactly and what constitutes its boundaries, philosophical investigation is restricted in this context by the empirical sciences. Our initial question raised a concern about whether our mainstream philosophical analysis of aesthetic judgement will be able to stand its own ground in the light of recent scientific evidence. To the extent that this discussion can represent the beginning of an answer to this problem, our response has overall been a hopeful one.

From a philosophical point of view, adopting an empirical approach to matters aesthetic might not hold the key to a comprehensive account of why we pursue and value the aesthetic. But it does enable us to understand something about why it is that we can engage in aesthetic appreciation in the first place, and what, in that sense at least, it is to be a subject of aesthetic experience. One might say that this only constitutes the 'mechanics' of aesthetic appreciation, and as such covers an area that philosophers have the prerogative to set aside. But if we do, then we do so at the price of overlooking a wealth of readily available knowledge about that which lies at the very heart of what interests us all, namely the powers of the human mind.

---

[24] See Beardsley 1962 and Sibley 2001b.

# References

Beardsley, Monroe C. (1958). *Aesthetics: Problems in the Philosophy of Criticism*. New York: Harcourt.

—— (1962). 'On the Generality of Critical Reasons', *Journal of Aesthetics and Art Criticism*, 59: 477–86.

—— (1982). *The Aesthetic Point of View*. Ithaca, NY: Cornell University Press.

Budd, Malcolm (2003). 'The Acquaintance Principle', *British Journal of Aesthetics*, 43/4: 286–92.

Dewey, John (1934). *Art and Experience*. New York: Putnam.

Dickie, George (1988). *Evaluating Art*. Philadelphia: Temple University Press.

Dissanayake, Ellen (2000). *Art and Intimacy: How the Arts Began*. Seattle: University of Washington Press.

Humphrey, Nicholas (1999). 'Cave Art, Autism, and the Evolution of the Human Mind', *Journal of Consciousness Studies*, 6/6–7: 116–22.

—— (2008), *Seeing Red: A Study in Consciousness*. Cambridge, MA: Harvard University Press.

Kant, Immanuel (2001 [1790]). *Critique of the Power of Judgement*, ed. Paul Guyer and Eric Matthews. Cambridge: Cambridge University Press.

Levinson, Jerrold (1996). *The Pleasures of Aesthetics*. Ithaca, NY: Cornell University Press.

Livingston, Paisley (2003). 'On an Apparent Truism in Aesthetics', *British Journal of Aesthetics*, 43/3: 260–78.

Ramachandran, Vilayanur S. and William Hirstein (1999). 'The Science of Art: A Neurological Theory of Aesthetic Experience', *Journal of Consciousness Studies*, 6/6–7: 15–51.

—— and Diane Rogers-Ramachandran (2006). 'The Neurology of Aesthetics', *Scientific American Mind*, October–November: 16–18.

Sharpe, Robert (2000). 'The Empiricist Theory of Artistic Value', *Journal of Aesthetics and Art Criticism*, 58: 499–510.

Sibley, Frank (2001a). 'Aesthetic and Non-Aesthetic', in *Frank Sibley: Approach to Aesthetics: Collected Papers*, ed. John Benson, Betty Redfern, and Jeremy Roxbee Cox. Oxford: Clarendon Press, 33–51. First published in *Philosophical Review*, 74 (1965): 135–59.

—— (2001b). 'General Criteria and Reasons in Aesthetics', in *Frank Sibley: Approach to Aesthetics: Collected Papers*, ed. John Benson, Betty Redfern, and Jeremy Roxbee Cox. Oxford: Clarendon Press, 104–18. First published in *Essays on Aesthetics: Perspectives on the Work of Monroe Beardsley*, ed. John Fisher (Philadelphia, PA: Temple University Press, 1983), 3–20.

Solso, Robert (2003). *The Psychology of Art and the Evolution of the Conscious Brain*. Cambridge, MA: MIT Press.

Tooby, John and Leda Cosmides (2001). 'Does Beauty Build Adapted Minds? Toward an Evolutionary Theory of Aesthetic, Fiction and the Arts', *SubStance*, 94/95 (30/1–2): 6–27.

Tormey, Alan (1973). 'Critical Judgments', *Theoria*, 39: 35–49.

Turner, Mark (2006). *The Artful Mind: Cognitive Science and the Riddle of Human Creativity*. New York: Oxford University Press.

Walton, Kendall (1993). 'How Marvelous! Toward a Theory of Aesthetic Value', *Journal of Aesthetics and Art Criticism*, 51/3: 499–510.

Weitz, Morris (1956). 'The Role of Theory in Aesthetics', *Journal of Aesthetics and Art Criticism*, 15: 27–35; reprinted in *Aesthetics and the Philosophy of Art: The Analytic Tradition*, ed. P. Lamarque and S. H. Olsen. Oxford: Blackwell, 2004, 12–18.

Williams, Bernard (1985). *Ethics and the Limits of Philosophy*. Cambridge, MA: Harvard University Press.

Zaidel, Dahlia (2005). *Neuropsychology of Art: Neurological, Cognitive and Evolutionary Perspectives*. New York: Psychology Press.

Zangwill, Nick (1999). 'Feasible Aesthetic Formalism', *Nous*, 33/4: 610–29.

Zeki, Semir (1999a). 'Art and the Brain', *Journal of Consciousness Studies*, 6/6–7: 76–96.

—— (1999b). *Inner Vision: An Exploration of Art and the Brain*. Oxford: Oxford University Press.

PART IV

Imagination and Make-Believe

# 13

# Imagination Unblocked

*Aaron Meskin and Jonathan M. Weinberg*

> "Resistance is futile."
> — The Borg

## 1. The puzzle(s) of imaginative resistance

Some things are very hard to imagine—round squares, prime numbers evenly divisible by eight, and five and seven not adding to twelve are pretty plausible mathematical cases of this. Most famously, our imagination seems especially constrained in the moral realm (Walton 1994, Moran 1994). For although it appears fairly easy to imagine a world in which people falsely *believe* that the torture and murder of innocents is required, it is rather difficult (arguably impossible) to imagine a world in which the torture of innocents *is* morally required. Relatedly, it seems hard to make sense of a fiction in which it is true in that fiction that the torture and murder of innocents is morally required.

But it is a noticeable feature of artistic practice that talented authors can turn the unimaginable into the stuff of fiction. Graham Priest arguably succeeds in making it true in his story 'Sylvan's Box' that there is an absolutely empty box with something in it (Priest 1997). Tamar Gendler, whose essay 'The Puzzle of Imaginative Resistance' (Gendler 2000) initiated a flurry of interest in a range of aesthetic issues having to do with the limits of the imagination, composed a clever story in which it certainly seems to be true—and reported as imagined by at least some readers—that five and seven do not add up to twelve. And a range of philosophers sceptical of the puzzle Gendler presented have pointed to cases in which writers do seem able to get us go along with (i.e., accept as true-in-the-fiction and perhaps even imagine) moral impossibilities—Icelandic sagas, Mafia movies, the hard-boiled detective genre, and *Hamlet* have all been suggested as fictions which do not generate imaginative resistance in response to the morally problematic worlds they portray (Landy 2008; Todd 2009; Kieran 2010). Even (fairly) untalented authors can do the trick. Later in this chapter, we construct a story that is designed (and we think succeeds) in turning what initially appears to be unimaginable—Brian Weatherson's 'Wiggins World' example—into the imaginable by adding a few details (Weatherson 2004).

Work by Gendler and Weatherson, as well as recent discussion by others such as Gregory Currie (2002), Derek Matravers (2003), Shaun Nichols (2006b), Kathleen Stock (2003, 2005), Dustin Stokes (2006), Cain Todd (2009), Kendall Walton (2006), and Stephen Yablo (2002) has enriched our understanding of the first set of phenomena—the various forms imaginative resistance including *imaginative refusal* (an unwillingness to imagine) and *imaginative blockage* (difficulty or full-fledged inability in imagining). But the phenomenon of *un*blockage—the way in which various imaginative impediments may be avoided or overcome—has gone largely unnoticed and untheorized. We think this is a serious gap in the discussion. For it is a condition on a successful theory of imaginative resistance that it be able to explain the various ways that we can get round such resistance. That is what we propose to focus on in this chapter.

In an earlier work on this topic (Weinberg and Meskin 2006), we argued that philosophers' almost exclusive reliance on metaphysics and folk psychology (see Currie 2002 and Nichols 2006b for noticeable exceptions) has meant that many relevant phenomena are left unexplained. We remain convinced that the psychologically and (cognitive) architecturally informed theory we presented in that work—with some modification—can do a better job than any of the other contenders of explaining various aspects of imaginative resistance. In particular, we shall argue that our theory offers natural explanations of the various ways that imaginative blocks (or would-be blocks) can be circumvented. In the next section of this chapter we lay out that theory briefly. We then explain why it predicts the phenomenon of imaginative blockage. In the later sections of the chapter we turn our attention to two ways in which we may be able to avoid blockage—either getting around it temporarily or getting rid of it altogether.

Our central interest is in the phenomenon of imaginative blockage. That is, we are primarily interested in a psychological phenomenon rather than in artistic concerns. But like many other writers on this subject, we assume that there is an intimate connection between fiction and the imagination. In broad strokes, fiction may be characterized as a tool to direct the (cognitive) imagination (Currie 1995; Walton 1990). So fiction, and facts about our engagement with it, will provide us with rich source of data about the cognitive imagination. But what is the cognitive imagination? To get a handle on that, we need to turn our attention to issues of cognitive architecture.

## 2. The cognitive architecture of the imagination

Two important empirically supported results about the nature of the imagination are key to our account: (1) the *functional similarity* between believing and imagining and (2) the existence of a *distinct* cognitive system that underwrites the workings of the imagination. While we do not have room to present the empirical evidence for these results here, we can say a bit about how these two characteristics of imaginings are to be understood.

Beliefs and imaginings are functionally similar insofar as they interact with (largely) the same mental mechanisms. By and large, if the belief system takes input from or produces output to a cognitive mechanism, then the imagination system does as well (and vice versa). For example, there is plenty of evidence that various inferential mechanisms operate on both beliefs *and* imaginings (Leslie 1994). In addition, the cognitive mechanisms that do interact with both systems (e.g., our emotional systems) treat representations from either system in roughly the same way (Lang 1984). In Shaun Nichols' terms, imaginative states and beliefs states are in a 'single code' (Nichols 2004b).[1]

But despite the functional similarity between beliefs and imaginings, a separate system—distinct from the belief system—must be posited. To take an obvious point, imagining does not appear to drive the action system in the same way that belief does. Since systems are individuated by their functional role, this suggests that there really are distinct systems that subserve imagining and believing.

These results raise a crucial question. Which cognitive mechanisms interact with both imaginings and beliefs, and which ones interact with just one of the systems in question?[2]

We have already mentioned that various inferential mechanisms operate on both beliefs and imaginings. A particularly important piece of the cognitive architecture for our purposes is the mechanism (or mechanisms) that Nichols and Stich (2000) have termed the 'UpDater'. The UpDater handles the crucial task of adding and deleting beliefs in response to the receipt of new information. And this mechanism is clearly required to make sense of imaginative engagement just as much as belief revision. For example, we regularly update the contents of our fictively-generated imaginings in light of new fictive input.

Other largely automatic or 'modular' systems will plausibly interact with both imaginings and believings. For example, most fiction relies heavily on audience use of folk psychology to make sense of characters and their actions, so it is reasonable to suppose that the systems that underwrite those capacities are able to interact with the

---

[1] 'The core claim of the single code hypothesis is that a mechanism that takes pretense representations as input will process those representations much as it would process isomorphic representations' (Nichols 2004b: 131). A plausible explanation for this phenomenon is that the two sorts of representations exhibit the same representational format; hence, talk of a 'single code'. (The notion of 'code' here should be understood along the lines of the computational theory of mind which holds that cognitive processes are to be understood as formal operations performed on representations 'written' in something like a computer code.)

[2] The discussion in this section is heavily indebted to the work of Shaun Nichols and Stephen Stich (Nichols and Stich 2000; Nichols 2004b). See Weinberg and Meskin (2006) for a more detailed discussion.

imagination in much the same way that they interact with belief. In the context of our discussion of imaginative resistance, we are particularly interested in mechanisms that underwrite our moral capacities. For it is crucial to our engagement with ordinary narrative fiction that *some* moral mechanisms be engaged by the imagination. We could not make sense of the moral emotions of fictional characters and respond appropriately to them were we not able to make moral judgements about the fictive (and, hence, imagined) events which they face.

While the aforementioned mechanisms interact with both beliefs and imaginings, there is at least one important special-purpose mechanisms that must be posited to make sense of the workings of the imagination. Although we cannot generally make ourselves *believe* whatever we decide to, some mechanism must allow us to *imagine* just about whatever we decide to—*modulo* cases of blockage, of course. We will call the mechanism which subserves our capacity to do this the 'InPutter'.

With this rough sketch of the architecture of the imagination in place, we can turn to our account of the phenomenon of imaginative blockage.

## 3. Imaginative blockage: a diagnosis

Many of the usually automatic systems that interact with the imagination can either add representations to, or remove representations from, that system. In addition to the InPutter, various modular reasoning systems that add or subtract from our store of beliefs also add or subtract from our store of imaginings. And because of this, it is possible to get a conflict between these various systems—in particular, a situation may arise in which one system (most typically the InPutter) is trying to insert a representation even while another (most typically the UpDater) is trying to remove it. On our account, this is exactly what happens in cases of imaginative blockage.

Consider moral imaginative resistance. Suppose in the course of some exercise of the imagination we are confronted with an invitation to imagine some morally abhorrent proposition $p$ and that this results in blockage. Our explanation is that two systems have been put into conflict: as we attempt to comply with that invitation, the InPutter is accordingly trying to insert $p$ into the imagination, but at the same time, the UpDater registers a conflict between $p$ and some output of our moral judgement systems (not-$p$, since it detects the abhorrence of $p$). Importantly, since the moral judgement system works automatically—and is outside of the imagination—removing not-$p$ will not be effective. The moral system will automatically function to reinsert not-$p$ into the imagination in response to morally salient features of the imagined situation. So the UpDater's only way to resolve the conflict is to remove or reject the offending representation $p$—even while the InPutter is trying to add $p$ in. At that point, we can no longer proceed smoothly and automatically. And there is no obvious *non*-automatic way to proceed, either. We can cast about for a way to imagine $p$ without engaging the moral judgement system, but none will prove easily forthcoming. So, we are stuck: we are instructed to do something that we are simply unable to do.[3]

Our account easily generalizes to other cases of blockage reported in the literature. Most typically, one of the systems involved in the conflict will be the InPutter itself, although we do not believe that this is a necessary condition on blockage. (In fact, our theory raises the very real possibility of blockages generated by the inconsistent outputs of distinct automatic systems.) And note that conflict need not be generated by an initially imagined proposition, but may be generated by some other proposition that we automatically derive from it.

Under some circumstances, when we run into such a conflict in the imagination, we simply would end up with one of the relevant propositions removed and then be able to move on. Something similar would happen with a similar conflict in our beliefs, and the single-code approach considers imaginings and beliefs both to be generally subject to the same sorts of coherence-driven revision processes. But this is not always possible: some conflicts involve contents produced by automatic and modular processes and, hence, cannot be revised away. Nor, in many cases, can contents that the InPutter has already inserted be easily removed. For example, we tend to treat many of those contents as (almost) sacrosanct—only allowing the contents we input from engagement with fiction to be removed if we come to believe that we were dealing with an unreliable narrator or a dream sequences or some other 'epistemological twist' (Wilson 2006).[4]

So far, we have presented a general picture of the cognitive underpinnings of imaginative blockage. The account rests on an independently well-supported theory of cognitive architecture (see Nichols and Stich 2000 and Weinberg and Meskin 2006), and that theory of cognitive architecture makes its own predictions as to when we will experience blocks.[5] We turn now to a consideration of how this account of the architecture of blockage sheds light on two phenomena exhibited in our engagement with fiction: *imaginative deferral* and *blockage removal*.

---

[3] We would note that there is something not entirely right about this diagnosis; namely, we *can* on occasion enter propositions into the imagination without triggering various of the representation-management systems that are normally engaged. We take it that this is exactly what goes on when we do not try to fully *imagine* A, but merely try to *suppose* it (cf. Gendler 2000 and Weatherson 2004). We take it that the vast majority of imaginings with works of fiction are not merely suppositional, but rather involve full-fledged imagination. For a preliminary discussion of the supposition/imagination distinction see Weinberg and Meskin (2006); see also the discussion below on configuration of the imagination.

[4] In fact, it is because of the norm that underwrites this tendency (i.e., the norm that we should treat fictively-generated contents as sacrosanct unless confronted with evidence of unreliable narration) that we may end up positing something like unreliable narration ('doubling the narrator' as Gendler puts it in her (2006)) in response to certain blockage-inducing contents. See below for more on unreliable narrators.

[5] To take another example, see Nichols (2006b) for discussion of why, given that in ordinary cases we cannot believe obvious contradictions, it is to be expected that we will find it difficult—perhaps impossible—to imagine obvious contradictions.

## 4. Imaginative deferral

In many fictions, the putative necessary cognitive conditions for blockage obtain, and yet we are not blocked. One way this may happen is if we are able *configure* our imaginations so that various subpersonal and automatic systems that typically interact with it (and with belief) are temporarily disconnected (Weinberg 2008). That is, we have a capacity to adjust our imagination, often aided substantially by the construction of the work of fiction, so that it does not take inputs from various systems (e.g., some of the moral systems); and this capacity is plausibly what enables us to imaginatively engage with works in the various counter-moral genres mentioned above.

In some other cases the fiction is so structured as to enable us to *defer* the conflict between our cognitive systems. Such deferrals are usually paid off by the narrative later demonstrating that the conflict was spurious: what initially struck us as impossible is later revealed as possible, albeit in a surprising way. Apparently unfulfillable prophecies are perhaps the most famous version of this phenomenon. In *Macbeth*, for example, we seem to imagine all of the following: that the witches speak truly in their claim that 'no man of woman born' can harm him, nor can harm befall him 'until Great Birnam Wood to high Dunsinane hill shall come'; that these conditions are impossible to satisfy; yet also, that Macbeth will ultimately be overthrown. This is, after all, a Shakespearean tragedy, and we know in advance that matters cannot go well for the title character, and the proper appreciation of works in that genre requires that such knowledge be deployed in our readings and viewings.

We know that these cannot all be true together, yet we seem to imagine them nonetheless. It is clear that all of these propositions are in some way active in our engagement with the play, after all, or else we would not experience the admixture of foreboding and mystery that we do. Hence, cases like *Macbeth* cannot be explained away in the simple terms of our either just not noticing the conflict between the propositions, or ignoring it. Nor do we allow ourselves to become blocked—it is hardly the case that we throw the text across the room, decrying what a hack this Shakespeare fellow is! So we seem to have a case of an imagined acknowledged impossibility that nonetheless does not create blockage, and we must address the question of how this could be so.

Our suggestion is to take the following propositions to be the ones actually entertained in the imagination: (i) that the witches' prophecy will be true; (ii) that Macbeth will nonetheless suffer a downfall; and (iii) *it does not seem possible* that (i) and (ii) can both be true. It is important that this last proposition not be (iii'): *it is not possible* for (i) and (ii) to both be true, or else we'd still just have the contradiction.

But one might wonder why that is not indeed exactly what we imagine. For it does seem that, on our first reading or viewing, we typically do not find ourselves able to imagine just how it might be that the witches' prophecy could be fulfilled, consistent with other aspects of this particular imaginative project (e.g., that human reproductive biology is the same in the world of *Macbeth* as it is in the actual world). Or, at least, we cannot do so—until Shakespeare shows us how. He does this by ultimately presenting us with Malcolm's wooden tactics and Macduff's claim to be from his mother's womb untimely ripped. But we are not supposed to make use of those rather improbable ways of satisfying the witches' words until near the end of the play. So for most of the play, we are not to imagine any such way. Nonetheless, under normal circumstances, we quite readily make inferences along the following lines:

I cannot imagine how it could be possible that $p$.
Therefore, not-$p$.

So it might seem odd that we are so epistemically reticent with regard to propositions like 'the witches' prophecy will come true'.

The close resemblance between belief and imagination in a single code architecture can play a useful role here, however. For we can consider the existence of epistemically unusual, though far from extraordinary, circumstances in which we do not find ourselves making this inference from apparent unimaginability to the outright falsity of what cannot be imagined—namely, those in which one has independent strong reasons for $p$. (Bits of contemporary physics which we accept on the basis of testimony may be like this for many of us.) Compare to a typical transaction in perception, in which a vision system tokens $p$, and this leads to the tokening of a belief with content $p$. Under normal circumstances, this transition happens automatically, even unconsciously. But when we take ourselves to have very good evidence against $p$—suppose that $p$ is the proposition 'a large purple elephant has just appeared in the room'—then we do not seem typically to token $p$ itself in our beliefs, but rather only 'it seems that $p$' or 'it seems visually that $p$'. We take it that this representation-downgrading typically happens fairly automatically when it occurs. For example, when we see the Müller-Lyer figure while we know that the two lines are the same length, we unconsciously and effortlessly find ourselves in a state of the two lines merely seeming to be of different lengths. So our hypothesis is that the same mechanism of epistemic deflation that avoids cognitive meltdown in cases like perceptual illusions, also serves to help defer blockage in some cases that *prima facie* should put us into a state of imaginative blockage.

A key difference between cases like *Macbeth* and perceptual illusions is the source of the evidence for the relevant $p$ that causes the would-be tokening of 'not-$p$' to deflate to a tokening of 'it seems that not-$p$'. For the Müller-Lyer case, we have such evidence as our perception of the lines when the diagonal 'wings' are blocked; measurements of the lines themselves; and the trusted say-so of the vision scientists. We have nothing like that for the three witches, obviously. What we do have, however, is good metafictional evidence: our trust in Shakespeare as an author; our expectation that in general literary works that are disseminated to us will have been executed with at least minimal competency, and thus not have an imagination-blocking impossibility at their core; our understanding of such devices as apparently unfulfillable prophecies that always do, somehow, turn out to be fulfillable in unexpected ways. It can also help when a main character is in a similar epistemic position to the reader: Macbeth thinks he is unstoppable, but nonetheless fears the prophecy about Banquo's children. (*Mutatis mutandis* all these sorts of moves in cases of locked-room murder mysteries.) Such evidence leads us to expect that, despite appearances, there will not *ultimately* be an unimaginable contradiction in the fictional world. And it thereby leads our cognitive systems to posit as a seeming that which would be imaginatively fatal if tokened in full voice.

We therefore call this phenomenon 'imaginative deferral': both in the sense that we defer allowing the conflict to break down our imaginative engagement with the fiction, and in the sense that we are willing to defer to the author as to the ultimate coherence of his or her work. Deferral is a successful aesthetic tactic because it allows us a particular narrative pleasure of suspense, which is ultimately resolved with a satisfying sense of closure, indeed all the more satisfying because we could not see for ourselves how it would be possible. This pleasure is deeply connected to that of erotetic (that is, question-and-answer) narrative more generally, as described by Noël Carroll in *The philosophy of Homer* (Carroll 1990). Carroll is interested there in the notion of erotetic narrative to explain the attraction of monster stories: according to him, it is the conceptually incongruent, ontologically problematic nature of monsters (and our interest in solving the puzzles they raise) that makes stories involving them so compelling. We are suggesting that in cases of deferral, the narrative itself is 'monstrous' (at least until the resolution), and that our interest in solving the conceptual puzzles raised by the apparent inconsistencies (i.e., in figuring out how they will turn out to be not inconsistencies at all) is a significant part of our appreciation of them. Hence, an account that claimed that readers ignore or fail to notice the conflicts would thus leave out one of the most compelling aesthetic features of such fictions.

## 5. Paying off the deferral

A deferral is by its nature a temporary affair: at some point, that which was deferred comes due, and the *prima facie* unimaginable must be *ultima facie* imagined, or else the fiction revealed to be a sort of literary Ponzi scheme.[6] A deferral must be paid off, and the blockage of the imagination unblocked.

The easiest form of unblocking is when we no longer take ourselves to be invited to imagine one of the impossibility-generating propositions. As the fiction develops, it becomes clear that there is an unreliable narrator, or a dream sequence, or the like.

---

[6] Of course sometimes the creator of a work of fiction aims to generate literary payoff precisely by constructing a sort of Ponzi scheme—take, for example, the *mise en abyme* 'infinite loop' device used in some stories. In such fictions, it is the cleverness of the scheme itself that the reader appreciates, instead of and, indeed, in lieu of a plot. But most fictions are not to be understood in this way. (Thanks to Peter Goldie for encouraging us to think about these cases.)

We take it that there are no psychological or philosophical puzzles about such cases, which we will thus call cases of *simple unblocking*.

More interesting are cases in which we come to see that there is a possibility we had not foreseen, and which shows what had seemed impossible is not actually so. Kathleen Stock (2005) presents such an account. According to Stock, many cases of imaginative blockage stem from 'contingent imaginative failure'—in particular, a failure to find an appropriate context in which the blocked proposition would be warranted. Such blockages can be overcome when further content is added which serves to make the proposition intelligible. (She tells a very different story about the apparent overcoming of blockages that are generated by conceptual impossibilities and the non-contingent imaginative failures they induce; see below.) So, for example, Walton's (in)famous Giselda sentence, 'In killing her baby, Giselda did the right thing; after all, it was a girl' (Walton 1994), is initially unimaginable because readers cannot conjure a scenario in which that sentence would be true. But, according to Stock, the addition of background information about, for example, the awful fate of female infants in Giselda's culture, might make the sentence imaginable because a relevant context has now been supplied. We think Stock is on the right track here, though we might not put things as she does, in terms of the contingent *unintelligibility* of the proposition. (On our account, the propositions are perfectly intelligible, and must be such in order for the automatic systems to generate contents inconsistent with them.) But although this approach—which we will call *reinterpretation unblocking*—seems the right story about some cases, we think that there are other cases that it doesn't account for.

What simple unblocking and reinterpretative unblocking have in common is that the end-state of the imagination is self-consistent. Things look impossible early on, but are shown not to be such by the end. But in still other, rarer fictions, the addition of further content from the fiction can lead to the elimination of the blockage, but *not* by ultimately revising the contents to the point of consistency. The 'Tower of Goldbach' story is just such a one as these: we would be blocked in trying to follow the imaginative instructions of a shorter version of the story that included the claim that an arithmetical impossibility was made actual. But, with all the trappings of Gendler's story—especially the theological ones—we seem enabled to imagine it, *impossibilities and all*. How is that so? In particular, surely our ordinary reasoning systems that are generally engaged in the imagining of the story would reject that mathematical impossibility as, well, an impossibility. This is the phenomenon of *the non-monotonicity of imaginative blockage*: one can have a fiction with blockage, and add more fictional contents to it *even without rendering the imagined contents consistent*, and not necessarily end up with blockage in the new fiction. The rest of the story does not make it less of an impossibility—so how can the rest of the story nonetheless succeed in rendering it more of an imaginability?

Let us put another example on the table. As it stands, Weatherson's 'Wiggins World' story seems to be a case of imaginative blockage:

The Hogwarts Express was a very special train. It had no parts at all. Although you'd be tempted to say that it had carriages, an engine, seats, wheels, windows and so on, it really was a mereological atom. And it certainly had no temporal parts—it wholly was wherever and whenever it was. Even more surprisingly, it did not enter into fusions, so when the Hogwarts Local was linked to it for the first few miles out of Kings Cross, there was no one object that carried all the students through north London. (Weatherson 2004, 5)

But now consider the following extension of Weatherson's story, which we will call 'Parts & Parcels: The Attack on the Hogwarts Express', noting that it has none of the features of either simple or reinterpretative unblocking:

And it was a lucky thing for Ron and Hermione that Dumbledore's protective enchantment had given the Express these unusual mereological properties. When Voldemort's evil minion in the Department of Literary Theories and Other Dark Liberal Arts first let loose with Derrida's Devious Dismantlement—'deconstructing' any object into all its component parts—the Local was flung into an infinite number of pieces, and indeed further flayed into the arcane power set of that number. The Express, though adjoined to the Local, was never part of any larger train, and was thus spared its lethal effect.

Then, the spell was cast again, this time directly on the Express. But this assault fizzled as well. The Express having no parts to be deconstructed into, the students didn't even know that their trusty vehicle had been subject to an attack in the first place, arriving at Hogwarts without any further effects (though one student who had been working on a jigsaw puzzle later claimed that the puzzle strangely resisted any future assembly).

We take it that this further story *is* imaginable, and precisely because of the ways in which the deviant mereology plays a substantive role in the story—e.g., it protects the Express from a dark spell of Voldemort's that's meant to dissolve the target of the spell into its component parts. We take it that our story is thus rather Tower of Goldbach-esque, in particular in that what was once impossible-and-unimaginable is rendered impossible-yet-somehow-imaginable.

It may seem that what these cases relevantly have in common is the supernatural: in a fictional world with such a God, or with such magic spells, is anything truly impossible? But that only takes us part of the way there—we predict that similar stories in which we're just told 'God did it' or 'it's magic', without any further narrative stage-dressing, would still lead to blockage.[7] Rather, in such stories the supernatural element is part of a larger effort by the author to give the reader *a special way of complying with the author's instructions for the imagination*. As we have analysed them, cases of blockage are cases of wanting to follow an author's instructions, but simply not being able to see how to do so. One way of being shown how to do so would be to remove a presupposition that had been in the way—that's what's going on in simple or reinterpretative cases. But

---

[7] Not that magic is particularly blockage-prone—the invocation of magic most often does not induce any blockage in the first place. Our point is that in cases where *already* is blockage, merely being told that 'it's magic' is (usually) not enough by itself to *dissolve* the block. *Mutatis mutandis* for the fictional actions of deities.

one can also be told that one's compliance with the instruction may take a special, somewhat delimited form.[8]

We are told, in essence: 'imagine that $5 + 7$ does not equal 12', and at first we can do nothing that seems to comply with this instruction. The further developments of the story, however, show us some ways in which this can be done. For example, we can imagine that when five righteous souls and seven righteous souls are brought together, nonetheless God's conditions have not been met. Or we can imagine that a spell that was shown to decompose things into their component parts fails to have any effect on the Express. Once we receive these *further* instructions to imagine from the author, we can recognize how they are appropriate to the not-yet-fulfilled instruction to imagine the impossibility.[9] We are also open, if these stories were to continue, to being shown still more ways in which we are to comply with the instruction to the imagination, should those be enumerated within the work of fiction itself.

What exactly does complying with the invitation to imagine amount to in these cases? Do we, somehow, actually insert the (typically) blockage-inducing representation into our imagination in some special way; i.e., with various automatic sub-systems toggled off so as not to generate blockage (as may have been suggested by our discussion in Weinberg and Meskin (2006))? We suspect not. While there is good reason to think various automatic systems can be toggled on and off, continued full-blown imaginative engagement with fictions typically requires that such subsystems be left on. Rather, we comply with the instructions to imagine that $p$ (where $p$ is some blockage-inducing content) *by* placing a cluster of other relevant representations in the imagination. In 'Tower of Goldbach', for example, we do not imagine that $5 + 7$ does not equal 12 by placing that content in the imagination, but rather by placing contents such as *God can do the impossible* and so on in the imagination.[10] And it is in virtue of having a number of such representations in the imagination that we may be said to imagine the blockage-inducing representation. Do we, then, *strictly speaking* imagine such impossibilities? After all, on the account we have sketched, when engaging with Gendler's story we do not ever come to have a representation with the content '$5 + 7$ does not equal 12' in the imaginative system. But we suspect that ordinary usage of 'imagine' may nonetheless countenance such as cases that properly fall under it, just

[8] Note that Priest's 'Sylvan's Box' story does not rely on the mention of God or magic. Rather, Priest encourages readers to imagine the impossible by providing a detailed and compelling account of the effect on the narrator of perceiving a 'naked and brazen' contradiction (Priest 1997).

[9] The nature of this recognition will likely involve a separate, metafictional deployment of our imaginative faculties. But we think that this is not unusual in our engagements with even more ordinary fictions. For example, detective fictions will standardly call upon our powers of supposition and hypothetical reasoning. There is an open empirical question here as to just how many *parallel* deployments of the imagination are possible for typical human subjects.

[10] Similar mechanisms may also make possible some highly atypical believings of the impossible. Such believings—we will not say 'beliefs' here, since they may not ever get literally tokened in the belief system—would be predicted to occur fairly rarely, just as with non-monotonic fictions, and might well be restricted only to matters like 'mysteries of faith'. (Thanks again to Peter Goldie for encouraging us to think about this.)

as we sometimes countenance agents as having beliefs even when they are not explicitly tokened anywhere in the agents' cognitive workings.[11] Most importantly in this aesthetic context, we are in such cases succeeding in complying with the author's instructions regarding the imagination for such fictions, all the while cognizant that we are doing so. We have been instructed to imagine that *p*, and we are doing something that we recognize will count as satisfying that instruction—so there seems to us little point in denying that whatever we're doing, we're imagining that *p*.[12]

The explanation of the non-monotonicity of blockage that we have offered may remind some readers of Stock's account of the merely apparent imagining of conceptual impossibilities. Stock argues that we cannot, in fact, imagine conceptual impossibilities, and so when it seems to us that we are doing so, we are in fact imagining what she refers to as 'conceptually possible defeaters'; i.e., conceptually possible propositions that we mistake for the impossible one: '[I]f a reader thinks that she is imagining that twelve is and is not the sum of seven and five as she reads Gendler's story, the content of her imagining rather should be explicated in terms of one of these or some other conceptually possible "defeater"' (2003: 120–1).[13] While there is a structural similarity between this story and our account of what happens in blockage removal (viz., the idea of substituting one or more imaginable contents for a blockage-inducing content), there are, in fact, a range of instructive differences between the two views. In the first case, we believe that the focus on conceptual impossibility and possibility is a red herring. Full-fledged blockage is generated by irreconcilable conflict between the outputs of various cognitive systems (and the folk 'theories' they implement)—there is no need to make a tendentious appeal to conceptual impossibilities. In addition, Stock is insistent on denying that we do, in fact, imagine the problematic proposition, and that in such cases readers are often *mistaken* about what they are actually imagining. We resist taking such a firm line on the ascription of propositional imagining, and much more importantly, we would resist attributing any such error to the readers of such fictions. On our account, readers may recognize both what they are doing and that they are co-operating with the author in so doing. This brings us to the most important differences between our view and Stock's—a difference that can be seen in the failure of her account to explain an important aesthetic phenomenon in the area. For on Stock's account, it would not make sense to admire the skill the author has

---

[11] For a classic discussion of tacit belief see Lycan (1986). See Nichols (2004b) for discussion of tacit pretence.

[12] Which is entirely consistent with there being other contexts and projects for which it would make more sense to rule the other way. For example, someone with a rich modal epistemology of imagination might want to only countenance a content as properly imagined if that content does indeed get tokened in the relevant cognitive system. Our point here is not really that boundaries of the ordinary language term 'imagine' *must* include these cases, so much as it is that it *may* include them, and that such an inclusion best fits the aesthetic data.

[13] So, for example, in this case a reader might, in fact, be imagining 'that Solomon *said* that twelve is and is not the sum of seven and five' or 'that *most people believe* the twelve is and is not the sum of seven and five' (Stock 2003: 120).

exhibited in getting us to imagine the seemingly unimaginable. But we think that readers' appreciation of this sort of achievement may be central to their engagement with such fictions. For example, we take it to be a central source of the pleasure we take in reading Gendler's 'Tower of Goldbach' story: she has succeeded in getting us to imagine (in some sense) the previously unimaginable, and it is because of this that her story is enjoyable. We don't see how Stock can capture this key aesthetic explanandum.

We should note that the phenomenon we have described is possible because the InPutter is at least partially under our conscious control. We can simply *decide* to imagine various propositions, and thereby do so. This form of blockage removal, therefore, reveals further the importance of what we have called *active management* in our imaginative engagement with works of fiction: our ability to decide, using our extrafictional (but frequently metafictional) mainline cognition, what we ought to be imagining, and thereby come to imagine it. We have suggested elsewhere (Weinberg and Meskin 2005) that simple versions of simulation theory may be insufficient to capture the complex back-and-forth between what is imagined and what is believed. On our account, active management is also crucial in cases of non-monotonicity. Without this active management, we would have a simple case of blockage—we're asked to imagine that $p$ without being able to see any way to comply with that request. But when we're shown the way to do so, we can decide to imagine other contents and by doing so comply with the author's initial instructions.

With this picture in place, we can see how non-monotonicity is possible. It is not because the additional material induces a mistake in the reader (as Stock has claimed), or that it somehow distracts us from or disguises the impossibility (as suggested by Gendler in her (2000)).[14] As with many other cases of deferral, fully attending to the impossibility is a prerequisite for a proper appreciation of the work. And, unlike the simple and reinterpretative cases, we still take ourselves to be instructed to imagine the impossible, even at story's end. The additional material informs the reader as to the manner in which they are, for purposes of engaging with the story, to imagine the proposition. With a little extra help from the author, and with the appropriate management from resources outside the imagination itself, even the impossible can be imagined.

---

[14] It is worth noting that, on our architectural story, we have an explanatory advantage that Gendler did not avail herself of in her earlier paper: namely, the distinction between what is recognized by the agent, and what might nonetheless not be detected by some subpersonal modular system of the agent. There is a sense in which our 'active management' story is one in which the agent takes a direct role in hiding the impossibility from the subpersonal systems, while nonetheless being aware at all times that it is indeed an impossibility that is being thus hidden. Given Gendler's more recent substantial interest in subpersonal cognition (e.g., Gendler 2008), we expect that she would be amenable to our current story.

## 6. Conclusion

The psychologically and (cognitive) architecturally informed theory of the imagination that we have outlined here and in previous papers offers a natural and plausible explanation of various imaginative resistance phenomena. In this chapter we have focused on the theory's capacity to explain some of the ways that imaginative blocks (or would-be blocks) can be circumvented. The ease with which the account handles imaginative deferral and blockage removal is a significant point in its favour, and it provides a framework for simultaneously accommodating a range of both psychological and aesthetic data. It's not what the White Queen had in mind, but with a little help from the author, an active reader can indeed imagine six impossible things before breakfast.

## References

Carroll, Noël (1990). *The Philosophy of Horror: or, Paradoxes of the Heart*. New York: Routledge.

Currie, Gregory (1995). 'Imagination and Simulation: Aesthetics Meets Cognitive Science', in Martin Davies and Tony Stone (eds.), *Mental Simulation*. Oxford: Blackwell, pp. 151–69.

——(2002). 'Desire in the Imagination', in Gendler and Hawthorne (2002), pp. 201–21.

Gendler, Tamar Szabó (2000). 'The Puzzle of Imaginative Resistance'. *Journal of Philosophy*, 97/2: 55–81.

——(2006). 'Imaginative Resistance Revisited', in Nichols (2006a), pp. 149–74.

——(2008). 'Alief and Belief'. *Journal of Philosophy*, 105/10: 634–63.

——and John Hawthorne (eds.) (2002). *Conceivability and Possibility*. Oxford: Oxford University Press.

Hagberg, Garry (ed.) (2008). *Art and Ethical Criticism*. Malden, MA: Blackwell Publishing Ltd.

Hume, David (1987). 'Of the Standard of Taste', in E. F. Miller (ed.), *David Hume: Essays Moral, Political, and Literary*. Indianapolis: Liberty Classics, pp. 226–49.

Kieran, Matthew (2010). 'Emotions, Art and Immorality', in Peter Goldie (ed.), *The Oxford Handbook of Philosophy of Emotion*. Oxford: Oxford University Press, pp. 681–703.

——and Dominic McIver Lopes (eds.) (2003). *Imagination, Philosophy and the Arts*. London: Routledge.

Landy, Joshua (2008). 'A Nation of Madame Bovarys: On the Possibility and Desirability of Moral Improvement through Fiction', in Hagberg (2008), pp. 63–94.

Lang, P. J. (1984). 'Cognition in Emotion: Concept and Action', in C. Izard, J. Kagan, and R. Zajonc (eds.), *Emotions, Cognition and Behaviour*. New York: Cambridge University Press, pp. 192–226.

Leslie, Alan (1994). 'Pretending and Believing: Issues in the Theory of ToMM'. *Cognition*, 50: 211–38.

Lycan, William G. (1986). 'Tacit Belief', in R. J. Bogdan (ed.), *Belief: Form, Content, and Function*. Oxford: Clarendon Press, pp. 61–82.

Matravers, Derek (2003). 'Fictional Assent and the (So-Called) "Puzzle of Imaginative Resistance"', in Kieran and McIver Lopes (2003), pp. 91–106.

Meskin, Aaron and Jonathan Weinberg (2004). 'Emotions, Fiction, and Cognitive Architecture'. *British Journal of Aesthetics*, 43/1: 18–34.

Moran, Richard (1994). 'The Expression of Feeling in Imagination'. *Philosophical Review*, 103/1: 75–106.

Nichols, Shaun (2004a). 'Review of Currie and Ravenscroft, *Recreative Imagination*'. *Mind*, 113: 329–34.

——(2004b). 'Imagining and Believing: The Promise of a Single Code'. *Journal of Aesthetics and Art Criticism*, 62: 129–39.

——(ed.) (2006a). *The Architecture of the Imagination: New Essays on Pretense, Possibility, and Fiction*. Oxford: Clarendon.

——(2006b). 'Imaginative Blocks and Impossibility: An Essay in Modal Psychology', in Nichols (2006a), pp. 237–56.

——and Stephen Stich (2000). 'A Cognitive Theory of Pretense'. *Cognition*, 74: 115–47.

————(2003). 'How to Read Your Own Mind: A Cognitive Theory of Self-Consciousness', in Q. Smith and A. Jokic (eds.), *Consciousness: New Philosophical Essays*. Oxford University Press, pp. 157–200.

Priest, Graham (1997). 'Sylvan's Box: A Short Story and Ten Morals'. *Notre Dame Journal of Formal Logic*, 38/4: 573–82.

Stock, Kathleen (2003). 'The Tower of Goldbach and Other Impossible Tales', in Kieran and McIver Lopes (2003), pp. 107–24.

——(2005). 'Resisting Imaginative Resistance'. *Philosophical Quarterly*, 55: 607–24.

Stokes, Dustin (2006). 'The Evaluative Character of Imaginative Resistance'. *British Journal of Aesthetics*, 46: 387–405.

Todd, Cain (2009). 'Imaginability, Morality, and Fictional Truth: Dissolving the Puzzle of "Imaginative Resistance"'. *Philosophical Studies*, 143: 187–211.

Walton, Kendall (1990). *Mimesis as Make-Believe: On the Foundations of the Representational Arts*. Cambridge, MA: Harvard University Press.

——(1994). 'Morals in Fiction and Fictional Morality'. *Proceedings of the Aristotelian Society*, supp. vol. 68: 27–50.

——(2006). 'On the (So-Called) Puzzle of Imaginative Resistsance', in Nichols (2006a), pp. 137–48.

Weatherson, Brian (2004). 'Morality, Fiction, and Possibility'. *Philosopher's Imprint*, 4/3.

Weinberg, Jonathan M. (2008) 'Configuring the Cognitive Imagination', in Kathleen Stock and Katherine Thomson-jones (eds.), *New Waves in Aesthetics*. Basingstoke: Palgrave Macmillan, pp. 203–23.

——and Meskin, Aaron (2005). 'Imagine That!', in Matthew Kieran (ed.), *Contemporary Debates in Aesthetics and the Philosophy of Art*. New York: Blackwell, pp. 222–35.

————(2006). 'Puzzling Over the Imagination: Philosophical Problems, Architectural Solutions', in Nichols (2006a), pp. 175–202.

Wilson, George (2006). 'Transparency and Twist in Narrative Fiction Film'. *Journal of Aesthetics and Art Criticism*, 64/1: 81–95.

Yablo, Stephen (2002). 'Coulda, Woulda, Shoulda', in Gendler and Hawthorne (2002), pp. 441–92.

# 14

# An Attitude Towards the Possible: The Contributions of Pretend Play to Later Adult Consciousness

*Dorothy G. Singer and Jerome L. Singer*[1]

As Spinoza proposed, "The uses of imagination are also paths to freedom, alongside the uses of reason."

Hampshire (2005), p. viii

We suggest that imagination, the great evolutionary development reflecting our human ability to create private story-like structures in our thoughts, to reminisce about the past, and to spin out various more or less realistic scenarios for future events, is an outgrowth of enjoyable childhood play practices. Our goal is to point to some theoretical and research possibilities that can enrich our speculation about how childhood play may presage particular styles of adult conscious experience.

The atmosphere of early childhood education in the beginning years of the twenty-first century has been characterized by a trend among some government agencies and school administrations in the United States to devaluate, if not actually to ban children's play, from the classroom (Zigler and Bishop-Josef 2006; Zigler *et al.* 2004). Presumably such activity by preschoolers and early elementary grade youngsters is viewed as ephemeral, pointless albeit enjoyable, and counterproductive to the major task of early education, the acquisition of literacy and numerical skills. We want to emphasize the importance of experiential learning in a child's normal development. By experiential learning we refer to a child's manipulation of objects, use of senses such as taste, smell, touch, hearing, and vision, and the use of both small and large motor movements. This kind of learning is in contrast to formal lessons using rote techniques, drill, flashcards, workbooks, and so on—all of which are perceived by many children as

---

[1] Some portions of this chapter were published in Singer and Singer (2005–6).

impositions from adults (Singer *et al.* 2009). Children enjoy their normal desires of exploration and curiosity about their environment. Children want to play with dirt, water, and peek under a rock to see the bugs. These small adventures seem free of the demands of academic learning, which often seem to impede the natural inclinations of children for fun. In the course of such seemingly non-motivated play, children are learning a good deal about themselves and the world.

Consider the dilemmas that confront babies or preschool children striving to find their way in a complex world. Children must first cope with consummatory behaviors to survive, express emotions to signal hunger or pain, increase and focus their motor activities to master standing and walking, and find ways of organizing sensory experiences to gradually make the "booming, buzzing" world a space of increasing familiarity. The task demands of growing up call for motor skill masteries and each successful "step" yields a positive emotional response, often further reinforced by parental smiles, words of approval, or physical rewards of food and hugging, or kissing. Private positive emotions develop through reductions of confusion and fears and also through the experiences of gradual mastery of the complex world. Such mastery can include the physical and perceptual skills as well as the more internalized thinking capacities for planning and self-regulation.

## 1. The beginnings of imaginative play

Pretend play may emerge as a feature of the toddler's efforts to master the seeming ambiguities or not fully comprehended features of the surrounding physical and social environment. The earliest forms of play involve sensory-motor, repetitive skill development activities, e.g., pulling oneself up in a crib, dropping and retrieving rattles. All of these play forms stay locked to the immediate givens of the object world. By about two years of age, new capacities begin to become evident in the child's ability "to take an attitude toward the possible" in Kurt Goldstein's felicitous phrase (1939: 306). Early signs of such activities are evident when the two-year-old pretends to drink from an empty cup and says "Yum, Yum" or "Goody" (Fein 1981). This example of what has been called a transformation may soon become a "second" transformation when the child pretends to feed the "milk" in the empty cup to a soft toy doll or a plastic horse, or it may be an even more complex transformation when the child offers the supposed milk to an invisible imaginary playmate. This ability for establishing the beginnings of a fictional world or of a set of relationships which are solely under the child's control may be an evolutionary development that opens the way for the emergence of a distinct personal autonomy and of an eventual flowering of narrative consciousness (Gopnik 2009; Harris 2000; Kavanaugh and Harris 1999; Lillard 2001; Rosengren *et al.* 2000; Singer and Singer 1990).

It is very likely that some of the earliest signs of play emerge in the course of older babies' or toddlers' manifestations of what psychoanalyst Winnicott (1971) termed involvement with "transitional objects." Early on many children become attached to a soft cloth or to some combination of an old crib blanket and a "plush" toy, a cloth bunny rabbit, bear, or lamb. Actually, one might propose that the tenacity with which children cling to these objects even as they fade in color, shrink or become ragged, may reflect the very beginnings of an experience of autonomy ("my blankie") and personal ownership, a primordial evidence of our nearly universal adult sense of private property upon which whole societies and legal systems are constructed.

For many children, especially first born or only children, these transitional objects may soon lead to the phenomenon of a personification of the soft toy which is given a name and is treated as a living individual with whom one can converse. Even more dramatically, parents often observe the emergence for three- to five-year-olds of an invisible playmate or scapegoat, the imaginary companion (Singer and Singer 1990; Taylor 1999).

Researchers on the imaginary companions of preschoolers have agreed to combine vivid personifications of some dolls or soft toys along with invisible friends and have found this phenomenon prevalent in between one quarter to more than one half of children in various samples (Gleason 2002, 2004; Singer and Singer 1990; Taylor 1999). Despite trepidation by parents that children who insist on a setting at the breakfast table for an invisible friend may be emotionally troubled, even pre-psychotic, the research evidence indicates that those children who early on show transitional object attachments and those with imaginary companions fall well within the range of normal functioning (Litt 1986; Singer and Singer, 1990; Taylor 1999). Actually, our own work and that of Marjorie Taylor provides indications that children who show these phenomena appear to be less aggressive or impulsive, more self-contained, and more capable of divergent, potentially creative thought.

Very recent work by Michelle and Robert Root-Bernstein who are among the leading investigators of the personalities and characteristics of creative adults in the sciences and the arts has also provided evidence from interviews with Nobel Prize and MacArthur Foundation "Genius" Award winners of their development by middle childhood of imaginary worlds or societies (Root-Bernstein and Root-Bernstein 1999, 2006). Such childhood imaginary worlds, first labeled "paracosms" by Robert Silvey and Stephen MacKeith (Mackeith 1982–3; Silvey and MacKeith 1988), have been identified as precursors of the adult consciousness and story-telling capacities of successful literary contributors like the Brontë sisters. They have now been shown by the Root-Bernsteins to be early manifestations of the adult thinking of a broader group of creative persons, scientists, artists, and inventors.

In summary, pending more extended longitudinal research, it seems likely that a significant feature of our adult narrative consciousness is prefigured in the transitional object attachments and imaginary companion play of the early preschooler and in the somewhat less common feature of paracosm constructions of middle childhood. While many adults may think of children's make-believe, invisible friends as the erroneous trivialities of the youngsters' limited grasp of reality, are they not, after all, foreshadowings of our adult religious or other forms of spiritual consciousness? Think of how many adults carry on extended interior monologues with their deity or with patron saints, guardian angels, or deceased parents and mentors.

We agree that play seems to be "just for fun." We wonder if its emergence in toddlers as the psychologist Paul Harris (2000) has suggested, more or less at the same time as language, may not actually reflect an evolutionary development with adaptive import. The child's playful creation of tiny story-lines and of little virtual reality situations may serve to organize novel memory structures. These schemas are often linked to verbal labels combined with visual or auditory imagery in easily retrievable forms. We watched two-and-a-half-year-old Olivia, standing with her mother at a riverside, pick up a small tree branch and say "fishing." She then proceeded to cast an invisible line towards the water and excitedly hauled in an invisible fish. She repeated this action several times with some increasing complexity of verbalization as well as of the story-line by piling fish in a basket and eventually "eating" one and throwing the others back saying, "swim, swim!" She had observed adults fishing recently, an action that was at first incomprehensible to her. After some brief adult explanation, fishing still seemed too abstract for her limited vocabulary and social scripts until she could reenact this event on her own terms by *experiencing* the act of fishing. In effect, little Olivia had witnessed a scene of big people with large fishing poles, and perhaps wearing special clothing and with other large items of equipment for which she knew no verbal labels. She cut them all down to a manageable mental form and to the few words about fishing she had been provided by her parents. She could then use language to describe her little game.

It seems likely that children's early make-believe reflects an innate method of miniaturizing their physical and social milieu and practicing new words or mental representations in the form of visual, auditory, or other sensory images along with some motor activity. Their primitive story-telling seems to provide a structural support that holds the material together and increases the likelihood of encoding, retention, and rapid retrieval of the material. As the research of Berk *et al.* (2006) has suggested, such play activity may become the basis for a developing sense of self-regulation, autonomy, and individuality.

## 2. The flowering of imaginative play in the preschool years

By about three years of age, new capacities begin to become evident in the child's ability "to take an attitude toward the possible." Considerable research has examined the factors in the child's family life or in the settings, availability of toys, and companions that foster such play. Adult encouragement by regular bedtime story-telling or direct initiation of such play or even exposure to age appropriate TV programming have been shown in research to enhance the likelihood of such play. There is also a body of research studies that demonstrate how guided play encourages further spontaneous play in preschoolers or early school age children and influences the child's acquisition of imagery skills, new vocabulary, ability to use such play for impulse control or delay, and for the control of aggression. There seems to be a general agreement among the researchers on the adaptive features of imaginative play. Experimental studies controlling for possible mediating or moderating variable strengthen some of the benefits of play we shall describe below.

*Benefits of imaginative play*

**Imagery.** Our ability to reproduce the physical characteristics of objects, facial features or social events once experienced by our senses but no longer objectively in evidence is a remarkable gift of human evolution. Such reproductions or mental representations in the various sensory modalities are rarely as vivid as what can be achieved by art or by the electronic techniques of twentieth-century photography or sound recording. The transformations of objects and events that are features of children's pretend play depend upon imagery but the skill in using imagery is also enhanced by the continuing practice effect of make-believe games (Garvey 1979; Litt 1973; Singer and Singer 1990).

*Vocabulary, verbal fluency, and divergent production.* Since preschoolers generally accompany their play activities by verbal descriptions and spoken commentary they are, in effect, practicing language usage. They may occasionally show "cute" misuses of words but their very voicing of such malapropisms or phrases provides opportunities for corrections and explanations by overhearing adults or fellow child players. The pioneering training studies directed by Eli Saltz also demonstrated that imaginative play provided basic opportunities for children to develop verbal fluency and more complex divergent thought by fostering preschoolers' ability to connect separate events and to form new meaning structures (Johnson *et al.* 2005).

The ability of children during pretend play to transform unstructured objects such as sticks, kitchen utensils, or packing boxes into horses, airplanes, human or animal figures, trucks, beds, or chips has been linked in research to later evidence of *divergent thought*, a forerunner of creative abilities (Dansky 1980; Johnson *et al.* 2005; Russ 1993, 2004; Russ *et al.* 1999; Singer 1973). There is reason to believe from research observations that children who are "experienced" pretend players not only are especially facile at language usage and flexibility, but that they also show preferences for less structured playthings that afford opportunities for more transformations of objects into a variety of forms and uses in their games (Russ 2004; Singer 1961, 1973).

*Reality and fantasy distinction.* There has been a great proliferation of research about the concept of children's awareness of their own mental processes and the distinction of such recognition with some rough understanding that others' mental processes may differ. Research evidence suggested pretty definitely that before about age four children often lack a mental construct called "theory of mind," distinguishing one's own thoughts from those of others. Alan Leslie (1987) in an important paper proposed that children's imaginative play may have served to prepare preschoolers for developing the critical conception of self and others' mental activity. One can understand how important such a development can be since it provides a sense of individuality, it signifies the privacy of one's thoughts, and it may also help the child recognize the distinction between reality and fantasy (Schwebel *et al.* 1999; Singer and Singer 1990,

2005). We know from ample anecdotal reports and from the research of Kavanaugh and Harris (1999) that many three-year-olds can already recognize that the pretended thoughts and behaviors assigned to play figures are not "real." It may well be that in the course of engaging in pretend games children become aware of their own control of the narrative and, while they enjoy the story and their sense of control, they are learning that their inanimate playthings lack any true autonomy.

*Delaying capacity and self-restraint.* When children gain further experience in laying out story-lines for their make-believe play they are increasingly acquiring a sense of temporal structure and the inherent sequence of events. A case can be made that the consequences of these experiences is a heightened awareness of the necessity for the delay of gratification, for self-restraint and increased emotion regulation. As early as 1908 Freud (1908/1962) had proposed that a crucial feature of effective human functioning was the ability to defer immediate gratification in the interest of a more important later gain and avoidance of immediate frustration. The implications of thought trials as a means toward self-restraint first signalized by Freud were carried further in studies of adults' and children's imagination, pretend play, and waiting behavior (Singer 1955, 1961) and in the later experiments of Walter Mischel and his group on how playful transformations can enhance children's delay behavior (Mischel *et al.* 1972; Mischel and Baker 1975). The accumulating research evidence is integrated in a diagrammatic model offered by Russ (1993: 9) in which the emotional intensity found in play is linked to creative thought as well as to the practice of alternative solutions and evaluative abilities.

Children who had been identified from interview and Rorschach inkblot scores as imaginative did indeed show more fantasy play during both the initial modeling and later spontaneous floor play sessions (Singer and Singer 1981). The more imaginative players also showed a greater tendency to be reflective. They also attributed positive events to their own actions while assuming that negative events were externally caused, a result generally found for normal rather than depressed persons in studies of attribution. This "illusion of control" of happy events may well emerge from the way in which fantasy play provides the child with opportunities to practice manipulation and power over a miniaturized world.

*Empathy.* Children learn as they play to express sympathy and empathy for others. Think of how when they play "doctor" and affix the bandage on the doll you hear the child say, "poor dolly, you have a boo boo."

Many of these benefits result from the playful interactions with children described by Lev Vygotsky, a Russian psychologist (1978) who had been an early exponent in the late 1920s and the early 1930s of a critical role for parents and other child caregivers in fostering adaptive play. Diana Shmukler and Ida Naveh's research (1984–5) in the early 1980s is particularly relevant here. Working with 166 economically disadvantaged preschoolers in South Africa, they found that children made significant increases in imaginative play behavior and in other aspects of play, such as positive emotionality, social interaction, cooperation, and concentration as a result of play training when compared to children who were in control groups either receiving mastery training or no intervention. The children who received play training also improved in verbal fluency, flexibility, originality, imaginativeness of stories, and in verbal IQ.

Shmukler and Naveh report that adult encouragement, endorsement of imagination, protection, modeling, and warmth were the factors that were "powerful" in the experimental play intervention groups regardless of whether the type of play intervention approaches were structured or unstructured. They are careful to point out that a supportive atmosphere in itself did not account for the social gains in imaginative play, since a similarly supportive atmosphere was present in the control situations but without the play training component. Our own research corroborates this finding. More imaginative older children significantly more often reported to us that their parents told them stories or played fantasy games with them. In more recent research, we found that preschool children who were read to in the evening, or who had a settling-down time before bedtime, and whose television viewing time was controlled, were less aggressive and more imaginative than children without such soothing.

The research by Elizabeth Meins (2003) and her group in England indicates that when mothers talk to children in their first four years using language that reflects mental activity, the children subsequently show better verbal skills, more awareness of theory of mind, and a richer stream of consciousness in their talk. The research evidence seems to make it clear that closeness to at least one parent and the exposure to adult story-telling and reading are all regularly associated with fantasy play. This relationship pattern suggests that warmth and sensitivity of the grown-ups' language, their acceptance of children's playful expressiveness, the sharing of humor and, occasionally, even of frightening fictional themes, work to increase a sound attachment.

## 3. Two modes of conscious thought

There is an increasing coalescence among personality, cognitive, and developmental psychologists suggesting that human consciousness has evolved to reflect two modes of thought. These have been labeled by Jerome Bruner (1986) as (1) the *logical-scientific* or *paradigmatic mode* and (2) the *narrative* mode. The paradigmatic mode reflects what for some people may be considered the highest level of human thought, the capacity for organized sequential and abstract thinking as exemplified in rational mathematical and scientific processes, or careful rational thought about economics or business processes. Such thought is critical also for features of artistic production as in a composer's choice of instruments in orchestrating a symphony or an opera or in an artist's choice of oils and color shades from one's color palette. The tools include the ability to use mathematics, formal logic, or nowadays to rely systematically on computerized processes.

Narrative thought may well reflect a somewhat earlier evolutionary development, the forming of experiences into story-like sequences, which help sustain individuals and make communication simpler. Often such thoughts depend heavily on gross sensory associations which can lead to the kind of errors reported in studies of children's failures in object constancy and conservation. In older children or adults, excessive reliance on event memories may lead to so-called false memory because of an individual's unwitting interpolations of subsequent experiences or suggested events. These story-like forms of thinking afford us a sense of past, present, and possible futures and open the way for the richness of interpersonal imagination.

As the research of Seymour Epstein (1994, 1999) demonstrates, the narrative mode is not inherently less adaptive or socially more primitive than the paradigmatic mode. They are basically complementary systems that may work together to produce the highest level of thought. They operate effectively for different kinds of situations. Our mental "story-telling" can develop in complexity and differentiation in the same way as children's dreams and make-believe games do in those critical years between three and six. Bruner also has proposed that the paradigmatic mode of thought seeks for "truth"; the narrative mode of thought involves a striving for "verisimilitude," the appearance of truth, or the conveying of a sense of believability because of the use of story-like or pictorial manifestations in one's thoughts.

## 4. Imaginative play in the middle childhood

Within the period between ages six and nine children learn to inhibit their public vocalization of pretend play. They no longer voice the make-believe conversations, sound effects, or plot sequences that adults observe in preschoolers. While they may for the next few years continue to manipulate action figures or dolls alone or with a few friends, they are less likely in public settings to continue overt speech in the game format. This process may be somewhat parallel with their increasing ability to read silently, gradually to control their mouthing of the sounds of words, and eventually also the silent movement of their lips. In his interesting historical study of the origins of silent reading, Kivy (2006) has proposed that this behavior may be regarded as a "performance." Reading silently not only is inhibiting public vocalization but also may become something like the individualized cognitive response of a critic. As we read we also produce mental images of characters or scenes and even interpretative glosses on the content of the text. We would view a child's mastery of such silent reading as a comparable "skill" to non-vocalized ongoing pretend play that after a period of practice can become automatized and as out of awareness as most of our overlearned cognitive and motor skills (Singer and Salovey 1991). This great step of internalization and the creation of private consciousness that we see in reading may take a little longer in the case of very young children's play.

The internalization process, critical in the formation of a "private personality," presents a challenging avenue for future research in both the psychological and neuroscience domains. We need longitudinal studies to establish more clearly for various socio-demographic groups of children when and how the ability to restrain overt vocalization emerges as a cognitive and motor skill. What are the contingent circumstances? Do family structures, the children's attachment styles, or the early school play a role? Is sheer analytic intelligence (IQ) a factor or is it possible that the creative or the practical forms of intelligence are also contributory to children's voluntary restraint of overt speech and concomitant elaboration of internal conscious experience (Sternberg 1999)? We hypothesize that those children who have had less experience at imaginative play and who are, as the research suggests, more likely to be impulsive in action, will be later in showing internalization of vocalization and restraint in the persistence of early childhood play patterns. We suspect that those children who have had less experience with imaginative play may quickly be attracted to the more aggressive, action-oriented violent video games, while the experienced pretend players, used to their own more elaborate narratives, will choose games that call for more deliberation and story-telling skills. We are proposing that middle childhood may be an understudied but very critical period for the development of imaginative, narrative skills. The internalization of the story-telling of imaginative play during the early school years may be a critical feature in the eventual effective use of narrative thinking in the emerging adolescent and adult.

## 5. The adaptive nature of conscious thought

We can characterize consciousness and unconsciousness as endpoints along a dimension of awareness that itself involves a system of sensory processing, perceptual construction, and reflective encoding (Johnson and Multhaup 1992). A prizefighter full of sensory-motor alertness and motor activity takes a blow to his chin, and for at least a brief period, loses all awareness. A normal sleeper in some phases of the psychophysiological sleep cycle shows comparable loss of awareness. As Hamlet accurately surmises, however, "to sleep—perchance to dream. Aye, there's the rub." During the EEG-Stage 1, Rapid Eye Movement phase of the sleep cycle we seem to regain awareness not of the external environment but of the ongoing activity of our stored long-term memories and fantasies (Antrobus 1993, 1999).

During our daily waking state as we go about our usual chores or social interactions, we are for the most part fully conscious, using our senses and perceptual capacity, but also aware of the kind of fleeting mental glosses we mentioned above in connection with silent reading. William James's (1890/1950) important chapter on the stream of thought and its subsequent literary exemplifications in the works of James Joyce and Virginia Woolf among many other modern writers characterizes this normal waking consciousness. It also allows for awareness and even labeling of the external environment as well as some sensitivity to passing interpretations of ongoing events.

James also suggests a deeper level of consciousness in his references to the possessive quality of "my thoughts." These represent a fuller commitment to playing out of one's ongoing thought stream of memories, wishes, intentions, or fantasies even to the neglect often of processing external stimuli. This third aspect of consciousness is often represented as daydreaming or "brown study." It may become a primary focus of awareness under conditions of voluntary reduction of sensory processing as when one prepares for sleep or when one simply chooses to "take a break" from regular chores or to "tune out" a boring lecture or sermon. Recent brain research with functional Magnetic Resonance Imagery (fMRI) has identified a Brain Default System that becomes active when, on the one hand, the individual has reduced processing external stimuli and, on the other hand, is engaged in various manifestations of day-dreaming (Buckner *et al.* 2008; Mason *et al.* 2007). A person's tendency to engage more willingly and frequently in this extended awareness of one's thoughts can become one of the major empirically established human personality traits, Openness to Experience (Costa and McCrae 1995; Zhiyan and Singer 1997).

If we return now to the internalization of play we may detect a link to this more self-oriented third form of consciousness. In the various research studies with preschoolers or with early school age children, we find evidence that those youngsters who play more consistently at pretend games show more indications of self regulation (Berk *et al.* 2006; Russ 1993, 2004; Schwebel *et al.* 1999; Singer and Singer 2005). In effect, children who continue such play mentally may well develop a personality trait akin to the Openness dimension.

Bernard Baars (1997, 1998) has made an impressive effort to elaborate on the special role of consciousness for human adaptation. We find his approach a congenial starting point for our own effort to show how the processes he described may emerge from children's early practices of various forms of play, especially their games of pretending and story-telling. We might put somewhat greater emphasis than he does on the importance of imagery not only to orient oneself in relation to one's physical environment but also as a means of representing the important people in our lives and the possible interactions between those people and ourselves. He lists the critical adaptive functions of consciousness as follows:

1. *Prioritizing*: We need to entertain in consciousness, whether through interior monologue or imagery, the important goals and real or fantasized dangers that confront us. If we want ultimately to modify our behavior or to reorganize the values we have assigned to particular goals or dangers we must think these through to some extent in what he terms "the theater of consciousness."

2. *Problem-solving*: Consciousness is necessary for interpretation of stimuli and for-mation of meaningful connections. It serves as a gateway to drawing on working memory and to encouraging curiosity and search activities for dealing with an imminent perceptual situation or for planning a potential future situation. As we shall note, both logical and experimental or narrative thought play a role in such adaptive processes.

3. *Decision-making*: Consciousness plays an important role in coming to conclusions and in the executive control of one's own actions It is important, however, that one must have time to react. Decisions such as whether to purchase a house or change jobs usually necessitate extensive conscious rumination. Consciousness helps in determining how much weight to give to organized sequences of

behavior specific to a situation. Sometimes in emergencies we may produce flexible but often not entirely clear reactions since those may derive from over learned but not necessarily relevant tendencies.

4. *Control*: Our thoughts, by clarifying the *meaning* of particular situations, may actually help in recruiting and then, subsequently, controlling one's actions. Here we may actually guide our imagery to play out various scenarios and then their possible consequences,

5. *Identifying error*. Consciousness plays a critical role in helping individuals identify mistakes whether in written material or in social situations. While such thought often takes the form of balancing abstractions and logical alternatives, it may often also require imagined possible social interactions that draw upon our narrative thought capacities.

6. *Confronting novelty*: Consciousness is critical for many kinds of learning experiences. This is especially important where one encounters novel situations for which there may not have yet been extensive practice.

7. *Establishing contexts*: Consciousness is critical for establishing meaningful contexts for events that occur. As we have written elsewhere, a conscious process involving imagery can provide a broader context in which to relate new information to past experiences and settings (Singer 2006; Singer and Singer 1990).

Baars importantly also points to the critical role that consciousness plays in creating access to a variety of experiences of a sense of self, which, we would add, have emotional implications as well.

We began with a quote from Spinoza on the importance of imagination along with reason, or to use more modern terminology, paradigmatic-rational thought as well as narrative consciousness. The pretend play of early childhood and its association with imagery and story-telling makes a special contribution to the sense of possibility. It reflects our human capacity to create virtual realities that may be manipulable in adult consciousness as links to creative productions in the sciences or arts. Even for those of us who lack remarkable gifts of artistic ability, early imaginative play may have prepared us to appreciate and to benefit from the aesthetic productions of others.

# References

Antrobus, J. S. (1993). Thinking away and ahead. In H. Morowitz and J. L. Singer (eds.), *The Mind, the Brain and Complex Adaptive Systems*. New York: Addison-Wesley, pp. 155–74.

——(1999). Toward a neurocognitive processing model of imaginal thought. In J. A. Singer and P. Salovey (eds.), *At Play in the Fields of Consciousness: Essays in Honor of Jerome L. Singer*. Mahwah, NJ: Lawrence Erlbaum Associates, pp. 3–28.

Baars, B. (1997). *In the Theater of Consciousness*. New York: Oxford University Press.

——(1998). *A Cognitive Theory of Consciousness*. Cambridge: Cambridge University Press.

Berk, L. E., T. D. Mann, and A. T. Ogan (2006). Make-believe play: Wellspring for development of self-regulation. In D. G. Singer, R. M. Golinkoff, and K. Hirsh-Pasek (eds.), *Play = Learning: How Play Motivates and Enhances Cognitive and Social Emotional Growth*. New York: Oxford University Press, pp. 74–100.

Bruner, J. (1986). *Actual Minds, Possible Worlds*. Cambridge, MA: Harvard University Press.

Buckner, R., J. Andrews-Hanna, and D. Schacter (2008). The brain's default network: Anatomy, function and relevance to disease. *Annals of the New York Academy of Sciences*, 1124/1: 1–38.

Costa, P. T. and R. R. McCrae (1995). Domains and facets: Hierarchical personality assessment using the revised NEO Personality Inventory, *Journal of Personality*, 64: 22–50.

Dansky, J. (1980). Make-believe: A mediator of the relationship between play and creativity. *Child Development*, 51: 576–9.

Epstein, S. (1994). Integration of the cognitive and psychodynamic unconscious. *American Psychologist*, 49: 709–24.

——(1999). The interpretation of dreams from the perspective of Cognitive-Experiential Self-Theory. In J. A. Singer and P. Salovey (eds.), *At Play in the Fields of Consciousness: Essays in Honor of Jerome L. Singer*. Mahwah, NJ: Lawrence Erlbaum Associates, pp. 51–82.

Fein, G. G. (1981). Pretend play in childhood: An integrative review. *Child Development*, 52: 1095–1118.

Freud, S. (1908/1962). Creative writers and daydreaming. In *The Complete Psychological Works of Sigmund Freud*, vol. 9, ed. J. Strachey. London: Hearth Press, pp. 141–54.

Garvey, C. (1979). An approach to the study of children's role play. *The Quarterly Newsletter of the Laboratory of Comparative Human Cognition*, 1/4: 69–73.

Gleason, T. (2002). Social provisions of real and imaginary relationships in early childhood. *Child Development*, 38: 979–92.

——(2004). Imaginary companions: An evaluation of parents as reporters. *Infant and Child Development*, 13: 199–215.

Goldstein, K. (1939). *The Organism*. New York: American Book Company.

Gopnik, A. (2009). *The Philosophical Baby*. New York: Farrar, Straus and Giroux.

Hampshire, S. (2005). *Spinoza and Spinozism*. New York: Oxford University Press.

Harris, P. (2000). *The Work of the Imagination*. Malden, MA: Blackwell Publishers.

James, W. (1890/1950). *The Principles of Psychology*. New York: Dover.

Johnson, J. E., J. F. Christie, and F. Wardle (2005). *Play, Development and Early Education*. Boston, MA: Pearson Education, Allyn & Bacon.

Johnson, M. K. and K. Multhaup (1992). Emotion and MEM. In S. A. Christianson (ed.), *The Handbook of Emotion and Memory*. Hillsdale, NJ: Lawrence Erlbaum Associates, pp. 33–66.

Kavanaugh, R. and P. Harris (1999). Pretense and counterfactual thought in young children. In C. Tamis-Lemonda and L. Balter (eds.), *Child Psychology: A Handbook of Contemporary Issues*. New York: Garland, pp. 158–76.

Kivy, P. (2006). *The Performance of Reading: An Essay in the Philosophy of Literature*. Oxford: Blackwell Publishing.

Leslie, A. (1987). Pretense and representation: The origins of "Theory of Mind." *Psychological Review*, 94: 412–22.

Lillard, A. S. (2001). Pretend play as twin earth: A social-cognitive analysis. *Developmental Review*, 21: 495–531.

Litt, C. J. (1986). Theories of transitional object attachment: An overview. *International Journal of Behavioral Development*, 9: 383–99.

Litt, H. (1973). Imagery in children's thinking. Unpublished doctoral dissertation, Liverpool University.

Mackeith, S. (1982–3). Paracosms and the development of fantasy in childhood. *Imagination, Cognition and Personality*, 3: 261–8.

Mason, M. F., M. I. Norton, J. D. Van Horn, D. M. Wegner, S. T. Grafton, and C. H. Macrae (2007). Wandering minds: The default network and stimulus-independent thought. *Science*, 335/5810: 393–5.

Meins, E., C. Fernyhough, R. Wainwright, D. Clark-Carter, M. Das Gupta, E. Fradley, and M. Tuckey (2003). Pathways to understanding mind: Construct validity and predictive validity of maternal mind-mindedness. *Child Development*, 74/4: 1194–1211.

Mischel, W. and N. Baker (1975). Cognitive appraisals and transformations in delay behavior. *Journal of Personality and Social Psychology*, 31: 254–61.

——E. Ebbesen, and A. Zeiss (1972). Cognitive and attentional mechanisms in delay of gratification. *Journal of Personality and Social Psychology*, 21: 204–18.

Root-Bernstein, M. and R. Root-Bernstein (2006.) Imaginary worldplay in childhood and maturity and its impact on adult creativity. *Creativity Research Journal*, 18/4: 405–25.

Root-Bernstein, R. and M. Root-Bernstein (1999). *Sparks of Genius*. New York: Houghton-Mifflin.

Rosengren, K. S., C. Johnson, and P. L. Harris (2000). *Imagining the Impossible: Magical, Scientific and Religious Thinking in Children*. Cambridge: Cambridge University Press.

Russ, S. W. (1993). *Affect and Creativity: The Role of Affect and Play in the Creative Process*. Hillsdale, NJ: Lawrence Erlbaum Associates.

——(2004). *Play in Child Development and Psychotherapy: Toward Empirically Supported Practice*. Mahwah, NJ: Lawrence Erlbaum Associates.

——A. L. Robins, and B. A. Christiano (1999). Pretend play: Longitudinal prediction of creativity and affect in fantasy in children. *Creativity Research Journal*, 12: 129–39.

Schwebel, D., C. Rosen, and J. L. Singer (1999). Preschoolers' pretend play and theory of mind: The role of jointly conducted pretense. *British Journal of Developmental Psychology*, 17: 333–48.

Shmukler, D. and I. Naveh (1984–5). Structured vs. unstructured play training with economically disadvantaged preschoolers. *Imagination, Cognition and Personality*, 4/3: 293–304.

Silvey, R. and S. MacKeith (1988). The paracosm: A special form of fantasy. In D. C. Morrison (ed.), *Ongoing Early Experience: Imagination and Cognition in Childhood*. Amityville, NY: Baywood, pp. 173–97.

Singer, D. G. and J. L. Singer (1990). *The House of Make-Believe: Children's Play and the Developing Imagination*. Cambridge, MA: Harvard University Press.

——  ——(2005). *Imagination and Play in the Electronic Age*. Cambridge, MA: Harvard University Press.

——  ——H. D'agostino, and R. Delong (2009). Children's pastimes and play in sixteen nations: Is free play declining? *American Journal of Play*, 1/3: 283–312.

Singer, J. L. (1955). Delayed gratification and ego-development: Implications for clinical and experimental research. *Journal of Consulting Psychology*, 19: 259–66.

——(1961). Imagination and waiting ability in young children. *Journal of Personality*, 29: 396–413.

——(1973). *The Child's World of Make-Believe*. New York: Academic Press.

——(2006). *Imagery in Psychotherapy*. Washington, DC: American Psychological Association.

——and P. Salovey (1991). Organized knowledge structures in personality: Schemas, self-schemas, prototypes and scripts. A review and research agenda. In M. J. Horowitz (ed.), *Person Schemas and Maladaptive Interpersonal Patterns*. Chicago: University of Chicago Press, pp. 33–79.

——and D. G. Singer (1981). *Television, Imagination and Aggression: A Study of Preschoolers*. Hillsdale, NJ: Lawrence Erlbaum Associates.

——  ——(2005–6). Preschoolers' imaginative play as precursor of narrative consciousness. *Imagination, Cognition and Personality*, 25/2: 97–118.

Sternberg, R. (1999). The theory of successful intelligence. *Review of General Psychology*, 3: 292–316.

Taylor, M. (1999). *Imaginary Companions and the Children who Create Them*. New York: Oxford University Press.

Vygotsky, L. S. (1978). *Mind in Society: The Development of Higher Mental Processes*. Cambridge, MA: Harvard University Press.

Winnicott, D. W. (1971). *Playing and Reality*. Harmondsworth: Penguin.

Zhiyan, T. and J. L. Singer (1997). Daydreaming styles emotionality, and the Big Five personality dimensions. *Imagination, Cognition and Personality*, 16: 399–414.

Zigler, E. and S. Bishop-Josef (2006). The cognitive child vs. the whole child: Lessons from 40 years of Head Start. In D. G. Singer, R. M. Golinkoff, and K. Hirsh-Pasek (eds.), *Play = Learning: How Play Motivates and Enhances Children's Cognitive and Social-Emotional Growth*. New York: Oxford University Press, pp. 15–35.

——D. G. Singer, and S. Bishop-Josef (eds.) (2004). *Chilaren's Play: The Roots of Reading*. Washington, DC: Zero-to-Three Press.

# 15

# Unpacking the Boxes: The Cognitive Theory of Imagination and Aesthetics

*Kathleen Stock*

In recent years, a new approach to the imagination has emerged, sometimes labelled the 'cognitive theory' of imagination[1] (henceforth [CI]). It is rooted in cognitive psychology, and presented as able to do much that other approaches cannot. It offers solutions to problems in aesthetics, including imaginative resistance and the paradox of fiction. It's allegedly 'perhaps . . . the most productive idea about the propositional imagination that anyone has ever had' (Nichols 2006a: 459). In this chapter, I'll examine to what extent this is true.

## 1. General features of [CI]

Some background: [CI] understands the mind as computational, containing symbolic representations coextensive with the sorts of intentional attitudes picked out by folk psychology (Nichols 2006b: 5–6; Weinberg 2008: 204). The type-identity of any such state is characterized functionally, and not in terms of content (Nichols 2006b: 5–6). Cognitive processing of these representations—including the formation of inferences, affective responses, and moral judgements—involves transformations upon them by domain-specific mechanisms.

[CI]'s main explananda are as follows. First, in one thinker, imagining and belief can share the propositional content that *p*, diachronically or even synchronically. Second, imagining is significantly functionally similar to belief. One similarity concerns inferential transactions: if, on believing that *p* and *q*, one would infer that *r*, then, on imagining that *p* and *q*, one will imagine that *r* (Nichols and Stich 2000: 122). Additionally, imaginings and beliefs with the same contents generate apparently similar affective responses (Meskin and Weinberg 2003: 31; Nichols 2004: 131). Further

---

[1] For example by Weinberg (2008: 204).

similarities include: that both belief and imagining that *p* tend to produce further beliefs about themselves; and that, as one tends to eliminate one of a set of conflicting beliefs once aware of the conflict, so too, given an imaginative scenario, one allegedly tends to eliminate incoherent imaginings (Weinberg 2008: 205).

Given the commitment expressed earlier to functionalism about mental state-types, such similarities should not be so extensive as to eradicate any distinction between the respective roles of imagining and belief. Differences noted include: that imagining and belief that *p* do not interact with desires to produce the same behaviour, *ceteris paribus*; and that imagining but normally not belief can be produced directly in response to a decision (Weinberg 2008: 206). Moreover, the content of imagining and belief each typically bear a different relation to perceptual input (Weinberg and Meskin 2006: 178).

[CI] also has it that beliefs and imaginings are separately 'stored', respectively, in a 'belief box' (BB) and an 'imagination box' (IB) (also sometimes called a 'possible worlds box'). Despite appearances, this doesn't entail that each literally inhabits a distinct neural location; it merely marks distinct functional roles (Nichols and Stich 2000: 121; Meskin and Weinberg 2003: 23). Dissent over the point (e.g., Currie 1995) is superficial, since all parties agree about the functional differences (Nichols and Stich 2000: 133).

What then is [CI]'s explanation for the functional similarities previously noted? Beliefs and imaginings with the same contents are operated on by at least some of the same sub-personal cognitive mechanisms, in the same way. Similarity in inferential transactions is explained in terms of each being processed by the same inference mechanisms (Weinberg 2008: 204). Likewise, similarity in generated affect is explained by IB and BB each interacting with the same 'affect-producing mechanism' (Weinberg 2008: 204). That in both belief and imagining, inconsistent thoughts are allegedly eliminated, is explained by the action of an 'UpDater' upon both the BB and the IB (Nichols and Stich 2000: 124). That a belief and an imagining each tend to be accompanied by beliefs referring to themselves is explained in terms of 'monitoring systems' (Weinberg and Meskin 2006: 180).

Meanwhile, functional differences are explained in terms of different relations to particular mechanisms/systems. The failure of imagining to motivate action as belief does is explained by the IB's lack of interaction with 'action control systems' (Weinberg and Meskin 2006: 178; see Currie and Ravenscroft 2002: 70 for a variation). That decisions can generate imagining is explained by the fact that the IB but not the BB is connected to an 'InPutter': the 'mechanism or set of mechanisms . . . driven by our decision to imagine that *p*, for nearly any *p*, and to produce a token of *p* in the IB' (Weinberg 2008: 206).

An additional commitment of [CI] is the claim that imaginings and beliefs are in a 'single code' (Nichols and Stich 2000: 125; Meskin and Weinberg 2003: 31). What this amounts to will be investigated below.

## 2. Is [CI] scientific?

[CI] is often implicitly presented as inheriting the prestige and relevance of science, unlike traditional philosophy. However, on examination, the contrast is not clear-cut.

### A. The role of science in identifying explananda

Some of [CI]'s explananda derive from informal observation: for instance, the claim that imagining but not belief can be produced directly in response to a decision; or that imagining doesn't produce action as belief does. Others, though, are apparently more rigorously grounded. For instance, Alan Leslie's 'tea party experiment' (1994: 222–4) is widely cited as evidence that imaginings and beliefs share inferential roles, *ceteris paribus*.[2] Ten children aged between 26 and 36 months are provided the wherewithal for a pretend tea party. Each is encouraged to pretend that two cups are filled with liquid. The experimenter then picks up one cup and shakes it upside down, asking the child to identify the 'full' and the 'empty' cup. In a high proportion of cases, the child correctly identifies the looked-for implication.

Leslie designed this experiment to illustrate a certain developmental picture. Defenders of [CI], however, merely take it to demonstrate that thinkers generally tend to make inferences from an imagined scenario near-identical in content to those they would also make, were (they to believe) the scenario actually the case. It would be perfectly appropriate to establish this fairly limited conclusion via informal reflection. We are familiar enough with devices such as *modus ponens* in the context of hypothetical reasoning to draw the moral.

Nichols and Stich use a range of such empirical studies, including one of their own (detailed in 2003: 22). From such data are drawn conclusions such as: 'Typical episodes of pretence begin with an initial . . . set of premises'; 'Inference often plays a crucial role in filling out the details of what is happening in pretence'; 'In addition to inferential elaboration, children and adults elaborate the pretend scenarios in ways that aren't inferential at all'; 'pretenders actually *do* things—they engage in actions that are appropriate to the pretence'; and so on (2003: 24–7). Each of these conclusions is already accessible to the non-scientist via informal observation and reflection. Even if a reflective folk psychology sometimes get things wrong, it's hard to see how it could do so here.

Presumably no defender of [CI] would deny such points. Nonetheless, it's easy for the unwary to get the impression that [CI] is especially credible in virtue of the large-scale contribution of science to identifying its explananda. Hence it's worth dispelling.

### B. Models of argument

Weinberg and Meskin ascribe a 'paradox-and-analysis' (P&A) model of reasoning to traditional philosophy of imagination, in which one identifies a set of conflicting

---

[2] Similar conclusions are drawn by Harris (2000:11-20), and cited by Weinberg and Meskin (2006: 180).

propositions, and then rejects one, while 'reconfiguring' concepts in line with meta-physical and folk psychological considerations (2006: 177). They instead endorse a 'more empirically-oriented phenomena-and-explanation model' (P&E), in which science both provides the explananda and the explanans, and which allows us to see the source of a conflict rather than simply discarding one of the commitments which generate it (2006: 177).

In practice, the authors aren't averse to reconfiguring mental concepts (see their objection to analysing fictive affect as empathy (2003: 27); or their analysis of two kinds of imaginative resistance (2006: 185)). Nor should they be, since cognitive science generally cannot but rely upon 'philosophical reflection on our commonsense conception' (Von Eckhardt 1993: 93). Meanwhile, P&A is not unconcerned with explanation, as the terminological contrast might imply. Consider the puzzle of imaginative resistance. Effectively, this involves apparent conflict between two propositions: (a) imagining is not answerable to epistemic standards, and so should be unconstrained; (b) there are some propositions one cannot imagine. In reply, Gendler rejects (b) (at least, for many resisted propositions), arguing that resistance is due to unwillingness, not incapacity (2000). Stock in effect rejects (a), arguing that imagining that $p$ involves having a sense of what it would be for $p$ to be true (2005). Meanwhile Stokes argues that the truth of (b) doesn't entail the falsity of (a), since resistance involves failure to have certain second-order desire-like imaginings (2006). In each, an explanation is proposed, citing a particular antecedent circumstance.

Is [CI], *qua* exemplar of a P&E-style explanation, superior to P&A, as Weinberg and Meskin claim? Their chief example concerns the paradox of fiction: whether or not to classify the affect-like responses one has towards entities acknowledged as imaginary as of a kind with affective responses to existents. We are told that, while P&A-style explanations respond by *either* analysing such responses as genuine affect, *or* denying this—thereby unsatisfactorily having to jump one way or the other—their account, rooted in [CI], does better by characterizing the *source* of our mixed intuitions: they derive, on the one hand, from a desire to type-identify emotions in terms of their cause (and so to differentiate non-fictive from fictive responses); and on the other, from awareness that both belief and imagining engage one's affective systems alike (which would suggest that they are of a kind) (2003: 33).

I'll examine later to what extent this description is accurate. Meantime, note that even if right, it apparently would leave the paradox as insistent as ever. For now we want to know—*should* we type-identify emotions in terms of cause, or instead take as significant that they each engage affective systems alike? No reason is offered to think puzzlement abates simply because we can better characterize its source. Relatedly, it's not as if P&A-style responses must leave their advocates mourning the loss of a rejected position. Walton, for instance, thinks he has dismissed the intuition that fear-like responses to fiction are of a kind with fear via his arguments, and so presumably is happy to see the back of it, *qua* remnant of an erroneous picture of the mind (1990). That practitioners of P&A must do 'philosophical tap-dancing to distract . . . from the discomfort that stems from having to stipulate one way or another' is overstated (Weinberg and Meskin 2006: 176).

Further points are made, not so much against P&A specifically, but against 'traditional' philosophy of imagination generally. One point made in favour of [CI] and against traditional philosophy of imagination is that the latter usually draws either on folk psychology or metaphysics, and that neither are as well-suited as [CI] to explaining problems of the imagination, such as the puzzle of imaginative resistance (Weinberg and Meskin 2006: 186–8). Folk psychology cannot properly explain unconscious or tacit aspects of mind, because it 'focuses on and appeals to aspects of our psychology that have some sort of phenomenological presence' (2006: 185–6). Hence philosophy based upon it cannot account for, for instance, that imaginative resistance which is 'too experientially thin to fall within its explanatory ambit' (2006: 185–6).

It seems right that few interesting problems about imagining can be answered by exclusively appealing to the phenomenology of mental states. However, this doesn't threaten philosophy which substantially draws upon folk psychology, for it faces no such constraint. Philosophers often discuss phenomenologically hidden states, while adverting to considerations constrained at least partly by what the folk think: for instance, false belief and knowledge; self-deception about attitudinal avowals (Wright 1998: 16–17); or externalist mental content. It's true that the latter discussion often strays into metaphysics: either way, the approach doesn't seem particularly ill-suited to the subject matter. Meanwhile, the grounds for the authors' objection to the use of metaphysics in discussing the imagination are not clear. They argue that there is no room for pure non-psychologized metaphysics in explaining imaginative resistance, but presumably the point is not supposed to generalize; and even so, they suggest there may be a valuable role for the psychologized version (Weinberg and Meskin 2006: 186).

A final point offered is that if one is 'restricted to folk psychology, philosophy of mind, and the tools of philosophical analysis' one cannot provide an explanation of the paradox of fiction as nuanced as theirs (Weinberg and Meskin 2006: 176). However, there is nothing to stop a folk psychologist offering an explanation which shares the form of theirs, and so presumably its nuance. She might, for instance, describe mixed intuitions about how to classify affect-like responses to imaginings as due to conflicting tendencies to (a) type-identify emotions in terms of what causes them; and (b) type-identify emotions in terms of their phenomenology and physiological effects. This looks to possess whatever subtlety the authors' account does; indeed, it shares its first conjunct.

In practice, then, [CI] doesn't have obvious general methodological advantages over traditional-style philosophy of mind. The possibility remains, however, that it is successful as a scientific theory, and as such, superior to extant accounts of the imagination. I now will examine whether this is so.

# 3. Decoding [CI]

*The [SOM] claim*

Let D stand for a particular dispositional property shared by both imagining and belief that *p* (e.g., a disposition to produce certain inferences, or moral or affective responses). *Prima facie* [CI]'s commitment to 'sameness of mechanism' ([SOM]) looks underpinned thus:

(I) A mechanism is of type M iff it realizes D in the entities it processes.

(II) In certain contexts, imagining and belief that *p* each realize D.

Therefore:

(III) In those contexts, imagining and belief that *p* each are processed by a mechanism of type M.

(I)–(III) concern processing mechanisms which take imagining and belief as input. Weinberg and Meskin add that some mechanisms produce imagining and belief *as output* (2006: 178). I'll focus on the more restricted version, assuming that my points apply *a fortiori* to theirs. Note also that [SOM] is not the claim that, numerically, there is only one such mechanism involved; rather it's a claim that they are processed by a single *type of* mechanism. As the numerical claim implies the 'single type' point, again I'll focus only on the latter.

That [CI] type-individuates mechanisms roughly as (I) does is implied by its examples, e.g., 'inference mechanisms', including a mechanism identified as whatever performs a 'modus-ponens-performing process' (Weinberg 2008); a 'moral response mechanism' (Nichols 2004: 136); an 'affective mechanism' (Nichols 2004: 133); and so on. As stated, (I) might be taken to imply that, for every property D attributable to both imagining and belief that *p* at the personal level, there is a single well-formed mechanism-type responsible for the capacity in imagining and belief to realize D. However, one might be sceptical that the capacities identified by reflective folk psychology are thus underpinned by neatly associated mechanism-types (Currie and Ravenscroft 2003: Section 3.5). Defenders of [CI] acknowledge that, in fact, several mechanism-types might be jointly responsible for a single property D of both imagining and belief (Nichols and Stich 2000: 127). So [SOM] is better expressed thus:

(I*) A mechanism is of type M iff it is a member of the set of mechanisms which realize/contribute to the realization of D in the entities it processes.

(II) In certain contexts, imagining and belief that *p* each realize D.

Therefore:

(III) In those contexts, imagining and belief that *p* each are processed by a mechanism of type M.

However, with this alteration the possibility emerges more clearly that M-mechanisms, *qua* members of the set of mechanisms responsible for D, subdivide in non-overlapping fashion into two groups: those which process imaginings; and those which process beliefs. This is ruled out by [CI]. At the heart of [SOM], then, is the further claim that:

(IV)  No mechanism of type M makes any discrimination between imagining and belief as input.

[SOM], thus presented, is a 'self-evidencing' version of inference to the best explanation, of the form: H(ypothesis) explains E(ntity) while E partly justifies H. Another example would be the positing of a passer-by in snowshoes to explain some tracks; simultaneously, the tracks partly warrant belief in that passer-by (Lipton 2004: 24). The postulation of a processing mechanism of type M, which doesn't discriminate between imagining and belief as input, is supposed to explain, in particular cases, the shared possession of a property D by imagining and belief; meanwhile the existence of D provides limited evidence for M. Of course, in this kind of explanation, the postulation of M must be supported, not just by D, but also otherwise (in Lipton's example, we've general reasons to believe in the existence of passers-by wearing snowshoes, other than the evidence provided by snow-tracks).

[SOM], including (IV), is clearly central to all versions of [CI] (see Nichols and Stich 2000: 122; Meskin and Weinberg 2003: 31; Weinberg 2008: 204). Yet what evidence supports it, assuming that neuroscience is not yet in a position to do so? (Currie and Ravenscroft 2003: 69).

*General* arguments for domain-specific cognitive mechanisms do not support (IV), unless, of course, it is argued for or entailed by them. *Prima facie*, one might find promising in this regard any claim that a particular sort of processing of imagining and belief occurs (at least initially) without reference to the identity of the state concerned. For instance, Jenefer Robinson argues that both in imagining and belief, affect starts with a 'pre-cognitive affective appraisal', which sets off certain physiological responses and actions; 'cognitive monitoring' then informs the subject about the reality or otherwise of the object of her response, and this information can modify the original response, in terms of physiology and 'action tendencies' (2005: 145–6).

Does this support (IV), at least with respect to affect mechanisms? There are two reasons for caution. First, since the picture is concerned with processes and not architecture, it's compatible with the existence of distinct state-specific affective mechanisms to realize those processes. Second, the evidence presented for this picture consists of cases where we have affect-like responses to objects acknowledged as non-existent (Robinson 2005: 146). Such cases can do only limited work in supporting (IV), since at most they slightly expand our conception of functional similarities between imagining and belief which the postulation of M-mechanisms satisfying (IV) was supposed to explain (more on this point below).

Whether or not support for (IV) can be found in other authors' work, I think it reasonable to focus on points made by defenders of [CI] themselves. Weinberg and

Meskin (2006: 179) emphasize the fact that imagining and belief that $p$ are inferentially similar, as indicated by Leslie's tea party. However, this is a straightforward restatement of one of the basic explananda which postulation of M-mechanisms satisfying (IV) was supposed to explain, and so doesn't provide any independent support for that thesis. (Of course, if the theory turned out to be plausible for other reasons, we could admit such similarities as evidence for (IV) with respect to inference mechanism.)

Currie and Ravenscroft also focus on inference, with an argument which I assume is supposed to imply (IV). After noting that belief contents are typically available for inferential transaction with imaginative contents, they ask:

> If imagination and belief operated under a system of inferential apartheid—as the two-mechanisms view has it—how could this happen? (2003: 69)

The point is not convincing, however, since a rejection of (IV) is compatible with the described phenomenon: for instance, if the contents of various beliefs were replicated as that of imaginings, and then fed to imagining-specific mechanisms.[3]

Both Weinberg and Meskin (2006: 179) and Nichols (2004: 131–2) cite as evidence for (IV), as applied to affective mechanisms, that imagining and belief that $p$ can prompt autonomic and other physiological responses associated with the same emotion-type. In terms of (I\*)–(IV) above: let 'D' refer to the property, possessed both by imagining and belief that $p$, of producing autonomic response AR. What [SOM] wants to rule out, via (IV), is that the set of M-mechanisms subdivides into two: those that produce AR upon the inputting of imagining, and those that produce AR upon the inputting of belief. I cannot see that the observation that both imagining and belief produce AR does this. The moral here is that, generally speaking, the noting of functionally identical or similar aspects of imagining and belief in some domain is compatible with distinct mechanisms generating each. Certainly, functional similarity in a given respect does not imply [SOM]: after all, there are functional similarities between perceptions in different modalities, without any suggestion of identical processing (I owe this point to Dustin Stokes). Yet even the fact that two distinct states function identically in some respect does not compel [SOM]. For this reason, the oft-repeated point that [CI] has substantial success in accommodating existing observations about functional similarities doesn't, on its own, give it any advantage *per se* over a rival view which posits state-specific mechanisms.

So far I've been considering arguments in defence of (IV) in particular domains. Of course, even if successful, any such argument need not generalize to other cases. But are there additional general reasons to endorse (IV)?

Quite often, defenders of [CI] talk as if it had predictive power. For instance, after identifying four features of affect-like responses to fiction, Meskin and Weinberg

---

[3] Perhaps lurking here is the implication that a single-mechanism set-up is of greater adaptive benefit than a two-mechanism set-up. If so, it would be good to hear it formulated plausibly.

identify a constraint on [CI]; namely, it 'must predict...that we have affective responses as characterized. (2003: 20). However, as noted by Lipton:

a theory is more strongly supported by successful predictions than by data that were known before the theory was constructed and which the theory was designed to accommodate. (2004: 68)

The features of fictive affect identified by Meskin and Weinberg are already available to folk psychology. So to say that their theory should or does 'predict' them is of limited value. Similar uses of 'predict' are scattered throughout the literature.

What if new evidence were found that imagining and belief functioned alike? I can imagine a defender of [CI] conceding that individual cases cannot motivate (IV), and that data available prior to [CI]'s construction are of limited value; but suggesting that cumulatively, the more of such cases which emerge, the more support is built.

Note that—as was suggested during discussion of Robinson—the greater the similarity between a new phenomenon and one which [CI] was designed to accommodate, the less interesting it would be that [CI] explained the former. In any case, I think this strategy would have to accompany an argument from economy, since, as I've suggested, even the cumulative noting of functionally similar/identical aspects of imagining and belief in some domain is compatible with state-specific mechanisms being responsible for each of the aspects.

Is (IV) indeed supported via reasons of economy (see Currie and Ravenscroft 2003: 67)? This is hard to assess, since what [CI] gains in ontological parsimony (obviating the need to posit one mechanism subtype to handle imagining, and another to handle belief) it may, for all we know, lose in terms of the theoretical complexity required to characterize such multi-functional mechanisms. Furthermore, since it's admitted that, in practice, several mechanism-types might subserve the function of realizing a given property D, it's not clear whether arguing that *all* such mechanism-types handle both imagining and belief has consequences for *how many* such mechanisms need to be posited. Perhaps, the greater the complexity of a task assigned to a mechanism-type (e.g., handling imagining *and* belief to process moral response, rather than one or the other), the greater the reason to assume that the type will decompose into distinct subtypes. Of course, this is speculative—the point is, such matters need to be discussed before the virtue of parsimony is assigned.

In this section, I've not claimed that (IV) is false; but only that the considerations explicitly adduced for it are not particularly compelling. A further point is that, even if (IV) were satisfied by a given mechanism, it would not follow that the explanation furnished by [CI] of the relevant functional similarity was superior to any drawing on folk psychology or metaphysics. Traditional explanations might be equally or more satisfying, depending on the specifics of the case (including what exactly the question was). Furthermore, at least so far as we've seen, [CI] may not extend any successful instance of [SOM] more widely, given success in one case. Hence [CI] doesn't look especially virtuously wide-ranging in comparison to a traditionalist's piecemeal approach, as first might be thought.

Perhaps though, evidence of [CI]'s greater scope is found in a different commitment.

*The 'single code' hypothesis*

[SCH] is the claim that a belief and an imagining with the same contents are in the same code. By this is meant, at least, that the sub-personal representations co-extensive with beliefs and imaginings are in the same syntactic form.[4] As Nichols admits, the code in question is unknown (2006a: 461). In fact, there might be multiple codes involved, but at least, every imagining 'is in the same code as some parallel belief representation' (2006a: 461, footnote 4). So [SCH] looks to provide a much-needed piece of the picture, explaining why a mechanism need not differentiate between imagining and belief that *p* as input: namely, because it responds to the code of each, rather than to the state-type. Presumably, then, a representation's code is posited as (at least partly) responsible for mechanism-types interacted with, and the manner of interaction.

A problem arises here, however. [SOM] has been presented only as the claim that imaginings and beliefs interact with *some of* the same mechanism-types, in the same way; for in many respects imaginings and beliefs with the same contents differ in the processes apparently performed upon them. As noted earlier, there is a differential relation to action. Furthermore, imaginings but not beliefs with the same contents tend to produce beliefs about possible non-actual states of affairs (Nichols and Stich 2004: 128). Several other differences are noted by Weinberg (2008). For one, in imaginative engagement with surreal fictions, we seem relatively happy to accommodate inconsistent imaginings as we would not do with parallel belief contents (2008: 212). For another, in response to some fictions we do not respond morally as we would do, had we analogous beliefs (2008: 212). A related point is that, despite the ostensible similarities adverted to earlier, our affective responses to imagining often seem different to those we would have towards beliefs with the same contents (2008: 210).

One might wonder, therefore: if an imagining and a belief that *p* are in the same code, and that code is (partly) responsible for mechanism-types interacted with, and manner of interaction, then what explanation can be given of the apparent differences in both the sorts of processing mechanisms interacted with and the way in which such interactions take place? Nichols suggests that such differences are indeed problematic; they are 'exactly' what [SCH] 'says won't happen' (2006a: 465).

Nichols focuses on differences in affect: for instance, that in watching *Dr Strangelove*, we are amused that 'all human life is about to be destroyed' (2006a: 464), and not appalled as we would be, given a parallel belief. Meanwhile, during thought experiments involving such imagining, typically one has no affective response to it at all (2006a: 465). In response he claims, first, that a desire can interact with a thought that *p* to determine which inferences get drawn from *p*; and that sometimes those inferences are such as to produce affect. For instance, a desire 'for the survival of human life' can

---

[4] It seems reasonable to assume that their endorsement of [SCH] demonstrates a commitment of defenders of [CI] to the well-known Language of Thought hypothesis (see Aydede 2004). However, it is curiously difficult to find any explicit articulation of this commitment.

interact with a belief that *human life is about to end* to entail affecting inferences such as *billions of innocent people will die horrifically painful deaths* (2006a: 472). Second, different desires can accompany belief and imagining that *p*, respectively. Hence it may or may not be the case that the corresponding inferences from *p* are drawn in imagination (2006a: 472). In the *Strangelove* case, imagining that *human life is about to end* is not accompanied by any desire for human survival, and so the affecting inferences aren't drawn out. Meanwhile, where an imagining with that content occurs in a thought experiment, since our dominant desire is to solve a 'hypothetical problem', here too we do not 'draw out' the disturbing inferences which would strongly affect us in the belief case.

This is all quite puzzling. Nichols seems to be trying to save the thought that in such cases, imagining and belief are in the same code (see for instance, his final sentence, 2006a: 472), while claiming that it is a representation's connections to a particular set of inferences which determine which affective mechanisms it interacts with, and to what extent, so that two items in the same code can be processed differently depending on the inferences which accompany them ('the asymmetries arise because the affective mechanism is *sent quite different input* depending on whether one imagines that *p* or believes that *p*' (2006a: 472, my italics)). This looks like a significant departure from the single code theory. It looked committed to arguing that it was precisely a representation's code which determined which inference and affective mechanisms it interacted with, and to what extent. Yet here Nichols seems to suggest that two identically coded representations can be accompanied by different inferences, and can give rise to different affect, depending on what desires are concomitant. Furthermore, insofar as the original view held that imagining and belief that *p* produce similar output, Nichols's claim that different desires can accompany a belief and an imagining that *p* respectively requires further explanation, given that in many cases such desires aren't independent of the content of the belief/imagining in question.

Perhaps Nichols is *denying* that in relevant cases, imagining and the belief that *p* are respectively in the same code, precisely *because* each stands in differential relations to desire, and so produces different inferences and affect. If so, we need explanation of how the accompaniment or absence of desire can make a difference to the code of another representation. Moreover, since presumably functional similarities remain between, for example, imagining and the belief that *all human life is about to end* (for instance, they have at least *some* inferential connections in common), we need an explanation of them, now that [SCH] is off the table.

In other cases (pity for Anna Karenina, and so forth), it seems our affective responses to fictional characters *do* mirror those we would have to parallel beliefs; so a question arises about what determines whether a given affective response is directed towards the content of an imagining or not, in a given case. Such matters are rendered more opaque by Nichols's invocation of two different sorts of desires in his examples: an absent moral one (no desire for human life to be preserved) and a present purposive one (to solve a puzzle) (2006a: 472).

It seems, then, that Nichols cannot alleviate the problems that distinct 'output' relations of imagining and belief that *p*, respectively, apparently pose for the single-code claim. A different approach is offered by Weinberg (2008). He argues that such data force us to see the IB as 'configurable' in that, for instance, we can 'adjust' which mechanisms it interacts with at a given time (2008: 217). In support he draws upon the notion of:

the 'soft assembly' of complexes of processes and mechanisms that recruit from available resources to create a 'task-specific device'. (2008: 210)

I'm not able to assess here to what extent the notion of 'soft assembly' is legitimately carried over from the field of human movement to the imagination. The picture presented looks compatible with (IV): mechanisms are still generally indifferent as to whether imagining or belief is inputted, but in certain contexts, may take only one of these as input. However, it makes the notion of the single code as responsible for what mechanisms are interacted with rather obscure, since now beliefs and imaginings that *p* are in the same code, but interact with different mechanisms on particular occasions.

More basically, there is also a worry that the data to which the 'configurability' claim responds apparently imply rejection of a central explanandum which [CI], and (IV) of [SOM] in particular, was originally designed to accommodate: apparently widespread functional similarities between imagining and belief, of certain sorts. Once doubt is cast on the existence of this explanandum, even the limited 'self-evidencing' support it provided for [CI], and (IV) in particular, looks undermined. Hence the configurability claim, including its continued endorsement of (IV), had at least better find some productive new work to do. Weinberg uses it to give a theory of genre mastery, among other things. Whether the tasks he assigns to the configurable imagination warrant his continued endorsement of (IV) in light of noted significant functional dissimilarity is unfortunately something I cannot examine here, but I think it worth raising.

At this point a defender of [CI] may respond that my expectations for [CI] are unrealistically high: that it's a framework for theorizing, not a theory itself, so doesn't require its postulates to be unequivocally established. The real test for [CI] is to see how it fares in explaining philosophical puzzles: not least, in aesthetics. I finish by considering what resources it brings to one central problem.

## 4. The paradox of fiction

As noted, this is the issue of how to classify affect-like responses to imagined contents: whether they are of a kind with ordinary affective response to entities believed existent, or not. Nichols notes as significant that:

on the single-code theory, an affective system can accept as input the pretense representation that *Lear is watching Cordelia die*, and the affective system will generate the same affective consequence from this input that it would if the input were instead a belief that *Lear is watching Cordelia die.* (2004: 133).

There are two ways to read this. One is that such a claim helps us decide how to answer the paradox of fiction, by providing evidence that affect-like responses to imaginings are of the same kind as ordinary affective responses, since processed by the same mechanisms. Yet this answer is not compelled by the data that imagining and belief are processed alike, but rather depends on what one has already decided it is the job of the affect system to do; this is precisely what the paradox of fiction asks. In other words: even if an affect system produces the 'same affective consequences' for both imagining and belief, taking them both indiscriminately as input and thereby satisfying (IV), we still need to know how to analyse those consequences. Is what imagining and belief that *p* have in common that they produce only *affect-like* response; where those affect-like responses further subdivide into real emotions and quasi-emotions? Or do they both produce genuine affect of a single kind? This problem is left untouched by [CI] *even if successfully defended.*

A different way to read Nichols is as following an approach taken by Meskin and Weinberg, who, as discussed earlier, use [CI] to account for the fact the paradox troubles us at all (2003). They characterize their approach as superior insofar as, supposedly, it doesn't force one to choose between conflicting intuitions, but rather explains the source of them. Earlier I expressed doubt about whether doing the latter either obviated or was superior to rejecting one of the intuitions as ill-grounded. In any case, the explanation they offer is rather implausible: as I described earlier, it characterizes the source of our puzzlement in terms of, on one hand, a desire to individuate emotions in terms of their cause, and on the other, awareness that each engages our affect systems alike (2003: 33). Yet to attribute to the ordinary person awareness of sub-personal events, as the latter point implies, seems rather unsatisfactory, especially since [CI] is being presented as a novel approach contrasted with folk psychology.

What of the authors' use of [CI] to explain the remaining three features? One is the by now familiar case of a functional similarity between imagining and belief—the 'phenomenological and physiological robustness' of fictive affect, i.e. that it feels 'substantive' to the subject, and has observable behavioural effects—and the appeal to [CI], including (IV), to account for it (2003: 32). As argued above, since functional similarities of this sort are identical or closely related to those initially identified as explananda, that [CI] explains them is not of great help to the theory as a whole. Meanwhile, the power of [CI] over its rivals to explain such similarities depends on the plausibility of (IV), which I've suggested is not inferable from the noting of any such similarities alone, and is otherwise rather inadequately supported, as things stand.

A second claim is that [CI] explains the 'behavioural circumscription' of fictive affect—that is, that behaviour associated with fictive affect is limited in ways in which its 'non-fictive analogue' is not (e.g., we do not run screaming from the cinema even though 'afraid'). This I find puzzling, since, again, such circumscription is again a datum usually cited as partly responsible for the shape of [CI] (it is one of the differences which allows us to construe the functional roles of imagining and belief as distinct). In any case, we've seen that such differences aren't explicitly accommodated by [SCH]; so to characterize it as 'explained' by [CI] sits rather uneasily on both counts.

Finally, the authors claim that [CI] explains why fictive affect has intentionality: namely, because imaginings and beliefs are in the same 'syntactic and semantic form' (2006: 183). This is most puzzling of all. Why should the fact that *imaginings/beliefs* are in a particular code explain why *emotional states* distinct from them have intentionality? Perhaps the thought is that (a) the intentionality of imaginings/beliefs is due to their being in the same code; (b) the intentionality of affect generated from any such imaginings/beliefs is also thereby derived. If so, (b) needs much work. So does (a). Perhaps a belief's code is responsible for its semantic properties (though among endorsers of the Language of Thought hypothesis, there is much controversy about how, exactly—see Aydede 2004); so perhaps *if* an imagining and a belief that *p* are in the same code, somehow that code is responsible for the imagining's semantic properties too. However, in the face of the problems raised earlier, the 'if' looks rather too premature to allow that the intentionality of imagining is thereby 'explained'.

## 5. Conclusion

Space restrictions preclude further examination of the explanatory resources of [CI] in aesthetics, though there is much to say. However, I've at least shown that in a central case, they are more limited than one might initially think. We are urged to treat [CI] charitably as a promising research programme, whose fine details have yet to be worked out. Yet, I have suggested, in the case of the paradox of fiction, its explanatory virtues are far from obvious. I have also argued that [CI] does not attract any special credibility in virtue of its model of explanation; and, more seriously, that the case for two central tenets of [CI]—[SOM] and [SCH]—remains underdeveloped. The threat to 'traditional' philosophy of imagination from [CI], both in form and in content, remains unproven.[5]

## References

Aydede, Murat (2004). 'The Language of Thought Hypothesis'. *Stanford Encyclopaedia of Philosophy*. http://plato.stanford.edu/entries/language–thought/
Currie, Gregory (1995). *Image and Mind*. Cambridge: Cambridge University Press.
——(1997). 'The Paradox of Caring: Fiction and the Philosophy of Mind', in Mette Hjort and Sue Laver (eds.), *Emotion and the Arts*. Oxford: Oxford University Press, pp. 63–78.

---

[5] Thanks to Peter Goldie, Aaron Meskin, Dustin Stokes, and Jonathan Weinberg for very helpful comments. At least two of these don't agree with much of what I've written here!

Currie, Gregory and Ian Ravenscroft (2002). *Recreative Minds: Imagination in Philosophy and Psychology*. Oxford: Oxford University Press.

Gendler, Tamar Szabó (2000). 'The Puzzle of Imaginative Resistance'. *Journal of Philosophy*, 97/2: 55–81.

Harris, Paul L. (2000). *The Work of the Imagination*. Oxford: Blackwell.

Leslie, Alan (1994). 'Pretending and Believing: Issues in the Theory of ToMM'. *Cognition*, 50: 211–38.

Lipton, Peter (2004). *Inference to the Best Explanation*, 2nd edn. London: Routledge.

Meskin, Aaron and Jonathan M. Weinberg (2003). 'Emotions, Fiction and Cognitive Architecture'. *British Journal of Aesthetics*, 43/1: 18–38.

Nichols, Shaun (2004). 'Imagining and Believing: The Promise of a Single Code'. *Journal of Aesthetics and Art Criticism*, 62/6: 129–38.

——(2006a). 'Just the Imagination: Why Imagining Doesn't Behave Like Believing'. *Mind and Language*, 21/4: 459–74.

——(2006b). 'Introduction', in Shaun Nichols (ed.), *The Architecture of the Imagination*. Oxford: Oxford University Press, pp. 1–19.

——and Stephen Stich (2000). 'A Cognitive Theory of Pretense'. *Cognition*, 74: 115–47.

————(2003). *Mindreading: An Integrated Account of Pretense, Self-awareness and Understanding Other Minds*. Oxford: Oxford University Press.

Robinson, Jenefer (2005). *Deeper than Reason: Emotion and its Role in Literature, Music, and Art*. Oxford: Oxford University Press.

Stock, Kathleen (2005). 'Resisting Imaginative Resistance', *Philosophical Quarterly*, 55: 607–24.

Stokes, Dustin (2006). 'The Evaluative Character of Imaginative Resistance'. *British Journal of Aesthetics*, 46/4: 387–405.

Von Eckhardt, Barbara (1993). *What is Cognitive Science?* Cambridge, MA: MIT Press.

Walton, Kendall (1990). *Mimesis as Make Believe*. Cambridge, MA: Harvard University Press.

Weinberg, Jonathan M. (2008). 'Configuring the Cognitive Imagination', in K. Stock and K. Thomson-Jones (eds.), *New Waves in Aesthetics*. Basingstoke: Palgrave Macmillan, pp. 203–23.

——and Aaron Meskin (2006). 'Puzzling over the Imagination: Philosophical Problems and Architectural Solutions', in Shaun Nichols (ed.), *The Architecture of the Imagination*. Oxford: Oxford University Press, pp. 174–202.

Wright, Crispin (1998). 'Self-Knowledge: The Wittgensteinian Legacy', in Crispin Wright, Barry C. Smith, and Cynthia Macdonald (eds.), *Knowing Our Own Minds*, Mind Occasional Series. Oxford: Oxford University Press, pp. 13–45.

# PART V

# Fiction and Empathy

# 16

# Enacting the Other: Towards an Aesthetics of Feeling in Literary Reading

*David S. Miall*

## 1. The problem of empathy

Our evolutionary history shows us to be strongly social beings. We live in the light of our understanding of our fellow human beings, and in part in the light of their understanding of us. Thus, among any survey of the reasons why we value literary works, we might expect to find that empathy has a prominent place, perhaps even the most important. Through empathy we share the feelings and emotions of the characters we read about (whether a narrative or a poem) or watch on stage or screen. Through feelings and emotions we recognize the concerns and motives of others, and thus come to realize something about their values and why they act the way they do. This in turn may enable us to recognize a similar complex of feelings and motives in ourselves, thus illuminating or even helping shape an aspect of our own identity.

Empathy, of course, is central also to daily life. It develops early in the young infant; we know that its absence is an important part of autism; it constitutes what has been termed Theory of Mind, our capacity to understand what other people are feeling and thinking. Empathy is in requisition frequently, whether voluntarily or involuntarily: as I think about how to persuade my son to sit down and begin his homework; as I see my wife off to a dental appointment; as I see on television a victim of war in a refugee camp. So the importance of empathy in our reading of literature is not surprising. What may be surprising is how much critical discussion empathy has caused. It seems that the more closely readers' empathy is looked at the more problematic it becomes.

The problem is often stated in this form: Given that we know the characters about whom we are reading are not real, how is it possible to have real emotions about them? Why should I feel joy or sorrow for the fate of a character who never existed? One answer is proposed by Gregory Currie (1997). If we care about fictional characters, then our empathy towards them should be amenable to the same explanation as the empathy we feel towards real people. Since the actual beliefs and desires of another person are not possible for me, then I imagine the beliefs and desires of the other; my belief and desire are a simulation having a systematic resemblance to the other in terms of content, and a likeness in internal causal role—although not in their external role, which is unavailable (Currie 1997: 67). As a reader it is as though I am simulating the experiences of a reader who is reading a factual account, and I experience the same emotions except that my state is one of "make-believe," or what Currie calls "off-line" versions of mental states. Thus, reading fiction "works by persuading me to engage in a certain piece of imaginative role-play, not by getting me to have false beliefs" (Currie 1997: 69).

This is to assume a similarity with the other, however, that may not be possible. As Carroll (1997) puts it, there is often an asymmetry between myself and a fictional character: I am situated quite differently from the character and have quite different experiences. We cannot directly identify with characters in fiction or drama, then: we know more than they do, or we have a view of other characters that is unavailable to them. Thus we cannot exactly share in, or simulate, the emotions of a given character (Carroll 1997: 200). Carroll rules out the notion of simulation or make-believe. For him, experiencing emotion in fiction does not necessarily require beliefs; it involves thoughts or a pattern of attention. As Aristotle put it, merely to think about the fate of Oedipus can evoke fear. A thought can be held unasserted, yet raise emotions; and such emotions have the power to effect bodily changes (Carroll 1997: 209). Fiction is full of unasserted propositions (Carroll 1997: 210).

Currie's explanation, that as fictional readers we simulate the reading of a factual account, is however paralleled by a suggestion of Carroll (1990), who proposes the following thought experiment. You hear a story, and only later are told whether the story is fictional or real. According to Carroll, the emotion you feel remains the same (Carroll 1990: 77). This conclusion is supported by the empirical studies of Melanie Green (e.g., Green and Brock 2000). She looked at "transport" while reading, that is, readers' absorption in the texts she asked them to read, which she defined as partly an emotional effect. If the text was an emotionally powerful one, she found that it made no difference to degree of transport whether readers thought the story was a real one, fictional, or based on a dream. She referred to this as the textual hegemony effect. This is one indication (there will be others) that emotion, once instantiated, has its own inherent power regardless of reality.

Walton (1990) takes a similar view to Currie: he proposes that in experiencing feelings while reading fiction, we are engaged in a game of make-believe and that our feelings are "quasi-feelings" (Walton 1990: 214). This is not to underestimate the power of such experiences. As Walton suggests, "having or expressing certain feelings in a dream or fantasy or game of make-believe is the means by which one achieves insight into one's situation, or empathy for others, or a realization of what it is like to undergo certain experiences, and so on" (Walton 1990: 272). And, he adds, from within the experience, the world of the fiction seems real. This explains why we should care about experiencing fictional characters: the function of the experience has some similarity to that of dreams and daydreams. Fiction provides an opportunity to rehearse feelings in particular situations, to purge undesirable feelings, to work through conflicts (Walton 1990: 272).

This view is vulnerable to the problem that Carroll identified: the asymmetry between reader and character. In addition, it supposes that reading fiction is comparable to daydreaming in that both involve make-believe. The daydream typically involves rehearsing possible situations—although our fantasies may take us outside the realms of reality; and daydreaming enables us to consider alternative choices for action. A fiction, on the other hand, provides no such contact with our own reality, nor does it offer different potential actions. If there is a similarity, it seems to lie in the power of feeling to develop offline the dynamics of a specific feeling, so that we experience it fully in ways that are rarely possible in everyday situations. Beyond this, however, while the feeling may be welcomed or resisted, as the case may be, in a daydream we have the power to be receptive to a feeling and extend it for as long as we wish; in fiction as we read on, a given feeling may be called into question, modified, opposed, or thwarted, regardless of our wishes.

Another important contribution to understanding empathy is made by Oatley (1999). He argues for translating Aristotle's term "mimesis" as simulation rather than imitation, in the sense that a computer can be programmed to run a simulation. The reader inserts the plans and goals of the character into his or her own planning processor, with resulting emotions; hence readers identify or empathize with the character. In this conception Oatley (2002) suggests that reading is an enactment, or performance; and it is one, he says, which "prioritizes personal truth" (Oatley 2002: 50) in contrast to the passive models of reception theory or reader response. Through taking an active part, we are "potentially becoming different from our habitual selves in doing so" (Oatley 2002: 51). We do not copy a character's emotions, we enact them.

Oatley's proposal can be elaborated through a distinction Coleridge makes between copy and imitation. For Coleridge a copy is a mere reproduction and cannot be a work of art. An imitation (Oatley's simulation), on the other hand, calls for the artist to have understood the laws of nature inherent in the subject he is creating. For this purpose, Coleridge (1987: 222) says, the artist must first "eloign" himself from nature in order to discover within himself the corresponding laws, before returning to his subject with appropriate understanding of the dynamics that make it what it is. This is not to suggest that the reader must undertake eloignment, but that what the literary reader experiences, in line with Oatley's simulation view, are the productive powers of feeling, feeling as a process not as an accomplished state—as I will suggest later, feeling evocative of resonance, bodily implications, and incipient action plans. The formal structure of the work motivates the reader's simulative powers: literary texts "have an incompleteness that challenges the reader to engage in creative, and imaginative, construction" (Oatley and Gholomain 1997: 280). The challenge of incompleteness in the formal sense also suggests that a literary reader is not fully immersed at all times in her experience of the work, but will "move in and out along the continuum of emotional distance, be fully engaged emotionally at one moment, and then in the glow of that emotion, think about the experience in a more distanced way" (Oatley 2002: 64).

The arguments I have been considering here suggest, first, that for empathy to occur, make-believe—or the "suspension of disbelief," in Coleridge's phrase—is unnecessary. To experience an emotion we need only entertain the thought of its initiating object or event, not believe or make-believe in its reality (Carroll 1990: 79). Second, this also suggests that as readers experiencing empathy with characters, where what we know is more or different than what they know, we have the leeway to feel differently. For instance, we can have feelings that resonate directly with how a character is feeling while concurrently experiencing a different feeling due to a situation of which the character is unaware. Third, feeling once initiated has its own lawfulness in how it unfolds, in its implications and consequences (until deflected by a different feeling or impetus equally strong), and in this respect it provides the underlying dynamics in our enactment of a given character's narrative (perhaps for the length of a certain action or episode).

The discussion of empathy has raised questions about what feelings are and how they occur. I pursue these questions in the next section in order to show how far the view of empathy I have put forward is supported by neuropsychological evidence. In particular I focus on bodily feelings and how these are invoked by the response to text.

## 2. Empathy and the body in discourse

The psychological study of response to text (discourse processing theory) has recently taken a major turn towards understanding of the body. The discourse processing model is now being extended to investigate the role of sensory imagery in addition to the visual (i.e., touch, hearing, etc.), feeling, and other bodily states (kinaesthetic imagery, breathing rate, etc.). As Zwaan and Singer (2003) point out, recent research has challenged the assumption of "the disembodied construction of abstract propositional networks"; alternative approaches have focused on theories of modal representation, claiming that comprehension "involves analog, perceptual representations that reflect how we, as humans, interact with our environments" (Zwaan and Singer 2003: 114). Such theories include Barsalou's (1999) perceptual symbol system, Glenberg's (1997) indexical hypothesis, and the Theory of Event Coding of Hommel and his colleagues (Hommel *et al.* 2001). Zwaan himself has published a contribution towards such a new theory that he calls the "the Immersed Experiencer Framework" (Zwaan 2004). Here, as in the other recent theories I have mentioned, the body is found to contribute significantly towards language understanding.

Zwaan's approach is based primarily on the recent and rather striking finding that the same brain areas that are involved in experiencing a situation are also involved in imagining it or, especially, while reading about it. Thus his theory proposes that "language is a set of cues to the comprehender to construct an experiential (perception plus action) simulation of the described situation. In this conceptualization, the comprehender is an immersed experiencer of the described situation, and comprehension is the vicarious experience of the described situation" (Zwaan 2004: 36). And, he adds, we comprehend "the described events through the integration and sequencing of traces from actual experience cued by the linguistic input" (Zwaan 2004: 38).

This insight is echoed in a number of other proposals. For example, the narratologist Monika Fludernik refers to a similar concept, what she terms "immundation," in which "man's enmeshment or engagement with his environment operates as a central constitutive feature and as a fundamental cognitive frame" (Fludernik 1996: 7); hence, Fludernik remarks, in order to locate the reading process we must study "the *embodiment* of cognitive categories and . . . the reliance of higher-level symbolic categories on such embodied schemata" (Fludernik 1996: 19). Similarly, the psychologist Glenberg (1997) argues that conceptualization and memory are not instantiated in propositions or symbols, but in embodiment: "the world," he says, "is conceptualized (in part) as patterns of possible bodily interactions," such that "the meaning of an object, event, or sentence is what that person can do with that object, event, or sentence" (Glenberg 1997: 3). In Barsalou's (1999) account the perceptual symbol systems that support our understanding of language are derived from moments of perception in which a range of information is retained, not only perceptual, but proprioceptive, and emotional; thus, part of this information can later be reactivated, simulating what the original experience was like. As Gibbs (2005) puts it, summarizing a range of studies, evidence shows that "representation of a visual object includes not only description of its visual properties, but also encodings of actions relevant to that object" (Gibbs 2005: 60). This provides a much richer context for our response to the empathic quality of literary texts, as I will point out shortly.

What is the empirical evidence that supports these claims? Here are brief accounts of a few of the studies. The studies can be categorized as providing either direct or indirect evidence for the proposed role of bodily feelings in reading. The direct provide insight into a bodily component of language processing. For example, Hauk and Pulvermüller (2004) studied the activity in hearers' brains in response to words describing actions with the face, hand, or leg. Using EEG to measure response in the relevant areas of the brain, they were able to show that location-specific neuronal activity was occurring within 210–230 milliseconds (msec) of word onset. In other words, the motor areas that control actions by the face, arm, or leg are also activated when hearing a relevant word. These neurons, they suggest, "play a crucial role for identifying these words" (Hauk and Pulvermüller 2004: 199). This study shows how a reader has direct and immediate access to the bodily situation of a character—a basis for empathy in an appropriate descriptive context.

Fischer and Zwaan (2008) describe a study by Speer and his colleagues (2005) that involved reading connected narrative. Readers' brain activity was monitored by a scanner while they read a narrative about a day in the life of a boy. They found that activity in the motor areas involved in imaging and executing hand movements coincided with those points in the story when the boy interacted with an object.

The impact of reading on behavior was shown in a study by Bargh *et al.* (1996). Student participants were asked to make a series of sentences by rearranging sets of words. A number of the provided words related to the elderly (e.g., *old*, *stubborn*, *wise*, *Florida*, but not *slow*), although participants remained unaware of this (participants were told that the study involved language proficiency). A control group received neutral words. After completing the task participants were timed as they left the lab and walked down a stretch of corridor. Questioned afterwards, participants saw no influence from the words. Yet those who received the "elderly" words moved more slowly: they took 8.28 seconds to walk the corridor compared with 7.30 seconds for those receiving the neutral words.

Other studies of response to language provide indirect evidence for a bodily component. Glenberg and his colleagues (2008) demonstrated what they characterize as the action-sentence compatibility effect (ACE). In this view, "sentences are under-stood by creating a simulation of the actions that underlie them" (Glenberg *et al.* 2008: 907) In one study participants read concrete and abstract sentences implying deictic transfer away or towards the reader. As they heard each sentence, participants judged its "sensibility" (whether it made sense) by pressing a button either further away or nearer than a start button. Reaction time was recorded. Whether a sentence was concrete (e.g., "You give the pizza to Andy") or abstract (e.g., "Liz told you the story"), hand action moving to a button was faster when it matched the direction implied by the sentence.

Another finding to emerge from this research paradigm is that to recall a concept is usually also to recall a richness of situational and sensory information. Vallée-Tourangeau *et al.* (1998) asked participants to generate examples for a familiar category (such as "vehicle") and ad hoc categories (such as "things people keep in their pockets"); participants were then asked to describe what strategy they used. Three main strategies were found: experiential, based on episodic memory; semantic, deriv-ing from logical or propositional analysis; or unmediated, where no prior processing was required. The important finding here is that recall based on experiential knowl-edge occurred about three times more often than semantic knowledge or unmediated recall. This seems to confirm Damasio's claim that sensorimotor, affective, and other bodily aspects form an integral part of concepts in memory (1999: 147–8).

The direct evidence provided by the studies I have cited supports the claim that understanding of language is typically embodied: for example, sentences that describe action evoke a resonance in the premotor and motor cortex, and a motor potential in the limb or other body part, although action itself is inhibited. As the study with words relating to the elderly showed, behavioral changes can be induced through language although the participant remains unaware. The indirect evidence points to the same phenomenon: for instance, the study showing that hand movement is influenced by reading a sentence denoting action, even when the movement is only metaphorical.

These studies suggest that a range of bodily and affective responses are evoked during the act of reading, that the situation models we create to represent the characters and events we are reading about are richer, more sensuous, and more concrete than the largely abstract, amodal conceptions envisaged by the earlier work in discourse processing.

A preliminary account of empathy, in the context of these and similar findings, would suggest that descriptions of bodily movements are felt immediately in the reader's own body; that abstract events that are modeled on a sensory mode are also represented bodily; that character descriptions are adopted by the reader as though they described the self, with consequent bodily feelings; and that bodily feelings may then resonate with the reader's episodic memories and other meaning structures from the reader's own experience and understanding, perhaps evoking further feelings in turn (although the question remains how much of this felt experience reaches consciousness during normal reading).

An important context for interpreting the findings I have mentioned so far has been provided by the discovery of mirror neurons. First demonstrated by studying single cell neural responses in the monkey, it is now thought that mirror neurons play a major and more extensive role in human neural processes. In the classic observation (Gallese and Goldmann 1998) a mirror neuron fires when a particular action is either executed by a person or when it is observed being executed by another. In the monkey the mirror neuron systems that have been found are particularly dependent on the action having a specific goal, such as grasping an object. In humans this constraint appears to be somewhat relaxed, and mirror neurons are involved in contexts where experiences are not specifically goal-oriented, such as responding to the sight of a tool or reading its name (Grafton et al. 1997), or resonating to the emotional expression of another (Singer et al. 2004). Mirror neurons also fire during objectless, intransitive movements.

The role of mirror neurons has primarily been held to enable us to simulate the minds of others, whether the other is observed or only imagined, so mirror neurons have figured prominently in discussions of our supposed "Theory of Mind" capacity (Gallese and Goldmann, 1998). As Gallese and his colleagues put it, we have direct experiential knowledge of others that is not conceptual but gained from simulating the minds of others, since the mirror neuron system enables simulation of both action and emotion (Gallese et al. 2004). As they emphasize, it is through simulation that mirror neurons provide experiential knowledge of others' emotions, not just a conceptual knowledge of them. Rizzolatti and Craighero (2004: 183), indeed, remark that "messages . . . are understood by an observer without any cognitive mediation." These authors also point out the active role played by the body during reading. Experiments show that hand movements and mouth movements (including pronunciation of syllables) are closely linked in humans, and when listening to prose, subjects activate the lip muscle. In addition, they remark (a reminder of the work of Liberman, e.g., Liberman and Whalen, 2000), "experiments show that an echo-neuron system exists in humans: when an individual listens to verbal stimuli, there is an activation of the speech-related motor centers" (Rizzolatti and Craighero 2004: 186).

Another interesting implication is that the mirror neuron appears indifferent to whether an action or feeling is located in another or in the self. As Fischer and Zwaan (2008: 830) suggest, mirror neurons provide "direct evidence for common coding at the neurophysiological level"; thus their features include independence of perspective. Experience, in this context, is presented disinterestedly, without being associated either with the self or with the other (cf. Becchio and Bertone 2005). In other words, mirror neurons suggest that an action or feeling, at least during the first few hundred milliseconds, is understood independently of agency. This provides an important new perspective on empathy that may play a role in reader's response to narrative: a reader's sense (albeit fleeting) of a given feeling as prototypical and without agency.

Finally, if cognitive mediation occurs only later, mirror neuron findings suggest that processing during reading is immediate in experiential terms, activating both feeling and motor systems and, probably, other bodily responses such as kinesthetic functioning, muscle tension, heart rate, and breathing. Combined with the implication that the reader's imagination involves perceptions imbued with mnemonic and affective elements, we can suggest that a rich experiential matrix must be implicated in the early phases of literary reading, i.e., in the first 300–500 msec. To what extent these components and their interactions can specify what is distinctively literary about such reading remains to be considered. In the next section I outline a possible answer to this question. I look at how somatic and affective aspects may contribute to the process of literary reading.

## 3. A bodily based view of empathy

The perspective I have been developing so far, drawing on the theory of the immersed experiencer and the evidence of mirror neurons, suggests that not only concepts and imagery are evoked during literary reading, but that bodily aspects, involving motor and kinesthetic responses and feelings, also play a role. At the same time, such bodily aspects are little reported by readers; they appear to remain largely below the level of consciousness. Probably one reason for their status being more fugitive than concepts and images is the rapidity with which they unfold, especially when readers' experiences of empathy absorb attention, taking over consciousness. In the following examples, however, taken from an empirical study of reading, the complexity of the context and its literary aspects allow us to trace some of the bases for readers' empathic responses.

The evidence is gathered from readers (who were senior undergraduates in literature) asked to think aloud after reading each of four sections into which we had divided Kate Chopin's "The Story of an Hour." In the opening of this story Louise is told that her husband has died in a railway accident. After weeping in her sister's arms she retires alone to her bedroom. The next two paragraphs (part of the second section) are:

There stood, facing the open window, a comfortable, roomy armchair. Into this she sank, pressed down by a physical exhaustion that haunted her body and seemed to reach into her soul.

She could see in the open square before her house the tops of trees that were all aquiver with the new spring life. The delicious breath of rain was in the air. In the street below a peddler was crying his wares. The notes of a distant song which some one was singing reached her faintly, and countless sparrows were twittering in the eaves.

This second section shifts to a different mood from the first. It does so not only in subject matter but in stylistic qualities, as it describes trees, rain, distance voices, and birdsong. Among the 46 readers who read the story in our lab and made comments on this section, a number explicitly noted the contrast between Louise's grief and the account of the spring day that follows. For some the contrast seemed to be a fault: it "takes away from the grief" (A203), said one reader; another remarked that "the story talks about everything else going on as if nothing really bad just happened" (A210). But for several other readers the contrast is intriguing, suggesting some aspects of an aesthetic response to the text. One reader said "I enjoyed the small paradox with the beautiful day outside and the death that she's dealing with" (A225). A second said "It all sounds very refreshing; it doesn't sound at all depressing. So there's an interesting tension created and I'm intrigued by that" (A257). While these two readers explicitly comment on the contrast, standing as if outside the immediate situation, other readers describe it more empathically as though they situate themselves within the room. One reader says the passage depicts "how when you're sad and when you're going through an experience the world around you seems to go on, and seems to be unaware" (A204); another says "I almost feel like you're in the room, in a corner, watching this woman as she's looking outside the window" (A205). For this last reader the passage seems to involve physically relocating herself. Similarly, another reader places herself in the room when she says "I'm kind of lulled into the story, especially in opening the idea of sitting and looking out the window . . . absolutely being suspend[ed] in that moment" (A261).

The attention of readers has been caught by this passage in several different ways. The contrast in it provided by the description of the spring day seems to qualify the state of grief of Louise, and this anticipates the transformation in her that will begin in the next section. Although only one or two of the readers we have studied expect this, their remarks demonstrate an awareness that the situation is unusual and casts the grief in an odd light. Our sense of Louise's grief is modified by the description of the view from the window, a description that seems to call for a recontextualization—although how that is to be resolved only emerges in the story several paragraphs further on. The effect created can be compared to metaphor, where a vehicle term modifies its topic (e.g., in the expression "Jan was caught in the crossfire of her parent's divorce," the situation of Jan is modified through the term "crossfire"). In the story the feelings of spring qualify the grief, representing the potential for growth that Louise will realize shortly in her sense of freedom now that she believes that her marriage is over. In other words, we see a type of anticipation that plays a permanent role in our conceptions of human possibility. In the metaphor theory of Glucksberg and Keysar (1990) metaphor creates an ad hoc class or type, thus Louise's predicament facing the window can be seen as the token (or example) of its generalizing power (see also Miall 2006: 79), that is, grief's limitation in the face of the generative power of spring.

How far readers notice the metaphoric potential of this passage is apparent in their comments. Among the readers I have cited we can see three different types of response: first, a rejection of the contrast in the passage; second, an appreciation of the contrast that acknowledges the tension inherent in it; and third, the imaginative relocation of the reader in the room to experience the character's position; and it is with this third type that a metaphoric appreciation is particularly evident. In readings of the second type the role of the body would appear limited to representing the contrast and fostering an appreciation of it (readers refer to feelings of paradox and tension). In the third type, on the other hand, the body seems to provide a site for enacting the experience of the character, as suggested by phrases such as "when you're sad," "you're in the room," and "lulled into the story." This third type of reading seems enabled in particular by the feelings of the reader—feelings that the reader projects onto the passage rather than being found in it explicitly (the passage does not mention being sad or lulled).

In these three comments we can detect some of the powers of feeling that give it a primary place in directing the reader's response. For the reader who remarks "how when you're sad . . . the world around you seems to go on, and seems to be unaware" (A204), we see the generalizing power of feeling: she has taken a specific instance from the story and, by empathizing with it ("when you're sad") has made her experience of feeling into a general law. For the reader who said "I almost feel like you're in the room, in a corner, watching this woman as she's looking outside the window" (A205) feeling appears to direct her capacity for imagery—she has also just referred to being "entranced" by what the woman sees, suggesting that such focus is typical of grief. For the reader who remarks "I'm kind of lulled into the story" and that she is "absolutely being suspend[ed]," we see an instance of Frijda's Law of Closure, that is, the feeling takes precedence and is felt as all-inclusive, containing no indication that it is contingent (Frijda 2007: 15). These three responses, as I have indicated, are more radical than the others I have cited, and demonstrate most clearly the empathic response of the "immersed experiencer": not only do they involve empathy, but more specifically they operate like metaphors in promoting an ad hoc class, while the more active role of feeling they demonstrate seems to implicate the body (although in different ways for the different readers). Whether this combination of more active feeling and bodily implication is characteristic of literary readers, or only of some types of reader or some types of text, we have not yet investigated systematically.

## 4. Quiet sympathies: the fundamental analogy

Going beyond the neuropsychological studies I have cited, or the empirical evidence from our studies of literary reading, a wider context for the empathic capacity can be suggested. It can be understood as a part of the animistic conception of the world we inhabit, in which a primary purpose of literary experience (at least in premodern times) has been to evoke in us a sense of an animist dimension. While we may (now) implicitly reject this feeling for the events and objects around us, consciousness of such a meaning occurs only after it has already been established—thus it is a feeling that is hard to resist. The neuropsychological evidence points to a temporal gap between the immediate onset of feeling and its cognitive consequents that unfold several hundred milliseconds later; thus we can also regard the gap as occurring between the precategorical and cognitive phases of response, to adopt Tsur's term (1992: viii). The mirror neuron system, it will be recalled, invokes our capacities at the precategorical level. This shows that we have, at least in principle, a capacity to enact the entities, objects and events we perceive in ways that activate our motor and other bodily systems (especially if the perception involved is transitive, i.e., involving an action with a detectable goal); consciousness can be regarded as belated.

The mirror system thus not only represents within 200–300 msec the stance, feelings, and (possibly) the intentions of another human being through an immediate resonance within the motor system, kinesthetic and other bodily responses. The same system, although perhaps less powerfully, also enables us to represent the disposition of an animal, an insect, or a tree; and does so, we must recall, ahead of the conscious, cognitive response to an unfolding event. Thus, before we are aware of it, we have enacted, or proved "upon our pulses," as Keats would say (1958: I, 279), the life of the sparrow, and will "take part in its existence and pick about the gravel" (1958: I, 186). Among the English poets Wordsworth has provided several descriptions of this process (among his writings from 1797–9). For instance, in a fragment later revised for *The Excursion*, he wrote:

> Not useless do I deem
> These quiet sympathies with things that hold
> An inarticulate language (Wordsworth 1990: 678)

He primarily has in mind natural objects (he mentions the sky, clouds, and the ocean). Through such sympathy, he adds,

> All things shall live in us, and we shall live
> In all things that surround us. (Wordsworth 1990: 680)

Wordsworth also held that we are born with the capacity to sympathize with external objects: in *The Prelude* he refers to "those first-born affinities that fit / Our new existence to existing things" (Wordsworth 1990: 389). It was on the basis of such affinities that Wordsworth (and Coleridge, who shared a similar response to nature) developed a pantheistic philosophy that suggested a mental continuity between the human mind and every aspect of nature, however lowly (Piper 1962).

In evolutionary terms we can also see such a capacity as having adaptive value: to endow what may appear living entities with feelings and motives allows us to react promptly in anticipation of what they might do. While this will result in many "false positives," it facilitates survival: better to see too many illusory predators than not see the one that is really there. Although, in considering empathy and related feelings we have been discussing literature, the words on the page arouse feelings, and this appears to invoke the same "just in case" strategy that also constitutes empathy (cf. Miall 2006: 77–8).

In conclusion I have suggested that to understand literary reading and the role of empathy in particular, an enactive account involving the body is required—enactive, given that the human mirror neuron system appears to simulate in our motor systems and feelings the events, objects, actions, and emotions that we encounter while we read. In this bodily sense (resonance in the motor system, the dynamics of feelings, etc.), the mirror neuron system puts the action on stage, as it were, making us bodily participants in what we read; literary reading in particular, as I have suggested, then tends to complicate our response, introducing conflicts, ambiguities, and the like, which serve to modify our understanding (and perhaps by recursive processes modifying our physiological responses as well). The animist claim that I mentioned in relation to Wordsworth's writing is perhaps only a more comprehensive perspective on a participatory response exemplified in much of our literary reading—whenever we become absorbed, experience empathy, or feel the body resonating with affinities to what we read.

## References

Bargh, John A., Mark Chen, and Lara Burrows (1996). Automaticity of social behavior: Direct effects of trait construct and stereotype activation on action. *Journal of Personality and Social Psychology*, 71: 230–44.

Barsalou, Lawrence W. (1999). Language comprehension: Archival memory or preparation for situated action? *Discourse Processes*, 28: 61–80.

Becchio, Cristina and Cesare Bertone (2005). Beyond Cartesian subjectivism: Neural correlates of shared intentionality. *Journal of Consciousness Studies*, 12: 20–30.

Carroll, Noël (1990). *The Philosophy of Horror: Or, Paradoxes of the Heart*. New York: Routledge.

——(1997). Art, narrative, and emotion. In Mette Hjort and Sue Laver (eds.), *Emotion and the Arts*. New York: Oxford University Press, pp. 190–211.

Coleridge, Samuel Taylor (1987). *Lectures 1808–1819: On Literature*, Vol. II, ed. R. A. Foakes. Princeton: Princeton University Press.

Currie, Gregory (1997). The paradox of caring: Fiction and the philosophy of mind. In Mette Hjort and Sue Laver (eds.), *Emotion and the Arts*. New York: Oxford University Press, pp. 63–77.

Damasio, Antonio R. (1999). *The Feeling of What Happens: Body and Emotion in the Making of Consciousness*. New York: Harcourt.

Fischer, Martin H. and Rolf A. Zwaan (2008). Embodied language: A review of the role of the motor system in language comprehension. *Quarterly Journal of Experimental Psychology*, 61: 825–50.

Fludernik, Monika (1996). *Towards a 'Natural' Narratology*. London: Routledge.

Frijda, Nico (2007). *The Laws of Emotion*. Mahwah, NY: Lawrence Erlbaum Associates.

Gallese, Vittorio and Alvin Goldmann (1998). Mirror-neurons: In reflection. *Trends in Cognitive Sciences*, 2: 493–501.

——Christian Keysers, and Giacomo Rizzolatti (2004). A unifying view of the basis of social cognition. *Trends in Cognitive Sciences*, 8/9: 396–403.

Gibbs, Raymond W., Jr. (2005). *Embodiment and Cognitive Science*. New York: Cambridge University Press.

Glenberg, Arthur M. (1997). What memory is for. *Behavioral and Brain Sciences*, 20: 1–55.

——Marc Sato, Luigi Cattaneo, Lucia Riggio, Daniele Palumbo, and Giovanni Buccino (2008). Processing abstract language modulates motor system activity. *Quarterly Journal of Experimental Psychology*, 61: 905–19

Glucksberg, Sam and Boaz Keysar (1990). Understanding metaphorical comparisons: Beyond similarity. *Psychological Review*, 97: 3–18.

Grafton, Scott T., Luciano Fadiga, Michael A. Arbib, and Giacomo Rizzolatti (1997). Premotor cortex activation during observation and naming of familiar tools. *Neuroimage*, 6: 231–6.

Green, Melanie C. and Timothy C. Brock (2000). The role of transportation in the persuasiveness of public narratives. *Journal of Personality and Social Psychology*, 79: 701–21.

Hauk, Olaf and Friedman Pulvermüller (2004). Neurophysiological distinction of action words in the fronto-central cortex. *Human Brain Mapping*, 21: 191–201.

Hommel, Bernhard, Jochen Müsseler, Gisa Aschersleben, and Wolfgang Prinz (2001). The Theory of Event Coding (TEC): A framework for perception and action planning. *Behavioral and Brain Sciences*, 24: 849–937.

Keats, John (1958). *The Letters of John Keats*, 2 vols., ed. H. E. Rollins. Cambridge: Cambridge University Press.

Liberman, Alvin M. and Doug H. Whalen (2000). On the relation of speech to language. *Trends in Cognitive Sciences*, 4: 187–96.

Miall, David S. (2006). *Literary Reading: Empirical and Theoretical Studies*. New York: Peter Lang.

Oatley, Keith (1999). Meetings of minds: Dialogue, sympathy, and identification, in reading fiction. *Poetics*, 26: 439–54.

——(2002). Emotions and the story worlds of fiction. In Melanie C. Green, Jeffrey J. Strange, and Timothy Brock (eds.), *Narrative Impact: Social and Cognitive Foundations*. Mahwah, NJ: Lawrence Erlbaum Associates, pp. 39–69.

——and Mitra Gholamain (1997). Emotions and identification: Connections between readers and fiction. In Mette Hjort and Sue Laver (eds.), *Emotion and the Arts*. New York: Oxford University Press, pp. 263–81.

Piper, H. W. (1962). *The Active Universe: Pantheism and the Concept of Imagination in the English Romantic Poets*. London: Athlone Press.

Rizzolatti, Giacomo and Laila Craighero (2004). The mirror-neuron system. *Annual Review of Neuroscience*, 27: 169–92.

Singer, Tania, Ben Seymour, John O'Doherty, Holger Kaube, Raymond J. Dolan, and Chris D. Frith (2004). Empathy for pain involves the affective but not sensory components of pain. *Science*, 203 (20 February): 1157–62.

Speer, N. K., J. M. Zacks, J. R. Reynolds, and R. A. Hedden (2005). Neural activity during reading reflects changes in the situation described by the text. *Society for Neuroscience Annual Meeting*, Washington, DC.

Tsur, Reuven (1992). *What Makes Sound Patterns Expressive? The Poetic Mode of Speech Perception*. Durham & London: Duke University Press.

Vallée-Tourangeau, Frédéric, Susan H. Anthony, Neville G. Austin (1998). Strategies for generating multiple instances of common and ad hoc categories. *Memory*, 6: 555–92.

Walton, Kendall L. (1990). *Mimesis as Make-Believe: On the Foundations of the Representational Arts*. Cambridge, MA: Harvard University Press.

Wordsworth, William (1990). *Wordsworth: The Oxford Authors*, ed. S. Gill. Oxford: Oxford University Press.

Zwaan, Rolf A. (2004). The immersed experiencer: Toward an embodied theory of language comprehension. In B. H. Ross (ed.), *The Psychology of Learning and Motivation*, vol. 44. New York: Academic Press, pp. 35–62.

——and M. Singer (2003). Text comprehension. In A. C. Graesser, M. A. Gernsbacher, and S. R. Goldman (eds.), *Handbook of Discourse Processes*. Mahwah, NJ: Erlbaum Associates, pp. 83–121.

# 17

# On Keeping Psychology Out of Literary Criticism

*Peter Lamarque*

All human practices are amenable to psychological description—description in terms of motives, desires, beliefs, emotions, or expectations—and many are open to psychological explanation as well. The making up and telling of stories, the construction of poems, the reading and enjoying of literary products of all kinds, as activities in a practice or set of practices, are no exception. There is plenty of scope for psychological investigation of the literary realm. Empirical studies into what actually goes on when writers write or readers read might well yield informative and unexpected results. None of that is being questioned in what follows.

The question I want to pursue is not whether participants in the practices of literature do manifest distinctive psychological states, in individual cases or systematically as a class, but whether the occurrence of such states—in particular affective states—plays a significant role in literary critical judgements of meaning or value. My argument will be that they do not and that they should not, at least if literary criticism is to retain its focus on literature as art. My discussion will centre on emotions both in authors and in readers but I take my conclusions to range more widely over psychological states. My thesis indeed is that psychology should be kept out of literary criticism. Empirical facts about the psychological states of actual people and empirical theories about such states will not illuminate what is of value in individual works of literature.

## I

There have been uneasy relations between psychology and literature for over a hundred years. Of course one could go back two and a half thousand years when Plato was denigrating poetry for its dangerous play with emotions but it is not much more than a hundred years since criticism established itself as a serious academic pursuit. In the early days it was thought that linking criticism to a science like psychology would add to its respectability. This was perhaps partly behind the development of the psychological theory of criticism presented by I. A. Richards in his *Principles of Literary Criticism* (1926). Armed with the distinction between referential and emotive functions of language and convinced that poetry deals paradigmatically with the latter, Richards postulated a complex isomorphism between poetic structure and affective response. What makes literature valuable, on Richards's account, is that it can arouse and organize emotion to a degree that is not available in everyday life. In effect it is psychologically valuable in what it can do for the psychological well-being of those exposed to it.

Yet curiously at just that time in the development of criticism there was a striking move away from psychology and away from emotion, at least emotion centred on the author. Indeed T. S. Eliot's essay 'Tradition and the Individual Talent' that was first associated with that move was published in 1919, seven years before Richards's *Principles*. It was here that Eliot made his famous pronouncement about the 'extinction of personality' in poetry:

the poet has, not a 'personality' to express, but a particular medium, which is only a medium and not a personality, in which impressions and experiences combine in peculiar and unexpected ways. Impressions and experiences which are important for the man may take no place in the poetry, and those which become important in the poetry may play quite a negligible part in the man, the personality.[1]

This is a remarkable passage for its anticipation of many powerful currents of critical theory that came to dominate the twentieth century from New Criticism to Structuralism to Poststructuralism. Eliot goes on:

It is not in his personal emotions, the emotions provoked by particular events in his life, that the poet is in any way remarkable or interesting. His particular emotions may be simple, crude, or flat. The emotion in his poetry will be a very complex thing, but not with the complexity of the emotions of people who have very complex or unusual emotions in life ... Poetry is not a turning loose of emotion, but an escape from emotion: it is not the expression of personality but an escape from personality.[2]

So began a modernist criticism, which emphasized poetry as linguistic medium, in direct challenge to a romantic criticism which dwelt on poetry as personal expression and emotional resonance. The romantic vision had dominated the previous century and it had become a commonplace to endorse Wordsworth's sentiment that: 'all good poetry is the spontaneous overflow of powerful feelings'. Idealist philosophers like Benedetto Croce and R. G. Collingwood built their own expression theories of art round such an intuition. The two camps, the romantics and the modernists, jostled repeatedly through the century with some notable exchanges. One such exchange was between E. M. W. Tillyard and C. S. Lewis in their book *The Personal Heresy:*

---

[1] T. S. Eliot, 'Tradition and the Individual Talent', in David Lodge (ed.), *20th Century Literary Criticism* (London: Longman, 1972), p. 75.

[2] Ibid., p. 76.

*A Controversy* (1939). C. S. Lewis takes the modernist line in attacking the 'Personal Heresy'. He writes: 'when we read poetry as poetry should be read, we have before us no representation which claims to be the poet, and frequently no representation of . . . a personality at all'.[3]

By the time that Wimsatt and Beardsley wrote their two essays 'The Intentional Fallacy' and 'The Affective Fallacy' in 1946 and 1949 respectively most of these ideas had already been well-aired, if not universally accepted, in the critical community. I am not going to talk about intention *per se*—it is an overworked topic—but it is worth recalling that the explicit target of 'The Intentional Fallacy' was romanticism, in particular the expression theory of Benedetto Croce. The aim was to distinguish what the authors called 'criticism of poetry' from what they called 'author psychology', in other words to keep author psychology out of criticism properly so called. Famously their own credo, in contrast to Wordsworth's, proclaimed that a 'poem . . . is detached from the author at birth . . . belongs to the public . . . [and] is embodied in language'. But less often quoted is a wider rejection of author psychology: 'there is a gross body of life, of sensory and mental experience, which lies behind and in some sense causes every poem, but can never be and need not be known in the verbal and hence intellectual composition which is the poem'.[4] This is the autonomy view of poetry at its most striking. I will come back to the expression theory and its critics later.

In many ways the other paper, 'The Affective Fallacy', is more interesting for our purposes. This, as is well known, is an attack on 'trying to derive the standard of criticism from the psychological effects of the poem' and, among other things, directly challenges I. A. Richards's emotive theory of meaning. But again it is primarily an attack on importing psychology into criticism, this time from the perspective of the reader's responses: 'The report of some readers . . . that a poem or story induces in them vivid images, intense feelings, or heightened consciousness, is neither anything which can be refuted nor anything which it is possible for the objective critic to take into account.'[5] The critic should attend not so much to the emotion induced by a poem but to 'the reasons for emotion, the poem itself' and such attention 'will talk not of tears, prickles, or other physiological symptoms, of feeling angry, joyful, hot, cold, or intense, or of vaguer states of emotional disturbance, but of shades of distinction and relation between objects of emotion'. They go on: 'It is precisely here that the discerning critic has an insuperable advantage over the subject of the laboratory experiment and over the tabulator of the subject's responses. The critic is not a contributor to statistically countable reports about the poem, but a teacher or explicator of meanings.'[6]

---

[3] E. M. W. Tillyard and C. S. Lewis, *The Personal Heresy: A Controversy* (London: Oxford University Press, 1939), p. 4.

[4] W. K. Wimsatt and M. C. Beardsley, 'The Intentional Fallacy', in Lodge (ed.), *20th Century Literary Criticism*, p. 340.

[5] W. K. Wimsatt and M. C. Beardsley, 'The Affective Fallacy', in ibid., p. 353.

[6] Ibid., p. 354.

In other words no psychological experiments about how readers as a matter of fact respond emotionally to poetry will reveal what the critic can reveal about a poem's meaning and achievement. This, to anticipate, strikes me as right, but in recent years philosophers, notably, among others, Susan Feagin and Jenefer Robinson,[7] have wanted to reintroduce the tears, prickles, and physiological symptoms, the anger and joy and emotional disturbance, back into criticism, so the Affective Fallacy is on the agenda again. Of course merely stating that there is such a fallacy is not an argument but I believe there are arguments in defence of Wimsatt and Beardsley and I shall come back to them.

However, no survey of the pro- and anti-psychology dialectic in twentieth-century critical theory can quite end there. There would be a huge and deplorable gap without mentioning psychoanalysis. For a sizeable chunk of the twentieth century the branch of psychology most closely associated with literature and criticism was psychoanalysis in its various manifestations. Many current psychologists might lament this influence but like it or not here was a systematic attempt to apply psychological theory to literature. Furthermore, it was based on a deceptively simple premise, as stated by the erstwhile psychoanalytic critic Frederick Crews: 'The simple fact that literature is made and enjoyed by human minds guarantees its accessibility to study in terms of broad principles of psychic and social functioning.'[8] In his seminal paper 'Creative Writers and Day-Dreaming' (1908), Freud had sought to identify some general motivation behind creative writing:

A strong experience in the present awakens in the creative writer a memory of an earlier experience (usually belonging to his childhood) from which there now proceeds a wish which finds its fulfilment in the creative work. The work itself exhibits elements of the recent provoking occasion as well as of the old memory. (S.E. 1908, IX, p. 151)[9]

This postulated link between writing and wish-fulfilment epitomizes many of the dangers of appeal to psychology in criticism. It looks reductive, speculative, indifferent to the particularity of the work, and difficult to verify. In fact, to be fair to Freud, he was much more cautious in *The Interpretation of Dreams* (1900), when he first mooted the connection between Hamlet and Oedipus: 'all genuinely creative writings,' he stressed, 'are the product of more than a single motive and more than a single impulse in the poet's mind, and are open to more than a single interpretation' (S.E. 1900, IV, p. 206). In his essay 'Psychopathic Characters on the Stage' (1905), Freud reflected on what we now know as the paradox of tragedy, why tragedy gives pleasure: tragic portrayals, he thought, are 'based on an illusion', the viewer's 'suffering is mitigated by

---

[7] See Susan Feagin, *Reading With Feeling* (Ithaca, NY: Cornell University Press, 1996); Jenefer Robinson, *Deeper than Reason* (Oxford: Oxford University Press, 2005).

[8] Frederick Crews (ed.), *Psychoanalysis and Literary Process* (Cambridge, MA: Winthrop, 1970), p. 1.

[9] All references to Freud's work will be to *The Standard Edition of the Complete Psychological Works of Sigmund Freud*, 24 vols., ed. and trans. James Strachey (London: Hogarth, 1953–74). In the text the date of the work will be given, followed by the volume in the *Standard Edition*, and the page reference.

the certainty that, firstly, it is someone other than himself who is acting and suffering on the stage, and, secondly, that after all it is only a game' (S.E. 1905, VII, p. 306).

The appeal, such as it is, of psychoanalysis lies in its aim to provide a general explanation across the board, not just of why works are written but of why readers enjoy certain genres—notably tragedies and romances—and also why particular works have an enduring value. Interestingly such overarching explanations in the arts have been sought in recent years through evolutionary theory.[10] But it is precisely this appeal to generality that also displays the weakness of such accounts. Could we really expect there to be a unified explanation for why Homer wrote the *Iliad*, Milton *Paradise Lost*, Trollope the Barchester Chronicles, and Philip Larkin 'The Whitsun Weddings' and is there any substantial psychological explanation of why these works continue to be enjoyed (an explanation beyond the fact that they possess unique literary qualities)? More on that as we proceed.

Psychoanalytic criticism is an extension, although not an exemplary case, of romantic theories, at least in its appeal to the states of mind of authors and readers. Even if these states are unconscious they are nevertheless real and thought to be determining factors in what is produced and what is valued. Anti-romantic attacks came not just from New Criticism with its general rejection of psychologizing but also from an unholy alliance of Marxism and Poststructuralism. For Marxists social determinants on literary production and literary value are more important than psychological ones. The Marxist idea that appealed to Poststructuralists was that the autonomous self is largely a fiction or social construct. Literary works cannot be thought of as products of pure mental processes, conscious or unconscious, on this view, because mental life is not an autonomous sphere but rather a site of conflicting social forces—or discourses for the Poststructuralists—lacking any kind of unity or anything that could count as the romantics' seat of personality or individual genius. For the Poststructuralists— just as for the Marxists in a slightly different context—the extinction of personality that T. S. Eliot had spoken of becomes an ontological fact not just a postulate for criticism.

I take it that in a broad sense this attack on autonomy is a further manifestation of modernism in its fight against romanticism. The unity or autonomy of the self, under this conception, becomes an illusion so no reference can be made to it in any genuinely informative account of literary practice. If psychology, like liberal humanism in general, presupposes a self, sufficiently coherent to engage in expression or reception, then, on such a view, there can be no psychology-based criticism. The death of the author is indeed the death of psychology in criticism but it is not, as Roland Barthes predicted, the birth of the reader in any recognizable sense, for, in following through the consequences, the reader too has no psychologically real point of view from which

---

[10] For a useful survey, see Denis Dutton, 'Aesthetics and Evolutionary Psychology', in Jerrold Levinson (ed.), *The Oxford Handbook of Aesthetics* (New York: Oxford University Press, 2003).

to respond to a text.[11] On so radical a scenario even meaning itself becomes a victim of depersonalization, at which point meaning strictly vanishes altogether.

Against this background, any anti-romantic stance about literary criticism, such as the one I am inclined to support, must tread a delicate path. It could scarcely be more important that different strands of anti-romanticism should be distinguished. It is all too easy to be trapped in guilt by association. My own position is not at one with any of those so far advanced. It is far from that of Marxist criticism, which has never quite shaken off the charge of reductivism and in any case relies on externalist or causal accounts of literary practice, as does, typically, psychoanalytic criticism. It is equally far from Poststructuralism which needlessly and groundlessly rejects the very bases of any coherent kind of criticism such as the self, meaning, objectivity, and aesthetic value. Nor finally is it very close to New Criticism which overemphasizes linguistic meaning in criticism, based on notions like 'semantic density' or 'irony', and thus gives undue weight to debates about the sources of meaning, notably intention, which I, like many literary critics, think is not of central importance. Some of the arguments for the Affective Fallacy are more relevant, as I will show, but to reject all notions of reader response is clearly a mistake.

# II

To develop and defend my own point of view I am going to focus the remainder of the discussion on certain arguments in Jenefer Robinson's book *Deeper than Reason* (2005) partly because I believe it is a very good book and rewarding to get to grips with, but partly because by examining the disagreements between us—some of them deep—in relation to literature our respective positions should become clearer. Robinson explicitly calls her theory, in particular her theory of artistic expression, a 'romantic' one and much of what she says about the role of emotion in literature will be congenial to those who think psychology has something to contribute to literary criticism. (Or at least it might *seem* congenial. I wonder in fact when the details are examined just how congenial it is to psychologists.)

Let us look first at Robinson's defence of expression theory. Her discussion of Collingwood and Alan Tormey's attack on Collingwood is exemplary and should be required reading for anyone studying expression in art. It brings out the issues with perfect clarity. I will not have anything to say on her expository and exegetical analysis. I am interested, though, in her own position. She calls this a 'new romantic theory of expression' but I do wonder if it really is a theory of expression at all. Here are the five necessary conditions she identifies for an artist to express an emotion in a work of art:

---

[11] It seems that Barthes noticed this himself when he characterizes the reader as 'without history, biography, psychology; he is simply that *someone* who holds together in a single field all the traces by which the written text is constituted': Roland Barthes, 'The Death of the Author', in *Image-Music-Text*, Essays Selected and Translated by Stephen Heath (London: Fontana/Collins, 1977), p.148.

1. the work is evidence that a persona (which could but need not be the artist) is experiencing/has experienced this emotion;
2. the artist intentionally puts the evidence in the work and intends it to be perceived *as* evidence of the emotion in the persona;
3. the persona's emotion is perceptible in the character of the work;
4. the work articulates and individuates the persona's emotion; and
5. through the articulation and elucidation of the emotion in the work, both artist and audience can become clear about it and bring it to consciousness.[12]

The first striking thing about these conditions is the insistence that possession of the expressed emotion is attributed not to the artist—except entirely contingently—but to a 'persona'. In other formulations Robinson speaks of an 'implied author'. There is thus no implication that the author has any real emotion to express and indeed the only reference to any actual person's real psychological state, if such it be, is to the author's *intention* to 'put the evidence [of a persona's experiencing an emotion] in the work', and for that evidence 'to be perceived *as* evidence of the emotion in the persona'. There is little here that the anti-romantic need take issue with. Of course we expect a work that genuinely expresses an emotion to be the product of an intention that that should be so. It also seems exactly right that any emotion expressed in a work be attributed to a persona, implied author, or dramatic speaker. This is a literary critical commonplace even if not always acknowledged by philosophers.

However, a reader of Robinson's account of artistic expression and her elaboration of it, might well detect a sense of discomfort on her part with this distancing of author and emotion even though she remains consistent in the account itself. After all, the book is about real emotions as psychological states of real people—on which she offers a penetrating and insightful analysis—and she sees a clear parallel between people expressing their emotions through actions, gestures, or facial expressions, and artists expressing emotions in their work. She writes, for example: 'The person's or persona's emotional state is expressed in the character of the artwork, just as the expressive character of a person's face or gestures or tone of voice may express the emotional state of that person.'[13] Note the use of 'person's or persona's', as if there were little difference. More importantly, is there not an obvious disanalogy between the artistic and non-artistic cases? When we see someone expressing their unhappiness or depression in their gestures and tone of voice we have no inclination to attribute the emotion to a persona or anything analogous to an implied author; we attribute it directly to the person concerned (unless of course we think they are dissembling but then there is no genuine expression). In the literary case, though, Robinson warns us not to make that direct connection.

---

[12] Robinson, *Deeper than Reason*, p. 270.
[13] Ibid., pp. 270–1.

The paradigm cases that Robinson refers to, quite naturally, in the literary context are romantic lyric poems and she uses examples like Keats's 'Ode to a Nightingale'. One of the emotions she identifies in this poem is a 'yearning for a timeless world of art and beauty'. It is significant, though, that in the page immediately following that in which she insists this emotion be attributed to a persona not to Keats himself, she writes: 'we should not be too quick to assert that it doesn't matter whether it is the author or his persona who is expressing his emotions in a poem ... [W]e are often quite interested in the fact that Keats himself probably yearned for a timeless world of art and beauty, and that it is perfectly appropriate to identify the poetic voice with that of Keats himself ... It is not unreasonable to enjoy the feeling that one is engaging with the actual emotions of a great poet.'[14]

This is no doubt right for we do have interests in the personality of poets. But if true it is a biographical not a literary interest. From a literary point of view it is the emotion attributed to the persona that matters. That is where the expression lies. A psychologist interested in the psychopathology of a poet might well go to the poem with the biographical focus in mind. But no one seeking to engage with the poem as a poem need seek help from a psychologist. Why? Because the emotion expressed is not an occurrent emotion, only an emotion attributed to a dramatic speaker constructed in the text. To understand the emotions expressed in lyric poetry we need to know not about psychology but about poetry, its conventions and powers. The emotions we examine are not psychological but literary; any intensity or power they exhibit is a property of the work explicable through the rhetorical devices employed not through the mind that created them. This is the insight of modernism over romanticism and it does seem to be an insight that Robinson endorses, in spite of designating her theory 'romantic'.

Take another type of case, poems written about the death of a child, where one might suppose the emotion to be both real and especially intense. Dylan Thomas's 'A Refusal to Mourn the Death, by Fire, of a Child in London', is a good example. The final two stanzas are:

> . . .
> I shall not murder
> The mankind of her going with a grave truth
> Nor blaspheme down the stations of the breath
> With any further
> Elegy of innocence and youth.
> Deep with the first dead lies London's daughter,
> Robed in the long friends,
> The grains beyond age, the dark veins of her mother,
> Secret by the unmourning water
> Of the riding Thames.
> After the first death, there is no other.

[14] Robinson, *Deeper than Reason*, , p. 255.

There is no doubting the intensity of emotion in the poem but it is far from an uncontrolled outpouring of grief tied to an occurrent emotional state. The poem is more reflective than that, more controlled, more self-conscious. It is indeed a 'refusal to mourn', it rejects any simple 'elegy of innocence and youth', which normally characterizes the genre. The poem seems to address—and challenge—the very possibility of poetry on this subject. The critic David Daiches notes the poem's 'deliberately sacramental imagery ['blaspheme', 'stations of the breath', recalling 'stations of the Cross', etc.], while at the same time the emotion is controlled and organized by the cadences of the stanza'.[15] The poem expresses grief by turning away from it. As with all the greatest poems on this theme, 'A Refusal to Mourn . . .' transcends the circumstances of its origin and reaches for something more universal in the human spirit: 'After the first death, there is no other.'

Ben Jonson's 'On My First Son' is also expressive of grief, even more poignantly so in speaking of the death of the poet's son aged seven. Its first two stanzas are again quietly but powerfully intense:

> Farewell, thou child of my right hand, and joy;
> My sin was too much hope of thee, loved boy.
> Seven years thou wert lent to me, and I thee pay,
> Exacted by thy fate, on the just day.
>
> Oh, could I lose all father now! For why
> Will man lament the state he should envy?
> To have so soon 'scaped world's and flesh's rage,
> And if no other misery, yet age!

Laurence Lerner notices the 'subtle rhythms, capturing the broken but controlled voice of the sorrowing parent' and insists, surely rightly, that we distinguish 'the meaning of the poem when written, and the meaning of the act of writing it'.[16]

What survives in both poems is the expression of grief, not the grief expressed. While the titles in each case indicate the specificity of the originating cause, the contents rise about this. How do such examples bear on Robinson's expression theory? First, as she admits, the emotion of grief in the poems is attributable to a persona, not directly to the authors (whatever the biographical circumstances). The poems readily satisfy her conditions: they are 'evidence that a persona . . . is experiencing/has experienced this emotion', the 'persona's emotion is perceptible in the character of the work', and 'the work articulates and individuates the persona's emotion'. The reader's attention is directed not to any real psychological state (however intense the originating cause) but, in both cases, to tightly, almost claustrophobically, structured linguistic artefacts. To understand the poems *as poems* the reader need not explore the poets'

[15] David Daiches, 'The Poetry of Dylan Thomas', in C. B. Cox (ed.), *Dylan Thomas: A Collection of Critical Essays* (Englewood Cliffs, NJ: Prentice Hall, 1966), p. 18.
[16] Laurence Lerner, 'Subverting the Canon', *British Journal of Aesthetics*, 32 (1992), p. 354.

states of mind, only the linguistic expression in the poems themselves, recognizing paradigmatic features of the elegiac lyric, both realized and challenged. The power and interest of the poems lie not in what they tell us about an individual on a particular occasion—why should that be of interest so many years later?—but in how they portray an emotion, one might say a literary emotion, in a timeless fashion.

The relation between the poets' actual states of mind and the poems is radically unlike the relation of a person suffering from grief and that person's overt behaviour. Indeed it is really only here that reservations arise about Robinson's expression theory, namely, in its emphasis of the analogy between poetic expression and ordinary behavioural expression. Otherwise the theory seems right in its distancing of author and emotion, even if this makes the evocation of 'romanticism' problematic. My concern, as it were from her point of view, is only that the theory sits oddly in a general account of emotional expression precisely because it has so little to do with real psychological states or with psychology tout court.

## III

Turning now to the other aspect of Robinson's account of literature we do find real psychological states—not states attributed to fictional personae—taking centre stage. Here my disagreements are deeper. Robinson's view is that for at least some literary works it is necessary for a reader to experience real emotional responses in order to understand the works. This view is developed in a chapter of *Deeper than Reason* aptly titled 'The Importance of Being Emotional'. As a theory of literary understanding or literary interpretation the account offered does not seem persuasive. Unlike in her expression theory, with its emphasis on implied authors, Robinson, in her emotion theory of understanding, is radically at odds with mainstream literary critical opinion. That might not worry her but it is at least noteworthy that professional critics give little attention to emotional responses to literature. No doubt there are a number of reasons for this, partly just that critics are wary of responses that might seem subjective, variable, and unmeasurable, partly, and perhaps more deeply, because if you study a work in detail, with repeated re-readings, and fine analyses of particular passages, any strong emotional responses associated with a first-time reading are likely to have worn off.

There are two parts to Robinson's theory. The first affirms the appropriateness, even the inevitability, of responding emotionally to some works of fiction; the second affirms the necessary role of such responses in literary understanding. Thus, speaking of a scene in Tolstoy's *Anna Karenina*, Robinson writes: 'we feel an intense urge to help Anna, an intense distress and sorrow at her predicament, an intense desire and hope that her predicament will be resolved. The passage is so poignant indeed that it easily provokes tears and other physiological symptoms of sadness and distress.'[17] The

---

[17] Robinson, *Deeper than Reason*, pp. 110–11.

emphasis is on strong and 'intense' emotional responses. But who is the 'we' referred to in this quotation, the 'we' who feels intense urges, intense distress, intense desires and hopes? What do we say of readers who do not respond with such intensity? Is it taken to be just a fact of the matter that readers will respond this way? Or true of sensitive readers? Or readers properly informed about literature? Robinson knows enough about emotions to know they are not always easy to predict, and depend on complex sets of circumstances both in the psychology of individuals and in surrounding conditions.

What is significant is that Robinson is here talking about actual psychological states of actual readers. There is an asymmetry then between readers and authors. In the case of authors their own personal emotions are bracketed off from the emotions expressed in the work. But if we need an *implied author* for expressed emotions why should we not postulate an *implied reader* for response emotions? Why insulate a work from authorial emotions but not from readers' emotions? Might we not say that the passage from *Anna Karenina* is intensely moving without implying that any reader must feel some intense emotion? Some readers might, others might not. These seem to be just contingencies. All of the emotions that Robinson mentions could be attributed to the passage rather than to the reader. It is a passage that is sad, distressing, of the kind to give someone an urge to help, and so on. These are characteristics of the work, not necessarily of any actual person.

This brings us to the second strand of Robinson's theory, the idea that a reader who does not have these strong affective responses has failed to understand the work. Robinson has several arguments for this view but they all relate back to a master argument, which is this:

Understanding character is essential to understanding the great realist novels... understanding character is relevantly like understanding real people, and... understanding real people is impossible without emotional engagement with them and their predicaments.[18]

The argument looks deceptively simple and persuasive but the trouble lies with the middle proposition, 'understanding character is relevantly like understanding real people'. Realistically drawn characters, like Anna Karenina, are indeed similar in certain respects to real people. We imagine them to be real people and in filling out the narratives of their lives we make inferences based on common assumptions about what people of that kind are like. But the notion of 'understanding character' is equivocal; it can mean understanding characters as imagined people and it can mean understanding them as elements in a literary work. Perhaps—although I am not entirely convinced—to understand them in the first sense, as imagined people, readers need to engage emotionally with them. But understanding them in the second sense, as elements in a literary work, surely does not require any actual emotional response. It is the second sense that concerns literary critics. The point about the first sense, concerning merely imaginary people, is that the manner of their presentation in a narrative is of only contingent significance. Your recounting to me the story of Anna Karenina in your own words—or anyone's retelling of the story—would be just as likely to stir my emotions as the account in the novel. All that matters is that the imaginary person—Anna—is recognizably the same character in each case.

But when Anna is thought of as an element in Tolstoy's novel then the manner of the presentation is not contingent but essential. Now we attend to the character as an integral part of a linguistic artefact. Other elements, literary elements, come into play. To understand Anna, on this conception, is to understand the thematic, symbolic, and meaning-laden relations that the character-as-described enters into with other characters and other incidents in the novel. On this conception emotional engagement from a reader is at best a contingent by-product of reading, not an integral part of a literary response and as likely to cloud understanding as to illuminate it.

Yes, the scene with Anna's son Seryozha must be recognized as poignant, distressing, and sorrowful. It must be recognized as an emotional scene. That is the way it is presented to us. If we read it as humorous or ironic we would be misunderstanding the passage. But from a literary perspective we must view it as an element in the construction of Anna's character, as resonating with other scenes in the novel, as elaborating on the desperate state of Anna's predicament, even perhaps as expressive in the sense that Robinson proposes for the lyric poem. We must locate the emotion in the scene, just as we did with the poetic expressions of grief. When Robinson says: 'if I laugh and cry, shiver, tense, and relax in all the appropriate places, then I can be said to have understood the story' she is not speaking as a literary critic but as someone simply reflecting on an imaginary person in an imaginary world.

This takes us back to the Affective Fallacy and the passage where Wimsatt and Beardsley instruct us to 'talk not of tears, prickles, or other physiological symptoms, of feeling angry, joyful, hot, cold, or intense . . . but of shades of distinction and relation between objects of emotion'. A final example is shared by both Robinson and Wimsatt and Beardsley and reveals what might be meant by 'objects of emotion'. It is the example of Macbeth. Robinson tells us that when attending to the scene in the play where Macduff is told that his wife and all their children have been murdered on Macbeth's orders, she responds with horror and disgust, 'by shuddering, turning cold, and tensing [her] muscles'.[19] Many readers or viewers might feel the same. But for Robinson it is only with some such response that a reader or viewer could genuinely *understand* the scene. But that, I have argued, is not *literary* understanding, not least because it does not draw on distinctive or specific features of the work as a work of art. After all, hearing of any premeditated murder of a whole family will induce a similar sort of revulsion.

---

[19] Robinson, *Deeper than Reason*, p. 111.

When Wimsatt and Beardsley discuss the murder of Duncan in the play they do offer a literary understanding that draws on literary specifics: 'Set in its galaxy of symbols—the hoarse raven, the thickening light, and the crow making wing, the babe plucked from the breast, the dagger in the air, the ghost, the bloody hands—this ancient murder has become an object of strongly fixed emotive value.'[20] One implication seems to be, in contradiction to Robinson's view, that any emotive response to this scene far from being a precondition of understanding actually *presupposes* understanding. Without first grasping the embeddedness of the action in a 'galaxy of symbols', no reader will be able to respond appropriately to the specific object identified. For the event described is not just the cold-blooded murder of a king but a literary scene of considerable complexity. An emotional response to an object of *that* kind will be quite unlike an emotional response to any real-life event.

# IV

Let me end by drawing out some conclusions. The specific, albeit negative, view I have defended is that the actual psychological states of authors and readers, notably affective states like emotions, do not and should not play a significant part in literary critical practice. Intense emotions can be expressed in works, particularly lyric poetry, but these emotions are ultimately properties of the works not of actual people; they are attributable to personae or implied authors or they are a characteristic of described scenes and actions. Authors and readers might well have emotions in producing and responding to works but this will always be a contingent matter inessential to an appreciation of the works themselves.

We can broaden out this conclusion to reflect on empirical studies by psychologists or cognitive scientists interested in the literary domain. Take the work that cognitive scientists have done on the mechanisms for responding emotionally to fictional characters.[21] I entirely approve this work—indeed some of it reinforces ideas that I came up with a long time ago *a priori*. But I don't think it has anything to contribute to literary criticism, to the analysis and appreciation of particular literary works. The theories themselves are neutral as to literary value and apply equally to fictional narratives of all kinds. Likewise, empirical studies that examine, as did psychoanalysis, motives for writing fiction or the satisfactions of reading will not illuminate critical practice. Critical practice is concerned with literary works of art, how they work, what they achieve, what values they exemplify. Responding to a literary work *as literature* is a distinctive, broadly convention-bound, activity.

In a recent issue of the *Journal of Aesthetics and Art Criticism* there is a forceful exchange between the cognitive scientist Laura Sizer and the philosophers Peter

---

[20] Wimsatt and Beardsley, 'The Affective Fallacy', p. 357.
[21] See e.g., Aaron Meskin and Jonathan M. Weinberg, 'Emotions, Fiction, and Cognitive Architecture', *British Journal of Aesthetics*, 43 (2003): 18–34.

Kivy and Noël Carroll on music and emotion.[22] Sizer claims that experiments in cognitive science have shown that a certain version of arousal theory is true—in particular the view that music arouses moods in its listeners. Kivy takes issue with this on the grounds that the experiments fail to attend to the right kinds of listeners in the right kinds of circumstances (e.g., listening in the appropriate manner). I admit to being sympathetic to Kivy's scepticism. Listening to music merely as a stimulus in a laboratory and listening to it in an informed, serious, and engaged manner in a concert hall are not the same. I extend that analogy to literature. One could read canonical works of literature simply to emote over love stories or tragic endings, just as one could read lyric poetry to dig out biographical insights into poets' minds. But neither is a good basis for literary criticism, nor takes seriously the peculiarities of literary appreciation. Literary criticism that focuses on literature as art is not a branch of psychology and psychological explanations concerning states of mind are the wrong kind of explanation to shed light on it.

---

[22] Laura Sizer, 'Moods in the Music and the Man: A Response to Kivy and Carroll', *JAAC*, 65/3 (2007): 307–12; Peter Kivy, 'Moodology: A Response to Laura Sizer', *JAAC*, 65/3 (2007): 312–18; Noël Carroll and Margaret Moore, 'Not Reconciled: Comments for Peter Kivy', *JAAC*, 65/3 (2007): 318–22; Peter Kivy, 'Moodophilia: A Response to Noël Carroll and Margaret Moore', *JAAC*, 65/3 (2007): 323–9.

# 18

# Mirroring Fictional Others

*Zanna Clay and Marco Iacoboni*

In this chapter, we discuss recent neuroscience evidence that suggests mechanisms for how we empathize with other people and with fictional characters. We propose that the same neural mechanisms we use to empathize with real people make us also empathize with fictional characters. While these neural mechanisms enable us to empathize with fictional characters of all kinds, in movies, plays, literature, and so on, we focus, in this chapter, specifically on fictional characters from novels.

The neural mechanisms that we discuss here can be broadly defined as 'mirroring neural mechanisms.' Mirror neurons, as we will later discuss, are cells with motor properties that fire not only when we perform an action, but also when we observe somebody else performing the same action or an action somewhat related to the action we performed (Rizzolatti and Craighero 2004). These cells may enable our capacity to put ourselves into somebody else's shoes.

At the beginning of the last century, Theodor Lipps proposed a concept of empathy, or *Einfuhlung*, according to which we achieve the ability to share and understand the emotions and feelings of others by using some sort of projection of the self into the other. As he noted, 'When I observe a circus performer on a hanging wire, I feel I am inside him' (as cited by Gallese 2001: 43). Lipps proposed that at the basis of our ability to empathize there is a process of *inner imitation*. Mechanisms of neural mirroring have functional properties, as we discuss later, that seem ideally suited to support this process of inner imitation. Interestingly, Lipps adopted the concept of *Einfuhlung*—which can be translated as 'in-feeling' or 'feeling-into'—from Robert Vischer's doctoral thesis 'On the Optical Sense of Form: A Contribution to Aesthetics' (1873). Lipps himself was mainly concerned with conceptions of art and aesthetics.

We focus specifically on fictional characters taken from novels because the feeling of connecting with such fictional characters can be an authentic and enduring experience. In fact, it is not uncommon for readers to remark that they feel they know fictional characters as genuinely as people within their actual lives. We propose that the foundations of this sense of connection lie primarily in our profound capacity for empathy, where the reader comes to experience the thoughts, actions, and perceptions of the fictional characters as if they were experiencing themselves. Because of their functional properties, neural mirroring mechanisms may underlie the ability to connect emotionally with fictional others in the same way that they help us relate to real people in our daily lives. We also discuss here empirical evidence in support of some concepts that are critical to our claim. First of all, the role of mirror neurons in imitation and empathy. Second, the links between mirror neurons and language, a necessary link to empathize with fictional others described in novels. We also take several salient examples of passages from novels to explore the relationship between our current understanding of the properties of neural mirroring mechanisms and the process of connecting with fictional others.

## 1. Mirroring responses in individual neurons

Neuroscience practices are strongly limited by ethical, financial, and technical considerations. While in rather exceptional cases it is possible to obtain some data on individual neurons in the human brain, almost everything we know on cellular brain mechanisms derive from animal research. Indeed, almost everything we know about individual neurons exhibiting mirroring responses comes from depth electrodes studies in monkeys. The main facts and concepts that emerge from the monkey literature are as follows:

**Mirror neurons are specialized for actions**: Actions involving three body parts, the hands (di Pellegrino *et al.* 1992; Gallese *et al.* 1996), the mouth (Ferrari *et al.* 2003), and the eyes (Shepherd *et al.* 2009), have documented mirroring responses at the level of individual neurons. Mirror neurons for hand actions, such as grasping, tearing, holding, and manipulating, are the most frequently reported in the literature. Most frequently studied are the grasping mirror neurons, which can be divided in two main categories: mirror neurons for precision grip and mirror neurons for whole hand grasps. Precision grip is the type of grasp that is required to grab small objects with two fingers, for instance a peanut. Whole hand grasp is the type of grasp required to grab a large object like an orange. Mirror neurons for grasping obviously fire when the monkey grasps, but also when the monkey observes somebody else, either a human or another monkey, grasping. Precision grip mirror neurons fire at the sight of a precision grip, regardless the type of object grasped. Whole hand mirror neurons also fire at the sight of a whole hand grasp, regardless the type of object grasped (Rizzolatti and Craighero 2004).

Mirror neurons for mouth actions have been associated with two main kinds of actions: ingestive (for instance, biting a banana) and communicative (for instance, lip-smacking, a gesture of lip protrusion with a positive communicative valence) (Ferrari *et al.* 2003). Mirror neurons for gaze have been recently reported in the literature and it is likely that other kinds of actions involving other body parts are associated with specific mirroring responses.

**Mirror neurons are not simply monkey-see-monkey-do cells**: While the term 'mirror' suggests a complete equivalence between the performed action and the perceived action, the majority of mirror neurons code the motor aspect of our own actions and the perceptual aspects of the actions of other people in more complex ways. Indeed, there are two major classes of mirror neurons: strictly congruent mirror neurons and broadly congruent mirror neurons. Strictly congruent mirror neurons— which correspond to approximately one-third of recorded mirror neurons—fire at the same action, either performed or perceived (say, precision grip). Broadly congruent mirror neurons—which correspond to approximately two-thirds of recorded mirror neurons—code also perceived actions that are different from the performed action. The perceived actions that trigger a response in broadly congruent mirror neurons are related to the performed action in two main ways: they either achieve the same goal or they belong to a motor sequence, as for instance grasping food and bringing it to the mouth (di Pellegrino et al. 1992; Gallese et al. 1996; Rizzolatti and Craighero 2004).

**Mirror neurons code actions at a fairly abstract level**: Mirror neurons do not respond only to seen actions. In fact, around half of mirror neurons that fire while performing or observing an action that produces a sound, also fire at the sound associated with that action (for example, the sound of breaking a peanut), even when the action is not seen (Kohler et al. 2002). Other mirror neurons, again approximately 50 per cent of the cells recorded in the relevant experiments, fire even when the action cannot be completely seen (mirror neurons for partially occluded actions) (Umiltà et al. 2001). Most importantly, the majority of mirror neurons, approximately three-quarters of recorded neurons in the relevant experiments, seem to code not simply the observed action, but rather the intention associated with it, the goal of the action (Fogassi et al. 2005). Taken together, all these properties suggest that mirror neurons code the actions of other people at a fairly abstract level.

**Mirror neurons are defined by physiology, not anatomy**: In the monkey, mirror neurons for hand and mouth actions have been recorded so far in two cortical areas: area F5 in the ventral premotor cortex and area PF/PFG in the rostral part of the inferior parietal lobule (Rizzolatti and Craighero 2004; Rizzolatti and Fabbri-Destro 2008). These two areas are anatomically connected, suggesting that mirror neurons belong to a specific neural system. Mirror neurons for gaze have been described in area LIP (Shepherd et al. 2009), within the intraparietal sulcus, a major sulcus dividing the posterior parietal cortex in superior and inferior parietal lobule. In principle, however, mirror neurons may be located in other cortical areas of the monkey brain. Indeed, detailed investigations of mirroring properties at single neuron level have been performed for years only in area F5. The recordings in area PF/PFG (Fogassi et al. 2005) and area LIP (Shepherd et al. 2009) of the parietal lobe are relatively recent. The neurophysiological exploration of other cortical areas may also reveal neurons with mirroring properties.

## 2. Mirroring responses in human neuronal ensembles

The neuroscience techniques used to study the human brain typically measure the activity of neuronal ensembles. Although these techniques present some interpretational limitations, the human studies seem compatible with the monkey data, suggesting the existence of a human mirror neuron system coding actions of the self and of other people, responding to action sounds, and coding the intention associated with observed actions (Iacoboni and Dapretto 2006). The human studies, however, have also linked activity in the mirror neuron system to imitation (Iacoboni *et al.* 1999; Koski *et al.* 2002; Koski *et al.* 2003; Iacoboni 2005) and investigated the relations between mirror neuron system activity and human behaviour. These studies suggest strong ties between the human mirror neuron system and empathy (Carr *et al.* 2003; Kaplan and Iacoboni 2006; Pfeifer *et al.* 2008).

A relatively early study (Carr *et al.* 2003) had suggested that neural mirroring may be relevant to our ability to empathize with other people. This early study tested a simulation-based model of empathy according to which when we see somebody else's facial emotional expression, activity in mirror neuron areas provides an inner imitation of the observed facial expression. Neural signals from mirror neuron areas are subsequently sent to emotional brain centres such as the limbic system, and activity evoked here make us feel what others feel. For instance, when we see somebody else smiling, our mirror neurons for facial expressions fire as if we were smiling ourselves (simulation or inner imitation of smiling) and send signals to the emotional brain centres to evoke the feeling that we typically have when we smile. More recently studies have confirmed this model and have demonstrated correlations between the tendency to empathize and activity in mirror neuron areas during observation and execution of facial emotional expressions (Pfeifer *et al.* 2008), observation of grasping actions (Kaplan and Iacoboni 2006), and even while listening to action sounds (Gazzola *et al.* 2006).

Relevant to our proposal that neural mirroring is critical in empathizing with fictional characters, is the body of research investigating the links between language and the human mirror neuron system. The anatomical location of area F5, where mirror neurons were originally discovered in the monkey, and the functional properties of mirror neurons, both suggested very early on that this neural system might have played a central role in language evolution (Rizzolatti and Arbib 1998). Indeed, an evolutionary hypothesis suggests that area F5 in the monkey is the homologue of Brodmann area 44 in the human brain (Rizzolatti and Arbib 1998). Brodmann area 44 corresponds to the posterior part of Broca's area in the left cerebral hemisphere. Broca's area is an important human brain area for language. Lesions in this area are typically associated with language disorders, and brain imaging studies using language activation tasks invariably activate this brain region.

There is also a functional argument linking mirror neurons to language. Indeed, well before mirror neurons were discovered, some linguists proposed that for communication to occur, there must be a common code between the sender and the receiver of a message (Liberman *et al.* 1967; Liberman and Mattingly 1985; Liberman and Whalen 2000). Mirror neurons, active during both production and perception, seem to provide an excellent neural substrate of such common code. For example, human studies have demonstrated that premotor areas active while we speak are also active while we listen to other people speaking and that the activation of these areas is essential to our *perception* of somebody else's speech (Wilson *et al.* 2004; Wilson and Iacoboni 2006; Meister *et al.* 2007; Iacoboni 2008).

Furthermore, research on how language conveys meaning has suggested that linguistic meaning must be grounded in perceptual and motor experiences associated with bodily activity. The abstract symbols of language cannot relate only to other abstract symbols, but must be mapped to the world, if they are to convey meaning (Glenberg and Kaschak 2002). This embodied semantic framework has generated many experiments providing links between language and action (Hauk *et al.* 2004; Pulvermüller *et al.* 2006; Tettamanti *et al.* 2005). After the discovery of mirror neurons, brain imaging studies investigated the links between neural mirroring and language. For instance, subjects watched actions performed with different body parts, the hands, the mouth, and the feet (Aziz-Zadeh *et al.* 2006). Action observation, as expected produced strong activation in premotor cortex, a finding typically interpreted as reflecting mirror neuron activation. Along the premotor cortex, the body maps—albeit fuzzy—show some level of separation, such that premotor activity associated with mouth movements is more ventral than premotor activity associated with hand actions, and in turn hand-related premotor activity is more ventral than the activity associated with foot movements. Premotor activity during action observation reflects such maps, suggesting that indeed this activity reflects mirroring of actions performed by specific body parts (Aziz-Zadeh *et al.* 2006; Buccino *et al.* 2001). When subjects are asked to read silently sentences that describe actions of the mouth, of the hand, and the foot, they specifically activate the sector of the premotor cortex that contains the map of the corresponding body part (Aziz-Zadeh et al. 2006). This suggests that while we read a sentence describing, say, a grasping action, our neural mechanisms of mirroring simulate (or produce an inner imitation of) the action we are reading about.

The same logic can also be applied to emotions. When we read about a fictional character experiencing a powerful emotion, neural mechanisms of mirroring may re-evoke the neural representation of the facial gestures and bodily postures typically associated with that emotion, and trigger activity in emotional brain centres such that we end up experiencing the emotion associated with those facial gesture and bodily postures.

## 3. Emotional response when connecting to a fictional character

Here we discuss some specific examples taken from the literature, and suggest that the description of actions and emotions that fictional characters perform and experience make us empathize with them through a simulation-based form of empathy that is enabled by neural mechanisms of mirroring. This feeling of being connected with the fictional others is a vicarious form of empathy that enriches the reading experience and likely underlies the great satisfaction people take from reading fictional literature.

Take for example, the following description from Tolstoy's *War and Peace*, of a gaze interaction between a mother and daughter:

'Speak, Mamma, why don't you say anything? Speak!' said she, turning to her mother, who was tenderly gazing at her daughter and in that contemplation seemed to have forgotten all she had wished to say.

While clearly describing an eye gaze interaction, this passage also provides an emotional context towards which the reader can empathize. The 'tender' gaze of the mother towards her daughter depicts something many readers will themselves have experienced in their own lives. We have previously briefly discussed that mirroring mechanisms for gaze have been described in the neuroscience literature (Shepherd *et al.* 2009). Here, the daughter turns and looks at her mother, who is in turn tenderly gazing at her. Thus, it is possible that this scene produces simultaneously two forms of neural mirroring: on the one hand, the mirroring of the tender gazing of the mother; on the other hand, the mirroring of the daughter turning to her mother and looking at her and her 'tender gaze'. By activating eye gaze mirror neurons simultaneously from two different perspectives (the mother and the daughter), the readers have a powerful emotional experience, and deeply empathize with the two characters and feel attuned to the relationship that binds them together.

Primary social tools such as gaze following and eye contact often feature heavily in fictional literature. These kinds of social capacities fall far back in our evolutionary heritage, and provide us with a crucial means to share intentions and thoughts with others. It is therefore unsurprising that we find that descriptions of eye contact and gaze following enable the reader to gain a closer connection with the character in question.

While emotive passages of course stimulate a strong emotional response in readers, passages simply detailing the actions surrounding a character's activities also serve to stimulate the mirroring process required for relating to fictional others. Take for example, the following passage from D. H. Lawrence's *Sons and Lovers* which describes a character in his workplace:

Now he had the packing up and addressing to do, then he had to weigh the sacks of parcels on the scales. Everywhere voices were calling weights, there was the chink of metal, the rapid snapping of string, the hurrying of old Mr Melling for stamps. And at last the postman came with his sack. Then everything slacked off, and Paul took his dinner basket, and ran to the station to catch the eight twenty train.

This passage provides a vivid picture of the activities of the workplace. The author achieves this by using numerous action-based descriptions which are likely to elicit mirror neuron activity in the brain. Thus, when we read 'he had to weigh the sacks of parcels on the scales', activity in our premotor cortex most likely simulates that action, as if we were actually weighing the parcels ourselves. An additional reason why a reader may be able to connect with this passage is the author's use of several onomatopoetic phrases, such as 'chink of metal' and 'snapping of string'. As well as being action-based, these kinds of phrases also make a direct link with sounds associated with those actions, and thus should in principle have the capacity to activate auditory mirror neurons in the brain, that we have also previously described briefly. Thus when we read the phrase 'snapping of string', our brain responds as if actual string could be heard snapping. With the same mirror neuron response, we therefore are able to experience this string snapping ourselves.

The discovery of auditory mirror neurons provides a neurobiological mechanism for why the use of sound-based phrases is a frequent tool adopted by authors to bring their readers into closer connection with their fictional characters. Obviously, the writers did not know about mirror neurons, but presumably had the intuition that sound-based sentences were very powerful. The following passage, taken from F Scott Fitzgerald's 'The Age of Jazz', is full of action-related sound descriptions, which presumably induce the activation of auditory mirror neurons in the reader, and help to paint a vivid scene of a character tensely waiting in darkness.

Long after midnight John's body gave a nervous jerk, he sat suddenly upright, staring into the veils of somnolence that draped the room. Through the squares of blue darkness that were his open windows, he had heard a faint far-away sound that died upon a bed of wind before identifying itself on his memory, clouded with uneasy dreams. But the sharp noise that had succeeded it was nearer, was just outside the room—the click of a turned knob, a footstep, a whisper, he could not tell; a hard lump gathered in the pit of his stomach, and his whole body ached in the moment that he strained agonizingly to hear.

When we read 'the click of a turned knob, a footstep, a whisper' we presumably activate the premotor areas controlling the hand (turned knob), the leg (footstep), and those speech areas that are activated during both speech production and perception, as we have discussed earlier.

## 4. Mirroring fictional others may be modulated by experience

Perhaps one of the most alluring properties of fictional literature is its capacity to meaningfully mirror real life events that the reader themselves has previously experienced. This is perhaps why classic literary plots and characters endure through time, as they manage to touch on deeper themes that flow through many people's lives.

There is growing evidence that experience plays an important role in shaping the human mirror neuron system. When observing someone performing a familiar action, your mirror neuron system automatically simulates these already well-practised actions internally, which then reactivates the emotional systems related to that action. The notion of experience-dependent mirroring has been demonstrated in a recent fMRI study examining the brain activity of experts and novices watching a series of specialized activities. Ballet dancers and capoeira dancers were studied with fMRI while they observed classical ballet and capoeira videos (Calvo-Merino *et al.* 2005). Activity in premotor areas was higher when subjects were looking at the activity they were more familiar with. In a more controlled follow-up study, male and female ballet dancers (who tend to make different kinds of moves during ballet) demonstrated the same patterns of activity (Calvo-Merino *et al.* 2006). Male dancers had higher premotor activity while watching male-specific ballet moves, whereas female dancers had higher premotor activity while watching female-specific ballet moves.

Being rich in descriptions of actions, perceptions, and emotions that a reader will have themselves already experienced, the concept of experience-dependent mirroring can be easily mapped onto our relationship towards fictional others. For example, we can take a smoker's mirror neuron response to experiencing somebody else, real or fictional, smoking a cigarette. Preliminary data from our lab suggest that mirror neuron activity in smokers is stronger when observing somebody smoking, than for a non-smoker. Thus, when a smoker, or even ex-smoker, reads a passage describing somebody smoking, as a result of their previous experience, there may be a stronger mirroring response compared to non smokers.

We will use the following passage from Cormac McCarthy's *All the Pretty Horses* as an example:

John Grady sat up and took his tobacco from his shirt pocket and began making a cigarette. He wet the cigarette and put it in his mouth and took out his matches and lit the cigarette and blew the match out with the smoke.

This passage is rich in descriptions of the sequence of actions involved in preparing and smoking a hand-rolled cigarette. As the imaging literature on language and mirroring and on experience and mirroring suggests all these sentences should induce premotor activity associated with the representation of those actions, in particular the explicit description of the hand-to mouth action of smoking. By internally imitating the already well-practised action of smoking, smokers (particularly those who hand-roll themselves) are able to directly relate their own experiences to those on the page.

As with this previous example, many people have habits in their daily lives that require a series of well-practised but specialized skills. Owing to our current understanding of experience-dependent activity of mirror neurons, the disparity between readers' prior experience with an activity described in a book is likely to alter the level at which they respond to the passage.

We could take, for example, a horse rider versus a non-horse rider reading another passage from Cormac McCarthy's *All the Pretty Horses*, describing actions associated with saddling a horse.

He lifted the blanket and placed it on the animal's back and smoothed it and stood stroking the animal and talking to it and then he bent and picked up the saddle and lifted it with the cinches strapped up and the off stirrup hung over the horn and sat it on the horse's back and rocked it into place. He bent and reached under and pulled up the strap and cinched it. The horses ears went back and he talked to it.

Even to a non-horse rider, the copious use of action-based descriptions of saddling a horse potentially elicits a strong simulative response in the mirror neuron system. This is because many actions using the same body part share similar features. However, as well as describing the actions required, the author also highlights the sensitive manner in which the character behaves towards the horse. As anyone experienced with horses knows, the manner in which you behave around horses is as important as the actual actions you perform. This is a sensitivity that can only be gained after acquiring experience interacting with horses. Thus, although the actions described in this passage should trigger a response in the average reader, this passage would be particularly salient to somebody already experienced with the activity of saddling a horse.

## 5. Romance and physical intimacy: internal mirroring of our deepest drive to connect with a loved one

Romance and intimacy are some of the most enduring themes in fictional literature, and our capacity for empathy can leave readers with a profound sense of connection to the fictional characters involved. The foundations of our literary obsession with romance lie in the fact that, thanks to our capacity to empathize with fictional others, romantic fictional relationships serve to tap into our deeper human drive to connect with loved ones. The small gestures that lovers perform to each other, and that are often described in detail in novels, are the vehicles that make such connection possible. Thus when readers follow the intrinsic and extrinsic perceptions of the fictional lovers, the activation of internal mirroring mechanisms in the brain enables the reader to fully engage and empathize with fictional others.

Take the following example, an excerpt relating an interaction between two characters in the book *War and Peace* by Leo Tolstoy

Natasha without knowing it was all attention: she did not lose a word, no single quiver in Pierre's voice, no look, no twitch of a muscle in his face, nor a single gesture. She caught the unfinished word in its flight and took it straight into her open heart, divining the secret meaning of all Pierre's mental travail.

. . . Pierre finished his story. Natasha continued to look at him intently with bright, attentive, and animated eyes, as if trying to understand something more which he had perhaps left untold. Pierre in shamefaced and happy confusion glanced occasionally at her, and tried to think what to say next to introduce a fresh subject.

This passage captures a brief but intense moment of connection between two characters. Through his perceptive use of language, Tolstoy enables the reader to able to fully empathize with the subtle communicative interactions between these two fictional characters. The neural mechanism underlying this kind of empathic connection relates to the internal mirroring taking place within the reader. This passage is rich in language that could potentially stimulate mirror neuron activity across multiple modalities within the reader's brain. For example, facial expressions, hand gestures, and speech perception all feature heavily, with the reader being privy to these both from the listener and the speaker's perspective. All three of these processes are demonstrated as being intimately related to mirror neuron activity in the brain. Indeed, as previously discussed, mirror neurons specialized for facial expressions most likely play a crucial role in the process of empathizing with others. By internally imitating the facial expressions of others, mirror neurons enable the reader to activate the neural pathways for the associated emotions and directly 'feel what the character feels'. This mirroring process is what enables us to gain an understanding of the mental states of another individual, whether they are real or fictional. Furthermore, not only is the reader able to connect with each of the characters individually; the explicit descriptions of the facial expressions of both Natasha and Pierre enable the reader to fully engage with the bidirectional flow of mirroring activity that creates the special connection between these characters themselves.

The following is an example of an intense moment captured between lovers and it also gives us the opportunity to discuss an open issue in the neuroscience literature on mirror neurons:

As she stood under the drooping thorn tree, in the darkness by the roadside, he kissed her, and his fingers wandered over her face. In the darkness, where he could not see her, but only feel her, his passion flooded him. He clasped her very close.

This passage is clearly emotionally evocative in its use of phrases such as 'fingers wandered over her face', 'feel her', and 'passion flooded him'. Furthermore, it may also tap into our neural capacity for tactile mirroring. Brain imaging studies have suggested that while we watch somebody else touched, we activate the areas in our brain that are active when we are touched ourselves (what is called the 'somatosensory cortex'; see Keysers *et al.* 2004). However, given that the monkey literature has not yet reported mirroring responses for touch, it is currently unclear whether neural mirroring for touch does exist. Assuming that it does, as the imaging literature suggests, when we read that the man in question is unable to see his lover, so instead feels her using touch and embrace, the mirroring mechanisms at work in the human brain should also evoke in the reader the feeling of being touched. By providing the neural simulation of the actions and perceptions performed on the page, mirroring mechanisms make us able to fully engage with the emotionally intimate moment between the two fictional characters that are interacting in complete darkness.

Even when the language of a novel is seemingly focusing on desires and beliefs, rather than concrete actions, brief descriptions of acts and feelings seem to provide the bridge for a strong emotional connection between the character and the readers. What follows in taken from *The English Patient* by Michael Ondaatje.

He sweeps his arm across plates and glasses on a restaurant table so she might look up somewhere else in the city hearing this cause of noise. When he is without her. He, who has never felt alone in the miles of longitude desert towns. A man in a desert can hold absence in his cupped hands knowing it is something that feeds him more than water.

...

He lies in his room surrounded by the pale maps. He is without Katharine. His hunger wishes to burn down all social rules, all courtesy.

Her life with others no longer interests him. He wants only her stalking beauty, her theatre of expressions. He wants the minute and secret reflection between them, the depth of field minimal, their foreignness intimate like two pages of a closed book.

The gesture of 'sweeping his arm' and the feeling of being alone 'without her' set the tone for what follows, and make the reader attuned with the character wanting the stalking beauty, the intimate foreignness. Not a lot happens here, but we still feel a strong emotional resonance with the character. This seems all prepared by the initial gesture, by sweeping his arm across the restaurant table. The simulation or inner imitation of that sweeping gesture that is provided by neural mirroring mechanisms makes us ready to feel the intense feeling of loneliness and longing of the character.

## 6. Is mirroring the only way of relating to fictional others?

Readers' empathic responses to fictional others are certainly complex and nuanced. A critical question here is whether the mechanisms of mirroring discussed so far can support all these complex empathic responses. A survey of the philosophical, psychological, and neuroscience literature on mind-reading reveals that in all these fields there is often a dichotomy between mirroring processes (or low-level mind-reading) and mentalizing (or high-level mind-reading) (Goldman 2006). Some have proposed that these processes are fundamentally different and may rely on different neural structures. Mentalizing or high-level mind-reading would be more reflective and less reflexive than mirroring, more controlled and less automatic, and rely on medial frontal cortex structures often implicated in 'theory of mind' sort of tasks (Goldman 2009). In other words, high-level mind-reading would be qualitatively different from mirroring, or low-level mind-reading. While this is possible, parsimony invites us to consider the possibility that both high- and low-level mind-reading may rely on relatively similar mirroring mechanisms. But how can this work?

We propose that mirroring can implement complex and nuanced forms of empathy via three mechanisms: layers of mirroring, varieties of mirroring, and control of mirroring. With layers of mirroring we mean that some mirror neurons may exhibit more complex responses than previously described. Indeed, data suggest that some mirror neurons respond to execution and observation of the same action with opposite firing rate changes, a neuronal behaviour never reported previously (Mukamel *et al.* 2010). That is, a cell may increase its baseline firing rate of, say, 5 Hz to, say, 10 Hz, during grasping execution. The same cell, during grasping observation, may decrease its firing rate to 1 Hz or to zero (no spiking activity at all). These opposite mirroring responses (that have been called super mirrors), recorded in humans with depth electrodes implanted for a medical procedure, at the very least seem to provide a simple neuronal mechanism for the control of unwanted imitation and for self/other differentiation. Their existence, however, also suggests that the mirror neuron system may be organized in neuronal layers, with a layer composed of the more 'classical' mirror cells and another layer composed of these more complex neurons. Complex interactions between the elements of these two layers can in principle support more complex forms of empathy.

Furthermore, there is also evidence—from the same depth electrode recordings in human neurological patients—that mirror neurons may be located in many different neural systems (Mukamel *et al.* 2010). The functional significance of mirror neurons may vary according to the location of neurons in brain areas. For example, mirror neurons in the insula may support the capacity to understand a specific emotion (disgust) in others, whereas mirror neurons in the classical mirror neuron areas (the parieto-frontal circuit PF/PFG-F5) may help understanding the goal of observed actions and the intentions behind them. Mirror neurons in brain areas important for movement selection and sequences of movements, as in the supplementary motor area (SMA) may mirror those aspects of human behaviour, whereas mirror neurons in memory-related brain areas, such as the medial temporal lobe, may be relevant to memory mechanisms (the sight of two people kissing may evoke the memory of a kiss in the observer).

Finally, while they have not yet been clearly identified, there must be mechanisms of control for mirroring outside the mirror neuron system itself. The main question here is whether this putative mechanism of control is a general purpose cognitive control mechanism or is specifically dedicated to the control of mirroring responses. Given that mirror neurons are specialized cells for actions, it is tempting to speculate that they require also specialized mechanisms of control. Large lesions in the prefrontal cortex are associated with imitative behavior (Lhermitte *et al.* 1986; De Renzi *et al.* 1996), suggesting that the lesion may have disrupted a mechanism of control specific to imitation.

Taken together, the three mechanisms briefly discussed above (layers of mirroring, varieties of mirroring, and control of mirroring) can conceivably implement more complex and nuanced forms of empathy. While it is entirely possible that higher forms of empathy for fictional others may be implemented via non-mirroring mechanisms, we believe it is more parsimonious to propose a model that relies entirely on some forms of mirroring and their control. For instance, in some cases authors seem to encourage the reader not to empathize with specific characters. We propose that the reader first feels what the unsympathetic character feels, and then suppresses the mirroring either via control mechanisms or via 'super mirror neurons' (or 'anti-mirror neurons').

For instance, in this example from *War and Peace*, Pierre in interacting with a rather unsympathetic character:

'I'll kill you!' he shouted, and with a strength as yet unknown to him, he seized the marble slab from a table, took a step towards her, and swung. Hélène's face became frightful; she shrieked and sprang away from him. His father's blood told in him. Pierre felt the enthusiasm and enchantment of rage.

With the clear descriptions of facial expressions in this passage we are quite able to feel what this 'unsympathetic' character is feeling: 'Hélène's face became frightful; she shrieked and sprang away from him.'

It seems that even in order to be unsympathetic towards a fictional character, the reader must first mirror how the character feels and then most likely modulate this mirroring in order to feel unsympathetic towards the character.

## 7. Intensity of mirroring: the written page vs. the screen

An interesting issue relates to the degree or intensity of mirroring evoked by the written page compared to the sight and the sounds of actions of other people. As we have discussed above, written sentences describing actions activate premotor areas most likely containing mirror neurons. However, both spatial extent and magnitude of activation differed slightly when compared to activation of the same areas in response to videos (Aziz-Zadeh *et al.* 2006). One of the problems in making these comparisons is that while we watch somebody grasping a cup of coffee, we perceive a specific hand, a specific cup, and a specific grasping action. In contrast, when we read the sentence 'He grasped the cup of coffee', we are given a much more abstract description of somebody grasping a cup. Indeed, while there is a large overlap in premotor activation for both videos showing actions and sentences describing actions, the activation associated with the latter tends to shift slightly anteriorly and is slightly reduced in magnitude. This may be due to the fact that when reading the sentence describing a grasping action, we may simulate only some aspects of the grasping action without simulating the action in all its details.

Does this mean that novels will always be second best in evoking the mirroring of fictional others, for instance when compared to movies? Not necessarily. Indeed, the dimension of time should be taken into account. While the intensity of evoked mirroring may be very high during the roughly two-hour period of a typical movie, readers take much longer to read a novel across multiple time periods. Whenever they resume reading, they most likely evoke the memories of what they have read previously. The longer temporal unfolding of reading a novel may completely offset the reduced intensity of mirroring produced by the more abstract nature of language.

Thus, while less intense than in movies, the mirroring induced by reading novels is more extended in time, and may even result in a stronger 'neural signature' of this form of mirroring.

## 8. Conclusions

We have argued here that the recent discovery of mirroring neural mechanisms in the primate brain suggests a unitary framework for empathizing with both real people and fictional others. The automatic, pre-reflective form of empathy that mirror neurons enable is most likely at work also when we are engaged in one of the most typically reflective behaviours, reading a novel. While there is no direct data in support of our claim (and most likely there won't be direct data in the near future, given the constraints of neuroscience investigations and the complexity of real life behaviours such as reading a novel), the well-controlled data obtained in the lab make our claim quite plausible.

Neural mechanisms of mirroring map extremely well with philosophical claims that were proposed almost a century before neuroscience discoveries. While the level of description of the inner workings of the brain provided by neuroscience studies cannot yet be fully translated into psychological mechanisms at work during the appreciation of art, the concept of *Einfuhlung* proposed by Theodore Lipps seems highly compatible with the functional mechanisms that mirror neurons most likely support.[1]

## References

Aziz-Zadeh, L., S. M. Wilson, G. Rizzolatti, and M. Iacoboni (2006). 'Congruent Embodied Representations for Visually Presented Actions and Linguistic Phrases Describing Actions'. *Current Biology*, 16/18: 1818–23.

Buccino, G., F. Binkofski, G. R. Fink, L. Fadiga, L. Fogassi, *et al.* (2001). 'Action Observation Activates Premotor and Parietal Areas in a Somatotopic Manner: An Fmri Study'. *European Journal of Neuroscience*, 13/2: 400–4.

Calvo-Merino, B., D. E.Glaser, J. Grèzes, R. E. Passingham, and P. Haggard (2005). 'Action Observation and Acquired Motor Skills: An fMRI Study with Expert Dancers'. *Cerebral Cortex*, 15/8: 1243–9.

——J. Grèzes, D. E. Glaser, R. . Passingham, and P. Haggard (2006). 'Seeing or Doing? Influence of Visual and Motor Familiarity in Action Observation'. *Current Biology*, 16/19: 1905–10.

[1] For generous support Marco Iacoboni thanks the Brain Mapping Medical Research Organization, Brain Mapping Support Foundation, Pierson-Lovelace Foundation, The Ahmanson Foundation, William M. and Linda R. Dietel Philanthropic Fund at the Northern Piedmont Community Foundation, Tamkin Foundation, Jennifer Jones-Simon Foundation, Capital Group Companies Charitable Foundation, Robson Family, and Northstar Fund.

Carr, L., M. Iacoboni, M. C. Dubeau, J. C. Mazziotta, and G. L. Lenzi (2003). 'Neural Mechanisms of Empathy in Humans: A Relay from Neural Systems for Imitation to Limbic Areas'. *Proceedings of the National Academy of Sciences USA*, 100/9: 5497–5502.

De Renzi, E., F. Cavalleri, and S. Facchini (1996). 'Imitation and Utilisation Behaviour'. *Journal of Neurology, Neurosurgery & Psychiatry*, 61/4: 396–400.

di Pellegrino, G., Fadiga, L., Fogassi, L., Gallese, V., and G. Rizzolatti (1992). 'Understanding Motor Events: A Neurophysiological Study'. *Experimental Brain Research*, 91/1: 176–80.

Ferrari, P. F., Gallese, V., Rizzolatti, G., and L. Fogassi (2003). 'Mirror Neurons Responding to the Observation of Ingestive and Communicative Mouth Actions in the Monkey Ventral Premotor Cortex'. *European Journal of Neuroscience*, 17/8: 1703–14.

Fitzgerald, F. Scott (2003 [1922]). *Tales of the Age of Jazz*. Pennsylvania : Pine Street Books.

Fogassi, L., P. F. Ferrari, B. Gesierich, S. Rozzi, F. Chersi, and G. Rizzolatti (2005). 'Parietal Lobe: From Action Organization to Intention Understanding'. *Science*, 308/5722: 662–7.

Gallese, V. (2001). 'The "Shared Manifold" Hypothesis'. *Journal of Consciousness Studies*, 8/5–7: 33–50.

——L. Fadiga, L. Fogassi, and G. Rizzolatti (1996). 'Action Recognition in the Premotor Cortex'. *Brain*, 119/Pt 2: 593–609.

Gazzola, V., L. Aziz-Zadeh, and C. Keysers (2006). 'Empathy and the Somatotopic Auditory Mirror System in Humans'. *Current Biology*, 16/18: 1824–9.

Glenberg, A. M. and M. P. Kaschak (2002). 'Grounding Language in Action'. *Psychonomic Bulletin and Review*, 9/3: 558–65.

Goldman, A. I. (2006). *Simulating Minds: The Philosophy, Psychology, and Neuroscience of Mindreading*. New York: Oxford University Press.

——(2009). 'Mirroring, Mindreading, and Simulation', in J. A. Pineda (ed.), *Mirror Neuron Systems*. New York: Humana Press, pp. 311–30.

Hauk, O., I. Johnsrude, and F. Pulvermüller (2004). 'Somatotopic Representation of Action Words in Human Motor and Premotor Cortex'. *Neuron*, 41/2: 301–7.

Iacoboni, M. (2005). 'Neural Mechanisms of Imitation'. *Current Opinion in Neurobiology*, 15/6: 632–7.

——(2008). 'The Role of Premotor Cortex in Speech Perception: Evidence from fMRI and rTMS'. *Journal of Physiology–Paris*, 102/1–3: 31–4.

——and M. Dapretto (2006). 'The Mirror Neuron System and the Consequences of its Dysfunction'. *Nature Reviews Neuroscience*, 7/12: 942–51.

——R. P. Woods, M. Brass, H. Bekkering, J. C. Mazziotta, and G. Rizzolatti (1999). 'Cortical Mechanisms of Human Imitation'. *Science*, 286/5449: 2526–8.

Kaplan, J. T. and M. Iacoboni (2006). 'Getting a Grip on Other Minds: Mirror Neurons, Intention Understanding, and Cognitive Empathy'. *Social Neuroscience*, 1/3–4: 175–83.

Keysers, C., B. Wicker, V. Gazzola, J. L. Anton, L. Fogassi, and V. Gallese (2004). 'A Touching Sight: SII/PV Activation during the Observation and Experience of Touch'. *Neuron*, 42/2: 335–46.

Kohler, E., C. Keysers, M. A. Umiltà, L. Fogassi, V. Gallese, and G. Rizzolatti (2002). 'Hearing Sounds, Understanding Actions: Action Representation in Mirror Neurons'. *Science*, 297/5582: 846–8.

Koski, L., M. Iacoboni, M. C. Dubeau, R. P. Woods, and J. C. Mazziotta (2003). 'Modulation of Cortical Activity during Different Imitative Behaviors'. *Journal of Neurophysiology*, 9/1: 460–71.

——A. Wohlschläger, H. Bekkering, R. P. Woods, M. C. Dubeau, *et al.* (2002). 'Modulation of Motor and Premotor Activity during Imitation of Target-Directed Actions'. *Cerebral Cortex*, 12/8: 847–55.

Lawrence, D. H. (1994 [1913]). *Sons and Lovers*. London: Penguin Books.

Lhermitte, F., B. Pillon, and M. D. Serdaru (1986). 'Human Autonomy and the Frontal Lobes. Part I: Imitation and Utilization Behavior. A Neuropsychological Study of 75 Patients'. *Annals of Neurology*, 19: 326–34.

Liberman, A. M. and I. G. Mattingly (1985). 'The Motor Theory of Speech Perception Revised'. *Cognition*, 21: 1–36.

——and D. H. Whalen (2000). 'On the Relation of Speech to Language'. *Trends in Cognitive Science*, 4: 187–96.

'F. S. Cooper, D. P. Shankweiler, and M. Studdert-Kennedy (1967). 'Perception of the Speech Code'. *Psychological Review*, 74: 431–61.

McCarthy, C. (1993). *All the Pretty Horses*. London: Picador.

Meister, I. G., S. M. Wilson, C. Deblieck, A. D. Wu, and M. Iacoboni (2007). 'The Essential Role of Premotor Cortex in Speech Perception'. *Current Biology*, 17/19: 1692–6.

Mukamel, R., J. T. Kaplan, A. Ekstrom, M. Iacoboni, and I. Fried (2010). 'Single Newon Responses in Humans during Execution and Observation of Actions'. *Current Biology*, 20: 750–6.

——M. Iacoboni, and I. Fried (2008). 'Visuo-Motor Mirror Responses in Human Medial Temporal Lobe'. *Journal of Cognitive Neuroscience*, 20: 1096.

Pfeifer, J. H., M. Iacoboni, J. C. Mazziotta, and M. Dapretto (2008). 'Mirroring Others' Emotions Relates to Empathy and Interpersonal Competence in Children'. *Neuroimage*, 39/4: 2076–85.

Pulvermüller, F., M. Huss, F. Kherif, F. Moscoso del Prado Martin, O. Hauk, and Y. Shtyrov (2006). 'Motor Cortex Maps Articulatory Features of Speech Sounds'. *Proceedings of the National Academy of Sciences USA*, 103/20: 7865–70.

Rizzolatti, G. and M. A. Arbib (1998). 'Language Within Our Grasp'. *Trends in Neuroscience*, 21/5: 188–94.

——and L. Craighero (2004). 'The Mirror-Neuron System'. *Annual Review of Neuroscience*, 27: 169–92.

——and M. Fabbri-Destro (2008). 'The Mirror System and its Role in Social Cognition'. *Current Opinion in Neurobiology*, 18/2: 179–84.

Shepherd, S. V., J. T. Klein, R. O. Deaner, and M. L. Platt (2009). 'Mirroring of Attention by Neurons in Macaque Parietal Cortex'. *Proceedings of the National Academy of Sciences USA*, 106/23: 9489–94.

Tettamanti, M., G. Buccino, M. C. Saccuman, V. Gallese, M. Danna, *et al.* (2005). 'Listening to Action-Related Sentences Activates Fronto-Parietal Motor Circuits'. *Journal of Cognitive Neuroscience*, 17/2: 273–81.

Tolstoy, L. (1869). *War and Peace*. Digital Edition, Project Gutenberg (http://www.gutenberg.org)

Umiltà, M. A., E. Kohler, V. Gallese, L. Fogassi, L. Fadiga, *et al.* (2001). 'I Know What You Are Doing: A Neurophysiological Study'. *Neuron*, 31/1: 155–65.

Wilson, S. M. and M. Iacoboni (2006). 'Neural Responses to Non-Native Phonemes Varying in Producibility: Evidence for the Sensorimotor Nature of Speech Perception'. *Neuroimage*, 33/1: 316–25.

——A. P. Saygin, M. I. Sereno, and M. Iacoboni (2004). 'Listening to Speech Activates Motor Areas Involved in Speech Production'. *Nature Neuroscience*, 7/7: 701–2.

# PART VI

# Music, Dance, and Expressivity

# 19

# Moving in Concert: Dance and Music

*Noël Carroll and Margaret Moore*

In 1962 in *The Philosophical Review*, George Dickie published an article entitled "Is Psychology Relevant to Aesthetics?" His answer was "no." His argument was based on examining three types of psychological research that some might claim were relevant to aesthetics and then showing that none of them are. The three types of research were: (1) experiments designed to show convergence among subjects in their attribution of meaning—that is, of expressive properties; (2) experiments designed to establish preference orders among objects of aesthetic interest; and (3) psychological characterizations of aesthetic experience. Dickie concluded that none of this research could contribute to the solution of any of the problems of philosophical aesthetics.

According to Dickie, polling people about the expressive properties they attribute to a piece of music does not address the philosophical problem of whether it is possible for music to possess expressive properties. Likewise, people's preferences are irrelevant to establishing normative standards. And finally psychology has little to offer by way of an account of aesthetic experience, because that is not a scientific question, but a matter of conceptual analysis.

Obviously a lot has changed in both psychology and philosophy since Dickie wrote that article, and some of it would seem to render his dismissal of the relevance of psychology obsolete. Much of the psychology that aestheticians rely upon today does not involve introspection and self-reports, but fMRIs. Similarly, views of the nature of philosophy have also expanded, especially in the area of the philosophy of mind. Post-Quine, the boundary between the conceptual and the empirical is more porous as philosophers avail themselves of the findings of, for example, evolutionary psychology.

However, we wonder whether Dickie was even justified in his rejection of psychology when he wrote the article, especially with reference to the description of aesthetic experience. For even in 1962, any theory of aesthetic experience would have had to be constrained by what is psychologically possible (not to mention actual).

Of course, the kind of account of aesthetic experience Dickie is after may also be a creature of the past. Dickie appears to think that a theory of aesthetic experience will be a uniform account across the arts—an account that covers literature as well as architecture and music, i.e., both concrete artifacts and abstract artifacts in very different media, addressing often very different sense modalities and cognitive faculties. But can such a characterization be anything but insufferably vague and threadbare?

Instead, a more informative approach might be to consider the ingredients that go into the experience of understanding specific art forms. And this is what we intend to attempt in this chapter. We will examine one kind of music—music that engenders the impulse to move in listeners—in relation to one kind of dance—which we regard as a performative interpretation of the music—for the purpose of illuminating how this kind of artistic symbiosis can affect the audience's experience of it. To that end, we will exploit the resources of recent psychological research in order to substantiate our claim that the experience, which we suggest results from the combination of the relevant sort of music with the relevant type of dance, is possible. Dickie may charge us with aesthetic revisionism here. Yet we believe that our approach is in keeping with Baumgarten's original definition of aesthetics as "the science of how things come to be cognized by means of the senses."

On our view, some music inspires feelings of movement. Likewise does some dance, often by activating certain mirror reflexes in viewers—that is to say, certain muscular, motor impulses that correlate to the movements observed in the pertinent dance. In this way, the movement in the dance clarifies, enlarges or expands upon the feelings of movement already available in the music. Thus, the dance enables the spectator to sharpen, deepen, or otherwise develop the intimation of movement she intuits in the accompanying music. And this, we maintain, is fundamental to the aesthetic experience of this sort of choreography, which mandates attentiveness to the movement impulse qualities in the dance-cum-music.

In order to defend the credibility of this hypothesis, we need to argue for the correlation between music and the impression of movement, on the one hand, and then go on to establish the likelihood that dance not only has the resources to hone this impression of movement, but that it often does. Such will be the burden of the next two sections. While our account may be relevant to the aesthetic experience of performers, composers, and choreographers, our primary focus is on the experience of the audience member. We will conclude with some remarks about the similarity between our approach and the expression theory of yesteryear.

## 1. Movement in music?

It is a commonplace that music moves. However, there is little consensus about how music moves, or what precisely is meant by "movement" with respect to music. Part of the problem lies in trying to reconcile what we know about sound waves and the way they move, with our subjective experience of music as moving. Many philosophers and music theorists would argue that these two things simply cannot match up. We know that sounds are created by vibrations that travel through the air as waves, and so clearly all music requires that there be something moving, but it is not the motion of these waves that we have in mind when we say that music moves. Instead, we talk of scales that ascend and descend, of rhythms that march along, and of music's pulse—something that we don't just move *to*, but *with*. It is hard to deny the conviction that there is a way that music moves that we can imitate with the movement of our bodies.

While the metaphysical niceties of movement in music are both interesting and important, for our purposes we need not claim that every case in which we can coherently talk of motion in music is a case in which something literally moves. All that we require is that the motion perceived in the music is often central to our experience of the music. For example, we often describe the musical structures we hear as expressive of feelings of movement, as if we detect those movements in the music the same way we detect the movements of the tide in the ocean. Moreover, these feelings can be systematically traced to central features of the music itself.

There is overwhelming anecdotal evidence that people do in fact perceive music as moving. That is how people frequently describe music. Indeed, research projects in the psychology of music take this as a basic presupposition.[1] Furthermore, even music theorists who have a specialized vocabulary with which to describe music use phrases like "oscillating triplets" and other movement terms to refer to musical events. In addition, fMRI studies have shown that music is processed in the same parts of the brain that are responsible for the processing of movement, and that listening to or imagining music results in activation of the premotor cortex.[2]

The perception of movement is fundamental to our hearing music as *music* rather than a collection of noises. In discussing what is required to hear something as a unified piece of music rather than as a mere succession of sounds, Roger Scruton proposes that we must hear "the experience of a musical unity across time, in which something begins, and then moves on through changes in pitch—perhaps to an audible conclusion. A melody has temporal boundaries, and a musical movement between them."[3] Edward T. Cone makes the same point about musical phrases, pointing out that "the typical musical phrase consists of an initial downbeat, a period of motion, and a point of arrival marked by a cadential downbeat."[4] The point is not only that we happen to hear a great deal of music as moving through time, but also that in order to hear sounds as music at all, we must in general hear these sounds as relating to each other in a temporal

[1] Many articles that make this presupposition can be found in *Music Perception*. Examples include R. W. Mitchell and M. C. Gallaher "Embodying Music: Matching Music and Dance in Memory," *Music Perception*, 19 (1991): 65–85; E. G. Schellenberg, A. M. Krysciak, and R. J. Campbell, "Perceiving Emotion in Melody: Interactive Effects of Pitch and Rhythm," *Music Perception*, 18 (2000): 155–71.

[2] Noël Carroll and Margaret Moore, "Not Reconciled: Comments for Peter Kivy," *Journal of Aesthetics and Art Criticism*, 65/3 (Summer 2007): 318–22; Laura Sizer, "Moods in the Music and the Man: A Response to Kivy and Carroll," *Journal of Aesthetics and Art Criticism*, 65/3 (Summer 2007): 307–11.

[3] Roger Scruton, *The Aesthetics of Music* (Oxford: Clarendon Press, 1997), p. 40.

[4] Edward T. Cone, *Musical Form and Musical Performance* (New York: W.W. Norton and Co., 1968), p. 27.

succession that is *directed*—which is to say: to hear music is to hear musical movement.[5] That is, insofar as time, or at least the experience of time, is unidirectional, we will unavoidably experience a succession of musical notes as going somewhere. Music is closely tied to time, which it structures, and since time is experienced as moving, so is music.

It seems, then, that the most natural way to describe what music does is to say that it moves. We describe the ways in which it moves in the same terms we would use to describe physical movement. For example, a piece might be marked *andante grazioso*, indicating that the tempo should be a walking tempo, and that the style of walking should be gracious. Or the marking could be *sehr rasch*, meaning very hurried. These directions for performance are able to indicate both the tempo and the character of the music at once precisely because it is so easy for the musician to understand how to play music in a way that is hurried, or is gracefully walking. If the performer heeds these markings, the listener will hear the music as hurried or as graceful.[6]

Since it has been established that we do in fact mean something by saying music moves, it is important to distinguish all the different ways in which music can move, linking these to the various technical devices or features that can contribute to this movement. These devices include pulse, meter, phrase structure, changes in dynamics and instrumentation, patterns of accents and articulation, harmonic motion, and others. Pulse is perhaps the most fundamental element that contributes to musical movement, since it is the pulse that creates temporal order in music by establishing a pattern of beats which becomes a background against which melody and harmony play out. Pulse also contributes to the impression of musical movement, since it is generally the pulse we are enticed to move to.[7] The aforementioned neuroscientific studies support the hypothesis that we process the music we hear in part by activating the portions of the brain that would be involved in producing those sounds. Thus, it is no wonder that we want to move to the music, since hearing the music primes us to move in time.[8]

But there are other elements of music less tied to pulse and time that nevertheless contribute to the experience of music as moving. In almost every culture, music

---

[5] Some aleatoric music may be an exception to this claim. Yet it is the exception that proves the rule, for the point of aleatoric music is to have sounds that appear to occur randomly. The expectation that we have for organized, directed sound is thwarted.

[6] There need not be a precise correspondence between the marking in the score and the words a listener might use. The point is merely that it is movement terms that are used, and there is general agreement about whether the marking is being followed or not.

[7] One feature of pulse that makes it of cardinal importance is that to interrupt the pulse is to interrupt the music itself. Composers often exploit this feature for dramatic effect, as is the case with the first movement of Beethoven's *Fifth Symphony*.

[8] B. Calvo-Merino, D. E. Glaser, J. Grezes, R. E. Passingham, and P. Haggard (2005) "Action observation and acquired motor skills: an FMRI study with expert dancers," *Cerebral Cortex*, 15 (2005): 1243–9;Ricarda I. Schubotz and D. Yves von Cramon, "Functional-Anatomical Concepts of Human Premotor Cortex: Evidence from fMRI and PET Studies," *NeuroImage*, 20 (2003): 120–31;Ricarda I. Schubotz, D. Yves von Cramon, and G. Lohmann, "Auditory What, Where and When: A Sensory Somatotopy in Lateral Premotor Cortex," *NeuroImage*, 20 (2003): 173–85.

consists of rhythms and melodies, and these melodies are constructed out of scales. As the pitches get higher one talks of ascending the scale, and of descending into the lower-pitched notes.[9] But it is not enough to combine a lower note and a higher note to produce upward motion; we have to hear these notes in a temporal sequence. Once this is done, we hear the music as moving towards the higher note, and thus hear the melody or phrase as rising.[10]

Most classical pieces exploit a combination of elements in order to create highly sophisticated musical structures. For example, the graceful, swaying waltzing character of the third movement of Tchaikovsky's *Sixth Symphony* is created by the juxtaposition of melody and rhythm. The melody ascends through one bar, and then turns back in the next, and this sequence continues in the next two bars, adding to the feeling that the waltz moves as a dancer would across the floor. The unusual feature of the Tchaikovsky waltz is that it is in five rather than the typical triple meter. We feel the first and third beats as emphasized, and so this rhythmic background confers a lilting feeling onto the melody. Of course, not every person who listens to this piece would be able to explain why the waltz moves in the way it does, in part because some structural elements adding to the motion of music are more readily identifiable upon hearing than others. Also, which patterns are felt will depend upon the attention and experience of the listener, and the particular interpretation put forth in performance.

Needless to say, as the preceding example illustrates, another reason it is natural to describe music in terms we use for bodily movement is that many musical forms were created for dancing. While it might be difficult to dance a minuet of a Beethoven string quartet, his minuets retain many of the characteristics of the Baroque musical form that developed along with the dance of the same name. Despite the fact that minuets by Beethoven were not written to be danced, it still makes sense to think of the music as "mincing," a term that might better describe the steps of the original Baroque dance. The parallel developments of the music and dance make it impossible to tell whether it is the dance that lends the music its characteristic grace, or whether the gestures of the dance developed in response to the graceful character already perceived in the music. While the minuet is perhaps the most familiar example of a musical form developed from a dance, there are many other forms that have characteristic musical gestures that match their dance counterparts, including the Baroque Sarabande, Gavotte, Bourrée, and Gigue, the Polish Mazurka, the gypsy Czardas, and so forth.

So far, we have shown a way in which we can legitimately describe music as moving. At the same time, it is widely reported that certain music makes people feel like

---

[9] The exception is in Ancient Greek music, which is exactly backwards. But this is because "up" and "down" the scale were thought of in terms of up and down the neck of a stringed instrument. It is easiest to explain this to modern readers in terms of the bass or the cello. As the cellist moves his finger *down* the string or fingerboard towards the bridge, the pitches get higher, not lower. The Greek scales were described in terms of the motion of the musician's hand, which results in a system that is backwards with respect to ours.

[10] For an additional discussion of movement in music, largely in agreement with ours, see Stephen Davies *Musical Meaning and Expression* (Ithaca: Cornell University Press, 1994), pp. 229–39.

moving. This is obvious with dance music designed to encourage, regulate, and even propel the prospective dances. Here one supposes that there is some relation between the movement patterns in the music and the feelings of movement it inspires in the dancer. To a certain extent, the dancer tries to mimic the musical movement impulses where the imitation is guided by musical patterns. For example, her foot automatically taps to the beat, or her arms reach upwards with the rising melodic line.[11] Of course, not all music is made for dancing. Some is made for listening. But where the stationary listeners detect the impulse to move to music, it is likely that the same structures are in operation, and in fact studies have shown this to be the case.[12] They feel prompted in their musculature to mimic aspects of the perceived musical movement.[13] It is this feeling of being prompted that we have in mind by referring to "movement impulses" inherent in the music. The relevant musical structures, that is, operate as sonic cues.

## 2. Dance, music, and movement

With respect to certain types of music, listeners report that they are able to discern movement in the sonic array—that is, listeners maintain that they can detect the feeling of movement of which the musical contour is expressive. This may prompt a listener to imagine movement consonant with the music—to imagine either that one is moving, or to imagine others moving, or, more abstractly, to imagine simply that *something* is moving. As well, such music can often inspire or encourage movement in the listener. The movement impulse expressed in the music may be felt literally in the percipient's body. One may sway, clap one's hands, or stamp one's feet to the rhythm or, in the privacy of one's living room, one might indulge in broad sweeping gestures as the music on the radio appears to soar.

That music has the power to infect our muscles in this way, of course, explains why music and dance appear together worldwide in rituals of all sorts and in social dancing. Though the specific dances differ from tribe to tribe and from nation to nation, the phenomenon of dancing to music that incites the associated movement is as nearly universal as language is. From pre-modern rain dances through modern waltzes and on to contemporary breakdancing, dancing to or with or for the music is ubiquitous.

Professional choreographers and dancers often reaffirm their conviction that the dance they practice is inspired by the music. Moira Shearer argues "It is the music that

---

[11] This phenomenon is not unique to dance, as anyone who has found herself walking or jogging in time to music will recognize.

[12] Mitchell and Gallaher, "Embodying Music."

[13] This phenomenon is frequent enough that Daniel Levitin has ironically suggested that Lincoln Center rip out the seats in its concert halls in order to give the audience the opportunity to air the movement impulses they feel in response to the music.Daniel Levitin, "Dancing in the Seats," *The New York Times*, October 26, 2007 (http://www.nytimes.com).

has caused the choreographer...to want to compose movements and dances."[14] Alexandre Benois, summing up the project of the early Ballets Russes, asserted "For us it was the music which provided ballet with its centre of gravity. The moment had arrived when one listened to the music, and, in listening, derived an additional pleasure from seeing it. I think this is the mission of ballet."[15] And George Balanchine appears to agree: "I cannot move, I don't even want to move, unless I hear the music first. I couldn't move without a reason, and the reason is the music."[16] Hegel, for once, put it succinctly—the music "gets into our feet," making, as the ancients believed, feelings visible.[17]

With these artists, it seems fair to hypothesize that the movement of the dancers enables the participants to clarify the feelings of movement that they detect in the music by acting out those impulses. Suzanne Langer called dance "the gestural rendering of musical forms." This may not be true of all dancing, especially not all theater dance. But it surely pertains to a great deal of social dance, as most of us can affirm on the basis of our own experiences. Indeed, Sixties post-Twist, free-style dancing was explicitly predicated upon incarnating the movement one heard beckoning from the music.

In cases like these, it should be unproblematic to say that the dancer expresses the feeling of movement that she derives from the musical contour. She brings outside, in a manner of speaking, the inner feeling of movement that the music excites inside her. She embodies the feeling, thereby clarifying it in the process of making it manifest. But what is the effect of this performance on spectators?

It is our conjecture that the dancer's activity can also serve to clarify the audience member's intimation of the movement that he intuits in the music. For, in addition to the movement stimulation that the spectator receives from the music, there is also further stimulation streaming from the dancers' bodies which can affect the receptive viewer kinesthetically.

How is this possible? Here it is instructive to recall a readily observable, everyday fact of life. Who has not noticed that often when we are speaking to other people, we take on their behaviors? They clench their face in a mask of high seriousness, and we do likewise. They look off to the doorway; so do we. They punctuate their sentence with a laugh; we chuckle in concert. If you have never noted this in your own behavior, just look at the people locked in conversation as you pass down the hallway. Quite often, they will appear as mirror images of each other.

---

[14] Quoted in Barbara Newman, *Striking a Balance: Dancers Talk about Dancing* (Boston: Houghton Mifflin, 1982), p. 105.

[15] Quoted in Stephanie Jordan, *Moving Music: Dialogues with Music in Twentieth-Century Ballet* (London: Dance Books, 2000), p. 1.

[16] Ibid.

[17] G. W. F. Hegel, *Aesthetics*, trans. T. M. Knox (Oxford: Clarendon Press, 1975), vol. II, p. 906; and Francis Sparshott, *A Measured Pace: Toward a Philosophical Understanding of the Arts of Dance* (Toronto: University of Toronto Press, 1995), p. 216.

Moreover, that which obtains with respect to facial expressions and behaviors also occurs with regard to posture. When one's interlocutor bends forward to confide in us, we automatically follow suit and lean inward. When we watch a football player stretching forward in order to catch a pass that is just barely within his reach, we sense our muscles tugging slightly, but insistently, in the same direction.

Needless to say, we are not doing this as a matter of reflection or deliberation. It is a reflex, as were our other examples, all of which were meant to substantiate the pedestrian observation that we humans have an involuntary tendency to mirror automatically the behavior of our conspecifics. Call this phenomenon the "mirror reflex."[18]

One function of the mirror reflex is to gather information about the inner states of others. By involuntarily mimicking the facial disposition of our interlocutor—by furrowing our eyebrows ever so gravely when he does—we gain an inkling of what is going on inside of him. The feedback from our own muscles stirs our own autonomic nervous system in a way that is roughly parallel to what is happening in him (that is, as long as he is not dissembling). We get an inward taste, so to speak, of some of what he is feeling by feeling something very like it in our own bodies.

Mirror reflexes are an indispensable feature of human life. Children on their caregiver's lap learn automatically what feelings go with this or that stimulus by "playing" mother's grimaces and giggles on their own bodies.[19] Moreover, the mirror reflexes that manifest themselves in outward behavior *may* have a physiological substrate in what cognitive scientists have labeled mirror neurons.[20] Indeed, the activation of the mirror neurons suggests a physical basis for the claims, often dismissed as "mystical," by dancers that choreography involves a dimension of kinesthetic communication.[21]

Much theater dance since the early twentieth century—undoubtedly, in part, in an effort to liberate itself from the demands of narrative—has been, in one way or another, about the feelings engendered by the music that accompanies it, either by way of drawing attention to or expanding otherwise upon these experienced aspects of the music.[22] This is true not only in the modern dance movement—including figures such as Isadora Duncan, Denishawn, Doris Humphrey, and, at present, choreographers like Paul Taylor and Mark Morris—but also in the balletic tradition, ranging from Michel

[18] Sometimes this is also called emotional contagion. See Elaine Hatfield, John T. Cacioppo, and Richard L. Rapson, *Emotional Contagion* (Cambridge: Cambridge University Press, 1994), chapter 2.

[19] A. N. Meltzoff and A. K. Moor, "Imitation of Facial and Manual Gestures by Human Neonates," *Science*, 198 (October 1977): 75–8.

[20] The conjecture concerning mirror neurons is based on research with macaque monkeys. M.A. Umiltà, E. Kohler, V. Gallese, L. Fogassi, L. Fadiga, C. Keysers, and G. Rizzolatti, "I Know What You Are Doing: A Neurophysiological Study," *Neuron*, 31 (2001): 155–65; V. Gallese, L. Fadig, L. Fogassi, and G. Rizzolati, "Action Recognition in the Premotor Cortex," *Brain*, 119 (1996): 593–609; G. Rizzolatti, L. Fadiga, V. Gallese, and L. Rogassi, "Premotor Cortex and the Recognition of Motor Actions" *Cognitive Brain Research*, 3 (1996): 131–41.

[21] Not only would this claim demystify the phenomenon of kinesthetic communication, but it would also account for the similarity of responses by providing material grounds for claims of intersubjectivity.

[22] See Jordan, *Moving Music*, chapter I.

Fokine's *Chopiniana* through Leonid Massine's *Symphonic Ballet* to George Balanchine's abstract ballets, and those of his progeny (to cite only a few of the people interested in making dances that are intimately connected to the music).[23]

Historically, when choreographers began to avail themselves of pieces of the symphonic repertoire which had not been originally created for the dance, they supplied themselves with a basis for sustaining evening-long performances without a whiff of narrative.[24] Instead, their dances could be about the music or aspects thereof. And perhaps for fairly obvious reasons, one of the foremost aspects of the music to which choreographers mean to direct our attention involves the feelings of movement that the music engenders, in virtue of the kinds of sonic elements discussed in the last section.

In the pertinent examples, the music in question awakens a feeling of movement in the listener, who also sees the dancer literally moving to or with the music, thereby enabling the receptive listener to refine or enlarge upon that feeling through the addition of the somatic input derived from her mirror reflexes. Whereas in listening to the music apart from the dance, one relies solely upon one's own imaginative resources, music-cum-dance ideally provides the audience with an image of appropriate movement which, by enlisting our mirror reflexes, heightens or extends our apprehension of the evolving feeling of movement. Abetted by our mirror responses to the image of movement created by the dancers' bodies, the feeling of movement initiated in the music can be apperceived ever more precisely and richly due to the conjunction of a kinesthetic dimension in addition to the aural one.

To mention just a few of the ways in which choreographic movement qualities can further articulate—either by illustrating or by expanding upon—the feelings of movement of which the sonic profiles of music are expressive, recall that the dancer can move slowly, lightly, hurriedly, carefully, smoothly, softly, weakly, forcefully, flowingly, hesitantly, firmly, tensely, quickly, abruptly, gradually, tightly, jerkily, nervously, urgently, and evenly, where all of these movement qualities, and more, can echo, underscore, enhance, or contrastively modify the movement impulses manifest in the music.

The dancer can rise and sink, grow and shrink, circle and dissipate in response to the call of the score. Dance gestures may describe or depict comparable musical gestures: the dancer may turn abruptly, push, pull, sweep ahead, freeze, swell, oscillate, subside, flutter, swing, undulate, jerk, tap, jab, punch, confront, fight, prolong the moment or hasten it, float, spread, fluctuate, change cadence, retreat, speed up, reverse direction, slow down, recede, advance, crawl, fall, or suspend movement altogether. Moreover, the choreography can introduce these gestures in anticipation of the music, along with the music, or as a retrospective reflection upon it, or even as a counterpoint to the music. The dance movement can be heavy or light, ponderous or airy, staccato,

---

[23] Ibid.　　[24] Ibid.

syncopated, conflicted, tense, or equilibrated, either in synch with musical movement impulses or in contrast to the feelings of motion issuing from the orchestra. But in any event, the dance activity may serve as a provocation for a succession of mirror responses, which, in turn, can palpably refine or accent our grasp of the evolving sense of movement as it emerges in concert with the suggestions of motion intimated in the musical score.

In the simplest cases, the dance movement functions as a translation from one medium to another—from the musical movement impulse into flesh and blood movement. For example, the slow, restrained, processional music of *Air for the G String* is realized by the stately, regal movement of Humphrey's dancers in her choreography of the same name to this piece by Bach. As the intuited musical lines of movement blend into each other cyclically, the accompanying dance phrases seamlessly interlace—the continuous feeling of the movement in the music captured in evenly flowing gestures whose energy vibrates quietly and softly inside the receptive viewer.

The dance, in examples like this, is, in effect, a performative interpretation of the movement impulses expressed by the music.[25] Just as a dramatic performance of a play is an interpretation of the text—one which draws out and makes evident some of its various qualities—so the performance of a piece of choreography can function as a further articulation and amplification of certain qualities that are inherent in or that supervene upon the music.

As we have seen, dance and music can be correlated across a number of dimensions. Thus, a choreo-performative interpretation of music can elect to make visible many different features of the music from the association of the sounds of various instruments with certain shapes, or even body types, to the imitation of musical movement (however that is explained). Of these dimensions of correspondence, of course, the ones that interest us most are those that involve the embodied translation of the musical motion impulses into moving choreographic forms and figures (for example, *climbing* toward a climax matched by a *grand jetée* which is then caught and frozen mid-air with dramatic finality). Or, as a musical phrase is passed sequentially from one group of instruments to another, a corresponding dance phrase moves from one group of dancers to the next.

A great deal of choreography is best thought of as a performative interpretation of the music that accompanies it. It is a *performative* interpretation, rather than a *critical* one, since it is a sensuous realization of the features of the music, rather than a propositional elucidation. It is an *interpretation*, at the very least, in that it selects only some of the features in the music for bodily emphasis instead of all of the features it could embroider through overt action. That is, as a matter of fact, no choreo-performative interpretation of music has, to our knowledge, ever attempted to visualize every element of its

---

[25] On the notion of performative interpretation, see Jerrold Levinson, "Performative vs. Critical Interpretation in Music," in Michael Krausz (ed.), *The Interpretation of Music: Philosophical Essays* (Oxford: Clarendon Press, 1993), pp. 33–60.

corresponding piece of music which could be illustrated, and, furthermore, perhaps no piece of choreography could. Choreo-performative interpretations are perforce selective practically and maybe even theoretically.

Moreover, the dances or parts of dances we have in mind are choreo-performative interpretations of *the music*, since they are about the musical experience (even if they are also involved in simultaneously advancing some story line, character trait, atmospheric mood, or theme). And lastly, undoubtedly related to their selectivity, a very large number of choreo-performative interpretations of the same piece of music are equally tolerable, since different interpretations of this sort may highlight different features of the music.

The choreo-performative interpretations we care about are those that cast into bold relief—those that literally give added dimensions to—the intimation of movement available in the music. Such choreo-performative interpretations realize the movement impulses of the music by finding bodily gestures and behaviors that correspond to or augment them. In this way, the dances make the impressions of movement proposed by the music more accessible and more perspicuous to audiences by providing the opportunity to us to fill them out or to color them further with the activity of our own mirror reflexes, as those are thrown in gear by the dance.

Of course, a dance may not just interpret the movement impulses expressed by the music by way of selectively imitating or echoing them. The dance may go beyond merely translating the intuited musical motions. The dance may expand upon the feelings of movement suggested in the music by either completing some sonic movement tendency in the music or by counter-pointing, complementing, supplementing, or evolving a contrast to it (as Balanchine does in *Agon* where the regular dance beat is posed against Stravinsky's jerky rhythms).[26] In any dance, the music may stop, and, in the silent interval, the dancers may stamp out a brace of steps that either resolves, subdivides, or colors what we have just heard. This too counts as a choreo-performative *interpretation*, inasmuch it goes beyond the musically given.

Mark Morris's *L'Allegro, il Penseroso ed il Moderato* is, first and foremost, a performative interpretation of the oratorio of the same name by Handel. Notice how in the second movement, initiated by the introduction of the male voice, the choral *entrances* are marked by the entrances of dancers; as more voices enter, more dancers enter. The leg movements imitate the orchestral ornaments. As the music delivers the impression of speeding up, the dancers appear, exaggeratedly, to be running in place exaggeratedly. Throughout the section, the music has a lively, highly animate character, ingeniously implemented by the dancers in a way that can touch viewers kinesthetically. When a *skipping* laugh rhythm punctuates the singing, two dancers bounce up and down like pogo sticks. Obviously, the audience does not follow suit precisely; we stay seated. But the receptive spectator also feels a ripple of that

---

[26] Marcia B. Siegel, *The Shapes of Change: Images of American Dance* (New York: Avon Books, 1979), p. 228.

enthusiasm swell in her legs, thereby integrating what she sees and hears in her own body, undoubtedly as a result of the synthesizing powers of the central nervous system. Of the piece in general, Joan Acocella observes "When the music, runs, plods, skips, sweeps, glides, meanders, so do the dancers"[27] whose gamboling we track as our own mirror reflexes are awakened.

## 3. Concluding remarks

The purpose of this chapter has been to place the aesthetic experience of one very prominent type of combination between dance and music in a philosophical frame-work ramified by speculations suggested by research in cognitive science. The frame-work we propose is a customized version of the expression theory. Needless to say, we are not endorsing the expression theory wholesale, but only helping ourselves to parts of it—and even those parts are being modified to suit our purposes.

The dancer nurtures the movement impulse she finds in the music—she visualizes, articulates, expands upon, completes, or otherwise develops it. The receptive viewer, moreover, is likewise involved in clarifying the feeling of movement she intuits in the music, but also takes advantage of the matching choreographic movement which further parses the musical movement impulses by energizing our mirror reflexes. The choreography functions to focus and define the feeling of movement which fixes the feeling in the receptive spectator and assists her in clarifying both it and the musical structures that prompt it.[28] Here the concept of clarification, inspired by the expression theory, is crucial. So let us try to suggest some of the components involved in the receptive viewer's experience. First of all, it is a participatory experience: the viewer makes an active response to the dance-cum-music, though part of that activity is automatic. In the process of response, the spectator's experience of the movement qualities become more articulate—the selectivity and emphasis of the choreo-perfor-mative interpretation afford a more simplified, inflected, oriented, and, therefore, more graspable characterization of the movement qualities than that which is available solely through the music. This abets the clarity of the experience by rendering it more coherent in outline.

But the dance not only makes the feeling of movement clearer. It also makes it more distinct, because it connects the aural impression of movement with a visual and kinesthetic image or interpretation of it. Thus, the dance quite literally makes the movement quality more concrete by embodying it externally. In this way, the impression of movement we imagine we hear in the music is integrated with our visual system, yielding a more embedded and unified experience than what may be procured

---

[27] Joan Acocella, *Mark Morris* (New York: Farrar, Straus, & Giroux, 1993), p. 241.
[28] In his "Dancing in the Seats," Daniel Levitin suggests that "Music can be a more satisfying cerebral experience if we let it move us physically." But even when we do not move, the movement impulses that course through our bodies via our mirror responses to the dancers serve to heighten our grasp of the music.

from the music alone. And in virtue of this unity—this integration of sight and sound—the receptive viewer develops a firmer hold on the relevant feeling of movement. Through reflecting upon these perceived motion impulses, the viewer may discover just which structural elements in the music are responsible for them, thereby deepening his grasp of the music itself.

Though with our emphasis on the spectator and our speculative invocation of cognitive science, it may seem that we have drifted far afield from any recognizable version of the expression theory, it should be noted that we have remained committed to one of the traditional aims of expression theories of various stripes. Such theories typically presume, as we do, that there are strata of human feeling for which we lack linguistic symbols and which we find virtually impossible to describe adequately with satisfying specificity. According to many expression theorists, the role of art is to find ways of grasping those feelings by other means—ways of marking them or showcasing them for reflection. On our view, that is one function that dance in consort with music discharges. It is a way of making the ineffable, if not effable, than, at least, a little more perspicuous.

# 20

# 'I'll Be Your Mirror'? Embodied Agency, Dance, and Neuroscience

*David Davies*

## I

When the Irish poet W. B. Yeats asked, 'How can we know the dancer from the dance?',[1] he traded for metaphorical effect upon a distinctive feature of dance as an art form. He could not have enquired, to similar effect, how we could know the painter from the painting, or the musician from the music, or even, for traditional theatre, the actors from the play. It is natural to characterize this distinctive feature of dance by saying that in the latter the performer uses her own body as the artistic vehicle through which an artistic content is articulated. Martha Graham, for example, wrote that the solitary aim of dance training has always been 'so to train the body as to make possible any demand made upon it by that inner self which has the vision of what needs to be said'.[2] It is because a dance seems to just be the movements executed by the dancer's body that we can raise the question posed by Yeats.

This is not to say that it is only in dance that the artistic content of works can be in part a function of what the artist does with her body. Jerrold Levinson, for example, contends that some of the expressive qualities of musical works depend upon the kinds of movements required of the musicians if they are to generate the designated sequence of sounds on the prescribed instruments.[3] And the notion of 'facture' in the visual arts—the visible indications in the artistic vehicle of how it was produced by the artist—provide the basis for something similar, as in the case of abstract expressionist canvases by painters like Jackson Pollock. In these cases, however, the expressive properties in question derive from the ways in which the artist manipulates a vehicular medium distinct from herself. In dance, on the other hand, it seems that the artist's own

---

[1] W. B. Yeats, 'Among School Children', in Peter Allt and Russell K. Alspach (eds.), *The Variorum Edition of the Poems of William Butler Yeats* (New York: Macmillan, 1965), pp. 443–6.

[2] Martha Graham, 'A Modern Dancer's Primer for Action', in Selma Jean Cohen (ed.), *Dance as a Theatre Art* (New York: Dodd, Mead, 1974), p. 139.

[3] Jerrold Levinson, 'Authentic Performance and Performance Means', in *Music, Art, & Metaphysics* (Ithaca, NY: Cornell University Press, 1990), pp. 393–408.

body serves as the vehicular medium through which the artistic content of her performance or of the work is articulated.[4]

However, Graham's way of characterizing the distinctive role of the body in dance carries with it certain philosophical preconceptions that can be challenged in light of empirical work on the relationship between agency, perception, and cognition. To suggest, as Graham does, that the dancer *uses* her body as an *instrument* is to subscribe implicitly to a 'dualistic' conception of the 'mindedness' of the human agent. On such a conception, the agent—or, in the present case, the dancer—is identified with the 'inner self' who is distinct from her body but able to act in virtue of her ability to make demands upon and control that body. The 'dualism' here is not Cartesian. It holds just as clearly if we identify the 'inner self' with something definable in neurological terms. It consists in the idea that the self stands in an instrumentalistic relation to the body. Such a dualism actually provides us with an easy answer to Yeats's question. The dancer, we can say, is the person responsible for those bodily movements that constitute the dance. And, in another sense of 'know', we can know the dancer from *observing* the dance by reading into the movements of the body the states of the 'inner self' that is directing those movements.

The instrumentalistic way of putting things seems very natural if, as Graham is doing, we consider what is involved in dance training and rehearsal. For, as she points out, dance training aims at providing the dancer with the ability to use her body in ways that are unavailable to those who lack such training, and this seems to require an instrumental conception of the relationship between the dancer and her body. The dance educator Margery J. Turner, for example, writes that

the human body, as the instrument of communication, has to transcend its personal limitations; it must be trained . . . to make neuromuscular discriminations; to sense degrees of action, textures, qualities . . . It must respond sensitively to the dancer's feelings and needs and to the demands of the choreographer.[5]

And a text on dance technique states that through the latter 'you learn how to control your body and make it your instrument'.[6]

Another philosophical tradition, however, appeals to work in cognitive and developmental psychology and cognitive neuroscience in questioning such a dualistic

---

[4] The position of the dancer *qua* performing artist might be compared here to the position of the ethnologist *qua* scientist. While scientists generally explore the world by manipulating different kinds of measuring instruments, the ethnologist who investigates the meanings of the behaviours of a culturally remote ethnological group is her own measuring instrument. On the challenges that this poses to the ethnologist's claims to be doing science, see Clifford Geertz, *Works and Lives: The Anthropologist as Author* (Stanford, CA: Stanford University Press, 1988).

[5] Margery J. Turner, *New Dance: Approaches to Nonliteral Choreography* (Pittsburgh: Pittsburgh University Press, 1971), p. 23.

[6] Sandra Minton, *Modern Dance: Body and Mind* (Englewood, CO: Morton, 1984), p. 3.

conception of human agency in general, and its application to dance in particular.[7] The French phenomenologist Maurice Merleau-Ponty, to whom many writers in this tradition trace their ideas, drew upon the cognitive sciences of his day to challenge the idea of the physical body as an instrument for the use of the mind/brain. We can express this challenge in two ways, which provide two perspectives on the same phenomenon. First, Merleau-Ponty maintained that the body itself is a 'lived body' whose engagements with the world are always inflected by the 'intentionality'—the purposes, projects, and perspectives—of the agent. The human body encounters objects in its world in ways that reflect both its capacities for embodied agency and the agent's intentionality. My hand shapes itself to grasp the glass in front of me without any explicit awareness on my part of its so doing, for example. This is what Merleau-Ponty termed 'primary consciousness', our embodied ability to negotiate our lived world successfully without the need for explicit awareness of that world. When we walk across a room to greet someone, we are conscious of what we are doing in terms of this purpose, with no explicit awareness of the ways in which we navigate around the furniture. The 'lived body' relies upon what can be termed a 'body schema', a system of sensory-motor capacities that function without conscious awareness or the need for perceptual monitoring. These capacities operate in ways that can be precisely shaped by our intentionality, as in the preceding examples.[8] The psychologist J. J. Gibson talks here of the 'affordances' in terms of which creatures like us perceive and interact with their environments, an 'affordance' being a way in which something fits with our projects and purposes given our physical capacities.[9]

Complementing such talk of the 'lived body' is talk of the 'embodied mind', whose cognitive and practical activities are structured by the intelligence of the lived body. In *How the Body Shapes the Mind*, Shaun Gallagher reworks the Merleau-Pontian project by drawing upon recent work in psychology and cognitive neuroscience. He argues that our conscious apprehension and understanding of the world depends on experiences that are informed in their very structure by *a body with various perceptual and motor capacities*. To understand our cognitive engagement with the world, Gallagher argues, we must focus not merely on the brain but also on the body understood as embedded within physical and social environments and situations that motivate thought and

---

[7] See, for example, Sondra Horton Fraleigh, *Dance and the Lived Body* (Pittsburgh: University of Pittsburgh Press, 1987); Maxine Sheets-Johnstone, 'Phenomenology as a Way of Illuminating Dance', in Sheets-Johnstone (ed.), *Illuminating Dance: Philosophical Explorations* (Lewisburg: Bucknell University Press, 1984); Richard Shusterman, *Body Consciousness: A Philosophy of Mindfulness and Somaesthetics* (Cambridge: Cambridge University Press, 2008). All of these texts draw upon Maurice Merleau-Ponty, *Phenomenology of Perception*, trans. Colin Smith (London: Routledge & Kegan Paul, 1962).

[8] See Merleau-Ponty, *Phenomenology of Perception*, and Shaun Gallagher, *How the Body Shapes the Mind* (Oxford: Oxford University Press, 2005), chapter 1.

[9] J. J. Gibson, *The Ecological Approach to Visual Perception* (Boston: Houghton Mifflin, 1979).

action. Relatedly, Richard Shusterman characterizes what he terms 'body consciousness' as 'the embodied consciousness that a living sentient body directs at the world'.[10]

On such a phenomenological picture of human cognition and agency, what sense can we make of the idea—central, as we have seen, to writings on dance training and dance technique—that the dancer trains her body as an instrument to be used to execute her artistic intentions in the dance? Writers sympathetic to the phenomenological account have addressed this question in different ways.[11] Sondra Fraleigh, for example, argues that, while there is an indissoluble lived unity of body and mind, it is possible, either in states of personal disintegration or through deliberate effort, for a person to take her physical body as an object, abstracting, in so viewing it, from its lived nature. She cites Merleau-Ponty, who writes of the body as 'the bearer of a dialectic' which can lead to a rupture in the lived unity of embodied agency:

Our body does not always have meaning, and our thoughts, on the other hand—in timidity, for example—do not always find in it the plenitude of their vital expression. In these cases of disintegration, the soul and the body are apparently distinct; and this is the truth of dualism.[12]

The dancer who wishes to train her body to perform must bring about such an objectification voluntarily. As she learns the dance, such a dualism

grows of necessity from an objectification of the body in rehearsal and performance through creative experiment with, and critical observation of, the body in motion. A psychic distance from the body is necessitated in the dialectical creative process of dance. It is significant, though, that such a phenomenal (or lived) duality is formulated upon a basic unity and according to intent, as existential phenomenology has held.[13]

# II

Gallagher's work, and work on dance that falls within the broadly Merleau-Pontian tradition, suggests how empirical work in psychology and neuroscience can bear indirectly upon our most fundamental assumptions about dance and the terms in which we describe what is going on in dance performance. As noted above, both Merleau-Ponty and Gallagher ground their claims about the 'lived body' and the 'embodied mind' in the empirical studies of their time in various areas of cognitive science. Gallagher, for example, draws upon a broad range of research in developmental psychology and cognitive neuroscience, including extended studies of pathological conditions such as acute sensory neuropathy in which he himself participated. If we

---

[10] Richard Shusterman, 'Body Consciousness and Performance: Somaesthetics East and West', *Journal of Aesthetics and Art Criticism*, 67/2 (2009): 133–45.

[11] We shall examine, below, Richard Shusterman's response to this question in his 'Body Consciousness and Performance'.

[12] Maurice Merleau-Ponty, 'The Relation of the Soul and the Body and the Problem of Perceptual Consciousness', in *The Structure of Behaviour*, trans. Alden L. Fisher (Boston MA: Beacon, 1963), p. 209.

[13] Fraleigh, *Dance and the Lived Body*, p. 13.

take our philosophical interest in dance to comprise questions about the nature of the artistic vehicle in dance and the ways in which the dancer is able to articulate an artistic content through her performance, where this involves an interest in her achievement in so doing, the bearing of this kind of empirical work on the philosophy of dance seems clear. In any case, I do not want to call this into question here. What does interest me are recent philosophical explorations within this tradition that draw upon a particular strand in contemporary research in cognitive neuroscience. Reflection on these 'case-studies' may, I think, help us to develop criteria to assess the legitimacy of appeals to such empirical resources in the attempt to answer questions in aesthetics.

Richard Shusterman raises questions similar to the ones canvassed above about how the phenomenological picture of the 'lived-body' can accommodate the kinds of demands made upon the performing artist both in training and in actual performance.[14] He acknowledges what he views as Merleau-Ponty's insight that, in our everyday dealings with the world, it is the spontaneous bodily intentionality of the 'lived-body' that enables us to successful negotiate our way around. In such contexts, explicit attention to our movements can get in the way of ordinary functioning, as when the bike rider thinks about exactly how she is propelling her vehicle and promptly loses her balance. But, Shusterman insists, while the 'habits' comprised by the 'lived body' play an essential part in human agency, these habits sometimes need to be corrected or refined if we are to flourish in our projects. The golf player, for example, needs to 'relearn' his swing when his spontaneous activity leads him to shank the ball to the left. In the same way, the dancer needs to 'train' her body so that its spontaneous activity achieves what she desires. This requires that she explicitly attend to the movements that her body is making in order to *change* the bodily intentionality that enables her to spontaneously generate such movements. Then, once she has 'retrained' her body, she can once again rely on spontaneous agency. Indeed, this is how we generally proceed in acquiring a bodily skill such as a new dance step.

Shusterman raises an interesting question, however. Is it possible to achieve such an explicit awareness of what one's body is doing—to in this sense treat one's body as an object—while also *exercising* the sort of embodied skill involved in the performing arts? Merleau-Ponty, as we have seen, thinks that such explicit awareness will hamper the exercise of the skill in question. Shusterman disputes this, however. He looks at the kind of training given both to dancers and to performers in Japanese Noh theatre. He argues that, for the skilled performer who trains herself properly, the best performances may involve both the exercise of a spontaneous embodied skill and an explicit awareness of what one is doing.

His argument however, as he acknowledges, draws in a speculative way on recent work in cognitive neuroscience, and in particular on work on so-called 'mirror neurons'. We should briefly say something about the latter before sketching

---

[14] Shusterman, 'Body Consciousness and Performance'.

Shusterman's argument.[15] Mirror neurons are neurons that are activated both by my execution of a given movement and by my observing another person executing the same type of movement. They play a crucial role in the explanations that some have offered of puzzling phenomena, such as the neonate's apparent ability to mimic facial expressions without any opportunity to visually observe its own face.[16] Mirror neurons, it is claimed, are involved in certain kinds of cross-modal neurological connections which 'translate' between our visual apprehension of the world and our acting on the world through our motor systems.

Shusterman appeals to mirror neurons in defending the possibility, proposed by Zeami Motokiyo, a renowned teacher of Noh theatre, that an actor, while acting, should not only 'look ahead' to see the other actors, the audience, and his place the full theatrical performance, but also 'look behind'. To 'look behind' is to 'see' how one appears to those spectators who are behind one, and to modify one's performances accordingly. Shusterman considers three hypothetical accounts of how such 'looking behind' might be possible. First, an actor might use literal mirrors, properly configured, to view his back in various postures, and note through proprioception how the different postures 'feel'. By associating different postures with their different feels, the actor could then infer how he looked from the back from how his posture felt. Second, an actor $A$ could enlist another actor $B$ to adopt various postures and could observe these postures from behind. The mirror-neuronal system would produce a firing of the same neurons in the observing $A$ as are firing in the posturing $B$, and this could generate in $A$ 'a proprioceptive feel of that action, a felt understanding that the actor could confirm perhaps by then imitating the posture and seeing whether his taking this postural attitude indeed produces this kind of proprioceptive feelings'.[17] The third possibility attempts, via a 'highly speculative and improbable' strategy, to make literal sense of Zeami's talk about the actor *seeing* himself as the audience views him from behind:

If proprioceptive feelings of posture could generate through mirror-neuron systems a corresponding visual input of that posture, then in principle someone very skilled in vivid proprioceptive awareness might be able to generate a visual image in his mind of how his posture would look . . . from his own proprioceptive self-observation of his posture or movement.

We need to say something briefly about proprioception, which plays a role in all three of Shusterman's scenarios. We noted above that Merleau-Ponty and Gallagher share a conception of the 'body schema', as the unconscious basis of spontaneous bodily

---

[15] Mirror neurons are discussed in a number of places in Gallagher, *How the Body Shapes the Mind*, esp. pp. 220–3. For recent critical reviews of the work on mirror neurons by some of the principal researchers in the field, see Vittorio Gallese, 'Motor Abstraction: A Neuroscientific Account of How Action Goals and Intentions are Mapped and Understood', *Psychological Research*, 73 (2009): 486–98; Giacomo Rizolatti and Corrado Sinigaglia, 'The Functional Role of the Parieto-Frontal Mirror Circuit: Interpretations and Misinterpretation206', *Nature Reviews*, 11 (2010): 265–74.

[16] See Gallagher, *How the Body Shapes the Mind*, chapter 3, for an argument to this effect.

[17] Shusterman, 'Body Consciousness and Performance', p. 142.

intentionality. This is to be contrasted with what Gallagher terms the 'body image', as a system of perceptions, attitudes, and beliefs pertaining to one's own body that are accessible to consciousness. In the case of both body schema and body image, a crucial role is played by proprioception, the means by which we obtain information about, and awareness of, the positions and movements of our own bodies. Proprioception operates by means of receptors situated throughout the body—in the tendons and ligaments, for example—which provide information to the brain as to how the body is disposed at any given moment. It is this information that enables the body schema to direct our actions in a monitored way without our being consciously aware of how this is being accomplished. More significantly in the present context, the same receptors that provide the *information* necessary for the operation of the body schema ('proprioceptive information') also provide us with an *awareness* of how our bodies are positioned, or how we are moving our bodies, at a given time ('proprioceptive awareness'). But—and this will be significant in the sequel—proprioceptive awareness is not an awareness of the proprioceptive information, but an awareness of the bodily state that is the source of the latter. This awareness is usually only at the periphery of consciousness, but it can be brought into focus when we deliberately attend to our bodies—when, for example, we close our eyes and concentrate on the position of our arms.

Barbara Montero has argued that proprioceptive awareness plays a crucial role in both dance performance itself and the appreciation of dance performance.[18] She argues, first, that proprioception can function as an aesthetic sense—a sense whereby we are able to grasp aesthetic properties of things. In this case, what we are able to grasp through proprioception are aesthetic properties such as the grace or beauty of bodily movements. Proprioceptive beauty and visual beauty are closely related but distinct aesthetic properties—proprioceptive beauty is a felt property of the movement that is not reducible to the ways in which, *qua* movement, it would aesthetically affect an observer. Rather, our judgements of visual beauty reflect our judgements of proprioceptive beauty and vice versa:

In some cases, one might proprioceptively judge that a movement is beautiful because one knows that the movements, if seen, would look beautiful. But in other cases one might visually judge that a movement is beautiful because one knows that, if proprioceived, this movement would feel beautiful.[19]

Dancers, Montero argues, can sense directly whether their movements possess such aesthetic qualities by the way those movements 'feel', without having to see, or imagine seeing, them.

---

[18] Barbara Montero, 'Proprioception as an Aesthetic Sense', *Journal of Aesthetics and Art Criticism*, 64/2 (2006): 231–42.

[19] Ibid., p. 236. One might also read Montero as saying that beauty is a uniform property of bodily movement that applies to certain movements on the basis of both their 'look' and their 'feel'. If we are only aware of one of these things, then our aesthetic judgements may be mistaken. I don't think anything hangs on this in the present context.

The claim that proprioception can be an aesthetic sense goes against a long tradition that has restricted our experiential access to the aesthetic properties of things, including artworks, to those senses that most obviously provide us with access to objects distant from us, namely vision and audition. Hegel, for example, claims that 'art is related only to the two theoretical senses of sight and hearing, while smell, taste, and touch remain excluded from the enjoyment of art'.[20] Montero argues, however, that proprioception, insofar as it can *mis*represent the disposition of my body—as in the case of 'phantom limb' experiences, for example—has the power to represent its object as being a certain way, and thus does not differ from vision and audition in this respect.

However, if proprioception were to be an aesthetic sense, this seems to imply that there are aesthetic properties of some artworks—dance performances—that are accessible only to a single individual—the performer herself. Montero argues, however, that proprioception gives the *spectator* the ability to experience proprioceptive aesthetic properties of the movements of others. Like Shusterman, she appeals here to mirror neurons. Her claim is that, when an appropriately qualified spectator observes a dancer executing a particular sequence of movements, the neurological activity in the spectator will mirror the neurological activity in the dancer. Thus, she argues, they can share a proprioceptive awareness of what it is to perform that sequence of movements, and thus a proprioceptive awareness of its aesthetic properties. An 'appropriately qualified' spectator, Montero suggests, must have had training in dance in order for the relevant mirror neurons to be activated in response to the dancer's movements.[21]

Both Montero and Shusterman admit that their theses are speculative extensions of the relevant current literature in neuroscience. But what constraints are there on such speculations if they are to advance our philosophical understanding of the performing arts? How far, we might ask, do they extend what has been established in the relevant neurological research, and how does this bear on the explanatory force of their accounts? Four kinds of concern might be identified:

First, one might be concerned that the work on visuo-motor mirror neurons was done on macaque monkeys, and has not been verified on human subjects. What has been verified in humans—indeed, it is difficult to see how this kind of research could be done on non-humans—is another kind of mirroring linking engaging in a given activity and imagining that one engages in that activity.[22] But the relationship between this work and the work on mirror neurons remains to be established. Nonetheless, it is generally agreed among those scientists who work on mirror neurons that mirror neurons do indeed operate in humans much in the way that they do in macaques. So I shall set aside this concern in the present context.

---

[20]  G. W. F. Hegel, *Aesthetics: Lectures on Fine Art*, 2 vols., trans. T. Knox (Oxford: Clarendon Press, 1975), cited in Montero, 'Proprioception'.

[21]  See Gallese, 'Motor Abstraction', p. 7, for a survey of research on the bearing of past motor experience on the operation of mirror neurons.

[22]  For example, Daniel Levitin's work on the imaginative activity of musicians, using the musician Sting as one of his subjects.

Second, and more significantly, the work that has been done on mirror neurons in macaques only applies to movements of the face and arms—in particular, various kinds of grasping behaviours. This makes sense in evolutionary terms given the importance of being able to mimic certain kinds of arm and facial movements, especially for the neonate. But clearly many of the movements that bear upon the aesthetic qualities of dance are leg movements. Here it seems that no parallel evolutionary story is likely to be forthcoming. This is not to say that there are not other kinds of 'mirror' systems that are more generally operative—for example, the system that relates action to the imagining of action. If imagining is a neural activity, it seems plausible that imagining performing a particular activity would activate those motor areas of the brain enlisted in the performance of that activity. But this isn't evidence for a broader range of visuo-motor mirrorings.

Third, and crucially, both Montero and Shusterman assume that the firing of mirror neurons in the observer of a given action provides the observer with proprioceptive *awareness* of that action, and not merely proprioceptive *information*. For Montero, this is essential to her argument for third-person knowledge of proprioceptive aesthetic properties. It is only if I am aware of those proprioceptively given qualities of the movement that form the supervenience base for the proprioceptive aesthetic properties that I can experience the beauty of the movement. And for Shusterman, this is an explicit assumption in his second strategy for explaining viewing from behind. In watching another adopt a posture, I am proprioceptively aware of how the posture feels, he maintains. But the experiments on mirror neurons provide no basis for this claim. First, we have no way of telling whether the macaques whose motor areas fire when given visual input of grasping behaviour 'feel' what it is like to grasp. Gallagher himself notes that there is no evidence linking mirror neuron activity to awareness: 'studies of mirror neurons are clearly studies of *non-conscious*, automatic processes that may or may not be experienced at a conscious level, although they surely shape conscious behaviour'.[23,24] Second, given the role that mirror neurons play in coordinating visual input and motor activity as part of 'primary consciousness', it isn't clear what purpose would be served by proprioceptive awareness, since the relevant coordination proceeds at the level of the body schema rather than the body image.[25]

Fourth, as we saw, Shusterman's third account of 'looking behind' requires that an actor's proprioceptive awareness of the particular posture that he adopts can stimulate his visual system to produce the (virtual) visual experience of seeing himself from

---

[23] Gallagher, *How the Body Shapes the Mind*, p. 221, stress in the original.

[24] Shusterman and Montero are not the only authors to posit proprioceptive awareness where it appears that we have no basis for positing more than proprioceptive information. Gallagher's own explanation of neonate imitation (*How the Body Shapes the Mind*, chapter 3) maintains that it requires ascribing proprioceptive awareness to the neonate, whereas it seems possible to explain all of the data purely in terms of proprioceptive information.

[25] Another problem for Shusterman's second scenario is that, according to the research on mirror neurons, it is goal-oriented activities such as grasping that trigger such neurons. It isn't clear that posture by itself will trigger mirror neuronal activity. See Gallese, 'Motor Abstraction'.

behind adopting that posture. However, all of the empirical evidence on mirror neurons runs in the opposite direction—from seeing someone perform a given action to activation of the motor circuits involved in the performance of that action. This is not a problem for Montero, for whom the claimed mirror-neuronal connections at least run in the 'right' direction. But it is a serious problem for Shusterman.

To be fair, he acknowledges this anomaly in his explanation, granting that there are no experimental studies that deal with proprioceptive generation of visual stimulation. He cites, however, an e-mail correspondence with Gallese where the latter grants the possibility in principle of proprioceptive stimulation producing stimulation in the visual areas of the brain. But, as Shusterman also concedes, this doesn't give us any basis for ascribing visual *awareness*, let alone clear visualization of a particular posture. Nor, indeed, does this deal with the need for the visual image to be perspectival, of the actor viewed from the back. The firing of the mirror neurons involved in observing an action is presumably not perspectivally coded, but reflects a classification of the bodily motions under some goal.[26]

We may feel that Montero's claims are less speculative than Shusterman's and have genuine explanatory value. After all, Shusterman's ventures into mirror-neuron territory are an attempt to show how something proposed by Zeami might be *possible*. There are no data here to be explained. In this respect, Shusterman's third scenario is more of a thought experiment than an explanatory appeal to empirical findings. The 'mirror neuron system' to which he appeals shows the possibility of literally 'seeing' one's back for creatures who have neurological capacities that we surely lack. But Montero's claims do seem to explain the admittedly anecdotal evidence of dance practice on which she draws. And it seems that it does, or should, make an aesthetic difference to one's ability to appreciate a dance that one has had training in the discipline. This would fit with our judgements in other areas of art. For example, we assume that painters are able to 'see' facture in paintings that escapes the eye of the untrained viewer, however aesthetically sensitive that eye, and that only a trained musician can properly appreciate the virtuosity of certain performers.

But it would be mistaken, I think, to find here grounds to endorse, even provisionally, Montero's proposed account of proprioception as an aesthetic sense that, through the operation of mirror neurons, provides us with access to proprioceptive aesthetic properties of a dancer's movements. For we can be sceptical about the idea of proprioception as an aesthetic sense of this sort, yet still uphold the idea that only one who has the relevant training in dance can properly appreciate dance performance. Such knowledge may be necessary to appreciate *what the performer has achieved*. If we think that the artistic achievement of the artist is one element entering into the artistic value of the artwork, then, just as a knowledge of the practice of painting is necessary to appreciate a painter's achievement, so a knowledge of dance technique might be

---

[26] See again Gallese, 'Motor Abstraction'.

necessary to appreciate the artistry demonstrated by the dancer in executing a given sequence of movements. While the spectator who has such a knowledge of dance technique may perhaps also experience a proprioceptive response to the observed movements of the dancer, this response is not itself relevant to the appreciation of the dance, but simply a consequence of something else that is—namely, the history of dance training.

Let me briefly draw some lessons as to the kinds of constraints that should govern the appeal to empirical work in our attempts to answer philosophical questions about the arts.

First, as our brief excursion into theories of the 'lived body' and the 'embodied mind' may have made clear, empirical work can bear crucially on our understanding of the arts when it supports one of a plurality of possible philosophical representations of our artistic practice. In this case, the 'embodied mind' view may provide us with a better conceptual framework than the 'instrumental' view of the body in terms of which to represent dance practice. Of course, empirical work cannot play this kind of role if a plurality of competing philosophical accounts are equally grounded in empirical evidence. And this is arguably the case in many philosophical debates about the arts where our interest is not in what we can do but in what we should do. Second, where we appeal to particular scientific theories in an aesthetic cause, as in the 'mirror-neuron' examples, caution is necessary. Obviously, we need to be sure that the theory in question is well respected by those working in the relevant branch of science, which does indeed seem to be the case with the work on mirror neurons in general. But, more crucially, we need to respect the scope of the empirical findings. This is the requirement that, I suggest, both Shusterman and Montero fail to meet.

# 21

# Music and Emotion: Psychological Considerations

*William Forde Thompson and Lena Quinto*

Music is experienced in many different contexts and its significance for human behavior is not always obvious. Music plays an important role in many social contexts such as weddings, funerals, and parties, but its appeal cannot be fully explained by such functions. Music affects us in ways that are personal and require psychological explanation: music energizes, surprises, soothes, delights, and otherwise shapes our emotional states. Research in cognition and neuroscience supports the idea that pleasure and emotions are key motivations for listening to music. Not only does music activate "pleasure centers" in the brain (Blood and Zatorre 2001), it can communicate and induce a range of powerful emotions (Juslin and Sloboda 2001).

This latter capacity—to communicate and induce emotional states—has been the subject of intense scientific investigation. Emotional interpretations and experiences of music are extremely common and play a significant role in our appraisals of music. Indeed, whenever emotions are evoked by stimuli, they are combined with appraisals of those stimuli occurring "on multiple levels of processing ranging from automatic and implicit to conscious conceptual or propositional evaluations" (Scherer 2005: 701). This pairing of emotion and evaluation occurs because, from a biological standpoint, stimuli that elicit emotional responses are (or were, at an earlier point in evolutionary history) relevant to the major concerns of the organism (Huron 2005).

The aim of this chapter is to provide a psychological explanation for the link between musical activity and emotional states. To the extent that aesthetic evaluations are motivated by and intertwined with emotional systems, our discussion contributes to a psychological account of musical aesthetics. However, we take for granted that aesthetic evaluations are based on more than gut feelings. The complex decision-making processes that lead people to assign *value* to phenomena reflect multiple considerations that extend beyond their emotional attributes and the emotional states they induce. For example, humans may be genetically predisposed to value images or sounds depicting or derived from adaptive contexts, such as healthy mates, safe environments, and food sources (Davies 2009). Artistic phenomena may also acquire value by virtue of "making special" the social patterns, conventions, and experiences that allow life to prosper (Dissanayake 2000). Nonetheless, behavioral and neuroscientific evidence indicates that emotional systems are always implicated in such preferences and appraisals of value (Damasio 1994; Lehrer 2009). As such, understanding the capacity of music to communicate and induce emotional states is an essential step in developing a psychological model of musical aesthetics.

A number of theories have been proposed to account for links between music and emotion but fundamental questions remain. Are there general principles that might account for the connection between music and emotion across cultures and historic periods or is musical significance unique to every time and place? Does music influence emotions directly or do cognitive and motor processes mediate this link? Can broad principles of human interaction account for connections between music and emotion?

We first discuss general theories of emotion and how they view the relation between emotion and cognition. We next discuss empirical evidence demonstrating that specific attributes of music are individually associated with distinct emotional interpretations, and may be manipulated by performers and composers to convey complex and dynamic emotional messages. We also describe empirical investigations that attempt to disentangle the contributions of cross-cultural and culture-specific associations between music and emotion. Finally, we introduce a recent body of theory and data concerning the cognitive-motor implications of music, and review an emerging framework for conceiving the link between music and emotion. This conception focuses on the capacity of music to resonate with psychological processes that function in human *synchronization*, and to elicit emotional effects related to these processes. Such effects may be particularly powerful because music accommodates synchronization on multiple levels, including movement (clapping, tapping), attention, and imagination (Livingstone and Thompson 2009; Overy and Molnar-Szakacs 2009). Effects arising from the motor system, in turn, may influence aesthetic judgments (Topolinsky 2010).

## 1. Emotion and cognition

The relation between emotion and cognition has been the subject of considerable debate, and views on the matter have informed psychological theories of music and emotion. Are emotions entwined with cognitive processes, such as reasoning, planning, and remembering, or is there a distinct emotional system that operates independently from "cold" cognition?

One view is that emotional and cognitive processes are independent of one another (Zajonc 1980). Goleman's (1995) concept of "emotional intelligence" implies two distinct types of intelligence: one rational and the other emotional. These two types of intelligence are presumed to operate independently and need not be consistent with one another. Research on implicit memory supports the idea that preferences do not depend on cognitive processing. For example, mere exposure to stimulus patterns (e.g., melodies, random dot patterns) can lead to increased preference for such patterns, even when there is no explicit recall of them (Zajonc 1980, 1984). Presumably, these unconscious preferences arise because previously encountered stimuli, even if they are not explicitly represented in memory, can still evoke a positively valenced emotion (for a psychological explanation of the mere exposure effect, see Huron 2006).

A second view is that emotional responses are the outcome of a sequence of cognitive processes in which features are coded, classified, and finally appraised. According to this *post-cognitive* conception, emotion is the end state in a causal chain of information processing in which an event occurs, followed by sensory registration, perceptual processing, and finally an appraisal. Emotions arise at the appraisal stage (Lyons 1980; Zajonc 1980).

A third view is that emotions are intertwined with cognitive processing. According to Damasio (1994, 1999), all images are infused with affective tags or "somatic markers" that link those images with emotional associations. Through experience, images and events become tagged with particular emotions. Somatic markers function to bias cognitive processing in a way that is maximally adaptive. For example, a person may decide against a course of action if the images associated with that course have a negative connotation. Somatic markers increase the efficiency of decision-making.

A connection between emotion and cognition is also assumed in a theory of emotion proposed by Carver and his associates (Carver and Scheier 2009). The model begins with the assumption that much of behavior, and hence cognition, is goal-directed and feedback-controlled. Feedback control describes the process by which psychological or physical acts are monitored, compared to a desired state (a goal), and adjusted to decrease the discrepancy between current and goal states. Emotional experiences are thought to arise as part of this feedback control process.

Whenever there is a gap between goals and outcomes, feedback mechanisms register the discrepancy and adjust plans accordingly. The registration of a discrepancy in itself does not generate an emotional experience; it is a neutral error signal that triggers behavioral adjustment. However, the unfolding pattern of adjustments that bring the system towards or away from goal alignment is experienced phenomenally as a positive or negative experience. From an adaptive perspective, such emotional consequences function to reinforce behavioral and psychological adjustments that bring an organism toward greater alignment with goals, and to extinguish adjustments that are ineffective or counter-productive to goal attainment. We will return to this model later, suggesting that its basic components and assumptions can account for some important emotional effects that arise when listening to music.

## 2. Empirical studies of music and emotion

Listeners are highly sensitive to the emotional aspects of music, and they have broadly convergent emotional interpretations of music. Results from a wide range of investigations over the past century suggest that the various attributes of music, such as intensity (loudness), tempo, dissonance, and pitch height, are strongly associated with emotional expressions. In particular, changes in any of these attributes are correlated with changes in emotional interpretation (Ilie and Thompson 2006) and affective experience (Husain, Thompson, and Schellenberg, 2002; Ilie and Thompson 2011; Thompson *et al.* 2001). Such attributes contribute to an emotional *code* that may be employed by composers and performers to communicate emotions in music, or by speakers when they communicate emotions in their tone of voice (Juslin and Laukka 2003).

One important cue is *tempo*. Melodies that are played at a slow tempo tend to evoke emotions with low energy such as sadness, whereas melodies that are played at a fast tempo tend to evoke emotions with high energy, such as anger or joy. To scientifically investigate the emotional significance of tempo, Hevner (1935) presented listeners with several pieces of classical music performed at slow (63–80 bpm) and fast (102–152) tempi. Listeners heard the performances and selected from a list of adjectives the terms that best described the character of each piece. Although the two versions of each piece were identical in all respects except tempo, the emotions implied by the two versions were strikingly different. The slow tempo performances were described using terms such as serene, calm, sad, tender, and dreamy, whereas those same pieces performed at a fast tempo were described using terms such as joyous, happy, exciting, and restless.

The emotional connotations of tempo might have been learned through passive exposure to the conventions of Western tonal music, but it is also possible that they reflect natural correlations that exist between pace and emotional states. Indeed, there is strong scientific evidence that the emotional consequences of manipulating acoustic attributes such as intensity and pitch height are not restricted to Western listeners or Western music but appear to tap into universal links between the auditory system and emotional responses. This evidence has emerged from two lines of research.

First, the emotional effects of manipulating such attributes in music overlap the effects of manipulating those same attributes in speech. That is, many of the attributes that comprise an emotional code in music are equally effective at communicating emotion by tone of voice, also referred to as the *supralinguistic* dimension of speech or *prosody*. Such findings implicate an emotional communication system that functions effectively across auditory domains (Juslin and Laukka 2003; Thompson and Balkwill 2010).

In support of this idea, Ilie and Thompson (2006) presented listeners with excerpts of instrumental music and spoken passages and asked them to evaluate the emotional connotations of each excerpt along three affective dimensions: valence (pleasant–unpleasant), energy arousal (awake–tired), and tension arousal (tense–relaxed). In both domains, excerpts were manipulated in intensity (loud and soft versions), rate (fast and slow versions), and pitch height (high-pitched and low-pitched versions). Two manipulations had strikingly similar emotional effects in the two domains: for both music and speech, increases in intensity led to reliable increases in both energetic and tension arousal, and increases in rate led to reliable increases in energetic arousal. Manipulations of pitch height had different emotional effects in music and speech, however, illustrating the importance of domain-specific emotional cues.

More recently, Ilie and Thompson (2011) extended this paradigm with longer excerpts of music and speech (7 minutes). In this case, the authors administered the *Profile Of Mood States* (POMS) to evaluate emotional *experiences* induced by the music and speech, and they also evaluated two types of cognitive skill: speed of processing and creative problem-solving. Once again, manipulations of intensity, pitch height, and tempo had overlapping emotional effects following exposure to music and speech. For example, for both music and speech, participants were more energetic after listening to fast stimuli than after listening to slow stimuli. Moreover, they were able to detect and respond to visual patterns more rapidly after listening to fast music or speech than after listening to slow music or speech. Thus, not only do attributes of music and speech communicate emotional messages; they induce emotional states and alter cognitive function.

Second, the emotional effects of manipulating acoustic attributes in Western music overlap with the effects of manipulating the same attributes in non-Western music. Although the significance of genre- and culture-specific emotional cues cannot be overstated, certain acoustic attributes may tap into deep-seated interactions between auditory and emotional neural areas, providing a source of cross-cultural emotional communication within the domains of music and speech prosody (Thompson and Balkwill 2010).

Balkwill and Thompson (1999) asked Western listeners to judge the emotional content of field recordings of Hindustani ragas, and to rate structural attributes in the music. Hindustani ragas were performed with the explicit intention to evoke specific emotions. Although listeners were unfamiliar with Hindustani music, they were able to decode emotional intentions. Ragas intended to convey joy/*hasya* were assigned high ratings of joy; ragas intended to convey sadness/*karuna* were assigned high ratings of sadness; and ragas intended to convey anger/*raudra* were assigned high ratings of anger. Judgments of emotion correlated with perceptions of musical attributes. For example, joy was associated with perceptions of fast tempo and sadness was associated with perceptions of slow tempo.

This ability to decode emotional intentions in unfamiliar music is not restricted to Western listeners. In another study, Balkwill *et al.* (2004) examined judgments by *Japanese* listeners of Japanese, Western, and Hindustani music. Again, listeners were sensitive to the intended emotion in Japanese, Western, and Hindustani music, and judgments were correlated with perceptions of musical attributes. As for Western listeners, joy was associated with perceptions of fast tempo and sadness was associated with perceptions of slow tempo.

These and other studies implicate the existence of an emotional code that is instantiated in music and speech and operates across cultures. Such evidence parallels the landmark studies by Ekman and his colleagues illustrating pan-cultural facial expressions of emotion (e.g., Ekman *et al.* 1969). Positive emotions are associated with smiling whether in Britain, China, Brazil, or the Congo, just as energetic emotional states are associated with rapid and high intensity speech or music.

## 3. Music as a multimodal emotional signal

When speaking or singing emotionally, emotional facial expressions and gestures are often combined with auditory signals of emotion, creating a powerful multimodal affective experience (De Gelder and Vroomen 2000; Thompson *et al.* 2008). Indeed, researchers are increasingly recognizing the important role of movement in the communication of emotion in music. Singers frequently use facial and body movements to reinforce or supplement emotional messages conveyed in music (Thompson *et al.* 2005). Visual cues associated with body movements may also nurture a sense of emotional connection between musicians and audience members (Kurosawa and Davidson 2005).

Body movements provide an important source of expressivity even in the absence of sounded music.

Davidson (1993) asked musicians to perform excerpts of music in a deadpan, projected and exaggerated manner while their performances were video recorded. Silent videos of these performances were then presented to experimental participants, who provided judgments of expressivity based on the visual information alone. Marked differences in body movements were observed between the deadpan and exaggerated performance conditions, and judgments confirmed that such movements provide reliable signals of expressivity.

Facial expressions also provide viewers and listeners with emotional information. Livingstone *et al.* (2009) recorded singers with motion capture or electromyography (EMG) as they imitated phrases of emotional singing. All singers were shown audiovisual recordings of sung phrases performed with happy, sad, or neutral emotional expressions and were asked to imitate these recordings. Singers made clear and reliable facial movements during their imitations, supporting the emotional message conveyed by the sonic dimension of vocal production. Empirical studies have confirmed that such facial movements significantly influence emotional interpretations of music (Thompson *et al.* 2005, 2008). Facial expressions provide a powerful supplement to vocal signals of emotion because they can occur not only during vocal production but also before and after it. Pre-production facial expressions and gestures function to *prime* the intended emotion for listeners, facilitating accurate interpretation and encoding. Post-production facial expressions and gestures reinforce a stable representation of the emotion that was conveyed during vocal production.

## 4. Theories of music and emotion

What features of music are capable of inducing emotional responses, and what is the basis for this capacity? Can specific properties of music trigger emotional responses?

If so, what are they? To date there is no one theory of music and emotion with which everyone agrees. A number of theories have been proposed to address such questions and include influential discussions by Aristotle, Charles Darwin, Suzanne Langer, Leonard Meyer, Peter Kivy, and many others.

One view considers music to contain a large number of "cues" that have referential properties, such that it is possible to identify various features that composers can use to communicate fairly specific emotional connotations (for a review, see Juslin and Laukka 2003). Cooke (1959) proposed that music consists of various melodic features and patterns that have recognizable emotional significance. He argued that composers draw on these features and patterns in order to capture the nuanced and dynamic emotions that they wish to express. In effect, music is viewed as a *language* of emotion, with melodic features signifying distinct emotions.

According to Cooke, melodic intervals—the pitch distance between two consecutive notes—provide a particularly important cue. An ascending major third interval (i.e., consecutive notes separated by four semitones) represents joy and triumph; an ascending major sixth (nine semitones) implies a longing for pleasure; the minor sixth (eight semitones) suggests anguish, and the augmented fourth (six semitones) connotes hostility and disruption. Cooke supported his arguments by examining the lyrics that accompany music, observing remarkable consistency in the adjectives that occur in conjunction with particular intervals. The interval of an ascending major third is typically accompanied by words describing positive emotions, whereas the interval of an ascending minor third is more often accompanied by words implying negative emotions.

According to this *language of emotion* perspective, associations between melodic intervals and emotions can be observed across cultures, so are not merely a quirk of Western tonal music. Although Cooke's theory represents a landmark in the study of music and emotion, there is little evidence that the melodic features he identified are consistently associated with specific emotional connotations across or within genres and historic periods. The main limitation of Cooke's theory appears to be that the emotional associations he proposed were too specific. His essential argument— that music can be broken down into a collection of auditory attributes that have emotional connotations—has considerable empirical support (for a review, see Juslin and Laukka 2003).

A second view focuses on the role of expectation in music (Huron 2006; Mandler 1984; Meyer 1956). Expectancy theories are powerful because they do not rely on a referential system for generating meaning. Anything acquires meaning if it is associated with something beyond itself. With designative meaning, symbols and referents are different in kind. Language has this feature in that words are different in kind than the objects and events to which they refer. With embodied meaning, symbols and referents are the same in kind. According to Meyer (1956: 35), "one musical event...has a meaning because it points to and makes us expect another musical event." Thus, the emotional power of music lies in the expectations that it creates in the listener. Music has the capacity to generate complex and nuanced emotions because it continuously deviates from our expectations.

According to Mandler (1984), such responses to music instantiate a more general biological response that occurs for all unexpected events. The ability to anticipate events is essential for human survival, and all behavior is guided by anticipatory responses. Failure to predict an event can be life-threatening, and hence leads to heightened arousal and increased attentional resources. Arousal alone does not fully define the emotional experience, however. It is a bodily reaction that includes increases in heart rate, breathing, and blood pressure to put an organism into a state of heightened alert or readiness. Following this bodily response is a process of appraisal that clarifies the precise nature of the emotion experienced. That is, emotional experiences of music reflect a process of appraising bodily reactions to fulfillments and violations of expected musical events. This idea draws from William James's view that "*the bodily changes follow directly the perception of the exciting fact,*" and "*our feeling of the same changes as they occur IS the emotion*" (James 1983 [1890]: 449). However, Mandler's theory focuses on physiological changes that occur in response to expectancy violations, and how music capitalizes on such expectancy effects.

In his ITPRA theory of musical expectancy, Huron (2006) extended the ideas proposed by Meyer and Mandler. He identified several ways in which expectations associated with music generate complex and nuanced emotions. Pre-outcome responses (feelings prior to an expected/unexpected event) include imagination and tension responses; post-outcome responses include prediction, reaction, and appraisal responses. *Imagination* entails contemplating future states and acting in a way that makes those states more likely if they are positive, and less likely if they are negative. *Tension* is an immediate physiological preparation for an imminent event and involves changes in arousal. *Prediction* is a transient state of reward or punishment that arises in response to the accuracy of expectation. *Reaction* and *appraisal* are emotional states that arise from assessments of the event itself independent of whether that event was anticipated. *Reaction* is a rapid "knee-jerk" process that occurs automatically and pre-attentively and activates bodily actions and/or visceral responses. *Appraisal* is more considered and need not be compatible with the reaction response.

A third view is that there are multiple mechanisms underlying the connection between music and emotion. For Juslin and Västfjäll (2008), music is capable of inducing emotion through expectancies, by directly stimulating the brain stem (a part of the brain that controls arousal and other basic functions), or by association with other emotional stimuli. The latter process of inducing emotion may be further broken down into associations with emotions themselves (classical or *Pavlovian* conditioning) and associations with events or stimuli which themselves have emotional connotations, including (a) past events (episodic memory), (b) visual imagery, and (c) the human voice.

The *multiple mechanisms* framework is an important theoretical advance because it identifies and differentiates possible mechanisms and provides suggestions for how each might be examined systematically. The framework highlights the importance of conditioned triggers of emotion in establishing links between music and emotion. Although associations can account for many emotional responses to music, they can occur for any type of stimulus and therefore have limited value as an explanation of the *unique* power of music to communicate or induce emotions. Of the remaining two mechanisms—expectancies and brain stem responses—we emphasize the former mechanism. Expectancies provide a rich and pervasive source of musical emotion, and may even account for some of the emotional effects associated with brain stem responses (Huron 2006; Krumhansl and Agnes 2008; Meyer 1956).

One of the most significant proposals by Juslin and Västfjäll (2008) is that *emotional contagion* underlies the link between music and emotion (see also, Davies 1980, forthcoming). Juslin and Västfjäll (2008) focused their discussion of this mechanism on the *voice-like* quality of certain melodies and instruments. In their view, emotional contagion is activated because at certain levels of processing, melodic patterns are registered as a "super-expressive" human voice (Juslin and Västfjäll 2008: 566). Thus, while excited individuals tend to speak rapidly and in a high-pitched voice, an exciting violin melody typically unfolds with much greater extremes in rate and pitch.

Other authors surmise that effects related to emotional contagion and mirroring are even more ubiquitous and, as such, may be relevant to many of the attributes of music, not just the voice-like qualities implied by melodies and instruments (Livingstone and Thompson 2009; Overy and Molnar-Szakacs 2009). An important instance of contagion effects is observed in behaviors that involve synchronizing with music. Synchronization is linked to the expectancies that are generated in music (Huron 2006). Physical responses, action tendencies, and mental events associated with music listening are manifestations of synchronization.

The construct of synchronization subsumes many of the issues surrounding music and emotion into a broader domain of inquiry. Synchronization in its most general sense is pervasive and essential to all human interaction, and depends on continuous and dynamic monitoring or "feedback" processes for its maintenance. Synchronization often entails physical movement (e.g., dancing, clapping, tapping, head nodding, ensemble performing), but it can also occur implicitly, that is, without overt movement. Implicit forms of synchronization include entrainment of attention with the dynamic properties of the music (e.g., rhythm, melodic accents), and alignment of mental representations with the unfolding musical structure (Jones 2009; Large and Jones 1999). According to Overy and Molnar-Szakacs (2009), the precision with which synchronization occurs is guided by activity in the *mirror neuron* system (a system of motor neurons that are activated when performing or observing an action).

Music can be construed as a technology that builds on the capacity of humans to synchronize with external sources. Its structure is optimally tailored to recruit and sustain mechanisms of synchronization. As argued by Carver and Scheier (2009), it is reasonable to surmise that emotional responses arise as experiential manifestations of feedback processes for synchronization. In this view, the error signals and appraisal processes arising from feedback loops for effective synchronization—which are engaged and manipulated so effectively by music—are manifested phenomenologically as feelings of emotion. However, just as the relation between expectancy and affect is complex and must be theoretically unpacked (Huron 2006), so too are the affective consequences of feedback processes in synchronization, and their intricate relation to musical structure and performance. We now elaborate on some of the assumptions of this model.

## 5.  Synchronization as a pervasive construct

Although we celebrate the many differences between people, from a biological standpoint such differences are a source of tension and, presumably, are responsible for much of human conflict. Counteracting this tension is a fundamental instinct to assimilate with others and our environment. This process of assimilation takes many forms, including instinctive mimicry of other people. Synchronization of behaviors is an extreme form of assimilation and has received relatively little attention by researchers. In contrast, mimicry has been vigorously examined in social psychology and is thought to nurture a sense of similarity with other people (Chartrand and Dalton 2009). More generally, mimicry leads to improved social interactions, rapport, empathy, and bonding. It extends from simple actions such as yawning to complex behaviors that can be analyzed on psychological, social, political, and economic levels.

Mimicry refers to a set of behaviors whereby interacting individuals adopt similar speech patterns, bodily positions, gestures, and mannerisms. For example, individuals who are having a conversation tend to use the same words and clauses as their interaction partners, even when other words and clauses could just as easily be used (Levelt and Kelter 1982). They also tend to adjust their bodies to increase postural congruence, and they adopt similar mannerisms to their interacting partners. The logic and flow of human interaction and communication prohibit full synchronization of actions and vocal patterns, but the instinct to assimilate pushes in that direction. Many psychological, social, economic, and political phenomena can be viewed as a compromise between the instinct for synchronization and the constraints of goal achievement in human–environmental interactions.

The discovery of *mirror neurons* suggests a possible neural basis for this instinct (Iacoboni *et al.* 1999; Koski *et al.* 2002). Brain-imaging techniques have revealed that certain cortical regions are automatically activated when people empathize with others. Nummenmaa *et al.* (2008) showed threatening and neutral images to participants, who rated their emotional reactions to those images. Threatening images portrayed an attacker and a victim. Neutral images portrayed a benign social exchange between two individuals. As expected, participants reported experiencing negative emotional reactions to threatening scenes. Participants were also asked to imagine what it felt like to be one of the individuals depicted in the images. During this empathy phase of the experiment, changes in blood flow to regions of the brain were recorded with functional magnetic resonance imaging (fMRI). When participants empathized with others in emotionally charged situations, activation was observed in brain areas associated with facial and gestural processing, as well as the premotor mirror-neuron area. Activation of such areas may help individuals to coordinate their actions in emotionally charged contexts.

What are the benefits of a tendency to synchronize actions with others? Early theories posited that mimicry functions to nurture understanding and togetherness which lead to social benefits. However, mimicry and synchronization can also be observed in individuals who are alone, for example as they are watching a video or listening to music. When individuals hear pleasant music in isolation, they automatically exhibit activity in the zygomatic muscle—a muscle associated with the expression of a smile. Conversely, listening to unpleasant music leads to greater activation of the corrugator muscle—a muscle associated with a frown (Lundqvist et al. 2009). If mimicry and synchronization serve social goals, why would mimicking behavior occur in lone individuals? One interpretation is that the tendency to mimic others occurs automatically as part of a hard-wired perception–action link.

Originally proposed by James (1890), *ideomotor theory* suggests that the act of thinking about an action increases the likelihood of that action. Extending this idea, Prinz and his colleagues proposed *common-coding* theory (for a review, see Prinz et al. 2009). According to this view, perceiving events and planning actions are accomplished through shared neural resources, resulting in a common representational domain for perception and action (Prinz 1990, 1997). More specifically, action is represented in terms of its perceivable effects, and these representations generate observable behavior once a certain threshold of neural activation is reached.

Research on mirror neurons implies that common-coding theory is not merely a functional model but is instantiated in individual neurons in the brain. It has also been speculated that such a system has adaptive value (Chartrand and Dalton 2009). If members of a group of hominids suddenly start running for the hills, an individual with a built-in perception–action link who instinctively synchronizes her behavior with the group activity will likely survive a charging predator. Survival is less likely for an individual who evaluates the situation, scans the environment for possible sources of sprinting behavior, and rationally decides on the most sensible course of action. In short, a synchronization instinct, undergirded by rapid and automatic perception–action links, may have deep evolutionary roots because of its survival value. Although such an instinct is no longer needed to avoid predators, its genetic encoding means that effects related to synchronization persist, permeating all levels of modern society. As we will argue below, they are especially relevant to musical behaviors and the emotional effects they proffer.

Musical synchronization can occur in obvious ways, such as choral singing, ensemble performance, clapping or tapping in response to music, and dancing to music. In line with common-coding theory, however, synchronization also occurs at the level of attention and imagination. Common-coding theory implies that the perception of any action-based event will also trigger mental representations of those actions. Because actions are required to produce all musical sounds, it stands to reason that the perception of music will result in representations of possible actions for producing such musical sound. For musically trained listeners, these may include representations of specific actions associated with the details of music performance. For other listeners, performance actions are less specified but still function to predict events along the multiple dimensions of time and pitch. For example, hearing an electric guitar may increase the likelihood of simulating the act of playing guitar ("air guitar"). The details of such action-representations will depend, however, on one's experience and knowledge of the electric guitar. In any case, the result is synchronization with music.

Rhythmic expectancies—predictions about temporal location—are associated with a tendency to synchronize movements with stress points in time. The accuracy and complexity of rhythmic synchronization vary with music training and experience. It is also possible to synchronize with non-temporal features of music, however, by forming mental representations of those features to coincide with their occurrence. When engaged in musical behaviors, including music listening, synchronization can occur in several ways that afford a degree of tight behavioral and perceptual coupling that is not possible with most if not all other stimuli. That is, music is unique in its capacity to permit precise and sustained synchronization. Synchronization is permitted because of the strong use of rhythm, but can also occur for other dimensions of music.

Overy and Molnar-Szakacs (2009) proposed a framework for explaining emotional responses to music called *Shared Affective Motion Experience*, or SAME. They emphasize that music is perceived not only as sound but also in terms of the intentional, hierarchically organized sequence of the motor acts that are required to produce the signal. Auditory features are processed in the superior temporal gyrus and are combined with movement information in the mirror neuron system. The anterior insula then connects the mirror neuron system with the limbic system, ultimately allowing a neural mapping of acoustic input onto an emotional state (see also, Carr *et al.* 2003). Depending on the listener's musical experience, they will extract differing degrees of motor information, ranging from a broad intentional level for untrained listeners to the muscular level for highly trained performers.

What is the process by which mirror neuron responses are mapped onto affective experience? Why is this mapping particularly potent for music? Overy and Molnar-Szakacs surmise that music is powerful because of its capacity for *minimized prediction error*, where prediction is a prerequisite for synchronization. They note that, "familiar, predictable music can be enjoyed to the fullest" whereas "the violation of expectancies can be more emotionally dramatic" (Overy and Molnar-Szakacs 2009: 494). In addition, they argue that movements used to produce music often reflect emotional states, and these states can be induced in the listener by a process of emotional contagion. We share many of these ideas, and propose that feedback control may provide a bridge between the tendency to synchronize our movements, attention, and imagination with music and the tendency to experience music as a powerful emotional stimulus.

# 6. Synchronization guided by dynamic feedback control

If music engages the instinct for synchronization, how is synchronization sustained? How are errors in synchronization corrected? Although the underlying mechanisms of synchronization remain to be fully understood, the changing nature of sensory input in general and music in particular means that synchronization requires feedback control mechanisms that continuously register discrepancies between actions and events and transmit signals to initiate a dynamic process of correction.

According to Carver and Scheier's (2009) model of emotion, all signals arising from feedback control mechanisms are experienced as feelings of emotion. Feedback about goal-directed behavior can account for a wide range of affective experiences, from joy or relief after attaining a goal to frustration, sadness, or anger when attempts to achieve goals are thwarted. Emotional experiences arise whenever the attainment of a desired condition or the avoidance of an undesired condition is facilitated or impeded. In the case of active music listening, an implicit goal is synchronization with the music (and/or other participants in the musical activity) in movement, attention, and imagination. What is unique about music is that it instantiates goal-directed behavior in the form of an especially tight coupling of action–attention–imagination with perceptual input: synchronization. This potential for detailed and accurate synchronization is carefully controlled and manipulated by composers and performers and requires continuous and rapid feedback control for its maintenance.

A feedback control mechanism has four components: an input, a reference value, a comparison, and an output (Carver and Scheier 2009; Mackay 1966). The input is the perception of target points of synchronization whereas the reference value is the goal of aligning behavior to these target points. The comparison is a measure of the degree of alignment, also called the "error signal." The output is an adjustment in response to the detected error. If the comparison process detects no error, current behavior is unchanged. Synchronization feedback is always controlled by discrepancy-reducing loops, so if a discrepancy is detected, behavior is adjusted to diminish the discrepancy.

Musical synchronization can occur on many levels, from activities that mirror the surface or tone-to-tone details of music to social forms of synchronization that account for musical movements. Some levels of synchronization are defined by simple action sequences such as tapping or clapping to the beat. Other levels are defined by brief action sequences such as singing along with a familiar phrase of music. Still other levels are characterized by synchronized social and economic behaviors such as attending concerts and purchasing musical products. Ultimately, all synchronization is related to action, but it can also occur with no observable bodily movement.

Synchronization also occurs at the level of attention (Jones 2004, 2009; Jones and Boltz 1989; Large and Jones 1999). Dynamic attending theory (DAT) defines *entrainment* as a biological process that leads to synchronization between mechanisms that control our attention and unfolding environmental events. These mechanisms are driven by oscillations of neural activation. Neural oscillations readily entrain to temporally regular patterns such as music that has a steady beat, but they may also guide the timing of attention for all biologically significant environmental phenomena that are potentially predictable. When listening to music, time spans at a metric level elicit a neural oscillation that has an internal periodicity that aligns with that metric level. In this way, neural oscillations "tune into" temporally predictable events by adjusting their phase in response to entrainment feedback (Jones 2009). Although attentional synchronization need not entail observable movement, it is a prerequisite for action synchronization. When attentional synchronization occurs without overt action, it may be viewed as an *action tendency* aimed at synchronization (see also, Frijda 1986).

## 7. Feedback and affect

Affective states are generated in response to goals and whether or not they are attained. When the achievement of a significant goal is thwarted, we may feel sad or frustrated. When an important goal is met we may feel a sense of relief or joy. Such feelings reflect the operation of feedback processes for goal-directed behavior. Carver and Scheier (2009) identify two processes that operate to assist with goal-directed behavior. The first is a behavior-guiding feedback process that registers error signals and acts to correct that error. The second is a feedback loop that monitors discrepancy reduction over time, essentially supervising the first process. Mathematically, the output from the second feedback loop is equivalent to the derivative of the output from the first feedback process. The simultaneous operation of both feedback systems, one controlling position and the other controlling velocity, allows for rapid and effective control of goal-directed behavior.

Figure 21.1 illustrates the model. The figure shows that acoustic input and perceptual analysis lead to processes by which perceivers synchronize their mental and physical state with the input. Synchronization occurs on motor, attentional, and imaginative levels and is guided by the behavior-guiding and monitoring feedback-control mechanisms described above. Experiences associated with the behavior-guiding process are equivalent to the tension and prediction responses identified by Huron (2006) in his ITPRA theory of expectancy. In the tension response, an arousal response is elicited as a target point of synchronization is approached, and the intensity of that arousal varies with the imminence, rate of approach, and significance of the point of synchronization. Changes in basic parameters of the acoustic input such as intensity (loudness) and tempo influence the tension response by altering the perceived significance of points of synchronization and the rate at which they are approached. In the prediction response, positive or negative feedback arises depending on whether

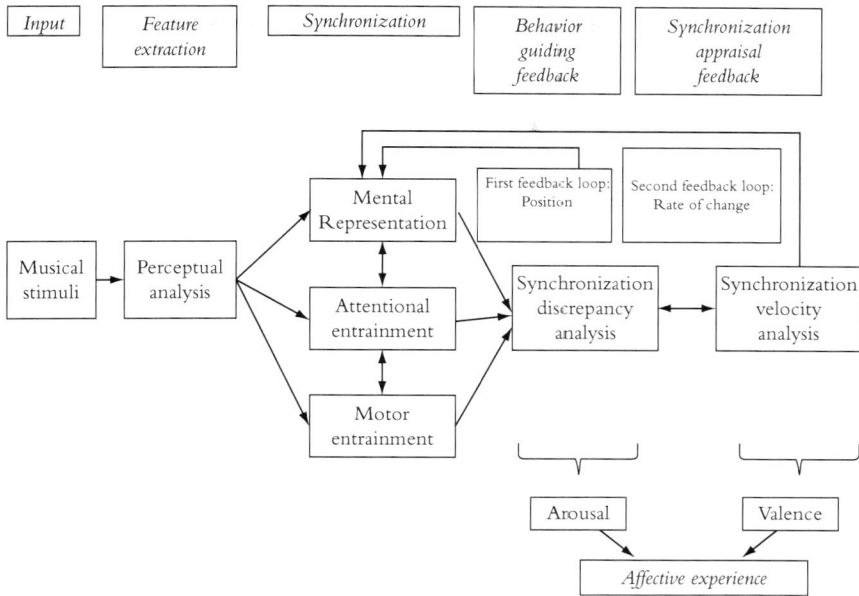

Figure 21.1 An illustration of the synchronization feedback model

synchronization with the target event is correctly aligned. Positive feedback rewards and reinforces alignment with the target; negative feedback motivates increased effort in synchronization.

The second *monitoring* feedback process is also manifested by affective experience. Specifically, if the system determines that there is an increase in the accuracy of synchronization over time, positive feedback results. If the system determines that there is a decrease in the accuracy of synchronization over time, then negative feedback results. The intensity of this second feedback signal is influenced by the significance and rate of increase or decrease in synchronization, which are determined by basic parameters of the acoustic signal. Thus, there are two sources of affective experience generated by feedback loops in synchronization. Moment-to-moment *arousal* and *reward* generated by the (first) behavior-guiding feedback process are combined with positive or negative experiences (*valence*) generated by the (second) monitoring feedback process.

On first glance, such a proposal might appear to be restricted in scope. After all, how often do we synchronize our actions with music, and can feedback mechanisms account for the subtleties of emotional responses to music? Although this is a valid concern when only one level of synchronization is considered (e.g., clapping to music), synchronization takes place along several dimensions and multiple levels of analysis. Synchronization at the level of the tactus—the pulse of the music—may generate only subtle effects when considered in isolation. However, the effects of metric synchronization must be considered in conjunction with higher-order rhythmic levels on which synchronization occurs, and with synchronization effects for other dimensions of the music, including melodic, harmonic, tonal, and phrasing structure. These immediate synchronization effects of music then interact with social synchronization effects that permeate and shape the political economy of music.

Because synchronization relies on prediction and expectation, it follows that any type of emotional response that can be explained by *expectancy mechanisms* can also be explained by synchronization feedback. As demonstrated by Meyer (1956), Huron (2006) and others, the unfolding patterns of violations and fulfillments of expectations that occur while listening to music can account for powerful and complex emotional responses, especially when multiple levels of expectancy are considered simultaneously. As an example, the experience of "awe" may be evoked when low-level violations of expectancy, which generate arousal responses, combine with high-level fulfillments of expectancy, which generate feelings of reassurance. As an analogy, standing at the edge of the Grand Canyon may generate a visceral elevation of arousal because of low-level links between visual perception and brain stem responses, mixed with high-level feelings of reassurance generated by an appraisal of the circumstances as non-life threatening. The combination of feedback from multiple levels of processing generates the emotion of awe.

It is important to note that feedback processes for human synchronization cannot account for all emotional responses to music. The model ignores responses to music that arise from learned associations between music and emotion, or other *mediated* responses. A composition may induce an emotional or aesthetic response because it reminds us of a death or a birth, or lends itself to social and political analyses, or because of its sheer artfulness. These responses are not produced directly by the music but are mediated by associations or cognitive appraisals. In other words, music is not the *object* of these emotional reactions. Such emotional experiences may be powerful but they are not generated directly from the music, and are not our focus.

Instead, our account combines arguments and evidence derived from psychological discussions and investigations of emotions, including Juslin and Västfjäll (2008), Jones (2009), Huron (2006), Carver (Carver and Scheier 2009), Overy and Molnar-Szakacs (2009) and others. We suggest that the unique power of music to elicit emotion lies in its capacity to engage participants in tightly controlled synchronization at multiple levels of abstraction. Music optimally recruits processes of synchronization that are ubiquitous in human behavior and that greatly influence our emotional lives.

## References

Balkwill, L.-L., and W. F. Thompson (1999). A cross-cultural investigation of the perception of emotion in music: Psychophysical and cultural cues. *Music Perception*, 17: 43–64.

——and R. Matsunaga (2004). Recognition of emotion in Japanese, Western, and Hindustani music by Japanese listeners. *Japanese Psychological Research*, 46/4: 337–49.

Blood, A. J. and R. J. Zatorre (2001). Intensely pleasurable responses to music correlate with activity in brain regions implicated in reward and emotion. *Proceedings of the National Academy of Sciences of the United States of America*, 98/20: 11818–23.

Carr, L., M. Iacoboni, M. C. Dubeau, J. C. Mazziotta, and G. L. Lenzi (2003). Neural mechanisms of empathy in humans: A relay from neural systems for imitation to limbic areas. *Proceedings of the National Academy of Sciences of the United States of America*, 100/9: 5497–5502.

Carver, C. S. and M. F. Scheier (2009). Action, affect, and two-mode models of functioning. In E. Morsella, J. A. Bargh, and P. M. Gollwitzer (eds.), *Oxford Handbook of Human Action*. Oxford: Oxford University Press, pp. 298–327.

Chartrand, T. L. and A. N. Dalton (2009). Mimicry: It's ubiquity, importance, and functionality. In E. Morsella, J. A. Bargh, and P. M. Gollwitzer (eds.), *Oxford Handbook of Human Action*. Oxford: Oxford University Press, pp. 458–86.

Cooke, D. (1959). *The Language of Music*. London: Oxford University Press.

Damasio, A. R. (1994). *Descartes' Error: Emotion, Reason, and the Human Brain*. New York: Avon Books.

——(1999). *The Feeling of What Happens: Body and Emotion in the Making of Consciousness*. New York: Harcourt Brace.

Davidson, J. W. (1993). Visual perception of performance manner in the movements of solo musicians. *Psychology of Music*, 21: 103–13.

Davies, S. (1980). The expression of emotion in music. *Mind*, 89: 67–86.

——(2009). Life is Passacaglia. *Philosophy & Literature*, 33: 315–28.

——(forthcoming). Music-to-listener emotional contagion. In Tom Cochrane, Bernadino Fantini, and Klaus Scherer (eds.), *The Emotional Power of Music*. Oxford: Oxford University Press.

de Gelder, B. and J. Vroomen (2000). Perceiving emotions by ear and by eye. *Cognition and Emotion*, 14: 289–311.

Dissanayake, E. (2000). *Art and Intimacy: How the Arts Began*. Seattle: University of Washington Press.

Ekman, P., E. R. Sorenson, and W. V. Friesen (1969). Pan-cultural elements in facial displays of emotions. *Science*, 164: 86–8.

Frijda, N. (1986). *The Emotions*. Cambridge: Cambridge University Press.

Goleman, D. (1995). *Emotional Intelligence*. New York: Bantam Books.

Hevner, K. (1935). The affective character of the major and minor modes in music. *American Journal of Psychology*, 47: 103–18.

Huron, D. (2005). The plural pleasures of music. In William Brunson and Johan Sundberg (eds.), *Proceedings of the 2004 Music and Music Science Conference*. Stockholm: Kungliga Musikhögskolan Förlaget, pp. 65–78.

——(2006). *Sweet Anticipation: Music and the Psychology of Expectation*. Cambridge, MA: MIT Press.

Husain, G., W. F. Thompson, and E. G. Schellenberg (2002). Effects of musical tempo and mode on arousal, mood, and spatial abilities: Re-examination of the "Mozart effect." *Music Perception*, 20: 151–71.

Iacoboni, M., R. P. Woods, M. Brass, H. Bekkering, J. C. Mazziotta, and G. Rizzolatti (1999). Cortical mechanisms of human imitation. *Science*, 286: 2526–8.

Ilie, G. and W. F. Thompson (2006). A comparison of acoustic cues in music and speech for three dimensions of affect. *Music Perception*, 23: 319–29.

——————(2011). Experiential and cognitive changes following seven minutes exposure to music and speech. *Music Perception*, 28: 247–64.

James, W. (1983 [1890]). *The Principles of Psychology*, with introduction by George A. Miller. Cambridge, MA: Harvard University Press.

Jones, M. R. (2004). Attention and timing. In J. G. Neuhoff (ed.), *Ecological Psychoacoustics*. San Diego, CA: Academic Press, pp. 45–89.

——(2009). Musical time. In S. Hallan, I. Cross, and M. Thaut (eds.) *Oxford Handbook of Music Psychology*. Oxford: Oxford University Press, pp. 81–92.

——and M. Boltz (1989). Dynamic attending and responses to time. *Psychological Review*, 96: 459–91.

Juslin, P. N. and P. Laukka (2003). Communication of emotions in vocal expression and music performance: Different channels, same code? *Psychological Bulletin*, 129: 770–814.

——and J. A. Sloboda (eds.) (2001). *Music and Emotion: Theory and Research*. Oxford: Oxford University Press.

——and D. Västfjäll (2008). Emotional responses to music: The need to consider underlying mechanisms. *Behavioral and Brain Sciences*, 31: 559–75.

Koski, L., M. Iacoboni, M. C. Dubeau, R. P. Woods, and J. C. Massiotta (2002). Modulation of cortical activity during different imitative behaviors. *Journal of Neurophysiology*, 89: 460–71.

Krumhansl, C. L. and K. R. Agnes (2008). Musical expectancy: The influence of musical structure on emotional response. *Behavioral and Brain Sciences*, 31: 584–5.

Kurosawa, K. and J. W. Davidson (2005). Non-verbal interaction in popular performance: The Corrs. *Musicae Scientiae*, 19/1: 111–36.

Large, E. W. and M. R. Jones (1999). The dynamics of attending: How we track time-varying events. *Psychological Review*, 106: 119–59.

Lehrer, J. (2009). *The Decisive Moment: How the Brain Makes Up Its Mind*. Melbourne, Australia: The Text Publishing Company.

Levelt, W. J. M. and S. Kelter (1982). Surface form and memory in question answering. *Cognitive Psychology*, 14: 78–106.

Livingstone, S. R. and W. F. Thompson (2009). The emergence of music from the Theory of Mind. *Musicae Scientiae*: 83–115.

Livingstone, S., W. F. Thompson, and F. A. Russo (2009). Facial expressions and emotional singing: A study of perception and production with motion capture and electromyography. *Music Perception*, 26: 475–88.

Lundqvist, L.-O., F. Carlsson, P. Hilmersson, and P. N. Juslin (2009). Emotional responses to music: experience, expression, and physiology. *Psychology of Music*, 3/1: 61–90.

Lyons, W. (1980). *Emotion*. Cambridge: Cambridge University Press.

Mackay, D. M. (1966). Cerebral organization and the conscious control of action. In J. C. Eccles (ed.), *Brain and Conscious Experience*. Berlin: Springer-Verlag, pp. 422–45.

Mandler, G. (1984). *Mind and Body: Psychology of Emotion and Stress*. New York: Norton.

Meyer, L. B. (1956). *Emotion and Meaning in Music*. Chicago: University of Chicago Press.

Nummenmaa, L., J. Hirvonen, R. Parkkola, and J. K. Hietanen (2008). Is emotional contagion special? An fMRI study on neural systems for affective and cognitive empathy. *NeuroImage*, 43: 571–80.

Overy, K. and I. Molnar-Szakacs (2009). Being together in time: Music experience and the mirror neuron system. *Music Perception*, 26: 489–504.

Prinz, W. (1990). A common coding approach to perception and action. In O. Neumann and W. Prinz (eds.), *Relationships Between Perception and Action: Current Approaches*. Berlin: Springer, pp. 167–201.

——(1997). Perception and action planning. *European Journal of Cognitive Psychology*, 4: 1–20.

——G. Ashersleben, and I. Koch (2009). Cognition and action. In E. Morsella, J. A. Bargh, and P. M. Gollwitzer (eds.), *Oxford Handbook of Human Action*. Oxford: Oxford University Press, pp. 35–71.

Scherer, K. R. (2005). What are emotions? And how can they be measured? *Social Science Information*, 44/4: 693–727.

Thompson, W. F. and L.-L. Balkwill (2010). Cross-cultural similarities and differences. In Patrik Juslin and John Sloboda (eds.), *Handbook of Music and Emotion: Theory, Research, Applications*. Oxford: Oxford University Press, pp. 755–88.

——P. Graham, and F. A. Russo (2005). Seeing music performance: Visual influences on perception and experience. *Semiotica*, 156/1–4: 203–27.

——F. A. Russo, and L. Quinto (2008). Audio-visual integration of emotional cues in song. *Cognition & Emotion*, 22/8: 1457–70.

——E. G. Schellenberg, and G. Husain (2001). Mood, arousal, and the Mozart effect. *Psychological Science*, 12/3: 248–51.

Topolinsky, S. (2010). Moving the eye of the beholder: Motor components in vision determine aesthetic preference. *Psychological Science*, 21/9: 1220–4.

Zajonc, R. B. (1980). Feeling and thinking: Preferences need no inferences. *American Psychologist*, 35: 151–75.

——(1984). On the primacy of affect. *American Psychologist*, 39: 117–23.

# 22

# Cross-Cultural Musical Expressiveness: Theory and the Empirical Programme

*Stephen Davies*

## I

Psychologists have described a set of six basic affect programmes: those for fear, anger, happiness, sadness, surprise, and disgust (Ekman 1992). Affect programmes are characterized as involving appraisals, affective states, and distinctive behavioural displays of these. They are programmatic in being automatically triggered and universal.

We should be careful not to equate affect programmes with full-blooded emotions. Affect programmes are common, perhaps even necessary, elements in emotional episodes of happiness, disgust, and the like, but there can be more to these emotions, especially cognitively, than is covered by the affect programme. Moreover, emotional episodes are themselves often only parts within a complex and temporally extended state that is the emotion proper. Nevertheless, in what follows I begin with affect programmes and go on to discuss emotions.

Because of their distinctive behavioural displays, we can predict that we should be able to detect the basic affective states of members of other cultures so long as the automatic displays of their states are unimpeded, and empirical evidence bears this out.

Though the display is automatically triggered, it might be suppressed or 'restructured'. If this occurs quickly, it is unlikely that cultural outsiders will be able naturally to read the affective significance of whatever behaviour takes place. The suppression or restructuring of standard behavioural displays of affect can be fast when it is no less automatic than the behaviour it supplants. And it can become automatic as a result of implicit or explicit socio-cultural training or conditioning. Nevertheless, because of the value of being able to communicate and recognize these fundamental affective states, we might anticipate that their distinctive displays are not all or always immediately cloaked by culturally shaped substitutes. The anticipated upshot is this: for the most part, we should be able to recognize the basic affective states of individuals from other cultures by the universal behavioural displays that characterize them, but we should not presume that this cross-cultural recognition will always be possible.[1]

# II

I now turn to the case of music and focus on 'pure' or 'absolute' music, which is to say instrumental music without literary titles, sung words, or accompanying pictorial depictions or verbal descriptions. Such music is widely recognized as being emotionally expressive, by which I mean that it seems to embody a certain emotional tone, appearance, or character in the way it sounds, independently both of how it arouses the listener (if it does) and of associations, whether shared with others or idiosyncratic, that it has for the listener. The range of emotions such music expresses is limited: happiness, sadness, anger, and their cognates are common; pomposity or sassy sexuality might also be possible.[2] Notice that happiness, sadness, and anger belong to the set of basic affect programmes. And for that matter, behavioural patterns of sassy sexuality and pomposity may also be cross-culturally recognizable, because they deal in aspects of sexuality and status that have long had significance in the evolution of our species.

An aside: some people suggest that the attribution of sadness and other emotions to music must be metaphoric, because plainly it is not literally true that music is sentient. By contrast, I regard this usage as secondary, derivative, and literal. It is no less true that the music is sad than that the mask of tragedy and the face of the basset hound present sad appearances, that bottles have mouths, and that the exchange rate moves up and down. Most dictionaries record this secondary use of emotion-terms in relation to the character and mood of artworks, which is a good sign that the relevant attributions are not live metaphors.

We might now speculate as follows: the widely made claim that music is a universal language often includes the idea that perception of the expressive character of music is unaffected by both the listener's and the music's cultural origins. In other words, we can be expected to recognize the affective character of the music of other cultures fairly often. (Given that we do not understand anything of their language, we might now be listening to songs and the like, not solely to instrumental works.) And experience also suggests that some kinds of music in other cultures can be expressively opaque to the outsider. So, in both these respects, the cross-cultural recognition of the expressive quality of music parallels the cross-cultural recognition of basic affective states. Moreover, certain universal principles of structure, organization, continuation,

---

[1] This prediction is borne out by the empirical data summarised in Elfenbein and Ambady (2002) and, for vocal displays of emotion, in Juslin and Laukka (2003).

[2] Empirical studies confirming these observations are too numerous to cite. The following are representative: Krumhansl (1997), Juslin and Sloboda (2001), and Gabrielsson (2002, 2003).

and closure are universal to all musics (see Higgins 2006).[3] So, if these play a role equivalent to that of the characteristic behaviours that universally betray basic affective states, and if these musical universals can also be subject to cultural suppression or restructuring, so that sometimes their fundamental expressive import becomes disguised, we might try to develop the analogy yet further.

We arrive at this conjecture: some (systematic) applications of universal musical principles somehow play the role of invoking, representing, or referring to the primitive behaviours that universally display basic affective states, and this is one, fundamental route by which music gets to have an expressive character. The universal significance of these musical applications usually facilitates the recognition of musical expressiveness across cultural boundaries and musical genres, styles, and kinds, though these applications can be subject to local inflections that make the expressiveness of the music then produced unfathomable to all but those steeped in the particular musical tradition and culture in which the music is made.

# III

There are two reasons for being wary of the fantasy that was just sketched. Here is the first: it is widely held that languages are structured according to deep, universal principles and, of course, languages are universal among humans, but it does not follow that we can understand each other's languages. Even if music is universal in its occurrence and is governed also by universal structural-cum-perceptual principles, it cannot be assumed that the expressive character of foreign music will be any more accessible to us than is the import of utterances made in the foreigner's native language.

Some of the differences between music and language mitigate this first concern, however. The structural universals displayed by languages do not require semantic transparency between languages. This is not an issue with 'pure' music, however, because it has no semantic content; its 'meaning' depends purely on its syntactic, tonal, and timbral properties. Besides, the structural universals characterized for language by Chomsky are deep indeed, not part of the phenomenology of following linguistic utterance, whereas what is universal to different musics and how they are experienced is accessible and much nearer the surface.

The second reason for doubting that music's expressiveness might be modelled in terms of the basic affect programmes is that it expresses only some of them. Music can be sad, happy, or angry. Despite its non-sentience, we say the music is sad, or that it expresses sadness, or that its expressive mood is one of sadness, and we do not mean by this merely that it is saddening, though it may be that too. But the other basic affect programmes do not seem to be susceptible of expression in pure music. Music can be

---

[3] Of course, opposed to this line of thinking there is a long tradition of scepticism regarding musical universals, based on an anthropological perspective that sees all biological grounding overruled and superseded by contingent cultural considerations. For an example, see Walker (1996).

surprising, disgusting, or even frightening—that is, it can elicit (and even be the object of) surprise, disgust, or fear—but we would not say of it that it is surprised, disgusted, or frightened.[4] Haydn's Surprise symphony is designed to startle the audience, but the symphony is surprised by nothing. And if someone expressed the view that a musical piece was disgusted, we would be hard pressed to guess what he might be trying to say.

This runs against the view implied earlier. If music expresses, say, sadness through exemplifying acoustic structural or perceptual principles that operate to display sadness by invoking, representing, or referring to the primitive behaviours that universally display the basic affective state of sadness, then, one might think, it should be able to do the same for each of the other basic affective states.

Consideration of the musical means by which musical expressiveness is achieved, and comparison then with basic affect-programme expressions, allows us to address this concern and to refine our proposal. The primitively expressive behaviours highlighted by psychologists in discussing the operation of affect programmes concern expressions of the face, but the expressiveness of music does not seem to be physiognomic in its genesis. For instance, if a certain kind of smile, as opposed say to a grimace, is characteristic of the unreflective display of happiness, it is not as if music is happy by imitating or depicting such a smile, and this might allow us to explain why it expresses only some affect-programme emotions. In music, expressiveness seems to be rooted in dynamic patterns or processes of tension and movement, rather than in the relative disposition of elements like those found in a facial array or expression. So, by way of filling out the account proposed earlier, it is plausible to suggest that the universally expressive behavioural displays that music is experienced as resembling (and thereby, the emotions it is experienced as presenting) have a temporally extended, processional, dynamic character, rather than a static physiognomy. Now, if besides their distinctive facial expression, some but not all the various basic affects have other expressive displays more akin to the musical kind, this would explain why only some of the basic affects are amenable to expression in music.

Surprise is typically short-lived. And while disgust and fear might persist, they do not possess distinctive patterns of behavioural expression over the longer term. Fear behaviours, where the fear's object is not immediately present, indicate a general nervousness or anticipatory tension. These are states that music can express—for instance, with disjointed, darting phrases, or with throbbing discords that call for future resolution—but these states are too general to count distinctively as of fear or disgust. And while aversive behaviours are also typical of fear and disgust, whether movement amounts to fleeing from or drawing towards depends on the location of its target or object, and nothing sufficiently specific counts as the object of musical expression. By contrast, happiness and sadness do have characteristic demeanours, carriages, gaits, ways of moving. Happiness tends to be fast rather than slow, tension-free, light rather than

---

[4] Music often plays a vital role in horror movies, but it does so typically by building tension and suspense or by being brutal, not by expressing fright as such.

heavy, whereas sadness is the reverse, dragging, clouded, heavy with unresolved tension. What is more, the expressive significance of these ways of moving is apparent even to the observer who sees another's expressive movement yet does not know the object to which this is a reaction. Anger is similar, though usually more short-lived.

In light of this, it seems plausible to suggest that music presents the appearances of sadness and happiness because it is experienced as progressing in ways that are typical of the non-physiognomic expression of such states in a person's carriage.[5] And we can now also explain why it does not express disgust or fear. These do not have distinctive gaits or carriages, or do not have them at least unless the third-party observer is aware also of the emotion's object and its location. And to return to the previous argument, if the gaits of sadness and happiness are universally distinctive, we should be able to recognize these emotions in the progress of foreign kinds of music, unless the music in questions alters or subverts the universal musical principles that most naturally shape its dynamic character.

# IV

Notice that, while many of the earlier claims about music's expressiveness were agnostic about how it is expressive, replying to the worry that music expresses only some of the affect-programme emotions forces engagement with that issue. So it is important to acknowledge that experimental work by psychologists sometimes assumes other models for musical expressiveness.

One alternative locates the musical features that are the source of music's expressiveness not in the way music is experienced as moving but in the way it is experienced as resembling prosodic features of expressive speech.[6] If the expressiveness of spoken utterances depends not only on their semantic content but also on prosodic features of pattern, duration, accent, volume, tempo, pitch variation, and contour, and if different basic affective states are matched by distinctive groupings of prosodic features, perhaps music is expressive by being experienced as presenting the relevant prosodic cues. And again, if the affective import of these prosodic cues is universal, we should be able sometimes to recognize the relevant affects in the progress of foreign kinds of music, unless the music in question alters or subverts the universal musical principles that most naturally shape its dynamic character.

---

[5]  I have defended such a view at length in Davies (1994, 2003, 2006).

[6]  See Juslin and Laukka (2003). They hold that vocal expression is an evolved mechanism based on innate and universal affect programmes that develop early and are fine-tuned by prenatal experiences. They predict: (a) communication of emotions is cross-culturally accurate in vocal expression and music performance, (b) the ability to decode basic emotions develops early in ontogeny, and (c) similar patterns of emotion-specific acoustic cues are used to communicate emotions in both vocal and musical communication channels. To test these claims they reviewed 104 studies about the vocal communication of emotion and 41 about the communication of emotion in music.

In favour of this view, there is strong evidence that verbal and vocal displays communicate their expressive tones (especially where these are the affect-programme emotions) to people of other cultures who have no semantic clues about what is being uttered. Though these data are suggestive for what we might expect in the musical case, there are insufficient data regarding that case to test whether cross-cultural communication of musical expressiveness depends on music's imitating expressive prosodic features (Juslin and Laukka 2003: 280).

This theory is clearly plausible, but how does it tackle the worry that only some affect-programme emotions are expressed in music? Earlier, I suggested that this could be explained by the facts that music is expressive via its pattern of movement and that only some affect programmes typically have temporally extended expressive displays. Is a similar argument available to support the prosodic account of music's expressiveness? Are the temporal and dynamic structures of the characteristic vocalizations of only some affect-programme emotions sufficiently extended to permit the expression of only some affect-programme emotions by musical means? I doubt this. Prosodic features can be extended through repetition and the like, but expressive prosodic features tend not to be temporally extended. Overall, it is less clear on this account of music's expressiveness than on the one presented earlier why music is limited in the range of affect-programme emotions it expresses.[7]

# V

I now briefly consider a further approach to the study of what if anything is universal in musical expressiveness. Instead of comparing adult listeners raised in different cultures, one might study neonates. If they are innocent listeners, and if they detect the expressive character of the music they first hear, whatever their culture, it looks as if music has a pre-cultural expressive dimension.

Though I am not aware of specific studies of neonates' reactions to 'foreign' music, there is work on their responses to 'good' and 'bad' melodies and to 'concords' and 'discords', and their reactions are sometimes characterized as having (or detecting) an emotional character, for instance because of the frontal hemisphere in which they are

---

[7] Most tests of the prosodic theory adopt a method that filters the expressive effects of structural features, such as the pattern of melodic and harmonic succession, which are responsible for the temporal play of tension and resolution. They do this by holding those factors constant; they use as examples different performances of a single piece, with the musician instructed to play it sadly, angrily, happily, and so on. In consequence, proponents of the theory give pre-eminence to prosodic over structural features in contributing to music's expressiveness and they attribute the expressiveness to *performance* properties rather than to *work* features. There is no reason why the two theories are not complementary, however, and many of the prosodic features identified as expressive could belong to the piece rather than to its individual interpretation if they are called for by the piece's composer. For other criticism of the prosodic theory, see Patel (2008: 345–8), who also notes the lack of neuroimaging data in favour of the theory.

processed, the one being associated with negative evaluations or experiences and the other with positive ones.[8]

Nevertheless, I think there are significant problems with the interpretation of the results of such experiments. To begin, it is not clear that neonates are musical innocents. They receive a fair amount of exposure to their culture's music while in the womb. And it is not obvious that their reactions are to music as such, as opposed to revealing biases related to speech processing or to auditory processing more generally. In addition, the interpretation of the behaviours or brain scans observed is surely controversial.[9]

Similar issues arise with studies of individuals whose musicality is affected by specific neural deficits (whether accidental or congenital). It is not accepted that such studies point to what in undamaged participants would be universal and innate capacities that are specifically musical (Justus and Hutsler 2005; McDermott and Hauser 2005; Patel 2008). In any case, few of these studies deal with music's expressiveness and none is cross-cultural or based mainly on people in non-Western musical cultures.

## VI

We are not out of the woods yet, but we are some way towards establishing a theoretical underpinning for an experimental programme. And it is noteworthy, I think, that psychologists have pursued the analysis of music's expressiveness along the lines I have indicated, by considering if music has a prosodic character and by considering the affective relevance of what I have called its carriage or gait.

The programme I have envisaged relies on two empirical claims: that we can often correctly identify the expressive character of foreign music and that sometimes we cannot do so because of ways in which the normal modes of musical expression are tweaked within the local musical tradition. Psychologists have ignored the second, taking no interest in the ways musical cultures set out to disguise or mask their music's expressiveness to outsiders. But they have attempted to study the first claim, that is, to look for cross-cultural correlations in judgements and reactions to music's expressiveness. As I shall show later, the results of this research programme have so far been limited, inconclusive, and inadequate. Before I get to that, though, I indicate some lines of research that I think should be put to one side.

---

[8] For instance, see Justus and Hutsler (2005); Trainor and Trehub (1994); Trehub (2000, 2003); Trehub *et al.* (1990).

[9] For elaboration of some of the reservations expressed here, see Mcdermott and Hauser (2005) and Patel (2008: 377–86).

# VII

There is cross-cultural recognition of lullabies, as distinct from other kinds of song, and it has been suggested that expressive communication is part of what makes lullabies distinctive.[10] The experimenters found that prosodic features in the style of presentation (see Trehub *et al.* 1993b) rather than dynamic pattern and structure appeared to be responsible for the recognition and the expression. I doubt, however, that this supports the prosodic theory of musical expression. Whereas that theory holds that music is expressive by imitating prosodic features of natural vocal expressions of basic emotions (by adults, under the force of those emotions), the prosodic features that account for this lullaby effect more likely derive from the inflections of Motherese, a sing-song, exaggerated vocal style adopted by mothers of neonates in all cultures. Fernald (1992) observed that descending pitch contours, which are characteristic of lullabies, dominate in speech used to soothe infants. As a result, the expressive effect of lullabies is more likely a result of their elaboration of Motherese than of their specifically musical character. So, these studies should not be offered in support of the hypothesis that *musical* expressiveness is cross-culturally recognizable.

Similar doubts are likely to arise with respect to cross-cultural recognition of the grief expressed in musicalized renditions of wailing and keening. Unless the musical intrusion is highly stylized, it is possible that the expressiveness lies more in the universal manner of vocalizing grief than in anything the music contributes to this.

The point I have been making is this: even where there is cross-cultural recognition of expression and that expression involves music or has a musical character, before one can credit the music with even partial responsibility for the transmission of affect it is necessary to control for other modes of universally recognizable auditory expression that could mediate the communication of affect. This was one reason for focusing on instrumental as against vocal music. I suggest that a similar consideration should lead us to discount results based on lullabies and laments.

# VIII

I now turn to empirical studies that offer the hope of confirming the cross-cultural transmission of musical affect. Some of these do seem to bear out the phenomenon. Balkwill and Thompson (1999) had thirty Western participants listen to twelve Hindustani raga excerpts that were agreed by Hindustani experts to express joy, sadness, anger, and peacefulness. These listeners were sensitive to the expression of joy and sadness, somewhat less so for anger, and least for peacefulness. Their judgements of the emotions expressed related significantly to judgements of psychophysical dimensions (tempo, rhythmic complexity, melodic complexity, and pitch range). A similar result was found with Japanese listeners to Japanese, Western, and Hindustani

---

[10]  See Trehub *et al.* (1993a) and Unyk *et al.* (1992).

music (Balkwill *et al.* 2004). Meanwhile, Krumhansl (2002)[11] compared British folk, Chinese folk, and atonal songs, and compared Western musicians with Finns with respect to Finnish spiritual folk hymns and vocal Saami music. The results she lists come close to what I have suggested. She concludes: 'In sum, these results support the idea that music draws on common psychological principles of expectation, but that musical cultures shape these in unique ways' (Krumhansl 2002: 49).

If these studies are suspect, they are so in the ways that most psychologists' studies are. They rely on a limited set of musical examples. The examples are brief and are stripped of their musical context. As well, they are presented under laboratory conditions that are not normal for (or conducive to?) the appreciative enjoyment of music. And they typically require choices between descriptors provided by the experimenter.

It should be noted that the brevity and absence of a temporally extended musical context for the excerpts is likely to be especially unfortunate in the study of cross-cultural responses. Whereas one can easily pick up and make sense of a musical excerpt when the style and kind of music is already native to one, access to the organizational principles and expressive character of unfamiliar styles of music can be expected to require a much longer exposure. In addition, the use of forced choice alternatives may be problematic in assuming that all cultures apply the same affective categories to music (Benamou 2003). And it is not sufficient to point to the 'successful' cross-cultural identification of music's expressive character, supposing this occurs, as the sign that these worries are misplaced. The thesis that expression may rely on universal musical elements is supported only if the participants have an appropriate experience of the music, and not if entirely inappropriate modes of listening or categorizations of musical affect fortuitously elicit the 'correct' identifications.

## IX

In other published studies, methodological flaws cast doubt on the credibility of the results claimed. Sometimes these flaws are widely found and are not specific to cross-cultural studies. For instance, while the goal of Gregory and Varney (1996) was to compare what Western and Indian listeners identified as the music's mood and character, instead of asking about that they asked about what the listener felt on hearing the music. It was plain throughout that they took these two very different questions to mean exactly the same. A similar confusion was present in the design of the trials conducted by Darrow *et al.* (1987), in which participants matched descriptors to the music. Some of the descriptors (mournful, dignified) had implications for the music's expressive character. Others (exciting, soothing) concerned the evocation of response as against expressive character. And yet others (fanciful, dramatic) fell in different categories.

---

[11] Reporting on Krumhansl (1995) and Krumhansl *et al.* (1999, 2000).

Unlike some philosophers, I do think that music can elicit an emotional response that echoes its own expressive character and that this process parallels other cases of emotional contagion as described by psychologists.[12] But I doubt that a thirty-second excerpt is likely to elicit this response usually, and in any case, it is surely obvious that the listener's response need not correspond to the music's expressive character. What does (thirty seconds of) Vivaldi's 'Spring' express? A certain joie de vivre. What does the 'Spring' excerpt make you feel? Perhaps frustration because the movement is cut short, or disappointment at the musicians' poor interpretation, or boredom because you have already heard the piece a dozen times this week, or irritation because that excerpt, like Barber's Adagio, is used so often by experimental psychologists, or sadness because this was the music playing when your child died.

A second fault is that of assuming music's expressiveness is always and solely a matter of contingent association. A particularly striking example of this occurs in an experiment done by Gregory and Varney (1996), who believe that expressiveness is based on learned association. So, in asking their participants what season is depicted by Vivaldi's 'Spring' and the monsoon raga 'Rag Kirvani', they equated spring with the monsoon season because there is 'the same association with renewal and joyfulness' (1996: 47). But if the expressiveness of music depends on its dynamic character, as I have already suggested, and if spring in Italy and the monsoon in India manifest dynamically distinct patterns of weather, as seems likely, that both are associated with renewal might be irrelevant to their expressive characters. So, the lack of a significant correlation, which was the outcome of this part of the experiment, should not be interpreted as proving a failure of cross-cultural agreement about the music's expressive character, though this is how the experimenters read it.

Other methodological problems are specific to cross-cultural studies. One is the limited number of musical cultures that have been compared and the tendency to concentrate on 'high', literate musical cultures, such as those of the West, of India, and of Japan, as against small-scale, oral, tribal traditions. Balkwill and Thompson (1999) and Gregory and Varney (1996) compare Western and Indian musics. Balkwill *et al.* (2004), Darrow *et al.* (1987), and Hoshino (1996) compare Western and Japanese subjects. A further methodological risk is that of confusing political with musico-cultural boundaries. Contrasting French with German listeners does not produce a musically significant cross-cultural comparison, for example, because the national styles present in their musics differ more as dialects than as languages. The relevant comparisons must be across musical divides. This may be an issue with the studies by Krumhansl and others (1995, 1999, 2000) comparing British folk and Finnish spiritual folk hymns with Saami yoiks.

Another difficulty results from the globalization of (popular and film) Western music: non-Western participants are already musically bicultural (McDermott and

---

[12] For detailed discussion, see Davies (2011).

Hauser 2005), whereas Western participants tend to be musically monocultural, and thereby are ignorant of the non-Western music the experiment exposes them to. In consequence, most studies are not fully cross-cultural and they lack the symmetry and two-directionality that would be required for the most satisfactory tests. Of course, the problem might be avoided if the comparison were between, say, the musics of Inuit and of tribal Australian aboriginals, but all studies so far involve Western music.

Here are some examples: Darrow *et al.* (1987) compare non-music majors in both the US and Japan with respect to excerpts of various styles of Western and Japanese music. As they allow, while the US listeners were unfamiliar with Japanese music, the Japanese listeners had considerable experience of Western music. They suggest this familiarity might explain the higher agreement in descriptors chosen for the Western examples, but in that case the comparison is not genuinely cross-cultural. The same problem arises also in a study by Hoshino (1996) involving female Japanese, who associated emotional characters with Western major and minor modes and various Japanese modes. (For another example, see also Balkwill *et al.* 2004.)

A more glaring instance is by Gregory and Varney (1996), who were supposedly comparing subjects from European and Asian cultural backgrounds. Whereas the Europeans were students of the University of Manchester, the Asians were of Indian descent but bred and raised in Bradford, England. They were enrolled at a college of further education. In addition to the issue of the lack of genuine biculturality raised above, this selection of participants introduces predictable differences in the socio-economic status of the two groups (ethnic majority at university versus ethnic minority at a college) that may be relevant to how subjects respond to music (or to psychologists).[13]

Gregory and Varney's conclusion was that there is a significant correlation between Western and Indian listeners for Western classical music and New Age music and also between male and female listeners, but that there is a lack of agreement over the season for which music is appropriate. For the reasons given, however, it is hard to accord this conclusion much credibility.

# X

Conclusion: cross-cultural studies of listeners' reactions to 'foreign' music are in their infancy. When one discounts methodologically questionable experiments, few remain. These do appear to support the hypothesis argued here, that cross-cultural recognition of musical expressions of basic affect-programme emotions is sometimes possible, but that conclusion is far from established.

---

[13]   McKay (2002) faults Gregory and Varney (1996), and also the study by Hoshino (1996), on this score.

# References

Balkwill, Laura-Lee and William Forde Thompson (1999). 'A Cross-Cultural Investigation of the Perception of Emotion in Music: Psychophysical and Cultural Cues'. *Music Perception*, 17: 43–64.

————and Rie Matsunaga (2004). 'Recognition of Emotion in Japanese, Western, and Hindustani Music by Japanese Listeners'. *Japanese Psychological Research*, 46: 337–49.

Benamou, M. (2003). 'Comparing Musical Affect: Java and the West'. *The World of Music*, 45: 57–76.

Cooke, Deryck (1959). *The Language of Music*. London: Oxford University Press.

Darrow, Alice-Ann, Paul Haack, and Fumio Kuribayashi (1987). 'Descriptors and Preferences for Eastern and Western Musics by Japanese and American Nonmusic Majors'. *Journal of Research in Music Education*, 35/4: 237–48.

Davies, Stephen (1994). *Musical Meaning and Expression*. Ithaca: Cornell University Press.

————(2003). *Themes in the Philosophy of Music*. Oxford: Oxford University Press.

————(2006). 'Artistic Expression and the Hard Case of Pure Music', in M. Kieran (ed.), *Contemporary Debates in Aesthetics and the Philosophy of Art*. Oxford: Blackwell, pp. 179–91.

————(2011). 'Infectious Music: Music-Listener Emotional Contagion', in P. Goldie and A. Coplan (eds.), *Empathy: Philosophical and Psychological Perspectives*. Oxford: Oxford University Press, pp. 134–47.

Ekman, Paul (1992). 'An Argument for Basic Emotions'. *Cognition and Emotion*, 6: 169–200.

Elfenbein, H. A. and N. Ambady (2002). 'On the Universality and Cultural Specificity of Emotion Recognition: A Meta-analysis'. *Psychological Bulletin*, 128: 203–35.

Fernald, A. (1992). 'Meaningful Melodies in Mothers' Speech to Infants', in H. Papousek, U. Jurgens, and M. Papousek (eds.), *Nonverbal Vocal Communication: Comparative and Developmental Aspects*. Cambridge: Cambridge University Press, pp. 262–82.

Gabrielsson, Alf (2002). 'Emotion Perceived and Emotion Felt: Same or Different?' *Musicae Scientiae*, Special number 2001–2: 123–47.

————(2003). 'Music Performance Research at the Millennium'. *Psychology of Music*, 31: 221–72.

Gregory, A. H. and N. Varney (1996). 'Cross-Cultural Comparisons in the Affective Response to Music'. *Psychology of Music*, 24: 47–52.

Higgins, Kathleen Marie (2006). 'The Cognitive and Appreciative Impact of Musical Universals'. *Revue Internationale de Philosophie*, 60: 487–503.

Hoshino, E. (1996). 'The Feeling of Musical Mode and Its Emotional Character in a Melody'. *Psychology of Music*, 24: 29–46.

Juslin, Patrik N. and Petri Laukka (2003). 'Communication of Emotion in Vocal Expression and Music Performance: Different Channels, Same Code?' *Psychological Bulletin*, 129/5: 770–814.

————and John A. Sloboda (eds.) (2001). *Music and Emotion: Theory and Research*. Oxford: Oxford University Press.

Justus, Timothy and Jeffrey J. Hutsler (2005). 'Fundamental Issues in the Evolutionary Psychology of Music: Assessing Innateness and Domain Specificity'. *Music Perception*, 23: 1–27.

Krumhansl, Carol L. (1995). 'Music Psychology and Music Theory: Problems and Prospects'. *Music Theory Spectrum*, 17: 53–80.

————(1997). 'An Exploratory Study of Musical Emotions and Psychophysiology'. *Canadian Journal of Experimental Psychology*, 51: 336–52.

Krumhansl, Carol L. (2002). 'Music: A Link Between Cognition and Emotion'. *Current Directions in Psychological Research*, 11/2: 45–50.

——J. Louhivuori, P. Toiviainen, T. Järvinen, and T. Eerola (1999). 'Melodic Expectation in Finnish Spiritual Folk Hymns: Convergence of Statistical, Behavioural, and Computational Approaches'. *Music Perception*, 17: 151–95.

——P. Toiviainen, T. Eerola, T. Järvinen, and J. Louhivuori (2000). 'Cross-Cultural Music Cognition: Cognitive Methodology Applied to North Sami Yoiks'. *Cognition*, 76: 13–58.

McDermott, Josh and Marc D. Hauser (2005). 'The Origins of Music: Innateness, Uniqueness, and Evolution'. *Music Perception*, 23: 29–59.

McKay, Cory (2002). 'Emotion and Music: Inherent Responses and the Importance of Empirical Cross-Cultural Research'. Course Paper, McGill University, Canada.

Patel, Aniruddh D. (2008). *Music, Language, and the Brain*. Oxford: Clarendon Press.

Trainor, L. J. and S. E. Trehub (1994). 'Key Membership and Implied Harmony in Western Tonal Music: Developmental Perspectives'. *Perception & Psychophysics*, 56: 125–32.

Trehub, S. E. (2000). 'Human Processing Predispositions and Musical Universals', in B. Merker and N. L. Wallin (eds.), *The Origins of Music*. Cambridge, MA: MIT Press, pp. 427–48.

——(2003). 'The Developmental Origins of Musicality'. *Nature Neuroscience*, 6: 669–73.

——L. A. Thorpe, and L. J. Trainor (1990). 'Infants' Perception of Good and Bad Melodies'. *Psychomusicology*, 9: 5–19.

——Anna M. Unyk, and Laurel J. Trainor (1993a). 'Adults Identify Infant-Directed Music across Cultures'. *Infant Behavior & Development*, 16/2: 193–211.

——(1993b). 'Maternal Singing in Cross-cultural Perspective'. *Infant Behavior & Development*, 16/3: 285–95.

Unyk, Anna M., Sandra E. Trehub, Laurel J. Trainor, and E. Glenn Schellenberg (1992). 'Lullabies and Simplicity: A Cross-Cultural Perspective'. *Psychology of Music*, 20: 15–28.

Walker, Robert. (1996). 'Open Peer Commentary: Can We Understand the Music of Another Culture?' *Psychology of Music*, 24: 103–30.

# PART VII

# Pictorial Representation and Appreciation

# 23

# Neurology and the New Riddle of Pictorial Style

*Mark Rollins*

"Style is an easy way of saying complicated things"
— Jean Cocteau

In his well-known introduction to *Art and Illusion*, "Psychology and the Riddle of Style," Ernst Gombrich described what he took to be the problem of pictorial style: "Why is it that different ages and different nations have represented the world in such different ways?" (1956: 3). In using these words, he construed styles as *manners of representation*, and he took the challenge to be to explain why pictorial contents have been given such diverse forms. His response was to propose a cognitivist theory of pictorial art. Pictures convey knowledge. In particular, they convey the knowledge on which perception depends. Styles vary, then, because knowledge varies across times and places, but also because artists and cultures differ in regard to the forms they believe best express the knowledge that is available to them. The riddle of style is thus a riddle of induction, and the solution involves showing how styles contribute to the representation of objects and events. To show that, Gombrich appealed to perceptual psychology. Pictures embody perceptual schemas or stereotypes. Those are acquired through experience, and they reflect the perceiver's knowledge and beliefs. Insofar as style is an aspect of the embodiment of mental schemas in pictures, some stylistic differences will derive simply from differences in schematic content. Others will be due to the ways the schemas provide psychological access to content and facilitate the processing of it in the artist's or perceiver's mind.

Recently a number of cognitive scientists and art historians have reiterated Gombrich's belief that psychology can shed light on the nature of style, appealing now to neuropsychology, which is heavily infused with research on the brain. For instance, historians and theorists Norman Bryson (2003), Michael Baxandall (1994), David Freedberg (2007), Barbara Stafford (2007), and John Onians (2007) have argued that cognitive neuroscience can contribute to our understanding of style and its history. On Stafford's account, neuroscience can open the door to a cognitive account of images; for Onians, it provides the foundation for what he calls *neuroarthistory*. Similarly, scientists such as Margaret Livingstone (2002), Semir Zeki (1999), V. S. Ramachandran (1990), Eric Kandel (2006), Dahlia Zaidel (2005), and Stephen Palmer (2006) have analyzed aspects of art in ways that suggest that stylistic features can be explained in terms of the organization and functioning of the brain. Although in some of this work the concepts of pictorial representation and perceptual knowledge reflect new ways of thinking that have emerged with recent scientific discoveries, on the whole the work implies that styles contribute to the development of knowledge, just as Gombrich believed. At the same time, stylistic features are distinguished from the representational elements by which content is conveyed.

There are reasons for thinking that style and content work together, but also that they play distinct epistemic roles. For instance, that stylistic and representational features function differently is suggested by the fact that there can be "synonymy" across styles: A photograph of Mount St. Victoire and a painting of it by Cezanne are, at a basic level, about the same thing. They refer to the same object, and that fact constrains the further meanings they can be said to have. But only the Cezanne painting exhibits his characteristic use of color and geometric forms, as against the realism of the photograph. Thus one might think, as Arthur Danto has put it, that "style . . . [is] what remains of a representation when we subtract its content" (Danto 1991: 197). The claim that style and content are distinct has also lately received empirical support. Studies of artists who have damaged brains suggest that there are dissociable mechanisms and processes for the production of content and style.

At the same time, it is clear that the understanding of content and style must go hand-in-hand. This interpretive interdependence becomes evident when the relation is misunderstood. A critic once described Renoir's painting, *Woman in Sunlight*, as a picture of a woman, not in dappled sunlight with shadows on her arms and face, but with bruises and rotting flesh, "like a corpse." In this case, he misapplied the principle articulated by Jenefer Robinson, that "identifying the stylistic features of a work of art depends upon understanding its aesthetic significance, and . . . understanding the aesthetic significance of a work (its subject matter, its form, its expression) depends upon identifying its style" (Robinson 1981: 12). There is also empirical support for this link. Brain imaging and psychophysical research on picture perception suggest that, while there are perceptual clues to the stylistic or representational identities of features, those drive a common, interactive process, from which distinctive functional roles only emerge at the end. It is not surprising that understanding style and understanding content are interdependent if the very status of features is the outcome of a kind of bootstrapping perceptual response.

In what follows, I will discuss three lines of argument, including Gombrich's own, that can be taken to explain how stylistic features might contribute to the grasping of pictorial content in distinctive ways. Each line embodies what I call the *Engagement Hypothesis*; the view that style contributes to the cognitive function of pictures by engaging the mind of the picture perceiver, encouraging and guiding investigation to a certain extent. In ascribing this function, these views avoid the trap of treating styles as merely ornamental, i.e., as the attractive clothing that bare abstract ideas put on. Nonetheless, I will argue that, in wedding style to content as they do, these views are vulnerable to a *New Riddle of Style*. The very relation between style and content becomes relative to the way or context in which interpretive processes are deployed. As a result, both the empirical warrant for pictorial content, as a kind of visual hypothesis, and the adequacy of style for the expression of it, are up for grabs. The evidence that is available for depicting objects in a certain way and thus categorizing them perceptually can be equally compatible with two different hypotheses, both of which a particular picture can be taken to represent. In contrast to Goodman's New Riddle of Induction, however, the New Riddle of Style is not a logical conundrum, to be solved by appeal to the entrenchment of predicative practices. Rather, it is a problem that derives from the nature of perceptual plasticity and the variations in neural resource recruitment that it allows. It is neurology that gives rise to this New Riddle of Style, and it is through a philosophical analysis of neurological research that a solution is to be found.

Some preliminary comments about the scope of my project before I begin. First, it is often noted that the term 'style' does not have a univocal sense. It can refer either to individual or to general styles, the latter including period styles, schools, and universal styles (in the sense of realism or naturalism). The question then is whether a general theory of pictorial style is possible. Richard Wollheim (1979, 1995) has argued that only individual styles are grounded in psychological reality and have explanatory value. The analysis that I develop here amounts to a rejection of that claim and treats individual and general styles as having the same neuropsychological basis. Gombrich (1968) also expressed skepticism about general style categories on the grounds that the features associated with them can change over time. I will argue that the changes themselves can be understood in psychological terms and that Gombrich's own view in *Art and Illusion* provides a candidate explanation of that fact. Thus my aim is to offer a general theory of pictorial style.

Second, there are important questions about the relation of style, as a manner of representation, to form, technique, and genre. Arthur Danto for one would reject the term "manner of representation," in referring to styles on the grounds that manners can be learned but styles cannot. In addition, style is sometimes distinguished from genre by treating genres as defined by type of subject matters (landscapes, portraits), which can be represented in more than one style. My analysis will imply that, contra Danto, the capacity to produce pictures in a certain style can be developed in an individual, and to that extent are manner-like. In addition, a strong distinction between genre and style will be put in doubt by the argument that style and content are closely related in more ways than one. However, I will not address these issues in detail here.[1]

Finally, considerations of the role of schemas or other psychological factors are sometimes conjoined with an appeal to the picture maker's intentions as a way of individuating styles (Wollheim 1979, 1995; cf. Walton 1970). To the extent that I stress psychological processes that give rise to stylistic features, my account might be seen as intention-based. However, although my view is not anti-intentionalist, I analyze style in terms of subpersonal processes that would count as intentions only in a very extended sense. In addition, I focus on *perceptual* processes that are at work in the production of styles. In many ways, the techniques used by the picture maker have to also be understood as evoking a perceptual response. Thus I offer a different perspective on style than those theories that make understanding pictures depend on an *imaginative* response by the viewer, in which the goal is to understand the beliefs and intentions that could have led to a picture looking as it does. As a result, my account of grasping the relation between style and content does not depend on the viewer imagining the hypothetical intentions of an implied maker, as theories of imagination tend to do (Robinson 1985; Currie 1995). While I do not believe that style can be fully explained in perceptual terms, a goal of my account is to show that perception can carry considerably more weight in that regard than theories emphasizing imagination have allowed, and my view is that the notion of pictorial style must be defined partly in terms of perceptual processes.[2]

## 1. The evolution of style

Each of the views I want to consider treats art and artistic style as having a natural basis. Specifically, these accounts explain the development and nature of style in terms of

---

[1]  There are also questions about the relation between expression and style that go beyond the issue of the relation of representational content and style. This would be so, for instance, if what are taken to be expressed are emotions or personalities. I set the issues of expression and style aside in the interest of space. Among other things, a consideration of expression and style would require an assessment of recent arguments that reason and an understanding of pictorial content depend on emotion, which is beyond the scope of the present topic.

[2]  Because of my emphasis on perceptual rather than imaginative engagement, there are certain lines of thought in cognitive science that can be taken to pertain to style which I ignore in this essay. In particular, Currie (2004: 110–11) has drawn upon the concept of "relevance" in the work of Sperber and Wilson and on simulation theories of mind-reading to shed light on the nature of imaginative engagement. According to the former, relevance in a representation is a matter of the probable cognitive or affective rewards that might be derived from efforts to understand it. On Currie's view, grasping relevance requires envisioning a hypothetical maker's communicative intentions. According to simulation theory, we can do that to some extent without theorizing *per se*, but rather by putting ourselves in the maker's shoes and running the beliefs that are prompted thereby offline (i.e., without causing action). Simulationism has lately been linked to the discovery of mirror neurons, which fire when a real or depicted action is observed rather than performed. Perhaps, then, the engagement of styles depends on our grasping relevance by way of simulation in this sense. Nonetheless, my view is that it also depends on a certain kind of perceptual response. Focusing on that, I set the topic of simulation aside.

evolutionary biology. However, the appeal need not be taken to imply that there are brain structures or capacities that have been selected and preserved specifically for producing stylistic features. Rather, the assumption is that the nature and history of pictorial style can be understood in terms of evolved structures and capacities that serve other ends. In particular, in the case of pictorial art, the structures and capacities on which styles depend are the same ones that are employed in the production of representations of objects and events. This possibility is explained in three different ways. On the first view, Gombrich's ancestral account, styles are said to evolve in a manner that is analogous to both the evolution of species and the testing and selection of scientific hypotheses. The latter process is taken to be "evolutionary" in Karl Popper's sense; thus do biology and evolutionary epistemology meet. On the second theory, stylistic features function like *ethological triggers*; i.e., features that cause us to automatically categorize objects as being of a certain type and to behave accordingly. This is a survival-enhancing response that carries over to pictures of objects, where survival is not at stake. This view is suggested by the research of Ramachandran, although it is not explicitly espoused by him. The third model asserts that pictorial styles pose problems that elicit perceptual strategies that depend, not only on evolved perceptual abilities, but also on evolution-like neural plasticities; i.e., evolution writ small, in individual brains. Such a model is compatible with much of Ramachandran's, Zeki's, and Livingstone's research. I will describe and comment on each of these views in turn, arguing that none of them will quite suffice. I will then propose my own alternative at the end, which is a variation on the third approach.[3]

*The ancestral view*

The basic idea that underwrites Gombrich's conception of the style/content relation is that there are perceptual schemas or stereotypes, which provide the bare bones of pictorial content, so to speak, as an index to what the picture denotes. Such schemas conjure up associated knowledge of features typical of the category, and the fuller meanings of pictures must be compatible with that. The first question then is how schemas come to be adopted and stored as psychological representations in the artist's and perceiver's minds and embodied in works of pictorial art. To this question, Gombrich proposed a Popperian response. We always begin with some schema or other, which experience then puts to the test. Those schemas that resist falsification are deemed to be acceptable, at least within a certain niche or milieu. Styles of picture then change as knowledge grows or different beliefs are acquired.

However, this theory allows for styles and stylistic features to be identified in more than one way. First, differences in pictorial style may simply reflect differences in

---

[3] Myer Schapiro (1994: 69–81) has argued that evolutionary models of style are historically deterministic. However, he has in mind the views of German historians influenced by Hegel. The sense in which Gombrich invokes evolution is explicitly anti-deterministic, and I hope it will be clear that the appeal to evolution-like neural processes in the brain is non-deterministic as well, given the way the "evolution" is construed.

perceptual knowledge or beliefs. Insofar as those are encoded in perceptual schemas and stereotypes, different styles should be constituted by differences in the schemas themselves. These occur most obviously across cultures and eras. For instance, Gombrich focused on ways of representing the human figure in ancient Egyptian art, which are very different from the representation of such figures in the art of the European Renaissance. Stylistic differences can also be identified with variations in schemas within a period or society. Aside from the fact that different groups of artists may emphasize different features selectively, artists may also produce pictures that, in effect, *contest* accepted manners of representation as being inappropriate to experience in certain respects. Insofar as they are reflected in perceptual schemas or stereotypes, some variations in style will reflect disagreements about the accuracy or veridicality of a form in expressing what is known or believed, based on the evidence available at the time. On Gombrich's account, those artworks that come to be predominant in a period will be the ones that have some competitive advantage in the environments in which they arise; for example, they make a wider range of experience comprehensible. In that respect, a style has an ecology within which it may thrive and outside of which it may die out. In any case, whether variations in style are measured across or within cultures and periods, style and content are closely related on this part of Gombrich's view. According to it, styles engage us because we believe that they convey knowledge accurately and well.

The second dimension of Gombrich's account ascribes a more distinctive role to style. It derives from his understanding of pictures as visual hypotheses, analogous to the hypotheses of science. As I have noted, Gombrich was influenced by Popper, and on Popper's view, in addition to resistance to falsification by the evidence, a standard for the acceptability of hypotheses is their adherence to non-evidential constraints. Of particular importance is the constraint that simple hypotheses should be seen as more acceptable than complex ones, because they are easier to put to empirical test. Simplicity is a notoriously slippery notion, and for Popper it is described partly in terms of content (in the sense that simple representations are said to contain more information than complex ones do). At the same time, simplicity can be construed as being manifested in form and as greasing the wheels of epistemic evolution, so to speak. Thus we might say that it functions as a standard for the acceptability of a representation in a *structural* or *procedural* sense; i.e., it facilitates the evolutionary process by which hypotheses are selected and knowledge grows. Simplicity in hypotheses is adaptive in that respect, but at a higher level than the ideas which the hypotheses represent. It is a feature, the object of a first-order preference itself; yet by virtue of its role in promoting the testing of ideas, it can be said to take on a criterial function. It becomes a second-order standard for preferring representations of various kinds.

Gombrich's treatment of pictures as visual hypotheses implies that there may also be second-order, structural standards at work in the evolution of pictorial art. The various ways in which pictures adhere to such standards could thus be said to have something to do with differences in style. Styles would contribute to knowledge and be related to content in that respect; but their contribution would be of a distinctive, second-order kind. The engagement that is proposed on the Engagement Hypothesis would then be a matter of inducing and facilitating a testing process; i.e., an assessment by comparison to perceptual experience of whatever a picture purports to show. To that extent, styles can be said to function *heuristically*, in one sense of the word. Stylistic features are diagnostic of the nature or extent of processing that is likely to be required to get access to content and evaluate it. They thus motivate an investigative process without demanding much preliminary effort on the perceiver's part.

What sort of features might play this role in pictorial art, and in what ways, remain to be seen. A case might be made that simplicity itself is sometimes the standard that is at work. For example, it may be part of what draws us to caricatures or pictures by Paul Klee. With such pictures, simplicity serves the testing of visual hypotheses by enabling the quick categorization of objects perhaps. As a general standard, then, we might say that styles differ in terms of relative simplicity. However, simplicity is obviously not the only measure of style, nor will it trump other features as a matter of preference in every case. We can thus get some further insight into how Gombrich thinks stylistic features work in the structural or procedural sense by considering another candidate proposed by him; viz. symmetry in buildings, pictures, and artifacts. Here Gombrich adds another dimension to his account of style. He describes our preference for symmetry as deriving, in the first instance, from our attraction to it in human bodies as a sign of fitness and health. That preference is then unwittingly extended to a love of symmetry in art and architecture, applying a biological "rule" outside its proper domain. In contrast to simplicity, which signals the assessability of representations, symmetry functions diagnostically in nature, where it motivates evaluation and action that promotes the survival of the species. In pictures, symmetry is not indicative of fitness or of the potential value of a picture to perceivers, and it does not elicit corresponding action. Yet we find it to be of interest nonetheless. While symmetry in pictures might be seen as inviting perceptual exploration and analysis, that is coincidental to what might be called a *Pygmalion effect*; i.e., when an artifact is valued for having features that we value in the living world. This effect may seem mysterious. However, I suggest that it can be explained by taking symmetry to work heuristically in a second sense: its motivational force is the result of an economical use of resources. Rather than cluttering the mind with a lot of principles specific to narrow domains, nature is frugal. It provides us with a few principles that are somewhat reliable for a variety of tasks. In this way, it avoids over-taxing the brain. We thus use symmetry as a basis for distinguishing one type or genre or style of picture from another because we use it for distinguishing one type of person from another and then for evaluating the picture or person accordingly.[4]

---

[4] Thus in his chapter "Pygmalion's Power" in *Art and Illusion*, Gombrich describes the effect as due to more than mere imitation: "The test of the image is not its lifelikeness but its efficacy within a context of action" (p. 110). We feel the pull to act even where the act is impossible.

As interesting as Gombrich's account of style is, I do not think that it is adequate to the task. There are problems, I will argue, with both aspects of style that his analysis suggests: as features that facilitate evolution in a structural or procedural sense, and as reflecting differences in content or in the ways that content is schematized. In regard to the structural/procedural aspect, some account is needed of why different styles that vary in regard to it come to be predominant at different times and places. I do not think that a satisfactory, non-question begging account can be given in Gombrich's evolutionary terms. The problem is evident when variations are considered both across and within domains.

Across domains, Gombrich's analysis depends on comparisons of two kinds: of pictures to scientific hypotheses and of pictures to objects in the natural world. Yet disanalogies come readily to mind. While simplicity may be a desideratum of scientific hypotheses, a certain complexity is often what attracts us to depicted scenes. It is not *ease* of access that is always what draws us into a work of art. Likewise with symmetry. Attractive as it may be in the animal kingdom, it may not be the best way to convey information pictorially. Even ignoring aesthetics, a picture might better compel attention if its subject is offset and not counterbalanced with anything interesting on the other side.

Of course, it might be said in response to these observations that, while the relevant features are domain specific, the type of role they play is the same. Simplicity in science only serves to illustrate the role, which happens to sometimes be played by complexity in our response to works of pictorial art. The problem is that, in explaining why the role is played in different ways, the appeal to evolution is too easy to make. For instance, we might say that a degree of complexity is valued in pictorial art, because the process that artworks encourage is not merely a matter of testing a visual hypothesis, but rather of exploiting its fertile potential in imagination. But this seems ad hoc and suggests that the thesis is rather empty as it stands. To say that a picture has potential for fertilizing imagination in this context, without an independently developed theory of imagination, is just another way of saying that the picture has a degree of complexity. Put generally, the risk is that the relevant features will always be identified within a domain as those that engage the mind in ways that are characteristic of that domain.

In any case, the problem of variable second-order standards also arises within domains, and some explanation of that is required. It could be argued, for instance, that along with symmetry, simplicity is valued in nature as well. Gombrich claims that the fact that "our mental make-up favours simplicity both in perception and in making" can be explained in terms of the survival value of these tendencies (cf. Onians 2007: 168). Viewed as the absence of concealing and distracting ornament, simplicity in form might have survival value because it signifies trustworthiness in a fellow being. Yet perceived complexity may also be valued in nature, for instance, as providing camouflage. The ability to hide behind the cloak of complex features or, for that matter, to deceive fellow beings, can have adaptive value for a species and lead to reproductive success. The point is not that Gombrich's particular examples of features that play structural/procedural roles do not work, but rather that it is too easy to explain the existence of opposing structural features as the engines of evolution in one or another case. Thus the evolutionary explanation of stylistic features in structural/ procedural terms would seem to rule very little out.

With respect to the idea that different styles reflect different contents or ways of schematizing contents, which is the second aspect of Gombrich's account, it is here that Gombrich confronts a New Riddle of Style. The problem is that perceivers have no real way to judge the acceptability of competing manners of representation. Any manner can be said, under some interpretation, to fit the evidence as well as another. Moreover, it is a familiar point of Goodman's that non-evidential criteria, such as simplicity, cannot be brought to the rescue here. The reason is that simplicity is relative to a perspective or starting place. "All emeralds are green" is not simpler than "all emeralds are grue," if *green* is defined as "grue prior to time t, when emeralds appear blue." Thus some justification must be given for privileging one starting place over another. This is impossible, because the turn to non-evidential criteria is motivated in the first instance by the fact that competing hypotheses fit the evidence equally well. Since competing hypotheses always compete from within a perspective or conceptual scheme, it follows that alternative perspectives can both fit the evidence, too. Going beyond Goodman, I suggest that, with Gombrich's account, the New Riddle also contains a special twist: The very *relation* of style and content, the manner of represen- tation and what it represents, will depend on a way of thinking, and competing ways of thinking that are compatible with the evidence can always be described.

For instance, a Fauvist portrait of a man whose face is painted purple or green, on one description, exemplifies the use of atypical colors as a stylistic device that is extraneous to face recognition. We might think of that use of colors as stylistic in the structural, heuristic sense; i.e., it adds a degree and type of complexity that is charac- teristic of Fauvist art. But we might also think of it as a manner of representation that is taken to fit a certain content particularly well; for instance, the belief that color is to be celebrated for its own sake, quite apart from the interest of the object to which it belongs. However, a second picture, visually identical to the first, could also be described as a realistic portrait of a man with green or purple skin; a manner of representation that is appropriate to beliefs about how men ordinarily look. Against it, a Sargent portrait would be seen as deploying deviant color in a celebratory way which Matisse's *Green Stripe* painting of Mme. Matisse would not be seen to do. Thus two visually identical uses of color can be viewed as an aspect of two different manners of representation, each appropriate to different types of content or belief, and there will be no way to judge this use of color as constituting one or another style. On the style- as-manner-of-representation model, the style–content relation will be as relative to a characterization or conceptual scheme as are representational contents themselves.

This suggests that Gombrich's account of variations in style as the result of perceptual plasticity is vulnerable to Goodman's conventionalist turn. This result depends on Gombrich's construal of perceptual plasticity. His theory explains pictorial representation in terms of perceptual processes that are modulated by background knowledge and conceptual frameworks. That in itself does not entail that making and understanding pictures requires knowledge of special symbolic conventions as Goodman's account requires. However, it opens the door to it, because background knowledge is context-dependent, and local knowledge can become embedded in representational conventions in the relevant locale. The next two lines of thought I will consider can be understood as rethinking the nature of scope and nature of perceptual plasticity. The question then is whether they can avoid Goodman's problem in that way and, if so, at what cost.

*Toward an ethological account of style*

It is an interesting fact that a number of neuroscientists writing about art have argued that, not only does pictorial art convey knowledge, it conveys knowledge of the *essences* of things. Thus Kandel, who won the Nobel Prize for his research on marine snails, says that in Matisse's painting, *The Snail*, Mattise "realized in a brilliant reductionist advance, that he could completely reconstruct the basic elements of a snail with only 12 simple blocks of color . . . The colored surfaces capture both the essential form and movement of the snail" (Kandel 2006: 3). Ramachandran cites Zeki in making a similar claim: "As the physiologist Zeki . . . has eloquently noted, it may not be a coincidence that the ability of the artist to abstract the 'essential features' of an image and discard redundant information is essentially identical to what the visual areas themselves have evolved to do" (Ramachandran and Hirstein 1999: 17). Indeed, Ramachandran suggests, it is the essence of art to do that, and the capacity of art in that regard can be explained in terms of functions of the perceiver's visual brain.

One way to understand this neurological essentialism is as implying that artistic techniques and styles have the power to strongly activate perceptual modules, which ordinarily respond to the non-accidental features of objects, on the basis of which real objects are categorized. Thus Zeki suggests that Malevich, Calder, and Mondrian, in various ways, try to isolate color, movement, or line in order to enhance the capacity of their artworks to stimulate neural systems dedicated to one or another feature. The features are abstracted by these artists from any depiction of objects, but a case can be made that stylistic devices work the same way in representational art; for instance, the use of bold contour lines emphasizing the geometrical shapes of objects in the work of Cezanne. In so far as the response of modules to the relevant features is fast, automatic, mandatory, and cognitively impenetrable, invoking them has the effect of diminishing the role of background knowledge in the perceiver's response to style. Thus this approach to understanding style sidesteps the problem I described in regard to Gombrich's view. It provides the basis for a naturalistic theory of style in terms of native abilities with which the visual brain has been genetically endowed.

However, while the appeal to modularity provides an account of how style and content are linked, it does little to explain the distinctive role that stylistic features might play. At most, the implication is that styles differ in the features they emphasize in order to activate modules selectively. While that may be true of some types of pictorial art, it is inadequate to account for all. An interesting variation on this approach has been suggested by Ramachandran, which can be viewed as potentially adding a new dimension to the theory of style and expanding it scope, although he does not develop it himself. According to him, various types of art involve, not just selective representation, but exaggeration and enhancement of the distinctive features or non-accidental properties. This is explained in terms of the *peak shift effect*: pigeons trained to peck at a rectangular shape in order to get food will peck more frequently when the length of the rectangle relative to its width (the essence of rectangularity) is exaggerated. He argues that artistic devices function in the same way. In that sense, he claims, all art is caricature. My suggestion then is that one might try to understand stylistic devices in these terms. Stylistic features could be said to function as ethological triggers to which we automatically respond, no matter where they are found. In that case, the visual systems of picture perceivers would respond to a style like Tinbergian gull chicks who open their mouths when they see a red stripe above them, whether its appears naturally on the mother gull's beak or is painted on a dangling stick.

This ethological approach calls to mind the Pygmalion effect that is suggested by Gombrich's account of our response to symmetry in art. However, the views are importantly different in two respects. First, on the present theory, stylistic features are explicitly not designed to replicate attractive features of things in the world. Rather, they distort standard features and engage the perceiver thereby. They thus contribute to the production of perceptual knowledge in a distinctive way. Second, because such representations activate an automatic recognition response by which objects or properties are categorized, they are not diagnostic in the sense that symmetry or simplicity are on Gombrich's account. Stripes on a beak are not treated by the visual system as like spots on a face, which indicate measles with only a certain degree of reliability. Likewise, Ramachandran suggests, our response to an exaggerated rectangle in a Malevich painting is not a matter of probabilistic inference, and the impact of background knowledge on the perception of it is minimized. The distortions and enhancements that Ramachandran has in mind thus do not function heuristically in the first sense that Gombrich thinks that symmetry does, i.e., by providing *evidence* that a certain response to an object is appropriate. Rather, they simply cause the response. That mitigates the problem that the style/content distinction is relativized to local theories and practices. As a consequence, this approach, too, would seem to avoid the New Riddle of Style.

However, there are a number of objections that can be raised to this view as an account of style as it stands. First, the general theory of art on which it rests has been criticized as being both overly general and false to the facts. For one thing, there are reasons to think that human perceptual categories are prototypical, and what are taken to be prototypical shapes can vary with experience. Even if such categories are rule-like, we might question the claim that a very long and narrow rectangle exemplifies the rule better than a somewhat shorter and wider one is, i.e., is really more rectangular than the other or even that it is more readily identified by humans as a rectangular shape. Finally, as an account of style, the theory would obviously be too narrow. In what sense, we might ask, can the Fauvists' use of atypical colors in portraits be seen as exaggerating essential features of faces so that they drive a more powerful face recognition response? The theory seems implausible in that regard. In any case, the perceptual triggering model really does not fit well with the general thought that stylistic features draw us in to picture processing, thus engaging our minds. A triggered response is not a flexible or deep response of the sort that we might expect style–content relations to provoke.

Some of Ramachandran's own research points to yet another approach, one in which the emphasis on ethological triggers is largely left behind. He thinks of the automatic responses as produced at the level of individual neurons, but he also makes perceptual categorization a function of the orchestration of very large numbers of them. There is thus some potential for a theory of richer modes of processing. The potential is illustrated by Ramachandran's experiments on motion capture. For instance, apparent motion can be produced for a subjective contour by the flashing of a pattern of lights arranged in a square, when the patterned lights alternate back and forth between two locations in space. If a transparent yellow patch is then superimposed on the pattern in one position and the patch is equiluminant with the background, it will appear in peripheral vision to move along with the pattern, even though it remains stationary as a matter of fact. The reason is that the system responsible for spatial location can only respond to luminance contrast, so it is unable to precisely locate the color patch; whereas the systems that detect color *per se* (hue) and motion remain active, and color and the motion of the lights are seen as going hand-in-hand. This is a top-down effect, in the sense that the perception of local features is affected by global relations with other features; but that is due to interactions among form, motion, and color systems, rather than to the perceiver's beliefs. There may be built-in "assumptions" made by the visual system in this case, such as that objects are generally rigid and that textures adhere to the surfaces of moving objects. Nonetheless, in these studies, the effects are produced too quickly to be explained in terms of higher-order cognitive processes.

The question then is whether such form–motion–color relations can be seen as stylistic features in some sense. I turn now to a closer consideration of this model with that question in mind.

*An interactive theory of content and style*

As I have noted earlier, there is evidence that points to the conclusion that style and content are subserved by different processes or systems in the brain. One body of evidence comes from studies of brain-damaged visual artists, which have been surveyed by Dahlia Zaidel (2005). This research shows that there can be various injuries to the brain of an artist which result in important changes in content and technique, but which have no effect at all on the artist's style. For instance, lesions in temporal/parietal regions of the brain of a certain designer caused him to shift from using many small strokes and cross-hatchings in his pictures to using fewer strokes and bold lines angled differently. Nonetheless, he used the new technique to continue to draw in the same realistic representational style. Given several such studies with damage in various locations, one implication is that the capacity for style is not localized: there is no style module in the brain. But the larger point is that style and technique seem to depend on different neural capacities, however localized or distributed those capacities might be.

That point can be extended to representational content and style. The capacity to depict objects in a certain style may be unaffected even if brain damage to one or another region impairs the ability to produce pictures of objects of certain kinds. For example, lesions may make it impossible for a Fauvist to depict faces in atypical colors in the characteristic Fauvist way, but leave the ability to use unnatural colors with objects of other kinds unimpaired. Not every type of content will be served by brain functions as localized as face recognition is. Still, the evidence initially suggests a dissociation of some kind, between the ability to represent recognizable objects and the ability to paint in a recognizable style. How is this dissociation to be understood?

The most straightforward way would be to hold that style, technique, and content are supported by distinct capacities or systems. However, that oversimplifies what the evidence implies. Zaidel discusses a patient with bilateral parietal wounds who is able to recognize depicted objects at different orientations but cannot report the orientation or egocentric location of the object he can see. In light of this, she argues, "different orientations . . . are not critical visual features for gaining meaning from pictorial re-presentations" (Zaidel 2005: 128). She has suggested that other features, such as color, are not necessary for the purpose of object recognition, either. These claims are not entirely surprising since it is known that there are neurons that respond to non-accidental properties of objects independently of point-of-view and (within limits) of orientation, and it is also known that color and shape are processed by different systems in the brain. If orientation and color are thought to make some contribution to style, then the implication of Zaidel's claim is that style and content are processed differently. But there are reasons to think that the difference in function is not entirely clear cut.

For instance, it's true that a capacity for distinguishing different orientations is not necessary to recognize what a picture depicts. Yet orientation can affect the *ease* of recognition at least. And with respect to color, in some paintings, color interacts with shape and surface properties, supporting our ability to recognize what a picture represents. Margaret Livingstone (2002) describes a work of Cezanne in which there is a color spreading effect. Color is experienced, she argues, as being more homogeneous across surfaces than it is in fact; surfaces defined by an object's contour lines, which are themselves incomplete. This spreading is due to the coarse way that the color system's neurons code color, giving the location of the color a certain indeterminacy. While the bold contour lines serve to constrain the spreading of color, that spreading enhances the perceived continuity of color across the surface, reinforcing the perception of shape by which the objects are recognized. In that case, the processing of a putatively stylistic feature contributes to the processing of a representational one.

Thus the apparent dissociations of content and style will have to be explained in another way. Zaidel herself suggests another approach. She argues that the capacity to produce pictures in a certain style depends on a type of neural plasticity in the adult brain: the ability of new regions to take on functions they did not previously have. The discovery of this kind of plasticity is important because it may come into play, not only in response to gross brain damage, but in various ways in the normal brain. In that case, it could underwrite manners of depiction that result in different styles. The capacity to produce work in a certain style could thus be vested in patterns of activity across regions that respond to ordinary features, and style would persist simply because the patterns are recreated across features other than those to which damaged regions would ordinarily respond. Zaidel suggests that styles depend on abilities or skills, and it might be argued that this can be understood, not solely at the behavioral level, but in terms of the brain's facility in deploying its own perceptual and cognitive resources; a kind of neural know-how, in effect. Thus in pictorial art, styles depend on something like the strategic deployment of representational resources in characteristic ways.

This possibility is illustrated nicely by Zeki's (1999) claim that artists such as Vermeer and Michelangelo represent situations to which several different event schemas might be applied; for instance, Vermeer's *Woman with a Gentleman at the Virginals* and Michelangelo's Rondini *Pietà*. Each work has features that activate a number of systems including those for texture, color, spatial location, and shape. The vagueness or multivocity of these images depends on the fact that the scenes that are represented are compatible with more than one narrative schema or event category. Events are categorized, in the first instance, by ways of segmenting them into action or movement patterns (implicit in a static picture). Thus, not only the imagination, but also the visual system, is presented with a categorization puzzle, and the perceiver is drawn in to a processing task that encourages her to deploy her visual abilities in certain ways. But the two works are distinctively different in that regard. With the Michelangelo sculpture, the perceptual completion of shape is of central importance. That completion may depend on a process of perceptual filling-in that derives from an interaction of shape-from-shading with a partial categorization process, e.g., involving face recognition activity in the fusiform gyrus. The Vermeer painting also provides opportunities to segment objects using shape discontinuities defined by shading patterns. But that is combined with a use of color–form relations that creates a different kind of task, one in which the results of various types of processing must be reconciled. This contributes to a distinctive mood or tone that makes the experience of this work very different from that of the Michelangelo.

On this model, then, putatively stylistic features would be defined as in some ways like the distortions, enhancements, or exaggerations of object properties described by Ramachandran. They would be caused by techniques, such as chiaroscuro or a partial bas relief effect, that elicit various interactive processes in response to impoverished or stimuli, engaging the mind. The relevant systems are the ones also used for perceptual categorization, and they are activated by stylistic features in the service of diverse perceptual categorization tasks. Thus, as on the other two models I have considered, style and content are related, but style contributes to perceptual recognition in a special way. However, in contrast to ethological triggers that cause object recognition behavior automatically, stylistic features are diagnostic of a process. In that respect, they are heuristic in both senses of the term that apply to Gombrich's account: they allow for the efficient use of resources and they promote the quick engagement of a line of processing.

In these respects, too, the model has an evolutionary cast. It explains style in terms of uses of evolved structures and gives stylistic features a facilitating role in an evolutionary process that is like that played by certain features in the natural world. Beyond that, however, this third model has an evolutionary dimension of a new kind. It has been argued by a number of writers that biological evolution is not a well-oiled machine. In nature, the development of organs is often a matter of the accidental modification of existing structures, and the genetic basis for the modification is then passed on if the modification helps its possessors to survive. This "making do" construal of evolution (as Ramachandran has called it) applies not only to the evolved structures in the brain, but on the present account, it also applies to the use of those structures as well. That is, the short-term neural plasticity that underwrites the appropriation of structures and processes for various tasks, for which they are sometimes not especially well designed, is governed by principles of competition in which short-cut, secondary functions are assigned to the structures and processes. These tend to be preserved within the ecology of the brain to the extent that they get the job done. This is evolution on a micro-scale; of viable patterns of neural activity and of the perceptual knowledge that depends on them.

So for example, spatial imprecision is one characteristic feature of Impressionist art. In Monet's painting, *Poppy Field Outside of Argentueil*, there is a sense of movement, as if wind were blowing across the flowers in the field (Livingstone 2002). This is produced by the use of bright red-orange hues for the flowers against the obviously different grey-green background of the grass, but where the different colors are equiluminant. As I have noted, the system responsible for spatial location depends on luminance contrast, so that in this painting, the "where" system is unable to precisely locate the flowers in the scene and their position is registered by the color system instead; and that is a system that is not well-suited to perform that task. The result is a kind of spatial instability. Thus a distinguishing mark of Impressionism is explained in the following way: The nature of the perceptual task creates conditions in brain's environment to which existing structures cannot respond well. To preserve the healthy functioning of the visual system and facilitate the flow of information, a structure is pressed into service, and its function is modified. The process involves an interaction in the sense that the appropriation of the color system for spatial location creates a relation between color processing and spatial perception in which the latter depends on the former. This is born out of a relation between the color system and the system for spatial location, in which the where system is, in a sense, turned off for the task, while the color system is turned on. This modification is relatively effective, in so far as objects in the picture are spatially located in a coarse-grained way, sufficient to distinguish the position of one flower from another in space. Because the registration of motion where there is none is harmless in this case (there being no negative consequences for the overall functioning of the brain), and similar perceptual tasks recur, the relevant modifiability is preserved. Thus do the uses of neural structures evolve.

There are a number of virtues with this sort of interactive account. Note first that, as the examples I have given suggest, it implies a shift in focus when stylistic features are identified. They are no longer viewed as the basic elements of a picture such as color and shape, but rather are emergent features that depend on those elements as they interact. The question then is not, as Zaidel suggests, which basic features are stylistic in the sense of being unnecessary for the representation of objects; color, for instance, as against shape. The question is how color spreading, shape-from-shading, spatial imprecision and the like are produced and function stylistically. This shift to a level of emergent properties is consistent with the claim that that is sometimes made, that style has a *physiognomic* quality; i.e., it is not explicable in terms of isolated features but depends on a holistic combination of features that make style a property of a picture overall.[5] One reason for thinking that style is physiognomic in this way is that it explains why we are able to quickly recognize the style of a painting without close scrutiny, as we walk through the museum or gallery. There is a certain "look" that, with some exposure, we can learn to identify. Spatial imprecision may not be found at every point in an Impressionist painting, but it is a general or diffuse quality that can be seen, without having to look in a particular place. This phenomenon fits well with the interactive model in two respects: physiognomic features function heuristically, in the sense that they promote a quick and easy response to a perceptual categorization task; and the model provides an explanation of why and how such features can be so construed. In addition, the explanation in terms of interactions among structures and systems gives meaning to the claim that pictures can have properties that are "holistic" in some sense.

Moreover, because of the nature of neural plasticity that is presupposed by this account, the same perceptual categorization task can be performed using different sets of resources, which are strategically combined. Thus, while flowers are recognized in the Monet painting as small patches of color, in another painting in which there is more luminance contrast the flowers may be recognized as localizable shapes. Because engaging different systems and structures is what underwrites the different styles on

---

[5] This is a corollary to other ideas that the physiognomic view of style may imply; i.e., that styles are expressive of individual personalities or their cultural analog (Meskin 2002: 494). As I have noted earlier, my concern here is with the relation of style to representational content rather than to expressive content. So in citing the physiognomy of style, I do not have these other ideas in mind.

this account, there is a natural sense to the claim that there can be a synonymy of styles. The interactive model tells us *what* can be different, even where representational content is the same.

Nonetheless, I suggest that the interactive account faces a number of problems in which virtue seems to turn to vice. The first problem concerns the claim that stylistic features serve to signal to the visual system something of the kind of processing that the picture would require and to present challenges that encourage the process to begin. That claim would seem to be undermined by the argument that styles have a physiognomic nature and function heuristically to provide for the quick recognition of style. That function, in effect, would seem to forestall perceptual engagement rather than encourage it. It amounts to relying on holistic qualities with which styles are associated to perform a task, instead of undertaking further processing. Furthermore, it looks as if stylistic features, such as spatial imprecision, are themselves the result of processing; i.e., they depend on interactions among systems such as color and form. Thus they cannot be said to induce a processing effort, at least to that extent. They are the effect of the process in question and not the cause.

Second, the claim that synonymy of styles can be explained by the fact that different perceptual strategies can be used to identify the same representational content would seem to have an unwanted corollary. Given the construal of neural plasticity on which that claim rests, it should also be possible for the same stylistic feature to be produced through different perceptual strategies. For instance, along with the presence of equiluminance between object and background to create a sense of spatial instability, a similar sense can be produced by using small coarse brush strokes to represent a highly variegated or textured scene, such as leaves on trees or many multi-colored flags along an avenue. In this case, there is a complex correspondence problem (determining which brush strokes represent the same color or a certain leaf on a tree) and the viewer's eye movements create many different matches. This gives the leaves and flags a dynamic quality that makes them seem to move. The problem then is that, if different strategies can give rise to the same style in this way, it follows that styles cannot be individuated by the type of strategies they tend to induce.

Third, representational and stylistic features often arise from a common process in which, in its early stages, any of the more basic features that are involved can be said to control and provide direction. By extension, it is natural to think that, once they have been produced and perceived, stylistic and representational features themselves interact in subsequent interpretive processing, such that control is distributed across the two emergent types. It comes as no surprise, of course, that recognition of the objects and events that are depicted can serve to encourage the investigation and interpretation of pictures. So it would seem that there is nothing special about style in that regard.

Fourth, the interactive account of style does not escape the New Riddle that I have described. It only gives it a different ground. While the relation of style and content no longer derives from a perceptual plasticity due to variable conceptual schemes, it is still dependent on variable ways of appropriating perceptual and cognitive resources.

Because the perception of representational and stylistic features derives from a common, interactive process, there may be no way to say under what description stylistic features should be identified. Monet's painting might be taken to represent poppies, not as having a location at any moment and swaying as the breeze blows through the field, but rather as vague objects with no fixed contours; something like diffused smoke rings or diaphanous clouds. The painting could be a realistic one for all we can tell. In that case, spatial imprecision loses its status as a stylistic feature and becomes part of what the picture represents. For the world depicted by a painting like that, it would be pictures of finely outlined flowers that employ spatial anomalies, and not the Monet. Such pictures would give an unnatural sense of timelessness and cold, we might say, as of flowers made rigid by a freezing rain. Emphasizing rather than diminishing luminance contrast, the flowers in these pictures would be depicted in a semi-abstract and unrealistic guise.

Finally, in so far as the account focuses on neuropsychological processes in individual picture makers and perceivers, it might be objected that it ignores the *historicity* of pictorial styles, i.e., the ways in which the nature of a style depends on the historical context in which it arises and, in particular, on its relation to other styles that have gone before, to which it may be a response. The same might be said for the very distinction between content and style. I have argued that visually identical pictures might be seen as being either Realist or Impressionist in style depending on the context, and it is natural to think that what is required for a proper understanding of such pictures is knowledge of their location in the history of art. Moreover, the turn to this account was motivated partly by a rejection of Gombrich's evolutionary epistemology as a model for pictorial art history and the development of styles over time, However, it is not clear whether the interactive theory provides an alternative view of how the dynamics of pictorial art history might be understood. It might thus be inferred then that the turn to a theory of styles in terms of perceptual strategies and neural plasticity amounts to a rejection of historical accounts generally. To be sure, the interactive model implies that the style/content distinction is relative, if not to beliefs and cultural practices, at least to ways of using perceptual resources in particular times and places. Still, it says little about how ways of using resources come to be preferred or how they might change over time.

Thus, while this model of style and its relation to content is promising, I think that it must be further elaborated and reconstrued. I believe that each of these problems can be successfully addressed. But that requires pursuing some new lines of thought.

## 2. Short-term plasticity and style

In general, the problems noted above have a common source; namely, the fact that both stylistic and representational features derive from low-level processes in which two or more systems are involved. The systems work together, but they also compete. For instance, the use of shading in pictures is a technique that can be associated with various styles, depending on how pronounced the contrast is between the background and the figure whose shape is represented through shading patterns falling across its surface. The effects range from the strong light–dark contrast in the *tenebrism* of Caravaggio to the light chiaroscuro modeling of Raphael. In the shape-from-shading process that plays a role in these works, shading patterns initially indicate partial shape. However, the patterns are typically ambiguous, and there is gradual fading toward their edges. Thus, the initial representation of shape is influenced by prior experience, and its fit with the shading patterns can serve to reinforce them in a certain way, pushing the process toward a resolution. At the same time, some modification of the shape representation may be required by the effort to define the shading patterns. In this way, there is a trade-off or dynamic distribution of control that evolves over a very short period of time. In response to the paintings of Caravaggio and Raphael, it would seem, the perception of stylistic features is the result of low-level processes that cannot be said to be caused by the perception of style and that are also involved in the recognition of pictorial content.

Nonetheless, several considerations suggest that stylistic features can be understood as engaging the visual system in a special way. For one thing, the processing of information does not stop once style is perceived. The perception of stylistic features must be sustained; thus there are ongoing interactions among the relevant systems. In light of that, there is a sense in which such features could be described as being present implicitly at the outset, namely, as dispositional causal powers embodied in the relevant techniques. At the same time, to say that a point has been reached at which the perception of style must be sustained also reflects the fact that some stability in the distribution of control across the systems has been achieved. In that respect, style has a distinctive role. At the neurological level, style *is* that distribution of control. Moreover, beyond the ongoing processes by which the perception of style is sustained, there will be subsequent interpretive processes of other kinds, which grasping the style of the picture can be said to prompt.

For example, in Georges de La Tour's painting, *Joseph the Carpenter*, the young boy Jesus looks at Joseph as he works, their faces illuminated only by a candle that Jesus holds. It may be, as Robert Solso (1996) has argued, that a believer who knows the title of the painting will infer that the boy is Jesus and then see the light reflected from his face as amplified by a divine inner glow. However, if so, I suggest that the inference is fueled by the more basic processes that depend on light–dark contrasts that makes the boy's face seem brighter than anything else in the scene. These processes are prior to the effects of beliefs, and activation of the beliefs is encouraged by them. In this way, shading effects are stylistic features that engage the perceiver and promote further reflection and thought.

In addition, in those instances in which pictures are categorized quickly by their stylistic features as a result of the viewer's familiarity, the fact that there is limited engagement is precisely what would be expected on this account. According to it, what style signals to the viewer is an extent and type of investigation that is likely to be rewarded, given a level of facility with a particular task. In any case, familiarity does not preclude the influence of style on subsequent processing for new perceptual tasks. The fact that stylistic features are sometimes not used in that way does not mean that they should not be understood in terms of this power.

In response to the problem that the same stylistic feature can be produced by pictorial techniques that elicit different types of perceptual strategy, it may be said that the range of strategies will be limited as a matter of fact. In that respect, a particular style will supervene on whatever strategy is responsible for it, and it will be identical to a finite disjunctive set of interactive processes. This variability is important, since the concept of engagement implies that the nature and extent of engagement will be partly a function of the viewer's level and type of perceptual expertise.

In reply to the objection that there is nothing special about stylistic features as far as engagement is concerned, I reiterate a similarity between the interactive theory and Gombrich's ancestral view: both treat stylistic features as diagnostic of the kind of processing a picture will require. On the ancestral view, in doing this, such features are distinctive because they facilitate the evolution of knowledge in a structural or procedural sense. I suggest that the interactions on which stylistic features depend can be viewed in that way as well. The difference is that, for Gombrich, the processing in question is a matter of testing the visual hypotheses for accuracy, whereas for the interactive theory, it is a matter of first resolving the relation between content and style; i.e., defining the aspects of the picture itself. Nonetheless, the spreading of color in a picture is like simplicity in a hypothesis. It invites further processing and signals the promising line to take. In that sense, it is style rather than content that exercises control, since the second-order structural/procedural status of a feature is defined precisely by way of contrast to the first-order semantic status of properties by which content is identified. Of course, I have argued that, on the interactive approach, there is a dynamic allocation of control among the systems on which stylistic features depend and, by extension, that we would expect similar trade-offs between content and style themselves. But that does not undermine the theory. It only means that the status of a feature can change. When a putatively representational feature dominates or guides the perceiver's response to a picture, it then assumes the mantle of style.

Of course it may seem far-fetched to think that, when we recognize the events depicted in Poussin's *Rape of the Sabine Women* or Gericault's *Raft of Medusa* and that causes us to reflect on what the pictures mean in a larger sense, the representations of events then become aspects of style. But two considerations show that this is a plausible idea. The first is that there is a puzzle about the style/content relation; viz. that sometimes styles are identified with types of content, as for instance in the regional landscapes of the Barbizon School. Moreover, certain types of content in paintings by a particular artist in his individual style can have far more market value that pictures with other contents in that same style. It can be argued that, from the collector's perspective anyway, the full construal of his style includes paradigmatic content types. But the account of how content can assume the role typically played by stylistic features helps explain these facts.

The second consideration that supports the claim that representational features can become stylistic ones is that there is evidence that, when a feature is the object of focused attention, there is a modulation of activity of the neurons that fire in response to it. To that extent, there is an enhancement of the representational features by which we identify objects, which is like the modulation of the qualities of features by which styles are identified when two or more systems interact.

The problem is that it is thus that the New Riddle returns. For it is reasonable to think that, if content can function stylistically, then style can be seen as part of what a picture depicts. There is, in that respect, a neurological basis for the New Riddle of Style. But there is also an explanation in neurological terms of how it is resolved as a matter of fact. The resolution depends on the adoption of strategic patterns of resource use in the context of an ongoing competition for time, memory, and energy. It is, to that extent, not the result of social practices, nor is it the result of sheer conditioning, which is insensitive to the need to use resources efficiently and economically. It also need not be viewed simply as a matter of learning, even in a broader sense than a conditioned response. The appeal to learning results in an incremental model of stylistic change. And the problem is that new styles can appear abruptly and be radically different from what has gone before. This is where the concept of evolution can help. We can think of these changes as being the result of something like random mutations of interactive processes, which happen to coincide with and serve well new dimensions to the tasks that arise in our perceptual milieu. Thus they tend to be preserved and recur. In this way, the ideas of interaction and evolution provide an improved account of the development of pictorial style.

However, it is here that the matter of the historicity of style looms large. Surely, one might say, styles and their relation to contents do depend on social and cultural practices, and an acquired knowledge of the history of those practices is required for a full understanding of style. Moreover, some explanation is needed of how significant stylistic changes come to be accepted after they are introduced, a central aspect of the history of pictorial art. I think that two responses can be made to address this concern, which suggest ways in which the historical location of styles can figure in the interactive account.

First, it is important to note that the model is not at all inconsistent with the claim that historical knowledge can be required for a proper understanding of a work of pictorial art. On the contrary, it provides an explanation of how such knowledge might be brought to bear. According to it, where conceptual and theoretical knowledge is required for the identification and comprehension of styles, knowledge and belief can penetrate basic perception itself. Thus it is not the case that styles are identified by way of historical knowledge which is wholly separate from how the works appear visually. My view is that the change in wrought through the recruitment of perceptual systems in a dynamic process in which various features vie for control.

Second, while I have argued that a reliance on historical knowledge is often unnecessary for the identification or categorization of a style in a basic sense, the account I have given assumes that perceptual processes have histories themselves, in terms of which the promulgation of styles must be understood. The implication is that relations among styles over time, as well as our grasp of those relations, can take more than one form. Specifically, while the history of ideas about pictures and styles is important, the past forms of perceptual encounters with pictures are important as well and can affect our responses to stylistic features in the here-and-now. One way to make this distinction is to say that historical knowledge is encoded, not only in semantic memory, but in *episodic memory*, as well. In that case, the historical component of our understanding of pictorial style can take the form of context effects, such as the encoding specificities that have been associated with episodic memory. For instance, viewers will more readily categorize a picture as exemplifying a certain style when it is seen in a setting that is like the one in which the picture was initially seen and in which the style/content differentiation processes unfolded in a certain form. Cultural and social history then become relevant, insofar as the nature of our viewings of pictures can be manipulated by institutional procedures and available technologies. In museums and art history books, for instance, pictorial artworks are commonly grouped in accordance with familiar style categories. This affects how the pictures are perceived in other venues: facilitating or challenging style categorization, depending on how like or unlike the original setting the subsequent venue happens to be. The point, then, is that the relevant historical knowledge need not be sociological, but can take the form of response proclivities—biases in the use of perceptual know-how—that are the result of the viewer's perceptual past. The perceiver's knowledge of this past is embodied in its effects on his perceptual strategies.

## 3. Conclusion

One central issue in the theory of style is how the relation between style and content should be understood. I have argued that it can be explained in terms of interactive processes in the visual brain. Having considered and rejected two other ways in which science might be said to provide models for both the distinctiveness of style and its intimate connection to content, I have developed a version of the interactive model in some detail. It explains how style and content are related but also distinct. Stylistic features are implemented in the brain in an evolution-like process in which they serve as prompts and guides to the processing of pictorial content. Thus neurologically speaking, style and content are intertwined.

## References

Baxandall, Michael (1994). "Fixation and Distraction," in J. Onians (ed.), *Sight and Insight: Essays in Honor of E. H. Gombrich*. London: Phaidon.

N. Bryson (2003). "The Newal Interface." *Blow-up: Photography, Cinema, and the Brain*. Warren Neidich Riverside, CA: University of California Press.

Currie, Gregory (1995). *Image and Mind: Film, Philosophy, and Cognitive Science*. Cambridge: Cambridge University Press.

——(2004).

Danto, Arthur (1964). "The Artworld." *Journal of Philosophy* 61: 571–84.

——(1991). "Narrative and Style." *Journal of Aesthetics and Art Criticism*, 49: 201–9.

David Freedberg and Vittorio Gallese (2007). "Motion, Emotion, and Empathy in Esthetic Experience." *Trends in Neuroscience*, 11(5): 197–214.

Gombrich, Ernst (1956). *Art and Illusion*. Princeton, NJ: Princeton University Press.

——(1968). "Style," in D. L. Sills (ed.), *International Encyclopedia of Social Sciences* vol. 15. New York: Macmillan.

Kandel, Eric and Sarah Mack (2006). "A Parallel between Radical Reductionism in Science and in Art." *Annals of the New York Academy of Sciences*, 1001: 272–94.

Livingstone, Margaret (2002). *Vision and Art: The Biology of Seeing*. New York: Harry N. Abrams.

Meskin, Aaron (2002). "Style," in Dominic Lopes and Berys Gaut (eds.), *Routledge Companion to Aesthetics*. New York and London: Routledge.

Onians, John (2007). *Neuroarthistory*. New Haven, CT: Yale University Press.

Stephen E. Palmer and J. S. Gardner (2006). "Aesthetic Issues in Spatial Cognition." *Spatial Vision*, 21: 431–49.

Ramachandran, V. S. (1990). "Interactions between Motion, Depth, Color, and Form: The Utilitarian Theory of Perception," in C. Blakemore (ed.), *Vision: Coding and Efficiency*. Cambridge: Cambridge University Press.

——and W. Hirstein (1999). "The Science of Art: A Neurological Theory of Aesthetic Experience." *Journal of Consciousness Studies*, 6: 15–57.

Robinson, Jenefer (1981). "Style and Significance in Art History." *Journal of Aesthetics and Art Criticism*, 40: 5–14.

——(1984). "General and Individual Style in Literature." *Journal of Aesthetics and Art Criticism* 43: 147–58.

——(1985). "Style and Personality in Literary Work," *Philosophical Review*, 94: 227–47.

Schapiro, Meyer (1994). "Style," in *Theory and Philosophy of Art: Style, Artist, and Society*. New York: George Braziller.

Schier, Flint (1986). *Deeper Into Pictures: An Essay on Pictorial Representation*. Cambridge: Cambridge University Press.

Solso, Robert (1996). *Cognition and the Visual Arts*. Cambridge, MA: MIT Press.

Stafford, Barbara (2007). *Echo Objects*. Chicago: University of Chicago Press.

Walton, Kendall (1970). "Categories of Art." *Philosophical Review*, 79: 334–67.

——(1979). "Style and the Products and Processes of Art," in Berel Lang (ed.), *The Concept of Style*. Philadelphia: University of Pennsylvania Press.

Wollheim, Richard (1979). "Pictorial Style: Two Views," in Berel Lang (ed.), *The Concept of Style*. Philadelphia: University of Pennsylvania Press.

——(1995) "Style in Painting," in C. Van Eck, J. McAllister, and R. Van de Vaal (eds.), *The Question of Style in Philosophy and the Arts*. Cambridge: Cambridge University Press.

Zaidel, Dahlia W. (2005). *Neuropsychology of Art*. New York: Psychology Press.

Zeki, S. (1999). *Inner Vision: An Exploration of Art and the Brain*. Oxford: Oxford University Press.

——(1993). *A Vision of the Brain*. Cambridge, MA: Blackwell.

# 24

# Varieties of Pictorial Judgement: A Functional Account

*Norman H. Freeman*

## 1. Current situation

The emergence of experimental psychology out of philosophy happened rapidly without general agreement on principles for reintegration of philosophy and psychology. In compensation, there are examples of cooperation. One thinks of philosophy of mind with psychological theory of mind (the package is sometimes known in the trade, after a comment by Adam Morton, as the theory of theory-theory). Auspicious conditions for that cooperation occurred when Bennett (1978), Dennett (1978), and Harman (1978) identified criteria for an empirical belief-test.

Where a theory of pictures is concerned, sporadic interchanges between philosophy and psychology have occurred. Thus, classes of psychology students have been startled by why a picture of you is not a picture of your identical twin, and its psychological importance in analyses of representation (e.g., Freeman and Adi-Japha, 2008). For general issues, let us glance at the labour of critics addressing the intuitive conceptions of members of the public. For performance arts, critics still circle around issues of *authenticity* and *authority* (Who has the right to decide what a dance may be said to mean? What is an authentic re-presentation of what Ibsen might have aimed at? Should 'period instruments' be used for Albinoni?). Central to such considerations is the gap between score and performance, or between script and performance, lending focus to the work of dance critics, music critics, or theatre critics. Drafting somewhat analogous questions for pictorial art highlights the fact that pictorial art criticism remains a dispersed endeavour. What is *the* central issue for pictorial art critics? I propose below that the psychology of the pictorial must necessarily be analysed as an account of a dispersed endeavour.

Psychology must account for viewers' engagement with pictures, from glancing at sketches to contemplative sessions in a gallery. Further, undeniable failures in pictorial engagement occur, and psychologists also must explain the significance of people's antipathies, even. One cannot explain pictorial success without attempting to explain pictorial failure, or viewers' adoption of excellent insights that harden into fallacies until they make the dreary list in Beardsley (1981). The suggestion made later is that our minds are so shaped that propensity towards failure necessarily attends success when viewers face some challenges.

The main theme next is the representational function of pictures; but it would be an impoverished account that left representation isolated from other pictorial functions (isolation was one limitation on the generalizability of Schier 1986). We begin with an everyday 'general-purpose' conception of pictures.

## 2. Brief consideration of some viewers and some pictures

Maybe 'we ordinarily look to art for beauty, expressiveness, style and formal qualities. Our aesthetic understanding consists precisely in coming to understand concepts like these in increasingly adequate ways' (Parsons 1987: 13). Many pre-adolescents find it difficult to comprehend how an unattractive scene could possibly inspire an attractive representational picture: ugliness in the scene seemingly transparently transfers onto the picture plane thereby marring the picture (Freeman and Sanger 1993). It is straightforward for interview-based research to identify symptoms of the development of 'increasingly adequate ways' of understanding (Freeman 2004; Freeman and Parsons 2001). What is hard is to discern how the criteria for 'adequate' should be formulated. That would seem to be a service best provided by philosophical aesthetics.

Parsons's functional approach to what we might expect of art, does not depend much on giving a causal account of how any given picture supports any particular function. As long as viewers find aesthetically relevant qualities, that picture will have worked on the viewer's mind. Such an approach evidently puts the viewer's mind at the centre of an analysis, compared with putting the picture at the centre (Freeman 2000). The aim of picture-centred research is to be meticulous about explaining how any given picture either causes effects or falls short. Such an approach overlaps with Parsons's approach when specifying primary functions; except that where Parsons formulated the matter as one of what we might ordinarily look for, one now asks what pictures themselves might do for us. Pictures can be 'emotionally engaging, eye-catching, and memorable' (Willats 1997: 25). Willats focused on representational formal properties, such as perspective lines, but extended to the attractiveness of some wilful violations of rules, particularly by Klee. For non-representational pictures, it may also be feasible formally to identify how they attract viewers. The paintwork of Pollock, gratifyingly anarchic though it may appear, is organized around fractals that not only may be reliable enough for settling authenticity in attributions (Abbott 2006) but might explain some of the pictures' visual allure. In an ultra-naturalistic stance, the fractal statistics of chaotic systems seem to 'display the fingerprints of nature' (Taylor et al. 1999: 25). Part of pictorial satisfaction might be sought in some ancient fit between people and visual environments. So might part of pictorial aversion to 'uncomfortable images in art and nature' (Fernandez and Wilkins 2008: 1098). But though ancient visual history explains something non-arbitrary of what some painters might exploit, it cannot either be normatively binding on us viewers, or in itself yield a developmental account.

Nor can recent viewing history within one's lifetime be altogether dealt with by picture-centred analysis. Freeman and Parker (1973) showed viewers a succession of abstracts, then in a second session half the shapes re-occurred mixed with shapes hitherto unviewed. Viewers preferred shapes that they erroneously thought they hadn't seen before rather than shapes that they really hadn't seen before. The variable that controlled attractiveness was not individual viewing history for a particular abstract but whether the viewer categorized that abstract as triggering a recognition. That categorization consideration helps in analysis of the question of the viewing history of quasi-recognizable pictures. Hekkert (1995) displayed Cubist portraits where some were rather easy to decipher as being human-figure portrayals; other portraits more obscured the portrayal. For untrained viewers with readily recognizable portrayals (e.g., Picasso's *Clovis Sagot*) how beautiful the pictures were found was dominated by representational function of how recognizable the picture was. For slow-recognizable portrayals (e.g., Braque's *Man Smoking a Pipe*) how beautiful the pictures were found was dominated by complexity of lines in the picture itself. The latter finding accords with one aim of Cubism, namely to manipulate denotation and projection rules so as to force attention to the picture plane: slow recognizability led untrained viewers to concentrate on the complexity of picture plane markings. Even more revealing of the process of engagement with Cubism was a criterion shift in vocationally expert viewers: assessed beauty was dominated neither by recognizability nor by formal complexity of the marks but by how typical a picture was categorized to be as an exemplar of that genre. The experts had put their viewing histories consciously in the service of vocational interest, whence a categorical system led to a new aesthetic stance linking recognition of subject matter and viewers' attraction to a picture.

In sum, a psychological account of pictorial engagement must mediate between analyses of the viewer's mind and of the marks on the picture surface as an object of regard. It is not clear how psychologists identify criteria for mediation between mind-centred and picture-entered analyses.

To set constraints for a psychological account, we provisionally characterize representational depiction as:

(a) representation of something as having a visual appearance, by means of
(b) intentional display of another visual appearance in a marked surface.

That raises questions which were of great concern to us as children, whose early engagement with intuitive art criticism launched our iconophilia:

How we can tell when a representational response to a picture is warranted?
How far can we allow a representational interpretation to proceed?
Does anyone have the authority to tell a viewer when their interpretation is right?
And if someone does, how is pictorial authority earned?

Perhaps we may think of such functional questions as reflecting concerns with *representational reliability*, covering issues of representational *authenticity* and responsibly exercised *authority*. The concerns can be instantiated by even homelier questions than the above, questions such as:

Is this picture clear enough for the viewer to recognize the white horse that it seems to portray?

If the recognition has not occurred, could it be that either the picture or the scene has somehow degraded?

If the recognition seems at all in doubt, to whom can the viewer turn for trustworthy help?

No one wants to mistake a windblown pattern in the sand for an authentic portrait of Winston Churchill (see Putnam 1981), nor to be misled by an inconsiderately given caption to a picture (see Goodman 1976). We turn to such considerations for direct implications for psychological analyses.

## 3. Minimal ontology for pictorial representation

The minimal ontology needed to organize the above representational questions comprises artist, viewer, picture, and state of affairs. Relations between those four in Fig. 24.1 form a net, where all six bidirectional relations are psychologically important (Freeman 1995).

   We can use the net as a sort of map to locate conceptualizations that can be tested for. How do people think that pictorial beauty arises? We noted earlier young children's transparency assumption that a picture can only be as beautiful as the state of affairs it depicts: one cannot have a beautiful picture of a rusting car. Later, children come to see the artist as the beautifier irrespective of the state of affairs being depicted (late childhood for city children, early adolescence for rural islanders: Freeman and Sanger 1993). Finally, it is hard for children to reckon with the grain of truth in 'beauty is in the eye of the beholder' (Freeman and Parsons 2001). And so forth: a mature theory of pictures would give due weight to all the relations possible in Fig. 24.1. Certainly in interview about pictorial quality, informants' minds do range over relations (Freeman 2004, 2006). Perhaps one can say that *the functions of a picture may be dispersed over the intentional net of relations*. A developmental account would eventually explain how and why children's minds come to encompass the relations.

   Let us assume not only that Fig. 24.1 maps the mental working space of pictorial reasoning, but that adults become so accustomed to letting their minds range over the space that they notice when anything in a situation impedes the process. That enables us to guess about conditions which provoke viewers' resistance, or, more optimistically, provide 'educational challenges' (Freeman 2004). Presentation of an objet trouvé as though it were a self-evident artwork might obscure the role of an agent. Even with some rearrangement of the object(s) so that an artist can claim some agentive role,

STATE of AFFAIRS

PICTURE

ARTIST ..........      ..... VIEWER

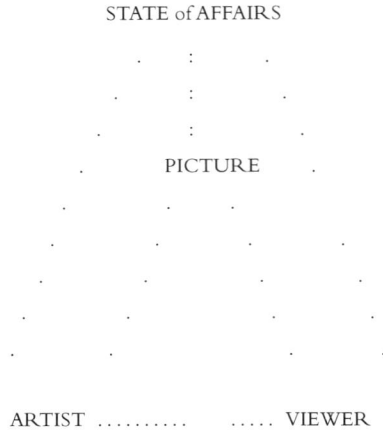

Figure 24.1  Four entities contract six bidirectional relations

viewers might resist. Such was the fate of Carl André's *Equivalent VIII*: unframed bricks tastefully piled on the gallery floor (see Eaton 1988, for discussion). Viewers were often scathing. Regardless of the rights and wrongs of such a viewer stance, there is the following attractive aspect to incorporating evidence on an artist into one's inspection of the putative artwork. Putnam (1981) drew attention to the need for constraint in applying a concept of pictorial representation, by contrast with the sparking off of capricious recognitions by natural patterns in the sand. Inclusion of an artist along with viewer and picture is an enrichment of the restricted viewer–picture relationship. Even preschool children spontaneously attend to evidence of an agent when evaluating the possibility of a picture representing something. Gelman and Ebeling (1998) showed preschoolers a set of vague shapes and then asked the children to say what had they seen. When the children had been told that the pictures had been made by accident with a paintpot, representational labelling (e.g., a 'teddy') did occur on many trials; yet when told that the pictures had been done on purpose, that level roughly doubled. Conceivably, 'Children might call a picture that looks like a bird "a bird" not merely because it looks like a bird, but because its appearance makes it likely that it was created with the intent to represent a bird. In general, appearance—and shape in particular—is seen as an excellent cue to intention' (Bloom and Markson 1998: 203). That is a case example of trying to balance a picture-centred against a mind-centred analysis. Young children incorporate respect for agency into their emerging intuitive judgment of pictures (Freeman 2008).

For untutored adults, it is not enough for agency merely to be claimed, or for a minimal trace of an artist to be vaguely detectable: a 'folk theory of art' encompasses a notion that a pictorial artwork should present an appearance of being well crafted (Hekkert 1995). It might be feasible to amend the earlier characterization of representational depiction, to representational pictorial artwork:

(a) the representation of something as having a visual appearance, by means of
(b) intentional display of another visual appearance in a marked surface, such that
(c) evidence of the role of an agent is intentionally displayed.

How defensible that unrefined position may be is a matter for debate. Certainly an emphasis on craftsmanship can on occasion impede pictorial engagement. Gross (1973) argued that viewers are right to expect evidence on why the artist chose as she did, allowing viewers to admire art by admiring artistry on display. The predictability of viewers' resistance and incomprehension can be deduced by playing thought-experiment 'deletion games' with the net, by interfering with any and many of the relations in different combinations. That seems to be common within philosophical aesthetics, as follows.

One can remove the relation between picture and state of affairs. Thereby the representing relation fails: a really rough scribble of a frog 'simply does not represent her as having any visual properties—properties she may be seen to have' (Lopes 1997: 98). That phrase 'properties she may be seen to have' raises the question 'seen by whom?' thereby making the viewer integral to the thought experiment. Let us add another thought experiment: 'If I tell you I have a certain black horse, and then I produce a snapshot in which he has come out a light speck in the distance, you can hardly convict me of lying; but you may well feel that I misled you' (Goodman 1976: 29). Note how Goodman posed the issue as one of the viewer's unwarranted reliance on the artist (Goodman) as provider of a caption to the picture. The artist had misused his pictorial authority while keeping just this side of the law on the question of pictorial authenticity. What is interesting about the way you might negotiate with Goodman for another picture is the way in which you might articulate your demands to bring your recognitional capacities concerning real horses into line with your recognition of what is in the photo. In accord with the functional analysis of Schier (1986), a marked surface iconifies a referent if and only if (a) the picture triggers a recognition of the referent in (b) a non-privileged viewer who has (c) the disposition to recognize the referent itself (see also Lopes 1997: 178). You might well make the practical picture-centred suggestion that Goodman reconsider the distance between camera and horse, but you would do so via putting your mind centre-stage as a viewer of states of affairs and pictures in your relation with the artist. I propose that most of the interesting cases in everyday encounters with pictures involve the mind ranging over the intentional net. The term 'intentional' is worth expanding: 'Intentionality is that property of many mental states and events by which they are directed at or about or of objects and states of affairs in the world' (Searle 1983: 1). As a communicative artefact, a representational picture *of* Charles I *as* Caesar may simultaneously be a portrait *of* Charles, be *about* the artist's conception of kingship, and be *directed towards* viewers whom the artist hopes to influence. That diversity may be thought of as *intentional dispersion*. That is what the pictorial realm affords, and it is why viewers' minds need to range over so many relations in engaging with the pictorial realm.

It may have been noticed that a role was attributed to the artist 'hoping to influence', a role in conceiving of a viewing public, thus forming a direct link to a viewer in the relational net. It may so happen that the viewing public is very restricted, maybe to someone who commissions, or hopefully will select, the picture for display. Little is known, empirically, about how a viewer's untutored conception of pictorial art comes to encompass such considerations. What is known, though, is that adolescents have a concept of what makes up an exhibition piece that someone commissions or selects. In interview, informants commented on the role of the framing and exhibiting of a picture as a celebration of the work of the artist and as an index of the taste of the exhibitor (Maridaki-Kassotaki and Freeman 2000). Those insights were offered almost unsolicited. Certainly for adolescents, there is a sort of intentional theory of pictures with inferential links readily activated, en route to becoming intuitive art critics (Freeman 2010).

Finally, the inference that exhibitors may unwittingly put their taste on display via the act of exhibiting is a component of an overcritical stance towards the pictorial realm. Perhaps all that some exhibitors display is the size of their art budget. Certainly, adolescents are notorious for their propensity to take up a critical stance. But it was earlier suggested that adversarial criticism of pictures can easily be provoked by interference with processes running over the intentional net, as in the case of Goodman's white horse. Consider what happened when it was announced at Tate Britain that the 2001 Turner Prize was won by Martin Creed who displayed an empty room with lights flickering now and then. The installation 'had people spluttering and complaining that anyone could have done it' (Searle 2001: 3). The role of the artist had been cut out of viewers' model of thinking. To fill the place of the missing artist with 'anyone' is not remotely satisfying. It is of limited use blankly telling viewers that they could have done it, because they hadn't wanted to have done it. The point animating protesters is to know what made the installation worth doing. That seems a worthy moral stance. How does morality get into the picture? Is it built in, emergent, or just tacked on?

At first sight the moral question is too broad. Surely any sort of challenge or perceived failure may be met with disapprobation. As an account of the meaning of art, Dissanayake (1988) opted for an anciently established, adaptive activity 'making special'. If the 'making special' is perceived to be impeded, generalized indignation might well result. We should do well to search out any particularity to pictorial admiration, since there might be some particularity to pictorial disapproval worth considering.

## 4. What an explanation of pictorial psychology might encompass

Interviews have been done by Kindler and Darras (1998) with children in that interesting phase between 7 and 14 years where a critical stance is being built. Let us select some findings and then note aspects of more than anthropological interest.

In explaining what makes a drawing good, 18 per cent of the French children spontaneously specified colour qualities, thereby referring to properties in the picture fitting a picture-centred account, as would 'being realistic' (16 per cent). More congenial to a mind-centred account were the rest of the admirable qualities: being 'well done' (31 per cent), 'beautiful' (29 per cent), even 'pleasing quality' (the latter does sound better in French). For Quebequois children, picture-centred terms were lower—'colour' did not figure as a criterion and 'realism' was at 10 per cent—with being 'well done' at 12 per cent clearly involving artist effort, 'expressive' at 13 per cent and very pleasingly for a mind-centred approach, 'conforming to expectation' at 12 per cent. Children in British Columbia mentioned the picture-centred 'detailed' as a desideratum (14 per cent), and thereafter no surprises, with 'effort put in' at 10 per cent. The most evident aspects are as follows.

First, no answer even remotely approached the conventional 70 per cent threshold that alerts researchers to probe for the possibility of a single dominant consideration (embedded in noise) about what makes a picture a good one.

Second, there was respect for signs of the artist's investment of labour as a reason for appreciating a picture, along with qualities of the picture, the relation between picture and states of affairs ('realism') and, occasionally, the mental set of the viewer (that irresistible 'conforming to expectation'): the foundation ontology in Fig. 24.1. Children's minds are ranging widely within the realm's constraints. That diversity of unsolicited ideas should be the object of explanation.

Can the diversity of the pictorial realm be forced down to a main function? 'Many species generate internal representations, but there is something about the architecture of the human mind that enables children and adults also to produce external notations, that is to use cultural tools for leaving an intentional trace of their communicative and cognitive acts' (Karmiloff-Smith 1992: 139). Figure 24.1 evidently captures the ground-plan of communicative action. One can replace 'picture' with 'utterance': 'When noises have meaning they do not only have distinctive relations with human beings who use them or respond to them but also distinctive connections with some . . . states of affairs . . . in the world' (Heal 1978: 367). Linguistic communication *of* something is from an agent *to* an agent *via* an utterance. Those four entities are the irreducible minimum needed for defining communication. It might be well to take literally an idea that pictorial engagement is akin to other forms of communication in which we 'leave an intentional trace' and, indeed, display our expertise in the medium. Any analysis taking referential acts as the communication of representation would be congenial. Let us briefly look at what such an analysis covers.

The paradigm case of a referential act is when an agent communicates a belief about a state of affairs in a way that enables someone else to identify or to describe or to attend to the state of affairs or a relevant aspect. Communication may not be of explicit readily formulatable belief, but may encompass the variety of epistemic indefiniteness (supposition, guess, assumption) congenial to a view of pictorial intelligence (as in Harrison 2006). Anything that an agent can communicate and a recipient receive falls within the ambit of the relational map in Fig. 24.1. Thus, a scowl might be no more than is needed for an expressive communication of a state of affairs, namely the state of the scowler in being angry. It is often not too difficult for communicators to add a non-linguistic indication of what they are angry about. Again, desires which are so readily linguistically communicable, are in principle pictorially communicable, though there are necessary constraints on the scope of any message. Thus, one can readily deploy universal quantification linguistically, in a variety of ways (with or without distributive predication: All tigers are green; the tiger is widespread) but such universals cannot be directly depicted. Depiction is constrained to particulars of what is put on the canvas. The immediate question is not about what cannot explicitly be pictorially communicated, but whether children's developing pictorial theory encompasses communicative reasoning about conceptions of belief, desire, and emotion that make up a theory of mind (Freeman 2000). Let us take emotional expressivity as a focus.

Expressivity as a topic in children's pictorial thinking was identified in interviews by Parsons (1987) and Lin and Thomas (2002). Freeman and Sanger (1993) questioned 11-year-olds and 14-year-olds on whether an artist's or a viewer's feelings affect evaluation of a picture. We shall adapt the summary in Freeman (2000). With the younger children, 9/12 held that a happy artist would produce a happy picture: expressivity was treated as though it were a transparent relation. But 9/12 older children thought that the artist's skills could override feelings. Again, when the children were questioned about the feelings that a viewer brings to the situation, the pattern of answers reversed: 9/12 younger children denied that a viewer's feelings were relevant and 8/12 older children held the opposite. The younger children regarded a viewer's feelings as irrelevant because they again treated the viewer–picture relation as transparent. Parsons (1987) argued that a concept of an expressivity function was acquired later than a concept of referential representation. Certainly within theory-of-mind research there is typically something like a two-year lag between referential and emotional reasoning (Bradmetz and Schneider 2004; de Rosnay et al. 2004; Freeman and Jackson 2005).

In sum, there develops a sort of intentional theory of pictures, en route to becoming intuitive art criticism (Freeman 2010). But there is a disadvantage to the viewer in having communicative reasoning at the heart of the theory. In linguistic communication, it is often feasible for the speaker to claim authority over what words she used and what they meant. In pictorial communication, agents have pushed such claim to authority beyond its limit: there is no discernible merit in 'This is an artwork because I say it is, and my assertion is sufficient.' Viewers often react with fury to such a claim, but viewers' communicative model of reasoning rather disarms them.

The pictorial domain is shaped by communicative principles, but that does not entail that we should give an explanation in terms of the pictorial being 'precipitated' from our nature as communicative beings. Instead, the pictorial domain might be a cobbled-together affair that people shape towards communicative ends. To that we now turn.

## 5. Explaining pictorial engagement

Within psychology, a long era of attempts to subjugate psychological explanations to formalized general principles ran into the problem of inter-individual and intra-individual inconsistencies. During a research interregnum of computer-simulation modelling, realization dawned that the acquisition of judgement is a cobbled-together affair, with epistemological advance in one domain, e.g., intuitive physics or biology, occurring with different developmental pacemakers from other domains, e.g., folk psychology (or, indeed, graphic arts: Karmiloff-Smith 1992). Realization that the mind is immensely decentralized was naturally congenial to students of evolution, which is itself a cobbled-together process par excellence. Evolutionary thinking then honed current formulations of why matters should be so in psychology (Barrett *et al.* 2002). The leading journal of debate, *Behavioral and Brain Sciences*, still contains intermittent exhortations not to impose unities but to seek recipes for integrating diversities. An evolutionary perspective which holds promise of generating integrative recipes is too easy to misapply, yielding just-so stories or reductionisms. There are guidelines on avoiding just-so stories, avoiding seeking a univocal answer to each research question as though there were some rule doling out one answer to each question. Instead the task is to tessellate no less than four levels of analysis to each question asked by a researcher.

So conventional are the four levels now, that the introductory textbook by Barnard (2004) advertises them on its cover: 'mechanism, development, function and evolution' as 'complementary' answers, not 'rivals for the truth' (2004: 10). 'Mechanism' denotes 'causal explanation': why you do something is because some mechanism is caused to operate at the time (e.g., the triggering of quasi-recognition by some Cubists forces attention to the marks which both promise and impede recognition). 'Development' (ontogenesis) gives the answer 'because something in your lifetime caused the activity' (e.g., prior encounters with art provoked an increase in adequacy of engagement with the artwork). 'Function' gives an answer in terms of what the activity might be for nowadays (e.g., assessing the value of displays as a record of intentional acts). 'Evolutionary' (phylogenesis) gives an answer in terms of something that occurred with your ancestors (e.g., ancestral selection pressure to celebrate likenesses).

Our visual systems evolved to detect natural regularities of biological significance. Automatic processing serves the purpose of recognizing others of our species. Maybe it is no accident that human figure drawing is just about universal for young children as artists. Our visuo-motor systems are hives of representational activity ready to be exploited; and our species eventually found out about that exploitable resource. Artists operate on optic constraints to turn them into visual prostheses, grappling with the problems of how a single shape on the page can denote multiple forms in a state of affairs (a circle can denote a ring, hole, sphere, disc), and how shape combinations constrain the denotations. Pictorial art occurred late in our species history, yet has evolutionary ancient roots in early evolving core domains. Phylogenetic analysis claims no more than that we are as we are because something of adaptive significance happened to our ancestors to make us so (Dennett 1995). Core domains are those that were once biologically advantageous to the development of our species. Art itself does not constitute a unitary core domain, unlike intuitive physics or intuitive mathematics. As Fig. 24.1 suggests, pictorial competence is communicative in nature: we now add that it springs from emergent cross-talk between mechanisms serving two core domains: (a) domain-specific representations of theory of mind, and (b) one strand of domain-specific naïve physics, namely intuitive optics. A prime function of intuitive optics is to understand the minds of other users of that same optics. Understanding how one's own line of sight can be impeded helps to predict the knowledge of someone else whose view gets blocked. Intuitive optics from the core domain of physics seems to conduct cross-talk with the core theory of mind domain (Freeman 2008).

It is always hard to tessellate the four levels of analysis. It makes one uneasy when a writer holds up one level without even nodding towards tessellation with the others. It is easy to misplace one level into the slot reserved for another level (Sherman 1988). Thus, 'It is logically incorrect (to) equate current utility with reasons for historical origin' (Gould 1987: 10). And, explaining why a competence arose phylogenetically cannot tell us how it arises developmentally, nor is there a prior indicator for what any two explanations necessarily have in common. From a developmental perspective, where one learns to take concepts of fundamentally mind-altering change in one's stride, there can be nothing demeaning about grounding aesthetic functions in even very lowly functions, nothing entailing an ontogenetic 'purification' device. Maybe a sense of disinterested beauty needs sexual selection as a phylogenetic permission condition. There is no 'conservation of function axiom' in biological development, no reason why feathers which phylogenetically emerged before flight should not come to serve flight. There is no principled reason why an initial function cannot act as a sort of booster rocket launching something into a new niche, and then just functionally falling away. That sort of occurrence is probably involved in development in all mental domains. Thus, it cannot be a calumny on higher mathematics that it is ontogenetically launched from a mechanism that limits its operations to cardinality. Higher mathematics is not reducible to any sort of jumped-up accountancy. In that light, it cannot be a calumny on our aesthetics that they might be launched from ancient mechanisms promoting things like conspecific recognition and appreciation, and range over a most cobbled-together mental terrain.

## References

Abbottt, A. (2006). 'In the Hands of a Master'. *Nature*, 439: 648–50.

Barnard, C. (2004). *Animal Behaviour: Mechanism, Development, Function and Evolution*. Harlow: Pearson.

Barrett, L., R. Dunbar, and J. Lycett (2002). *Human Evolutionary Psychology*. Basingstoke: Palgrave Macmillan.

Beardsley, M. C. (1981). *Aesthetics*. Indianapolis, IN: Hackett.

Bennett, J. (1978) 'Some Remarks About Concepts'. *Behavioral and Brain Sciences*, 1: 557–60.

Bloom, P. and L. Markson (1998). 'Intention and Analogy in Children's Naming of Pictorial Representations'. *Psychological Science*, 9: 200–4.

Bradmetz, J. and R. Schneider (2004). 'The Role of Counterfactually Satisfied Desire in the Lag between False-Belief and False-Emotion Attributions in Children Aged 4–7'. *British Journal of Developmental Psychology*, 22: 185–96.

de Rosnay, M., F. Pons, P. L. Harris, and J. M. B. Morrell (2004). 'A Lag between Understanding False Belief and Emotion Attribution in Young Children: Relationships with Linguistic Ability and Mothers' Mental-State Language'. *British Journal of Developmental Psychology*, 22: 197–218.

Dennett, D. C. (1978) 'Beliefs about Beliefs'. *Behavioral and Brain Sciences*, 1: 568–70.

——(1995). *Darwin's Dangerous Idea*. New York: Simon & Schuster.

Dissanayake, E. (1988). *What is Art For?* Seattle, WA: Washington University Press.

Eaton, M. (1988). *Basic Issues in Aesthetics*. Belmont, CA: Wadsworth.

Fernandez, D. and A. J. Wilkins (2008). 'Uncomfortable Images in Nature and Art'. *Perception*, 37: 1098–1113.

Freeman, N. H. (1995). 'The Emergence of a Framework Theory of Pictorial Reasoning', in C. Lange-Kuttner and G. V. Thomas (eds.), *Drawing and Looking*. Hemel Hempstead: Harvester Wheatsheaf, pp. 135–46.

——(2000). 'Communication and Representation: Why Mentalistic Reasoning is a Lifelong Endeavour', in P. Mitchell and K. Riggs (eds.), *Children's Reasoning and the Mind*. Hove: Psychology Press, pp. 349–66.

——(2004). 'Aesthetic Judgment and Reasoning', in E. W. Eisner and D. M. Day (eds.), *Handbook of Research and Policy in Art Education*. Mahwah, NJ: Lawrence Erlbaum Associates, pp. 359–78.

——(2006). 'Psychological Analysis of Deciding if Something is Presented in a Picture', in R. Maniura and R. Shepherd (eds.), *Presence: The Inherence of the Prototype within Images and Other Objects*. Aldershot: Ashgate, pp. 135–44.

——(2008). 'Pictorial Competence Generated from Crosstalk between Core Domains', in C. Milbrath and H. M. Trauttner (eds.), *Children's Understanding and Production of Pictures, Drawings and Art*. Cambridge, MA: Hogrefe & Huber, pp. 33–52.

——(2010). 'Children as Intuitive Art Critics', in C. C. Milbrath and C. Lightfoot (eds.), *Arts and Human Development*. Boca Raton, FL: Taylor & Francis, pp. 249–73.

——and E. Adi-Japha (2008). 'Pictorial Intention, Action and Interpretation', in C. Lange-Kuttner and A. Vinter (eds.), *Drawing and the Non-Verbal Mind*. Cambridge: Cambridge University Press, pp. 104–20.

——and L. Jackson (2005). 'Belief-Emotion Lag and the Child's Idea of Heroism: Can the Curse of Knowledge be Lifted for Attributional Inference?' *Hellenic Journal of Psychology*, 2: 46–58.

——and D. M. Parker (1973). 'Affective Preference and Misclassification in a Novel/Familiar Identification Task'. *British Journal of Psychology*, 64: 77–81.

Freeman, N. H. and M. J. Parsons (2001). 'Children's Intuitive Understanding of Pictures', in B. Torff and R. J. Sternberg (eds.), *Understanding and Teaching the Intuitive Mind*. Hove, UK: Erlbaum, pp. 73–92.

——and D. Sanger (1993). 'Language and Belief in Critical Thinking: Emerging Explanations of Pictures'. *Exceptionality Education Canada*, 3: 43–58.

Gelman, S. and K. Ebeling (1998). 'Shape and Representational Status in Children's Early Naming'. *Cognition*, 66: 35–47.

Goodman, N. (1976). *Languages of Art*. Indianapolis, IN: Hackett.

Gould, S. J. (1987). 'Stephen Jay Gould Replies'. *Natural Historian*, 96: 4–6.

Gross, L. (1973). 'Art as the Communication of Competence'. *Social Science Information*, 12: 115–41.

Harman, G. (1978) 'Studying the Chimpanzee's Theory of Mind'. *Behavioral and Brain Sciences*, 1: 515–26.

Harrison, A. (2006). 'What is "Presence"?', in R. Maniura and R. Shepherd (eds.), *Presence: The Inherence of the Prototype within Images and Other Objects*. Aldershot: Ashgate, pp. 161–72.

Heal, J. (1978). 'On the Phrase "Theory of Meaning"'. *Mind*, 87: 359–75.

Hekkert, P. P. M. (1995). *Artful Judgements*. The Hague, Netherlands: Cip-Gegevens Koninklijke Bibliotheek.

Karmiloff-Smith, A. (1992). *Beyond Modularity*. Cambridge, MA: MIT Press.

Kindler, A. M. and B. Darras (1998). 'Culture and Development of Pictorial Repertoires'. *Studies in Art Education*, 39: 147–63.

Lin, S. F. and G. V. Thomas (2002). 'Development of Understanding of Popular Graphic Art: A Study of Everyday Aesthetics in Children, Adolescents, and Young Adults'. *International Journal of Behavioral Development*, 26: 278–87.

Lopes, D. (1997). *Understanding Pictures*. Oxford: Clarendon Press.

Maridaki-Kassotaki, K. and N. H. Freeman (2000). 'Concepts of Pictures on Display'. *Empirical Studies of the Arts*, 18: 151–8.

Parsons, M. J. (1987). *How We Understand Art*. Cambridge: Cambridge University Press.

Putnam, H. (1981). *Reason, Truth and History*. Cambridge: Cambridge University Press.

Schier, F. (1986). *Deeper into Pictures*. Cambridge: Cambridge University Press.

Searle, A. (2001). 'Judges Switched on as Turner Prize Goes to Creed of Nothingness'. *The Guardian*, 10 December, p. 3.

Searle, J. R. (1983). *Intentionality*. Cambridge: Cambridge University Press.

Sherman, P. W. (1988). 'The Levels of Analysis'. *Animal Behaviour*, 36: 616–19.

Taylor, R., A. Micolich, and D. Jonas (1999). 'Fractal Expressionism'. *Physics World*, 12: 25–8.

Willats, J. (1997). *Art and Representation*. Princeton, NJ: Princeton University Press.

# 25

# Pictorial Representation and Psychology

*Derek Matravers*

'Aesthetic questions have nothing to do with psychological experiments, but are answered in an entirely different way.'

Wittgenstein (1970: 17)

The question of the nature of pictorial representation has enjoyed much debate in the recent philosophical past. Prominent in this debate has been the work of Richard Wollheim, one of whose essays on the topic was entitled: 'Representation: The Philosophical Contribution to Psychology' (Wollheim 1977). Hence, a volume such as this seems the appropriate place to discuss Wollheim's contribution. This chapter is divided into three sections. The first outlines, very briefly, Wollheim's account; the second comprises some general remarks about how Wollheim conceived the relation between philosophy and psychology; and the third attempts to make sense of how psychology could be brought to bear on the account.

## 1. Wollheim's account

Wollheim defines pictures in terms of the kind of experience to which they give rise, combined with a standard of correctness for the particular experience. The experience is complex. According to Wollheim:

There are three fundamental perceptual capacities that the artist relies upon the spectator to have and to use. They are ... (one) *seeing-in*: (two) *expressive perception* and: (three) the capacity to experience *visual delight*. (Wollheim 1987: 45)

These correspond roughly to the capacity to see the representational content, the capacity to see expressive content, and the capacity to experience pleasure.[1]

I shall take each in turn. Wollheim gives a succinct characterization of 'seeing-in' in the paper just mentioned:

Confronted with a configuration on a two-dimensional surface, we should think of representation whenever we assign spatiality or a third dimension to what is in front of us—in so far, that is, as this assignment does not derive directly from the spatial properties of the stuffs of which the configuration is constituted. (Wollheim 1977: 160)

There are some objects (the surface of the wall of a room, perhaps) which are two-dimensional painted surfaces, and which we experience as two-dimensional painted surfaces. There are other objects (visual representations) which are two-dimensional painted surfaces, but in which depth can be seen.[2] Not real depth, of course, but illusory or pictorial depth. Wollheim claims that this—which he calls 'seeing-in'—is a complex experience with two aspects: the first modelled on our experience of the surface of the picture (the 'configurational aspect'), and the second modelled on our experience of the 'absent object' in the picture (the 'recognitional aspect'). It is important to bear in mind that the capacity to see-in is a distinctive visual capacity: Wollheim is describing the content of our visual experience. Finally, the standard of correctness is supplied by the intention of the artist: if what we see in the picture corresponds with what the artist intended we see in the picture, then what we have in front of us is a picture of that thing.

Expressive perception is also a distinctive visual capacity—another 'genuine species of seeing' (Wollheim 1987: 80). Wollheim draws on the notion of projection, familiar in psychoanalysis, in which we project our mental state (anger, say) onto someone in our environment and form the false belief that they are angry. This Wollheim calls 'simple projection'. In 'complex projection', by contrast, we project our mental states onto the world, and, as a result, end up experiencing those parts of the world in a way different to that which we would have experienced them had we not projected our emotions. In slightly more detail: the look of certain parts of the world has an affinity with our mental states. We project our mental states onto those parts of the world and they take on a different look; we see them as possessing certain 'projective properties'. How would we describe this look? Wollheim thinks we can do no better than saying that the world is 'of a piece' with the person's mental states (Wollheim 1991: 151).

The third notion, of which Wollheim says least, is that of 'visual delight'. Indeed, discussions and reformulations of seeing-in and of expressive properties can be found in several places in Wollheim's work but there is, to my knowledge, only one discussion

---

[1] There are additional sources of meaning for a painting: meaning arising the through the employment of the device of the internal spectator, textual meaning, historical meaning, secondary meaning, and metaphorical meaning.

[2] This is not quite right as there are some pictures (for example, Jasper Johns's *Flag*) where the content of the picture is up against the picture plane. Wollheim is aware of these difficulties.

of visual delight (Wollheim 1987: 98–100). Wollheim claims that he is not going to define visual delight or explain its nature. Rather, he will answer the following two questions: 'What is the source of visual delight?' and 'What aspect of painting gives us the pleasure that we characteristically derive from it?' Wollheim speculates that the best answer to this might be given on a case-by-case basis, but instead identifies three systematic sources of visual delight. First, the world affects how we see representations, and, in a more interesting manner, representations affect how we see the world. The first is clear; in looking (say) at a Chardin we might think to ourselves that the content of the picture 'is congenial . . . is full of life like a kitchen' (Wollheim 1987: 98); Wollheim is quoting Proust's essay 'Chardin', in his *Contre Sainte Beuve, suivi de Nouveaux Melanges* (Paris, 1954). The reverse arrangement is more opaque:

Pleasure now seeks a Chardin-like quality in domesticity, or a quality which can be discerned only by having looked at Chardin: more generally, a quality which can be discerned only by having looked at representation. Proust makes clear, without making explicit, that his quality is to do with expressive perception. It is to do with projection controlled by a great artist. We now have access to the 'unnoticed life of inanimate objects': unnoticed, but not contingently unnoticed. (Wollheim 1987: 99)

The second source of visual delight is a particular kind of case of moving between the two aspects of experience that define 'seeing-in'. That is, moving between at the one moment an image, and the next moment a paint surface without meaning. However, it is more specific than this: visual delight lies in 'the perception of what is apprehended as detail: detail relative to a more comprehensive, a more distanced view of the marked surface' (Wollheim 1987: 100). The third and final source of visual delight is, superficially at least, clearer: that much of the pleasure of painting 'draws upon synaesthetic associations to what we see: that is, the way in which the motifs and images of painting can stir remembered sensation of smell, taste and hearing' (Wollheim 1987: 100).

## 2. The relation between philosophy and psychology on Wollheim's account

Let us begin by considering, in more general terms, the relation between philosophy and psychology in thinking about the nature of experience. One view, dominant in philosophy in the last half of the last century and exemplified (for aesthetics, at least) in the quotation from Wittgenstein that heads this chapter, is that there is a question specific to each discipline.

1. What is constitutive of an experience?
2. Through what process can such an experience be generated?

The first question—the philosophical question—attempts to throw light on the intrinsic nature of the experience; to provide some grasp of what it is like to have the experience. The answer to this question might surprise people familiar with the experience, but that is only because we are not always good at grasping the nature of our experiences (familiarity, after all, is not understanding). However, the terms in which this question is answered should in principle be available to the person who has the experience by them reflecting on their experience—it should be something that they know, even if they do not know they know it until told by a philosopher. The second question—the psychological question—has no such constraint. David Marr's account of the process underlying our visual experiences includes talk of such notions as 'the primal sketch', 'the 2.5D sketch' and 'the 3D sketch' (Marr 1982). These will be unfamiliar to almost all who are familiar with visual experiences, and not available to them through their reflecting on their visual experiences. Rather, the answer to the psychological question rests on empirical discovery, or speculation on the best explanations of observed psychological phenomena. The philosopher could claim that this tells us nothing about what it is like to have visual experiences, and the psychologist can claim that reflecting on the nature of visual experiences could only result in our rather pointlessly coming up with redescriptions of those experiences.

Such a way of dividing the two enquiries has come under increasing pressure recently. One source of such pressure is that there are many areas where it is not clear what of interest the philosopher could say. Consider, for example, the (so-called) 'basic equation' for colour (for example, red).

X is red if and only if X is perceived as red by qualified observers in the right perceptual circumstances.

The right-hand side of this definition is not contentless; it at least tells us something about what it is for an object to be a certain colour. That is, not every experience we have of an object counts towards determining its colour; it is only experiences of 'qualified observers in the right perceptual circumstances' (provided those can be specified in a non-circular manner). Hence, the colour something seems may not be the colour it is. However, we do not learn much about red itself as the term 'red' appears on the right-hand side of the definition. We can reflect all we like on the experience of red but we will not learn more than that it is an experience of red. It looks as if it is the second, psychological, question that we need to make progress towards understanding colour perception. Generalizing, we might conclude that the psychological question is the more interesting the more limited the scope for illuminating the nature of an experience simply by reflecting upon it. Optimistically, one might hope that answers to each of the two questions illuminate the other.

What, then, of Wittgenstein's view as stated above? It is in the nature of aesthetic experiences that they are internally rather complicated. Hence, the philosophical question (of making progress by reflecting on what it is like to have such experiences) seems apposite. My claim is not, incidentally, that this is the only resource available to philosophy in attempting to grasp the nature of experience. There are also matters such as whether the purported constituents of the experience are metaphysically respectable, are plausibly present in experience, and (as I said above) are available to the person having the experience.

With this in mind, I shall begin by attempting to clarify Wollheim's own views on what the relation is between his account of visual representation and psychology. There is only one place in his writing where he explicitly discusses issues that psychology might take up in relation to his work. He proposes that psychological studies of representation should have the appropriate scope, should have the appropriate consequences, and the appropriate flexibility (Wollheim 1977: 166–8). He uses these three headings (the details of which need not detain us here) not to speculate as to psychological processes which might provide evidence for or against his account, but to argue that some psychological experiments are flawed in not taking the distinctive and introspectable nature of pictorial representation seriously.

Putting this aside, and looking instead at whether psychology could provide evidence for or against his account, we can phrase our two questions more specifically:

1. What is constitutive of the experience of pictorial representation?
2. Through what process is such an experience generated?

The complex nature of the experience of pictorial representation suggests that illumination might well come through attempting to answer (1). However, that is compatible with attempting to answer (2). Given Wollheim's interest in both disciplines, we need to consider two possible relations between the philosophy and the psychology. The first (A) holds that the two questions are separate, that philosophy should restrict itself to answering (1) and should have no commitments as to the answer to (2). The second (B) holds that the questions are not separate, and an answer to each of them involves an answer to the other.

It is not clear which of A or B Wollheim held. When he addresses the point explicitly, he appears to hold B. The title of the essay alluded to above is indicative: 'Representation: The Philosophical Contribution to Psychology', and the opening paragraph explicit:

It is now, I hope, accepted as the outmoded view that it is that philosophy and psychology are totally independent disciplines [sic]. It seems to me that there are many philosophical questions that cannot be answered unless we know the relevant psychology, and there are many psychological questions whose answers await the relevant philosophy. I think that one of the many reasons why the topic of representation is so interesting is that it illustrates extremely well the interdependence of the two disciplines. (Wollheim 1977: 159)

Much later, in 2003, he seems not to have changed his mind, claiming not to interpret the distinction 'between the philosophical task of saying what it is to see x in y, and the psychological task of discovering when, or in what circumstances, we may expect to see x in y' very rigidly (Wollheim 2003: 139).

However, this is rather puzzling because, as Robert Hopkins points out, at least with reference to the account of seeing-in, Wollheim's theory is directed at (1) and has no

resources with which to answer (2) (Hopkins 2003b: 159). As claimed above, Wollheim defines pictures in terms of the kind of experience to which they give rise.
A complete answer is given to this by providing a perspicuous description of that
experience: that is his answer to (1). How such an experience is generated (that is, an
answer to (2)) is an empirical matter. There might not be one such process—the
processes might, as Hopkins claims, 'be many and variable, with nothing common at
anything like the level of generality that philosophical claims require' (Hopkins 2003a:
661). Furthermore, in reply to criticism of his views on expressive perception by
Malcolm Budd, Wollheim explicitly distinguishes between (1) and (2), and argues
that implausibilities in (2) do not attach to (1) (Budd 2001; Wollheim 2001: 255).

The absence of consistency in Wollheim's view of the relation between philosophy
and psychology makes the task of discovering how the latter could support his view of
pictorial representation more difficult than it might have been. Any account that
attempts to answer (2) will have definite psychological commitments, which can be
assessed against rival explanations of the same process. It is much less obvious that an
answer to (1) will be threatened or supported by the psychological evidence.

## 3. Bringing psychology to bear on Wollheim's account

*Seeing-in*

Wollheim's account of seeing-in has been the subject of significant criticism from
philosophy; in particular, Budd and Hopkins have pointed out some serious problems
with the view (Budd 1992; Hopkins 2003b). Criticism or support from psychology
is less common. This is not surprising, as there is a structural feature of Wollheim's
account that makes it unclear what form such criticism or support could take. We can
divide Wollheim's account of the experience of paintings (as we could divide any
account) into two: the features which are distinctive of the account ('seeing-in'), and
the features which are common to a number of plausible accounts. The features that are
distinctive of the account are the division of the experience of pictorial representation
into two: the 'configurational aspect' (modelled on a face-to-face experience of the
surface of the painting) and the 'recognitional aspect' (modelled on the face-to-face
experience we would have of the 'absent object' in the painting), and the claim that
these are two aspects of a single experience. The features which are common to a
number of plausible accounts are that we are in some way simultaneously visually
aware both of a surface and of illusory three-dimensional space.

One might hope, for example, that psychology could attempt to investigate subjects'
experience of pictorial representation in order to discover whether any evidence could
be found of the subject having either the configurational aspect or recognitional aspect
as Wollheim describes it. The problem is in getting any independent grasp of these two
aspects. Each aspect is distinct from its face-to-face counterpart; indeed, incommensurable with it (Wollheim 1987: 47). The structural problem—put generally—is this: the

two aspects that make up the twofold experience are not defined independently of the way the experience of pictorial representation seems to us. Hence, whatever features this experience has just will be the features possessed by these two aspects. Hence, there is no point in psychology attempting to find features of the experience that may or may not match those of the aspects, as the two are not independently defined.

Intriguingly there has been some empirical research into the perception of pictorial space, and how it differs from our seeing the world face-to-face.[3] Koenderink and van Doorn have developed a technique of tracking the gradients of the surfaces as we see them in a picture (Koenderink and van Doorn 2003). Consider a scenario in which the observer is face-to-face with a flat surface on which there is a depiction of a figure. Using Wollheim's terminology, they see a flat surface and they see an object in the surface: they have a visual experience of an illusory space and an object in that space. Koenderink and van Doorn have developed a figure—roughly a circle with a line drawn from its centre out beyond its circumference—that is seen as being in the same illusory space. This figure (which they call a 'gauge figure') can be changed such that the change we see it undergoing in the illusory space is a change in its curvature (its slant and tilt). Observers can change the figure such that it clings to the surface of the object as seen in the picture (Koenderink and van Doorn 2003: 255). In short we can map the three-dimensional aspects of the objects seen in the picture; we can get a map of the illusory pictorial space.

There is much of interest in Koenderink and van Doorn's findings, not least that pictorial space is not Euclidean. However, these need not detain us here; for the moment, I am interested in whether this particular psychological research supports any one account of pictorial representation over any other. It would rule out any account that was incompatible with the claim that our experience of depicted figures is an experience of something we can still call, despite it not being Euclidean, three-dimensional. There are accounts that appear to entail the experience of a figurative painting is not what we pre-reflectively take it to be. Ernst Gombrich's account strikes many this way (despite him invoking the authority of Kenneth Clark as evidence). Gombrich held that we can experience the qualities of the picture surface as the picture surface, or we could experience the depicted content as the depicted content, but we could not have the two experiences simultaneously (Gombrich 1977: 4–5). One problem—one of a number of problems—with this account is that it does not seem true to our experience: we do not alternate between these two different, and independently characterizable, experiences. Koenderink and van Doorn's account may be problematic for Gombrich's account if it entails that our experience is not consistently one of a three-dimensional space.

The plausible accounts in the literature, however, are compatible with the claim (indeed, some, such as Wollheim, begin with the claim) that the experience of the

---

[3]  I am grateful to Robert Hopkins for referring me to this literature.

illusory space of pictures includes an experience of three-dimensional space, and therefore that the figures therein will have surfaces whose gradients could be mapped by Koenderink and van Doorn's techniques. In short, Koenderink and van Doorn will not provide psychological evidence that will support one of these philosophical accounts of depiction over another.

*Expressive perception*

Wollheim's account of expression is perhaps the most prominent aspect of his view where he attempts to blur the boundary between the constitutive and causal questions discussed in section 2 of this chapter. Once again, and partly because of this blurring, the view has been the subject of serious criticism by philosophers, again by Budd (2001). Wollheim takes an explicitly psychoanalytic stance over this matter: the core notions are of complex projection (the phenomenon of our projecting our mental states onto inanimate parts of the world) and correspondence (the phenomenon of seeing that part of the world as being 'of a piece' with our mental states). This is not the place to sort out the debate as to whether or not psychoanalysis is scientifically respectable; however, the claim that it assessable via the usual methodology of psychology is surely a minority opinion which would be sufficient explanation for the absence of discussion within psychology of Wollheim's view.[4]

Indeed, it is not even clear that Wollheim's use of 'projection' is defensible within the psychoanalytic literature. In his later discussion, Wollheim refers us to *The Thread of Life* as the definitive statement of his view (Wollheim 1991: 150). There, Wollheim boldly introduces his claim: 'Projection takes two different forms: simple and complex' (Wollheim 1986: 214). By 'simple projection', Wollheim takes over the Kleinian notion: that is, her notion of 'projective identification' in which some part of an agent's psychology is unknowingly projected onto another. Classically, an agent has hostile feelings towards another and 'projects' those feelings onto the other resulting in the false belief that the other has hostile feelings towards the agent: 'I hate him' becomes 'he hates me'. This is part of a defence mechanism; the hostility causes the agent anxiety, and the projection lessens that anxiety. There are two substantial differences between this and 'complex projection' in which the agent projects their mental state onto some part of the inanimate world. First, there has to be 'a real match, or correspondence' between the world onto which the mental state is projected and the mental state. This is not the case with simple projection; the paranoid, for example, can project their hostile feelings onto anyone. Second, the result is not a false belief about the world, but rather the world taking on a certain look; a look that corresponds to the mental state.[5]

---

[4] See (Noordhof 2008) for brief discussion of this and further worries about Wollheim's account.
[5] There is a worry here that correspondence enters twice: first as the suitability for projection, second as a result of projection. See Budd (2001).

The problem for Wollheim is that the notion of 'complex projection' does not occur in the psychoanalytic literature.[6] In as much as he is taking over a notion familiar in psychoanalysis, and trading on the explanatory power it has from its place in that explanatory scheme, it matters that it is that familiar notion. Clearly, there are some problematic differences between simple and complex projection. Simple projection describes a mechanism that results in a false belief: the belief that a minded individual (and therefore an individual who could have mental states, including hostility to the agent) in fact has the mental state of hostility to the agent. Complex projection has a much more complicated outcome: the phenomenon of the world looking a certain way—namely, being 'of a piece' with the agent's mental state. It is not clear that the story told of the first can transfer across to the second (that is, the claim that 'projection takes two different forms' covers a multitude of possible differences between the familiar first form, and the unfamiliar second). The worry is further exacerbated because, as we shall see shortly, complex projection does not require the agent actually to be in the mental state projected. However, if this is the case, then the rationale for simple projection—namely, the externalization of an actual mental state as a defence mechanism—is simply lacking in the case of complex projection. What is there to cause or sustain it?

The second issue is whether psychology could be used to support or criticize Wollheim's constitutive account. That is, Wollheim gives us an account of what it is to see an object[7] as expressive: it is to experience it as having an appearance that corresponds to an inner state (let us call this 'expressive perception'). Once again, the same problem looms as we encountered with attempting to evaluate 'seeing-in': expressive perception is supposed to capture exactly the phenomenology of our seeing an object as expressive (a caveat is entered below), hence any evidence that a person is experiencing the latter will equally be evidence that they are experiencing the former.

The caveat arises because of Wollheim's deliberate failure to distinguish the causal from the constitutive accounts.[8] The simple version of the view is that expressive perception is the result of complex projection. However, that is too simple: it would entail that expressive perception could only occur in the immediate aftermath of projection. This is absurd; as Wollheim himself says, 'we can and do perceive nature as of a piece with our feelings in cases where we can no longer recall having projected those feelings onto it' (Wollheim 1991: 153). Hence, expressive perception can take place in the absence of complex projection, which casts doubt not only on complex projection being a constitutive part of expressive perception, but also it being part of the causal history of expressive perception. To block this, Wollheim claims the

---

[6] This paragraph is based on conversations with Malcolm Budd. Whether Budd would endorse the use I have made of his ideas is another matter.

[7] Wollheim changes his mind as to whether his account covers art and nature, or whether a different account is needed for each. See Budd (2001: 102).

[8] All the points in this and the following paragraph are taken from Budd (2001).

following: 'those experiences of projective properties which do not intimate their own history nevertheless intimate how experiences of such a sort originate: they intimate that such experiences originate in projection' (Wollheim 1991: 153). Let us call this 'the intimation thesis'.

The intimation thesis is surely too strong to be plausible. As Budd claims, if complex projection really were intimated in the experience of expressive perception, it would entail that anyone capable of expressive perception possesses the concept of complex projection. Although this seems clearly false, Budd reports that Wollheim himself embraced the entailment, as he was (for other reasons) committed to the view that some knowledge of psychoanalytic theory is innate (Budd 2001: 110). It is difficult to know what to make of Wollheim's claim that an intimation of complex projection is a part of our experience of expression in the face of the fact that anyone (or almost anyone) who has an experience of expressive perception fails to register this fact.

*Visual delight*

If psychology is to have a role in aesthetics, it would seem most suited to illuminating the pleasure we take in works of art. That aesthetic judgements are grounded in pleasure has a venerable history: such a claim was standard during Enlightenment. This would seem to open the door to a 'science of aesthetics'; all we need to do is establish those psychological laws that connect certain inputs with pleasure, and we put aesthetics on an objective footing. Whether the same inputs would have the same effects on any of us would determine whether aesthetic judgements were universal, or whether they needed to be relativized.

A lot of work has been done by psychologists on beauty, particularly on people's attractiveness to other people. There are laws connecting attractiveness to features of ourselves such as facial symmetry, hip-to-waist ratio, and shoulder-to-hip ratio where attractiveness is measured by 'positive affect-laden appraisals of beauty' (Prinz, this volume, p. 71). Such an approach has fallen out of favour in aesthetics, particularly since the 1950s, although recently it has been revived by Jesse Prinz.[9] Prinz argues that works of art are beautiful for us, if they cause in us a sentiment of appreciation. There are complications in what exactly Prinz means by 'sentiment of appreciation' (see Prinz, this volume, pp. 71–88) which need not worry us here; for our purposes, it only matters that it is some positive affective state.

Prinz's view answers the question of the relation between psychological research as to the basis of attraction, and aesthetic judgement; the relation is direct. There is, however, a *prima facie* worry with this. Take a familiar case in which one might consider whether (for instance) Rothko is a good painter. One might consider whether one's reaction to Rothko's paintings is merely a reaction to large areas of colour (a kind of visual shock), or perhaps whether one's reaction is overly influenced by what one

---

[9] See the chapter in this volume, and the references therein.

knows about the melancholy facts of Rothko's life. It seems to me that considering whether Rothko is any good is not the same as considering whether the paintings cause in us some positive affective state. To be fair, Prinz does not maintain that our reaction to works of art stops with the positive affective state; that, in turn, might provoke states of awe and reverence. However, puzzling about whether a positive aesthetic judgement is merited does not have much to do with puzzling over whether it provokes an affective state, so much as whether the work provides grounds for the value of some non-instrumentally valuable experience, where such value goes much beyond affect and into the realms of reason-giving and understanding (Budd 1995: ch. 1).

In short, I find Wollheim's notion of visual delight more conducive to the notion of aesthetic judgement than can be got from psychological work on the basis of attraction. To take visual delight in a picture is, in part, seeing the picture as a construction that provides a certain expressive appearance (putting aside Wollheim's analysis of expressive appearance for the moment). That is, it is to see it as something deliberately constructed such that our visual experience of it has a certain complexity; we have access to the 'unnoticed life of ordinary objects' (Wollheim 1987: 99). Wollheim's is an odd notion of 'delight'. It does not seem to have much to do with positive hedonic states; more to do with an experience of a certain complexity that provides grounds for value of our experience of the work. This experience is not a matter of having our sentiments provoked, but rather a matter of there being a certain intentional state; of our bringing one experience to bear on another experience, and it is very unclear to me how psychology could have a hand in illuminating that.

What I have tried to show in this chapter is that the experiences of painting that Wollheim describes stand at some distance from psychological evidence. Wollheim himself is inconsistent in his attitude to psychology; sometimes regarding the process through which one comes to have an experience as part of the experience and sometimes distinct from the experience. I have not covered (and am not sceptical about) an issue that was important to Wollheim: namely, the extent to which the spectator needs to be familiar with 'the hypotheses of psychology and psychoanalysis' in order to 'retrieve' the mental states of the painter of the picture (Wollheim 1987: Preface).[10]

# References

Budd, M. (1992). 'On Looking at a Picture', in J. Hopkins and A. Savile (eds.), *Psychoanalysis, Mind and Art: Perspectives on Richard Wollheim.* Oxford, Blackwell, pp. 259–80.

——(1995). *Values of Art: Pictures, Poetry, Music.* Harmondsworth, Penguin.

——(2001). 'Wollheim on Correspondence, Projective Properties and Expressive Perception', in R. Van Gerwen (ed.), *Richard Wollheim on the Art of Painting.* Cambridge: Cambridge University Press, pp. 101–11.

---

[10] I am grateful to Peter Goldie for comments that did much to improve this chapter.

Gombrich, E. (1977). *Art and Illusion: A Study in the Psychology of Pictorial Representation*. London: Phaidon.

Hopkins, R. (2003a). 'Pictures, Phenomenology and Cognitive Science'. *The Monist*, 86/4: 653–75.

——(2003b). 'What Makes a Representational Painting Truly Visual?' *Supplementary Proceedings of the Aristotelian Society*, 77: 149–67.

Koenderink, J. J. and A. J. van Doorn (2003). 'Pictorial Space', in H. Hecht, R. Schwartz, and M. Atherton (eds.), *Looking into Pictures: An Interdisciplinary Approach to Pictorial Space*. Cambridge, MA: MIT Press, pp. 239–300.

Marr, D. (1982). *Vision: A Computational Investigation into the Human Representation and Processing of Visual Information*. New York, W. H. Freeman and Company.

Noordhof, P. (2008). 'Expressive Perception as Projective Imagining'. *Mind and Language*, 23/3: 329–58.

Wittgenstein, L. (1970). *Lectures and Conversations on Aesthetics, Psychology, and Religious Belief*. Oxford, Blackwell.

Wollheim, R. (1977). 'Representation: The Philosophical Contribution to Psychology', reprinted in *The Mind and Its Depths*. Cambridge, MA: Harvard University Press, 1993, pp. 159–70.

——(1986). *The Thread of Life*. Cambridge: Cambridge University Press.

——(1987). *Painting as an Art*. London: Thames & Hudson.

——(1991). 'Correspondence, Projective Properties and Expression in the Arts', reprinted in *The Mind and its Depths*. Cambridge, MA: Harvard University Press, 1993, pp. 144–58.

——(2001). 'A Reply to the Contributors', in R. Van Gerwen (ed.), *Richard Wollheim on the Art of Painting*. Cambridge: Cambridge University Press, pp. 241–61.

——(2003). 'What Makes Representational Painting Truly Visual?' *Supplementary Proceedings of the Aristotelian Society*, 77: 131–47.

# Index

Printed and bound by CPI Group (UK) Ltd, Croydon, CR0 4YY